A
Communications
Cornucopia

A Communications Cornucopia

Markle Foundation Essays on Information Policy

Roger G. Noll
Monroe E. Price
Editors

BROOKINGS INSTITUTION PRESS
Washington, D.C.

About Brookings

The Brookings Institution is a private nonprofit organization devoted to research, education, and publication on important issues of domestic and foreign policy. Its principal purpose is to bring knowledge to bear on current and emerging policy problems. The Institution was founded on December 8, 1927, to merge the activities of the Institute for Government Research, founded in 1916, the Institute of Economics, founded in 1922, and the Robert Brookings Graduate School of Economics and Government, founded in 1924.

The Institution maintains a position of neutrality on issues of public policy. Interpretations or conclusions in Brookings publications should be understood to be solely those of the authors.

Copyright © 1998 by
THE BROOKINGS INSTITUTION
1775 Massachusetts Avenue, N.W., Washington, D.C. 20036

Library of Congress Cataloging-in-Publication data

A communications cornucopia : Markle Foundation essays on information
  policy / Roger G. Noll and Monroe E. Price, editors.
      p.   cm.
  Festschrift in honor of Lloyd Morrisett, president of the John and
Mary R. Markle Foundation from 1969 through 1997.
  Includes bibliographical references and index.
  ISBN 0-8157-6116-3 (alk. paper). — ISBN 0-8157-6115-5 (pbk. :
alk. paper)
    1. Communication policy.   I. Price, Monroe Edwin, 1938–
  II. Noll, Roger G.   III. Morrisett, Lloyd, 1929–
  P95.8.C59   1998
  302.2—dc21   97-45380
                                                            CIP

9 8 7 6 5 4 3 2 1

The paper used in this publication meets the minimum requirements of the
American National Standard for Information Sciences—Permanence of Paper for
Printed Library Materials. ANSI Z39.48-1984

Set in Sabon

Composition by Harlowe Typography, Inc.
Cottage City, Maryland

Printed by R. R. Donnelley and Sons Co.
Harrisonburg, Virginia

Contents

Preface

THE FIELD OF communications policy encompasses economics, engineering, law, psychology, political science, and many other disciplines. Too often these areas are tightly cabined; essays and articles from one discipline are seldom read by scholars and students in another, and they and policymakers are disadvantaged by this segregation. Our objective in assembling this volume is to act as gatherers and synthesizers. We seek to provide a survey of the best of these disciplines, a choir of policy analysis in which the different disciplines have their own voices yet together yield something with its own strength and cohesion.

This book is dedicated to Lloyd Morrisett, who served as president of the John and Mary R. Markle Foundation from 1969 through 1997. The essays reflect the amazing sweep and outstanding quality of the work that was supported by Markle during Morrisett's presidency. For three decades, the Markle Foundation has been one of the most influential philanthropic institutions in communications policy. That achievement is largely attributable to Morrisett's vision and judgment as the architect of the foundation's program. The essays included here, while representing the scope and depth of contemporary scholarship on communications policy, also emphasize the concerns of authors who have worked with the foundation in one way or another. Therefore we, and the authors included, wish to make this volume a testimony to Morrisett's energetic and imaginative leadership.

The Markle Foundation

The John and Mary R. Markle Foundation was created in 1927 with a gift of $3 million from John Markle. The foundation's original charter establishes as its objective "to promote the advancement and diffusion of knowledge." Upon John Markle's death in 1933, the foundation's endowment increased to $15 million. From 1927 to 1935, the focus of the foundation's grant program was social welfare; in 1935 the emphasis was changed to medical research. Then, in 1947, the major program of the foundation became Scholars in Academic Medicine, which provided five-year grants to young faculty in medical schools.

When Lloyd Morrisett became president, he shifted the foundation's focus from medicine to mass communications. In his first year, based on his own path-breaking role in being one of the founder's of Children's Television Workshop, the creators of *Sesame Street*, the foundation supported CTW in developing sound research methods to undergird its bold and nationally important new programming initiatives. In the same year Markle also initiated the communications policy research program at the Rand Corporation, which for three decades has been the most influential economics research program on telecommunications policy. Morrisett later served as the chair of the board of both CTW (a position he still holds) and the Rand Corporation.

In the second year of its new communications program, Markle helped to establish the Aspen Institute Program on Communications and Society and New York University's Alternate Media Center and gave its first of a series of grants to Peggy Charren's Action for Children's Television (ACT), the *Columbia Journalism Review*, the National Association of Educational Broadcasters, and the United Church of Christ.

Since this auspicious beginning, Markle has spent its annual appropriations of two to eight million dollars with wisdom and effectiveness, and with no visible biases or limitations in the kinds of activities that it will support. The foundation's program is multidisciplinary, supporting researchers in the social sciences, law, applied science and engineering, and the humanities. The foundation supports a complete range of activities, from basic academic research on the information sector to new for-profit companies that seek to introduce high-risk information products. Under Morrisett's guidance, the staff has placed bets on neophytes in addition to well-placed scholars, and not a few academics have enlarged their impact precisely through Markle's largesse. Markle defines information technology and communications policy broadly, sometimes supporting work on institutional relationships in distantly related areas, such as regulatory methods in other infrastructural industries, that might have application in communications.

Issues in Communications Policy and Plan of the Book

This book is intended to provide a comprehensive introduction to the broad spectrum of the issues that are likely to dominate the communications policy debate during the first few years of the next millennium. In chapter 1, we describe the historical background of the current debates, placing the evolution of policy issues within the context of the management decisions of the Markle Foundation. This chapter has two substantive themes. The first is the key characteristic of the evolution of information technology and the mass media: convergence and choice. The second is the strategic decisions by the Markle Foundation in carving out an important niche in carrying forward these developments.

The theme of convergence and choice permeates the entire book. Convergence refers to the trend in the underlying technologies of all communications, from mass media such as newspapers and television to computers. Technology is causing these disparate means of managing information and communicating to converge in the sense that society now faces the opportunity to use a single technology, combining computers and telecommunications networks, to provide all information-related services and to create new methods of communications that combine the features of the separate old media. Choice refers to a seemingly contradictory feature of a converging information infrastructure, which is that businesses and consumers are experiencing ever greater choice in both the form of information services and the providers of those services. In short, convergence to a single, ubiquitous medium for information technology has been accompanied by greater diversity in the number of service providers and the substance of the services that they supply. Interestingly, a foundation that is minuscule compared with the size of the information technology sector has nevertheless managed to play a significant role in the creation of opportunities for convergence and choice and the policy decisions that made these developments more than an unexploited technological opportunity.

This book deals with major themes in contemporary communications policymaking. Each one represents a primary interest of the Markle Foundation as well as a category of policy issues arising from developments in the information sector. These main themes are the relationship between the media and democratic society, including both political processes and the protection of individual rights; the effect of television on children; the communications policymaking process; and the rapidly evolving economics of information technology and services.

Part one includes essays that assess issues about mass media and the public sphere. Robert M. Entman surveys the gulf between media descriptions of affirmative action and public attitudes toward the problem of distribution of employment opportunities in the society. Both Benjamin R. Barber and Elihu Katz examine the implications of segmentation and technological abundance for democratic discourse and definitions of political and social community. Ellen Mickiewicz surveys how broadcasting has been redefined in Russia in the post-Soviet era and how that redefinition affects political debate. Monroe E. Price posits a theory relating broadcasting regulation to national identity. Matthew L. Spitzer discusses the inconsistencies and commonalities of the three most significant Supreme Court decisions that attempt to confront a trade-off between regulation of information technology and First Amendment guarantees of freedom of speech and the press. Marc Raboy discusses the need for transnational regulatory approaches in light of a globalizing media. Bruce Murray explores the potential of the World Wide Web to offer unprecedented opportunities for deliberative discourse on a local and global scale.

Part two discusses children and television. Daniel R. Anderson, Aletha C. Huston, John C. Wright, and Patricia A. Collins offer important new information on the impact of watching *Sesame Street* (and other CTW productions) on children's performance in school. Shalom M. Fisch addresses the opposite causal relationship: how research on the effects of television on children affects programming at the Children's Television Workshop. Jay G. Blumler reveals the findings of a recent survey of trends in production and performance of children's television programs on European public broadcasting entities. Finally, Donald F. Roberts provides background and analysis of the debate over the question of whether—and how—to engage in rating and labeling programs to protect children, within constitutional bounds, from programming that has sexual or violent content.

Part three examines topics in communications policy. Elizabeth E. Bailey explores changes in public sector priorities toward telecommunications regulation during the twentieth century, documenting the change in emphasis from "client politics" and universal service to "entrepreneurial politics," interest group pluralism, and majoritarianism. She also evaluates the 1996 Telecommunications Act from this perspective.

Robert W. Crandall systematically unpacks the century-long debate about the pursuit of universal service through subsidized access for residential customers, concluding that these policies have only a tiny effect on income distribution and telephone penetration, yet are very expensive and distort the structure of the industry. Frank A. Wolak examines how electronic technologies, such as facsimile and e-mail, have reduced the demand for first-class postal service and may undermine the future financial viability of the post office. Charles L. Jackson, John Haring, Harry M. Shooshan III, Jeffrey H. Rohlfs, and Kirsten M. Pehrsson describe an important problem arising from the use of spectrum auctions to allocate licenses for satellite services. Because satellite services are not naturally confined to national boundaries, the failure among different countries to coordinate these auctions can distort the efficient evolution of the industry. Charles R. Shipan examines the history of broadcast regulation to promote public interest content as primarily an exercise in limiting the entry of new competitors. James N. Dertouzos and Steven S. Wildman study the development of standards for television signals of cable television, addressing the question of how advanced video technologies can most efficiently be introduced in the medium that most Americans use to gain access to television. Gerald R. Faulhaber projects the history of telecommunications policy debates about pricing, entry, and industry structure on to the emerging converged digital infrastructure, providing a cautiously optimistic view about the continued evolution of choice in an era of convergence. Henry Geller discusses the history of policies to ensure that broadcasters serve public interest objectives and observes how these policies fare under the 1996 Telecommunications Act. Steven S. Wildman examines how the public goods characteristics of media content and the demand for advertising by both consumers and advertisers complicates the application of antitrust policy to media markets. Finally, Bruce M. Owen investigates the underlying core economics of digital technology and what this implies about how mass media will evolve and whether the market is likely to support a digital delivery system that provides all or virtually all communications. Owen argues that, because of the nature of consumer demand for light entertainment and the relative cost of information products in a digital medium, new technologies are unlikely to spell the end to passive mass communications like television and newspapers. He says that many, if not most, American households are unlikely to be willing to pay for multimedia capability in the backbone telecommunications network.

The Role of Markle in Communications

Both the technological possibilities and the policy issues that they have created have been strongly influenced by the Markle Foundation over the past thirty years. The foundation has made grants to all of the important education and research programs at leading American universities and nonprofit research institutions. Besides numerous project grants to universities, Markle established long-term programs at Carnegie-Mellon, Columbia, Duke, Harvard, the Massachusetts Institute of Technology, New York University, Stanford, the University of California at Los Angeles, and the University of California at San Francisco. The foundation has financed projects at the American Enterprise Institute, the Brookings Institution, the Manhattan Institute, the Rand Corporation, and the Urban Institute.

Markle has supported the media and communications policy activities of many public interest organizations, including Action for Children's Television, the American Film Institute, the Fund for Investigative Journalism, the League of Women Voters, the Media Access Project, the National Association of Educational Broadcasters, the National Citizens Committee for Broadcasting, the National News Council, the Public Agenda Foundation, and the United Church of Christ. It has helped create professional associations and ethical standards for broadcast executives, independent radio producers, and television critics.

The foundation has underwritten entrepreneurial ventures in new media technology and their socially beneficial applications in the nonprofit and for-profit sectors. Markle has a long history of support for CTW, WNET in New York, National Public Radio, the Eastern Public Radio Network, and many other organizations in public broadcasting. It has financed the development of several public television programs about education, the media, public health, local public affairs, national policy issues, and the arts. In recent years, it has invested part of its own endowment in start-up companies that seek to develop new multimedia products for education and entertainment.

Markle grants are wide ranging in their scope. Here is but a partial list of the purposes of funded projects and their purpose: to televise events from Lincoln Center in New York; to establish *Channels*, a magazine devoted to critical analysis of television and related technologies; to create a multimedia package to teach the piano; to test methods of nonjudicial dispute resolution mechanisms to resolve libel claims against media organizations; to develop SeniorNet, a system of communications networks for senior citizens; to provide start-up investments for new companies that develop educational software; to establish the Broadcasting Research Unit, an independent communications policy research organization in the United Kingdom and to establish a program in comparative media law and policy at Oxford University; to create handbooks or other training materials for producers trying to market audio productions or video material to public television, citizens desiring to participate in broadcasting regulation or cable television franchising, local groups seeking access to broadcast media, and journalists desiring background information on the national politics they cover; to develop new methods of measuring television audiences that would take into account their evaluations of programs; to facilitate the use of information technology in political campaigns and voting; to create video games to encourage community involvement through cable television, simulate national policymaking about health care, reflect the national elections process, and educate citizens about issues in a presidential campaign.

The Markle Foundation has supported many conferences on telecommunications policy. The usual method of support is a one-shot, single-purpose event in response to a project proposal. But there are also two notable continuing activities. First, the foundation has been a stalwart supporter of the Aspen Institute Program on Communications and Society. Aspen has developed, to a fine art, the skill of bringing together a small group of people who have disparate experience and giving them an opportunity to develop common approaches to public policy questions. Second, Markle has provided continuing support for the annual Telecommunications Policy Research Conference. The TPRC brings together about two hundred communications scholars, government officials, and representatives of businesses and nonprofits in the communications and information technology sector. In the communications policy community, an invitation to TPRC is a very hot ticket. Attendance is by invitation only and is granted by an independent committee of leaders in the field for presenting scholarly papers on some aspect of communications or for participating in intensive, off-the-record panel discussions of the relationships between research and policy.

The editors of this book have a long, happy relationship with the Markle Foundation and Lloyd Morrisett, culminating with the honor of organizing this *Festschrift*. We have attended numerous conferences and seminars that Markle has sponsored and personally have enjoyed generous support for our research. But these experiences hardly make us unique; dozens of scholars have similar tales to tell. We are all deeply grateful to the Markle Foundation for supporting our work and the work of our students, colleagues, and friends. No useful idea or innovation in communications policy escaped the foundation's attention, and every scholar who has made a significant intellectual contribution to communications policy has somehow, at some time, been involved in a Markle-supported activity. We cannot imagine how scholarship about mass communications could have evolved as far as it has without the Markle Foundation's support, nor how Markle possibly could have done more for communications policy during Morrisett's tenure. We hope that this book serves not only as an expression of our appreciation but as a reflection of the importance of Lloyd Morrisett's legacy.

A
Communications
Cornucopia

CHAPTER ONE

Communications Policy: Convergence, Choice, and the Markle Foundation

Roger G. Noll and Monroe E. Price

B<small>Y THE LATE</small> 1960<small>S</small> information technologies had begun to exhibit two characteristics that have become increasingly significant during the last third of the twentieth century. The first is choice: more options—numbers and diversity—for those seeking communication, information, and entertainment. The second is convergence: ever greater overlap in the capabilities of different information technologies. This essay examines how, in the postwar era, these significant new characteristics emerged. But it does so primarily to come to understand a wholly different history: that of the Markle Foundation as it evolved from 1969 to 1997. During those years, Lloyd Morrisett was its distinguished president and had the enviable position of leading the only philanthropic institution that was devoted to understanding and encouraging choice and convergence during the era in which wondrous new opportunities emerged in the communications sector.

The history of the Markle Foundation is important because of its extraordinary relationship to communications policy over three decades. But it is also an exemplar for nonprofit practices. There is little understanding of how a foundation board or management picks a tax-exempt function in which it can make a difference and how it imposes some measure of self-accountability to determine whether it is performing well the function that it elected to perform. Like for-profit firms, these foundations face the problem of ensuring that management acts in the best interest of the firm, rather than pursue the manager's own personal agenda. In a public company, shareholders, or shareholders acting through a board of directors seek to maximize profits and can use measures of financial performance to evaluate managers. Indeed, corporate law requires that managers act in the financial interests of stockholders, within the bounds of legal behavior. Nonprofit organizations lack such a simple measure of performance, and charitable law does not require that foundations and managers pursue a foundation's objectives with reasonable efficiency. In most states, the attorney general seeks to ensure adequate performance by charitable institutions, but the record is not promising as to the adequacy of review. In many cases, weak boards or boards stocked by members with personal agendas yield underperforming nonprofits.

The Markle Foundation, both historically and under Morrisett's management, is a case study in surmounting these special distinguishing features built into the unusual legal architecture of nonprofit entities. At the Markle Foundation, a maximizing discipline was built in from the beginning. When John Markle created the first board, he appointed as members a select group of individuals—J.P. Morgan was one—steeped in a maximizing philosophy. A self-discipline that was begun then and continued in the Morrisett era ensured that the foundation always has a working definition of what needs to be done and a method to measure the foundation's effort or contribution. The annual reports of the Morrisett era are efforts to articulate this goal and, over time, to clarify and sharpen this goal and the strategy for achieving it.

Take the question of "line of work." When the Markle Foundation was established, its founder and his friends initially decided that social services were to be the foundation's focus. But nothing required that the focus remain constant, and, indeed, within a few years the foundation changed its focus to medical research. Just like a firm, a foundation might need to change, and change radically, in order to pick activities in which it can have a measurable impact. To do this, a modern foundation needs to take into account the activities of government and other institutions. In most public service activities, government is an overwhelming presence. Even a very large foundation has very small annual expenditures compared with federal, state, and local government; hence, the first task of a foundation leader is to identify areas that the government is ignoring or grossly mismanaging. Also, if a foundation duplicates the activities of private businesses or several other foundations, its expenditures are likely to make a minimal contribution.

For a relatively small foundation, these problems are magnified. A small foundation must not only find an activity in which its contribution will not be overwhelmed by the activities of government, business, or a larger foundation, but also one in which significant progress can be made with modest expenditures. The Markle Foundation is relatively small. When Lloyd Morrisett assumed its presidency, the market value of Markle's assets was less than $50 million, and its annual budget for philanthropic purposes was less than $2 million. At the end of Morrisett's term, the foundation was larger in nominal dollars. In 1997 the market value of its assets was $172 million, and its annual budget was $7.7 million. Considering the effects of inflation, the 1997 figures are roughly equal in purchasing power to the 1969 numbers. To obtain some sense about just how limited these resources are, consider the following statistics: the federal government spends about $75 billion on research, about a third of which is accounted for by national laboratories and two-thirds by grants and contracts. The National Science Foundation spends more than $2 billion annually. Stanford University's budget for 1997 was about $1.5 billion, of which more than $200 million came from government research grants. Indeed, the annual expenditure of Stanford's Department of Economics and Center for Economic Policy Research alone is roughly equal to the budget of the Markle Foundation.

Before September 1969, the foundation's biggest program, Scholars in Academic Medicine, provided five-year grants of $30,000 to about thirty young medical school professors and an annual conference for these scholars. By 1969 a program of this size was not likely to make a dent in the field of medical research and education. Since the inception of the Markle Scholars program in 1947, and its predecessor program for providing project support in medical research that began in 1935, federal government medical research programs had become enormous, and state support for medical schools at public universities was immense compared with Markle's budget. In addition, numerous other foundations, including some an order of magnitude larger than Markle, had been established in the postwar era with a primary mission in medicine. If anything, the field was destined to receive still more attention in the years to come as the federal government assumed responsibility for health care for the poor and the elderly through Medicaid and Medicare. In this environment, it was highly implausible that anything cheap but important would be persistently overlooked for long.

Mass communications provided a sharp contrast with medical education and research. On the research front, government was not supporting any significant amount of research on either communications policy or the effects of mass media. The federal government clearly was an 800-pound gorilla in supporting relevant science and engineering research and development (R&D), with its basic research programs in the National Science Foundation and its applied projects in operating agencies like Defense and the National Aeronautics and Space Administration. But in social sciences, the NSF programs were small and aimed at "basic" methodological topics, and the operating agencies had minimal research budgets and largely ignored the economic, social, and psychological implications of information technology. Markle, despite modest annual expenditures, could become a major factor in this area of research.

On the applications side, the foundation faced only a slightly less difficult problem in finding a niche in which it could have a major impact. The advantage of communications over medicine was that the former was not a primary focus of any competing foundation. Nevertheless, there were other impressive players. The communications sector contained numerous large organizations that were perfectly capable of developing new products and participating effectively in public debates about communications policy. In addition, the Corporation for Public Broadcasting was being launched for the purpose of substantially improving noncommercial television. Although the government's financial support for CPB was not generous, it was still large compared with anything the Markle Foundation could spend. The challenge was to find niches in the area of mass communications that were not occupied by any of these institutions.

In 1969 the connection between mass communications and children was a promising arena for a small foundation. Although public education is an enormous sector, it has neither the budget nor the institutional flexibility to do very much in exploring the use of electronic technologies in education. Both public and commercial television were focused primarily on providing services for a general audience. Commercial television derived its incentives from the need to sell advertising, which was accomplished most effectively through light entertainment, even on Saturday mornings, when TV oriented its programs toward children. Public television, with a modest programming budget and a financial structure that required obtaining voluntary contributions from business and adult viewers, had little discretionary money to spend on experimenting with educational programs that could not generate private donations.

A Brief History of Choice and Convergence

Before examining the evolution of Markle's grant policies, it is useful to examine the communications history in which they fit. Before 1960, significant choice was not a feature of electronic communication technologies. In the United States, a single, ubiquitous firm—the American Telephone and Telegraph Company—enjoyed a virtual monopoly in long distance telephony and controlled more than 80 percent of local telephone service and the manufacture of telephone equipment. Only slightly less impressive was the position of IBM, with more than three-quarters of the computer market. Television, which had vaulted past motion pictures, newspapers, and radio as the most important mass communications medium, enjoyed only a little more competition, with two strong commercial networks (CBS and NBC), a weaker third network (ABC), and a few almost invisible commercial independent and educational stations.

The old fashioned technologies—print media, motion pictures, and recordings—were not so concentrated, and therefore offered more choice. The motion picture industry was somewhat diverse, but a handful of studios still controlled almost all film production and distribution. The industry had not responded effectively to the rise of television as the primary means for providing light entertainment. Recorded music exhibited a similar structure to motion pictures, although small, independent companies were somewhat more important. In addition, recordings and radio, unlike movies and television, had created a symbiotic relationship that offset their natural competition as a source of musical entertainment. Record companies had discovered that giving their products to radio stations, and even occasionally paying stations and disc jockeys to play their releases, was an effective strategy for increasing record sales. In the print media, metropolitan daily newspapers were merging and dying, causing many major American cities to have but one source of in-depth news. Finally, national circulation general audience magazines like *Colliers* and *Life* also were dying.

Although communications technologies exhibited some overlap, the overriding feature of these industries was that they operated largely independently. Computers were used as a superior means of storing information and making arithmetic calculations. Telephone networks were used almost entirely for conversation beyond shouting distance. Newspapers, radio, and television were means of delivering current information, but they had already become quite specialized: newspapers for in-depth information and features, radio for music and opinions, and television for headline news and light entertainment. Audio recording was used for home musical entertainment and by radio; home audio recording was cumbersome, expensive, inferior in quality, and therefore economically unimportant. Video players and recorders for consumers were nonexistent, and the only connection between telecommunications and television was that network programs were delivered to local affiliates over the long distance telephone network.

Communications policy in 1960 was as fragmented as the technologies. The Federal Communications Commission (FCC) regulated telecommunications and broadcasting, but in wholly different ways arising from both statutory and constitutional considerations. The underlying law for regulating communications was passed in 1934, but its essential features had been adopted earlier—in 1910 for telephones and in 1927 for radio.

When the 1934 legislation was passed, telecommunications was viewed as a natural monopoly, so the primary issues were how to prevent it from exploiting consumers through high prices, low quality, and insufficient investment in capacity, and how to allocate regulatory authority between federal and state regulators. TV was still in the design stage, so radio was the only commercial broadcast medium, and it was presumed sufficiently competitive to make economic regulation unnecessary.

The new act raised only two constitutional issues. For telephone regulation, the constitutional constraint was the prohibition against imposing regulations that, in effect, expropriated the property of telephone investors without compensation. For radio, the constitutional issue was the extent to which the First Amendment protections of the press applied to the new medium.

Radio and television policy was primarily an issue of frequency allocation, which determined the number and geographic reach of stations. The FCC made these allocation decisions but was substantially constrained by two policies. First, most of the spectrum was controlled and allocated by the national security agencies. Second, Congress strongly preferred that the FCC allocate most radio and all TV licenses so as to create relatively low-power stations that each serve a single metropolitan area. The alternative policy, which is practiced in most of the rest of the world, is to create fewer but more powerful stations that can serve a larger geographic region. These two constraints caused consumers to have access to fewer stations than the market could sustain and made the creation of more than three national TV networks impossible.

Given this policy-created scarcity in stations, a second concern of the FCC was how to decide who should receive the scarce broadcast licenses. Out of this concern grew the continuing conflict between imposing program performance requirements and respecting the First Amendment rights of broadcasters. The essence of the FCC's approach was to hold licensing contests among competing applicants, and to favor applicants who had local ownership, who were not affiliated with other media companies (especially disfavoring newspapers in the same locality and "chains" that were or might become networks), and who promised the most news, public affairs, and locally produced programs.

In the print media, policy in 1960 focused almost exclusively on the First Amendment protection of the press, although on occasion antitrust issues also arose. Freedom of expression and the press raise fascinating, thorny, but superannuated policy questions, such as those concerning censorship regarding material that is sexually explicit, a threat to national security, or recklessly harmful to others. In 1960 the reigning legal theory was that First Amendment issues had much less application in broadcasting than in print media, based on the view that the spectrum was a scarce public resource, the use of which could be closely regulated by the government as long as regulators did not prescribe the content of programs.

Other aspects of communications were essentially off the table from the perspective of public policy except for an occasional antitrust case. The most important of these was *U.S. v. Western Electric*, filed in 1947, which sought to force AT&T to separate its equipment manufacturing business from telephone services. This case required that the federal government consider the relationship between computers and telecommunications. AT&T was an early player in experimenting with electronic computers, although no commercial computing existed at the time the case was initiated. Through its patent on semiconductors, AT&T had promising opportunities to enter the computer business successfully; however, in the settlement of the antitrust case in 1954, AT&T was permitted to keep its telecommunications equipment manufacturing affiliate, Western Electric, in return for allowing others to use its semiconductor patents without royalties and promising not to enter the computer business. A fair assessment is that neither the government nor the company understood at the time that these technologies were destined to converge. The decision to prohibit AT&T from making computers would profoundly affect both industries.

The 1960s Revolution

When Markle decided to enter the communications field, both technology and policy were changing, the first creating and the second responding to opportunities for convergence and choice. Early in the decade, the space race with the Russians led the United States to consider how satellites might be used for something other than international prestige. Because it financed satellite R&D, controlled launches, and allocated spectrum for communicating with satellites, the federal government controlled the market structure of the U.S. satellite services industry. Internationally, the government established Comsat as a monopoly; however, domestically the government decided not only to allow competition in satellite services, but initially to prohibit telephone companies from entering the business.

In ordinary telecommunications, policy was also changing. The computer industry had solved two technical problems of enormous significance. One was parallel processing, enabling computers to perform several tasks simultaneously. The other was remote access, which allowed users to connect to computers, and computers to connect to each other, using telephone lines or other physical connections over substantial distances. These innovations enabled networks to combine many smaller computers and related equipment into one large system. An important feature of this development was that it gave the designer of a network new choices about where to put different kinds of information and intelligence. For example, while a file was being printed, would it be stored in the computer, the printer, or the network that connected them? Would a user store both data and a computational program in the same computer, or different ones? Would errors in a file be corrected by a computer, or by the features in the network transmission system that detected and corrected transmission errors? The opportunities to make these choices began the process of blurring the boundaries among the computer, its peripheral devices, and the network that connected them.

These new technical possibilities forced the FCC to reconsider its entire regulatory structure for the telephone industry. Historically, the FCC had allowed telephone companies to manufacture all equipment that connected to the telephone network, and the technical characteristics of all the services that used the network. But the 1954 settlement of *U.S.* v. *AT&T* prohibited AT&T from making computers, which were now being connected to the network for the purposes of offering remote computer services. The FCC launched a major investigation of the relationships between computers and telecommunications regulation, and in 1968 decided to favor convergence with choice. The FCC would not regulate computers or computer services that merely used the network for interconnection; it would let telephone companies become regulated monopolists of computer services only if the service was primarily telecommunications in nature. For the first time, end users of the telephone system could own their terminal devices and decide exactly how they would be used, including, within a loose limit, the role that the public telephone network would play in their system.

In rapid succession, other important impediments to consumer choice in telecommunications were eliminated. *Carterfone* allowed consumers to own their own speaker phones, and by implication other terminal devices, as long as customers acquired a protective device that prevented their "foreign attachments" from harming the network. (A few years later, the requirement for a protective device was replaced by a much simpler and cheaper standard and certification system for competitive manufacturers.) In *MCI* and *Specialized Common Carriers*, the FCC decided to allow competition in "private lines" for long distance telecommunications, which enabled large companies to lease lines between cities and thereby to avoid long distance toll charges. Several companies (including IBM) quickly made use of the new policies regarding satellites, computers, and private lines to launch an entire new business: constructing computer services networks that were completely independent of the public telephone network. Moreover, within a few years the camel's nose of leased lines had become full-fledged competition in long distance telephone calls for all customers, including residences.

Another dramatic change was the emergence of a nascent cable television industry. Cable began in the 1950s as a mechanism for overcoming reception problems in areas that were remote from television stations or that, owing to local topography, had signal reception problems. In the 1960s, cable systems began to emerge in all but the largest cities for the purpose of importing the signals of distant stations. This service allowed citizens in cities with a small number of stations to gain access to a full complement of all three networks, a public television station, some commercial independents, and, through "network duplication," the local news and sports from an economically powerful station in a different city.

Initially the FCC found this development shocking and froze further growth of signal-importing systems on the ground that it threatened the historical policy of making television a localized mass medium. If citizens in San Diego watched Los Angeles stations, the FCC reasoned, then television could not succeed as a means for informing San Diegans about local public affairs and otherwise broadcasting programs to suit their specialized needs. San Diegans and their cable company disagreed. They sued the FCC, questioning the view that the FCC knew better than San Diegans what San Diegans ought to watch; however, the Supreme Court sided with the FCC, allowing regulation to protect broadcasters by preventing distant signal importation.

Nevertheless, by 1969, cable television was sufficiently established in enough communities that the industry could not simply be put out of business without causing a serious protest. Hence, the issue of how to regulate it had to be treated seriously, and the FCC began to consider the future role for cable. By 1972 the commission would remove the freeze on cable development and would allow cable systems to import some distant signals—enough, it turned out, to allow the industry to develop.

Cable policy issues were faced in an era when Americans were recognizing the revolutionary nature of television as a mass communications medium. By the mid-1960s, scholars began speculating that TV was more than a way to deliver news and entertainment, much as newspapers and radio had done before. Full-motion video, especially after the development of color TV, could affect people's attitudes and behavior far more profoundly than other mass communications media. Some saw this possibility as a promise: TV could be used to educate, to make people better citizens and parents, and to provide a common experience that could galvanize large numbers of individuals for a common purpose. Some saw TV's ability to affect people as a threat, contending that TV made viewers passive receptacles of a supremely effective form of propaganda, destroyed meaningful interpersonal relations within families and communities, and elevated popular culture beyond an entertainment to an addiction. One particularly powerful and influential view, expressed by former FCC Chair Newton Minow, accepted the promise, but saw the threat in the reality of TV programming, which he termed a "vast wasteland" that had forsaken the destiny in its promise.

In 1968, in the midst of the debate about the value of television, the federal government created the Corporation for Public Broadcasting. Whereas the FCC had created a substantial number of noncommercial television stations, the industry that emerged was underfinanced and weak. Many licenses were held by educational institutions, which placed strong emphasis on televised instructional programs that were produced on a shoestring budget and so were little more than video recordings of classroom lessons. CPB was created to infuse the system with new funds for national programs, and its spin-off, the Public Broadcasting Service, was created to operate as a national noncommercial network, much like ABC, CBS, and NBC.

It would be hard to overstate the significance of the events of 1968 and 1969 in shaping the future of the communications sector and the course of public policy. Technological developments in the early 1960s had forced a complete reconsideration of all important policy issues affecting the industry. It would also be hard to overstate the unique state of interest and excitement that was generated by these developments. Communications experts, whether in industry, government agencies, or universities and think tanks, realized that, all of a sudden, everything was up for grabs: who would offer what services to whom under what regulatory rules were no longer settled questions. Convergence with choice was just beginning and had created chaos that offered both threats and promises to everyone.

The Revolution That Just Won't End

As the twentieth century draws to a close, the world is much different from the state of affairs in 1969. Telecommunications is now the domain of many large firms. Every aspect of the industry is now reasonably competitive except cable television systems and local telephone service for residences and small businesses.

In telecommunications, long distance is now reasonably competitive for all users, and for certain types of users, so is local telephone service. Office buildings, apartment houses, and businesses with more than a few telephones now can and do create their own local telephone networks, and no longer use local telephone monopolies for calls among members of their local mininetwork or for access to long distance carriers. These developments still leave most local calls and virtually all long distance termination in the hands of local monopoly telephone companies, but with the passage of the Telecommunications Act of 1996 the remainder of local service also is targeted for competition.

Cable television, now serving 70 percent of all households, usually with thirty to one hundred channels, has induced dozens of new television networks (including three hybrids, Fox, UPN, and Warner, that combine off-air affiliates with cable distribution to reach a national audience). Most motion picture studios (Disney, Fox, Paramount, Universal, Warner Brothers) have entered the network television business. Whereas many new networks provide light entertainment (including sports) very much like the programming of the old over-the-air stations, others, like CNN, the History Channel, the Discovery Channel, the Learning Channel, Home Shopping Network, and Bravo, have substantially diversified the range of video services. Collectively, new networks have caused the combined audience shares of ABC, CBS, and NBC to fall below half, and one, Fox, now achieves prime time audiences that are comparable to those of the three older networks.

In the 1990s, a new medium, the Internet, arrived that holds the promise of completing the convergence of all communications media. The Internet was made technically feasible by the convergence of computers and the telephone network, and institutionally feasible by the introduction of substantially more competition—hence, choice—in telecommunications infrastructure. In a modern telephone network, the switches are computers that can store and process data. The connecting links, owing to digitalization as well as advances in transmission, have far greater capacity for carrying information, and so can be enhanced to carry pictures as well as sound to every household. As a result, newspapers, broadcasters, motion picture studios, book publishers, and direct mail advertisers—and many others who are new to mass communications—can all deliver their products over telephone lines, cable television systems, off-air multipoint distribution systems, and direct satellite transmissions to a user's combined television and home computer.

Technological advances have also begun to change public services. In 1960 public education extensively used only one medium—printed text. Gradually, first television and now computer software and the Internet are enabling students to learn through video instruction and to gain easy, inexpensive access to far more information than was ever available in the school library. In addition to providing marketable skills in the use of computers, the use of electronic hardware and software in the classroom is just beginning to exploit its potential for rapidly improving educational performance. Similar changes are beginning to emerge in health care (remote diagnostics), law enforcement (criminal database and identification), and transportation (computerized traffic control and highway toll systems).

Technological convergence will not necessarily lead to a single, ubiquitous technical method for delivering all forms of communications services. Different technical systems have different strengths, weaknesses, and costs for performing the same communications function. In any case users who do not desire the full fire-hose of information flow may find specialized backbone systems easier and cheaper to use for years to come. In the next decade, we will learn how complete convergence will be; however, we have learned enough in the 1990s to know that the communications sector has changed permanently and fundamentally, most obviously in the choices that have become available for almost all services.

To date, the most important companies in connecting businesses and residences to national services—local telephone companies and cable television systems—have not made the investments necessary to enable them to deliver the full range of mass communications services, and perhaps they never will. But the barrier to far greater diversity in services is no longer technological. Instead, the key issues are, first, how much service customers want and will pay for, and second, whether public policy will facilitate or retard giving customers the opportunity to choose how many and which services they will have. The key public policy issue is about the last mile in the delivery of telecommunications and video services. Will policy protect the two specialized monopolies, cable and telephone, or encourage competition and diversity? The war for convergence and choice is nearly over; the final battle is over the last mile.

The Morrisett Window on Communications Policy

It is against this rich historical setting that the Markle Foundation acted during the three decades of Lloyd Morrisett's presidency. Morrisett was hardly new to communications issues when he assumed Markle's leadership and had been deeply and personally involved, during his previous position at the Carnegie Corporation, with the founding of Children's Television Workshop and the Corporation for Public Broadcasting. His academic training, his professional exposure, and his personal interests meant that he was well prepared not only to think about the future of communications and society but to seek to affect that future, as well, through the efforts of the foundation. He recognized, more than most, the quality of the technological moment and the necessity for serious policy analysis. He recognized that this was a time for public understanding and public debate since the new technology could have a profound impact on democratic practices. Finally, he realized that the foundation would provide more than a bully pulpit: he could seek to identify and support initiatives that would nudge the uses of the technology in ways that might not occur if the marketplace of ideas were wholly left to itself.

Researchers into the philosophy of the Markle Foundation are fortunate in that every Markle annual report during the Morrisett era begins with an essay by the president, reflecting on a contemporary issue in communications. These were opportunities for the president to articulate his understanding of the impact of new technology for regulation and for civic concern. We cannot deal with all the important themes in communications policy that received attention in these documents, but we emphasize two areas, one—television policy—which received concentrated attention in the earlier years of the Morrisett presidency, and another, the shift to electronic publishing and multimedia technology during the last years of his tenure. In the final section of this chapter, we then turn to the programmatic aspects of the foundation's work to explore the relationship between Morrisett's articulation of the problems and the actions taken in the form of grants and related practices.

On Television

Three of the first four annual reports during the Morrisett presidency focus on television: the societal effects of television, the relationship of TV to children and education, and the role of public broadcasting. Together they set forth the interesting issues that would dominate policy discussions for the rest of the century. These three essays discuss the basic issues regarding the rise of television as the most influential mass medium, the promise of cable television for expanding diversity and choice and for facilitating convergence of the media, and the role of public television. The baseline concern is the performance of the over-the-air television industry. What television did well then, and would do even better in the future, is provide light, escapist entertainment. Morrisett set forth the problems arising from the direction that television has taken: it was (and still is) a passive medium that may affect people's behavior adversely, and in any case fails to educate and inform up to its capabilities or to provide entertainment to other than a mass audience.

Morrisett also identified how policy and economics have interacted to produce this result. First, policy was designed to make broadcasting local, thereby sacrificing numerical options and competition for a system in which virtually all metropolitan areas with a population of more than 50,000 have at least one local television station, but few have more than five. Second, economics overcomes policy localism because it favors national programming. Television programs, like all information products, are "public goods" in that the cost of producing content is independent of how many people have access to it. Hence, the cost per consumer is minimized when content is distributed nationally. For this reason, book publishers, news services, magazines, and networks all tend to be national in scope rather than localized. Moreover, most consumer tastes are not defined by geography—interest in sports teams being a notable exception. Instead, as soon as one gets beyond national mass audiences, consumer demand for both entertainment and information tends to be based on commonalities of education, occupation, and culture, rather than geography.

In plain language, Morrisett outlined the basic economic argument about the relationship between market structure and content diversity, which is known as the Steiner model because Peter Steiner first articulated it in the 1950s in the context of the choice of formats by radio stations. The essence of the argument is that if a mass medium has few competing outlets, the optimal content choice for private entrepreneurs is likely to be homogenized entertainment that is designed to appeal to a very large audience. As the number of competing outlets increases, eventually the best available strategy for a new entrant will be to appeal to a narrower audience by designing content that appeals more to their special tastes.

Morrisett explained a second implication of the Steiner model: that a multichannel monopolist would offer more diverse programming than a competitive industry operating the same number of channels. The reason is that independent firms will compete for and divide the mass audience; however, a monopolist, having attracted the mass audience in the first one or two channels, would operate additional channels to try to attract viewers to whom mass audience programs did not appeal. After observing that this philosophy is reflected in most foreign broadcast systems, with one or two entities operating all channels, Morrisett indicated why this model is not really relevant in the United States because Americans have dedicated themselves, in Learned Hand's immortal words, to the "marketplace of ideas"—that is, a reliance on free choice among many independent voices as the best means to provide information products to the public. The problem, then, for improving choice, diversity, and information content in American television is to expand opportunities for aggregating specialized national audiences, rather than heterogeneous, localized audiences, by increasing the number of independent choices available to a viewer.

Finally, Morrisett discussed the implications of financing television by advertising. The system is not all bad, because advertiser-supported television outlets are quite adept at providing mass entertainment that viewers find very attractive. The problem is that some types of viewers are uninteresting to advertisers. Morrisett explained why advertiser-supported television was especially unsuited to serve children. Children can be an attractive target for advertising, but light entertainment as a means of attracting their attention is far more problematic than it is with adults. The first priority for children is their emotional and intellectual development. While educating them can be more effective when the material is presented in an entertaining way, the purpose of children's programming should be its educational value, not simply its ability to produce consumers of cereal, candy, and toys.

Morrisett's description of the future of cable television is a magnificent example of policy analysis that is firmly rooted in knowledge about the industry, including its basic economics. After observing that cable television will require enormous investments and at least a decade to begin to supplant over-the-air broadcasting, his essay addressed the key issues: how is the industry likely to develop, and what can policy do to encourage the most beneficial form of development? Morrisett formulated the key issue as posing two questions: for citizens, "What's in it for me," and for the social critic, "Is it any good?"

The answer to "What's in it for me?" is implied by the Steiner model. More options means more choice among more diverse offerings, some of which may appeal to an individual's more specialized tastes than the mass audience fare. Applied to cable, the implication is that once cable gains a large enough foothold among the population, companies will begin to provide programs exclusively for cable distribution, most likely financed primarily by national advertising. Thus, in expanding viewer choice, cable will evolve from importing distant broadcasting stations to delivering completely new source of programs.

As to "Is it any good?" Morrisett saw more uncertainty. One problem is that multiple channels fragment the audience and therefore generate less advertising revenue per viewer. Lower revenues are likely to lead to lower investments in program quality. Morrisett singled out news programs as especially vulnerable; and in 1971, he presciently forecast the rise of CNN and its followers, stating: "In the long run this problem should be overcome by the growth of specialized news services over cable television, perhaps in the form of all news channels."

Another problem is that channel growth may not be as extensive as society would find most beneficial. Cable systems are likely to be successful once they offer a few more options than over-the-air broadcasting, and so might not have a financial incentive to offer as much choice as the market could support. Moreover, it may not be attractive to advertisers to serve some specialized audiences (owing to either their small numbers or their low purchasing power) with commercial programming. To solve these problems, Morrisett proposed regulatory changes to ensure adequate cable capacity, access to cable systems by program sources, and a broader base of financial support for cable programming, including pay-TV (viewer payments for access to programs that can not be financed by advertising), paid access, and subsidies for producing and distributing certain types of programs that may be socially desirable but commercially unsustainable. Morrisett focused on how new forms of revenue can expand choice through private, commercial ventures. Access to the possibility of subscriber fees frees program producers from having to rely exclusively on advertisers, and thereby increases the financial viability of programs that appeal to smaller audiences with an intense taste for a particular type of program, thus increasing choice and diversity. Here Morrisett predicted that cable TV pricing would evolve toward a per channel subscription fee, or a single payment for an additional bundle of channels that provides several services.

Paid access is another way to deliver programs to consumers that has emerged in the modern cable business. Paid access refers to a circumstance in which someone who wants to obtain access to consumers pays for the right to use the cable channel. Normally we think of payments going the other way: broadcasters pay program sources for programs, and then either sell advertising in and around the program, or sell pro-

gram access to viewers. Paid access reverses this payment flow, with
program producers paying broadcasters for the right to deliver their
message to viewers. Contemporary examples include the Home Shopping
Network and "infomercials" in which advertising is built directly into a
program. Morrisett correctly predicted that this source of revenues for
cable television would likely be smaller than advertising and fees from
viewers, but he argued that, nevertheless, it should be permitted to expand the range of program choice.

Morrisett described how with minor enhancements cable television
could be made into a two-way communications system, allowing viewers
to pick programs in real time, or to respond to inquiries from the programmer. This development makes feasible the convergence of communications media. Two-way communications over a video delivery system
permits interactive television programs, thereby terminating the complete
passivity of the medium that so many social critics find threatening.
Among the other potential uses mentioned in the essay are in education
and politics, both of which eventually received high priority in the foundation's programs in the 1980s.

In analyzing public television, Morrisett applied with clarity the same
arguments that he used to forecast the future of cable. After summarizing
alternative visions of public television, he made two key points. First,
public television can not expect to command an audience comparable to
that of a national commercial network unless it provides essentially similar programming: light entertainment appealing to a broad spectrum of
tastes. Second, it is far from obvious why the government should support
public television of this form, rather than hand over the public network
to a commercial operator. National subsidized mass entertainment is
against U.S. traditions and policy regarding the proper role of government, and in any case it is susceptible to political interference that would
detract from its quality.

If a mass audience public system (like those in Europe) is ruled out,
what, then, is the role for American public television? The answer is to
find and serve special audiences that are overlooked by the mass entertainment orientation of commercial television, which in turn is derived
from FCC policies to promote local television stations at the expense of
giving viewers access to a greater number of independently programmed
outlets. Morrisett began his prescription by advocating the abandonment
of local service in public broadcasting. Instead, he proposed that public
television find specialized but national audiences that are not served

by a commercial system built on few (three) networks and many local affiliates.

To implement this recommendation, Morrisett proposed specifying a target audience and a purpose (entertainment, education, information), and developing program ideas to match these goals. To implement this plan requires two activities. The first is to find a mechanism for determining what viewers want that is not now being provided. Morrisett proposed detailed surveys of audience desires and an audience rating system that would enable public television to assess its ratings within the target audience. The second activity is to make a value judgment about which of the candidates that emerge from this process ought to be selected, based on technical feasibility and the inevitable necessity to allocate scarce resources among competing uses.

Perhaps the most remarkable (and at the time controversial) part of Morrisett's analysis of public television is his analysis of the importance of incentives in improving public television. Morrisett advocated abandonment of cost-reimbursement contracting for public television programs, instead proposing rewards to producers that are based on their success in reaching their target audience. He focused on how more specialized audience ratings might be used to pay bonuses to especially effective program producers. His line of reasoning, however, also applies to the financial mechanism for public television that emerged in 1973 through the PBS "station program cooperative." In this system, producers proposed programs at a price (not necessarily equal to cost), and public television stations, through a computerized polling system, responded by voting for the programs that they wanted at that price. Meanwhile, stations, in seeking private donations, began to organize periodic "pledge week" campaigns around the theme of viewers contributing annual dues to support particular programs, thereby connecting viewer tastes through contributions to the PBS program selection process. This approach simultaneously implemented two of Morrisett's recommendations: First, the creation of incentives for producers and stations to supply the programs that viewers want, and second, the implemention of a means for measuring the intensity of viewer demands for programming that differs from the eyeball counts that motivate advertiser support.

The analysis of television in these three essays stands as an exceptionally clear example of why policy research is important. Morrisett applied simple but nonobvious economic analysis to new developments in the industry and made reliable predictions about how it would evolve, and to explain why the policy emphasis should be on facilitating choice, including allowing anyone—program supplier or viewer as well as advertiser—to help pay for new services. The policy implications, with powerful arguments against the policies in place in 1971, are carefully drawn out, including by implication a persuasive case for how government can shape the incentives of public, nonprofit, and for-profit entities in socially desirable ways.

The Multimedia Future

In 1994 Morrisett turned to the convergence of computers and television in multimedia. The theme of his essay that year is that the convergence of computers and television will reinvigorate print communications—the use of words and numbers as opposed to visual images. Electronic publication and storage of printed material is already cheaper than hard copy publication. High definition TV makes electronically produced text as easy to read as hard copy. And the use of computer search routines is vastly superior to an index and table of contents as a means for locating specific parts of a text. Electronic technology allows annotation without defacing or damaging the original material. Annotations can be inserted into a copy of the text, in a way that makes visual access to them optional.

The reemergence of printed text also is facilitated by the growth of electronic communication. On-line computer services companies have found that e-mail and computer bulletin boards devoted to specialized topics are in extremely high demand. Even the Imagination Network, designed for interactive video games, provides extremely popular chat rooms where its customers compare notes about the games.

The multimedia producer also can make use of the informational advantages of print—its ability to convey a great deal of information with minimal use of time and space. Multimedia products make use of all communications media, including electronic transmission and storage. This enables a consumer to combine a mass-produced product (like a television program) with other private files to create an individualized product. Television networks have recently begun to use digital technology to insert scores and other information into the picture of a game. High definition television can enable viewers to have access to the vast array of player and team statistics that so enrapture the true sports fan, even allowing the viewer to create a private insert from this database pertaining to the action at hand. While one viewer calls up the batter's success in hitting against the pitcher (or all left-handed pitchers or in the same ballpark), another viewer can inquire about the success of the player on first base in stealing second against the same pitcher or team, or in the same ballpark.

Morrisett's 1995 essay takes one more step forward in analyzing the future of multimedia. The foundation for this essay is the passivity of most previous mass communications media. Whether reading, listening, or viewing, the act of consuming information from mass media does not invite deliberation. Moreover, it gives the content producer control of the agenda. Whereas many see agenda control as leading to ideological bias, in practice competition among many sources of content enables the consumer to pick and choose among this source of bias, or to select sources that seek to maximize objectivity. Another type of agenda control may be far more important: the selection of the order in which information is presented and questions are answered. Indeed, some information may never appear in media content because the creator just never thought of it.

The mass communications media that are not passive and subject to unilateral agenda control are those that are used in personal communication, like the telephone and the postal service. These two-way media are democratic in that each party is equally empowered to raise a new issue. The main liability of these media relate to their relationship to time. Mail is slow, which facilitates reasoned, deliberative communication but is subject to long interruptions. Telephone conversations are immediate, thereby facilitating experimentation with new topics that can be abandoned quickly, but they do not promote deliberation. Telephone technology, by not easily accommodating silence or lengthy, detailed communication, demands continuous conversation in the form of brief statements.

Morrisett argues that our initial experiences with multimedia conversation, through e-mail and chat rooms, holds forth the promise that we can capture the best attributes of all the mass media in the new converged technology. Multimedia communication is instantaneous when we want it to be but accommodates pauses and long discourse. It converts the extremes of agenda control and pure democracy into a continuum that the user controls. One can construct a multimedia environment that is as passive or interactive as one wants, depending on the purpose of the communication and the preferences of the user. Chat rooms illustrate an intermediate point on this continuum. Participants can offer opinions, ask questions, or just read what others have to say on the same topic.

Morrisett observes two significant features of these developments. One is that they encourage the honing of analytical and deliberative problem-solving skills, and so increase individual competence at independent reasoning and informed choice. The second is that they enhance freedom, partly by expanding the range of choice and partly by improving our ability to be effective citizens and to make collective decisions about governance and policy. His first-step policy proposal is universal e-mail, implemented through the provision of an inexpensive computer and modem, plus supporting software to provide access to a simple computer service. After summarizing the rather modest cost of such a proposal, he concludes that it is economically feasible for these reasons: it can reduce other costs (such as hard copy mail delivery); others may be willing to pay for it; and if it is offered as a new service with a monthly billing charge (freeing the consumer of the necessity to buy a computer), its price can be substantially less than the monthly cost of cable or phone service.

Morrisett's arguments about why new technologies are favoring printed communications over video, how multimedia communications are likely to develop, and what government can do to facilitate the process, are based on a firm technical knowledge of the new media combined with an understanding of their economics. We do not know whether the forecasts in these essays will prove accurate, but they represent a distillation of the best information that is currently available in a highly imaginative but sound prognostication.

Implementing the Vision: Thirty Years of Grants Policies

Against this background of communications policy and the commentaries of the president, the programs of the foundation, primarily its grants practices, can better be understood. The formal program statement for Markle's new venture first appeared in the foundation's fiscal 1970 annual report: "The goal of the current program is to strengthen educational uses of the mass media and communications technology." The section of the report that more fully described the foundation's activities also emphasized education, and the first year's appropriations mostly reflected this focus. Grants were made for studying the needs for professional education in journalism, undertaking research on television and children, training young film makers, supporting an internship program on urban affairs for journalists, and, of course, supporting the Children's Television Workshop, creators of *Sesame Street*, in undertaking a research project to develop a greater understanding of how CTW could most effectively reach inner city children.

Two important first-year grants demonstrated Morrisett's commitment to better communications policy research. A small grant initiated the foundation's long tradition of supporting research on the effects of mass media on attitudes and behavior. A much larger package of two grants, one for general support and the other to study cable television, established the communications policy research program at the Rand Corporation. These awards enabled Rand to commission work on telecommunications issues by a long list of strong scholars, such as Stanley Besen, Leland Johnson, Bridger Mitchell, Richard Posner, and Rolla Edward Park. In explaining these grants, which amounted to more than a quarter of the foundation's new commitments that year, the annual report accurately describes the agenda of the first significant comprehensive research program on the economics of communications policy as focusing on communications regulation. To connect the grants to the foundation's mission statement, the report states that "as the program develops," its researchers "hope to examine new and expanded uses of communications technology in education and instruction" as well as in attacking other social problems. (This hope was not forlorn, as within a few years Rand scholars produced several studies in this area; however, the major contribution of the Rand program has been on the economics of broadcasting and telecommunications policy.)

The main motivation for the Rand grant was derived from the 1968 report of the President's Task Force on Communications Policy, named the Rostow Report after the task force chair, State Department Undersecretary Eugene Rostow. This report received little immediate attention in the media or in formal Washington, but it contained a prophetic message. The Rostow Report tentatively and cautiously endorsed using new technologies to introduce more competition and diversity in communications, and it urged the creation of what became the White House Office of Telecommunications Policy to provide independent advice to the president about policy issues facing regulators, antitrust officials, and operating agencies in the communications arena.

Good policymaking in a technical area like communications depends on good information and analysis, as the 1970 Markle annual report recognized. True, the Carnegie, Ford, and Sloan foundations were supporting a small amount of policy research in this area, most notably the grants from Ford and Sloan to the Brookings Institution to initiate its Studies in the Regulation of Economic Activity. And, by the summer of 1970, a few important studies had emerged from scholars at several universities, including MIT, Michigan, Stanford, and Yale. Still, the Markle grant to Rand represented an enormous increment to research on communications regulation and substantially expanded the information base for making communications policy. Given the size of the emerging need for public initiatives, it was not too far from the mark to suggest, as the 1970 Report did, that "policy making on every level is . . . hampered by the lack of systematic, objective, and independent studies of policy alternatives and their implications."

By the second year of the new Markle program, projects dealing with mass media and communications policy, rather than specifically with education and children, accounted for most new financial commitments. Only one grant dealt specifically with children, although it was a very important one: $171,200 of general support for Action for Children's Television. With one or two exceptions, all of the other new projects were either for studying the mass media or some aspect of communications policy, developing new programs for public television, or promoting broader participation in the industry and the communications policy process.

Telecommunications and new directions in the use of technology emerged as well in the second year program. The foundation made a major grant to the Mitre Corporation to develop the use of two-way communications in cable television. The focus of Mitre's work was on making cable a broadband telecommunications service. In the next few years, additional work in telecommunications received support through grants to establish the Harvard Program on Information Technologies and Public Policy, the MIT Communications Research Program, and the University of California, Berkeley, program on communications for the elderly. All of these programs included studies of both mass media and telecommunications.

The focus of the Berkeley program on the elderly also was an element of still another revision in the foundation's focus. The initial orientation toward children was soon perceived as exemplifying a broader opportunity: to extend the reach of the communications revolution to improve the lives of all specialized groups that might be ignored by business and government. The elderly were one such group; women and minorities were others.

In the first two years of the new program, Markle had found its niche: an area of policy research, policymaking, and product development where a small foundation could have a major effect. Three major themes had been established. The first was to develop a large community of high-quality scholars who would study the mass media and communications policy. The second was to support broader public participation in the industry and its policymaking processes, partly by supporting public interest organizations, partly by helping the industry to develop professional watchdog groups, and partly by assisting women and minorities in career enhancement. The third was to support the development of new products, with an emphasis on special groups like children, the elderly, minorities, and women. Initially, the program emphasized education and television, but eventually its focus broadened, and by the 1990s had become almost totally redirected to educational and public service applications of computer software, including Internet services.

Adapting to Change

Once a niche has been found, the task of finding a useful role does not end. One problem is that early success may bring copy-cats with fatter wallets. An example is CTW. The first year of *Sesame Street*, 1968–69, was financed by grants from the Carnegie and Ford foundations, plus additional support from the newly created Corporation for Public Broadcasting. Markle chipped in a year later with support for evaluating CTW programs. History should record in bold type that without support from Carnegie, Ford, and Markle, Big Bird, Ernie, Kermit, Miss Piggy, and Oscar the Grouch may not have become the enduring stars that they are. But very quickly the world recognized that CTW was on to something. Viewers, corporate sponsors, and the public television network were all willing to help pay for CTW programs, and CTW successfully marketed offshoot children's products, with the profits plowed back into more children's programming. A small operation like Markle was destined to become a drop in the Muppet bucket, so other overlooked niches offered greater opportunities. The key to continued success was to be flexible and responsive to change, to recognize that success required redirecting resources within the set of issues identified as important. The genius of finding the right field must be followed by the continuing genius of knowing when to quit and recognizing promising new opportunities. Markle's history through the 1970s, 1980s, and 1990s shows that it possessed the second genius as well as the first.

One self-policing mechanism used by Morrisett was to issue a program statement as a means of informing the field and to match grant priorities to articulated vision. For example, beginning in fiscal 1977, the program section of the annual report contained a quite specific list of topics of interest to the foundation. "In its efforts to improve the mass media," the statement said, "the Foundation supports projects that expand research on the role of mass communications in society; analyze public policy issues and questions of public interest; improve the performance of professionals involved in the mass communications industry; develop better media services to specialized groups (for instance, children, the elderly, minorities); explore the relationship between the media and politics; and enrich the quality of print and electronic journalism." What was emphasized were those issues identified in the presidential essays: the need for better policy research to understand the relationship between communications and society, efforts to intervene where the market failed, for some reason or another, and increasing the capacity of professionals to use the new technology in ways that served the public interest.

A Pause in Telecommunications Policy Research Support

Despite Morrisett's commitment to research, for several years Markle deemphasized research in telecommunications policy. In fiscal 1976, the foundation made grants to MIT and Rand that continued the work at these institutions on telephone regulation, but no new telecommunications projects were initiated. In fiscal 1977, all of the new appropriations were aimed exclusively at mass media. Institutional support for MIT continued, but with an exclusive focus on television. The Rand program was dropped when its multiyear grant ended in 1977. Harvard's program was dropped when its multiyear grant ran out in 1979. The timing of the withdrawal from telecommunications requires some scrutiny. Telecommunications policy hardly had become a dead letter. The Department of Justice had filed another antitrust complaint against AT&T. Congress was actively considering mooting the antitrust case by passing legislation that would more clearly define the role of regulation and the boundary between monopoly and competition. New telephone switches were computers that were capable of data processing as well as telephone functions, so the FCC revisited its earlier decision about separating computer services and telecommunications. Cable television was booming and was experimenting with telecommunications services. Surely the importance and utility of objective, independent research had not diminished.

Nevertheless, other changes had occurred. The government had institutionalized policy research in telecommunications by establishing the National Telecommunications and Information Agency in the Department of Commerce and the Office of Plans and Policy at the FCC. The National Science Foundation had moved extensively into supporting policy-oriented research by creating such programs as Research Applied to National Needs, the Program on Regulatory Policy, and the Program on Information and Society. Scholars could now receive grants from NSF to study telecommunications policy. Hence, in the mid-1970s, Markle may have faced something like the old *Sesame Street* problem: the success of its earlier grants drew the attention of the 800-pound gorilla, threatening to convert the foundation from the leading role to a bit player.

In any case, the election of Ronald Reagan quickly led to massive reductions in policy-oriented research throughout the government, especially at the National Science Foundation. The NSF program on information studies survived, but it was smaller, more narrowly focused, and more purely academic. The other policy programs at NSF died. The vacuum, if it had been filled before, was certainly reestablished.

Telecommunications projects returned to Markle in fiscal 1981, when the foundation established a telecommunications policy research program at Duke University's Washington Center. This grant initiated a long, happy relationship between the foundation and Henry Geller, who had been the FCC's general counsel in the Nixon administration and the assistant secretary of commerce and director of NTIA in the Carter administration. When the Reagan revolution arrived at NTIA, Markle provided an institutional home for Geller. In 1982 a small grant of $37,000 to the Harvard program was given substantial attention in the annual report, signaling sustained interest despite little new spending. Then, in 1983, the foundation supported work on the divestiture of AT&T, the use of telecommunications to increase political participation, the possibility of teleconferencing, and how telecommunications and computer developments should affect job preparation by the educational system. In 1987 a telecommunications research and education program was established at Stanford, and in 1989 the old Rand program was again given substantial support. Telecommunications was back.

Program-Related Investments

Another significant policy change, which occurred in 1982, also illustrates the Morrisett philosophy. Without elaboration in the body of the report, the notes to the financial statement disclose a foundation "program-related investment" of $300,000 (to be increased by a further $66,625) in Family Radio Programming, a company that intended to develop and distribute programs for young people and their families. Here was an intervention by the foundation, using an innovative technique, to try to meet goals identified in the president's essays and in the program statement. The foundation, by acting through program-related investments rather than grants, would become a venture capitalist, providing not only financial but managerial assistance that sought to help build an enterprise. Program-related investments by nonprofit institutions are not well understood. The issues raised by critics include whether the public interest can be advanced by investment in a company that seeks to maximize its profit, regardless of how interesting the product, and whether using investments to influence private market developments is a legitimate activity for a nonprofit institution. But the proper response may be found in the Morrisett vision as articulated in the annual report essays and in the variety of ways to come closer to achieving the foundation's goals.

Private companies have financial and informational assets that a public interest organization can find useful. From the beginning Markle has sought to develop new information products, starting with *Sesame Street*. In some cases, a private organization will have intellectual property rights that are extremely useful for purposes that fill the foundation's mission and may have skills in developing and marketing products in formats that are especially attractive to users. In addition, a product that might be very useful for a target constituency of a foundation may fall just short of having expected profits high enough for a private firm to want to develop it. In all of these cases, program-related investments represent a way to combine the special talents of a private company with the financial resources and special objectives of a foundation. The program-related investment can be a foundation's least expensive way to obtain its objectives.

In some cases, projects that foundations support have been highly successful financially to the people involved. *Sesame Street* is certainly one example. In the admittedly unusual case where the resulting product is highly profitable, a program-related investment enables the original sponsor to reap some of the financial rewards, which then can be used for still more expenditures in pursuit of its public interest goals.

For these reasons, program-related investments should not be ruled out in principle as a useful pursuit by a foundation. Nevertheless, program-related investments have an important down side: foundation officials may not be very adept at evaluating the financial prospects of an investment. In essence, a foundation that makes a program-related investment is operating as if it were a venture capital firm, and it may not be very effective in this role. This problem is not so much an argument against these investments as it is a caution in how they should be treated in the budget process.

Treating program-related investments as just another part of a portfolio is a clear mistake, because they are less likely than standard investments to retain their value and to earn a return. Yet treating them as annual grants may be too pessimistic, because, unlike a grant, they have some prospect for retaining value and earning returns. Markle's formal policy in this regard is not explicitly stated; however, notes to the financial statements indicate that its program-related investments are treated in the second, more conservative manner.

In 1985 Markle made its second program-related investment. The foundation invested $560,000 in Television Audience Assessment, Inc., a start-up company that sought to develop technology for measuring the response of audiences to television programs. The focus was on measuring reactions and attitudes, not just whether the set was on or the viewer was watching. Better audience measurements had been identified by Morrisett as an important element of improved decisionmaking. In 1986 the foundation invested another $500,000 in the effort.

Venture capitalism has its harsh realities. In 1987 Family Radio Programming and Television Audience Assessment both failed. The foundation lost all but $32,302 of its $1.4 million investment in these companies. Nonetheless, in the 1990s, the foundation continued its experiment with program-related investments. These projects reflect Markle's strong commitment to enhancing multimedia technology and the social uses of electronic publishing. The most important investments were $272,000 in Voyager Company in 1989 for the development of optical technology with potential software applications; $1,068,100 in MultiMedia Corporation in 1990 for the development of multimedia software; $750,000 in Infonautics Corporation in 1994 to develop a new on-line educational software system, *Homework Helper*; and $756,800 in Night Kitchen, LLC in 1997. The MultiMedia investment was soon written off, but the others remain active. From a programmatic perspective, the most successful to date has been Infonautics. In 1995 *Homework Helper* was made available on the *Prodigy* on-line service system and was rather extensively used.

The 1997 financial statement reports revenues of $2,977,055 from the sale of a program-related investment that had previously been written off. This windfall substantially alters the overall picture concerning the Markle investment program. Had the foundation's earlier $1.4 million loss been invested in a standard portfolio, it would have approximately tripled in value by 1997, to about $4 million. The more recent investments have a present value in 1997 of about $3 million, for an amount of program-related investment totaling $7 million in 1997 dollars. Thus, taking account of the 1997 windfall, the foundation has a net investment of about $4 million. The foundation's annual budget equals about 4 percent of its net asset value, so the implicit cost of these investments is equivalent to annual grant expenditures of $160,000.

Six investments hardly establish a reliable estimate of the annualized financial cost of program-related investments; however, at the end of fifteen years, this figure represents a rough estimate of the annual amount by which program-related investments have, at the moment, crowded out other expenditures. In an $8 million annual budget, the implicit cost of these investments is hardly extreme.

Further Broadening: Politics and Democracy in the Computer Age

In the annual reports after 1986, the expression of program interests provides for renewed interest in telecommunications and a broader, more sophisticated interest in computers. For example, the annual report covering fiscal 1986 and 1987 neatly summarizes the programmatic implications of the goals now set forth in the president's essay: The foundation, the report announced, should focus on "the potential for communications and information technologies to enhance political participation; the benefits of communications and technologies for an aging population; an analysis of public policy issues in communications; the educational and entertainment use and value of computer software on the home; and developments in electronic publishing." The notable fea ture of the statements in this period is that children and education have almost disappeared from the foundation's focus. In the annual report covering fiscal 1984 and 1985, less than 10 percent of the foundation's new commitments dealt with public education or media effects on children, and by fiscal 1987, no new grants were made in these areas. In fiscal 1987, nearly 20 percent of the foundation's new commitments were for projects directed at senior citizens. In prior years, the relationship between communications and the elderly had been a minor part of the foundation's activities.

More than 20 percent of the budget in 1987 was allocated to another item: the role of the media and information technology in politics, and especially the feasibility of using electronic technology in voting. The relationship between media and politics had received substantial support for a long while, but the combined 1984 and 1985 reports reflect an expanded interest that also includes telecommunications and computers. In fiscal 1982, the inventory of the foundation's grants on politics reveals almost exclusive attention to the coverage of public issues in the mass media and the role of presidential debates. The sole exception was an inexpensive conference on "The Communications Revolution and the Transformation of Politics." The next year, the foundation made four grants totaling over $350,000 (about 10 percent of the budget) to study the effects and uses of new communications technologies in politics. This theme has remained an important part of the foundation's program to the present.[1]

The 1989 annual report contains a new paragraph that remained with few alterations through 1995. This paragraph clearly articulates the theme of convergence and choice that we have used as the organizing principle of this essay. "The convergence of the media has transformed communications and our ability to manipulate, store, and gain access to information and knowledge. As new services become widely available, they are changing the ways in which we live and work, and altering our perceptions, beliefs, and institutions. It is essential that we understand these effects in order to develop our electronic resources for the benefit of society." The next year, the paragraph was tightened and focused, and the revised version survived unchanged through 1995. The phrase "and knowledge" was dropped from the first sentence, no doubt because it was redundant. In the next sentence, "technologies" replaced services, emphasizing the importance of technological progress in driving service innovations. The last sentence lost its passivity and reasserted the issue of potentially overlooked groups. "We need to understand these effects in order to exploit our electronic resources for the benefit of the many and diverse sectors of society." Some might interpret the new ending to the last sentence as giving excessive attention to using mass communications to protect differences that do not deserve preservation; however, another implication is that technological progress is more valuable if it offers more choice. Diverse sectors need not be warring tribes; they can be people with different tastes, students who learn in different ways, or even alternative ways to package information and entertainment that a single person might flit among, seeking personal diversity in acquiring knowledge or being entertained. In either reading of the meaning of diversity, the crucial element is choice.

The 1990 annual report makes a few minor changes in the statement of areas of program interest. The "emerging" role of information technology in the lives of older people is changed to the "expanding" role. The phrase "electronic publishing" is now "multimedia and electronic publishing," and the phrase about educational and entertainment software has been dropped. Most important, the last phrase abandons "communications policy" for "telecommunications policy." The last three changes reflect convergence. By 1990 visionaries in the field realized that the different mass communication media all can be delivered by telecommunications networks.

This feature of convergence has two implications. The first is that the mass media should be considered as variations of one thing—arriving by wire, cable, air, or printed page. The second is that to optimize the development of the mass media in the new technological age, society must adopt sensible policies governing the main delivery system, which is an electronic network. Regulation of the delivery system has elevated importance because it is no longer just about stopping a monopoly from charging too much for telephone service and cable television. In addition, it is about ensuring that these backbone systems are neither too simple nor too elaborate, and that new ideas about how to use them are given a chance to fail on the merits, rather than because some company or regulator fears them or just does not understand them.

The combined reports for 1991 and 1992 make one further change, which is to add "for home learning and entertainment" to modify multimedia and electronic publishing. Again, this change corrects erroneous inferences that might have been drawn from the simplification of the previous year: that the foundation had lost interest in education or had shifted the focus on education and entertainment in the home to include the school or office. This message correction was short-lived. In the combined 1993 and 1994 report, the reference to the home disappears for good.

The technological bullet train makes its presence felt again in the report for 1993 and 1994. Multimedia is now too narrow, so the relevant phrase in the statement of program interest is rephrased: "the developing role of interactive communications technology, including advances in multimedia and electronic publishing." In the 1996–97 report, the last under Morrisett's leadership, "computer networks" are added to the list. The technological convergence that holds out the possibility of merging the media also can facilitate education and entertainment that is not passive. Traditional education is largely passive: one reads texts, listens to lectures, and otherwise allows information and analytic methods to be poured into one's head. Also, except for pinball machines and video games, entertainment is mostly passive: reading a novel, watching TV, a play on the stage, or a movie screen, or listening to the radio or a recording. Technology convergence brings the possibility of "telephone entertainment" in which the relationship between user and producer is bilateral, like a telephone call.

Maybe students and consumers mostly will prefer passive reception of information. If so, converged communications will probably arrive in an evolutionary way—more snazzy and exciting versions of pretty much the same old stuff, in which case existing institutions probably will do a good job developing them. But maybe interactivity will make entertainment more enjoyable and education more effective, in which case converged technology may be more radical. If so, an important lesson from economic history is that radical technological innovations rarely come from those who perfected the technologies that were replaced. Apple and Microsoft, not IBM, developed the user-friendly operating system that caused computers to become a mass consumer good rather than a tool reserved for a technical elite. Risk-taking private philanthropy is far more likely to have a useful role under the second scenario than the first.

The last budget of the Morrisett era, published in the 1996–97 report, contains old friends and new arrivals. In the former category, the Aspen Institute Program on Communications and Policy, the longest continuing beneficiary of the grant program, received $175,000. Other old friends that continue to be supported are Columbia, Duke, MIT, Rand, the Telecommunications Policy Research Conference, and UCLA. Carnegie-Mellon, where research on learning through electronic technologies has been supported for more than a decade, remains on the list, as does Stanford University, which received support in the 1970s to study media effects on children and since 1987 to study telecommunications policy. Some newer grantees are Boston University, the Brookings Institution, the California Institute of Technology, Northwestern University, the University of Massachusetts, and a host of organizations that are developing interactive software. The mix of expenditures reveals the same pattern as before: diversity, continuity, and change, all within the original niche. The program continues to reflect sensitivity to convergence and dedication to choice.

By 1997, on its website, Markle could organize and display its program areas and recent projects in a manner that used new technology to force an articulation of long-gestating themes of foundation activity. In the area of Media and Political Participation, there were experiments in deliberative democracy, including on-line policy simulations. There was also applied research on such subjects as political advertising and voter motivation, and the presentation of political news. Similarly, the theme of Interactive Communications Technologies included not only the program related investment experiments in game development, but also interactive storytelling and the development of educational products. Communications policy included a wide array of efforts to explore the potential for universal e-mail and its consequences and a raft of targeted policy projects. These included a sustained effort at MIT to explore media in transition, a new program on comparative media law and policy at Oxford, continued support of the Aspen Institute's Media and Society Communications Seminars, sustained research at Stanford's Center for Economic Policy Research, research at Duke on communications policy in the former Soviet Union, and research at the Universities of Kansas and Massachussetts on the long-term effects of childhood television viewing.

Conclusion

Revolutions are threatening, but they offer dramatic new possibilities. Technological progress creates especially exciting revolutions because, while it may cost some their fortunes, it rarely leaves many dead bodies and always expands human capabilities. The revolution examined in this book is enduring. Information technology is the dominant economic force of the last half of the twentieth century, and promises to continue this role far into the twenty-first. The revolution would have been profound had each communications industry been confined to its own turf, with innovation simply allowing them to do what they do better and cheaper. Cable television, the personal computer, and virtually costless long distance telephone connections by themselves have changed our work place productivity and personal lives immensely. But the gods of technological change have not stopped there. In addition, modern technology has brought us to the threshold of picking and choosing among the methods of mass and personal communications, mixing them in whatever manner appeals to us.

We do not know whether society will decide to exercise this choice, although in the information sector no new capability has yet gone unexploited for very long. We also do not know fully the implications of this choice after it is exercised. The role of scholars and innovators in communications is to try to answer these questions. Fortunately, for three decades the Markle Foundation has facilitated this search for answers. We believe that the history of this small but influential foundation sheds a great deal of light on how and why philanthropy can make a significant difference in exploring the implications of new technologies and the policy issues that they bring with them. We also hope that this book lays out the possibilities for the future as well as the Markle presidential essays have done in the past.

Note

1. The wording of the description of program interests has evolved through the years in a fascinating way that reflects underlying changes in technology. In 1988 the changes seek more precise explanation, rather than some more cosmic programmatic purpose. "Facilitate" replaces "encourage" as a modifier of political participation, "for the home" modifies the interest in educational and entertainment software, and "public" replaces "nation's" to define the interest at stake in policy. Only the return of "in the home" is significant in that it again signals lesser interest in public education inside the school.

Part One

Media and Democracy

CHAPTER TWO

Manufacturing Discord: Media in the Affirmative Action Debate

Robert M. Entman

D URING 1995, as periodically in the past two decades, affirmative
action became a leading policy controversy. Judging by much of the
media coverage, in fact, the issue sparked a popular uprising, an intense
outcry of opposition from white Americans based on their perceptions
of the policy's injustices and failures.[1] *Newsweek* ran a cover showing a
black fist and white fist pushing against each other under the headline
"Race and Rage," and in another issue proclaimed that affirmative action
"could dominate the 1996 election year." On NBC *Nightly News* (July
19, 1995), Tom Brokaw said, "Affirmative action: two words that can
start an argument just about anywhere in America. . . . We'll be hearing
a lot more about this in the months leading to the 1996 election." Such
depictions of intense racial conflict framed the media's construction of
public opinion and policy substance on affirmative action. This chapter
explores the affirmative action debate in the news and its implications
for race relations and media theory.

News frames are composed of the themes that are selected, highlighted, and reinforced through repeated prominent display, vivid illus-
tration, and emotion-arousing vocabulary.[2] The framing messages, as
revealed especially by qualitative textual analysis, emphasized that affirmative action arouses profoundly negative emotions among whites,
who suffer grievous losses under the policy—feelings met by equally

A condensed version of this chapter appears in the *Harvard International Journal of
Press/Politics*, vol. 2 (1997). The research reported here was supported by grants from the
Markle Foundation and the Chicago Human Relations Foundation. I thank Andrew
Rojecki for insightful comments.

strong reactions from blacks, who gain at white expense. The conflict frame doubly misleads. First, it does not describe the actual state of public opinion, insofar as journalists, politicians, and the rest of us can know it through the imperfect mechanism of sample surveys. Second, it misrepresents the conflict of interest created by affirmative action policies, which does not exist exclusively or even mainly between whites and African Americans, and which may not exist at all if viewed from a long-term, comprehensive perspective. Making these two points does not imply an unqualified endorsement of affirmative action. Specific implementations have exhibited serious shortcomings, and some have imposed unfair losses on individual whites. This chapter is an attempt to assess the media's version of affirmative action; it is not an *apologia* for all programs categorized under the affirmative action rubric.

The typical citizen does not carry around a firm, well-considered ideological philosophy that guides his or her specific positions. Rather, whites are typically ambivalent. Whites can go either way, depending on the context and the specific political stimuli in the environment. White Americans have a range of beliefs and feelings potentially relevant to affirmative action. They possess sentiments that can bolster support for affirmative action, and sentiments that can reinforce opposition.[3] Many white Americans cling to negative stereotypes and exhibit anxiety, resentment, and fear toward African Americans.[4] Yet data discussed below show that majorities also respond with considerable acceptance for the principle of affirmative action and for leaders who support it. This ambivalence and complexity are generally missing from media coverage.

To take just one example of a positive marker, in many polls during 1995 and 1996 white Americans expressed substantial support for a black man, Colin Powell, to become president. A *Time*/CNN poll in June 1995 asked respondents: "Do you have a favorable or unfavorable impression of the following people?" Colin Powell received the highest favorable rating (56 percent) and lowest unfavorable (10 percent) of any political figure named.[5] Another CNN poll asked how Powell's position on affirmative action ("he says he does not believe in quotas but supports continuing many affirmative action programs") would affect people's support for him; 37 percent said it would make them more likely to vote for him and 32 percent said it would make no difference; just 27 percent said less likely.[6] It is difficult to square these results with an insistence that whites are nothing but antiaffirmative action bigots. Rather, they are of two minds.

This is where "social capital," a concept of growing importance in political science and sociology, comes in.[7] Social capital refers to the level of trust and empathy in a society. The more social capital, the better able a society is to work out its problems; the more trustful communication and interaction, the more social capital grows, and the more effective and satisfied a society can be.[8] A widespread perception that people of other races are trustworthy and possess goodwill and understanding encourages white Americans to express their more positive sentiments. However, low social capital, marked by a general feeling among whites that they cannot trust or understand blacks (and vice versa), encourages a pinched, anxious, negative response—heightening the salience in this case of antiaffirmative action considerations. Such negative predilections exist alongside the positive ones, awaiting entrance into working memory and active expression, given the relevant stimuli.

Social capital requires a sense that group membership has limited rather than comprehensive significance. It embodies widespread feelings that boundaries between groups and individuals are blurry and permeable. Such a fluid perception of the social structure allows for subjective sharing, for empathy and trust across group lines. When all outgroup members seem to possess fundamentally different traits, it becomes difficult for ingroup members to trust and empathize with them. And that feeds a downward spiral: members of the outgroup recognize the dominant group's distrust and the media's signals of exclusion; the outgroup's own sense of trust and goodwill erodes, their suspicion and resentment mount. Such conditions make for hostile communication in public spaces—which further feeds each side's negative emotions.

Media influence on levels of social capital transcends the meaning of the words and images in the news. The deeper messages of the conflict-exaggerating, simplistic coverage of affirmative action told audiences that blacks and whites may hold fundamentally incompatible values and interests, sharing only a tenuous cultural bond. Although research shows considerable overlap in values held by both groups, media are replete with insistent reminders of fundamental *difference* between those categorized as black and white, bolstering the assumption that racial identity determines individuals' behavior and values.[9]

As the coverage of affirmative action reveals, all this can occur within news texts meeting conventional journalistic standards of balance and accuracy. Thus, beyond what it tells us about race relations, the social capital framework can provide new insight into the media's influence more generally. For example, scholars have frequently described the news media's predilection to seek out, simplify, and emphasize political conflict. Yet observers have thoroughly dissected the impact of this orientation only as it relates to election campaigns.[10] In summarizing white feelings as dominated by resentment and anger, in failing to note the nuances when they framed their narratives of racial conflict over affirmative action, journalists' highlighting of the negative obscured the positive side of the white public's complicated feelings. Standard operating procedures of the media may work to break down the positive cognitive and emotional elements needed to sustain social capital.

These procedures also shape the rest of the media's message; news of affirmative action did not appear in a vacuum. Research suggests local news reinforces anxiety-provoking negative stereotypes of blacks among whites, while both local and network news arouse hostility toward black political activity.[11] The news closely links poverty to African Americans without providing an understanding of the structural reasons that people become and remain poor.[12] Television advertising conveys images that suggest whites and blacks occupy profoundly different realms of values and experience.[13] Given the media's general tendency to lower interracial social capital, it is perhaps predictable that journalists would frame affirmative action as they did.

The news media were sampled by selecting via computer search all items that mentioned "affirmative action." These were then filtered to exclude items that offered only passing reference to the policy. Inclusion required that a majority of paragraphs discuss affirmative action. While quantitative content analytical data were generated, qualitative analysis of the text and visual images proved equally important for getting at the framing of news about affirmative action. The sampling process covered all items in *Newsweek* and *Time* on news events between January 1 and July 21; all stories shown on ABC's *World News* between January 1 and July 21; and a random sample of half the stories about affirmative action on the CBS and NBC evening news programs between the same dates.[14] The ending date of July 21 was selected because of two climactic events in the debate: a highly anticipated and highly publicized speech by President Clinton (July 19) announcing his new affirmative action policy, and the meetings of the University of California Regents (July 20–21) at which affirmative action in admissions and hiring was abolished.

Overall Slant and Themes of Affirmative Action News

The quantitative analysis coded every assertion in the newsmagazines and the network coverage that expressed an evaluation of affirmative action, a total of 278. (Details on the content analysis can be found in appendix A. Coding was performed by the author and a trained student, with average intercoder reliability at .89). The slant of the different media diverges substantially. Newsmagazines tilted against affirmative action, by a ratio of about 3:1, with *Time* slightly less negative than *Newsweek*. All three network news programs, however, came out at almost exactly a 1:1 ratio.

The content analysis also recorded 217 expressions of *reasons* for opposing or endorsing affirmative action in the magazines and network coverage. Taking the newsmagazines and TV coverage together, these balanced quite evenly between supportive and oppositional reasons, dividing into eight categories. The most common oppositional considerations were that affirmative action constitutes reverse discrimination (55 mentions, 25 percent of all reasons); and that it violates meritocratic values (25 mentions, 11.5 percent). In addition, there were eight claims that affirmative action stigmatizes intended beneficiaries (3.7 percent), nine that affirmative action programs are unworkable or absurd (4.1 percent), and 13 that affirmative action fails to achieve its objectives (6 percent). On the supportive front were 45 claims that discrimination remains a problem (21 percent); 42 that affirmative action achieves its important objectives (19 percent); and 21 that affirmative action helps the entire society, not just blacks, other minorities, or women (9.6 percent).

It might be argued that the media did a reasonably good job on this issue. While the newsmagazines energetically attacked affirmative action, the networks offered a balanced depiction. Looking only at the reasons, the coverage was almost equally distributed between pro- and antiaffirmative action considerations. The quantitative content analysis thus suggests that the information environment was rich enough to enable elites and the mass public to reason through the issue.

However, the quantitative counts do not clarify the framing, the dominant impressions promoted by the texts. Research suggests that merely counting the sheer number of times the media air a message can distort understanding of its likely effects. Not only frequency of repetition, but the vividness, recentness, and distinctiveness of images contained in the message all affect its impacts.[15] In ways subtle and overt, the media selected and highlighted with vivid and distinct verbal and visual messages the dominant theme of high-intensity conflict of interest between mutually antagonistic whites and African Americans. By so doing, they fortified two major misimpressions that could undermine social capital and rational deliberation.

Framing Opinion on Affirmative Action

In framing the story of affirmative action, journalists selectively emphasized manifestations of white public opinion that bolstered the dominant news theme, while neglecting contrary evidence. Coverage frequently referred to white opinion as a "tide of white anger" or "backlash," employing no data beyond anecdote and hunch. To be sure, "actual" public opinion toward something as vague and protean as affirmative action cannot easily be gauged. News texts, survey questions, and public discourse alike suffer from severe terminological imprecision. Discussion of affirmative action tended randomly to select, omit, and combine busing, racially motivated electoral districts, contract set asides, college recruiting, college admissions, government employment regulations, and private hiring and promotion programs. Given the uncertainty about what is meant by "affirmative action," poll questions can yield deceptive results. Survey data may convey the impression that the policy issue can be summarized simply, and that people have a clean, clear opinion toward it. Still, sample surveys offer mountains of evidence contradicting the media frame, information at least as valid as what reporters relied on.

Journalists, it seems, built their frame on claims by elite sources with an interest in promoting the impression of white arousal, filtered through the conflict norm that shapes story construction. In fact, journalists appeared to confuse *elite rhetoric* with the *average citizen's preferences* and *priorities*. It is clear that some of the most important political leaders who set the media agenda—especially presidential hopefuls—became more overtly hostile to affirmative action in 1995. It is far from clear that their views reflected the sentiments of ordinary white Americans.

A *Newsweek* column by Joe Klein on February 13, 1995, contained two of many media assertions that affirmative action had become an enormous political issue, a source of intense white emotion and opposition. *Newsweek* highlighted this view in large print: "A NEWSWEEK columnist says we may be hurtling toward the most sensitive point in race relations since the 1960s" is the article's subhead. A large-print caption accompanies the picture of University of California Regent Ward Connerly and his wife: "California's effort to end racial preference is just the first step—the issue could dominate the 1996 election year." Connerly, an African American, led the effort to rescind affirmative action at the university. Underneath the picture is a smaller-print quote: "I want to be judged by the quality of my work," implying that those covered by affirmative action programs are not. At the same time, the writer asserts (without empirical support) that emotions run high among blacks: "The reaction of the black community [to abolition of affirmative action] is likely to be cold fury, incendiary rhetoric—and a deep sense of despair." An equal opportunity pessimist, he continues "The response from white America is likely to be a disingenuous and slightly smarmy call for a 'colorblind society'." These predictions exaggerate the interracial gulf, depicting enmity in black-white relations without offering evidence that such sentiments dominate in either group.

Supporting the interpretation that the columnist conflates the opinions of average citizens and those of elites, in the two sentences about "reaction of the black community" and "response from white America," Klein actually referred to leadership elements, not the average individual (who does not speak in "rhetoric" or engage in "smarmy calls"). Equating elites' strategically chosen rhetorical positions with the mass public's opinions can lead journalists and their audiences, both mass and elite, to underestimate the zone of potential compromise.

Even if they are deeply flawed, sample surveys offer the only reliable data journalists or scholars have about general public sentiments toward policy issues. Mass sentiments as recorded in surveys are both more complex and more favorably inclined toward affirmative action than the public positions staked out by most political leaders. By neglecting to depict whites' stands carefully—by highlighting those dimensions that propel conflict and downplaying those that promise conciliation—media coverage may exacerbate interracial tension and misunderstanding, thereby diminishing social capital. This would be especially likely if depictions of other issues with implications for black-white relations also rely heavily upon elites and emphasize conflict (which is true in at least one other instance, that of black-Jewish relations).[16]

Yet four separate polls in mid-1995, around the time coverage peaked, revealed evidence of widespread support for the principle of affirmative action. In a 1995 *Los Angeles Times* poll, 21 percent favor affirmative action that "uses quotas," 50 percent favor affirmative action "without quotas," and 20 percent "oppose affirmative action altogether." This result implies that affirmative action with or without quotas is favored by 71 percent. On this question, even white men are 61 percent in favor of affirmative action (white women, 76 percent) when we combine the "without" and "with" quota categories. An ABC/*Washington Post* Poll (March), an NBC/*Wall Street Journal* poll (July–August), and a CNN/ *USA Today* survey (July, right after President Clinton's speech) all find 70 percent of respondents favoring either affirmative action as currently practiced or with reforms. (Question wording and details can be found in appendix B, part I.) These three, and the rest of the surveys discussed in this section, come from archives of the Roper Center P.O.L.L. database at the University of Connecticut. Every poll taken after January 1995 and stored in the P.O.L.L. archive that offers a reform alternative reveals about two-thirds of respondents favoring continuation of affirmative action as is or with reforms. Further, similar questions asked about affirmative action without quotas (in "business," "employment," or "industry") in 1982, 1988, and 1990 find virtually identical percentages. In showing this, Charlotte Steeh and Maria Krysan's comprehensive review of survey data concludes that whites' attitudes on affirmative action have remained virtually unchanged since 1965, despite journalists' and politicians' frequent claim of a massive shift in the mid-1990s.[17]

Polls do show, however, that a majority opposes "quotas" or "preferences." Thus the *Los Angeles Times* poll of March 1995 that found 71 percent support for the principle of affirmative action also asked if "qualified minorities should receive *preference* over equally qualified whites" (emphasis added). On this question it found 72 percent of all respondents opposed, 78 percent of whites—and also 50 percent of blacks. These results and others suggest not only widespread antagonism toward "preference" programs, but also that many African Americans share the antipathy.[18] Blacks and whites seem to occupy more similar moral worlds than news implied.

We should not leap from the data showing support of affirmative action programs without quotas or preferences to a presumption that every member of the majority would approve any one reformed affirmative action policy. We do not have a definitive sense of the public's opinions on what is actually a diverse range of policy solutions. We do not know how this general commitment would hold up under various conditions. In addition, whites may mask their true sentiments when responding to interviewers' probes on affirmative action. Some are probably unwilling to reveal hostile feelings to a stranger, to risk being perceived as racist. Paul Sniderman and Thomas Piazza argue that most whites do oppose affirmative action programs—though these authors treat affirmative action synonymously with "preference"—and they find that whites also oppose discrimination and sympathize with other attempts to help victims of discrimination.[19] In their comprehensive survey of poll data, Steeh and Krysan find, as suggested here, that the average public stance falls "somewhere between color blindness on the one hand and preferences on the other." Appendix B, part 2, displays additional polling data that support this reading.[20]

At the same time, polling evidence reveals considerable contradiction, uncertainty, and ambivalence. For example, part 3 of appendix B describes one survey in which the same sample endorsed by a slim margin a referendum repealing affirmative action and (by a larger margin) favored another referendum maintaining affirmative action. Part 3 also suggests that whites consider antiwhite discrimination a bigger problem than antiblack, but also seem to accept affirmative action as a remedy for the latter. The instabilities within and across representative samples suggest we cannot infer much about the details of public thinking—if indeed many Americans even possess detailed philosophies of affirmative action.

But we can combine the poll data to reach a reasonable synthesis (one that parallels the conclusions of Steeh and Krysan). A number of variously worded surveys reveals general support for the principle. They also show a widespread perception that current applications entail some undesirable costs or practices. Distinguishing among affirmative action programs, Lawrence Bobo and James R. Kluegel argue that whites support "opportunity-enhancing" affirmative action policies while opposing "preferential" ones.[21] These strands are congruent with a majority of white Americans wanting to "mend" but not "end" affirmative action.

The favorable majority might not be as robust as the polling data suggest, but at a minimum, the best available empirical evidence does not support the pessimistic image painted by the media. Rather, polls suggest a significant reservoir of sympathy and support among whites for redressive public policies, even if other, less friendly, sentiments coexist. We cannot determine which is *the* true reading of the white public's opinion toward affirmative action. In all likelihood, depending on circumstances and stimuli, whites can genuinely feel both sympathy and antipathy.[22]

In any case, the failure of the issue to catch fire in the 1996 election campaign, despite many pundits' expectations and politicians' calculations to the contrary, suggests white Americans were much less exercised over the issue than the news depicted. That leads to another misleading element in media framing of public opinion: the portrayal of intense white arousal over this issue. Beyond the fizzling of the issue in 1996, survey data suggest that, whatever their stance on affirmative action, whites and blacks alike have long considered it a low-priority issue. The best evidence we have suggests it was not bubbling at the surface of a seething white America's political consciousness in the mid-1990s. Nor were African Americans obsessing about affirmative action.

An NBC/*Wall Street Journal* poll (March 1995) asked about legislative priorities; affirmative action came in last (see appendix B, part 4), far behind the other six issues on which respondents were queried. Another asked an open ended question: "Is there any one issue that you care about that would make you vote against a candidate for president?" Affirmative action ranked near the bottom, named by just 1 percent. An April 1996 poll asking about issues people would "like to hear discussed by the candidates running for president" had a similar outcome. And none of the frequent polls that ask about the "most important problem facing the country" and recorded in the comprehensive Roper Center database from 1985 through 1996 showed "affirmative action" named as a top priority by more than 1 percent. (One poll in 1987 found 2 percent mentioning "affirmative action/civil rights.") Since about 12 percent of a representative national survey should be composed of African Americans, this figure reveals that hardly any whites *or* blacks during these years considered affirmative action a top-priority issue. (If, say, just one-fourth of blacks named affirmative action as their top issue, that alone would be enough to push the total national figure to about 3 percent.)

In 1995 the media did report some of the data suggesting that majority white sentiment exhibited elements of ambivalence, goodwill, and a desire to eliminate real flaws while retaining affirmative action programs. Yet the dominant framing of affirmative action emphasized high intensity, angry opposition among whites, confronted by obstinate, self-interested support among blacks. Bolstering the misleading depictions of

Table 2-1. *Affirmative Action Stands by Racially Identifiable Sources in Newsmagazine and Network News Coverage*

Sources	Favor affirmative action	Oppose affirmative action	Total responses
Black	72%	28%	68
	(n = 49)	(n = 19)	
White	29%	71%	120
	(n = 35)	(n = 85)	
Column total	84	104	188

public opinion were the mirror images in sentiments expressed by identifiably black and white sources. Table 2-1 displays the data. Among black sources, 72 percent of affirmative action evaluations expressed were positive whereas for whites, 71 percent were negative.

The source data combine both leaders and ordinary citizens of each race. They show significant numbers of white proponents and black opponents of affirmative action, so the depictions were not completely polarized. Nonetheless, the dominant impression is of a stark racial divide in sentiments toward affirmative action. Choices of sources among ordinary citizens—not elites (experts or political leaders)—compounded the image of division. According to the news, ordinary blacks endorsed affirmative action by a margin of 14 to 2; ordinary whites opposed it by 28 to 4. The coverage also contained 16 citations to general public opinion—*all* of them opposed to affirmative action. Yet as we have seen, evidence on "public" opinion generally, and white opinion specifically, is more complex and far less opposed than these representations imply. By depicting the races as more sharply polarized than they are, by showing most white citizens in opposition, and almost all blacks in favor, news messages could have deepened perceptions that each group lacks empathy and shared values with the other. That sense in turn established an unfavorable environment for balanced deliberation and instead opened the way to fearful, resentful responses.

Media coverage also strengthened the incentives and inclinations of elites to play on and respond to this imagined public arousal. Media depictions could have helped reinforce the moves by some judicial, legislative, and executive branch officials to restrict affirmative action programs more than most white Americans said they wanted. By spreading the notion that an angry white majority was fed up with affirmative action, the media also created disincentives to white politicians who might otherwise have publicly defended the policy. To justify it in this media-constructed environment could have made a politician seem unresponsive, even arrogant. Perhaps this is one reason that none of the twelve network stories on Clinton's affirmative action speech or the California Regents' decision showed a white political leader other than the president endorsing affirmative action. That absence, along with the presence of so many white opponents, transmitted a message that might well have reinforced African Americans' sense of isolation and alienation from the dominant ethnic group, deepening racial polarization despite the considerable overlap in positions on this issue.

Framing the Policy of Affirmative Action

Beyond public opinion, the media had much to say on the policy of affirmative action itself. Here, too, the coverage was misleading. The most prominent elements of the message—the headlines, the visuals, the highlighted quotes, and the journalists' narrative emphases—framed the policy dispute as a zero-sum conflict of interest between whites and blacks, in which only one group could win and one must lose. Although the spotlight occasionally fell on others, the emphasis, especially in visuals and in quoting of sources, was on blacks as beneficiaries, who purportedly gain at the direct expense of whites. Since the majority of immediate beneficiaries of affirmative action has apparently been white women,[23] the primary division might more accurately have been drawn along the gender rather than racial divide. Furthermore, treating affirmative action as necessarily a zero-sum conflict distorts the policy stakes and choices.

Television networks and newsmagazines imposed a black-white frame likely to compound misunderstanding and distrust across racial lines. Thus a *CBS Evening News* story of June 12, 1995, that called affirmative action "deeply divisive" also distinguished (in a quote from *Newsweek*'s Joe Klein) two camps on the issue: "Jesse Jackson and African Americans" on the one hand, and "the rest of the country" on the other. The *Newsweek* cover story (April 3, 1995) carrying the headline "Race and Rage" and the image of black and white fists colliding offered two subheads: "Affirmative Action" and "When Preferences Work—and Don't." Inside the magazine the headline "Race and Rage" appeared again to introduce the lead story, alongside a large picture of a demonstration that emphasized a black woman yelling. Because two-sided conflict is a primary value in constructing news frames, the networks and newsmagazines tended to emphasize the black-white division, potentially stirring more resentment between the groups than their real views would create.

The text that accompanied the inflammatory framing in *Newsweek* was by no means wholly misleading, nor completely hostile to affirmative action. In some ways, this *Newsweek* issue mirrored the ambivalence of public sentiment even as it reinforced the impression that negative emotion courses through the body politic. The lead story clarified important distinctions among different types of affirmative action programs (recruiting, goals and timetables, quotas). The coverage offered some useful case studies of affirmative action programs and provided space to the black sociologist William Julius Wilson and to a black *Newsweek* editor, Ellis Cose, supporting affirmative action. But this came in a section headed "Battleground Chicago/Report from the Front: How Racial Preferences Really Work—or Don't." The headline (like the cover) ignored the very distinctions just mentioned, by categorizing all policies as "preferences." The magazine further undermined accurate understanding— and social capital—by focusing only on *racial* (and particularly *black*) affirmative action, and by employing the war metaphor. Arguably it is these most vivid elements of the message that were most likely to remain in readers' minds.

Newsweek's lead piece read:

Never far from the surface of politics, race is rising with raging force in the presidential campaign now beginning. A quarter century ago the issue was busing. In 1988 it was crime.... But the most profound fight—the one tapping deepest into the emotions of everyday American life—is over affirmative action.... When is it fair to discriminate on the basis of race or gender? Louder than before, Americans seem to be saying, "Never."

Although the paragraph mentioned gender, it framed the issue "rising with raging force" as one of "race." It equated "Americans" with whites and misstated the unanimity and intensity with which they allegedly reject affirmative action. And it implied that affirmative action inherently discriminates.

The media-constructed gulf between blacks and whites is further illustrated by the quantitative content analysis, which recorded the race of each source making an evaluative statement about affirmative action.

The coverage heightened impressions of a specifically black-white confrontation through its choice of sources. Fully 188 of the 253 cited sources for evaluative statements in the quantitative analysis were identifiably African American or white, only 13 Asian or Hispanic American. (The rest of the evaluations cited general public opinion sources or were unattributed.) Although women are perhaps the primary beneficiaries of affirmative action, opinions of women as a group were never cited, another telling indicator of the black-white framing.

The visual dimension of coverage also depicted a largely black-white confrontation. Coverage conveyed this message through illustrations that connote the beneficiaries of affirmative action. Of the 26 stories in the NBC/CBS sample, 23 illustrated the debate by showing predominantly or exclusively black persons as beneficiaries or defenders of the programs; only three stories prominently featured nonblack beneficiaries. Eight stories showed pro-affirmative action demonstrations, all but one predominantly black,[24] and three stories showed black persons shouting at a white person.

It is unrealistic to expect news coverage of this issue to transcend the incentives and limitations imposed by the dominant purposes and practices of the news business. Consequently, even stories that set out to provide a sympathetic account wound up endorsing the dominant framing. For example, a story by Gwen Ifill, a black correspondent on NBC, focused on an *Asian* beneficiary of a minority contractor program. But Ifill justified her story by saying, "Today the country is in the middle of a violent mood swing" on affirmative action. And the story included House Speaker Newt Gingrich speaking at a table to black persons and concluded by showing a picture of a well-dressed anonymous *black* man—connotatively a success story of the program—on a street corner alongside other apparent executives who are white. Thus the account supported the notions that blacks are the prime beneficiaries and that public opinion had undergone a "violent" shift toward opposing affirmative action.

Another more detailed story presented a seemingly supportive view of affirmative action that arguably subverts it. This story contributed to the positive side of the ledger in the conventional quantitative content analysis reported earlier and thus provides a good example of how such analysis can mask important subtleties. The CBS report (May 31, 1995) framed the issue in white versus black terms. It reported that "Blacks get ahead in the military not through the preferential treatment of affirmative action but because the military makes integration work." It went on to attack typical affirmative action programs as unnecessary and undesirable, though without saying so directly. The correspondent said, "The idea is to make the playing field level before the contest begins, so that ability not affirmative action is the key to promotion." In this way he implied that affirmative action programs and promotion according to ability or merit are opposites.

The story quoted the (black) secretary of the army saying the U.S. Army "refuses to simply order promotion boards to select a higher percentage of blacks." Rather, he said, "We will not force it artificially. When it happens, every soldier, every officer who views those promotions will say 'Yes, that was a fair thing'." Thus he implied that other affirmative action programs are artificial and unfair because they "simply order" more blacks to be promoted. The story defended this particular affirmative action program and thus suggests that not all affirmative action is bad. But even as it supported this one policy, the story implied that most other versions of affirmative action do "prefer" blacks (and only blacks), discriminate against whites, and violate what is otherwise an inviolate principle of meritocracy.

By way of lauding the program, the story showed a white soldier saying "It doesn't matter what color you are," or, as the correspondent reported, "Race is irrelevant." Yet the central purpose of the U.S. Army's program is to detect and encourage blacks and members of other under-represented groups who might attain success in the military. Race is not irrelevant. A more sophisticated journalistic policy narrative might make room to admit the paradoxes of affirmative action policy—such as its need to practice race, ethnic, or gender consciousness in order ultimately to minimize it—rather than simplifying in a way that may undermine whites' understanding of the intellectual and moral case for the programs. Given this kind of putatively sympathetic coverage of an affirmative action program, and the framing of the issue in mostly black-white terms, perhaps it is not surprising that Steeh and Krysan find white public opinion "most negative when [survey] questions about the policy mention blacks as the only beneficiaries."[25]

Beyond the black-white frame, the other misleading component in coverage was the notion that affirmative action policy creates irreconcilable differences, a zero-sum game, in which if one side wins, the other must lose. By narrowly defining self-interest in short-run, material terms—by casting the policy largely as taking away jobs, career mobility, contracts, or educational opportunity from the dominant group to benefit one minority—the coverage thwarted shared understanding of how all might benefit collectively from reformed affirmative action.

Media coverage highlighted "reverse discrimination" against whites.[26] The effect of this emphasis is suggested by surveys finding that a two-thirds majority of whites appear to believe that discrimination against them and in favor of blacks is a problem.[27] Similarly, a March 1995 survey showed respondents believed by a 2:1 ratio that whites losing jobs because of affirmative action was a bigger problem (46 percent) than blacks losing jobs owing to racial discrimination (23 percent) (see appendix B, part 3). Some might accept this claim, but empirical studies suggest otherwise: research reveals that few whites file employment discrimination complaints.[28] The authors attribute the perception that blacks frequently take jobs from whites to "the negative character of our current public discourse."[29] Presumably they mean to indict the media, but they might also point to the defects of survey research. The selective wording of survey questions and narrow range of specific opinions tapped prevent whites from expressing their ambivalence directly. Instead, scholarly observers must tease apart seemingly incongruous poll results to reveal the mixed feelings. Such sentiments should not be entirely unexpected given that American political culture itself has never reconciled its simultaneous commitments to both egalitarianism and individual freedom. But this kind of complexity in public sentiment rarely fits conventional news formats and reports.

The deeper inaccuracy of such reporting is that the costs and benefits of affirmative action flow across ethnic and gender lines in ways that belie the simplistic conclusion that it creates a zero-sum conflict. Even in strictly short-run individualistic and material terms, every white person is either a woman who potentially or actually benefits from affirmative action, or a man with close female relatives (wives, daughters, mothers) who may benefit. This fact illustrates the difficulty of determining exactly which racial groups benefit and which suffer in the short run. In the longer run, affirmative action could help distribute human capital to its most valued uses, thereby making all of society better off. The debate over this policy could quite accurately be framed as one among people who share fundamental moral values *and* long-run economic interests.[30]

These points do not gainsay serious problems and understandable criticisms of many programs that have risen under the banner of affirmative action. Among these are special college admissions treatment for children of immigrants who face no systematic discrimination resembling that still experienced by African Americans.[31]; contract preferences for firms whose minority owners are figureheads fronting for wealthy whites; and racially gerrymandered congressional districts that have arguably enhanced representation of forces antagonistic to policies favored by most African Americans and other ethnic minorities. There is no doubt that affirmative action, like all laudable principles, can in practice yield undesirable, perverse, or unintended consequences. For that very reason, debate and deliberation over this policy would benefit from rationality, terminological and conceptual precision, empathy, and goodwill. It would be naive to expect any political process to be dominated by these qualities, of course, but it may not be unreasonable to expect the media to refrain from undermining them.

Conclusion

Affirmative action exemplifies how the media's conventional practice of seeking out and dramatizing conflict may have consequences beyond merely leaving mass audiences uninformed or distracted. Three potential effects of the discord-emphasizing frame for affirmative action can be hypothesized. At the elite level, the frame likely affects the political calculations of public officials, enhancing incentives to exploit interracial tension and diminishing incentives to deliberate rationally on the problems underlying this complex issue. For the mass public, these repeated messages emphasizing the absence of common ground between whites and blacks could undermine longer-term feelings of social trust and empathy across racial lines. At the more general theoretical level, the findings here suggest that the media's well-known tendency to emphasize simplified, dramatic conflict as a way of generating interesting narratives may in some respects render this institution dysfunctional to social cohesion and stability.[32]

Elites' Strategic Use of Affirmative Action

The sudden leap in media attention to affirmative action during 1995 suggests that, however inadvertently, the media may indeed have augmented some elites' inclinations to use affirmative action as a political tool, or in the common parlance, a "wedge issue." Some politicians

Figure 2-1. *Items Mentioning "Affirmative Action," 1985–96*

Number of articles

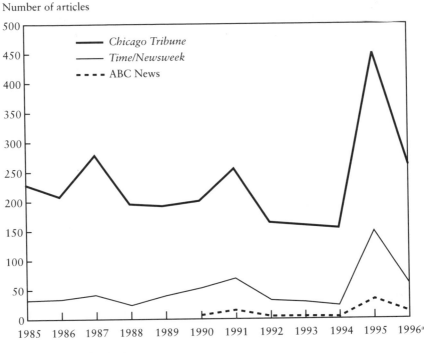

a. Through September 22 only.

apparently find electoral advantage in framing affirmative action as a conflict between the pure and safe American way—connotatively, the white way—and the impure, distorted, threatening way.[33] They supply the fiery quotes, the invocations of aroused "public opinion," and the media often follow along. Figure 2-1 graphs the number of news articles, editorials, and opinion columns published in the *Chicago Tribune* and *Time* and *Newsweek* that mentioned affirmative action, for the years 1985–96 (the latter year through September 22 only). Also shown are numbers of stories mentioning affirmative action from 1990–96, on ABC's nightly *World News.*

Two results stand out. First, a sharp increase in attention to this issue took place in 1995. The number of articles more than doubled in the *Tribune* and grew even more precipitously in the other outlets. Counting the total number of times the words "affirmative action" appeared in the *Tribune* articles makes the spurt even more striking: the term was invoked 436 times in 1994, and 2,710 in 1995. Mentions plummeted in 1996 (through September 22) to 511. The most obvious reason for the surge in 1995 was the publicity surrounding the important Supreme Court rulings on minority contractor set-asides and minority electoral districts. Both of these rulings marked a significant change in policy, restricting government actions intended to redress discrimination. However, an equally momentous decision involving university admissions (*Hopwood* vs. *State of Texas*) occurred in 1996 and failed to spark voluminous media discourse on affirmative action. This suggests an additional force behind the surge in coverage during 1995.

That force is indicated by an intriguing pattern in coverage: a peak in attention to affirmative action in the years before presidential elections: 1987, 1991, and 1995. The same pre-election year peaks occurred in all the media studied. The pattern might be random, or it could reflect some unmeasured variable. Still, the trend suggests that some political leaders use their power over the media agenda to elevate the affirmative action issue in pre-election years. The media usually frame the issue in black-white racial terms. During the campaigns, raising the issue might be more vulnerable to attack as pandering to prejudice to win votes. By heightening awareness of the issue before the campaign is under way, candidates can stimulate sensitivity among susceptible whites without seeming so purely motivated by electoral concerns. This does not mean discussion of affirmative action disappears during the elections themselves. Politicians raise this and other perceived racial issues during campaigns, often obliquely, by talking about "Willie" Horton and crime (1988), "family values" (1992), or "drugs" (1996).

Effects on the Mass Public

Rational deliberation about policy issues involving black-white relations has been in short supply for decades. The issue has tugged and torn at the national conscience, animated protest candidacies and mass movements, and variously aroused bitter antagonism and admirable altruism. This is a policy area that needs social capital more than most: a sense shared across racial lines that the human beings ascribed to each group possess goodwill and reason, that they share important values. It is just these perceptions that were challenged by the dominant framing of affirmative action in the news. The media have reported affirmative action as an arena of clashing racial interests rather than one of shared concern and overlapping interests. They have depicted a stark division between

African Americans and white Americans rather than highlighting many crosscutting group connections and identities implicated in affirmative action policy. Judging by the dominant emphases in the text, it does not seem farfetched to suggest that this kind of coverage could help bring the reality of race relations closer to the near-total alienation depicted in the news.

Yet it might reasonably be asked: if the media coverage has any impact beyond the elite stratum, why do the public opinion data remain generally supportive? After all, the media's often confident predictions in 1995 that affirmative action would become a major (even *the* major) political issue of 1996 did not prove valid.

Certainly a current in the literature emphasizes how the polysemy of media messages creates opportunities for oppositional readings, for people to find meanings that challenge the ones that seem to dominate the news text.[34] Significant numbers of white Americans could be reframing the media coverage of affirmative action, rejecting the version that emphasizes a zero-sum, black-white clash. Some of the poll numbers suggest as much.

But the assumption that the real and persistent condition of white public sentiment is ambivalence provides the more politically pertinent and empirically accurate interpretation. The white public can be cued by stimuli in the communication environment to respond favorably and empathetically to specific applications of the affirmative action principle. But where political communication cues the more negative considerations stored in their belief systems, whites may respond antagonistically. Being told repeatedly that most whites are angry and opposed, while blacks occupy a different moral universe and militantly demand total support for all affirmative action programs, could make the hostile, negative considerations more salient to whites. Such messages prepare the way for political advertising and campaign rhetoric that attempt to shape *voting decisions* by raising the salience of negative feelings toward affirmative action—and given the media's dominant frames, toward blacks more generally.[35] Individuals may cast ballots motivated in part by such top-of-the-head, recently activated considerations even though in other environments with different stimuli—say a pollster's question—they might support affirmative action.[36] Although the attempt to generate white votes in 1996 by attacking affirmative action did not seem to work in the presidential race, the tactic might have affected the outcome of other electoral struggles, including the California referendum banning the policy in state government activities.

Dysfunctional Media?

These points raise questions about any assumption that the dominant media inevitably function to stabilize society. Those media purportedly contribute to social and political stability by, among other operations, socializing citizens to a common culture, legitimizing governmental authority, and encouraging sublimation of conflicts among diverse groups in a larger identification with the nation-state. Yet in this instance, the coverage heightened the salience of racial identifications on both sides of the divide, discouraging a sense of shared culture and overlapping subjectivity. At least for this case and likely for black-white relations as a whole, the media's messages seem more prone to exacerbate group conflict, undermine authority, and diminish collective or communal identity than to help maintain the social fabric.[37] Rather than contributing to social integration and mutual adjustment, the media's conflict frame could make it more difficult for leaders to conduct a rational deliberative process that might help to produce legitimate and successful solutions to the real problems that underlie the affirmative action debate. As those problems fester unresolved, black and white members of the society—even blacks who "make it" economically—become increasingly alienated from each other and dubious about legitimizing promises central to American political culture.[38] These include the claim that opportunities are equal and that America is a pragmatic, effective society that solves its problems.

Adding to the complexity, however, in the very act of undermining support for affirmative action, the media's coverage (specifically the newsmagazines') arguably bolstered the hegemonic American ideology: individualism, individual responsibility for one's status, and suspicion of government programs that might promote equality. In this sense, perhaps, some of the media's messages might have contributed to the system's stability by boosting its core ideology even as at another level the messages promoted destabilizing intergroup hostility.

At the more practical level, could the media have performed in ways more nurturing of social capital and effective deliberation? The primary journalistic shortcoming here is failure, as usual, to contextualize: how many whites are harmed by affirmative action? How many deviations from pure merit are countenanced already, for reasons besides affirmative action—how many alumni children receive preferential college admissions, how many well-paying summer jobs or entry positions go to the offspring of the well connected? In California, for example, many of the University Regents and politicians who opposed affirmative action on grounds it violates meritocratic principles had successfully intervened in admissions processes to secure preferential treatment for children of associates and patrons. Most of these beneficiaries, apparently, were white and affluent.[39] How bad is continuing discrimination against blacks, women, and other beneficiaries? What are the benefits to all of society in prying open opportunities for those subject to severe discrimination, and what is the scope and distribution of real costs? Such questions did receive attention in some outlets but, judging from this sample, rarely in the mass-oriented news media.

To know context could enhance mutual understanding and trust across the lines dividing those who see themselves as helped or harmed by the policy. Context would not necessarily lead to consensus on policy antidotes. But a contextual narrative supportive of higher social capital would provide a more favorable climate for whites to reconcile their conflicted feelings about affirmative action and, perhaps, about African Americans more generally.

Appendix A: Coding Instructions

The unit of analysis is the source assertion within a paragraph. That is, each separate source who voices an evaluation in a paragraph is coded. If the same person is cited twice in a paragraph, code only once. If two different people in the same category (say two black politicians) are cited, code twice. If two different people in two different source categories are in one paragraph, code them both. Two types of assertion are coded. 1. The source in the paragraph utters an evalutive assertion, a claim that clearly supports or opposes affirmative action. 2. The source utters an assertion matching one of the thematic considerations. Often both will be coded: if Jesse Jackson says "I support affirmative action because discrimination still stymies black progress," the source code is 2, pro-con code is 1, and theme code is 4. If however Jackson simply says "I support affirmative action," leave theme code cell blank; or if he simply says "Discrimination still stymies black progress" and the context does not make it clear that this is an evaluative assertion (i.e. that the assertion implies "I support affirmative action because. . . "), then code only source and theme.

If the same source expresses two different considerations in the same paragragh, code each on separate lines. If the same source expresses two of the same pro-con evaluations in a paragraph, one with a codable consideration and one without, code twice (one with the evaluation only, one with the evaluation and consideration both coded). If the same source expresses the same evaluation twice with no considerations either time, code once. Do NOT code descriptions of court rulings (which tend to be ambiguous, confusing, technical, and refer to only one instance). Do code if a judge is quoted clearly opposing or supporting affirmative action as a general policy or utters one of the general considerations listed.

Do not code descriptions of positions as in "Sen. Gramm opposes Affirmative Action." Code only an expression of evaluative sentiment in a quotation, or one that carries a consideration. The goal is to code only those evaluative assertions that are actually themselves assertions, not to code descriptions that carry no evaluative valence or persuasiveness. A codable evaluative expression then is either a quotation from the actor holding the position; or a paraphrase of the position or description of it that comes with a consideration. You *would* code "Senator Gramm says, 'I oppose affirmative action'." And you would code "Senator Gramm says he opposes affirmative action because it violates meritocratic principles."

For TV: a paired correspondent comment followed directly by sound bite complementing, expanding, or illustrating the correspondent assertion is counted as 1 paragraph.

Appendix B: Survey Data on Affirmative Action

Note: All data displayed below are based on results of national sample surveys stored in the P.O.L.L. on-line archive administered by the Roper Center at the University of Connecticut.

I. Support for reformed affirmative action

1. What's the best thing to do with affirmative action programs giving preference to some minorities—leave them as they are, change them or do away with them entirely?

Leave	23%
Change	47
Do away with them entirely	28
Don't know/No opinion	2

Organization conducting survey: ABC News, *Washington Post*
Number of participants: 1,524
Beginning date: March 16, 1995; Ending date: March 19, 1995

2. What is your view of affirmative action today—it is fundamentally flawed and needs to be eliminated, it is good in principle but needs to be reformed, or, it is basically fine the way it is?

Fundamentally flawed, needs to be eliminated	22%
Good in principle, needs to be reformed	61
Basically fine	9
Don't know/Refused	9

Number of participants: 1,208
Survey Sponsor: Cable News Network, *U.S.A. Today*
Beginning date: July 20, 1995; Ending date: July 23, 1995

3. In your view, should federal affirmative action programs that give preferences to women and minorities be continued as they are, be continued but reformed to prevent reverse discrimination, or should they be ended?

Continued as they are	13%
Continued but reformed	57
Ended	26
Not sure	4

Number of participants: 1,005
Survey Sponsor: NBC News, *Wall Street Journal*
Beginning date: July 29, 1995; Ending date: August 1, 1995

4. If you had to choose, would you rather see the federal government's affirmative action programs mended—that is, changed in certain ways—or ended altogether?

Mended	65%
Ended altogether	24
Stay the same/No change (vol.)	1
Not sure	10

Number of participants: 1,000
Survey sponsor: *Time*, Cable News Network
Beginning date: July 19, 1995; Ending date: July 20, 1995

II. Evaluations of affirmative action fall "somewhere between color blindness on the one hand and preferences on the other."

When question does not define or contextualize affirmative action, support hovers near 50-50.

1. All in all, do you favor or oppose affirmative action programs for blacks and other minority groups?

Favor	44%
Oppose	49
Not sure	7

Number of participants: 1,005
Survey sponsor: NBC News, *Wall Street Journal*
Beginning date: July 29, 1995; Ending date: August 1, 1995

Same question asked in September 1995: 48% favor, 37% oppose; late October 1995: 42% favor, 45% oppose.

2. Do you think most government affirmative action programs in hiring, promoting, and college admissions should be continued or do you think these affirmative action programs should be abolished?

Continued	50%
Abolished	40
Don't know/No answer	10

Organization conducting survey: CBS News
Number of participants: 1,001
Beginning date: December 4, 1996; Ending date: December 5, 1996

Same question asked Oct. 23-27, 1996: 55% continued, 34% abolished; Aug. 3-5, 1996: 45% continued, 43% abolished.

Reference to discrimination increases support (although part of the increase may be due to the social desirability of support when the interviewer mentions discrimination).

3. In order to overcome past discrimination, do you favor or oppose affirmative action programs designed to help blacks, women and other minorities get better jobs and education?

Favor	58%
Oppose	36
Don't know/Refused	6

Number of participants: 1,476
Survey sponsor: *Times Mirror*
Beginning date: August 17, 1995; Ending date: August 20, 1995

When the question refers to "preferences" or "quotas," support shrinks, even when discrimination is mentioned.

4. In order to overcome the effects of past discrimination, qualified blacks, women and other minorities should be given special preferences in hiring and education.

Completely agree	8%
Mostly agree	28
Mostly disagree	37
Completely disagree	25
Don't know	2

Number of participants: 2,000
Survey sponsor: *Times Mirror*
Beginning date: October 25, 1995; Ending date: October 30, 1995

5. The next few questions are about the affirmative action programs both public and private that are intended to increase opportunities for minority groups that have been discriminated against. What about affirmative action programs that set quotas, that is, programs that give preference to minorities for a certain number of positions? Do you favor affirmative action programs with quotas, or do you favor affirmative action programs only without quotas, or do you oppose all affirmative action programs?

Favor with quotas	16%
Favor without quotas	47
Oppose all	28
Don't know	9

Number of participants: 1,006
Survey notes: Interviewing was conducted by I.C.R. Survey Research Group.
Beginning date: July 7, 1995; Ending date: July 11, 1995

III. Uncertainty/ambivalence about affirmative action

Whites perceive alleged discrimination against whites as a more serious problem than discrimination against blacks, and they'd prefer affirmative action be directed toward the poor rather than toward ethnic or gender groups. These results suggest the limits to many whites' appreciation of the continuing impediments to progress faced specifically and perhaps uniquely by African Americans; such understanding might boost whites' support for more vigorous affirmative action policies.

1. Which do you think is a bigger problem in the workplace today . . . blacks losing out because of racial discrimination or whites losing out because of affirmative action?

Blacks losing because of discrimination	23%
Whites losing because of affirmative action	46
Neither is a big problem (vol.)	6
Both equally (vol.)	11
Don't know/Refused	15

Number of participants: 752
Survey sponsor: *Newsweek*
Beginning date: March 23, 1995; Ending date: March 24, 1995

2. If you had to choose, would you prefer the current approach to affirmative action which targets women and minorities for benefits, or would you prefer a new approach to affirmative action which would target poor Americans, regardless of their sex or race?

Prefer current programs	10%
Prefer programs which benefit the poor	77
Not sure	13

Number of participants: 1,060
Survey sponsor: *Time*, Cable News Network
Beginning date: March 22, 1995; Ending date: March 23, 1995

But given a specific example, majorities of whites appear to support affirmative action for "well qualified" blacks, and to want President Clinton to enforce the policy.

3. In order to fill the hiring goals of an affirmative action program, suppose a company were to give a job to a well qualified black applicant rather than to an equally well qualified white applicant. Would you view this as discrimination against the white job applicant, or would you not consider this discrimination?

Yes, discrimination	24%
No, not discrimination	73
No opinion	3

Number of participants: 1,220
Survey sponsor: Cable News Network, *U.S.A. Today*
Beginning date: March 17, 1995; Ending date: March 19, 1995

4. I will read you some things Bill Clinton might try to do in a second term as President. (As I read each one, tell me whether you would like to see Clinton do this and whether you think he will try to do this in a second term.) What about . . . put more emphasis on affirmative action to improve educational and job opportunities for women and minorities? Is this something you would like to see Clinton try to do, or not?

Yes, would like to see	65%
No, would not	30
Don't know	5

Number of participants: 752
Survey sponsor: *Newsweek*
Survey notes: Registered voters who plan to vote in the 1996 presidential election
Beginning date: November 2, 1996; Ending date: November 4, 1996

Example of ambivalence/uncertainty: The same sample appears to support two referenda, one that repeals affirmative action and one that allows it.

5. Next year on the ballot in a number of states, there is likely to be a referendum to repeal the state's affirmative action laws. In general, would you favor or oppose repeal of affirmative action here in your state?

Favor	44%
Oppose	41
Not sure	15

Number of participants: 1,364
Survey sponsor: The Feminist Majority Foundation
Beginnin date: March 16, 1995; Ending date: April 3, 1995

6. Now let me read you the wording of a possible referendum that might be on the ballot next year in your state. Would you vote in favor or vote against this proposition: The state may use affirmative action programs designed to help women, minorities, and others who have not had equal

opportunities in education, employment, and in receiving government contracts to achieve equal opportunities?

Favor	68%
Oppose	25
Not sure	7

Number of participants: 1,364
Survey sponsor: The Feminist Majority Foundation
Beginning date: March 16, 1995; Ending date: April 3, 1995

IV. *Affirmative action as low priority*

1. Is there any one issue that you care about that would make you vote against a candidate for president? (If Yes, ask:) What issue is that?

Abortion—(most frequent response)	11%
Affirmative action	1%

Number of participants: 1,023
Beginning date: March 12, 1995; Ending date: March 14, 1995
Survey sponsor: CBS News, *New York Times*

2. I'd like to read you a list of seven possible legislative priorities. Please tell me which one or two you feel are the most important issues for Congress to address . . . health care reform, a balanced budget amendment, a middle class tax cut, welfare reform, a revised crime bill, cutting back affirmative action programs, an increase in the minimum wage?

Health care reform	40%
A balanced budget amendment	30
A middle class tax cut	19
Welfare reform	41
A revised crime bill	19
Cutting back affirmative action programs	7
An increase in the minimum wage	20
All equally important (vol.)	4

Number of participants: 1,011
Survey sponsor: NBC News, *Wall Street Journal*
Beginning date: September 24, 1995; Ending date: September 26, 1995

3. What issue or problem would you particularly like to hear discussed by the candidates running for president this year? Is there another issue or problem you would like to hear those candidates discuss?

Economy (most frequent response)   18%
Affirmative action/civil rights/fairness   1%

Number of participants: 1,374
Beginning date: April 13, 1996; Ending date: April 16, 1996
Survey sponsor: *Los Angeles Times*

4. I am going to read you some statements about Colin Powell's positions on some issues. For each one, please tell me if that position would make you more likely to vote for Powell, less likely, or whether it would not affect your likelihood of voting for Powell one way or the other.) . . . On affirmative action he says he does not believe in quotas but but supports continuing many affirmative action programs.

More likely   37%
Less likely   27
No effect   32
No opinion   4

Number of participants: 1,011
Survey sponsor: Cable News Network, *U.S.A. Today*
Beginning date: September 22, 1995; Ending date: September 24, 1995

Notes

1. See Benjamin I. Page, *Who Deliberates?* (University of Chicago Press, 1996).

2. See Robert M. Entman, "Framing: Toward Clarification of a Fractured Paradigm," *Journal of Communication*, vol. 43 (Autumn 1993), pp. 51–58; and L. J. Shrum, "Psychological Processes Underlying Cultivation Effects," *Human Communication Research*, vol. 22 (1996), pp. 482–509.

3. For the theory of variation in opinion response, see John Zaller, *The Nature and Origins of Mass Opinion* (Cambridge University Press, 1992); on ambivalence about race matters specifically, see John Dovidio and Samuel L. Gaertner, eds., *Prejudice, Discrimination, and Racism: Theory and Research* (Academic Press, 1986). See also Paul Sniderman and Thomas Piazza, *The Scar of Race* (Harvard University Press, 1993) and Donald Kinder and Lynn Sanders, *Divided by Race* (University of Chicago Press, 1996) on variations in white responses depending on stimuli. R. Michael Alvarez and John Brehm, "Are Americans Ambivalent toward Racial Policies?" *American Journal of Political Science*, vol. 41 (May 1997), pp. 345–74, maintain whites are uncertain, not ambivalent. The measures in the Alvarez and Brehm article offer only problematic support for its argument. Uncertainty is measured by a two-item index of level of general political information (number of Supreme Court justices and maximum number of

presidential terms). This measure does not tap the specified concept of uncertainty well. To test their claim, the authors would need to measure uncertainty *about affirmative action and related matters*—for instance, how much antiblack discrimination still exists, how much whites suffer from implementations of affirmative action, how effective past affirmative action programs have been. Most people would have a high level of uncertainty about such matters because they have been inadequately measured and studied, and empirical studies have been underpublicized. Ambivalence appears to make better sense of the opinion data, though it is probably fed by the uncertainty that afflicts most observers.

4. Robert M. Entman, "Whites' Attitudes toward Blacks: Chicago and the Nation," Report to the Human Relations Foundation of Chicago (1994); Sniderman and Piazza, *The Scar of Race*; and Joe R. Feagin and H. Vera, *White Racism* (Routledge, 1995).

5. *Time*, July 10, 1995, p. 24.

6. See appendix A, part IV (4).

7. I regard the concept of social capital as a useful metaphor for psychological feelings of community and solidarity, of shared subjectivity, among members of different ascriptive groups. I do not mean to suggest it is quantifiable in the same way as economic capital, nor does my use of the concept imply an acceptance of Robert Putnam's entire argument in *Making Democracy Work* (Princeton University Press, 1993). For a critique see Pippa Norris, "Does Television Erode Social Capital? A Reply to Putnam," *P.S. Political Science and Politics*, vol. 29 (September 1996), pp. 474–80; and Sidney Tarrow, "Making Social Science Work across Space and Time: A Critical Reflection on Robert Putnam's *Making Democracy Work*," *American Political Science Review*, vol. 90 (June 1996), pp. 389–97.

8. Putnam, *Making Democracy Work*; and Francis Fukuyama, *Trust* (Free Press, 1995).

9. Sniderman and Piazza, *The Scar of Race*; Jennifer L. Hochschild, *Facing Up to the American Dream* (Princeton University Press, 1995); Feagin and Vera, *White Racism*; and William J. Wilson, *When Work Disappears* (Knopf, 1996).

10. Thomas E. Patterson, *Out of Order* (Knopf, 1993).

11. Robert M. Entman, "Blacks in the News: Television, Modern Racism, and Cultural Change," *Journalism Quarterly*, vol. 69 (Summer 1992), pp. 341–61; Christopher P. Campbell, *Race, Myth, and the News* (Sage, 1995); and Jon Hurwitz and Mark Peffley, "Public Perceptions of Race and Crime: The Role of Racial Stereotypes," *American Journal of Political Science*, vol. 41 (May 1997), pp. 375–401. See also Robert M. Entman, "Representation and Reality in the Portrayal of Blacks on Network Television News," *Journalism Quarterly*, vol. 71 (Autumn 1994), pp. 509–20.

12. Robert M. Entman, "Television, Democratic Theory and the Visual Construction of Poverty," *Research in Political Sociology*, vol. 7 (1995), pp. 139–59; and Shanto Iyengar, *Is Anyone Responsible?* (University of Chicago Press, 1991).

13. Robert M. Entman and Andrew Rojecki, "Advertising Boundaries: Race and Intimacy in Television Commercials," presented at the 1997 annual conference of the International Communication Association, Montreal.

14. Resource limitations constrained the study to this sampling of network outlets. Because all ABC transcripts were available without charge, and taped excerpts of network news from the Vanderbilt Television News Archives were costly, the analysis of both verbal and visual content was based on a representative sample of affirmative action stories on CBS and NBC. Analysis of ABC was confined to the verbal text.

15. Bradley S. Greenberg, "Some Uncommon Television Images and the Drench Hypothesis," in S. Okamp, ed., *Television as a Social Issue: Applied Social Psychology Annual*, vol. 8 (Sage Publications, 1988), pp. 88–102. See also Shrum, "Psychological Processes," and J. Shedler and M. Manis, "Can the Availability Heuristic Explain Vividness Effects?" *Journal of Personality and Social Psychology*, vol. 51 (July 1986), pp. 26–36.

16. Andrew Rojecki, "Deadly Embrace," presented at the annual conference of the International Communication Association, Chicago.

17. Charlotte Steeh and Maria Krysan, "The Polls—Trends: Affirmative Action and the Public, 1970–1995," *Public Opinion Quarterly*, vol. 60 (Spring 1996), pp. 128–58.

18. Steeh and Krysan, "The Polls—Trends," pp. 144–45.

19. Sniderman and Piazza, *The Scar of Race*.

20. Steeh and Krysan, "The Polls—Trends," p. 128; and see also James H. Kuklinski and others, "Racial Prejudice and Attitudes toward Affirmative Action," *American Journal of Political Science*, vol. 41 (May 1997), pp. 402–19.

21. Lawrence Bobo and James R. Kluegel, "Opposition to Race-Targeting: Self-Interest, Stratification, Ideology, or Racial Attitudes?" *American Sociological Review*, vol. 58 (August 1993), pp. 443–64.

22. John Zaller, *The Nature and Origins of Mass Opinion* (Cambridge University Press, 1992).

23. This does not imply that affirmative action policies have eliminated discrimination against women either. See U.S. Federal Glass Ceiling Commission, *Good for Business: Making Full Use of the Nation's Human Capital* (Washington: Federal Glass Ceiling Commission, 1995).

24. The reason for this might be that almost all demonstrations for affirmative action were in fact predominantly black. There is no empirical way to verify this possibility. Even if it is the case, the news images could promote an inaccurate perception that the primary group benefitting from and strongly committed to affirmative action was African Americans.

25. Steeh and Krysan, "The Polls—Trends," p. 138.

26. See also William Gamson and Andre Modigliani, "The Changing Culture of Affirmative Action," *Research in Political Sociology*, vol. 3 (1987), pp. 137–77.

27. Steeh and Krysan, "The Polls—Trends," p. 139.

28. See Susan Sturm and Lani Guinier, "The Future of Affirmative Action: Reclaiming the Innovative Ideal," *California Law Review*, vol. 84, no. 4 (1996), pp. 953–1036, for an exhaustive study of affirmative action complexities.

29. Steeh and Krysan, "The Polls—Trends," p. 140.

30. Sturm and Guinier, "The Future of Affirmative Action."

31. Douglas S. Massey and Nancy A. Denton, *American Apartheid: Segregation and the Making of the Underclass* (Harvard University Press, 1993).

32. See, for example, Herbert J. Gans, *Deciding What's News* (Pantheon, 1979); and David L. Paletz and Robert M. Entman, *Media Power Politics* (Free Press, 1981).

33. More on this binary opposition of purity and danger in media coverage of race relations can be found in Robert M. Entman and Andrew Rojecki, "Advertising Boundaries: Race and Intimacy in Television Commercials," paper presented at the annual conference of the International Communication Association, 1997; and Andrew Rojecki, "Deadly Embrace," paper presented at the annual conference of the International Communication Association, 1996.

34. See, for example, William A. Gamson, *Talking Politics* (Cambridge University Press, 1992); and W. Russell Neuman, Marion Just, and Ann Crigler, *Common Knowledge* (University of Chicago Press, 1992).

35. Kathleen Hall Jamieson, *Dirty Politics* (Oxford University Press, 1992).

36. Zaller, *The Nature and Origins of Mass Opinions*.

37. See Rojecki, "Deadly Embrace"; and Entman, "Blacks in the News " and "Television."

38. Hochschild, *Facing Up to the American Dream*.

39. Ralph Frammolino, Mark Gladstone, and Henry Weinstein, "UCLA Eased Entry Rules for the Rich, Well-Connected," *Los Angeles Times*, March 21, 1996, p. A-1; and U.S. Federal Glass Ceiling Commission, *Good for Business*.

CHAPTER THREE

The New Telecommunications Technology: Endless Frontier or the End of Democracy?

Benjamin R. Barber

T HE NEW TELECOMMUNICATIONS technologies are everywhere celebrated: celebrated as the key to the new global economy—this was Bill
Gates's theme at the 1997 World Economic Forum in Davos, for example; celebrated as the secret of America's new global economic recovery—
President Bill Clinton and Speaker Newt Gingrich agree on this much;
and celebrated as the beginning of a "new era in American Politics" and
of a new stage in the evolution of global democracy.[1] While the first and
second claims may be true, the third, linking the new technologies directly
to democracy, is far more controversial, palpably dangerous if not entirely false.

To be sure, innovations in communications and information technology do offer new technical opportunities for strong democrats and civic
republicans to strengthen civic education and enhance direct deliberative
communication among citizens. Only Luddites would dismiss the possibilities of the digital revolution as wholly nefarious. I was myself an early
advocate of exploiting the democratic potential of the new technologies,
and there are many responsible democrats who today are exploring in
theory and practice this potential.[2] Caution has, however, been outrun
by techno-Panglossians and cyberenthusiasts who seem to think that with
new technologies of communication we can overcome every defect of
communication our political system has experienced.

Historically, technology has always had a special if deeply ambivalent

A different version of this essay appeared in *Constellations*, vol. 4 (April 1997) and was
reprinted in Benjamin R. Barber, *A Passion for Democracy: American Essays* (Princeton
University Press, 1998).

relationship to democracy. Jean-Jacques Rousseau believed that the progress of the arts and sciences had had a corrupting effect on morals;[3] Frankfurt School critics from Adorno and Horkheimer to Marcuse and Habermas have warned that the Enlightenment's faith in progress has had costs that are the more severe for their invisibility.[4] The truth seems to be not so much that technology is averse to civic ideals than that it has run away from politics and morals, evolving so rapidly that its impact on democracy and vulnerability to undemocratic forces have gone largely unremarked.

Technology: Mirror of Democracy or Mirror of the Market?

The problem goes deep—to the very core of what democracy means. Democracy depends on deliberation, prudence, slow-footed interaction, and time-consuming (thus "inefficient") forms of multilateral conversation and social interaction that by postmodern standards may seem cumbersome, time consuming, demanding, sometimes interminable, and always certifiably unentertaining. Computer terminals, however, make process terminable, for electronic and digital technology's imperative is speed. Computers are fast as light, literally. Democracy is slow as prudent judgment, which is very slow indeed, demanding silences as well as communicative exchange and requiring upon occasion that days or months pass by before further thought or action can be demanded. Unlike our computers, we humans crash a lot. We often need to cool off, ponder, rethink, and absorb the consequence of previous decisions before we can make prudent new judgments. With human intelligence, "parallel computing" entails sociability and deliberative interaction and slows rather than hastens ratiocination and decision.

Digital reasoning is binary, privileging a simple choice between on and off, a and b, yes and no. It "likes" oppositions and dualism. Political reasoning is complex and nuanced, dialectical rather than digitally oppositional. It aims at escaping the rational choice games that computer modeled decisional processes prefer. To the question "A or B?" the citizen may reply "both!" or "neither!" or "those are not the right choices," or even "I don't care!" Imagine a computer that replies to a question "je m'en fou!" Our tools are in a certain sense out of synch with democracy, out of control. In an epoch of antipathy to government and antiregulatory passion, as the new technologies pass into the hands of corporations organized to secure maximum profits and little else, they are likely to become ever more so. Henry David Thoreau (perhaps in his anarchist incarnation) worried about how easily we can become the tools of our tools.

Perhaps it is even worse: we may be becoming the tools of the tools of our tools—guided not by the technology itself but by how it is being utilized as a consequence of market forces. It has been decades since Fred Friendly suggested Americans might need an "electronic Bill of Rights" to keep pace with changes in information technology that the American Founders could not possible have foreseen. Their Bill of Rights was designed for a world of print in which fast communication meant the pony express or a six-week sea voyage. The Progress and Freedom Foundation has promulgated a Magna Carta for the Information Age (1994), but there has been no serious mainline attempt to update the Federal Communications Act of 1934, devised for the then "modern" world of radio and quite properly concerned to "encourage the larger and more effective use of radio in the public interest." Indeed, the recently passed Telecommunications Bill of 1996 seeks only to move government out of the way, leaving it to the whims of money and markets of how the new technologies will affect our civic lives and our democratic society The only other advance has been the Communications Decency Act, aimed not at civic enhancement but civic censorship of Internet pornography.

While Europe has traditionally retained greater public control over its information and broadcasting utilities, it is currently under extraordinary pressure (in the name of global competition) to privatize. At the 1997 World Economic Forum in Davos, Bill Gates hectored the French for their cyberbackwardness and reportedly met privately with representatives of the Indian government to push them toward privatization (and perhaps a contract with Microsoft). The Munich Declaration of 1997 promulgated at the Academy for the Third Millennium's Conference on the Internet and Politics calls boldly for greater governmental and popular control and use of the new technologies for civic purposes, but it leans into the hard wind of privatization.[5] Indeed, the information superhighway is being built so fast that whatever residual regulatory powers survive the current regulatory mania, guaranteeing privacy and controlling monopoly are likely to be left far behind. President Bill Clinton has been reduced to high-minded jawboning in trying to persuade the private sector to control entertainment mayhem and link up public schools and libraries to the Internet.[6]

How long will the vaunted "wild west frontier" of the Internet hold out against the colonizing forces of commerce and corporatism? Point-to-point communication systems like the telephone and the Internet are, it has been repeatedly argued, lateral systems and hence more inherently democratic than vertical systems like broadcast radio and television. This is perfectly true, and it offers democrats the very real promise of technologically enhanced forms of civic interaction. But those who own conduits and software platforms, those who write programs and are systems' gatekeepers, still wield extraordinary power. We may wish there were no gatekeepers, although I would argue that there are forms of control and intervention like editing, facilitation, and education that are necessary to democratic utilization of the net and that amount to positive or legitimate forms of gatekeeping. In any case, the alternative to the regulatory state is not the free market but the regulatory market, whose choices and boundaries are powerfully delimiting, but as part of the "invisible hand" of the market, are largely invisible to us. Can any regulatory body hope in the name of the public good to bring a civic dimension to a 500-channel cable system, where the spectrum scarcity that once justified federal regulation has (in theory at least) vanished? Or curtail the inexpensive duplication (pirating) of cassettes, compact disks, and computer programs? Or influence telephone companies that now have the right to compete in cable television markets? Or track and regulate global satellite companies whose stations recognize no borders and can be picked up anywhere by a dinner-plate-sized dish? Such systems are, ironically, more susceptible to corporate than to government control and are likely to serve private rather than public interests.

What these somber reflections suggest is that technology is often less a determinant than a mirror of the larger society. Who owns it, how it is used and by whom, and to which ends: these are the critical questions whose answers will shape technology's role in the coming century. To be sure, technology bends a little this way, a little that, and it has intimations and entailments that obviously can modify human institutions and behavior. But ultimately it reflects the world in which it finds itself. Gunpowder helped democratize a Protestant, urbanizing Europe ripe for democratizing, but in feudal China it secured the hold of grasping elites; moveable type facilitated the democratization of literacy but also made possible mass propaganda and the extended thought control that marked the innovative tyranny known as totalitarianism. Interactive two-way television and keypad voting invite participation even as they expedite surveillance and marginalize thoughtfulness and complexity. But why should we finally expect our technologies to look much different than the society that produces and puts them to use?

Whatever entailments technology may have in the abstract, it still will reflect concretely the premises and objectives of the society deploying it. This is precisely the meaning of the key political idea of sovereignty: politics governs technique, society and culture always trump technology. Ends condition means, and technology is just a fancy word for means. The new telecommunications are less likely to alter and improve than to reflect and augment our current socioeconomic institutions and political attitudes. A commercial culture will entail a commercialized technology.[7] A society dominated by the ideology of privatization will engender a privatized Internet.

Wishful thinkers at outfits like the Electronic Frontier Foundation fantasize an Internet as free and democratic and horizontally organized as their own ingenuity and imagination. For Internet technology *is* point to point and certainly can be said to have a democratic potential. But it will take political will to allow such tendencies to emerge and modify traditional attitudes and institutions, which in the meantime are likely to be determinative.

The internal combustion engine and electricity did not absolutely mandate a privatized, highway-strip, suburbanized, overmalled America. Those late nineteenth-century technologies suited mass transportation systems (railways and buses, for example) equally well and thus could have also helped anchor an urban and town culture (as they did after World War II in Europe). It was not automotive determinism but specific political decisions taken in the first half of the twentieth century that translated the technologies of internal combustion and electric motors into a suburban society—perhaps most significantly, a critical decision by the U.S. Congress after World War II. Under pressure from the postwar steel, rubber, cement, and automobile industries, and possessed of a spirit of individualism that predated the new technologies, Congress voted to fund an immense interstate highway system that privileged the automobile and the social environment it mandated.

Who knows how different America might look today had that same Congress opted for an equally extensive interstate rail system? During the cold war, Deputy Secretary of State George Ball once justified investment in the Soviet Union's automobile industry by observing that an automobile is an ideology on four wheels. But it was not the automobile that created the ideology but the ideology that created the automobile. A car is radical individualism writ large, the internal combustion engine turned to the purposes of private liberty rather than (to name some alternative ideologies) to such ends as environmental protection, or the preservation of cities, or social cooperation, or war.

Is there then really any reason to think that a society dominated by profit-mongering and private interests will exempt the new telecommunications technologies from the pursuit of profit or constitute them in a more public-spirited manner than the society at large? Bill Gates's vision in *The Road Ahead* omits any reference to the civic good, prophesying instead a "shopper's heaven" in which "all the goods in the world will be available for you to examine, compare, and, often customize" and where "your wallet PC will link into a store's computer to transfer digital money."[8] And even where it can be shown that the technology inherently holds out the promise of civic and democratic potential, is it not likely to reflect the thin, representative, alienating version of democracy that currently dominates political thinking?[9] For without a will toward a more participatory and robust civic system, why should technologically enhanced politics not produce the same incivility and cynicism that characterize politics on the older technologies, radio and television, for example? (Recall that radio too once promised a more egalitarian and democratic form of communication.) Political chatroom banter on the Internet is as polarized and rude as anything you can hear on talk radio.

It remains true that technology can assist political change and may sometimes even point in new political directions. Interactive computer-based television hookups "point" in a certain sense to the feasibility of direct democracy, but unless there is a political will directed at greater participation, the potential remains just that. Nor will interactive technology do anything, on its own, to cure the primary defect of unmediated participatory politics—the danger of undeliberative majority tyranny and thus a kind of plebiscitary dictatorship. One-way information retrieval via the Net may expand for some the orbit of available resources; the Library of Congress has achieved an instant success by making millions of items including Matthew Brady's Civil War photographs, Gershwin's musical scores, San Francisco earthquake pictorials, and theatrical memorabilia from the Yiddish Theater available on its new Net site (www.loc.gov). Yet retrieval is at best an improvement on access to information, not a move towards genuine interactive communication.[10]

Indeed, while Umberto Eco uncritically assumes that new technologies will render obsolete many kinds of books,[11] publishers who were originally excited by the rush to digital publishing and CD-ROMs have recently pulled back from the brink, arguing that "the business has been a huge bust for book publishers."[12] If then technology is to make a political difference, it is the politics that will first have to be changed.

The New Media: Diversity or Monopoly?

Much has been made over the apparent diversification of media and the multiplication of communication spectra that have accompanied the evolution of advanced telecommunication technologies. In place of three networks in America, or two or three state networks in many other countries, we now have cable and satellite-based systems that can offer up to five hundred or more channels. Even the traditional broadcast media are soon to be subjected to a digitalization that will yield five or six channels for every one that currently exists on the broadcast spectrum—a change that led U.S. Senator Bob Dole, fearing the "giveaway of the century," to exempt the question of what is to be done with these new spectra from the recently enacted 1996 telecommunications bill, leaving it for the new Congress to debate. Moreover, the multiplication of available channels of communication is clearly abetted by an Internet that offers literally endless millions of interconnected sites that promote point-to-point communication of a kind that seems in turn to promise endless diversity.

In short, the technology is clearly capable of exerting a pluralizing influence on communications. Yet though the technology may be inherently disaggregating and devolutionary, ownership over the technology's hardware and software is aggregating and centralizing. As delivery systems diversify and multiply, program content becomes more homogeneous. As the laterally organized Net expands, commercial carpetbaggers move in, ready to turn its horizontal and interactive communications networks into an opportunity for vertical one-way "we-sell you-buy" commercial control (sometimes called "push" rather than "pull" techniques). So that kids logging onto playroom sites owned by companies like Toys-R-Us that are supposed to be educational and fun are in fact being used as unwitting subjects of cybertot market surveys they fill out as their password to play.

More conduits, more hardware, and more outlets do not mean more diversity. Imagine a one-hundred-channel cable system in Nazi Germany. "Yes, we Nazis prize diversity!" a Goebbels would say. But turn on the system and you find Himmler on channel 1, the Hitler Jugend on channel 2, the Oberkommando Wehrmacht on channel 3, Goering on channel 4, the Party Platform as Hypertext on channel 5, an exhibition of *Entartente Kunst* (Decadent Art) on channel 6, and so on. Some "diversity"!

Free market advocates defend this commodification of cyberspace by insisting on what they call the "synergy" between markets and the new technologies that supposedly turns markets into engines of efficiency that advantage public interests by maximizing competition and choice. But late capitalism is neither entrepreneurial nor competitive. It flourishes by selling singular, mass-produced goods like athletic shoes, electronic hardware, and colas to everyone on the planet: the same movie, the same book, the same burger—and the same software platform, the same program—to as many billions of citizens as can be turned into consumers. And when it can no longer push goods, it starts manufacturing needs so that there is a demand for the endless goods it must bring to the market if it is to flourish. No wonder that, as governments bow out of the communications regulation business and new technologies globalize in a manner that makes them resistant to regulation, ownership patterns are growing more rather than less monopolistic.

Software understood as computer programs, information and data banks, films and videos, entertainment, music, and images are at the heart of technological change in the postindustrial era. And in the sector that supplies the new technologies with this software, production is controlled by a small handful of powerful corporations that, quite literally month by month, grow fewer in number and more encompassing in scope and ambition. The concept that drives the new media merger frenzy carries the fashionable name "synergy."

The idea is to gather together the production companies turning out product, the phone and cable and satellite companies transmitting them, and the television sets and computers and multiplexes presenting them to the public all into the same hands.[13] Synergy, however, turns out to be a polite way of saying monopoly. And in the domain of information, monopoly is a polite word for uniformity, which is a polite word for virtual censorship—censorship not as a consequence of political choices but as a consequence of inelastic markets, imperfect competition, and economies of scale—the quest for a single product that can be owned by a single proprietor and sold to every living soul on the planet. (In the United States, the popular C-Span channel that allows Americans to watch Congress around the clock has been forced off some cable systems by the new Rupert Murdoch–owned Fox News Channel); or the search for a "safe image" that avoids all controversy in the name of broad consumer acceptance.

The quest for image safety manifests an all-too-common corporate anxiety about controversy and a tendency to support the bland and the plastic over the disputatious and the risk-taking. Postmodern capitalism is preternaturally risk-averse, anything but entrepreneurial. This means just as Hollywood makes sequels to successful megahits rather than experimenting with new "art" films, that publishers seeks megabooks by celebrities rather than serious nonfiction and new novels and that television is hostile to anything that seems too far out: too politically radical or too reactionary, too religious or too insistently atheist, too eccentric and thus too far from the mean, too (quite literally) unpopular.

The consolidation of ownership in the infotainment telesector, well documented by Ben Bagdikian and others for the period from 1945 through the 1980s, has accelerated as technologies have multiplied and the possibilities for transmitting information have diversified. Conglomeration had reduced the number of mainstage telecommunications players from forty-six in 1981 to twenty-three in 1991. And of these, a handful like Time Warner/Turner, Disney/ABC, Bertelsmann, and Murdoch's News Corporation dominate—genuinely intermedia corporations with a finger in every part of the business.[14] So that, for example, when Rupert Murdoch wanted to accommodate the Chinese on the way to persuading them to permit his Asian Television Network to broadcast, he was able to instruct HarperCollins (a News Corporation subsidiary) to withdraw its offer to Harry Wu—a dissident thorn in the side of the Chinese—for his political memoirs.[15]

The recent erosion of boundaries between telephone, cable, and broadcast transmission has accelerated the conglomeration process even more radically, and the orphans of Ma Bell, cut loose in 1984, are now threatening to supplant their aging mama as they are licensed by the government to enter and compete in the long distance telephone field. In fact, the new telecommunications bill allows any company to compete in more or less any field of communications so that AT&T (Ma Bell) can pursue cable television or satellite, the local phone companies can go after long distance or cellular, and people can buy pretty much anyone or anything as long as they can cut the deal and pay the freight. In February of 1997, sixty-eight nations agreed through the World Trade Organization to remove barriers that prevented private companies from competing with state telecommunication monopolies—good news for consumers in the short run, but better news by far for the powerful, technologically advanced American telecommunications cartels poised to take over much of the world's long distance business and further secure their hold on global communications.[16] In the name of free markets, private profit once again is permitted to displace public utility (or is assumed to be synonymous with it). An eighteenth-century version of free market ideology is thus used to legitimate antientrepreneurial monopoly practices of a twenty-first-century global capitalism that has lost its taste for real competition.

The Soft New Totalitarianism of Consumerism

The new trend toward monopoly signals then not synergy but vulnerability to a kind of commercial totalitarianism—a single value (profit) and a single owner (the monopoly holder) submerging all distinctions, rendering all choice tenuous and all diversity sham. Carriers want to control and profit from what they carry; cultural creators want to control and profit from the entities (stations and networks) that carry what they create; software purveyors want to control and profit from the hardware on which their wares are purveyed. Everyone wants a piece of the creative core, where the "content" that drives everything else is manufactured. The result is more talk about variety but far more uniformity in actual product and content. Why be a pipe for someone else's music, when you can own composer and composition alike? There may be one hundred or even five hundred channels on the new cable systems, but if the content providers are gargantuan monopolies, what difference does it make that the conduits are multiple? And so Bill Gates buys Washington pundit Michael Kinsley to put a magazine, *Slate,* on Microsoft's Internet network and purchases the rights to the Barnes's collection of art, taking an option on filmmakers at the same time by buying into Dreamworks, the new creative "content providers" production company constituted by director Steven Spielberg, record titan David Geffen, and ex–Disney magnate Jeffrey Katzenberg.

The men who dominate this extraordinary new world of technologized culture are mostly American (though there are the Murdochs and Bertelsmanns and Burdas to be reckoned with as well.) America may have been down in the eighties, but as power has softened and soft information and entertainment products have replaced durable industrial goods, it has become the world's economic superpower. American media moguls like Michael Eisner, Ted Turner, Sumner Redstone, Barry Diller, Martin S. Davis, George Lucas, Michael Ovitz, Bill Gates, Jeffrey Katzenberg, H. Wayne Huizenga, John C. Malone, and Steven Spielberg are surely as powerful today as Vanderbilt, Carnegie, Rockefeller, and their gilded age cousins were in the late nineteenth century.[17] Except the new titans of telecommunication exercise monopoly control not just over material goods like oil, coal, steel, and the railroads but over the essential instruments of power in an information-based civilization: ideas, images, words, and pictures. Such monopolies not only destroy capitalist competition, they also corrupt the diversity and pluralism of information on which democracy depends. Behind the beckoning diversity of their media empires lurks a new form of totalism all the more dangerous because it boasts of "choice" and is sold in the language of freedom. The claim is that in the marketplace, with government out of the way, we are all equals. I have a home page on the Net just like Bill Gates and the Disney Corporation. But does anyone really believe that the common capacity to produce a home page is the same thing as the common power to affect the world? Is power a question of who is speaking or who is listening (and who can get whom to listen)? In a world of communications leviathans, democracy requires more than home page equality.[18]

In a world where monopoly passes as synergy, why should we expect technology to produce genuine diversity? Or universal access—without which income and education disparities are likely to be reproduced by information and technology disparities, with cleavages between rich and poor being replicated as cleavages between the information rich and the information poor. Who represents the public good in a world of privatized information production? Is there a global equivalent of even so reluctant a defender of the public interest as the Federal Communications Commission? Which institutions can exert countervailing pressures on media monopolies in the name of quality or diversity or community? There appear to be no easy answers, even on the rare occasions when the questions get asked.

What Is Virtual Community?

In the solipsistic virtual reality of cyberspace, commonality itself seems to be in jeopardy. Not only does commerce tend toward monopoly, it mandates privatization, and privatization is the death of democracy. For democracy is always about *public* willing and *public* goods and the *common*weal. Decentralization can enhance democracy, privatization only corrupts it. Little is no better than big when it is private and for profit rather than public (but local) and for the common good (not personal benefit). You can be eaten alive by piranha as well as by a great white shark: it just takes a little longer.

Here commerce is reenforced by certain technical features of telecommunications technology, which in turn it reenforces. How can there be "common ground" when ground itself vanishes and women and men inhabit abstractions? There may be some new form of community developing among the myriad solitaries perched in front of their screens and connected only by their fingertips to the new web defined by the Internet. But the politics of that "community" has yet to be invented, and it is hardly likely to be democratic as a result of market imperatives. It has yet to be shown that anonymous screen-to-screen interaction can do for us what face-to-face interaction has done. The out-of-body nature of virtual communication is both a virtue and a vice. It can marginalize bodies—as when college roommates sit side by side conversing via their screens, or when on wired campuses social clubs and local recreational centers atrophy because students are glued to their computers. I will believe in the virtual community when someone shows me virtual community service.

Enthusiasts for Internet chatrooms or cybertot playpens prattle on about "community," but can an anonymous exchange with strangers whose identity is a matter of invention and artifice replicate the kind of conversations that occur spontaneously among fellow PTA members about a school board election or even mimic a gossip session across a back fence? If good fences make good neighbors, virtual neighbors may turn out to make good fences against real neighbors. The *New York Times* recently reported that "E-Mail is becoming a conduit of prejudice on many campuses."[19] Is the social trust that is eroding in our social and political world likely to be rekindled on the Internet, where identities can be concealed and where "flaming" and other forms of incivility are regularly practiced? Civility means taking responsibility for one's views (their virtues and their vices): the Net is far more anonymous than talk radio, and neither medium seems much interested in social responsibility. My own painfully vapid visits to the Internet in search of deliberative dialogue and meaningful political talk netted little that would support Lawrence K. Grossman's happy conclusion that "the transformation to participatory democracy has been helped by the remarkable increase in the speed of information, pushed along" most recently by "digital convergence."[20] Information seekers are mostly after porn and pulp while chatroom visitors, when not also pursuing sex, seem to be asleep. In a typical conversation:

> On Line Host: "You are in Town Square. . ."
> DeepPhaze: "Which guy wants to eat me out?"
> Jr. Twety: "What's everyone talking about?
> Iceburn 911: "Me." . . .
> Lodino: "OK."
> Iceburn 911: "Deep is a gay."
> Bjanyeats: "No way pal."
> DWJLY: "I'm a girl."
> Hulk Dog: "Hi."
> JMWICK001: "I am a new AOL User from Long Island, Where are any of you from?"
> BJANYEATS: "Big fat hairy deal."
> Lodino: "Bye"
> Lene77: "Dork."
> Iceburn911: "Let's have cybersex."
> Otterhawk: "Get a clue."
> Bjanyeats: "What clue?"

(This conversation is concluded by the posting of an ingenious digital image provided by "Kyoung Pro" of Hulkdog being apparently fellated by his "little sister.")

There are more serious sites of course, but the great preponderance of them dispense superficial information about political parties, platforms, and candidates or host polarized debates around the conventional talk radio extremes with little in the way of real discussion or persuasion. [21] And there are a handful of sites that have tried to create new formats for interactive political education, including Project VOTESMART and MINNESOTA E DEMOCRACY. But even these sites seem better geared to serve citizens during elections, and often do little in the long periods between them. There is no better guide to the apparent futility of hopes for cyberdemocracy and genuine political dialogue than John Seabrook's new account of his disillusionment with the medium he initially celebrated. In a memoir called *Deeper*, he confesses that his hopes for a "many-to-many" technology "uniquely capable of inspiring" new hope for human relations were dashed by the reality that the Net only offered people new ways to "be just as cliquish and exclusionary as they ever were."[22]

Finally, the economic trends of our world tend toward radical commercialization of values and behavior in a fashion that compromises not only civic politics but family values, education, and spirituality. The technology is not per se commercial or commercializing, but *commercialized*, and it becomes one more weapon in the arsenal of corporations for whom consumption is the only relevant human behavior. When *U.S. News and World Report* trumpeted on the cover of its special issue on the Internet "Goldrush in Cyberspace!" it mixed nineteenth-century frontier imagery with twenty-first-century cyberjabber on the way to revealing that for the telecommunication corporations the only significant question is how to make money from the innovations that utopians and idealists believe will usher in a new world of democracy.[23]

The frontier has been a powerful image in American political iconography, and it is no surprise that radical individualists and decentralist democrats like to deploy it in thinking about the Net—as with the Electronic Frontier Foundation. But in reality, the wild west frontier was opening up after the Civil War at the very moment when the concentration and conglomeration of capital in oil, coal, steel, and railways that defined the gilded age were getting under way. And by the end of the nineteenth century, it was not the frontier but the cartel that defined America, and the products of the cartel—railroads, industry, urbanization—had been the very commodities that closed the frontier down.

There is little reason to think that, in the absence of political will, the metaphoric electronic frontier will fare any better in the face of monopoly capitalism than did the territorial frontier. Are the new monopolists like Gates and Eisner and Malone any less ambitious or talented than Carnegie and Rockefeller and J. P. Morgan? Is capitalism any less interested today in the kinds of control that breeds big profits than it was a hundred years ago? The electronic frontier is not a metaphor, it is a dream, a myth, and a deeply misleading one at that: a perfect smokescreen for those busy closing it down.

The young history of music video offers a particularly instructive lesson for those who believe the Internet is likely to remain free from commercialization because it is a new, creative medium developed that was used in its early incarnation by electronic frontiersmen and cyber-pioneers. In the 1970s, music videos were the playground of artists and countercultural dissidents—a medium for new wave creative explorers working at experimental studios like 'The Kitchen' in lower Manhattan. Like moving pictures, which in their own time were celebrated as a democratization of aristocratic theater, music video was to be a peculiarly "democratic" medium. Its early experimental users insisted that, unlike film, videotape was inexpensive, flexible, erasable, and reusable and hence accessible to everyone.

Yet within ten years, the television, cable, and music industries had moved in and expropriated the "experimental" medium, and today MTV and its imitators are wholly owned subsidiaries as well as the selling arm of the global music industry: a twenty-four-hour-a-day advertisement for a globalizing and ever more homogeneous pop music, as well as for the software and hardware it takes to play that music. Why should it be any different with the Internet? Just because today it is the playground of intrepid cyberexplorers will not insulate it tomorrow from ambitious corporate profiteers.

Computer shopping has already become the fastest growing part of the World Wide Web. Even the usually technologically upbeat Aspen Institute, in a report celebrating "The Future of Electronic Commerce," warns that while "the business rush to colonize the Internet will surely invigorate cyberspace and make it more accessible to mainstream Americans . . . it may also marginalize the vast 'third sector' of nonprofits, civic groups and public institutions who generally do not have the money and expertise to participate fully in the on-line culture."[24]

Does this portrait of global commerce and growing monopoly mean then that all technological innovation is inimical to democracy? Not necessarily. It means only that without directives aimed at taking advantages of its democratic potentials, the global socioeconomic forces that are today shaping the world will also shape the technology's usages.

Is This Progress?

Science has been linked to progressive liberalism and democracy at least since the Enlightenment, when pioneers standing on the threshold of modernity believed that through their new science they could command the world and liberate the human race from prejudice, ignorance, and injustice. At the beginning of the century now ending, Bertrand Russell saw in scientific skepticism a source of democracy's epistemological humility even as he worried about technology's association with power and manipulation. Advocates of the consumer society might ponder his warning that having once "delivered man from bondage to nature" science was in danger of delivering him "from bondage to the slavish part of himself."[25]

Less cautious heirs to Russell have become Panglossian futurologists, unknowingly mouthing Candide's ditty "this is the best of all possible worlds." Taking their cue from the eighteenth-century Frenchman Condorcet (who died in a French revolutionary prison while writing a book about the Ten Stages of inevitable human progress), enthusiasts like Walter Winston, Alvin Toffler, John Naisbett, and Bill Gates have all composed odes to the emancipatory, democratic powers of the startling new technologies that drive McWorld and have transformed capitalism from a system that serves needs into a system that creates and manipulates them.[26]

Walter Winston thinks that "the information age is rapidly giving the power to the people," speeding us along on "our journey toward more human freedom,"[27] while Bill Gates is certain that "technology can humanize the educational [arena]. . . . The net effect [of the new technology] will be a wealthier world . . . (and) the gap between the have and have not nations will diminish. . . . Somewhere ahead is the threshold dividing the PC era from the highway era. I want to be among the first to cross over."[28]

Technology's mandarins are correct in seeing improved information and communication as potentially useful in improving democracy. From the time of the Greeks, who believed Prometheus's theft of fire from the gods lit the way to human civilization, technical gadgets have been made to support democratization. In ancient Athens, small machines that randomized the selection of white and black balls were used for jury selection. During the Renaissance movable type, gunpowder, and the compass helped society transform itself through forces that both equalized and mobilized the population. Democratic trends already under way were thereby reenforced.

Twentieth-century technologies have mimicked those of the fifteenth and sixteenth centuries, further democratizing transportation, communication, and war. Combat has become the democratic burden of civilians as well as soldiers, while the internal combustion engine has given everyman a horse and buggy and the mobility that goes with it. Most significantly, radio and television and in time mass-produced computers have offered an ongoing technically enhanced democratization of words and pictures that spreads effective literacy and political knowledge even to those who cannot read and thus strengthens the will to govern (if not necessarily the deliberative competence) of democratic electorates. Television, one might say, does not so much enhance literacy as render it irrelevant—bypassing the black and white of the word to bring a bright color world of pictures to everyman.

The Internet still seems wedded to words. Scrolling text with how-long-do-we-have-to-wait-to-get-them? pictures is the Internet's medium, suggesting a technology that is little more than a souped-up telegraph. But of course that is only a technical glitch resting on its immaturity. As its capacity to carry more information at greater speeds increases, it is likely to become motion picture based . . . just like television and the movies! Pictures are clearly the favored form of information on what are after all *moving picture* screens, whether they are found in quad cinemas or aboard laptop computers. Clever kids already use their keyboards to design character-generated graphics, using what are supposed to be the building blocks of words (and thus thought) to compose pictures. So obviously the technology is fairly wasted if all it does is transmit text. Yet many of the new technology's virtues have been associated precisely with this text-based character, its most retrograde feature.

Live picture interactive hook-ups beat electronic bulletin boards for some purposes of democracy, although agreement with this statement clearly depends on what we mean by democracy and whether we are looking for affective interaction or rational deliberation. Video teleconference capabilities allow people at a local town meeting to interact with others in similar meetings across a region, a nation, or the world, breaking down the parochialism of face-to-face interaction without entirely sacrificing its personalism. I recently hosted a four-site interactive discussion of immigration and American identity in Arizona, with groups participating from Tuba City, Flagstaff, Tempe, and Tucson, where it again was demonstrated how interactive television can transform a passive medium aimed at complacent consumers of entertainment and advertising into an active theater of social discourse and political feedback. Members of the World Economic Forum (the convening of economic and political elites at Davos each winter) are being offered their own communications network called Welcom (World Electronic Community) that promises to inaugurate a "secure, private, high-level, reliable network of active face-to-face global video communications" that will connect members "with cabinet members, heads of international organizations and central banks, and the foremost experts and knowledge-producing centers across the globe."[29] And of course "distance learning" facilitated by new technology is the latest rage on many college campuses.

The technology does then open up the possibilities of democracy. For example, home voting by interactive module can facilitate and personalize voting, if we are willing to pay the costs of privatization. Interactive technologies foster lateral as well as vertical communication. This means citizens can interact with one another and not simply listen passively to leaders and elites. Project Vote Smart, a national citizens' clearinghouse for election information, recently moved from 800 and 900 number technology to a "Vote Smart Web" on which the politically curious can access a welter of vital political and electoral statistics, data, and candidate information.[30] There are also web sites for the White House, Congress, and the new international CIVITAS network of global nongovernmental organizations.[31]

Satellite dishes the size of a dinner plate put a global ear at the disposal of peoples imprisoned in the most despotic regimes and have proved their worth in places like China and Iran where despite an official government ban, they continue to spread—and as they do, to spread unfettered images and words to information-starved consumers. To be sure, much of what is spread is consumer information and banal entertainment rather than political debate and news, but this is the fault of those who exhibit it rather than of the technology itself.[32]

Which Democracy? Progress for Whom?

In combination then, the new technologies and the software they support can potentially enhance lateral communication among citizens, can open access to information by all, and can furnish citizens with communication links across distances that once precluded direct democracy. Yet there is a formidable obstacle in the way of implementation of these technologies: unless we are clear about what democracy means to us, and what kind of democracy we envision, technology is as likely to stunt as to enhance the civic polity: is it representative democracy, plebiscitary democracy, or deliberative democracy for which we seek technological implementation? The differences among the three are not only theoretically crucial but have radically different entailments with respect to technology.

Do we aspire to further the representative system, a democracy rooted in the election of accountable deputies who do all the real work of governing? Most advocates of this form of indirect democracy are properly suspicious of the new technologies and their penchant for immediacy, directness, lateral communication, and undeliberativeness. Or is it plebiscitary majoritarianism we seek, a democracy that embodies majority opinions aggregated from the unconsidered prejudices of private persons voting private interests? New technology can be a dangerously facile instrument of such unchecked majoritarianism: the Internet affords politicians an instrument for perpetual polling that can aggravate the focus group mentality that many rue as Dick Morris's political legacy. Will any politician ever again gather the courage to lead in the face of a technology that makes following so easy?

Yet if we are in search of what I have called "strong democracy," a democracy that reflects the careful and prudent judgment of citizens who participate in deliberative, self-governing communities, we will need to tease other capabilities out of the technology. If democracy is to be understood as deliberative and participatory activity on the part of responsible citizens, it will have to resist the innovative forms of demagoguery that accompany innovative technology and that are too often overlooked by enthusiasts, and listen carefully to those like Theodore Becker and James Fishkin who have tried to incorporate deliberative constraints into their direct democratic uses of the technologies.[33] In other words, there is no simple or general answer to the question "is the technology democratizing?" until we have made clear what sort of democracy we have in mind. Home voting via interactive television might further privatize politics and replace deliberative debate in public with the unconsidered instant expression of private prejudices, turning what ought to be public decisions into private consumer-like choices; but deliberative television polling of the kind envisioned by James Fishkin can offset such dangers, while the use of the Internet for deliberation across communities can actually render decisionmaking less parochial.[34]

Strong democracy calls not only for votes but for good reasons; not only for an opinion but for a rational argument on its behalf. Those who once preferred open to secret ballots, who preferred open debate about justified viewpoints to closed votes aggregating personal interests, will today prefer technologies that permit frank interactive debate with real identities revealed, to technologies that allow game playing and privately registered, unsupported opinions.

Traditional proponents of Madisonian representative democracy are likely to find much of the new interactive technology intimidating, since it threatens to overwhelm what they regard as a pristine system assuring government by expert politicians with a free-for-all among "ignorant" masses who swamp the polity with their endless demands and overheated prejudices. Such critics already complain about traditional broadcast television as destructive of party identity and party discipline, and they will properly worry about technologies that further erode the boundaries between the governors and the governed. Plebiscitary democrats will be mindlessly enthralled by interactive instant polling and imagine a time when private consumers make precedent-shattering public choices with no more serious thought than they give to which button to hit when they are surfing a hundred-channel cable system. "Let's see," mutters the glib new Net-surfer, "do I want to play checkers or outlaw abortion? Do I prefer Sylvester Stallone to Bill Clinton? Shall we download the 'Playmate of the Month' or vote to expand NATO to the Russian border? Is it time for a mock battle with Darth Vader on my Star Wars simulation, or should I just declare war for real on Libya?" Deliberative democrats can only shudder at such prospects, insisting that they do more to destroy than to enhance democracy. Deliberation, on the other hand, does require intervention, education, facilitation, and mediation—all anathema to devotees of a anarchic and wholly user-controlled Net.

Technology can then help democracy, but only if programmed to do so and only in terms of the paradigms and political theories that inform the program. Left to the market it is likely only to reproduce the vices of politics as usual. How different is the anonymous flaming that typifies certain kinds of Internet chatter from the anonymous vilification that characterizes talk radio and scream television? Will the newer technologies be any less likely to debase the political currency, any less likely to foster sound-bite decisionmaking in place of sound political judgment?

By the same token, if those who deploy the technologies consciously seek a more participatory, deliberative form of strong democracy and a newly robust civil society, they can also find in telecommunications innovation an extraordinarily effective ally. The trouble with the zealots of technology as an instrument of democratic liberation is not their understanding of technology but their grasp of democracy. They insist that market-generated technology can, quite by itself and in the complete absence of common human willing and political cooperation, produce liberty, social responsibility, and citizenship. The viruses that eat up our computer programs, like sarin in the Tokyo subway, are but obvious symbols of technology's ever-present dark side, the monster who lurks in Dr. Frankenstein's miraculous creation.

With participatory interaction comes the promise of political and economic surveillance.[35] With interactive personal preference modules comes the risk of majoritarian tyranny. With digital reasoning comes the peril of adversarial modes of thought inundating consensus. Computer literacy cannot finally exist independently of life-long educational literacy. The age of information can reenforce extant inequalities, making the resource and income poor the information-poor as well.[36] The irony is that those who might most benefit from the Net's democratic and informational potential are least likely to have access to it, the tools to use it, or the educational background to take advantage of the tools. Those with access, however, tend to be those already empowered in the system by education, income, and literacy.

And how easily liberating technologies become tools of repression. As consumers tell shopping networks what they want to buy and tell banks how to dispense their cash and tell pollsters what they think about abortion, those receiving the information gain access to an extensive computer bank of knowledge about the private habits, attitudes, and behaviors of consumers and citizens. This information may in turn be used to reshape those habits and attitudes in ways that favor producers and sellers working the marketplace or the political arena. Moreover, the current anti-regulatory fever has assured that the new data banks being compiled from interaction and surveillance are subject neither to government scrutiny nor to limitation or control—a sunset provision, for example, which would periodically destroy all stored information.[37] The model of Channel One, an invidious classroom network founded by Chris Whittle's Whittle Communications (and now owned by the K III Corporation) that extorts classroom advertising time from needy schools in return for desperately wanted hardware, suggests that the public is likely to be served by the new technologies only in as far as someone can make serious money from it.[38]

It may be a cause of satisfaction, as Walter Winston insists, that nowadays it is the citizen who is watching Big Brother and not the other way around. But if Big Brother is no longer watching you, nor is he watching those who *are* watching you, and even adversaries of regulation may find reason to be disturbed by that omission. If the classical liberal question used to be who will police the police, the pertinent liberal question in today's McWorld ought to be who will watch those who are watching the watchers? Who will prevent the media from controlling their clients and consumers? Who will act in lieu of a government that has demurred from representing the public's interests? These are issues for democracy deliberation and decision, not for technological resolution. For technology remains a tool: allied to particular conceptions of democracy, if we know what kind of democracy we want, it can enhance civic communication and expand citizen literacy. Left to markets (and that is where it is now being left), it is likely to augment McWorld's least worthy imperatives, including surveillance over and manipulation of opinion, and the cultivation of artificial needs rooted in life-style "choices" unconnected to real economic, civic or spiritual needs.

If democracy is to benefit from technology, then we must start not with technology but with politics. Demanding a voice in the making of science and technology policy is the first step citizens can take in ensuring a democratic technology.[39] The new technology is still only an instrument of communication, and it cannot determine *what* we will say or to whom we will say it. There is a story about the wireless pioneer Marconi who, when told by his associates that his new wireless technology meant he could now "talk to Florida," asked, presciently, "and do we have anything to say to Florida?" Enthusiasts exalt over the fact that on the Net we can talk to strangers throughout the world. But many of today's problems arise from the fact that we no longer know how to talk to our husbands and wives, our neighbors and fellow citizens, let alone strangers. Will our blockages and incivilities locally be overcome by the miracles of long distance computer communication? Will virtual community heal the ruptures of real communities? Will we do on our keyboards what we have notably failed to do face to face?

If in the coming millennium—a millennium in which technology is likely to dominate our lives as never before—we want democracy to be served, then the bittersweet fruits of science will have to be subordinated to our democratic ends and made to serve as a facilitator rather than a corruptor of our precious democracy. And whether this happens will depend not on the quality and character of our technology but on the quality of our political institutions and the character of our citizens.

Notes

1. See Anthony Corrado and Charles M. Firestone, eds., *Elections in Cyberspace: Toward a New Era in American Politics* (Aspen: Aspen Institute, 1996).
2. More than a dozen years ago, I suggested that "electronic enhancement of communication offers possible solutions to the dilemmas of scale" and called for television town meetings, a "Civic Communications Cooperative," and a "Civic Videotext Service." See Benjamin R. Barber, *Strong Democracy* (University of California Press, 1984), chap. 10, pp. 273–80. Ted Becker and his colleagues in the televoting project have developed effective pilots in which electronic voting is tempered by various deliberative strategies. See Theodore L. Becker, "From Televoting to Teledemocracy," in A. Kiskinen, *Teledemokratia* (Helsinki, 1995).
3. Rousseau, *First Discourse, Social Contract and Discourses* (London: J.M. Dent and Sons, 1913), second part, p. 140.
4. See, for example, Theodore Adorno and Hans Horkheimer, *Dialectic of Enlightenment* (1947) and Herbert Marcuse, *One Dimensional Man* (Beacon Press, 1964).
5. See the "Munchner Erklarung," Akademie zum Dritten Jahrtausend, Munich, February, 1997.
6. President Bill Clinton's intervention with corporate executives from the entertainment industry at his February and July 1996 meetings can be seen as politically successful since it not only elicited the promise of a self-generated rating system and a commitment to the V-Chip (allowing parents to identify and screen out material unsuitable for children), and got a weak agreement to secure three hours of "educational television for children" ("educational" to be defined by the broadcasters, however!), but acted as an implicit threat: if you don't do this voluntarily, Congress and the White House might do it for you. The same is true of his efforts to applaud and encourage private industry's voluntary efforts at funding the wiring of schools and libraries. However, government-encouraged market initiatives will always play a secondary role to the primary corporate ambition to augment earnings, and this ambition will never be a sufficient source for securing public goods in the technological arena. In the case of hardwiring the nation's schools, for example, the industry has backed off from its early pledges, and the program appears today to be in jeopardy.
7. According to Gingrich in his ebullient 1984 book *Windows of Opportunity*, "breakthroughs in computers, biology, and space make possible new jobs, new opportunities, and new hope on a scale unimagined since Christopher Columbus

discovered a new world. . . . hope for a continuing revolution in biology . . . hope for jobs, opportunities, and adventures in space." Newt Gingrich, with David Drake and Marianne Gingrich, *Window of Opportunity: A Blueprint for the Future* (New York: Jim Baer, 1984), cited in Thomas M. Disch, "Newt's Futurist Brain Trust," *The Nation*, February 27, 1995. David Drake is a science fiction writer. His offhand suggestion that welfare might be licked by dropping portable computers into the laps of the poor is suggestive of futurological gusto and is fairly representative of the naivete with which many novices view the new technologies.

8. Bill Gates, *The Road Ahead* (Penguin, 1995), excerpted in *Newsweek*, November 27, 1995, pp. 59, 65.

9. This is why the most important section of the Munich Declaration alluded to above is Part III, called "Citizen Politics," in which the Academy calls for citizen participation—*Burger Engagement* not just on the Net but in all our civil and political institutions.

10. See R.W. Apple, Jr., "Library of Congress Is an Internet Hit," *New York Times*, February 16, 1997.

11. Umberto Eco, "Gutenberg Galaxy Expands," *Nation*, January 6, 1997, p. 35.

12. Chris Garske, senior vice president in charge of publishing at GT Interactive Corporation. Phyllis Furman, "Plugged In: Interactive Meltdown: Publishers Retreating from Digital Books," *Authors Guild Bulletin*, Fall 1996, p. 39. The book turns out to be a remarkable little technology of its own, packing an extraordinary amount of easily accessed information into a portable format that goes anywhere and makes reading an aesthetic pleasure as well (something no one claims for the Internet!).

13. For a full account of these tendencies, see Benjamin R. Barber, *Jihad versus McWorld* (Times Books, 1995), chapter 9.

14. Ben H. Bagdikian, *Media Monopoly*, fourth ed. (Beacon Press, 1993), p. 19.

15. The Disney Company seemed to exercise more autonomy when it resisted Chinese attempts to close down production of a Disney feature film on the Dali Lama and repression in Tibet, but the company is extremely anxious to do business in China, which has expressed interest in a theme park. The story is not over.

16. The agreement opens up the global telecommunications market and permits outside companies to buy into (though not take over or buy out) national companies. In the name of free trade and open markets, nations are being asked to permit international cartels to move in and take over communications. The idea of a public utility is apparently dead. See "68 Nations Agree to Widen Market in Communications," *New York Times*, February 16, 1997, p. 1.

17. Ted Turner is chairman of Turner Broadcasting, TNT; Sumner Redstone is CEO of Viacom and the feisty competitor for Paramount; for Barry Diller see text; Martin S. Davis is president of Paramount; Michael Ovitz was chairman of the Creative Artists Agency and a key player in the MGM–Credit Lyonnais deal and is now Disney Corporation president; Bill Gates is the power behind Microsoft; and John C. Malone is president of Tele-Communication, part-time chair

of Liberty media, as well as a one-quarter owner of Turner Broadcasting, which makes him a major force beyond Barry Diller's QVC Network.

18. When cable was first introduced, many thought that if communities were given access via public access studios, they could compete with the networks and corporations who were cable's primary vendors. It did not happen that way.

19. *New York Times*, February 16, 1997, p. 40.

20. Lawrence K. Grossman, *The Electronic Republic: Reshaping Democracy in the Information Age* (Viking, 1995), pp. 46–48.

21. One can visit web pages for White House or Congress or the British Labor Party or the Library of Congress and download information easily available through other sources.

22. John Seabrook, *Deeper: My Two Year Odyssey in Cyberspace* (Simon & Schuster, 1997). For the kind of cyberenthusiasm Seabrook is puncturing, see the vituperative and polemical account of the Net as a weapon of the young against the moralistic old by Jon Katz in his *Virtuous Reality: How America Surrendered Discussion of Moral Values to Opportunists, Nitwits and Blockheads like William Bennett* (Random House, 1997).

23. *U.S. News and World Report*, November 13, 1995, cover.

24. David Bollier, "The Future of Electronic Commerce" (Washington, D.C.: Aspen Institute, 1996), p. 39. Companies like Pepsico, Nabisco, Toys-R-Us, Nintendo, Time Warner, and Disney have all developed web sites on the Net aimed not only at selling their products but, in some cases, also designed to elicit market survey information from kids logging on. See Lawrie Mifflin, "Advertisers Chase a New Target: 'Cybertots,'" *New York Times*, March 29, 1996.

25. Bertrand Russell, *The Scientific Outlook* (London: Unwin Brothers, 1931), p. 279.

26. See Condorcet, *Sketch for the Historical Progress of the Human Mind* (Paris, 1794); Alvin Toffler, *Future Shock* (1970) and *The Third Wave* (1980); *Power Shift*, (1990); and John Naisbett, *Megatrends* (1982) and *Global Paradox* (1994).

27. Walter B. Winston, *The Twilight of Sovereignty* (Scribner, 1992), pp. 170, 176. Winston also thinks "modern information technology is also driving nation states towards cooperation with each other so that the world's work can get done," p. 174.

28. With him on his trek is of course Microsoft, a corporation the *New York Times* described in a Sunday magazine cover article title as "The Microsoft Monopoly"—with a subtitle asking "How Do You Restrain a 800-Pound Gorilla?" Gates, *The Road Ahead*, excerpted in *Newsweek*, pp. 66–67. See James Gieick, "The Microsoft Monopoly," *New York Times Magazine*, November 5, 1995, sec. 6.

29. From the inaugural brochure printed by World Electronic Community, 70 Blanchard Road, Burlington, Massachusetts 01803; e-mail: welcome@avcinc.com. Once again, corporate and elite uses of the Net for commercial purposes are light years ahead of civic uses.

30. See Project Vote Smart, "1996 Election Year Guide to the VOTE SMART WEB." http://www.votesmart.org

31. The Aspen Institute boasts of a "new era in American Politics," but turns out to be concerned only with traditional elections. See Anthony Corrado and Charles M. Firestone, *Elections in Cyberspace: Towards a New Era of American Politics* (Aspen: Aspen Institute, 1996).

32. A Western diplomat in China says, "The Chinese Government has decided and I think logically that it really can't shut out satellite television entirely, whatever the threat. We're not talking about a few dissident here. Hundreds of thousands of Chinese have now invested their life savings in these dishes, and there would be a nasty public uproar if the Government really forced the dishes down." And in Iran, the *Teheran Times* concludes that "the cultural invasion will not be resolved by the physical removal of satellite dishes." Both quotes from Philip Shenon, "A Repressed World Says 'Beam Me Up,'" *New York Times*, Sunday, September 11, 1994. Note that the danger is not of political propaganda but of pop cultural contamination. Murdoch willingly took the BBC World Service off of his China service, and in Iran the danger is not CNN, but *Dynasty*, which is the most popular program in Teheran today.

33. See Becker, "From Televoting to Teledemocracy."

34. James Fishkin has devised a deliberative technique that brings citizens together for several days and permits them to interact with one another and with experts, so that their views are not merely registered but pondered and modified. In 1993, Channel Four in the United Kingdom broadcast an exemplary weekend of Fishkin's project; a similar broadcast is being planned on public television (if there is still public television) for the 1996 American presidential elections. For details, see Fishkin's *Deliberative Democracy*. [Publisher, Date of publication?]

35. Precisely because it is interactive, new telecommunications technology "learns" about its users as its users learn about it. A system that "knows" what you buy, how you pay for it, what your consumer and political preferences are, and even (in programs providing home security) when you leave and when you come home, and which then stores and disseminates such information in the absence of any regulatory safeguards, is hardly a system political skeptics should trust.

36. Robert Reich has drawn an American portrait in which privileged information/communication workers increasingly withdraw public support from the larger society as they move to insular suburbs, buy private recreational, schooling, security, and sanitation services for their own walled communities that the public at large can no longer afford. Their withdrawal (Reich labels it the politics of secession) leaves the poor poorer, the public sector broke, and society ever more riven by economic disparities that technology reenforces. Robert Reich, *The Work of Nations* (Knopf, 1991), chap. 23.

37. An early and prophetic book about the problems of electronic surveillance is John Wicklein, *Electronic Nightmare* (Beacon Press, 1981).

38. Channel One is currently in about 12,000 junior high and high schools. It offers free televisions, VCRs and a satellite dish to schools (usually needy ones) willing to dish up two minutes of soft news, two minutes of commercials, and eight minutes of infotainment to its students during regular school hours. Channel One sells spots for up to $195,000 for a thirty-second ad and has attracted many

of the corporations on McWorld's frontier, including Pepsi and Reebok. In 1994 Chris Whittle sold the network for nearly 240 million dollars to K III, an "educational" publisher.

39. This suggests that science and technology policy needs to be subjected to democratic scrutiny. Technology should not try to produce an appropriate democracy, democracy should try to produce an appropriate technology. Experts in technology are not experts in the appropriate public uses of technology. Richard Sclove's project on community science boards speaks to these issues. See *Democracy and Technology* (MIT Press, 1995).

CHAPTER FOUR

And Deliver Us from Segmentation

Elihu Katz

IF ONE WERE DESIGNING a participatory democracy, one would make provision for a central space in which all citizens could gather together and for dispersed spaces in which they could meet in smaller, more homogenous groups. Ideally, the agenda would be agreed upon in the central space (forum, agora, town meeting), mulled over in the dispersed spaces (cafe, salon, club, trade union hall, party headquarters), and returned for debate and decision to the central space. In the era of mass society and mass communication, these spaces would be served, even cloned, by generalized media dedicated to the polity as a whole, and specialized media dedicated to the citizens' need to know what like- or right-minded others are thinking.

Making provision for a central space is not a totalitarian idea. All depends on who controls the space and who has access to it. If the space is publicly owned and independent of government, if it is free of commercial exploitation, if all have access and an equal chance, at least in principle, to hear and be heard, it provides an opportunity to set agendas,

This is one of an overlapping series of papers seeking to develop appropriate concepts for treating the social implications of new media technology. Previous unpublished papers were delivered at the World Congress of Sociology, New Delhi, August 1986; Intermedia Congress, Hamburg, 1985; the European Broadcasting Union symposium for the European Cinema and Television Year, Brussels, 1988; the Research Committee of European Broadcasting Union, Tel Aviv, 1989; and the International Conference on National Television and Globalization, University of Montreal, 1990. A version of this chapter was read at the colloquium on communication of the French-speaking Swiss Universities in Geneva, June 1995. It appeared in the *Annals of the American Academy of Political and Social Science* (July 1996) in a special issue on media and politics edited by K. H. Jamieson, and a a slightly revised version is reprinted here by permission.

to map the distribution of opinion, to legitimate the decisionmaking process, and to sense one's membership in the polity. If these conditions are met, it is obvious that multiple and particularistic spaces cannot substitute for the central space. It is shocking but true by this logic that one can defend the idea of a polity with only one channel of public television commanding attention from all and offering the gamut of views.

It is even more shocking to suggest that multiple and dispersed spaces may keep people away from the central space, unless these function as a feeder system that keeps the priority of the center clearly in focus. Dispersed spaces that lose sight of the center—or provide escapist alternatives—may even lead to the center's collapse. By now, we are well on the road to segmentation, and there is little hope for recovery of the center. We have all but lost television as the medium of national political integration. Not so long ago, most Western democracies had a very few national broadcasting channels that brought everybody together and a large number of specialized and local newspapers. This ideal was more closely approximated in Europe, where public broadcasting systems— officially independent of government and free of advertising—offered a menu of news and public affairs in the very center of prime time,[1] which were then chewed over by the flourishing party press and in the myriad places of political conversation. Comparing Italian and American television news—some years ago, even before segmentation—Daniel C. Hallin and Paolo Mancini portrayed the Italian viewer getting up from the national television news, putting on an overcoat, and rushing out to the piazza or union hall to discuss it.[2] Indeed, for the first decade of television in Britain, there was only one channel, public service in orientation and financed by a user's fee levied on set owners, along with three radio channels differentiated by brow level—all under the aegis of the British Broadcasting Authority. Other European countries followed suit. Israel— one of the more politicized societies—had a single, BBC-like television channel for two decades. Americans often dismiss these systems as government owned, unaware of the European history of courtly patronage of the arts and universities, which gradually wrested their freedom from their patrons but continued to benefit from a tradition of public patronage.

Land-grant colleges notwithstanding, Americans prefer entrepreneurship to patronage, and thus commercial and competitive broadcasting was established, albeit subject to some regulation. It is noteworthy that there emerged only three national networks that slowly added public affairs coverage to their entertainment programming and became forums for the American polity—distinguished ones, at that—even if the news never quite made it into prime time. Meanwhile, the British retreated somewhat—in part, because the government wished to bridle the BBC's independence—and a dual system was established whereby a network of franchised regional stations, no less public-service oriented but financed by advertising, was established alongside the BBC. Subsequently, both BBC and Independent Television (IT) have spun off second channels, and more is soon to come.[3]

But that was long ago, or maybe not so long ago. By now, there are hundreds of television channels to choose from—over the air, on the cable, off the satellite—not to speak of the video and multimedia systems in which television is implicated. Yet, from the point of participatory democracy, television is dead, almost everywhere. It no longer serves as the central civic space; one can no longer be certain that one is viewing together with everybody else or even anybody else, and the here-and-now of current affairs is being minimized and ghettoized and overwhelmed by entertainment. Television today is like a middle-sized video shop, offering the viewer an effortless choice of old and new movies, and soon it will be a MCGA video shop offering viewers home delivery of anything that exists on tape. Viewing of the national news on any of the networks stands at about 30 percent in the United States, and newspaper readership continues to decline.

Except for the occasional media event,[4] television has ceased to offer citizens the experience of shared contemplation of matters of state that demand attention. The polity was rejuvenated and rededicated by events such as the live broadcasts of the moon landing, the Kennedy funeral, the Olympics, the Watergate and Hill/Thomas hearings, and the fall of communist Europe. These political ceremonies were of such great moment that the networks virtually combined to take us there. Until the invention of the televised debates, citizens were unlikely to give equal attention to both sides in presidential campaigns.[5] However inadequate, it is the monopolistic coverage of the debates by the networks that mobilizes us to compare and consider—and feel that we belong. Television takes center stage and gives us a look at both sides—so that we discuss it the next day. It should not go unmentioned here that television has also emasculated party loyalty in the process.

Even media events may be on the wane. People seem increasingly cynical about political ceremony: the parade of premature Middle East peace celebrations is a current example.[6] True, the O.J. Simpson trial captured national attention, but its interest was mostly prurient (except at the finish), not issue oriented as was Hill/Thomas, for example. Only near catastrophe—the Persian Gulf War, the bombing in Oklahoma City—holds the whole nation in its grip. Otherwise, segmentation seems to be fast displacing national comings-together, and pleasure seems to be pushing public affairs ever more out of sight.

Media Technology and the Nation-State

The waning of television augurs ill not only for participatory democracy but also for the nation itself. The media had a lot to do with shaping the nation and holding it together—not just politically but also economically, socially, and culturally. Thus the newspaper contributed to the consolidation of European nationalism, inviting speakers of a particular vernacular to recognize their commonality and to imagine the polity that might result therefrom.[7] If the newspaper conquered space, the telegraph conquered both time and space, empowering investors in California and New York to compete on an equal footing on Wall Street, thus to establish a single national economy.[8] Radio in Britain gave voice to regional differences in the celebration of national occasions, and people became used to the idea of a united kingdom thereby.[9] Broadcasting in the United States—radio and television—also united the nation culturally, and television is said to have leveled social boundaries by providing easy glimpses into the lives of the other gender, the other age-group, the other class.[10]

Technological determinism or not, changes in the organization of the media seem to anticipate, or reflect, the changing structure of society. In Israel, war and severe crisis are marked by the pooling of the broadcast media—not only for reasons of security—so that, in effect, there is only one national channel of radio and television to cope with disaster. The public has repeatedly said that it likes this display of unity. The channels also combine to present great media events, such as the signing of a peace treaty. Their disassembly signals that the crisis or grand occasion is over.

Putting aside the question of whether one can speak of the teleology of technology or only of those who govern it, the theory underlying these observations is that media technology and its deployment affect social organization.[11] Applying this logic to contemporary media technology, it seems altogether clear that the new technology has two, albeit competing, tendencies, both of which overlook and thereby threaten the nation-state. One of these tendencies is toward increasing atomization, such that communication will be increasingly tailored to the measure of its individual consumers. People will be able to customize their electronic newspapers ("anything but the Middle East, please"); they will be able to phone for the movie of their choice and view it alone. The other tendency is toward globalization, such that everybody, everywhere, will be viewing *Dallas* or *Dynasty* or the Olympics at the same time. Neither of these tendencies matches the requirements of the participatory nation state. Technological determinists would say that the nation-state must therefore collapse in the face of this radical segmentation, on the one hand, and globalization, on the other. There is a lack of fit between geopolitical boundaries and the boundaries defined by the new media technology.

The Road to Segmentation: Why Take It?

As these tendencies accelerate, it is ironic to hear so much optimistic talk about electronic town meetings.[12] Perhaps it is possible for presidential debates to be more interactive, and it surely will be possible to announce a town meeting on health care on what remains of one of the networks or on CNN. But will anybody answer the summons? Are there any citizen viewers left? Or should the meetings take place on MTV?

It is all the more ironic because a town meeting or a national assembly was so much more possible before we gave in to segmentation. We threw away the real possibilities that we had, and now we want to reconstitute them. In short, we threw out the baby.

But why? The answers are not so difficult.[13] The first reason has to do with the pressure of technology or at least the way the technology is understood. The idea of limited frequencies—and thus the rationale for regulation—was made obsolete both by cable and by satellite; the number of potential channels is almost unlimited. Some nations are resisting this pressure, allowing for only a limited number of cable channels, and controlling the size of satellite-receiving dishes by license. But as plummeting prices invite mass ownership of the needed technology, this will become a lost cause.

A second reason for the rapid multiplication of channels is the mood of liberalism and privatization that is sweeping the world. The cost of financing the BBC, for example, is extremely high, and as the number of commercial channels multiplies, the compulsory license fee looms larger in the minds of those set owners who prefer the other channels anyway. This process has been evident since advertising-supported ITV forced the BBC to popularize its programming, for fear that a major drop in its ratings—below 50 percent—would foment a revolt among fee-paying viewers. By now, there is a constant call—sometimes from inside the organization itself—to allow the BBC to accept advertising or to solicit voluntary subscription in lieu of the license fee.

A closely related reason for rapid segmentation—that is, for failure to protect the major channels, especially the great public channels of Europe—has been the emergence of aggressive multinational entrepreneurship on the scale of Berlusconi, Murdoch, Turner, and others. It is remarkable that even conservative governments—ever ready to promote patriotism and national pride—are prepared to sell off their public channels, as in France, to the highest bidders.[14] Privatization overcomes patriotism, and joining the multinational economy seems a better bet than very expensive locally produced television productions. These governments then lament the low cultural level of imported American programs and raise the specter of cultural imperialism. It is also just possible that these governments become fed up with the criticism they receive from public channels, and believe, maybe rightly, that commercial channels will be kinder.

Israel: A One-Channel Polity

Since it is in the early stages of channel multiplication, Israel provides a good case study of this process. Television broadcasting was introduced late in Israel, after years of debate over its likely effects.[15] Opponents of the medium, led by Prime Minister David Ben-Gurion, thought that renascent Hebraic culture would be undermined by the introduction of alien values, that the people of the book would turn into the people of television, that ascetic and pioneering values would be uprooted by consumerism, that ideological politics would be displaced by personality politics. Religious elements feared secularization of the culture. Having seen television in the United States, opponents seemed to believe that *I Love Lucy* and *Kojak* were stored on a hard disk inside the set, and that

Israeli television would look just like American television. They were not altogether wrong.

Those in favor argued that the medium carried no intrinsic message of its own, that it would do whatever it was told: inform, educate, teach Hebrew, absorb immigrants, foster creativity, enfranchise marginal groups, show Israel to the world, and, altogether, promote national integration—political, economic, cultural, and social. But proponents who thought that Israel television would be free to do its own thing were only partly right, because television in a small country has very few degrees of freedom, being heavily dependent on inadequate budgets and too little talent to do all the things that richer and resource-full nations can do.[16]

The half-hearted efforts to establish television after Ben-Gurion stepped down led, first, to an educational broadcasting company, financed by a major gift from the Rothschilds and aimed primarily at schools. A general, BBC-like broadcasting station was established only in 1967, following the Six Day War, when enemy countries directed television broadcasts to Arabic-speaking Israelis, the more vulnerable sectors of the population. Thus television was inaugurated in Israel not only to right a propaganda disadvantage but because it was thought, wishfully, that the new medium might make for effective communication between Israelis and Arab residents of the newly occupied territories. This distorted beginning, however well intentioned, gradually righted itself, and by 1969—twenty years after most of the developed countries— Israeli television was on the air, as part of a BBC-like Broadcasting Authority, which also held a charter for the exclusive operation of radio.[17]

Television controlled by the Broadcasting Authority was the only show in town. Within two years of its inauguration, almost all households owned television sets, and almost everybody watched almost everything on the one monopolistic channel. From the beginning, strong emphasis was placed on news and public affairs. Even without the marketing survey that placed information well above entertainment and education in the ranking of public expectations of the new medium,[18] broadcasters were well aware that Israelis expected high-quality news and analysis on radio and television. The channel's flagship program was the 9 p.m. newsmagazine, one of the top programs of its kind anywhere, thanks to the political skills of both producers and viewers. That does not mean that government did not pressure broadcasters or attempt to intervene. Nor does it mean that the channel always resisted this pressure—in spite of its official independence—or that every one of the succession of directors-general stood his ground equally well. On the whole, however, the program was highly regarded by all sectors, and it was viewed nightly by some two-thirds of the population and by even more when there was special cause for concern.

Israel watchers, including some of its growing number of liberal politicians, regularly expressed pity for an aspiring democracy that was so impoverished or so constrained or both as to have to depend for televised information on only one channel and one newsmagazine. "Who would believe the news broadcast on a Government-owned channel, financed by a quasi-tax, even if publicly operated?" they asked. The answer: hawks and doves watched it—and largely believed it; Jews and Arabs watched it—and largely believed it; even Arabs across the borders paid attention. There is good research to support these statements.

Moreover, the shared experience of viewing often made for conversation across ideological divides. There were plenty of newspapers of all stripes and much political discussion, but the shared central space of television news and public affairs constituted a virtual town meeting. Everybody could reasonably expect his or her family, neighbors, co-workers, friends, and enemies to be in the audience. Indeed, the nightly 9 p.m. newsmagazine became a sort of civic ritual during which the society communed with itself.[19] There was an informal norm that attendance was required, and that no intrusions were allowed—no telephone calls, for example. The lesson of the first twenty years of Israeli television is that participatory democracy may be enhanced, rather than impeded, by gathering its citizens in a single public space set aside for receiving and discussing reliable reports on the issues of the day.

These achievements were reflected far less in the departments of drama and entertainment. As is the case everywhere, much light entertainment was imported, mainly from the United States, and indigenous drama—light or serious—was not a great success. Viewers did call for more entertainment, especially more homemade entertainment, but it was slow in coming. Twenty years of monopoly broadcasting had passed, and many viewers, back from touring abroad, felt that paternalism was depriving them of entertainment and cosmopolitan programming. But the symbiosis of Israelis and their national television station is renewed with every new crisis or holiday—or media event such as Sadat's visit to Jerusalem or Menahem Begin's funeral.[20]

Israel: Segmentation after All

Inevitably, technology and politics and privatization and what is said to be common sense prevailed, and multiple channels have come to Israel, late as usual. Hardly anybody spoke up to say that the society might be better off remaining with a single channel, however anachronistic. The old arguments were dusted off: democracy needs competition; a single channel—government-owned at that—cannot be credible; private ownership will increase the quality of programming on both channels; cable and satellite technologies are flourishing everywhere; neglected talent will finally be given its chance, with commissions from a second channel; and the people deserve more entertainment, don't they?

The committee that deliberated whether and how to establish a second channel decided to follow the British again by creating a second authority, chartered to award franchises to produce and buy programs and sell advertising. The days of the week are divided, as in London, among the three franchise holders and join together with the authority to underwrite a news-production company to produce the nightly news. The authority is unashamedly loaded with government officials and lackluster trustees. It took years before the second channel was approved by the parliament, where the most vociferous voices in opposition were the newspaper owners, fearing that their advertising revenue would be diverted to television. They settled for the right to own a minority share of the stock of the companies bidding for the three franchises.

By the early 1990s—twenty years after the establishment of the first channel—it became clear that there would be a second channel, as well as regional cable systems, along with commercial radio stations licensed in association with the second television channel. This was channel multiplication with a vengeance. It was also the moment when I made a public bet with the director-designate of the new authority that the combined audience for news on both channels would be lower than was the audience for the news on the first channel.

And so it is. News on the second channel—not very different from the first, of course—reaches about 15–20 percent of the audience, while the audience for news on the first channel has plummeted to 15–20 percent. Overall viewing of television news in this highly politicized society has dropped by almost half, from a nightly average of 65 percent in the 1980s to an average of about 35 percent now. Some people have moved to cable entertainment in lieu of either news broadcast; more are not watching at all.

It is possible, but unlikely, that this is an artifact of changing the news hour on channel one from 9 p.m. to 8 p.m., for fear of being scooped by its new rival, which had decided on the earlier hour. It is possible, but unlikely, that the sharp drop is an artifact of variations in measuring techniques.[21] It is also possible that Israelis suddenly became fed up with being slaves to the news and became tired of its frenetic downs and ups; indeed, a depoliticizing trend is in evidence. The most likely explanation, however strange it sounds, is that the choice between two news programs raised the possibility of a third choice: not to view either. Stated otherwise, the latent message of two competing news programs is that television news is no longer required viewing, because there is no knowing whether one's reference groups are in the audience. The latent message of moving the news to the earlier hour is that entertainment—not news—deserves to be at the center of prime time.

As expected, game shows, comedy, and other entertainments predominate on the second channel, and even the highly popular prime-time talk shows—originally oriented to public affairs—are becoming more freakish and prurient, even while continuing to play an important public role, at least so far. Action/adventure and other dramatic series are still largely imported, and late-night movies figure prominently as well. When the directors of channel two are reminded that the law specifies that it be a second public channel, it is evident that they have already forgotten this detail. One of the franchise-holders, before being dismissed by his board, managed to say that "the public has a right not to know."

Surprisingly, and against the argument of this chapter, the first channel has so far responded by moving in the direction of higher quality and a higher ratio of self-produced programming. It is acting as if oblivious to the fact that, after the news, there is a 2:1 ratio of viewing in favor of channel two for the remainder of the evening. It seems unlikely that this situation can last; defense of the license fee will require the two channels to be equally populistic as long as they are both trying to maximize their audiences. Further segmentation, which appeals to specialized audiences, is available, so far, only on cable.

Television and National Integration

In research on the functions and effects of broadcasting in the First World, too little attention is given to its role in national integration. The rare exception is David Cardiff and Paddy Scannell's study of the influence of early radio on British national unity.[22] A similar story can now be told for Israel from a study of the uses of leisure, culture, and communication conducted in 1970, shortly after the introduction of television, and again in 1990, when the era of monopoly was about to end.[23]

In 1970 the newspaper was the predominant medium. Asked to assess the utility of each of five media—radio, television, book, newspaper, cinema—in satisfying each of a variety of different "needs," the newspaper was given first place most often. In 1990 television had displaced the newspaper as the medium that best fulfills the greatest number of different kinds of concerns, whether overcoming loneliness, for example, or helping spend time with family. But in the minds of most Israelis, television takes only second place to books or cinema or both with respect to personal values such as knowing oneself, cultivating good taste, being entertained, aesthetic experience, spending time with friends, and improving morale. Where television's role is most prominent—where it has most clearly taken first place from the newspaper—is in the area of the collectivity, especially in the emotional aspect of attachment to nation. More surprising, perhaps, is that television is rated the medium most helpful in satisfying national values that are not only affective but cognitive—for example, not only do people say that television helps them the most "to feel pride in [their] State," but that it also best helps them "to understand the true character of [their] leaders."

Whether or not this would have satisfied Ben-Gurion is an open question. He would have to concede that television served Israel as a powerful unifying force. It deepened the sense of attachment to the center both in its focus on collective concerns and in its communal way of doing so. "But this is at the expense of reading," might be the retort, and indeed, the longitudinal study would reveal that there is some decline in the extent of reading books and newspapers, not in number of readers but in amount read. Alternatively, it might be objected, "Alien values have invaded Israeli society during these twenty years," pointing to evidence in the study that the values of self-interest and pleasure have increased between 1970 and 1990, at the expense of altruistic, collectivity-oriented values and activities and future orientation. But it is more likely that Israeli television, given its content, slowed these value changes, say the authors of the study.[24] Nevertheless, it remains possible that *Dallas* and *Dynasty*—not only the 9 p.m. news and holiday celebrations—have had a part in shaping the values of Israelis.[25]

The opponents of television also expressed concern that the medium would undermine the party-based politics of proportional representation and contribute to the personalization of politics in Israel. This is exactly what is taking place with the introduction of primary election contests, and the new provision for direct election of prime minister, which is strongly opposed by many academics and journalists. The allegation that television is implicated here is well supported by the unending parade of politicians in the news, in public affairs broadcasts, and on talk shows.

The years of monopolistic public television in Israel have almost certainly had an effect on the forging of national identity, enhancing the sense of belonging, promoting civil religion and the continuity of traditional sentiments, accelerating the spread of spoken Hebrew, and the absorption of immigrants. It may also have contributed to the personalization of politics, to a decline in the extent of reading, to a per capita drop in attendance at spectacles ranging from theater to football games, and perhaps even to relieving the frustrations of suppressing self in favor of obligations to collectivity.

But if the fears of opponents proved more wrong than right during the first twenty years of television in Israel, they are about to be confirmed in the next twenty years with a vengeance. The new era of segmentation will support the growing liberal spirit of individualism, self-fulfillment, hedonism, and privatization. By definition, it won't do much good for altruism, patriotism, collectivity orientation, ideological politics, or the civic need for a shared public space.

For a sad metaphor, consider the following: Memorial Day and Independence Day, which are celebrated on successive days in the Israeli tradition, are the occasion for a deep sense of coming together. For twenty years the Memorial Eve broadcast originated from the Wailing Wall and the Independence Eve broadcast from Mt. Herzl, following which Israel Television put on its festive show-of-the-year for all to smile and cry with, and to feel part of society and history. This year—the first year of the second channel—there were two shows, almost exactly alike, featuring the same politicians and artists, speaking the same communion, but in two competing voices.

Conclusion

Throughout the Western world, the newspaper was the first medium of national integration. It was followed by radio. When television came, it displaced the radio as the medium of national integration, and radio became the medium of segmentation. Now, following radio again, television has become a medium of segmentation, pushed by both technology and society. Unlike the moment when television assumed radio's role as the medium of national integration, there is nothing in sight to replace television, not even media events or the Internet.

Notes

1. Jay G. Blumler, "Public Service Broadcasting before the Commercial Deluge," in Jay G. Blumler, ed., *Television and the Public Interest: Vulnerable Values in West European Broadcasting* (Sage,1992), pp. 7–21. On news in prime time as a defining characteristic of public broadcasting, see Stephen Hearst, "Broadcasting Regulation in Great Britain," ibid., pp. 61–78; and Raymond Williams, *Television: Technology and Cultural Form* (Schocken Books, 1975).

2. Daniel C. Hallin and Paolo Mancini, "Political Structure and Representational Form in United States and Italian Television News," *Theory and Society*, vol. 13 (November 1984), pp. 829–59. By contrast, American broadcast news is thought to abort in the living room. See also Paul F. Lazarsfeld and Robert K. Menton, "Mass Communication, Popular Taste and Organized Social Action," in L. Bryson, ed., *Communication of Ideas* (Harper, 1948).

3. Hearst, "Broadcasting Regulation."

4. Daniel Dayan and Elihu Katz, *Media Events: The Live Broadcasting of History* (Harvard University Press, 1992).

5. Paul F. Lazarsfeld, Bernard Berelson, and Hazel Gaudet, *The People's Choice* (Duell, Sloan and Pearce, 1943); Elihu Katz and Jacob J. Feldman, "The Debates in the Light of Research," in Sidney Kraus, ed., *The Great Debates* (Indiana University Press, 1962), pp. 173–223; and Kathleen Hall Jamieson, *Eloquence in an Electronic Age* (Oxford University Press, 1988).

6. Tamar Liebes and Elihu Katz, "Staging Peace: Televised Ceremonies of Reconciliation," *Communication Review*, vol. 2 (September 1997), pp. 235–57.

7. Gabriel Tarde, *L'opinion et la foule* (Paris: Alcan, 1901); and Benedict Anderson, *The Imagined Community: Reflections on the Origin and Spread of Nationalism* (London: Verso, 1991).

8. James A. Carey, "Technology and Ideology: The Case of the Telegraph," *Prospects, An Annual of American Cultural Studies*, vol. 8 (1983), pp. 303–25.

9. David Cardiff and Paddy Scannell, "Broadcasting and National Unity," in J. Curran, A. Smith, and P. Wingate, eds., *Impacts and Influences* (London: Methuen, 1987).

10. Joshua Meyrowitz, *No Sense of Place* (Oxford University Press, 1985).

11. Harold A. Innis, *The Bias of Communication* (University of Toronto Press, 1951).

12. Jeffrey Abramson, *Electronic Town Meetings* (Washington, D.C.: Aspen Institute, 1994).

13. Blumler, "Public Service Broadcasting," pp. 14–19.

14. Dominique Wolton, "Values and Normative Choices in French Television," in Blumler, *Television and the Public Interest*, p. 149.

15. Elihu Katz, "Television Comes to the People of the Book," in Irving Louis Horowitz, ed., *The Use and Abuse of Social Science* (Transaction Books, 1971).

16. See Elihu Katz and E. G. Wedell, *Broadcasting in the Third World* (Harvard University Press, 1974).

17. Israel deviates from the BBC model in that the director general in Britain is appointed by the board of governors which is appointed by the queen, while in Israel, the director general is appointed directly by the government on recommendation of the board and the relevant minister. Membership in the Israeli board is also more politicized than in Britain, where party affiliation is overlooked, at least in principle.

18. Elihu Katz and Michael Gurevitch, *The Secularization of Leisure: Culture and Communication in Israel* (London: Faber & Faber, 1976).

19. Tamar Liebes, "Decoding Television News: The Political Discourse of Israeli Hawks and Doves," *Theory and Society*, vol. 21 (June 1992), pp. 357–81.

20. Elihu Katz, Daniel Dayan, and Pierre Motyl, "Television Diplomacy: Sadat in Jerusalem," in G. Gerbner and M. Seifert, eds., *World Communications* (Longman, 1983).

21. Unified ratings have still not been installed in Israel, although this will happen very soon. Two forms of telephone surveys are now prevalent, which either reconstruct "yesterday's viewing" or ask respondents what they are viewing at the moment. The comparison in the text is based on face-to-face interviewing in the 1980s with phone interviewing in the 1990s, both about "yesterday."

22. Cardiff and Scannell, "Broadcasting and National Unity."

23. Elihu Katz, Hadassah Haas, and Michaael Gurevitch, "Twenty Years of Television in Israel: Are There Long-Run Effects on Values, Social Connections, and Cultural Practices?" vol. 47 (Spring 1997), pp. 3–20.

24. Ibid.

25. Tamar Liebes and Elihu Katz, *The Export of Meaning: Cross-Cultural Readings of* Dallas (Oxford University Press, 1990).

CHAPTER FIVE

Media, Transition, and Democracy: Television and the Transformation of Russia

Ellen Mickiewicz

TELEVISION IS SOMETIMES mesmerizing, often trivial, occasionally grip-
ping, but, except during wartime and natural disasters, rarely heroic. The
story of television at the end of the Soviet Union and the transformation
of Russia had moments of heroism and incompetence, tragedy and comic
opera, war, but almost never peace. Prized by the powerful and invested
with an almost magical impact, the medium became the battleground,
literally and figuratively, for those who would retain or gain political
power. With institutions in disarray and a decentralizing impetus set in
motion by weakness at the center, whose laws and edicts were only
imperfectly and intermittently enforced, television at the end of the Soviet
Union was just about the only institution left standing. In post-Soviet
Russia, too, as the single most important information source in a country
virtually totally penetrated by its signals, television was called upon to
make extraordinary things happen.[1]

In the United States, the impact of television is of particular interest
during elections—and ballot issues, too, for that matter. Among scholars,
public officials, and the press, it is a constant subject for reform, criticism,
and, occasionally, praise. Less obvious, but no less important, the entertainment side of television is very much a part of the larger narratives,
lessons, myths, and values that viewers, especially children, learn. That
learning experience includes televised violence, and debates about its
effects on children have propelled the violence in the media issue to a

This chapter is partially drawn from Ellen Mickiewicz, *Changing Channels: Television
and the Struggle for Power in Russia* (Oxford University Press, 1997). Copyright 1997 by
Oxford University Press, Inc., used by permission of Oxford University Press, Inc.

prominent place in public policy discussions, especially during electoral campaigns. Although this chapter on the revolutionary impact of television in Russia devotes a great deal of attention to news and public affairs, where the focus of public policy was, the rest of television, including entertainment programs and advertising, was also part of television's capacity to reach its viewers, especially when political advertising began.

When I first started studying media audiences in Russia, the Soviet system of information guidance and control was in force. Yet, even then, in the late 1970s, it was clear that this pervasive new medium was associated with some important changes in leisure time use and that the public was certainly not reacting in the uniform (and wholly positive) fashion their leaders expected. It seemed to me unwise to ignore television, even if it was centrally controlled for furtherance of state interests. Whatever the intentions of the state, the medium presented a field of information that significantly exceeded perfect control. Enhanced by a new system of communications satellites, the reach and penetration of television would increase exponentially and present to the leaders in the Kremlin what they believed to be a formidable new instrument.

Television emerged during the time of Leonid Brezhnev. It was then that resources were poured into communications satellites and the production of television sets. Affordable and available, television sets soon became necessities of domestic life. By the time Mikhail Gorbachev came into office 93 percent of the population were viewers; that meant just about everybody in cities and 90 percent of rural households.[2] In St. Petersburg and Moscow in 1992, just under half the people had more than one television set.[3] Then, as now, it was the coveted prize for power holders and power seekers alike. The intrinsic properties of this medium were simply thought to produce an effect like no other. The poet Andrei Voznesensky once said that the Moscow television spire was a "syringe for ideological injections."[4]

Mikhail Gorbachev and his close advisers ordered television to implement an information revolution and render legitimate the practice of politics itself—a practice even the ordinary citizen could participate in through real, as opposed to theatrical, voting. What was surprising about the television revolution was that in the same institution (and usually the same building), at the same time, people who had come up in the same system, with the same rules of the game and the same vetting procedures, behaved very differently. Some kept as tight a ship as they could and punished the slightest deviation. Others took risks they knew would agitate the rulers, excite viewers, and push the limits of reform far beyond what was then permissible. Institutional boundaries limited individual behavior, to be sure, but the contest between leaders and the institutions they led was a bumpy ride over uncharted terrain. Waking the country to a new, more spontaneous conversation, unearthing long-suppressed history, and, not least, exposing viewers to an entirely new electoral process in which the vote really did matter were the tasks the reformers of television sought to accomplish.

Under Boris Yeltsin in his first term as president of (then-Soviet) Russia—acquiring television to challenge Mikhail Gorbachev made possible the country's first alternative, widely disseminated news coverage. Campaigning for his second term, he charged the medium with safeguarding the reform project from the challenge of the Communist Party. Television did much during an extremely short time to project a new and reformed version of the leader to a very divided country. But the Yeltsin administration, in its passionate attachment to television, often overlooked the fact, as had its predecessors, that television was no surrogate for the powerful reality of everyday life, whether in wartime or at election time.

Yeltsin and his advisers were also caught by surprise by how much the market had penetrated the media, both state and private, and by the de facto pluralization—or fragmentation—that was taking place. The market was hardly perfect; in television it began as entirely unregulated and, when the rules were made, the fortunes and interests were deeply rooted and corruption endemic. Television was still the most desirable of political tools, and parliament and president alike attempted to take it, but the old monolith had already cracked before Gorbachev was out of office. It was not until the market supported a separate structure that some degree of autonomy was institutionalized.

The dilemma of the 1996 presidential election—framed by Yeltsin in very stark terms (as in the April 1993 referendum) as either nullification of reform or retention and expansion of benefits—appealed to a new incentive structure: individuals and their self-interest matters, including that less easily defined interest of "expressive need."[5] Autonomy, especially of private television, became the jackpot in a wrenching bet: seek autonomy now by adopting a journalistically sound, analytically neutral stance toward all candidates and risk the end of autonomy in the future with a return to communist leadership. Or hope to guarantee autonomy later by adopting a journalistically doubtful policy of supporting one candidate during the campaign.

During elections, television is thought to be particularly valuable and particularly effective. In 1996 in Russia—as in the United States that year—the largest proportion of campaign expenditures went into the television campaign. In Russia nine critical elections and referenda in eight years brought voters to the polls, always with a turnout exceeding that of quadrennial presidential elections in the United States. Time after time, Russian voters attempted by lawful means to overcome their profound divisions. It is an astonishing record, but, not surprisingly, those divisions persisted and would continue to render politics dramatic and uncertain. It would be the task of future Russian administrations to heal those divisions, if they could, in large part by changing the structure of incentives and providing the benefits of reform to those who had been left out. It would be a challenging task to end zero-sum television, where the prize was the victor's and could not be shared when shared values were so few.

The Moscow-centered television networks reached a huge national audience. They were the sources of information for most people, especially in times of crisis, such as the war in Chechnya. At the same time, local privately owned television stations were growing vigorously, popping up in significant numbers and serving local constituencies. The rise of these local stations merits a separate study. This chapter discusses policy issues relating to the critical role national television played at key times and with key political actors and institutions. In part, that role is related to the tension between reformers seeking autonomy and their opponents propping up the political orthodoxy of the party in power. In part, the role is related to an entirely new political economy and market solutions. The viewing public is a central part of this equation, as the source of votes determining political fortunes and the source of rating points guiding programming.

In the decade following Mikhail Gorbachev's assumption of power in 1985, the basic mold of Soviet information policy was broken, but the deep social, economic, and political cleavages in Russia did not guarantee a fully protected, fully autonomous press. Indeed, perfect autonomy—from commerce and from the state—is granted to no press system anywhere, and the dilemmas and tensions are very much alive in Western democracies as well.

Two Snapshots: May Day 1990 and Chechnya 1995

In the seventy years of the Soviet Union, the annual May Day parade was always an opportunity for the power elite to be displayed, ranged along the balcony of Lenin's mausoleum to review the parade of Soviet citizens pledging loyalty to the party and its leader. Since the advent of television, the Moscow parade was transmitted to all locales, with small windows in the coverage to incorporate celebrations in remote areas. State television hosts introduced their colleagues across the country, showing slices of look-alike parades from other major cities. Parades were public displays, a visual statement of mass political purpose and bonding, and as in all Soviet rituals, public discourse was tightly controlled. In provincial towns—where the obligation to parade was accepted as a low-energy stroll in return for a day off—the exercise was lackluster and limp, but in Moscow, the country's camera lens, the procession was crisper and more muscular. It was expected that although the form might change with the times, respectful fealty to the reviewing stand would remain unchanged.

On the hundredth anniversary of the May Day holiday, the Soviet leader, Mikhail Gorbachev, was himself captive of the myth. In his advocacy of change, Gorbachev underestimated the depth of his countrymen's disaffection and the explosive power of the dissatisfactions that his policies had unleashed. Deprived of adequate sources of feedback, he expected support and gratitude for the changes he had initiated. He expected, too, that pressure for wider and more accelerated reforms would be tempered by a compliant understanding of the limits of compromise. May Day 1990 proved to Gorbachev that his assumptions about the effects of his reforms had been wrong. He lacked information to predict the outcomes of his policies, and he found these outcomes repugnant. He would respond to unwelcome feedback by attempting to short-circuit it. In time, he would have fewer and fewer instruments for reining in his own initiatives. In television terms, he could only pull the plug.

On that day in May 1990, Mikhail Gorbachev, president of the Soviet Union and Communist Party general secretary, mounted the tribune. With him were Nikolai Ryzhkov, chairman of the Council of Ministers, Anatoly Lukyanov, head of the parliament, the speakers of both chambers of parliament, and Gennady Yanayev representing the trade unions. Yanayev's shaking hands would later be televised to the country during his short-lived attempt to seize Gorbachev's place. Viewers heard

Yanayev say: "Today, under the May Day banners, those who preserve the solid faith in the strength of the working class, in the fighting traditions of its solidarity, unity, and brotherhood have come to historic Red Square."[6] Marchers moved past the reviewing stand, where Gorbachev and the other leaders stood, regarding the assembled labor force with benign approval. As usual, television cameras transmitted the ritual of the country's support of its leadership and new policies live to the entire country. All seemed to be going smoothly—until the newly permitted "unofficial" marchers came into view.

The country saw collective anger. The leaders atop Lenin's tomb were taken by surprise. Homemade banners and signs told Gorbachev: "The People no longer believe you—Resign!" They upheld Lithuania's right to independence and secession. They condemned the Communist Party and the KGB; Christian believers carried the image of Christ; the "cult of Lenin" was hooted down and the end of the Red Empire was proclaimed. Workers shouted their fear of unemployment and high prices and the deprivation that was already becoming their lot.

After watching some of the counterparade, the dismayed Gorbachev and his associates uneasily turned away from Red Square and disappeared down into the mausoleum. Yegor Ligachev, the strongest traditional party voice on the ruling Politburo, was standing close to Gorbachev when he saw the "crazies" come into Red Square. After three or four minutes, Gorbachev said to him that they probably ought to leave the reviewing stand. In 1993, recounting to me what he saw, Yegor Ligachev was still emotional and angry. He called those people who yelled at Gorbachev in front of the mausoleum, "hooligans, drunks, extremist forces."[7]

As the people in the news studio remembered it, the cameras were rolling, transmitting the official march. Then came the countermarch, and the cameras kept on rolling. After all, the leaders were still up there reviewing this less-than-docile demonstration. Then, according to Oleg Dobrodeyev, a longtime news director who recalled the moment vividly, a call came in on the direct Kremlin line. Hanging up, Reshetov ran full tilt down the corridors to the newsroom. He took off "like a deer," said Dobrodeyev, and screamed at the newspeople in the studio to shut down the broadcast immediately. "When the deputy chairman says 'cut,' you cut." There were no questions. Only a few minutes of the unofficial parade had been shown. As the nation watched, the parade was abruptly switched off.[8]

Two weeks later the Supreme Soviet, the USSR parliament, passed a law making it a crime to insult the president of the country. Hereafter, "the deliberate humiliation of his honor and dignity, expressed in improper form," by individuals was punishable by up to two years in a labor camp or up to three years in prison, or a three-thousand-ruble fine. For media organizations disseminating insults, the fine rose to twenty-five thousand rubles and two years in a labor camp or six years in prison.[9] But like the earlier attempt to assert control over the unofficial demonstration, this law could not be enforced. About a month later, police swooped down on hawkers of nested dolls on Arbat Street, ordering them to remove the ones that caricatured the president, but nothing happened. The "insulting" dolls were soon back on the street.[10]

It was supposed to be a warm welcome. It was mid-December in the Znamenskoye district of the Chechen republic, one of the ethnic regions of the Russian Federation. Though Chechens predominated in the republic, Russians made up about a third of the population and as much as three-quarters of the population of Grozny, the capital.[11] Both Russians and Muslim Chechens lived in the Caucasian region, which claimed sovereignty after the failed August 1991 coup and had successfully avoided collection of taxes and other incursions of Russian authority for three years. Three years earlier, Chechen leader (and former Soviet air force general) Dzhokar Dudayev had dismissed his parliament and crushed challenges to his power. This opposition survived, the most prominent members of which were in the pay of Moscow, and established a center in Znamenskoye, near the border of Chechnya and Russia. It was not surprising, then, that when the Pyatigorsk Division of the Ministry of Internal Affairs entered Znamenskoye, it had support from the population. People came out to greet the soldiers and, as welcoming custom dictated, the women scattered wheat in the tracks of the vehicles. In response, some drunken soldiers, possibly alarmed, fired on the crowd. Three died (a woman and two men); thirteen were wounded.

When Elena Masyuk, a twenty-nine-year-old field reporter for NTV, the largest private television station in Moscow, arrived to cover Chechnya, local Chechens told her about the incident. She found the division commander, who admitted on camera that the story was true and promised a court martial.[12] NTV's audience—at the time, not all of Russia by any means, but residents of Moscow and tens of millions in many cities beyond—was thus able to compare the story to official reports claiming smooth military operations.

In what looked like a replay of the Soviets' information management during the war in Afghanistan, the Yeltsin government's press center issued reports that Russian planes were only "pinpoint" bombing in the Chechnya conflict. Official information stated that damage had been confined to military targets. Meanwhile, some seven kilometers from the Chechen capital of Grozny, Elena Masyuk filmed the remains of a bazaar, what was left of the kiosks lining the street. This had been a place where mainly women sold whatever they could to passersby. In the Russian raid, vendors and their kiosks were destroyed. The women's bodies—or what they could find of them—were taken to the cemetery and laid on the ground so authorities could photograph them for identification by relatives and friends. Masyuk, who reached the area a few hours after the bombing, saw pieces of the kiosks, blood on the street, and women's corpses. In pictures that stunned the country, viewers of NTV saw vivid proof that the government's claim of "pinpoint" bombing was false.

Chechnya was the first war to be televised in Russia, and it was televised from several points of view, one of which—NTV—was institutionally and financially independent of the government. Of course, that independence was qualified: qualified by dependence on the government's control of signal transmission and by the government's ability to tear up a legally granted broadcast-license agreement or alter its conditions without effective opposition from the judicial system. Those news reports from the front catapulted NTV into the leading news position. With the tragic conflict in Chechnya, the world of Russian television had been transformed; Russia had broken, however imperfectly and incompletely, with the Soviet legacy of information control.

In the spring of 1996, as a momentous election drew near, the head of NTV voluntarily joined the presidential campaign team. Though not a reassertion of the old Soviet pattern of state control over the media, it removed much of that fragile wall of autonomy NTV had battled to achieve. The opposing communist campaign was covered on NTV's news and public affairs programs; its leaders got airtime and the chance to convey their positions in their own words—a notable departure from the state-controlled stations and from past practices. But they got far less airtime than did the incumbent, and much nonnews programming detailed the costly and cruel events of past Communist Party rule. Moreover, while there was abundant (negative) analysis of communist positions, there was no such analysis of the positions of Yeltsin. Nor was his health made a news issue during the period between the first and second rounds, when he disappeared from sight because of what was said to be a cold, but was, in fact, a serious heart attack. It was a controversial call and it affected NTV's postelection image and prestige, especially abroad.

Television and the Challenges of Democratization

Only four-and-a-half years had passed between the 1990 May Day parade and the winter of the Chechen war. On May Day Mikhail Gorbachev was surprised by the public's hostility and during Chechnya Boris Yeltsin was surprised by the low impact of his information policy. In both cases, the events taking place in a single, delimited space became nationally significant, in large part because of television. The old ways—on the screen and in the polity—did not work any more, if, in fact, they had ever worked as imagined. The battle for television reflects and explains much in the demise of the Soviet Union and the transformation of Russia. The enormous changes wrought there merit consideration because of the broader policy issues regarding the role of television in times that redefine the meaning of the nation and its future.

For leaders, as for the public, television is often the focus of obsessive interest, but it may produce different meanings for leaders than for viewers. In a democracy the two groups are inextricably intertwined because election to office depends on interaction with the public, in whose hands lies the voting decision. In an authoritarian society such interdependence is not recognized because the public's own construction of messages and the generation of its own interests are of little moment to those in power. Viewers as real people, not doctrinaire constructs, are unseen, but they are not absent. During the process of democratization, Russia's effort to convert to high-impact television tells us about the contradictions of control, the complexity of credibility, and the meaning of the nation that television does so much to define.

Controlling television appears to be a mixed blessing. In their stewardship of television the Soviet government repeatedly sought total control and in the process made itself the principal target for dissatisfaction. When conflicts and tensions inevitably arose between ethnic groups or regions or social classes, the government invariably became the butt of charges of bias and prejudice on the part of at least one of the aggrieved parties. Framing news stories to display the power of the state (Soviet or Russian) and the grandeur of its leader, the leadership set itself up for individual dissatisfactions, especially potent in the context and culture of a Soviet-style socialism that located the state as the source of individual welfare.

"Control" is, in any case, imprecise. How fully controlled is communication in a modern world freighted with messages carried by multiple channels? Apart from an only partially successful effort to eliminate intrusive foreign or other unapproved messages, Soviet leaders found it impossible to prevent multiple interpretations of the messages over which they thought they had full control. In their understanding of television messages, viewers brought to bear the baggage of their personal experiences and observations. They were less able to evaluate stories about foreign affairs and could only operate by analogy. When audiences deconstructed messages, it was a private act, and Soviet authorities believed the television public to be largely passive, inert, and malleable, because there was no public space for and no legitimation of unauthorized political views on the part of viewers. In only limited and informal ways could citizens know each others' views as worthy of consideration and as possessing weight.

The ancient Greeks believed that at the founding of every political system is a coercive act that renders the grounding of legitimacy always problematic, even as the heroic founding myth is reaffirmed through story and symbol. Without a constitution or norms governing relationships of power among the elites, control of status-affirming institutions in the Soviet Union was vital both to assist the leaders' climb to the top and to ratify it. The symbolic politics so essential to the Soviet system that had to craft legitimacy from violent beginnings played out on television as on no other mass medium. For Soviet leaders, this was the highest impact they could seek. The advent of mass ownership of television offered benefits that were unprecedented: instantaneous saturation of the country with visuals to persuade the skeptics and the unliterary (or functionally illiterate). The same understanding of television continued in post-Soviet Russia, where the stakes in the outcome of defining elections and referenda were very great. With a political system deeply divided about the legitimacy of democratization itself, the costs of granting television access to those who were not part of the consensus were considered infeasibly high. The state's attempt to monopolize television created a zero-sum environment in which those unable to exploit what was considered the chief political asset sought extralegal measures of violent protest or seizure. The battle over television in the fall of 1993 was the culmination of months of demonstrations and virtual siege. The conflict in Moscow that October was also about the power of appointment and oversight of content on the most powerful medium.

Insulating television from governmental intrusion should ultimately be rooted in the legal system, reinforced by the legal culture. Neither was effectively in place yet. Even when buffer councils or regulatory commissions exist, their membership is based at least in part on criteria of loyalty and ideology, particularly the ones directly nominated or appointed by a government. Perfect insulation from political pressure does not exist anywhere, and the journalists' vulnerability to rulers varies dramatically across the countries that once constituted the Soviet bloc. The journalists' battle for autonomy is also made difficult by an element of the law used frequently to stifle reporting. Free-wheeling charges of libel and defamation exposed journalists to trials with vague standards of evidence. The rabble-rousing politician Vladimir Zhirinovsky alone was reported to have filed nearly one hundred lawsuits from late 1993 through the summer of 1994. In 1996 a journalist in Hungary was sued for writing about an accusation one political figure made against another in a public press conference.[13]

The rash of defamation suits, though many were intended to have a chilling effect on journalists and circumscribe their freedom, signaled another problem. The new competition for readers, viewers, and advertisers put a premium on dramatic revelations and speed of reporting. The whole definition of newsworthiness and standards of reporting had changed with great suddenness. Rumor and gossip were often reported without adequate verification. Journalism education had not caught up with the new circumstances of reporting, and a whole new generation was learning on the job.

Credibility and objectivity are inseparable components of the canons of Western journalism. It was not always so, and there is much debate about the meaning of objectivity. Dependence on government-generated news and highly placed sources tends to undercut the notion of objectivity, as does an understanding of facts that fragments them into receiver-constructed, multiple meanings until they disappear in a swirl of equal and opposed truths.

Objectivity in television news may be a different thing altogether for countries shedding authoritarian pasts. Subjectively reported news was for many the first bold step toward accurate coverage and an alternative to the state-dominated message. The *subjective* was the credible and the tradition extended beyond the fall of the dictatorship. The ability of journalists to make themselves credible in the late Soviet period required them to present themselves as individuals separate from the institutions in which they worked. They told viewers their opinions; they reflected sarcastically or ironically on what they were told to say, what others said, and what they observed. They made of themselves stars and "personalities." Many did so for a political purpose: to provide viewers with a genuine alternative, to act as a counterweight to official pronouncements, and to educate the public. How well suited this strategy was to the construction of an independent, credible, modern media system remained very much at issue. The Russian public continued its affectionate connection to the emoting, judging anchors as the conscience of the country. The place reserved for the poet-seer of nineteenth-century Russia had been filled by the anchor-prophet at the end of the twentieth.

In seeking to make television credible and more effective in Russia, overt censorship ceased and live programming expanded. New modes of discourse and more natural personal bearing replaced the alienating abstraction of officials skilled in the language of the organization but unaccustomed to seeking public approval. The wooden style of Communist Party bureaucrats could not compete effectively on television and, except for Mikhail Gorbachev, these bureaucrats were unprepared to communicate in the new accents of the television revolution. Later, Yegor Gaidar, though a risk-taking, pioneering economic reformer, had little understanding of the new requirements, nor did his party, nor did most of the candidates vying for public attention in 1993, during the first multiparty competitive elections in post-Soviet Russian history. Vladimir Zhirinovsky was the first political communicator on Russian television to address specifically identified, largely neglected segments of the public in their own language. His success, it is true, was a relative one; the competition was decidedly weak in its ability to make contact with the long-ignored public. Zhirinovsky pioneered a new kind of electioneering and broke the mold. By the next elections, two years later, his "discoveries" had been appropriated by a wider field in the election races.

The removal of intrusive, identifiable, government censorship did much to enhance the credibility of Russian television. But the modern toolbox of methods for enhancing credibility is much richer and more problematic than that. The "technological" war of the Persian Gulf presented to American viewers a huge flow of information that was apparently comprehensive but controlled and light on reportage of civilian damage. Television docu-dramas, recreations of historical or current events, morphing, and computer-enhanced photographs all blur the line between news reporting and artifice. The diversions of celebrity and scandal can leave little room for more serious coverage and thus beg the issue of news credibility altogether: Who is, after all, interested in hard news? Soviet airbrushing was amateur in comparison.

If all politics is local, then is all truly effective television local? In Russia, the wrenching movement from the dictatorship of the past to the pluralism of the future went forward in the rhythms and packaging of the West. Whether or not the television principals preferred to convey precisely a Western appearance or content in their new wares, they had few alternatives with which to signal a radical, thoroughgoing change. Their distinctiveness had to be Western-looking since that was what had been forbidden for decades, what had so stunningly separated the controlled sameness of the past from a dynamic future, and what would be salient for a youthful generation opting out of the system. The Soviet government had short-sightedly adopted a dichotomous view of the world in which all that was not Soviet—politics, culture, economics—was generated directly or indirectly by the West. And so it appeared on television. Certainly, American models and collaboration, especially news footage from CNN and Ted Turner's personal interest and projects, played an important role in the process of reform.

But the issue was more complex and could be seen as a four-layered dilemma. First was the layer of contemporary international trade. American companies, like others, were in search of global markets and particularly well positioned in the rapidly developing television programming market. Like most other countries in the world, post-Soviet Russia was a consumer of American television programs and movies, and like other countries, it was concerned about the maintenance of local ways in a global market. As information markets developed, that tension became part of a worldwide process. The superimposition of the other three layers made the Russian case much more uncertain.

The second layer of the dilemma resulted from a severe contraction of the Russian economy. It had become very—usually prohibitively—costly for Russian firms to produce and air their own entertainment or large-scale public affairs documentaries. Later, as private money flowed into television, domestic production began to revive. Locally produced soap operas outdrew foreign imports as early as 1996. Domestic films also began to outnumber foreign ones, but film *premieres* were overwhelmingly foreign.

The third layer of the dilemma was the rise of product advertising, domestic and foreign, to support television stations the state budget could no longer afford. To Russian viewers the glitzy, rock-scored images in those ads looked and sounded distinctly American, or at least seemed to be what Soviet propagandists of the past called American, though by then the style had already been globalized.

Finally, the fourth layer regarded the notion of democracy. Democracy itself was associated with America, but in the minds of many in the public, the "American" principles of democracy and Americanized electioneering were not easily disengaged from the "American-looking" economic changes that had yet to produce wide benefits across social classes and regions. Of course, American democracy and the development of markets were not unconnected, but the arrival in Russia of both severe economic dislocation *and* drastic political change tended to displace, onto a construct called "America," the unwanted results of both. In the transitional period, the effects were most pronounced. Searching for a stable definition of the country, some viewers escaped into the varnished past of Soviet films, a past that never was. Others moved into a competitive future in which individuals expected little from the state—not even legal protection—and acquired benefits, often by successfully converting state assets into personal ones.

During the late 1980s and into the early 1990s, the institutions of the Soviet system eroded or actually imploded, and new structures were not yet in place. Institutional instability, the fragmentation of power, and the delegitimization of old patterns of control and conformity provided space for a nascent journalistic community to function in new ways with new norms.

Journalists pushed the boundaries of press freedom and won invaluable concessions. Though not uniformly, in many of the countries of the old Soviet bloc, journalists experienced a new corporate identity in opposing the old regime, and, for a group lacking the usual unifying attributes of a profession, began, in fact, to function with a considerable degree of shared norms. They not only tended to see themselves as exerting a salutary influence on politics, but also self-consciously began to use the levers of power in the political system. That this period and this influence were possible only because of a vacuum during the transition and the *weakness* of institutions, was not immediately apparent to the reformist journalistic community. Nor did the reform-minded journalists fully grasp the fact that their own new cohesion and community were themselves related to the fragmenting of the political and economic environment. The breakdown of elite consensus and the old central organizing ideological framework enabled the media to illuminate and also to widen the divisions.[14]

In looking back over the difficult road to legitimated press pluralism and attempts at guaranteeing autonomy, various models of journalism came into play. Some retained the expressive patterns and *engagement* of the early struggles against a decaying Soviet-era system. For these journalists, the role of overt socializer had not changed; the content had. Others sought maximal revenue and ratings, often through sensationalism and scandal. But, for some journalists—such as those at NTV, Russia's largest private network—there was a highly self-conscious effort to impose Western journalistic values and styles. Elites responded positively, but the imposition of what appeared to be foreign, ahistorical norms was itself problematic. The Moscow-based station, whose motto was "news is our profession," became the most respected news organization in the country. Yet it appeared to some to be an alien missionary. As a highly regarded television critic wrote in an elite liberal Moscow newspaper:

> Our "lighthouse" has become NTV. [It is] a superbly professional channel. [It is] beyond state, beyond popular, beyond ethnic. It is done intelligently and professionally, and with determination it destroys the state domination and mentality of the people in order to create a new state and a new people.
>
> But this is idealism. And strangely, even Bolshevism. The Bolsheviks tried to change the nature of the Russian person and created a generation of Soviet people. The new Bolsheviks are doing just about the same thing. They think we—this provincial, undisciplined, unnecessarily emotional, unable to organize ourselves—people need to adopt a western intellect and then Russians finally will learn how to live, work, think and feel, as in America.[15]

If the nation was in flux even about its boundaries, if many of its cultural precepts had been delegitimized with great suddenness, if economic change had arrived with such force that many were disadvantaged, what kind of impact could television have for this "nation"? What was the public, and what was in its interest? How could television function in the public interest as the state moved to reform its institutions, even if not along a straight path?

In some of the most serious crises in the fragile post-Soviet period, television connected people all across the country. At those times indigenous accents, points of view, and symbols had the greatest impact. The stolid square figure of Prime Minister Viktor Chernomyrdin negotiating in the broiling heat for thousands of lives held hostage by Chechen terrorists in the southern Russian town of Budyonnovsk in June 1995 was exactly the right image. The public understood it. Russian television's unrehearsed marathon of drop-ins to a modestly appointed reserve studio under fire during the revolt of October 1993 was the common thread connecting a country that had yet to make up its mind about the two sides of a contested future. These were television events that brought together most of the people of the country, no matter where they lived or how much they earned. This was television in which viewers saw themselves as collective and connected.

Television portrays the nation to itself and defines the polity. Yet, dislocating change can make the definition of nation elusive. This was fundamentally at issue after the break-up of the Soviet Union, and Moscow-dominated television did little to address the separate lives of regions and ethnicities. Differentiation in other respects was also increasing. The public was sharply divided by generation and by rapidly diverging economic interests and opportunities, ranging from the conspicuous consumption of the "new Russians" to the bare subsistence existence of pensioners.

In Soviet times, television officials played to a public imagined to be, in most important respects, homogenous. Viewers were not a uniform mass, but there were far fewer inequalities than later in Russia. The different demands and needs of the stratified public suggested that a wider range of messages and products was essential. Choice was developing briskly, ahead of an adaptable infrastructure and without a legal process of transparent procedures and competitive access. As elsewhere, both vectors—the integrative potential of national television and the fragmenting, customized, expensive new services—operated at the same time. In a resource-constrained environment, who would have access to information, culture, and entertainment on the most important medium? For most people the world of global interface had not yet arrived; the world of basic channel choice had *just* arrived.

But is access to channel choice enough? The development of market-based television pluralism—real choice among channels—was indeed a notable achievement in the new Russia. Opportunities for the expression of differing points of view were clearly enhanced, but did the market provide all the solutions? Some Western observers, aware that their own huge array of channel choice did not bring in its wake a correspondingly broad range of opinion, have argued that the market is a poor guarantor of the kind of diversity of speech and expressions of minority opinions that democracy needs.

If we equate "free speech" with maximum diversity of views, then, strictly speaking, "free speech" involves not only the negative government function (that political views be protected from government sanctions), but also the positive one (that government be "held responsible for ensuring the expressibility of all views, including the misguided, the shocking, the hurtful, and the irreverent").[16] Yet, even if it were possible or desirable, this expansive principle of government activism cannot guarantee that hostile public opinion will easily make room for views it regards with contempt. Given the often chilling effect of majority opinion on expressions of minority views and the failure of even a highly developed market to guarantee the widest possible expression of views, how interventionist should a government be to ensure diversity of views?

In the formative years of post-Soviet television policy, such an intrusive role for the state was not desirable. Market-based pluralism was a breakthrough; it brought alternative views on critically important issues to a mass public. The new commercial stations, not the state, served to broaden expressive choice. The range of choice was far from complete, and and the media were far too concentrated and less buffered from government than desirable. But bringing the state back in to rule on content was, at this stage, the much more pernicious alternative.

Throughout eastern Europe and the countries of the former Soviet Union, economies plunged immediately after the end of Soviet rule, along with the ability of household incomes to support newspaper subscriptions, especially during a period of rapid inflationary increases. The subscription base plummeted, leaving television as the dominant information source. In 1996 in Hungary ten of Budapest's eleven daily newspapers were verging on bankruptcy.[17] In Russia, only three newspapers could claim national circulation by 1996, and one of them, *Izvestia*, had seen circulation decrease from 12.5 million in 1990 to only 600,000.[18] At the same time, the ability of the government to support media declined. State-owned and -operated television subsidies were cut and wage arrears grew. To protect freedom of speech, the newspapers argued, state financial help was needed. However, the distribution of governmental subsidies inevitably raised questions of criteria and whether those criteria were or ought to be political.

To many, the answer was foreign help in the form of partnerships with commercial media enterprises, but the partnerships were very unequal. The Czech government under the leadership of Prime Minister Vaclav Klaus encouraged a free market in media and the participation of foreign investment. At the regional level particularly, most newspapers were supported by foreign capital and, according to a 1993 report, the Bavarian media firm Passauer Neue Presse had "become the most extensive foreign presence in the Czech media, having purchased nearly all daily and weekly regional publications."[19] Investment opportunities in the electronic media were equally open. In the former German Democratic Republic some thirty-one of thirty-four daily newspapers found West German partners, with the ultimate result that the twelve largest West German publishers owned more than 85 percent of the former East German papers.[20] In Poland, German media magnates—and some other foreign players—took over so many newspapers that a Warsaw daily ran an article entitled "Are There Polish Papers in Poland?"[21]

Except for the Czech Republic and Romania, most countries had limits on foreign investment in broadcasting, but even so, the stations with foreign partnerships tended to outperform the older media. The Central European Media Enterprises Group, mainly owned by U.S. investor Ronald Lauder and Mark Palmer, former U.S. ambassador to Hungary, created TV Nova in the Czech Republic and by the mid-1990s had captured more than two-thirds of the market and was engaged in starting up Pro-Tv in Romania and partnerships in Slovakia and Hungary. The case of Russia was different: the size of the market made it possible for domestically generated investment to challenge the primacy of foreign investors, especially as concern with national identity increased and the forging of new cultural commonalities rose on the public and political agendas.

In Russia's large media market, the banking industry and the partially privatized extractive industries and utilities acquired media properties energetically, and, by 1997, the major Moscow-based television networks and a number of newspapers and radio stations had a highly concentrated pattern of investment with much crossownership. In the summer of that year, the results of a telecommunications auction disadvantaged two of the largest media barons. One of them was the major private partner in ORT, a private/public television station, the nation's most watched station. In a notorious week-in-review commentary, the station's leading news analyst charged the winners of the auction with a host of illegal activities.

The tension between efficiency of ownership strategies and assurance of multiple, especially unpopular, points of view remained serious, because of the pressure of the unfinished revolution and the methods of rapid privatization used to wrest control of the economy from the communists, while lodging it in relatively few players.

Whether the new media market was adequately open even to reasonable diversity of ownership was very much in question in Russia.

Under Mikhail Gorbachev the impact of television was projected to be nothing less than undermining the stranglehold of the dead hand of bureaucracy. This it did with consummate effectiveness. Obstacles to change—though Gorbachev had an impossible kind of contained change in mind—were attacked and discredited, a striking event in the Soviet Union, where there was no sanctioned challenge to high officialdom before Gorbachev came to power. Dethroning an oppressive system of colonial or authoritarian rule may unite disparate and contradictory elements on a provisional basis, but applying television to building new institutions is incomparably more difficult than setting about to dismantle the old order.

The dynamic of attack was difficult to harness for other outcomes. Soviet-style news and public affairs programming had always served up an overly positive version of reality. This menu was no longer available to a ruling group determined to dissociate itself from the past and to a public weary of the exhorting dissonance. The polarized drama of exposé and the unleashing of criticism had an invigorating effect, but in vain did Gorbachev and Yeltsin charge television with producing effective constructive programs. When television officials attempted to obey, the output was all too reminiscent of the past.

Elections are critical moments. In Russia, the power of television was considered so great that it was an exceptionally valuable prize for those in power to monopolize and those not in power to acquire—by the rules if possible and by force if not. State television was crudely biased during what was considered a crucial referendum campaign in April 1993, and in the December 1993 and 1995 parliamentary electoral campaigns, it was wanting in expert analysis or genuine debate.

In 1996 gravely threatened by a weak candidate, a strong communist challenger, and the potential nullification of the reform project itself, the television networks framed the election as a referendum, just as it had done in April, three years before. Television—public and private—returned to open partisanship. Significantly, three factors made a difference: free time was given fairly to all candidates on the state stations; the candidates could buy additional advertising time; and a private station, NTV, provided considerable access to opposing candidates, even though it suspended analytic reporting critical of their candidate, the president. The weight of so many elections designed to solve so many systemic crises impaired the fragile birth of autonomy.

Toward Democratic Television

Russians use the word "normal" (*normalny*) very often, and when they do, to outsiders the term seems to describe not the quotidian but the exceptional. What isn't *normalny* for Russians is something sudden and extraordinary. Persisting conflict, bad news, problems, tragedy, all became *normalny*. The test for television—as for society—is to establish democratic criteria for more truly normal times.

Political leaders as well as television officials would be well advised to draw a distinction between a tight grasp and a bully pulpit. As long as politicians—of whatever stripe—believe they have to keep television tightly in their grip, they likely forfeit the kind of impact they seek. Failure to communicate to the public effectively deprives political leaders of what Richard Neustadt called the American president's most powerful asset.[22] Used appropriately, television is indeed a bully pulpit, but leaders need to know how to use it. The real issue is not one of technique; it is not merely a matter of adopting a professional on-screen presence and uniforms of tasteful suits and hair helmets. The most powerful impact of television on Russia in recent times came from an extemporizing, unglamorous actress in a makeshift studio under siege during civil strife in Moscow and a sweating bulky prime minister trying to save hostages in a small provincial town. Because viewers are voters, television becomes a political asset to leaders who understand and connect with the viewers' values and concerns. Effective leadership does more, as it not only reflects but shapes these concerns.

The task of leadership is immeasurably more difficult when viewers are deeply divided along so many fault lines, and in the early days of a new country it is especially difficult to forge coalitions. Coalitions and compromise are necessary modes of behavior in the political arena, and also on the nation's greatest educational medium, television. A zero-sum approach is ill suited to a media market in which the private sector provides a multiplicity of news and public affairs options. Television could do much to legitimate a game in which there are payoffs for many and more than one side wins, but it should do so as a result of professional judgment without governmental intrusion over content.

For generations the Russian public was basically a cipher for the people who run the country and television. Still, those leaders should have understood that even with few choices, viewers were telling political leaders where their interests lay by switching to each new more challenging option as soon as it arrived. They did this in Soviet times with *12th Floor*, *Vzglyad*, and *Vesti*, the Yeltsin-partisan news program, and in post-Soviet times with NTV's coverage of the Chechen war.

That the public also enthusiastically opted for game shows and soap operas should not obscure the fact that it could mix escapism with discerning judgments about information. Vladimir Zhirinovsky's success was by no means solely the result of his televised ranting, but was also a representation of his voters' insecurities and negative evaluations of the competence of his rivals, most particularly incumbents. Alexander Lebed was popular because he acted decisively and talked little, and he singled-handedly arrested the war in Chechnya. Gennady Zyuganov's formidable challenge was turned back primarily because most people did not believe in the future the communists promised and did not want to change course, however harsh the journey. Many now had a stake in the future and, retrospectively (always less suspenseful than prospectively), it is entirely possible that they did not have to be battered by partisan television to make their choices. Perhaps post-Soviet political executives—and those in the television industry—should learn to appreciate the complexity of the public and be less dismissive of the mass they like to term "lumpen."

New television stations sprang up with amazing rapidity in Russia. Practically everybody had television sets; many households had more than one, and some had a wide range of channels from which to choose. For most people, choice—especially in news and public affairs—was still limited and few stations reached very large audiences. Because of these limitations, the public-interest responsibility of the leading national channels may be considered unusually great, which means that television officials have a critical duty to understand the needs of the public. Ratings numbers tell them only who watches in the contest of a limited array of contenders for a given time slot, obviously critical to an advertising-driven bottom line—and survival. Yet reputation and prestige are also part of the more intangible profit picture. Taking only the soap-opera-loving side of the numbers obscures both the public's other interests and the differences among various sectors of the public, not to mention the role television might play in a "national conversation."

As the twenty-first century approaches, some of the old combative habits the stations adopted to achieve credibility and assist democratic reform in a hostile environment may have to give way to a lower temperature, a more "normal," way of operating. What to throw overboard and what to retain of the "homegrown" ways will not be easy decisions.

Television officials and legislators pondering their role in helping to forge a newly rediscovered nation are often tempted to substitute protectionism for creativity. Under conditions of diminished domestic program production the danger of foreign saturation appears enormous. Applying quotas to imports raises all sorts of problems: what, exactly does "foreign" mean? Are the states of the former Soviet Union to which Russia wants to build ties and in which reside large numbers of coethnics, as foreign as others across the Atlantic? Does delivery of programs by direct broadcast satellite leapfrog rules? Does foreign investment, with locally formed consortia? And isn't there another, more fundamental question: competing for one's own domestic public is not only a question of rich production values and internationally recognized stars; it is much more about crafting programs that connect to the public with integrity, veracity, and artistry. Viewers do not need to be forced to recognize achievements of this rank; they do not need to have other choices eliminated.

To address the public in ways that matter, television must be able to tackle problems of great moment, and it cannot do so as long as vaguely worded, intermittently enforced laws prohibit much speech relating to war, religion, social class, ethnic differences, and other profoundly important questions. The prohibitions do not forbid people from talking about these issues in their private lives. They do not restrain the extremists in their bids to unleash popular frustration.

The prohibitions *do* restrain television from introducing responsible discourse and developing a way of illuminating the issues in a fashion that does not seek to annihilate the opponent or arouse bigotry. It is not just a matter of talking-head panels and television used as radio; such television cannot possibly reach the emotions and minds of the national public. It takes the pictures and sounds of compassion and discerning understanding to do this. In perhaps no other country in the world is there a greater opportunity and greater role for television than in rapidly changing, transitional Russia.

Notes

1. During the course of my research on television and democracy in Russia, I have been privileged to work with an extraordinary group of media leaders, government officials, and academic experts in the Commission on Radio and Television Policy. Former president Jimmy Carter and Eduard Sagalayev, founder of the first private television station in Russia, cochaired this nineteen-nation nongovernmental organization, which began in 1990, and I served as director of the commission. The commission began as a bilateral, U.S.-Soviet body. The first steps in its formation took place when television was beginning to play a uniquely central role in the changes that the policy of *glasnost* initiated. For the American participants, the experiments and changes in the Soviet Union often led to reflection on U.S. television practice and policy. In the course of our meetings on television policy in Russia, Kazakstan, Austria, and at the Carter Center in Atlanta, some of the most critical issues of television were discussed and six Working Groups, conducted in association with the Aspen Institute, brought together more than one hundred experts and practitioners for an often contentious and always stimulating analysis of the issues at stake, the solutions attempted in a variety of contexts, and policy proposals for the future. The process of identifying a range of policy options and working out the trade-offs each one represented made very clear and compelling the central issues of electoral campaign coverage, coverage of minorities and ethnic conflict, privatization, and press autonomy. The policy guidebooks we wrote have been translated into over a dozen languages and have been distributed from Kazakstan to Romania, Hungary, and Bosnia, from Latvia and Lithuania to Morocco and the West Bank, and, of course, in Russia. They have become part of the process by which rules and practices evolved. Thus I have had the chance not only to study the course of the development of television policy, but also to hold discussions in a variety of settings about real options for policy choices that have to be made when a framework of rules and practices has not yet been established.

This project of policy research and consultation would not have been possible without the support of the John and Mary R. Markle Foundation. When the project was in its very first stages, the fate of the Soviet Union was unknown. Nor was it apparent at the time how enormous a role television would play in the events in that country and its largest successor state, the Russian Federation. Lloyd Morrisett's understanding of the potential of the project and his and the foundation's commitment to it as supporting democratization and, in the process, learning about our own system were fundamental to the achievement of its goals.

2. Ellen Mickiewicz, *Split Signals* (Oxford University Press, 1988).

3. Data for December 1992. *Mass Media Audience*, Postfactum News Agency, Moscow–St. Petersburg, 1993.

4. Quoted by Sergei Muratov in "Television and Democracy: Who Will Prevail," *Moscow News*, no. 14 (August 7–14, 1991), p. 10.

5. On the importance of "expressive need," see Timur Kuran, *Private Truths, Public Lies: The Social Consequences of Preference Falsification* (Harvard University Press, 1995).

6. S. Bogatko and Iu. Kazmin, "Solidarnost liudei truda," *Pravda*, May 2, 1990, p. 1.

7. Interview with Yegor Ligachev, 1993.

8. Interview with Oleg Dobrodeyev, May 1992.

9. "V Verkhovnom Sovete SSSR," *Izvestia*, May 23, 1990, p. 4.

In post-Soviet Russia, a law forbidding the media to insult the head of state was also on the books. In 1995 this provision of the criminal code was used by the attorney general to initiate action on behalf of President Yeltsin against NTV for its "Puppets" program of political satire. The suit was dropped, and the prosecutor dismissed (he had also brought criminal charges against NTV's Chechen war reporter Elena Masyuk for interviewing a terrorist). When Mikhail Gorbachev was asked his view of the matter of the alleged insult to President Boris Yeltsin, he answered, "I like all kinds of parodies in general very much, and specifically about myself. If of course, it is not insulting." Mark Deich, "Mikhail Gorbachev: master varit kashu," *7 Dnei* (August 21–27, 1995), no. 34, p. 38.

10. Simon Midgley, "Around the World," *Independent*, June 26, 1990, p. 12.

11. I thank Professor Vladimir Treml for these estimates.

12. This and the following three incidents from covering the Chechnya war are drawn from an interview with Elena Masyuk, March 1995.

13. "World Press Freedom Review 1996," *IPI Report*, December 1996–January 1997.

14. Philip Schlesinger, "From Production to Propaganda," in Paddy Scannell, Philip Schlesinger, and Colin Sparks, eds., *Culture and Power* (London: Sage, 1992), pp. 293–316; and Daniel Hallin, *The "Uncensored War:" The Media and Vietnam* (University of California Press, 1986).

15. Valery Kuchin, "Kogda kriveet zerkalo," *Obshchaya gazeta* (December 11–18, 1996), p. 12.

16. Kuran, *Private Truths, Public Lies*, p. 85.

17. "World Press Freedom Review 1996," *IPI Report*, December 1996/January 1997.

18. A fourth, *AIDS Info*, was a sex tabloid.

19. Tracie L. Wilson, "Press Systems and Media-Government Relations in the Czech and Slovak Republics," *Gazette*, vol. 54 (1994), pp. 145–61.

20. Slavko Splichal, *Media beyond Socialism: Theory and Practice in East-Central Europe* (Westview, 1994).

21. "World Press Freedom Review 1996," *IPI Report*, December 1996–January 1997. For an extended discussion of these issues, see Ellen Mickiewicz, "Transition and Democratization: The Role of Journalists in Eastern Europe and the Former Soviet Union," in Doris Graber, Denis McQuail, and Pippa Norris, eds., *The Politics of News: The News of Politics* (Congressional Quarterly Press, 1998).

22. Richard Neustadt, *Presidential Power* (John Wiley, 1960).

CHAPTER SIX

The Market for Loyalties in the Electronic Media

Monroe E. Price

THIS CHAPTER IS about a market—I call it the "market for loyalties"—in which large-scale competitors for power, in a shuffle for allegiances, often use the regulation of communications to organize a cartel of imagery and identity among themselves. Government is usually the mechanism that allows the cartel to operate and is often part of the cartel itself. This market produces "national identity," to use the European term, or "community," to use the less discriminating Americanism.[1] Management of the market yields the collection of myths, ideas, and narratives employed by a dominant group or coalition to maintain power. For that reason alone, control over participation in the market has been, for many countries, a condition of political stability. Because of a frenzied explosion of communications technology that transcends existing national boundaries, the power to manage output and maintain political stability is diminishing.

The market for loyalties has existed everywhere and at all times. What differs about today's market is the range of participants, the scope of its boundaries, and the nature of the regulatory bodies capable of establishing and enforcing rules for participation and exclusion. This market metaphor may help explain the legal and political responses to the gigantic transformations now taking place in media industries as telecommunications become more global, confounding national borders and the reach of national legislation. New forms of communication—satellites, electronic highways, relentlessly global telephony—have qualities that

Reprinted by permission of the Yale Law Journal Company and Fred B. Rothman and Company from *The Yale Law Journal*, vol. 104, pp. 667–706.

make them seem unregulable by traditional organs of power; bursting from existing political boundaries, they put historic ties into question and can undermine existing legal regimes.[2]

In this essay, I first describe the workings of a market for loyalties, distinguishing it from a market for goods and a marketplace of ideas. I show how the media structures of selected countries, particularly in Western Europe, exemplify the operation of such a market. Next, I focus on constitutional, statutory, and administrative aspects of media regulation in the United States to demonstrate that the market for loyalties functions within the context of the First Amendment. Finally, I suggest how changes in media technology are creating new global pressures in the various specific markets for loyalties, affecting the capacity of governments to perform their historic function of regulating those markets, and compelling a transformation of local, national, and global regulatory arrangements.

Defining the Market

The market for loyalties must be contrasted with the "marketplace of ideas," the compelling metaphor that has played so substantial a role in the development of First Amendment jurisprudence in the twentieth century. The marketplace of ideas is a particular incarnation of the market for loyalties, one that has an established definition and a history of proponents and detractors.[3] An active, thriving bazaar with atomized buyers and sellers, the marketplace of ideas is, in its purest form, free from anticompetitive conduct. Ease of entry is assumed, and the government plays a limited role, if it plays any role at all. Because truth is thought to prevail in the resulting competition among ideas, no governmental regulation of competition is justified. The market for loyalties, as a model, is a closer approximation of actual market practice than is the marketplace of ideas. Like the market for goods, the world of ideological discourse is frequently characterized by monopolistic and oligopolistic practices, including efforts by competitors to exclude new entrants.

It is easier to describe a market for goods than a market for loyalties. In a market for automobiles or sugar, well-developed traditions identify buyers and sellers, determine a market-clearing price, and describe the means for settling accounts. Prolific literature exists on monopolistic and oligopolistic practices affecting markets for goods and the use of law, regulation, and agreement to fix prices and divide those markets. A centuries-old discussion surrounds the power of the state to nourish and favor domestic products and shield industries from foreign competition. Even in countries that pride themselves on their commitment to a free market economy, government has an often dramatic role in establishing the rules of the game, encouraging production, and mediating between protectionism and unregulated competition. The collaboration of government and business to organize markets has had a recent renaissance as part of "industrial policy," including efforts to cope with the meaning of borders through the General Agreement on Tariffs and Trade (GATT), North American Free Trade Agreement (NAFTA), and the European Union.

In contrast, there is little in the way of a similar literature identifying the buyers and sellers of ideology and the nature of transactions among them.[4] For example, the supply side in the market for loyalties has a structure that is badly served by reductionist terms like "state," or "government," or "political party." In the market for loyalties, the major "sellers" or "producers" are a wide range of manufacturers of identities—classically states or governments, but other sources include interest groups and businesses. The sellers in this market are all those for whom myths and dreams and history can be converted into power and wealth. The "buyers" are citizens, subjects, nationals, consumers—individuals or their surrogates—receivers of the packages of information, propaganda, advertisements, drama, and news propounded by the media. The consumer "pays" for one set of identities or another in several ways that, together, we call "loyalty" or "citizenship." The amount the buyer pays is not expressed in the ordinary coin of the realm: The buyer's payment for loyalties includes not only compliance with tax obligations but also the obeying of laws, readiness to fight in the armed services,[5] or even remaining within the country.[6] The buyer also pays with his or her own sense of identity.

Media Law and Restrictions on Competition

Legislation is commonly used by the controlling group or groups in the market to enforce and reinforce its ideal of the people's identity. This is done through the allocation of market shares, with the intent of creating cartels of allegiances where possible. As in the market for goods, competitors in the market for loyalties seek to use the force of law, as well as collusion among themselves, to restrict supply and establish barriers to entry.[7] Worldwide, government-operated and -controlled companies with established monopolies over communications technology have fought the introduction of private competition and the expansion of cable television. A narrow funnel for expression, created by controlling which viewpoints have access to the means of mass communication, could be used to function as an integrating, assimilating influence, subtly reinforcing a vision of cohesion, or to support existing cultural divisions in society.[8] In Italy, for example, the very architecture of public broadcasting was once designed to accommodate the existing system of political parties, with the Christian Democrats controlling the first channel, the Socialists the second, and the former communist PADS the third. In Germany, by constitution and statute, public broadcasting corporations are obliged to adhere to a rule of "internal pluralism" supervised by the *Rundfunkrat* so that all of the opinions, values, interests, and perspectives of the society are adequately represented.[9] The statutory ideal is for broadcasting to mirror society's composition, but the consequence has been a rough parceling out of licenses among dominant political parties.[10]

Europe's increased involvement in the media field began with the European Convention on Human Rights and Fundamental Freedoms of 1950. The Convention provided in article 10(1) that the right to freedom of expression would include the right to receive information and ideas without regard to frontiers.[11] In 1990 the European Court of Human Rights added teeth to this provision in the *Groppera Radio A.G.* v. *Switzerland*[12] and *Autronic A.G.* v. *Switzerland*[13] cases. In those cases, the court decided that article 10 rights applied not only to the printed press but also to radio and television. Although the court recognized a limited right for receiving states to protect their technical licensing schemes, state-imposed barriers to transfrontier television would generally offend the principles set out in the convention. The policy of establishing a regional market was concretized in the Television Broadcasting Directive of the European Economic Community and the virtually equivalent European Convention on Transfrontier Television of the Council of Europe (implementing the cultural requirements).[14] In the 1990s the legal focus has shifted from protecting internal markets to protecting, through the imposition of quotas, European program production from foreign attack. All of this goes to show that the competitors in the market for loyalties often use the force of law to restrict the supply of competing perspectives. In the GATT negotiations of 1994, the European Union reserved film and television programming from the general lowering of trade barriers on the ground that a European cultural space ought to be preserved, strengthened, and protected from the influx of American entertainment.[15]

Law also has been used to protect domestic producers of national identity from international competition. For most of the twentieth century, the international order believed that radio transmissions should be contained primarily within the boundaries of one nation; the international function was to dispense frequencies to ensure that conditions of market division along national borders could be realized and enforced.[16] International regulations and arrangements were built to implement the policy of limiting broadcasting, in large part, to "national service of good quality within the frontiers of the country concerned."[17] In the interlude between the world wars, there were bilateral and multilateral agreements to control propaganda subversive to the state system. For example, the League of Nations–sponsored convention Concerning the Use of Broadcasting in the Cause of Peace provided that:

> The High Contracting Parties mutually undertake to prohibit and, if occasion arises, to stop without delay the broadcasting within their respective territories of any transmission which to the detriment of good international understanding is of such a character as to incite the population of any territory to acts incompatible with the internal order or the security of a territory of a High Contracting Party.[18]

The proper mediation between law as a device to protect national systems and law as a device to enhance international freedom to communicate remains a major issue today.

Advertising as a Competitor for Identity

In a market for loyalties, advocates for disparate national identities will predictably have different attitudes toward the use of ordinary commercial advertising on television.[19] European governments, long preoccupied with limiting advertising messages and protecting public broadcasters from competition, have assumed that the subtext of advertising is a substitute for more traditional packages of identity. To see why requires harking back to the modes of payment in social cohesion by the consumer. Assume, for a moment, that a citizen can express loyalty in terms of willingness to pay taxes. In this case, the seller (the government) of the product (a kind of patriotism) must persuade the voter to spend more disposable income on the product (through higher taxes). Taxpayers can resist, and instead decide that their religious salvation, for example, is more important than the public weal.[20] They can consequently vote to divert government expenditures from the defense industries or to lower the public revenues altogether. Or citizens can determine, through voting or through the articulation of public opinion, that they should spend more on local taxes and less on taxes for the federal government. Governments can see that—with consequences for visions of the public good—advertising can persuade individuals to consume rather than to save and invest, teaching the primacy of loyalty to self and satisfaction rather than community and sacrifice. In this sense, marketers of "pure" national identities or ideologies compete with sellers of consumer goods, who are trying to impress on the citizen another identity. The question is how a person decides, at the margin, whether a higher or lower percentage of disposable income should go to the state to pay for education or environmental protection, rather than for personal goods like food, television sets, and automobiles.[21]

In the market for loyalties, proponents of some patriotic identities recognize the indirect supporting role that the barrage of traditional commercials might play in connection with their own visions of future happiness. Take, for example, a rather simple one-dimensional view of the Republican Party in the United States, or the Conservative Party in the United Kingdom, or the parties advocating a more rapid transition to a marketplace economy in Russia. These aspirants for power may see the political benefits of a citizenry saturated with the culture of advertising and consumerism as containing indirect messages of political support. The message of the sellers of toothpaste and automobiles reinforces a national identity that claims that the opportunity to have maximum choice to consume is good. We see assertions of national identity in the interstices of commercials, in their depiction of an idealized home life, or their depiction of a certain idea of traditional family values.[22] If the images of a consumer society bolster the party in power, then that is reason enough for advocating an increase in advertiser-supported broadcasting.[23]

Alternatively, a ruling party may see the images of advertising and the foreign programs surrounding them as a threat both to its culture and, more centrally, to its continued hold on its government.[24] In some settings, foreign programs (usually labeled "American" for convenience and often originating in Hollywood) are characterized as subversive; through the basic aspects of their story lines they advocate a view of the individual that is wholly at odds with the reigning perspective.[25] These dominant forces fear that the successful penetration of the world view contained in Western advertising (and in Western news) yields instability and a call for internal political change.[26] Bearded leaders of Islamic societies are not the only ones who proclaim the subversive nature of Western broadcast imagery. Supporters of Radio Free Europe and Radio Liberty as well as avid proponents of free market television have argued that the images of Western society, including its advertising, are entitled to a large part of the credit for the great changes such as the collapse of the Soviet Union.[27]

Government as Speaker

Locating the government in the market for loyalty flirts with the edges of propaganda theory. Propaganda is the name that we give to the use of symbols to influence or manipulate public opinion,[28] at home or abroad. There is much to be learned about our conflicting attitudes toward this kind of speech, especially from those writers who recognize that propaganda does not necessarily imply a pejorative outcome and who see propaganda as a mainstay of all modern governments, including democratic ones.[29] But most writings on propaganda do not use a marketplace approach. Those who analyze propaganda are usually concerned with its behavioral implications. They may use the metaphor of competition, but not its analytic consequences.

The function of the government in a market for loyalties ordinarily goes far beyond its role as regulator and enforcer for a cartel of identity producers. The government is frequently a participant in the market for loyalties in its own right. By my earlier definition of national identity and its role in reinforcing the status quo, the government often depends on a specific range of outcomes for its very existence. Here, the relationship between the state as censor and the state as generator of images is important. Not only have governments sought to exclude a range of destabilizing narratives, but they have also insured that a reinforcing sense of national identity is available and, if possible, prevails. The preoccupation with flags, including their proper veneration, is the most obvious of such efforts. The establishment of churches, the investment in the writing of history, state patronage of the arts as a means of uniting a community—all of these are part of the process of reinforcement. Furthermore, much of what the state provides is a public good; for example, the benefits of security and peace are even available to those who do not pay taxes. The marketing of loyalty, however, does tend to increase the share of those who shoulder the costs of the state's undertakings. There are many other reasons for the government to become a speaker—maintaining cohesion, correcting for widely perceived unfairness, introducing missing narratives—and thereby strengthen its hold on power. Historically, the question is not whether government should be a speaker, but whether it becomes a monopoly supplier of national identity.[30]

To perform its functions in regulating and participating in the market for loyalties, government has a cluster of alternatives: it can subsidize messages that it deems important, censor messages that it deems antagonistic,[31] or even become a vocal contributor in the market.[32] And there is an interrelationship among these alternatives. Other things being equal, the pressure for censorship increases where the government and other dominant suppliers have not successfully agreed on an acceptable range of narratives and the state itself has limited power to generate images of cohesion and loyalty.

The United States and the Market for Loyalties

The "market for loyalties" approach is less evident in the United States, partly because law affects narratives of identity there in far less apparent ways than in Europe and elsewhere. Basic to the American sense of itself is the historical aversion to the idea that government shapes, or has any role in mediating, national identity. In other words, the state's role in the structure of speech and media is and ought to be minimal. From its revolutionary beginnings, the concept of the American central government is different from that of its European counterparts. The idea of the limitation of government, not powers, was at the heart of the founding vision of the United States. The articulation of denial, or an injunction against the *abridgment* of freedom of speech, shaped the constitutional definition of the role of Congress in relation to free speech. A nineteenth-century frontier mentality, still flaunted and still generative of the American character, has always been antigovernment. Gritty independence, in action as well as speech, has been one of the key elements of national identity.

Great spaces, protected by the insular nature of the continent, contribute to a history in which a comfortable dominant narrative of national identity persists, though now and then it is challenged by competitors. Unlike its European counterparts, the United States was buffered from attack. In the twentieth century, the continental United States did not suffer the debilitating wounds of bombardment, actual invasion, or occupation, either physically or culturally. Furthermore, the American experience was of a long-term, now-ending isomorphic relationship between dominant language and space. There was less of a perceived need for the state to intervene and mediate among contending cultures, except, as in the great periods of immigration, to engage in a process of acculturation.

Beneath the calm of a set of accepted stories, however, the national identity of the United States has always been subject to dispute. The disputes range from contested colonial settlement to sharp sectional disparities, through the Civil War, and the rise and decline of cities, to the current contests over race, gender, and language. For most of the twentieth century, broadcasting has provided an envelope of seeming homogeneity, helping to produce and reinforce a national identity of domestic security and economic growth. Even now, as history is told and retold, a struggle to redefine American national identity, to determine how plural it should be, is emerging.[33] Because each formulation of national identity has consequences for the distribution of power, the contest for the regulation of images arouses great passion.[34]

The First Amendment and the Market for Loyalties

In considering the place of law in structuring the market for loyalties in the United States, the First Amendment is the appropriate starting point, particularly because it is so commonly thought to limit, if not bar, a forceful governmental role in organizing and disciplining speech.[35] Throughout American history, however, the interpretation and application of the First Amendment has had a vital and surprising role in shaping the market for loyalties.[36] The First Amendment can be read as an allocation of regulatory authority among those who control the market for loyalties rather than a mandate for unfettered speech. Under this interpretation, the First Amendment represents an agreement among existing governors of identity (that is, the states and private enforcers of moral rectitude) to prevent Congress from competing with them.[37] Only Congress was precluded from "abridging freedom of speech and of the press." Despite the celebration of reason and liberty in the late eighteenth century, there were severe local limitations to permissible speech and conduct as well as harsh sanctions for breaching local bounds.[38] The then-existing process of setting and implementing standards was not effaced by the adoption of the First Amendment. To the young states and other cultural regulators like the eighteenth-century churches, the power to control speech and behavior was too important to be shared with the new central administration. The early First Amendment, as an artifact of federalism, determined what level or locus would be the forum for providing barriers to entry, restricting output, or dividing markets. Without the First Amendment, a new federal congress, reflecting a new assortment of interests, might have threatened then-existing power relationships between states, other cultural forces, and the press.[39]

The structuring role of the First Amendment changed as society changed. While the amendment reinforced the decentralized regulation of speech in the eighteenth century, it emerged transformed in the twentieth century. Through incorporation into the Fourteenth Amendment and by its application to state and local governments, the Free Speech Clause became a mechanism to inhibit the states and facilitate the development of a national market for speech and identity. As a result, state and local governments are constrained in their attempts to prohibit specific points of view, and their capacity to shield and nurture regional audiences is diminished by the First Amendment's prohibition against abridgement of speech.[40] In this transformed environment, the erosion of local impediments to the national market for speech was virtually inevitable.[41]

America's television service grew in soil so remarkably nourishing that the process of psychic integration took place much earlier and more rapidly in the United States than in Europe. This process, which has yielded the internal "cultural space" that is the hope of the Council of Europe, has largely been successful, for better or worse, in the United States. The creation of an interstate broadcast medium reinforced and integrated the whole's triumph over the identity of its local parts. The advanced state of the U.S. speech and broadcasting commonwealth may be a prototype for current European developments. Not only has the First Amendment created a common market for speech within the United States,[42] it has also protected internal competition for loyalties from foreign competition. Ultimately, the First Amendment allows the government to limit the entry of voices from abroad under specifically circumscribed and clearly authorized powers.[43] For example, the United States sought to limit, by multilateral treaty, directional broadcasting emanating from Mexico, Canada, and elsewhere, partly as a control on the content of those who use the powerful broadcast medium.[44] There are other reminders. Officials of the U.S. Information Agency, under legislation implementing the 1949 Beirut Agreement, must certify the "authenticity" and "accuracy" of Americanmade documentary films for duty exemptions in their intended country of import, prior to their export.[45] Under the Foreign Agents Registration Act (FARA),[46] Congress has required, *inter alia*, the labeling of certain imported films as "propagandistic."[47] National security considerations limit the flow of information into or out of the United States.[48] Thus the extent of the power of Congress to limit the flow of ideas in or out of the United States is, in terms of the structure of the market for loyalties, greater than the power to constrain and organize the internal market.[49] Nonetheless, the First Amendment continues to protect the internal dominant suppliers of national identity from challenges within and outside of the national territory. The ability of the national government and the First Amendment to continue to do so will be seriously challenged with advancements in communication technology.

Regulation of Media and the Market for Loyalties

The day-to-day work of shaping and regulating the broadcast market for loyalties falls to the Federal Communications Commission (FCC), an agency with a tight and traditional relationship with Congress, the White House, and the industry it oversees. While the Communications Act of 1934 prohibits the FCC from engaging in censorship,[50] the very process of licensing radio and television stations is a major constraint on the competition for loyalties.[51] Competition for federal licenses and the requirement of a renewal (every three years in television's "golden age") inevitably affects the range of views expressed. While that range has been quite wide, and renewal of licenses is typically automatic, the possibility that a valuable asset could be lost is an effective argument for conformity. The powers of the FCC, Congress, and the White House have all been used as weapons in the battleground for competing notions of the good, the ideal model for organizing and directing society, basic ideas of cohesion, and the definition of community.[52]

Government-mediated actions have had important consequences for the narrative of national identity.[53] During the McCarthy era, the authority of Congress and the commission was enlisted to sanitize the airwaves of left-wing sentiment. In the 1960s Presidents Lyndon Johnson and Richard Nixon used the "fairness doctrine" and the licensing process to intimidate broadcasters who challenged their views. Nixon, for instance, sought to punish the *Washington Post* by launching a threat to the economic security of the television stations owned by its parent company.[54] Nixon also sought to reduce the central power of public broadcasting because, in his view and that of Vice President Agnew, the noncommercial system was creating allegiances hostile to conservative values.[55] In the 1980s, through the introduction of preference rules, the FCC sought, at least cosmetically, and until the judicial mood changed, to ensure minority ownership of broadcast media on the understanding that ownership has implications for on-screen narratives.[56] In addition, during the 1960s and 1970s, the licensing process and the power of groups to petition to deny renewal were employed to change the practices (in terms of employment and representation of groups) by the licensees and the networks.[57] In these ways, to the extent they could manage to bring the power of the state behind their perspectives, law and regulation were deployed to strengthen the interests of one interest group or another and to limit entry by ideological competitors.[58]

Boycotts and Group Action

Now, as the deregulation spirit enlarges, there is a new ordering of the market for loyalties, reliant on a set of powers and constraints that are more ephemeral, less visible, and less subject to the old forms of analysis. With a diminution in the government's overt power to regulate markets, an enriched interaction between private organizations and government influence occurs. Government pressure to change television's stories takes the shape of the bully pulpit, not the censorial stick. George Bush's vice president, Dan Quayle, and Bill Clinton's secretary of health and human services, Donna Shalala, both decry the television character, Murphy Brown, as an overly romanticized depiction of single parenthood and birth out-of-wedlock. Congress votes antitrust immunity to the networks so that they can negotiate an agreement to lessen violence during the hours of family viewing. Well-organized private groups, each with their own agenda, have established outposts in Los Angeles with the aim of influencing the content of programming and using, or threatening to use, contacts with government if their objectives are not reached. Kathryn

Montgomery, the historian of this movement, attributes the expansion of intense, effective, and well-financed advocacy to television's power as "the central storyteller for the culture."[59] According to Montgomery, groups such as the Population Institute, the Alliance for Gay and Lesbian Artists, the Solar Lobby, the American-Arab Anti-Defamation League, and Justicia, have engaged in intense lobbying efforts because "fiction programming, even more than news and public affairs . . . most effectively embodies and reinforces the dominant values in American society."[60] Or as communications scholar George Gerbner has argued, those who write a nation's stories need not worry about who makes its laws.[61]

Using whatever leverage they can, through pressure on advertisers, corporate boards, and politicians, these associational representatives establish an agenda for public discussion and help to determine the limits of the ensuing debate.[62] From all sides of the political spectrum, they are concerned with the handling of environmental issues, the depiction of gays and lesbians, the construction of narratives concerning race, the representation of Jews and Catholics, and the stories that affect the agenda of the Christian Right. They engage in the process of jawboning and friendly persuasion, often using friendship ties and peer pressure. So effective have these advocacy groups been that, in the 1990s, it has become the practice, where sensitive questions are raised, for producers to vet scripts and seek input from the relevant organizations even before a program is shot.

The issues throughout the entertainment field now are not only ethical and legal, but ones of balance in the war of conflicting pressures. Some groups have more favorable access to writers and producers than others, a consequence of wealth, ideology, or the familiar networks of neighborhood and class. Other groups use their power not only to threaten consumer boycotts, but also to secure the intervention of the state (Congress or the courts).[63] It is difficult to conceptualize an arena in which advocacy groups passionately articulate ideas in which advantages of wealth or access to power are not invoked. In the era of deregulation, the impact of the government on the market for loyalties may become more dificult to detect, but it is not necessarily reduced.

Laissez-Faire and the Legal Structure

The most important way in which law affects the market for loyalties is not through the explicit actions of Congress and the FCC, but through the tolerance and protection of the status quo. Modern interpretations of the First Amendment maintain and enlarge the field for advocates of consumerism. Television now showcases a series of stories that celebrates the consumption of goods, promoting an idea of self that dominates competing allegiances and ancient ideas of citizenship.[64] The idea that commercial speech is to be treated identically to noncommercial speech, that cable television operators are speakers just as publishers of newspapers, all leads to a set of narratives that emphasize commercials while info-mercials replace documentaries and celebrities replace civic leaders.[65]

A First Amendment theory that denies the very absence of the capacity to regulate, or at least to regulate positively,[66] becomes the basis for structuring the market for loyalties in the United States. American television may provide more channels and choices than any other system, but ironically, it provides less diversity and a more uniform perspective on national identity than television in some countries with fewer channels. The United States, internally, could be viewed as the first example of globalization, a test run for some of the technological consequences now felt throughout the world. An institutional history of broadcasting in the United States, one that traced its national and international dimensions, would emphasize the development of the radio chains or networks that crossed local American cultures. In so doing, broadcasting exploited the trappings of localism but established a national market that eventually encompassed the vast and disparate regions of the land. The oft-told story—in which "American television" is the aggressor, becomes global, and engulfs the rest of the world with the United States as the subject, not the object of cultural change—may be too simple.[67] Broadcasting in America itself can be reinterpreted as a dress rehearsal for globalization, altering identities here first. It is as comedian Jay Leno joked during the inauguration of NBC's European Super Channel, "We're going to ruin your culture just like we ruined our own."[68]

New Technology, Globalism, and the Market for Loyalties

I have tried to show how law and technology interact and affect a state's power to organize the market for loyalties, and how a governing entity's use of law and regulation of technological advances allow it to foster or impede particular promoters of competing loyalties.[69] New and changing technologies—direct-to-home satellites, the spread of cable, and the rich potential of the electronic highway—increasingly limit one of the most important aspects of state power: the effectiveness of intervention by governments to protect an internal cartel from the destabilizing cacophony of the world. Even internally, government media policies that explicitly shape narratives appear as throwbacks to another era, one in which the bounds of competition for national identity could be contained.[70] Even more in jeopardy is the "bubble," the power of law to contain debate within traditional physical boundaries. The consequences for law are intriguing because the passion for using law to regulate loyalties, fence out competition, and fabricate or reinforce national identities will not disappear. The market for loyalties persists; what changes are the market's players, the mechanisms for control, and, finally, the future of the state.

Global Competitors and State Responses

The world is now moving from a well-regulated and divided market for loyalties to one in which constraint by national governments is almost impossible. If one way of understanding the political essence of society is to examine and calibrate its internal web of message sending,[71] then the new technologies mean that the society of reference requires reinterpretation as the codes of interconnection are modified. The satellite, the most modern form of communication, echoes "the older imagining," ancient forms of social organization "where states were defined by centres, borders were porous and indistinct, and sovereignties faded imperceptibly into one another."[72] Then, the technology and organization of imaginings contributed "paradoxically enough [to] the ease with which pre-modern empires and kingdoms were able to sustain their rule over immensely heterogeneous, and often not even contiguous, populations for long periods of time."[73] Now, again, kingdoms outside the established order have a similar capability to surmount self-contained national identities.

Who are the candidates for these new kingdoms? They can include dynamic and charismatic religious forces—Islamic or Christian. The possibilities also include a rejuvenated Voice of America, a BBC World Service given a new charter by Parliament, or other modernized extensions of a national and propagandistic past. But mostly, these new producers, reaching past boundaries, include the kind of ideology that springs from MTV, the recognizable Western package in which the appeal to the individual is the underlying drumbeat of advertising. Sometimes these potentates have names in the fashion of the monarchs of old, like Murdoch or Disney. Already, a global competition exists among the BBC, CNN, NBC, and News Corporation to establish hegemony over global news. Not all of these are kingdoms that have the emotional power to sustain the imagination of far-flung peoples, thereby replacing the current order. There is no national identity of Murdoch, no flag or loyalty to Disney. But between religious faith and consumerism, there seems to be passionate battle enough. The contest of imagery, in the next generation of global tensions, more likely will not be among nation-states, but rather among clashing civilizations, defined by history, language, ethnicity, and religion.[74]

The distinguishing characteristic of this market for loyalties is the decrease in state control. Countries that oppose, for religious or political reasons, the content of messages coming from the outside, must search for mechanisms that have either a more direct impact on the behavior of the suppliers of programming, or harsher, though less effective, measures directed at households. In the spring of 1994, after discussions between Rupert Murdoch and the People's Republic of China, Murdoch dropped carriage of the BBC from the relevant AsiaSat transponder.[75] Murdoch's action came in the wake of his statement in late 1993 that advanced technologies such as satellites, "have proved an unambiguous threat to totalitarian regimes everywhere."[76] The regimes with which he was dealing presumably did not appreciate the sentiment. In particular, China protested Star TV's carriage of the BBC, which had been critical of the regime. Star's penetration in the China market was threatened, and Murdoch acquiesced. In Singapore, a ban on the purchase or use of satellite-receiving dishes, absent a hard-to-obtain license, is designed to keep out those programs that are unapproved.[77] Several Egyptian governates, under pressure from the local imam, have established similar ordinances prohibiting the use of satellite dishes.[78] In many corners of the former Soviet Union, a strong central government has renewed its efforts to maintain a monopoly over imagery. This has entailed censoring newspapers, precluding the distribution of dissenting papers, tightly policing the entry of foreign broadcast television signals, and monitoring those who are considered frequenters of foreign messages.[79] Not surprisingly, Iran vigorously attempts to fence out foreign signals and criminalizes the watching of some foreign programs. In these and other places, states attempt a partial or complete withdrawal from the mainstream of world communications commerce in order to maintain national identity and culture.[80] It is often thought that censorship, the ancient and indispensable tool in shaping the market for loyalties, is rendered obsolete by the abundance of technology and ease of access. Intense partisans, however, will seek ways to enforce their norms. Where signals penetrate, snooping and snitching may replace systematic exclusion. Terror, too, may become the weapon of antimodernists whose views technology has rendered unenforceable.

While it seems certain that advanced technology and multiple channels will be introduced, it is less certain how quickly and in what technical form they will come.[81] States concerned with controlling loyalties will prefer the introduction of cable television to the spread of home satellite dishes, which can receive signals directly from abroad.[82] Since a cable monopolist is a domestic intermediary, states can more easily influence it.[83] Electronic information delivery systems allow creative governments effectively to monitor messages. The U.S. government has sought, so far unsuccessfully, to insert decoding chips into the new information infrastructure to enable eavesdropping when judicially or legislatively authorized.[84] Other less liberal governments may introduce such monitoring technology without public debate.

Those who ring the death knell of the state may ring too soon. I have already suggested that increased acceptance of commercialization and a probable denationalization of the media are also possible responses to imagery without boundaries. If confronted with a choice between a national identity that competes for authority and the weak product loyalties created by consumerism, governments will choose an influx of MTV over messages sponsored by meaningful, passionate critics of the existing political arrangements. Those in power prefer commercials to alternate identities offered by groups such as Islamic fundamentalists in Egypt, Basque separatists in France, or Kurds in Turkey. Commercialization may undermine historic cultures, but it may well be far less subversive than destabilizing political messages. In this sense—at least in the short run—governments benefit from allowing the entry of new and attractive commercial programming. Such programming fills the social space into which a hauntingly competitive national identity otherwise might emerge.

Global and Regional Regulation

In indistinct yet vital ways, global signals create more than unimpeded invasion of local markets for loyalties. The also create a global competition with a search for global rules, global cartels, and global regulation. For most of this century, as I have indicated, the international order was based on the assumption that national interests, constrained by borders, should be the overriding concern in determining regulation.[85] This assumption is changing. Public international institutions, which exist to serve their sovereign members, are criticized for failing to cope with transnational developments.[86] After a long period of desuetude, principles of human rights, which have always included a right to receive and impart information across borders,[87] are reappearing as the basis for striking down national ordinances.[88]

Communication specialists talk of enlarging the powers of existing international bodies, such as the International Telecommunication Union (ITU), or creating a new body that can establish and enforce rules to discipline a global market.[89] Because of new needs, radically different institutions for dealing with the new technology are most likely to survive this transformative period. Regional multilateral arrangements, epitomized by the 1989 European Convention on Transfrontier Television,[90] demonstrate how new technology spurs supranational forms of regulation in order to provide more effective market division and policing given the geographical sweep of new media,[91] and undermines national measures by which governments maintain monopolistic control of the media. In a recent case challenging a prohibition on private broadcasting, the Austrian government argued that its legislation was "aimed at preventing manipulation of the population and the concomitant serious disturbances of the public order."[92] The European Court of Human Rights, however, ruled that the public monopoly could not be maintained.[93] The locus for making these decisions—decisions about the extent and nature of permissible competition for audience—has shifted from the national level to that of the Council of Europe.

This shift, however, has not been sudden. The UN deliberations over international regulation of the direct broadcasting satellite twenty years ago foreshadowed such a change.[94] A central question of those meetings, particularly for the Western democracies, was whether a state should or could take responsibility for irresponsible or unwanted communications merely because the signals originated within its frontiers. A great number of countries, most fervently those of the Soviet bloc and the nonaligned members of the United Nations, sought a convention that would do one or more of the following: bar certain kinds of programs from direct broadcast satellite;[95] require consultation with the government of any state whose audience was a target of the broadcasts;[96] and require the prior consent of any such state before transmitting signals.[97] Only a nonbinding General Assembly Resolution resulted from the deliberations, and the resolution lacked a formal multilateral mechanism for enforcement.[98] The United States opposed the creation of an international standard that would establish prohibited categories of programming because it considered such regulation incompatible with human rights and First Amendment principles.[99] Exhausting discussions revealed the difficulty—in the face of technology indifferent to national borders—in achieving social control of new instruments of communication.

No match yet exists between a global market for loyalties and a global regulating entity. We are still at an early, frontier-like stage in the overarching competition among global voices, and as a consequence, the underlying consensus—the market-shaping impulse that is at the root of media law—does not exist. Familiar instruments of change—banks, giant telephone companies, international trade organizations—are beginning to find their way. Being more plastic, they mediate transborder markets for loyalties, responding to economic and political forces, providing technical and financial assistance, assuring step-by-step change. Since sovereignty is a difficult thing to cede, candidates for greater international power, such as the ITU, face the dynamic of reluctant sponsors. At some point, in the not-too-distant future, participants in the global market for loyalties will require a stronger regulatory presence, a global hand, invisible or not. But that moment is not yet here.

Conclusion

National identities are, of course, quizzical imaginings: a combination of the aesthetics of patriotism, romantic searches through the past, and the reinvention of old myths for sometimes benign, sometimes malevolent purposes. They can change rapidly. The nation-state has always been, as Eli Noam has written, "at tension with cross-border allegiances— whether proletarian international solidarity, rebellious youth culture, international financial capital, or ethnic minorities."[100] Now, however, new networks can weaken national cohesion while strengthening and internationalizing particular allegiances (often among globally distributed communities). Noam notes, "It is difficult for a state to extend its powers beyond traditional frontiers, but it is easy for the new networks to do so."[101] Thus, audiocassettes, with the recorded voice and message of the exiled ayatollah, which were smuggled from France to revolutionary strongholds in Iran, immediately transported the fiery zeal of the ayatollah and helped unite opposition to the shah. Radio gave to the people of Moscow the sense that they were a community, stronger and more independent than the organizers of the reactionary coup. The lesson demonstrated by these examples is not only one of freedom; it is also the lesson of imperiled narratives and susceptible regimes. A global market for loyalties increasingly supplements its local counterparts, and participants in the local markets tend, as in the market for goods, to be increasingly transnational. Great corporations, religious entities, and programmers of signals bind together scattered ethnic populations and others with defined interests.

The global drama of the programs and narratives that have been poured through the skies as a technique of the new era may have been captured best by the gifted Polish journalist and author Ryszard Kapuściński. Although describing Iran's turn to Khomeini after westernization under the shah, his words have a more general truth:

> A nation trampled by despotism, degraded, forced into the role of an object, seeks shelter, seeks a place where it can dig itself in, wall itself off, be itself. This is indispensable if it is to preserve its individuality, its identity, even its ordinariness. But a whole nation cannot emigrate, so it undertakes a migration in time rather than in space.[102]

In this passage Kapuściński was writing of resistance to messages from the West, a "walling in" that must use every technique possible to screen out the compelling, attractive, permeating voices from without. This theory of atavism, this turn against modernity, also suggests one of the strong motivations, conscious or not, for the West to project the enveloping narratives of its contemporary radio and television. There is a key here to the importance of the stories that are pumped into the transition societies and the periphery of the developed world, a key to the impact of the dream factories of Hollywood on the villagers of the Carpathians, pubkeepers in Wales, shepherds in the Basque Country, or workers in Azerbaijan. The rhythm and music of Western radio and television become a push toward modernity against competing forces. Alan Rusbridger of *The Guardian* caught this "full surreality of the New Media World Order" in a village located an hour from New Delhi.[103] There, while young people chant at the temple of the monkey-god, Hanuman, the family of Yogbal Sharma watches MTV with its "[l]egs, lipstick, kisses, jeans, fast cars, beaches, cafes, drink, [and] waterfalls," a representative sample of Star TV fare.[104] In the years to come, Rusbridger observes, children will choose whether to spend Tuesday evening singing to Hanuman or watching Dynasty.[105]

Imagine a world of hyperbolic interactivity, a home-shopping network not just of consumer goods, but of ideologies and movements. In this mythological telecommunications future, the boundaries that will count will be the footprints of satellites and the reach of computer system operators. They will demarcate the sway of the empires of production exerting their influence over the fealties of mere consumers. It is a future in which the third world becomes even more marginalized, unless it becomes more of a market for goods and therefore more relevant to the producers and distributors of imagery. The wiring of the world, and the expanding of the technology that enables the allegiances of consumerism, is akin to establishing the infrastructure for resource extraction in the colonies of old. Modern broadcasting devices, once the perfect instruments for capturing loyalties and maintaining the state, are becoming consummate devices for undermining the established order. The new technologies and the mechanisms that are evolving for their exploitation are reducing the capacity of existing states to regulate political discourse. Even in an era of more limited broadcast entry, some argued that Radio Free Europe, Radio Liberty, and Voice of America helped destabilize the Soviet regime. If abundant channels become easily accessible, universally available, and used by powerfully charismatic, unmediated voices, then the potential for novel, widespread, populist alliances will certainly be realized.[106] Whether the competitors will be the industries of faith, the distributors of blue jeans and alcohol, or empires yet unborn, the point remains the same. The ascendancy of the new players, the new media structure and allegiances, will weaken and ultimately replace the now-reigning oligopolies. It is in this transformed market for loyalties that the possibilities, however dim, of global coordination and regulation must be realized.

Notes

1. I develop this definition of national identity in *Television, The Public Sphere and National Identity* (Oxford University Press, 1995); see also Philip Schlesinger,

Media, State and Nation: Political Violence and Collective Identities (London: Sage Publications, 1991), pp. 137–75.

2. See Thomas L. McPhail, *Electronic Colonialism: The Future of International Broadcasting and Communication* (Sage Publications, 1981).

3. See *Abrams* v. *United States*, 250 U.S. 616, 624–31 (1919) (Holmes, J., dissenting) (advocating free exchange of ideas). For a critique of the marketplace metaphor, see Cass R. Sunstein, *Democracy and the Problem of Free Speech* (Free Press, 1993). (Hereafter, *Democracy and the Problem of Free Speech*.)

4. One example is Anthony Downs, *An Economic Theory of Democracy* (Harper and Brothers, 1957), pp. 207–76 (arguing that information always imposes some cost on the consumer, at least of time and attention; and the problem, in terms of efficiency, is to convert these costs into payments to producer); see also Charles Lindblom, *Politics and Markets* (Basic Books, 1977), p. 13.

5. This assumes consumer choice, exercised by an autonomous individual with some modicum of preference. For an example, see the discussion on personal choice in Mark Kelman, "Consumption Theory, Production Theory, and Ideology in the Coase Theorem," *Southern California Law Review*, vol. 52 (1979), p. 669. Loyalty becomes obedience in the most authoritarian of markets.

6. See Albert O. Hirschman, *Exit, Voice and Loyalty* (Harvard University Press, 1970) (studying alternatives open to citizens). For a review of human rights provisions concerning the right to emigrate and its relationship to state sovereignty, see Francis A. Gabor, "Reflections on the Freedom of Movement in Light of the Dismantled 'Iron Curtain,'" *Tulane Law Review*, vol. 65 (1991), p. 849.

7. It is possible to consider a number of techniques—defamation laws, discriminatory tax policies, ideology-based restrictions on travel—as methods of influencing the composition and operation of the market for loyalties. However, integrating all of these interrelationships between state and narrative is beyond the scope of this chapter.

8. The use of law to ensure market access has its benign face: The Republic of Ireland, in not atypical language, requires its public broadcasting system to "be responsive to the interests of the whole community, be mindful of the need for understanding and peace within the whole island of Ireland, ensure that the programmes reflect the varied elements which make up the culture of people of the whole island of Ireland, and have special regard for the elements which distinguishes [sic] that culture and in particular for the Irish language." Acts of the Oireachtas, Broadcasting Authority Act, § 17 (1960) (amended 1976).

9. See Vincent Porter and Suzanne Hasselbach, *Pluralism, Politics and the Marketplace: The Regulation of German Broadcasting* (Routledge, 1991), pp. 1–6. However, in practice, direct public participation is limited. Ibid., p. 56.

10. In Germany, the state regulating agencies have the obligation to assure that television, especially the public broadcasting system as a whole, represents the plurality of opinions and voices the views of the relevant political, ideological, and social groups of civil society. See Porter and Hasselbach, *Pluralism, Politics, and the Marketplace*, pp. 16–17. For examples of the parceling out of channel-time among interest groups, see ibid., p. 69.

11. European Convention for the Protection of Human Rights and Fundamental Freedoms, November 4, 1950, art. 10 ¶ 1, 213 U.N.T.S. 221.

12. 12 Eur. Ct. H.R. (ser. A) at 321 (1990).

13. 12 Eur. Ct. H.R. (ser. A) at 485 (1990).

14. European Convention on Transfrontier Television, May 5, 1989, Europ. T.S. No. 132; see Council Directive 89/552 of October 3, 1989, on Television without Frontiers, 1989 O.J. (L 298) 23 (Hereafter *Television without Frontiers Directive*); see also *Television without Frontiers: Green Paper on the Establishment of the Common Market for Broadcasting Especially by Satellite and Cable*, COM (84) 300 final. (Hereafter *Television without Frontiers Green Paper*.) See Eric Barendt, *Broadcasting Law:* A Comparative Study (Oxford University Press, 1993), pp. 222–36. (Hereafter *Broadcasting Law*.)

15. Laurence G. C. Kaplan, "The European Community's *'Television without Frontiers'* Directive: Stimulating Europe to Regulate Culture," *Emory International Law Review*, vol. 8 (1994), pp. 255, 341–45.

16. See R. H. Coase, *British Broadcasting: A Study in Monopoly* (London: Longmans, Green and Co., 1950), pp. 110–16 (explaining how national and international regulation in Britain was used to limit competition from radio signals originating in France and Luxembourg and to protect British nationhood).

17. Leonard Zeidenberg, "President Pushes TV Marti; ITU Pushes Back," *Broadcasting,* vol. 118 (April 9, 1990), pp. 37, 38 (concerning legality of TV Marti); see also Steven Ruth, Comment, "The Regulation of Spillover Transmissions from Direct Broadcast Satellites in Europe," *Federal Communications Law Journal*, vol. 42 (1989), p. 107.

18. International Convention concerning the Use of Broadcasting in the Cause of Peace, September 23, 1936, art. I, 186 L.N.T.S. 301. In the Litvinov Agreement between the United States and the U.S.S.R., both countries promised not to spread propaganda hostile to the other and not to harbor groups working toward the overthrow of the other. See "Exchange of Communications between the President of the United States and Maxim M. Litvinov People's Commissar for Foreign Affairs of the Union of Soviet Socialist Republics," *American Journal of International Law*, vol. 28, Supplement (1934), pp. 3–4.

19. See generally, Stuart Ewen, *Captains of Consciousness: Advertising and the Social Roots of the Consumer Culture* (McGraw-Hill, 1976) (discussing historical growth of advertising and its connection to mass culture); Michael Schudson, *Advertising, the Uneasy Persuasion: Its Dubious Impact on American Society* (Basic Books, 1984) (explaining current relationship between advertising and consumer culture). For a recent effort to rethink the relationship between advertising and free speech doctrine, see C. Edwin Baker, *Advertising and a Democratic Press* (Oxford University Press, 1994) (arguing advertising is threat to free press).

20. Because compliance with tax obligations is hardly ever wholly voluntary, individuals cannot freely substitute their predilections for the collection of goals established by the state.

21. The notion of elasticity of demand comes into play here. Sellers of ordinary goods often want to know whether and how much an increase in price will

decrease demand for their product. Manufacturers of national identities—including the state itself—must (in the economic model) ask the same question.

22. See generally Schudson, *Advertising, the Uneasy Persuasion*; and Cecelia Tichi, *Electronic Hearth: Creating an American Television Culture* (Oxford University Press, 1991).

23. The Conservative Party in the United Kingdom and the CDU in Germany favored the introduction of a competing private channel partly on these grounds. See Barendt, *Broadcasting Law*, note 14, p. 12; and Porter and Hasselbach, *Pluralism, Politics, and the Marketplace*, note 9, p. 7.

24. Marika N. Taishoff, *State Responsibility and the Direct Broadcast Satellite* (Pinter, 1987), pp. 12–13. (Hereafter *State Responsibility and the Direct Broadcast Satellite*.)

25. Certainly this is the view of the influence of Western television in Singapore, Malaysia, and much of the Islamic world. See, for example, Erhard U. Heidt, *Mass Media, Cultural Tradition and National Identity* (Fort Lauderdale, Fla.: Breitenbach, 1987), pp. 157, 160–63; James Lull, *China Turned On: Television, Reform, and Resistance* (Routledge, 1991), pp. 165–66. The BBC broadcast excerpts of recorded prayer sermons at Tehran University on September 16, 1994:

> Satellite transmission, broadcasting the programmes of foreign television networks, is not designed to increase the scientific knowledge of nations. Rather it has been developed to mislead the youth. . . . They sell obscene films either at a very low price or give it to you free of charge, whereas the scientific films are so expensive that one cannot afford to buy them. They [the West] do not transfer their knowledge . . . [or] their experience of modernizing technology. What they transfer is something which drags families into corruption.
>
> He [the Westerner] is planning to make the Islamic countries give up the ownership of their chastity . . . . [H]e wishes to make our young people addicted to drugs . . . irresponsible towards their parents, spouses and their living conditions.

BBC: Rebroadcast Excerpts from Around the World, BBC, September 17, 1994, available in LEXIS, News Library, BBC excerpts file.

26. According to an official at China's Ministry of Radio, Film, and Television, "International satellite dissemination conducted by Western developed countries threatens the independence and identity of China's national culture . . . [which includes] loving the motherland, hard work, advocating industry and thrift, . . . taking a keen interest in science, attaching importance to culture, . . . and stressing moral courage.

Precisely because of this, we take seriously the infringement of overseas radio and television and the influence they bring which hampers the national spirit to expand." Zhao Shuifu, "Foreign Dominance of Chinese Broadcasting—Will Hearts and Minds Follow?" *InterMedia*, vol 22 (April–May 1994), pp. 8, 9.

27. See, for example, *President's Task Force on U.S. Government International Broadcasting*, Pub. 9925 (Department of State, 1991), pp. 5–6.

28. Richard A. Falk, "On Regulating International Propaganda: A Plea for Moderate Aims," *Law and Contemporary Problems*, vol. 31 (1966), pp. 622, 623.

29. Jacques Ellul is certainly of this school. See Jacques Ellul, *Propaganda: The Formation of Men's Attitudes* (Knopf, 1965), as was Walter Lippman. See Walter Lippman, *Public Opinion* (London: Allen and Unwin, 1922); and Kevin Robins and others, "Propaganda, Information and Social Control," in Jeremy Hawthorn ed., *Propaganda, Persuasion and Polemic* (Baltimore, Md.: Edward Arnold, 1987), pp. 8, 16 (arguing that "propaganda and information management are normative aspects of modern democratic societies" but "inherently totalitarian").

30. For a general account of the monopoly over information in the former Soviet Union, see Brian McNair, *Glasnost, Perestroika and the Soviet Media* (Routledge, 1991), pp. 9–29. In the recent *Informationsverein* case, the European Court of Human Rights affirmed the invalidation of Austria's rule by the European Commission of Human Rights. Austria's rule maintained a state monopoly that protects a geographical area against competition. Austria did not license private radio and television stations, maintaining a monopoly for the public service provider. Austria argued that it was necessary, in a small country, to further democratic values by maintaining tight control over the market, including the market for advertising revenues. A monopoly could assure "the objectivity and impartiality of news, the balanced reporting of all shades of opinion and the independence of the persons and bodies responsible for the programmes." *Informationsverein Lentia v. Austria*, 276 Eur. Ct. H.R. (ser. A) at 150 (1993).

31. But see International Covenant on Civil and Political Rights, opened for signature December 16, 1966, art. 19, para. 2 (right to freedom of expression), reprinted in *A Compilation of International Instruments* (New York: Centre for Human Rights ed., 1993), p. 20.

32. See Steven Shiffrin, "Government Speech," *UCLA Law Review*, vol. 27 (1980), pp. 565, 571 (exploring ways to "integrate government speech into our constitutional constellation").

33. See, for example, Kenneth L. Karst, "Paths to Belonging: The Constitution and Cultural Identity," *North Carolina Law Review*, vol. 64 (1986), p. 303.

34. See Monroe E. Price, "Controlling Imagery: The Fight over Using Art to Change Society," *American Art*, vol. 7 (Summer 1993), p. 2; see also Edward S. Herman and Noam Chomsky, *Manufacturing Consent: The Political Economy of the Mass Media* (Pantheon Books, 1988), pp. 16–18 (providing a critique of pervasive control of national narrative).

35. As in most markets for loyalties, federal and state governments have been called upon to set the outer limits of who can compete and who presents a sufficiently "clear and present danger" to require exclusion. *Schenck v. United States*, 249 U.S. 47, 52 (1919); see, for example, S.C. § 2385 (1988) (criminalizing advocacy of overthrow of government). For state statutes on sedition, see Alfred H. Kelly and Winfred A. Harbison, *The American Constitution: Its Origins*

and Development (Norton, 1976), pp. 909–11. For a recent general discussion, see Alan I. Bigel, "The First Amendment and National Security: The Court Responds to Governmental Harassment of Alleged Communist Sympathizers," *Ohio Northern University Law Review*, vol. 19 (1993), p. 885.

36. See David Yassky, "Eras of the First Amendment," *Columbia Law Review*, vol. 91 (1991), p. 1699 (tracing understandings of the First Amendment in different periods); see generally Leonard W. Levy, *Emergence of a Free Press* (Oxford University Press, 1985). Consider, for example, the specific protection of the right of religions to participate in the market for loyalties in the Free Exercise Clause. The clause, as interpreted, has both expanded and limited the range of techniques religions can utilize. See, for example, *Reynolds* v. *United States*, 98 U.S. 145, 166 (1878) (holding that while Free Exercise Clause protects beliefs, it does not protect all practices). The Establishment Clause precludes Congress from following the British example of tying national identity to a single church. Yet there is no similar explicit prohibition against "establishing" a press or set of speakers through subsidy.

37. Richard A. Posner, "Free Speech in an Economic Perspective," *Suffolk University Law Review*, vol. 20 (1986), pp. 1, 3–7 (discussing jurisdictional and linguistic interpretations of the First Amendment).

38. See Yassky, "Eras of the First Amendment," note 36, pp. 1702, 1710–17.

39. Donald J. Boudreaux and A.C. Pritchard, "Rewriting the Constitution: An Economic Analysis of the Constitutional Amendment Process," *Fordham Law Review*, vol. 62 (1993), pp. 111, 135–36; see Wilfrid E. Rumble, "James Madison on the Value of Bills of Rights," in J. Roland Pennock and John W. Chapman eds., *Nomos*, vol. 20 (New York University Press, 1979), pp. 122, 136 (discussing rejection by Senate of bill limiting state restrictions on rights of press); see also Akhil R. Amar, "The Bill of Rights as a Constitution," *Yale Law Journal*, vol. 100 (1991), pp. 1131, 1147–52 (considering First Amendment's structural and historical purpose of safeguarding rights of popular majority against Congress); and Harry N. Scheiber, "Federalism and the Constitution: The Original Understanding," in Lawrence M. Friedman and Harry N. Scheiber, eds., *American Law and the Constitutional Order* (Harvard University Press, 1978), pp. 85, 87 (examining differing attitudes of Framers and antifederalists toward state sovereignty).

40. The practice of southern states censoring abolitionist literature, for example, is traced in W. Sherman Savage, *The Controversy over the Distribution of Abolition Literature 1830–1860* (Washington, D.C.: The Association for the Study of Negro Life and History, Inc., 1938). See also Russell B. Nye, *Fettered Freedom: Civil Liberties and the Slavery Controversy 1830–1860* (Michigan State College Press, 1949); Michael Kent Curtis, "The 1859 Crisis over Hinton Helper's Book *The Impending Crisis*: Free Speech, Slavery, and Some Light on the Meaning of the First Section of the Fourteenth Amendment," *Chicago-Kent Law Review*, vol. 68 (1993), p. 1113.

41. *New York Times Co.* v. *Sullivan*, 376 U.S. 254 (1964) (limiting state-authorized defamation and libel actions). Obscenity, as considered in *Miller* v.

California, 413 U.S. 15 (1973), is also affected by a "national" constitutional standard that limits the scope of local standards. See also *Captal Cities Cable Inc.* v. *Crisp*, 467 U.S. 691 (1984) (holding federal regulations preempted application of Oklahoma's alcoholic beverages advertising ban to out-of-state signals carried by cable operators).

42. In my view, the First Amendment is, in this narrow sense, a predecessor of the European Union's Broadcasting Directive.

43. See generally Burt Neuborne and Steven R. Shapiro, "The Nylon Curtain: America's National Border and the Free Flow of Ideas," *William and Mary Law Review*, vol. 26 (1985), p. 719 (looking at America's national border as barrier to free trade in ideas). In the Immigration and Nationality Act of 1952, Congress authorized the denial of visas to aliens who "advocate the economic, international, and governmental doctrines of world communism or the establishment in the United States of a totalitarian dictatorship." 8 U.S.C. § 1182 (a)(28)(D) (1988); see also *Kleindienst* v. *Mandel*, 408 U.S. 753 (1972) (upholding denial of visa to Ernest Mandel, a Marxist author invited to conference at Stanford University).

44. North American Regional Broadcasting Agreement (NARBA), November 15, 1950, 11 U.S.T. 413, T.I.A.S. No. 4460. See Stephen D. Bayer, "Comment, The Legal Aspects of TV Marti in Relation to the Law of Direct Broadcasting Satellites," *Emory Law Journal*, vol. 41 (1992), p. 541; and Pamela S. Falk, "Note, Broadcasting from Enemy Territory and the First Amendment: The Importation of Informational Materials from Cuba under the Trading with the Enemy Act," *Columbia Law Review*, vol. 92 (1992), p. 165.

45. See Scott Lewis Landsbaum, "Note, How to Censor Films without Really Trying: The Beirut Agreement and the Foreign Agents Registration Act," *Southern California Law Review*, vol. 62 (1989), p. 685.

46. 22 U.S.C. §§ 611–621 (1988).

47. For a discussion of FARA, see *Meese* v. *Keene*, 481 U.S. 465, 469 (1987); see also Brian C. Castello, "Note, The Voice of Government as an Abridgement of First Amendment Rights of Speakers: Rethinking *Meese* v. *Keene*," *Duke Law Journal* (1989), p. 654; Anne Dorfman, "Note, Neutral Propaganda: Three Films "Made in Canada" and the Foreign Agents Registration Act," *Communications/ Entertainment Law Journal*, vol. 7 (1985), p. 435; and Dorfman, "Note, Government Exclusion of Foreign Political Propaganda," *Harvard Law Review*, vol. 68 (1955), p. 1393.

48. Harold H. Koh, *The National Security Constitution: Sharing Power after the Iran-Contra Affair* (Yale University Press, 1990), pp. 200–01; see, for example, Pamela S. Falk, "Broadcasting from Enemy Territory and the First Amendment: The Importation of Informational Materials from Cuba under the Trading with the Enemy Act," *Columbia Law Review*, vol. 92 (1992), pp. 170–71, 182–84; and Thomas G. Havener, "Note, Assault on Grenada and the Freedom of the Press," *Case Western Reserve Law Review*, vol. 36 (1986), p. 483.

49. As Hollywood films and American mass media are perceived as reinforcing values important to American society and as the federal government attacks restrictions on their entry in foreign areas, reciprocity will require that America

lessen restrictions on its imports. For instance. the law prohibiting the licensing of broadcast stations to entities not controlled by American citizens, 47 U.S.C. § 310(b) (1988), is likely to be challenged.

50. 47 U.S.C. § 326 (1988).

51. Much of American regulation of broadcasting has rested on the scarcity rationale. See *Red Lion Broadcasting Co. v. FCC,* 395 U.S. 367, 376 (1969). The manufactured nature of the shortage has caused this ground to be derided. See, for example, Bruce M. Owen, *Economics and Freedom of Expression: Media Expression and the First Amendment* (Ballinger Publishing Company, 1975), p. 91.

52. See Lee C. Bollinger, *Images of a Free Press* (University of Chicago Press, 1991), p. 74 (discussing regulatory efforts to protect "quality of public discussion and decision making"); and Steven H. Shiffrin, *The First Amendment, Democracy, and Romance* (Harvard University Press, 1990), pp. 156–57 (discussing social engineering in the First Amendment area). Cass Sunstein's "New Deal" for speech explicitly proposes a closer match between permissible regulation and the objective of achieving certain societal goals. See Sunstein, *Democracy and the Problem of Free Speech,* pp. 81–88.

53. One could start with the issue of whether licenses should have been granted locally or regionally and what role government had, or could have had, in determining how powerful the national networks would become. Thus an FCC action as mundane as determining whether to enforce an obligation for local stations to serve as an outlet for local voices could favor Hollywood over Main Street, and in so doing, affect the mix of imagery.

54. See Marilyn A. Lashner, *The Chilling Effect in TV News: Intimidation by the Nixon White House* (Praeger, 1984), p. 189 (describing presidential requests for retributive antitrust investigation, threat of antitrust action, FCC monitoring, and tax investigation); and William E. Porter, *Assault on the Media: The Nixon Years* (University of Micigan Press, 1976) (describing wide-ranging government effort to intimidate, harass, regulate, and damage news media).

55. See Porter, *Assault on the Media,* p. 145 (describing Nixon White House attitude and efforts). Public broadcasting remains under severe attack to assure that it is restrained from being "nonobjective, unbalanced, indecent, or elitist." Howard A. White, "Fine Tuning the Federal Government's Role in Public Broadcasting," *Federal Communications Law Journal,* vol. 46 (1994), pp. 491, 501. The Corporation for Public Broadcasting now is obliged to review national public broadcasting programming and take necessary steps to facilitate objectivity and balance. 47 U.S.C. § 396 (Supp. IV 1992).

56. See *Metro Broadcasting, Inc. v. FCC,* 497 U.S. 547 (1990) (holding that FCC minority ownership program does not violate due process).

57. *Office of Communication of the United Church of Christ v. FCC,* 359 F.2d 994 (D.C. Cir. 1966). A television station in Jackson, Mississippi, in violation of the FCC's "Fairness Doctrine," determined, at the height of the civil rights movement, that it would favor programs advocating the preservation of racial segregation. When national news reports showed civil rights leaders in a favorable light, the station would put a card on the screen saying that weather, or circum-

stances beyond its control, interfered with the delivery of the national signal. The Citizens Communications Center sued, arguing that the station, a supposed instrument of discourse on the key issues facing the public, was in fact blocking discourse. The court found that representatives of the listening public did have standing to challenge the renewal of the license.

58. Patrick M. Fahey, "Comment, Advocacy Group Boycotting of Network Television Advertisers and its Effects on Programming Content," *University of Pennsylvania Law Review*, vol. 140 (1991), p. 647.

59. Kathryn C. Montgomery, *Target: Prime Time* (Oxford University Press, 1989), p. 6.

60. Ibid.

61. The exact quote is, "Scottish patriot Andrew Fletcher once said that if he were permitted to write all the ballads, he need not care who makes the laws of a nation." George Gerbner, "Liberal Education in the Information Age," *Current Issues in Higher Education, 1983–84* (1984), p.14.

62. For a discussion of the constitutionality of boycotts of media for their editorial policies, see *Environmental Planning and Info. Council v. Superior Court*, 680 P.2d 1086 (Cal. 1984).

63. The molding of narrative through collective action has become virtually institutionalized in terms of informal relations between groups and government. Pressure is placed on government officials, government officials put pressure on industry, and industry responds "voluntarily." Following the model now so well established in the motion picture industry, Senator Joseph Lieberman recently introduced legislation requiring regulation of imagery in video games. See S. 1823, 103d Cong. 2d sess. (Government Printing Office, 1994). In what is now a familiarly orchestrated set of actions and responses, the video-game industry established self-regulatory machinery to avoid more intrusive governmental intervention. See "Makers Say They'll Rate Video Games," *New York Times*, March 5, 1994, p. 48 (discussing video industry's proposed voluntary rating system).

64. See generally Neil Postman, *Amusing Ourselves to Death: Public Discourse in the Age of Show Business* (Viking, 1985), pp. 125–41 (describing television's contribution to the rise of image politics).

65. In sum, this leads to what might be called a home shopping of the mind.

66. See *Turner Broadcasting Sys. v. FCC*, 114 S. Ct. 2445 (1994), and accompanying text (discussing Justice Kennedy's opinion).

67. See Jeremy Tunstall, *The Media Are American*, pp. 38–40 (1977); Herbert I. Schiller, *Communication and Cultural Domination* (White Plains, N.Y.: International Arts and Sciences Press, 1976). ("What does it matter if a national movement has struggled for years to achieve liberation if that condition, once gained, is undercut by values and aspirations derived from the apparently vanquished dominator?"); Ibid., p. 24 ("The genesis and extension of the free flow of information concept are roughly coterminous with the brief and hectic interval of U.S. global hegemony.").

68. Richard W. Stevenson, "Lights! Camera! Europe!" *New York Times*, February 6, 1994, sec. 3, p. 1.

69. The destruction of European capacities to enforce barriers to entry (at least among European countries themselves) has been caused partly by the decisions of the Court of Justice of the European Economic Community determining that broadcasting was a service to be, by and large, held to the same Community competition standards as other services. See, for example, Ad Van Loon, "National Media Policies under EEC Law Taking into Account Fundamental Rights,"*Media Law and Practice*, vol. 14 (1993), p. 17.

70. At a time when the United States is seeking to open markets for its entrepreneurs worldwide, there is something anachronistic in a statute that prohibits aliens and corporations organized under the laws of foreign governments from acquiring a broadcast or common carrier radio license. See 47 U.S.C. § 310(b) (1988).

71. Karl W. Deutsch, *Nationalism and Social Communication* (MIT Press, 1953), pp. 70–71.

72. See Benedict Anderson, *Imagined Communities*, rev. ed. (London: Verso, 1991), p. 19.

73. Ibid.

74. See Samuel P. Huntington, "The Clash of Civilizations?" *Foreign Affairs*, vol. 72 (Summer 1993), p. 22. One response, although apparently difficult to accomplish, would be for the government to invest more in its own narrative of national identity. In Western democracies, however, the commitment to public broadcasting seems to be declining. See also Porter and Hasselbach, *Pluralism, Politics, and the Marketplace*, p. 170 (suggesting a renewed role for Germany's public service broadcasters).

75. See Raymond Snoddy, "Murdoch Cut BBC to Please China," *Financial Times*, June 14, 1994, p. 6.

76. Ibid., p. 6; see also Philip Shenon, "A Repressed World Says, 'Beam Me Up,' " *New York Times*, September 11, 1994, sec. 4, p. 4 (discussing Saudi Arabia and Singapore).

77. See Kieran Cooke, "Singapore Caught in Media Dilemma," *Financial Times*, September 6, 1994, p. 4 ("On one hand, Singapore's planners see the economic necessity of being plugged into the global information network. . . . But, on the other hand, the government is deeply concerned about losing control over information flows within Singapore."). Control over receiving technology to alter market structure is not new. In the 1960s Congress forced manufacturers of television sets to ensure that both UHF and VHF channels were available in order to increase the possibility of competition and to help support public broadcasters. During the third reich, Germany required the manufacture of radio receivers that could be tuned only to approved frequencies.

78. Mamoun Fandy, "Who Is Afraid of the Satellite Dish?" *Christian Science Monitor*, December 15, 1993, p. 23. The public pressure resulting in the prohibition of satellite dishes is only a small part of the general hatred that is aimed at the impact of foreign signals. Ibid.

79. See, for example, Jeri Laber, "The Dictatorship Returns," *New York Review of Books*, vol. 40 (July 15, 1993), p. 42 (describing persecution and censorship of dissenters by ruling regime in Turkmenistan).

80. The easiest and most obvious barrier to entry during the early television era is to limit the number of television channels available for public viewing. A dramatic example of cultural protectionism achieved through a maintained scarcity occurred in apartheid South Africa, where the government banned television until 1976. The National Party felt that American and British programming would threaten the Afrikaans language and undermine the "multinationalism" of its bantustan system. See Rob Nixon, "Keeping Television Out: The South Africa Story," *InterMedia*, vol. 20 (August–September 1992), p. 35.

81. In Turkey, for example, as elsewhere, the first break in the state media monopoly resulted from satellite technology and was tolerated because the new channels carried commercial and entertainment programming that reinforced the secular mandate of the parties in power. But the new channels were also used by a deported imam, fueling fear of political splintering and an intense fear of competition among the then-ruling parties.

82. In rural villages, even the location of receivers has hierarchical implications. Communal reception will affect authority less strongly than if each home has its own set. In the distant world of the interactive information structure, loyalties to the virtual communities of affinity groups will replace loyalty to the authority figures of the physical place. See David Morley, *Television, Audiences and Cultural Studies* (Routledge, 1992), pp. 214–15 (implying position of the set is an expression of hierarchy in both "advanced" and "primitive" cultures). According to Aksoy and Robins, in Turkey, satellite dishes became "symbols of how taboos and prohibitions [we]re being dismantled." See Asu Aksoy and Kevin Robins, "Gecekondu-style Broadcasing in Turkey: A Confrontation of Cultural Values," *InterMedia,* vol. 21 (June–July 1993), p. 16 (quoting Hasan Cemal, *Islamcilarin Televizyon Atagi*, Sabah, January 13, 1993), and informal, squatter-type radio stations soon followed.

83. In most cable systems, even those in the United States, whether there are fifty or five hundred channels might be less important than whether there is just one determiner of what is shown on those channels.

84. See Jaheen Nelson, Comment, "Sledgehammers and Scalpels: The FBI Digital Wiretap Bill and Its Effect on Free Flow of Information and Privacy," *UCLA Law Review*, vol. 41 (1994), pp. 1139, 1139–43.

85. See note 16.

86. See, for example, Walther Richter, "Wanted: A Satellite Communications Board to Sort out the ISOs," *InterMedia*, vol. 22 (August–September 1994), p. 40 (noting need for more centralized authority over International Satellite Organizations); Yoshio Utsumi, "Why the ITU Has Taken Only the First Step towards Transformation," *InterMedia*, vol. 22 (August–September 1994), p. 36 (arguing that International Telecommunication Union must resolve many issues to maintain its leading role in the face of recent international developments). For a general study of the International Telecommunication Union's reform efforts, see Audrey L. Allison, "Meeting the Challenges of Change: The Reform of the International Telecommunication Union," *Federal Communications Law Journal*, vol. 45 (1993), p. 491.

87. See, for example, Case 353/89, *Commission* v. *Netherlands*, 1991 E.C.R. I-4069.

88. See *Informationsverein Lentia* v. *Austria*, 276 Eur. Ct. H.R. (ser. A) at 8–12 (1993) (holding that Austrian cable monopoly violated the freedom of expression guaranteed by the European Convention of Human Rights).

89. See note 86.

90. See *Television without Frontiers Directive*, note 23 (implementing European Convention on Transfrontier Television); see also *Television without Frontiers Green Paper* (reviewing existing and foreseen developments in television broadcasting and outlining European response).

91. Under article 2.2 of the *Television without Frontiers Directive*, a receiving state may provisionally suspend broadcast transmissions after consultation with the transmitting state when certain limited standards are not met. *Television without Frontiers Directive*, note 23, art 2.2, p. 26. Article 22 requires member states to "ensure that broadcasts do not contain any incitement to hatred on grounds of race, sex, religion or nationality." Ibid., p. 29. See Andrew Clapham and Antonio Cassese, eds., *Transfrontier Television in Europe: The Human Rights Dimension* (Baden-Baden: Nomos Verlagsgesellschaft, 1990), p. 29.

92. Austrian radio cases II *(Informationsverein Lentia et al.* v. *Austria)* Council of Europe, European Commission of Human Rights, Report of the Commission (adopted on September 9, 1992), para. 77. This argument was fashioned to meet the standards provided by the European Commission on Human Rights Convention for the Protection of Human Rights and Fundamental Freedoms, December 10, 1948, art. 10, para. 2, Europ. T.S. No. 5 (providing for "such . . . restrictions or penalties as are prescribed by law and are necessary in a democratic society . . . for the protection of . . . morals").

93. European Court of Human Rights 36/1992/381/455–459 (24 November 1994), series A, vol. 276, published by Carl Heymanns Verlag KG, Luxemburgerstraße 449, D50939 Koln, Germany; see note 30 (discussing *Informationsverein* case).

94. See the Georgetown Space Law Group, "DBS under FCC and International Regulation," *Vanderbilt Law Review*, vol. 37 (1984), pp. 67, 98–140 (discussing international regulation of direct broadcasting satellites); and Monroe E. Price, "The First Amendment and Television Broadcasting by Satellite," *UCLA Law Review*, vol. 23 (1976), pp. 879, 883–86 (discussing U.S. role in negotiations). See generally Sara F. Luther, *The United States and the Direct Broadcast Satellite: The Politics of International Broadcasting in Space* (Oxford University Press, 1988).

95. *Draft Convention on Principles Governing the Use by States of Artificial Earth Satellites for Direct Television Broadcasting* (1972), U.N. Doc. A/8771 (1972), art. IV ("States Parties to this Convention undertake to exclude from television programmes transmitted by means of artificial earth satellites any material publicizing ideas of war, militarism, nazism, national and racial hatred and enmity between peoples as well as material which is immoral or instigative in nature or is otherwise aimed at interfering in the domestic affairs or foreign policy of other States."). One of the taboo subjects was "broadcasts undermining

the foundations of the local civilization, culture, way of life, traditions or language." Ibid. art. VI (e).

96. The Committee on the Peaceful Uses of Outer Space (COPUOS) proposed the following principles:

> 1. A direct television broadcasting service by means of artificial earth satellites specifically directed at a foreign State, which shall be established only when it is not inconsistent with the provisions of the relevant instruments of the International Telecommunication Union, shall be based on appropriate agreements and/or arrangements between the broadcasting and receiving States or the broadcasting entities duly authorized by the respective States, in order to facilitate the freer and wider dissemination of information of all kinds and to encourage co-operation in the field of information and the exchange of information with other countries.
>
> 2. For that purpose a State which proposes to establish or authorize the establishment of a direct television broadcasting service by means of artificial earth satellites specifically directed at a foreign State shall without delay notify that State of such intention and shall promptly enter into consultations with that State if the latter so requests.

Report of the Legal Sub-Committee, U.N. GAOR Comm. on Peaceful Uses of Outer Space, 17th Sess., Annex 2, p. 6, U.N. Doc. A/AC.105/218 (1978) (containing draft principles on direct television broadcasting).

97. *Draft Contention on Principles Governing the Use by States of Artificial Earth Satellites for Direct Television Broadcasting, supra* note 95, art. V; *see Broadcasting from Satellites*, U.N. GAOR Comm. on Peaceful Uses of Outer Space, 2d Sess., at 32–34, U.N. Doc. No. A/AC.105/PV.62 (1969) (discussing Soviet position); the Georgetown Space Law Group, note 94, p. 115; see also Taishoff, *State Responsibility and the Direct Broadcast Satellite*, note 24, p. 34 (describing Soviet fear of harmful propaganda).

98. The final vote was 108 to 13. The debate in the United Nations was related to the general controversy over a new international information order. See Anthony Smith, *The Geopolitics of Information: How Western Culture Dominates the World* (Faber and Faber, 1980), pp. 111–47.

99. The Georgetown Space Law Group, note 94, pp. 71–89 (discussing development of U.S. regulation of direct broadcast satellites in context of First Amendment).

100. Eli M. Noam, *Beyond Territoriality: Economics and Politics in Telesociety,* Working Paper 690 (Columbia Institute for Tele-Information, 1994), p. 10.

101. Ibid.

102. Ryszard Kapuciski, *Shah of Shahs,* translated by William R. Brand and Katarzyna Mroczkowska-Brand (San Diego: Harcourt Brace Jovanovich, 1985) (1982), p. 113.

103. Alan Rusbridger, "The Moghul Invasion," *Guardian*, April 8, 1994, p. T6.

104. Ibid.

105. Ibid.

106. As an analogy, consider televangelism's ability to gain access to viewers through cable television and its impact on American politics.

CHAPTER SEVEN

Turner, Denver, and Reno

Matthew L. Spitzer

Four supreme court decisions in the last three years have shaped the law of cable television under the First Amendment. Three of the four decisions, *Turner Broadcasting System, Inc. v. FCC (I)*, *Turner Broadcasting System, Inc. v. FCC (II)*,[1] and *Denver Area Educational Telecommunications Consortium, Inc. v. Federal Communications Commission*,[2] involved sharp disagreements among the justices, while the fourth, *Reno v. ACLU*,[3] saw the Court drawing together in consensus.

Through these four cases the Supreme Court has formally rejected testing cable television regulations under the First Amendment in the same way that ordinary economic regulations are tested. The Court has also rejected applying the same approach to cable television that it applies to broadcasting. However, a solid majority of the justices has not yet worked out the approach that will be used. Many of the justices disagree sharply with one another about how much deference the Court should show to congressionally enacted cable television regulations.

The justices' disagreements about the degree of deference to be shown to Congress's cable regulations stem from the awkward place of cable television regulation within the existing structure of constitutional law. Constitutional law currently requires the Court to show more deference to purely economic regulations than to speech regulations. Cable television regulations, however, often involve both forms of regulation at the same time. Thus current constitutional law seems simultaneously to re-

Many thanks to Kathy Zeiler and Theodore Kevin Roosevelt for research assistance. This article is based, in part, on a chapter from a book that I am writing with Thomas Hazlett.

quire the Court to show great deference and little deference to the same regulations.

Through the first three cases, Turner (I), Denver, and Turner (II), the justices are trying simultaneously to work out an acceptable approach to cable regulation and to do little damage to the overall framework of constitutional law. Treating all cable regulation with the degree of skepticism usually reserved for speech regulation would invalidate the vast majority of cable regulation and might also invalidate regulating the telephone companies. However, treating cable regulation with the same degree of deference usually reserved for purely economic regulation would allow local governments to run cable as a monopoly and, through regulation, direct some of the monopoly profits to favored groups. I suspect that none of the Justices will embrace either of these alternatives. The Justices differ sharply over how to construct an intermediate position, and the disagreements are erupting into print.

The fourth case, *Reno* v. *ACLU*, presented itself in a way that allowed the justices to elide the underlying disagreements. The property used to support the Internet is owned as private property at the endpoints, and as common carriers in between. The government was attempting to regulate *only* the endpoints, and asserted nothing about the use of the privately owned computers at the endpoints that raised an economic regulation issue. Hence, all of the justices could approach *Reno* v. *ACLU* as a pure speech case.

Turner Broadcasting System v. *FCC* (I)

First I will give some background on "must-carry" rules, and then I will parse *Turner Broadcasting System, Inc.* v. *FCC* (I).[4]

The Genesis of Must-Carry Rules

Traditional TV broadcasting delivers electromagnetic signals to television antennas. All who are within the range of the broadcasting station may receive the signal. Cable television, on the other hand, requires that cables be laid throughout the area of operation and used to deliver signals into the subscriber's house via wire (metal or glass). The cable television system can choose, technically, whether to carry the signals of local terrestrial broadcasters. The question at issue in *Turner (I)* was whether the law may *require* cable systems to carry the signals of local broadcasters.

"Must-carry rules" require cable systems to carry local broadcaster signals. A series of FCC rulings between 1962 and 1972 provided the modern genesis of the must-carry rules. In the late 1960s cable television, a small interloper into the politically settled terrain of broadcasting, began to threaten the cozy arrangement between the broadcasters, the Federal Communications Commission (FCC), and Congress. Until the advent of cable television, the FCC guaranteed high profits to the broadcasters by issuing few broadcast licenses. In response, the broadcasters were well behaved and tolerated controls that newspapers and magazines did not have to countenance. When cable television threatened to inject competition into the marketplace, the FCC acted to squash the threat.[5] The FCC designed a complex set of rules to stop cable systems from carrying the fare that consumers valued most (distant independent broadcast signals, sports, and recent motion pictures). The reader may think of the rules that *stopped* cable as "must-not-carry" rules. The commission also adopted must-carry regulations. The basic idea was to keep cable as an adjunct to over-the-air TV, rather than let cable compete freely with broadcast television. Incremental FCC changes a decade later, spurred by the deregulation of private satellites and *Home Box Office, Inc.* v. *FCC*,[6] changed all that.[7]

First Amendment Challenges

Must-carry rules had been challenged and found wanting under the First Amendment in two important cases decided by the District of Columbia Circuit Court of Appeals prior to the *Turner (I)* case. In *Quincy Cable TV, Inc.* v. *FCC*,[8] the court, in a blistering opinion, struck down the must-carry regulations, mainly because the FCC had offered no proof that allowing cable operators the option to refuse to carry local broadcast signals would threaten over-the-air broadcasting. In response, the FCC formulated stripped down, temporary must-carry rules. Systems with fewer than 20 channels were exempt, while those with 21–28 channels had to reserve seven channels for local broadcast signals. Those cable systems with over 28 channels were required to reserve 25 percent of capacity for must-carry signals. The rules were to expire in five years, to give consumers a chance to become familiar with "A/B" switches. An A/B switch is a simple two-position switch that allows a consumer to choose between using the cable feed or using the rooftop antenna. The D.C. Circuit seemed to think that a normal ten-year-old child should be able to master using the switch in less than one minute. The seeming ridiculousness of allocating five years for consumers to learn how to use the switch led the court to strike down the must-carry rules in *Century Communications Corp.* v. *FCC.*[9]

Turner Broadcasting System v. *FCC (I)*

The Cable Television Consumer Protection and Competition Act of 1992[10] (the act) revamped the system of regulating cable television. Part of the measure reimposed broadcast signal carriage obligations. Cable television systems with fewer than 12 channels had to set aside three channels for must-carry signals, while cable systems with more than 12 channels had to allocate up to one-third of total signals to must-carry. In addition, the act defines which local signals must be carried. The obligations are different for commercial and noncommercial stations. Furthermore, the act allows broadcasters to choose between mandatory carriage obligations and retransmission consent—the so-called pay or play provisions. If the broadcaster chooses mandatory carriage, the local cable system must carry the signal but need not pay any money to the broadcaster. If the broadcaster chooses retransmission consent, then the cable system need not carry the broadcaster's signal. However, if the cable system *wants* to carry the signal of a broadcaster that has chosen retransmission consent, the cable system must secure the broadcaster's consent.[11] Finally, the act also gave jurisdiction[12] to hear challenges to the must-carry provisions (but not challenges to the rest of the act) to a special three-judge panel of the D.C. District Court, with direct appeal to the Supreme Court. Congress, seemingly weary of the beatings administered in *Quincy* and *Century*, took the District of Columbia Circuit Court of Appeals out of the judicial review loop.

Matters of General Agreement

Following a split decision in favor of the constitutionality of the must-carry rules by the special three-judge panel,[13] the Supreme Court took the case. The crucial issue was whether the must-carry rules constituted a violation of freedom of speech, or of the press.

All of the justices appeared to agree on a host of issues, some of which could have been quite contentious. Together, these issues seemed to define the analytical approach for testing cable regulations under the First Amendment. The agreed-upon issues were as follows.

(1) Cable television is protected by the First Amendment to the Constitution.[14]

(2) Cable, which frequently has a monopoly in its area, controls a type of bottleneck in transmission.[15]

The justices agreed that a single cable operator sits between many willing cable programmers and potential viewers, and alternative routes to viewers are unsatisfactory. This is the issue of market definition. If one were to include over-the-air broadcasting, video cassette, satellite broadcasting, microwave transmission, and other methods of bringing video into the home, then it would be much less obvious that cable represents, in general, a bottleneck facility.[16] Instead, one could argue, cable might achieve the level of bottleneck only in *some* markets. As a consequence, case-by-case analysis must support the application of the must-carry rules to any particular community. Further, one could reason, cable has no monopoly in the transmission of ideas. The government might or might not be able to weather this attack. Compelling data suggest that cable has significant market power,[17] and this might be enough to prove the existence of monopoly. The Supreme Court, however, was having none of that debate. Instead, the Court was quite deferential to Congress. Because Congress said there was a monopoly, there was a monopoly. Moreover, it was the sort of monopoly that was relevant to consider in the First Amendment analysis—a leap the Court firmly resisted in *Tornillo*, the prevailing content regulation case in the newspaper market.[18]

(3) Congress passed the Cable Act's must-carry provisions to curb the ability of cable to exercise monopoly power and thereby reduce the supply of over-the-air sources of programming.[19] This is the friendliest description of Congress's motive, and it flows, in part, from the acceptance of the bottleneck idea in the first place. A justice who was inclined to *realpolitik* might have described the must-carry rule as protectionist legislation, benefiting both existing, successful networks, and marginal UHF broadcasters who would be dropped by the local cable system.

Note that cable systems with severely limited channel capacity (for example, 24 or 36 channels) must make hard choices between services offered. Must-carry rules require such a cable operator to dedicate as much as one-third of its capacity to local broadcast signals, leaving two-thirds for cable-originated networks, such as MTV, ESPN, CNN, HBO, and so forth.

The real capacity crunch comes in instances where, owing to overlapping broadcasting contours, duplicative network signals claim must-carry status. If viewers in a cable system's area can get more than one version of a network signal over the air, then the cable system must carry all of those signals. If an area gets two NBC, two CBS, and two ABC signals,[20] the cable system must-carry all six stations. Brian Lamp, CEO of C-SPAN, a public affairs cable network, claims C-SPAN has lost carriage (since the 1992 Cable Act) on cable systems forced to carry as many as five PBS stations.[21] As of 1993 there were many video programming networks distributed by satellite, forcing choices upon even the high-capacity cable system. If a fledgling cable network were to start up, it would have to persuade a cable operator with limited capacity to drop an existing cable offering in order to gain carriage.[22] In the absence of must-carry rules, a start-up cable network need only convince the operator to drop a marginal UHF broadcaster. With must-carry rules, however, the cable operator must drop a much more attractive offering. In sum, then, the must-carry rules discourage new entry and protect existing networks. Local UHF broadcasters also gain protection under the act. Congressmen, concerned both about employment within the district and about editorials on local media outlets, would regard each small UHF broadcaster as an employer, and potential supporter, at risk from cable competition. The Supreme Court was seemingly unwilling to consider any of these arguments as *motivation* for passing the Cable Act. Instead, the Court considered the must-carry rules only as the regrettably speech-restrictive means of accomplishing the laudable industrial policy goal of the act—protecting the public's access to "free," local, over-the-air broadcast signals.[23]

(4) *The must-carry rules restrict speech.* Finally, the justices agreed that the must-carry rules restricted speech in two ways. "The rules reduce the number of channels over which cable operators exercise unfettered control, and they render it more difficult for cable programmers to compete for carriage on the limited channels remaining."[24] The first point, that cable operators lose control over the channels subject to the must-carry requirements, is obvious. The second point, that cable networks have fewer remaining channels available to carry their product, was the rejected *motivation* from the paragraph above. Here it was considered incidental to the otherwise laudable goal of Congress.

The justices thus appeared to have agreed upon a great deal. However, the Majority and Minority reached very different results while applying the agreed-upon approach. The different results reflect broader disagreements about the role of First Amendment law in cable television regulation.

Testing the Restrictions

Testing the must-carry rules under the First Amendment required a standard of review. Standards of review constitute a complex and subtle subject, but I will refrain from presenting any extended inquiry. Instead, I will present only the bare-bones outline, allowing the reader to appreciate this article's main points.

There were two obvious alternative standards of review confronting the Court in *Turner Broadcasting. Strict scrutiny* requires that a law be justified by a "compelling" state interest and that the law be very narrowly tailored to achieve the compelling state interest.[25] *Intermediate scrutiny* requires "only" an important or substantial state interest to support the law, and narrow tailoring will suffice if the regulations do not "burden substantially more speech than is necessary to further the government's legitimate interests."[26] Strict scrutiny, which is often used to strike down regulations of speech, usually applies to laws that are content based.[27] Content-based laws either explicitly discriminate between messages that say different things or are motivated by the desire to discriminate on the basis of the message. Intermediate scrutiny, which is much less restrictive, usually applies to content-neutral regulations. Content-neutral regulations neither explicitly discriminate nor are motivated by the desire to discriminate on the basis of what is communicated.[28]

The law contains one large, potentially relevant, exception to the content-based/content-neutral dichotomy outlined in the paragraph above. Content-based laws regulating *broadcasting* only need to pass intermediate scrutiny rather than strict scrutiny.[29] To justify regulating the content of broadcasting, the government must proffer an important reason, and the regulation must directly implement the reason. An important reason can be less important than a compelling justification needed for print regulations, and the regulation's connection to the important reason can be less precise in broadcasting than in print.

Why is there a difference between print and broadcast? Print publishers and broadcasters hold property rights in different forms. Print publishers hold title to printing presses, paper, ink, and (newspaper) delivery trucks as private property. Broadcasters use spectrum as a licensee of the federal government.[30] The broadcaster's license makes it a fiduciary and subjects the broadcaster to operate "in the public interest." The public interest includes an obligation to broadcast particular content, and this obligation may constitutionally be enforced by the Federal Communications Commission and the courts.

What justifies licensing broadcasting, but not print? The Supreme Court claims that "scarcity" makes spectrum different from newsprint. Spectrum scarcity, according to the Court, requires the licensing regime for broadcasting and the reduced First Amendment protection that flows therefrom.[31] The Court's reasoning runs something like the following. If two broadcasters try to broadcast at the same time on the same frequency, interference will destroy much of the value of both signals. To control the destructive interference, the Court has said, the federal government must license the right to broadcast at a particular place, time, and frequency. Because only a tiny subset of the population can get licenses, those who are fortunate enough to be licensed take their rights subject to a fiduciary obligation to serve the public interest.

The Court has acknowledged the near-universal academic denunciation of the scarcity rationale for differentiating broadcasting from print and has rejected attempts to extend the scarcity rationale to newspapers.[32] When litigants have complained that newspapers are characterized by economies of scale and scope, thereby limiting access to the newspaper publishing market to a greater degree than broadcasting scarcity limits competition in broadcasting, the Supreme Court has acknowledged the problem but rejected any reduction in First Amendment protections for print. The government may not become involved in telling newspaper publishers what to print.[33]

In *Turner (I)* the government claimed that intermediate scrutiny should apply to the must-carry regulations because cable is *like* broadcasting. The Court rebuffed the government by rejecting the claim that cable suffers from "physical scarcity."[34] Cable systems can carry ever-larger numbers of channels by simply duplicating wires or improving electronic repeaters, and incur minimal atmospheric interference. In sum, then, regardless of whether or not the scarcity argument makes any sense as applied to broadcasting, it makes no sense, said the Court, as applied to cable.

Next, the government tried to persuade the Court to apply the least demanding scrutiny (termed "rational basis")[35] that the Court ever uses, not because of scarcity, but because "the must-carry provisions are nothing more than industry-specific antitrust legislation."[36] Under the Court's precedents,[37] application of general economic regulation laws to remedy market failure in the press sometimes garners only minimal scrutiny.[38] However, the must-carry rules, by their terms, apply *only* to a segment of the *press*, the industry specifically protected under the First Amendment. As such, the must-carry rules had to face, said the Court, normal review under the First Amendment.

In sum, then, the *Turner (I)* justices appeared to have agreed upon a framework for testing cable regulation that included the following: (1) Cable television is presumed to garner full First Amendment protection, unlike broadcasting; (2) congressional regulations are to be construed in a friendly fashion, presuming Congress had good industrial organization purposes rather than bad protectionist or rent-extraction purposes; (3) content-neutral regulations seeming to be aimed at controlling market power will be tested under intermediate scrutiny; and (4) content-based regulations are to be tested under strict scrutiny. However, when we examine the majority's application of this framework, something seems to be very wrong.

The Majority Opinion

The majority (Kennedy, Rehnquist, Blackmun, Stevens, and Souter) held that the must-carry regulations are content neutral.

EXPLICIT DISCRIMINATION BASED ON CONTENT. First, the majority found that nothing on the face of the rules refers to the content of communications. Cable systems' duties to carry local broadcast signals depend only on the size of the cable system, not on the content of any cable program. Broadcasters' rights to be carried depend only[39] upon location, said the majority, not upon the content of the transmission.

The majority's argument founders because the federal government explicitly restricts the *content* of the broadcasters' signals—the stuff that must be carried—in several ways. Broadcasters must give candidates for federal elective office reasonable access to communicate with voters;[40] broadcasters must notify victims of personal attacks, made within the discussion of a controversial issue of public importance, and give the victims a chance to respond;[41] broadcasters may not transmit obscene, indecent, or profane programming;[42] broadcasters are obligated to air educational programs for children;[43] and, more broadly, broadcasters must operate in the "public interest." None of these restrictions apply to the print media or to cable television programming distributed by satellite. All are legally justified by the (alleged) special characteristics of broadcasting. Unless the test for whether a regulation is content based precludes looking up more than one statute or regulation at a time, the must-carry regulations would seem to be explicitly content based.

Indeed, this was the argument of Judge Williams's dissent in the court below.[44] The majority tried to avoid the force of this argument by doing three things. First, they dropped the most egregious content restrictions into a footnote. Second, they minimized the extent of control that the FCC has over broadcasting:

> The argument exaggerates the extent to which the FCC is permitted to intrude into matters affecting the content of broadcast programming. The FCC is forbidden by statute from engaging in "censorship" . . . "and, in fact, is barred by the First Amendment and [sec. 326] from interfering with the free exercise of journalistic judgment."[45]

Third, they transferred the discussion of the explicit controls on broadcast content into the analysis of whether the Congress was *motivated* by an intent to discriminate on the basis of content. In that context, the explicit controls of broadcast content could be balanced by other evidence of content-neutral intent.

CONTENT-BASED MOTIVATION. The majority held that the must-carry rules were not motivated by a desire to discriminate on the basis of content. Congress intended to protect *all* over-the-air broadcasting, a purpose unrelated to the content of the expression. Congress wanted to ensure that those consumers unwilling or unable to pay for cable could gain access to the full set of over-the-air broadcasters. This purpose was "substantial" enough to satisfy intermediate scrutiny.[46]

To make this argument stick, the majority had to resolve one major problem. The Cable Act justified the regulations by the need to ensure provision of the local news, public affairs, and informational *content* carried by local broadcasters.[47] This strongly suggests that Congress's *motivation* in passing the must-carry rules was to discriminate in favor of some (local) content. As a consequence, strict, rather than intermediate, scrutiny ought to apply. The majority attempted to explain away the problem in a couple of sentences:

> That Congress acknowledged the local orientation of broadcast programming and the role that noncommercial stations have played in educating the public does not indicate that Congress regarded broadcast programming as *more* valuable than cable programming. Rather, it reflects nothing more than the recognition that the services provided by broadcast television have some intrinsic value and, thus, are worth preserving against the threats posed by cable.[48]

This response cuts the traditional link between choice and motivation. Usually when someone chooses one of several alternatives, we say that the individual regards the chosen alternative as more desirable. This style of analysis is often applied to institutions, as well. But, the Supreme Court's response denies the connection between choice and desirability. Congress's choice of broadcast programming does not imply, according to the majority, "that Congress regarded broadcast programming as *more* valuable."

The Court's analysis, if applied to other legislation, would be moderately astonishing.[49] If the Court were to apply its reasoning more broadly to First Amendment challenges to statutes, the "motivation" branch of the test for content-based statutes would be completely cut off. After all, whenever Congress acts to protect a certain type of content, the Court could simultaneously assert that Congress chose one class of content over another but deny that Congress was motivated by the perception that the chosen content was more valuable.[50] However, the Court's reasoning likely will not be applied broadly. Instead, this was likely another bit of evidence that the majority was really applying a different test to cable regulation than it claimed it was applying.

The majority, having found must-carry regulations content neutral, chose intermediate scrutiny. Finding important governmental interests was easy; "(1) preserving the benefits of free, over-the-air local broadcast television, (2) promoting the widespread dissemination of information from a multiplicity of sources, and (3) promoting fair competition in the market for television programming"[51] all qualified as important interests.[52]

On the question of whether the must-carry rules are narrowly[53] tailored for these interests, the Court remanded to the District Court. The District

Court had to make two findings of fact to support narrow tailoring. First, the District Court had to find that without the must-carry rules significant numbers of broadcast stations would be dropped and, second, that stations denied carriage would either deteriorate or die. The District Court ultimately made these findings, and the case made its way back to the Supreme Court in *Turner (II)*. But, before we discuss *Turner (II)* we must look at the dissent in *Turner (I)*, and also at the intervening case, *Denver*.

Dissent in Turner (I)

The Dissent (O'Connor with Scalia, Ginsburg, and Thomas) found the must-carry rules to be content-based. The Cable Act's stated motivation to protect and prefer local news, information, public affairs, and so forth disposed of the issue.[54] Hence, the Dissent applied strict scrutiny to the must-carry rules, requiring a "compelling" state interest that is furthered by "narrowly tailored" regulations. The Dissent rejected protecting local programming as a compelling interest and rejected the interest in public affairs and informational programming because the must-carry rules are not narrowly tailored to that purpose.[55]

Under traditional First Amendment doctrine, the Dissent certainly got the better of the argument. The explicit justification for the must-carry rules, included in the Cable Act, rested on the *content* of local broadcasts. This should have been enough to trigger strict scrutiny. And once strict scrutiny is applied to the must-carry rules, they almost certainly fail. Nothing about them suggests narrow tailoring to a compelling state interest.[56]

Explanation

If the must-carry rules were so obviously content-based, why did the majority find otherwise? I believe the majority characterized the must-carry rules as content neutral, and then applied intermediate scrutiny in a very regulation-friendly manner, because the majority was unable to see this dispute as a real "press" case. As I will explain in greater detail below, the Court has demanded much greater justification for speech and press regulations than it has for economic regulations. The apparent agreement at the beginning of *Turner (I)* masked an underlying disagreement about how to resolve the tension between the two approaches. The majority implicitly treated the must-carry rules as closer to economic regulation than speech regulation. Admittedly, the majority rejected the government's attempt to characterize the must-carry rules as nothing more than antitrust rules for the cable industry. But, that was because the government overreached by trying to persuade the Court to apply only a rational basis test to the regulations.

At the time *Turner (I)* was announced, commentators tried to make sense out of what had happened. For example, Cass Sunstein believed that *Turner (I)* created a "new model" of First Amendment analysis with four elements:

> Under *Turner*, (a) government may regulate (not merely subsidize) new speech sources so as to ensure *access for viewers* who would otherwise be without free programming *and* (b) government may require owners of speech sources to provide access to *speakers*, at least if the owners are not conventional speakers too; *but* (c) government must do all this on a content-neutral basis (at least as a general rule); *but* (d) government may support its regulation not only by reference to the provision of "access to free television programming" but also by invoking such democratic goals as the need to ensure "an outlet for exchange on matters of local concern" and "access to a multiplicity of information sources."[57]

Thomas Krattenmaker and Lucas Powe were far more circumspect, suggesting that "a bare majority of the Supreme Court has tentatively and uneasily accepted" a new "intermediate model" of First Amendment jurisprudence in *Turner (I)*.[58]

Turner (I) did something other than the same old First Amendment analysis, just applied to cable television regulation. *Turner (I)* represents the Court's attempt to reconcile a laissez-faire approach to judicial review of economic regulation with the more demanding analysis of content regulation. The subsequent cases, Denver and Turner (II), suggest that there is a long way to go before the forging of a new, accepted analytical model.

Denver Area Educational Telecommunications Consortium, Inc. v. FCC

Denver Area Educational Telecommunications Consortium, Inc. v. *Federal Communications Commission*[59] upheld, in part, three portions of the Cable Television Consumer Protection and Competition Act of 1992[60] aimed at regulating sexual programming on cable television. The apparent agreement in *Turner (I)* did not hold; *Denver* produced six opinions with profound differences. The justices disagreed not only over how to apply existing First Amendment doctrine to the statute, but on whether any First Amendment doctrine ought to be invoked.

From 1984 to 1992 federal statutes had authorized two different forms of access to cable television systems. First, a cable operator had to set aside a small percentage of its capacity for leasing to unaffiliated entities (leased access channels).[61] Second, federal law authorized local franchising authorities to require cable operators to give access to public, educational, or governmental entities (PEG access channels). Virtually all local authorities chose to impose PEG access requirements. Federal law prohibited cable operators from exercising any editorial control of material on either leased access or PEG access channels. Cable operators were to take the access material and retransmit it to subscribers without altering the content.

During the eight years from 1984 to 1992 some pornographers chose to lease time on cable channels in New York City and some other large cities.[62] The pornographic leased access channels included nude talk shows, X-rated videos, and discussions of intimate sexual matters.[63] Neither the leased access nor the PEG access cablecasts were scrambled or blocked in any way. The cable operators were powerless, under federal law, to do anything about it. Cable operators and politicians received some complaints, but the number of genuine complaints remains unclear.

In response, Congress passed three sections of the 1992 Cable Act. The first two covered leased access programming and gave cable operators a choice. The first option was defined by §10(a)(2):

> This subsection shall permit a cable operator to enforce prospectively a written and published policy of prohibiting programming that the cable operator reasonably believes describes or depicts sexual or excretory activities or organs in a patently offensive manner as measured by contemporary community standards.[64]

The second option governed cable operators who chose not to prohibit indecent programming on leased access. Such cable operators had to require those who leased channels to inform the operator if any of the programming would be indecent under the standard quoted above, to segregate any indecent programming onto a separate, blocked channel, and to unblock the channel upon written request by a customer.[65]

The third challenged section of the 1992 Cable Act covers only PEG access and permits cable operators to prohibit indecent programming on PEG access channels.[66] There was no section requiring operators to segregate and block indecent programming on PEG access.

Plaintiffs sued, claiming the three provisions violated the guarantees of freedom of speech and press in the First Amendment. After the United States Court of Appeals for the District of Columbia Circuit, sitting *en banc*, upheld all three sections, the Supreme Court agreed to hear the case. Justice Breyer delivered the opinion for a plurality of the Court.

Breyer Opinion

Justice Breyer had at least three obvious alternatives for choosing a doctrinal approach for evaluating §§ 10(a)–(c): public forum doctrine, newspaper doctrine, and broadcasting doctrine.

PUBLIC FORUM DOCTRINE.   When the government owns or controls property, it may dedicate the property for expressive use by the public. There are two ways of dedicating property. Streets, parks, and sidewalks are regarded by the Court as dedicated to the public by long tradition.[67] Second, the government can affirmatively dedicate some other types of property for expressive use. Such a dedication can be limited by the government to certain topics or speakers, as long as the limitations do not offend the First Amendment.[68] The "property" dedicated as a public forum need not be real estate; school newspapers[69] and government charitable solicitation forms[70] have qualified.

The government loses some of its power to regulate speech in a public forum. The government may impose "time, place and manner regulations" that serve as traffic regulations for speech and that do not directly discriminate between content or viewpoint. The government may also discriminate between content or viewpoint if the government has a compelling interest in doing so, and the public forum regulation is narrowly tailored to effectuate the state's compelling interest.[71]

Justice Breyer could have invoked public forum doctrine in at least two different ways, but refused both options. First, he could have ruled that when a local franchising authority demands PEG access channels from the cable operator the demand serves as an express dedication of the channels to public expressive use. Justice Breyer instead construed the 1992 act's exceptions for indecent programming as establishing a limited public forum.[72] Second, Justice Breyer could have held that the rules and regulations imposed on the access channels made them into common carriers, and that common carriers transporting cable television programming were subject to the public forum doctrines. Instead, Justice Breyer stated that it was "not at all clear that the public forum doctrine should be imported wholesale into the area of common carriage regulation."[73] He also claimed that applying public forum doctrine would make no functional difference in the analysis.

PRINT MEDIA DOCTRINES. The print media receive the highest degree of protection under the First Amendment. Any content-based regulation of the print media must be narrowly tailored to accomplish a compelling state interest. To invoke these doctrines for cable television, one would have to analogize a cable television operation to a newspaper or magazine. Owning the studios, satellite dishes, and cables would be like owning the printing plant and distribution network. In each case, the owner would be able to claim the highest degree of protection under the First Amendment.

Justice Breyer refused to make the analogy, pointing to rapid legal, technological, and economic change in telecommunications.[74] New situations may, according to Justice Breyer, require new approaches.

BROADCASTING DOCTRINE. Recall that during our analysis of *Turner* (*I*) we explained that broadcasters get less protection under the First Amendment than do the print publishers.[75] To justify regulating the content of broadcasting the government must proffer an important reason, and the regulation must directly implement the reason. An important reason can be less crucial than the compelling justification needed for print regulations, and broadcasting regulations' connections to the important reasons can be less precise than those required for print. Note that the broadcasting standard is the same standard used to test *content-neutral* regulations of cable under *Turner* (*I*).

There is one other way in which broadcasting gets less protection than other media. Indecent material—the patent depiction of sexual or excretory activities or organs in a manner offensive to the relevant community—can be prohibited in broadcasting where there is an unreasonably high risk of children hearing or seeing the material.[76] The Court's opinions state that the unique pervasiveness of broadcasting, coupled to the accessibility of broadcasting to children, justifies the regulation. The Court has never explicitly settled the issue of whether broadcast indecency can be regulated for less compelling reasons than indecency in other media.[77] I suspect that it can. Regulations of indecency in print[78] and on the telephone[79] have been tested under strict scrutiny and struck down. The protected material, such as dial-a-porn, was quite pervasive and accessible to children. Because the stated rationales of pervasiveness and accessibility fail to distinguish broadcast indecency from other indecency, the distinction probably rests on property differences, which in turn are justified by the scarcity argument.

Justice Breyer refused to import broadcasting law directly into cable.[80] Just as in the case of print media doctrine, Justice Breyer pointed to rapid legal, technological, and economic change in telecommunications.[81] In addition, this issue had already been addressed and resolved in *Turner (I)*.[82]

So, what *did* Justice Breyer do? He refused to pick any established doctrinal framework, at all. The aforementioned need for flexibility in the face of great technological, legal, and economic change demanded something else.[83] Justice Breyer then announced a formulation that sounded a lot like a new test, but simultaneously denied that it was a standard to be applied to future cases: "Rather than [choose an established framework] we can decide this case more narrowly, by closely scrutinizing § 10(a) to assure that it properly addresses an extremely important problem, without imposing, in light of the relevant interests, an unnecessarily great restriction on speech."[84] Then he applied this test so as to uphold § 10(a) but strike down §§ 10(b) and (c). Section 10(a) passed muster because it protects children from indecency, but § 10(b) failed because it was overly restrictive, given technological alternatives, and § 10(c) failed because there are other institutional safeguards against PEG access channels showing indecency.[85]

Kennedy Opinion

Justice Kennedy, joined by Justice Ginsburg, disagreed strongly with Justice Breyer's refusal to use settled First Amendment doctrine:

> The plurality opinion . . . is adrift. The opinion treats concepts such as public forum, broadcaster, and common carrier as mere labels rather than as categories with settled legal significance; it applies

no standard, and by this omission loses sight of existing First Amendment doctrine. When confronted with a threat to free speech in the context of an emerging technology, we ought to have the discipline to analyze the case by reference to existing elaborations of constant First Amendment principles. . . . Rather than undertake this task, however, the plurality just declares that, all things considered, § 10(a) seems fine.[86]

Justice Kennedy proceeded to write several pages about the jurisprudential advantages of having a doctrinal framework, the relative disadvantages of ad hoc balancing, and the inadvisability of adopting a new standard—"properly addresses an extremely important problem, without imposing, in light of the relevant interests, an unnecessarily great restriction on speech"—without acknowledging it as such and explaining its relationship to other standards.[87]

Justice Kennedy chose public forum analysis. For §§ 10(a) and (b) he ruled that federal laws requiring leased access created a common carrier, and that regulations of speech on common carriers were subject to public forum analysis. For § 10(c) Justice Kennedy held that requiring PEG access channels in a franchise agreement was an express dedication of the channels as public fora. All of the sections failed under public forum doctrine, according to Justice Kennedy, because selective exclusions from a public forum are unconstitutional.[88]

Thomas Opinion

Justice Thomas also disagreed with Justice Breyer's refusal to use one of the existing paradigms, but his criticism was grounded in precedent:

In the process of deciding not to decide on a governing standard, Justice Breyer purports to discover in our cases an expansive, general principle permitting government to "directly regulate speech to address extraordinary problems, where its regulations are appropriately tailored to resolve those problems without imposing an unnecessarily great restriction on speech." . . . This heretofore unknown standard is facially subjective and openly invites balancing of asserted speech interests to a degree not ordinarily permitted. It is true that the standard I endorse lacks the "flexibility" inherent in the plurality's balancing approach, . . . but that relative rigidity is required by our precedents and is not of my own making.[89]

Justice Thomas analogized cable operators to newspapers. He claimed that *Turner I* had made this choice, but as we saw in the discussion above, this was an exaggeration. Because cable operators get, according to Justice Thomas, full First Amendment rights, leased and PEG access are intrusions on the cable operators' rights and produce no additional constitutional rights for programmers. Programmers, like freelance writers, have a First Amendment right to create whatever product they wish. But they have no First Amendment right to force anyone to distribute the product:

> A programmer's asserted right to transmit over an operator's cable system must give way to the operator's editorial discretion. Drawing an analogy to the print media, for example, the author of a book is protected in writing the book, but has no right to have the book sold in a particular book store without the store owner's consent.[90]

Cable programmers' rights are thus coextensive with their protections under statute.[91] Petitioners who want to program leased access indecency on a system that refuses to carry it have no right to force carriage. Justice Thomas refused to apply public forum doctrine or common carrier doctrines to this situation. Nothing could shake his conviction that the private property rights belong to the cable operator, and government intrusions create no constitutional rights for third parties.[92]

Turner (II)

Turner (II) affirmed the must-carry rules, concluding that the factual records assembled by Congress and the District Court supported Congress's reasons for adopting the rules.[93] The five-to-four split that produced this outcome also produced three opinions that reinforced my characterization of *Turner (I)* and *Denver*; the justices disagree deeply over how to analyze cable regulation. Some approach the issue as if it were more like a traditional economic regulation question, while others tend toward using traditional First Amendment approaches. Justice Breyer is groping toward some third ground.

Kennedy Opinion

Justice Kennedy, writing with Rehnquist, Stevens, Souter, and (for the most part) Breyer, upheld the must-carry regulations. Before Justice Kennedy could appraise the quality of the evidence that supported the reasons for passing the rules, he had to recharacterize the reasons. Kennedy, using something akin to the Goldilocks approach, rejected as too soft the position of the Department of Justice that "the loss of even a few broadcast stations 'is a matter of critical importance,' "[94] and rejected as too hard Turner's claim that "Congress's legitimate interest in assuring that the public has access to a multiplicity of information sources . . . extends only as far as preserving a minimum amount of television broadcast service."[95] Instead, Congress's real interest was just right: "Significant numbers of broadcast stations will be refused carriage on cable systems, and those broadcast stations denied carriage will either deteriorate to a substantial degree or fail altogether."[96] Justice Kennedy quickly signaled that he was going to be very deferential over the definition of "significant" numbers of station failures. If Congress thought that it was important for the existing structure of the broadcasting industry to be preserved, the Court ought not to second guess Congress under First Amendment analysis:

> Congress' evident interest in preserv[ing] the existing structure of the broadcast industry discloses a purpose to prevent any significant reduction in the multiplicity of broadcast programming sources available to noncable households. To the extent the appellants question the substantiality of the Government's interest in preserving something more than a minimum number of stations in each community, their position is meritless. *It is for Congress to decide* how much local broadcast television should be preserved for noncable households, and the validity of its determination does not turn on a judge's agreement with the responsible decisionmaker concerning the degree to which [the Government's] interests should be promoted.[97]

Kennedy first reviewed the evidence on whether significant numbers of broadcast stations would be denied carriage on cable systems, and made good on his promise of deference to Congress, often sounding like he was writing an opinion in an economic regulation case.[98] Congress had evidence of cable operators' market power, derived from both municipal franchises and from vertical integration. Vertically integrated cable operators would have incentives to drop broadcasters and replace them with affiliated cable programmers, and large multiple system cable operators would have incentives to drop broadcasters so as to garner some of the broadcasters' advertising revenues. In addition, there was a lot of anecdotal and survey evidence showing that many stations had failed to gain carriage on cable systems, and that many cable systems had refused to carry stations.[99] Evidence before the district court buttressed the evidence before Congress. Contrary theories about the incentives of cable operators and critiques of studies of broadcasters dropped from cable systems were rejected.[100] Justice Kennedy explicitly refused to involve the Court in the details of evaluating the best economic regulations for the industry, as the Court must do in antitrust cases. Instead, the Court was to defer to Congress's reasonable judgments, based on substantial evidence.

> This is not a case in which we are called upon to give our best judgment as to the likely economic consequences of certain financial arrangements or business structures, or to assess competing economic theories and predictive judgments, as we would in a case arising, say, under the antitrust laws. . . . The issue before us is whether, given conflicting views of the probable development of the television industry, Congress had substantial evidence. . . . We need not put our imprimatur on Congress' economic theory in order to validate the reasonableness of its judgment.[101]

Justice Kennedy took the same deferential approach to evaluating the evidence about whether stations denied carriage would "deteriorate to a substantial degree or fail altogether."[102] The theory is that broadcast stations depend on advertising revenues, which in turn depend on viewership. When a broadcaster fails to get carriage, its viewership falls because cable households cannot watch the station. The reduced advertising revenues will cause marginal stations to fail or to curtail their programming expenditures. Either outcome reduces the quantity and quality of broadcasting available to noncable households.

Justice Kennedy found that Congress had more than enough evidence to show that marginal stations would fail or reduce programming if not carried on cable. He acknowledged undisputed evidence showing that only 31 broadcast stations "went dark" during the years without must-carry, and that during the same period 263 new stations went on the air. In addition, cable systems voluntarily carried local broadcasters "accounting for about 97 percent of television ratings in noncable households."[103] However, this evidence would only be relevant if the Court were evaluating the actual need for the regulations, and Kennedy would have none of that. Instead, the Court was to defer to Congress; the question was whether Congress's judgment was reasonable and supported by substantial evidence. If so, the Court should defer.[104]

Having concluded that Congress could reasonably find that significant numbers of broadcasters would fail to gain carriage without must-carry, and that these unfortunate broadcasters would go dark or deteriorate, Justice Kennedy asked whether must-carry would promote "a substantial governmental interest that would be achieved less effectively absent the regulation," and would not "burden substantially more speech than is necessary to further that interest."[105] Justice Kennedy argued that 5,880 broadcast stations had gained cable carriage from must-carry, and most or all of those stations would be dropped without must-carry. Thus, must-carry also represented 5,880 instances of countermanding the decisions of cable operators—the burden of the must-carry rules. Benefits and burdens are thus "congruent."[106] This methodology relies on counting channels added and lost, rather than on computing their marginal value. Congress's burden of justification lightens considerably, as Congress need not worry about who is watching particular channels, whether they can get the same material through other means, and how highly valued the material might be.

Justice Kennedy also turned aside charges that the must-carry rules were overbroad, because they required carriage of stations even when there was no anticompetitive conduct or risk of station deterioration.[107] Purportedly less intrusive alternatives of leased access for broadcasters, switches that toggle between cable and outdoor antennas, and subsidies for marginal broadcasters all failed to impeach must-carry regulations. None of them fit Congress's objectives perfectly.[108]

Breyer Opinion

Justice Breyer concurred in everything except the unfair competition rationale. He regarded the congressional balance of competing First Amendment interests of viewers, cable operators, and broadcasters as reasonable and supported by substantial evidence. Cable's bottleneck control over programming, even if not used for any economically predatory purposes, provided enough control over the marketplace of ideas to allow regulation, at least if content neutral.[109] Justice Breyer's approach is slightly more deferential to Congress than Justice Kennedy's approach, for Congress need not make out a case for anticompetitive conduct for Justice Breyer.

O'Connor Opinion

Justice O'Connor, writing with Justices Scalia, Thomas, and Ginsburg, disagreed with almost everything in the Kennedy and Breyer opinions. Justice O'Connor first reaffirmed her conclusion from *Turner (I)* that the must-carry rules were really content based, and hence should pass strict scrutiny. Then she attacked the majority's application of intermediate scrutiny as being far too deferential to Congress.

Justice O'Connor was far more skeptical about everything in the government's case. She was untrusting of broadcasters' testimony about vertical integration in the cable industry,[110] was skeptical about the government's data regarding drops from cable systems,[111] was unaccepting of the government's failure to connect station drops to the stations' markets and the size of viewership,[112] and was highly skeptical of the purported connection between a station's being dropped and the station's deteriorating or going dark.[113] But Justice O'Connor saved her harshest critique for Justice Kennedy's equation of the benefits and the burdens from must-carry.[114] The only way Justice Kennedy's equation worked was to redefine the government's objective as identical to the statute's effect. This technique, of course, makes all statutes narrowly tailored.

Justice O'Connor rejected the must-carry rules as sufficiently tailored to an acceptable government purpose. She was particularly interested in alternatives, such as switches, leased access, and subsidies. A little bit of creative design would allow the government to achieve its ends with less First Amendment cost.

The strength of Justice O'Connor's dissent is found in her summation.

> In sustaining the must-carry provisions of the Cable Act, the Court ignores the main justification of the statute urged by appellees and subjects restrictions on expressive activity to an inappropriately lenient level of scrutiny. The principal opinion then misapplies the

analytic framework it chooses, exhibiting an extraordinary and unwarranted deference for congressional judgments, a profound fear of delving into complex economic matters, and a willingness to substitute untested assumptions for evidence. In light of gaps in logic and evidence, it is improper to conclude, at the summary judgment stage, that the must-carry scheme serves a significant governmental interest "in a direct and effective way." Moreover, . . . the undisputed facts demonstrate that the must-carry scheme is plainly not narrowly tailored to serving the only governmental interest the principal opinion fully explains and embraces—preventing anticompetitive behavior .[115]

Reno v. *ACLU*

In *Reno* v. *ACLU* the Court appeared to close ranks.[116] The Court, unanimously as to some of the issues, seven to two as to others, struck down parts of the Communications Decency Act of 1996 (CDA). The CDA, a last-minute addition to the Telecommunications Act of 1996, contains two provisions designed to limit the availability of indecent and obscene material to minors over the Internet. The first criminalizes the knowing transmission of obscene or indecent messages to those under 18.[117] The second prohibits the knowing sending or displaying of patently offensive material so that it is available to those under 18.[118] The CDA provides two affirmative defenses. Those who take "good faith, reasonable, effective, and appropriate actions" to screen out minors will escape criminal liability. Similarly, those who use verified credit cards or adult identification numbers or codes to screen out minors escape liability, as well.[119]

Although *Reno* was not labeled a "cable televsion" case by the Supreme Court, it should be regarded as such. The technology of the Internet relies on distribution of video and audio by wire and display on a cathode ray tube and through speakers. There are a number of important distinctions, of course. At the present most Internet connections cannot support a bit rate needed to produce good quality full motion video. In addition, the Internet's structure is fully distributed; every user can be a publisher and a consumer. Traditional cable television consists of one headend and a lot of receivers. And these differences were crucial to the decision in *Reno*. But the Internet should be regarded as something fundamentally different from cable television. Instead it is a version of cable television or perhaps what cable television can become. In this sense *Reno* is a cable television case and gives an insight of how cable television's role under the First Amendment may change as the structure of cable television changes.

A three-judge District Court struck down these sections of the CDA, and a direct appeal to the Supreme Court followed. Justice Stevens, writing for Scalia, Kennedy, Souter, Thomas, Ginsburg, and Breyer, upheld the District Court.[120]

Stevens Opinion

Justice Stevens had little trouble deciding that this case should be treated in the same way that the Court would treat content-based regulations of a pamphleteer or a speaker on a soapbox:

> Through the use of chat rooms, any person with a phone line can become a town crier with a voice that resonates farther than it could from any soapbox. Through the use of Web pages, mail exploders, and newsgroups, the same individual can become a pamphleteer. As the District Court found "the content on the Internet is as diverse as human thought." We agree with its conclusion that our cases provide no basis for qualifying the level of First Amendment scrutiny that should be applied to this medium.[121]

Broadcasting, which gets reduced First Amendment protection, is different. There is no history of regulating the Internet, there is no use of "scarce" frequencies by the Internet, and the Internet is not as intrusive as broadcasting.[122]

Because the regulations seemed so clearly content based, Justice Stevens went directly to the central issue: narrow tailoring. The regulations seemed likely to reduce the amount of indecent material available to minors *and* to adults. Because there is, as yet, no low-cost way for anyone posting material on the Internet to determine the age of those accessing the material, many providers would likely just withdraw questionable material.[123] Information providers most likely to find themselves at the margin were nonprofit institutions or individuals, providing such things as AIDS information, breast self-examination instructions, prison rape prevention sites, and other material with clear First Amendment value to adults.[124] Given the situation, parents must rely on user-based software packages that screen Internet content out of the user's computer. In sum, the regulations were fatally overbroad.[125]

The government tried several defenses, the most aggressive of which was the claim that even if the CDA does make chat groups, newsgroups, and mail exploders totally unavailable for indecent material, the CDA is constitutional because speakers can always set up a Web site and do age verification. The Court rejected the defense, making a direct analogy to the protection for print publications:

> The Government's position is equivalent to arguing that a statute could ban leaflets on certain subjects as long as individuals are free to publish books. In invalidating a number of laws that banned leafletting on the streets regardless of their content—we explained that one is not to have the exercise of his liberty of expression in appropriate places abridged on the plea that it may be exercised in some other place.[126]

O'Connor Opinion

Justice O'Connor agreed that portions of the CDA regulations were overbroad, and hence unconstitutional, but thought that they could be applied constitutionally in certain circumstances. The CDA's prohibition of any display "available" to a minor was overbroad, but the prohibitions on sending indecent material to a person the sender knows to be under 18 could survive, in part.[127] Such a prohibition is constitutional if "applied to a conversation involving only an adult and one or more minors—e.g., when an adult speaker sends an e-mail knowing the addressee is a minor, or when an adult and minor converse by themselves or with other minors in a chat room."[128]

An Explanation

What can explain the highly fractionated and at times heated disagreements among the justices over how to approach cable television regulation under the First Amendment? And why did they close ranks in *Reno*? I reject any notion that the particular regulations at issue in the cable cases were momentous. Allowing cable operators to keep pornographic and indecent material off of the access channels is not a major social issue. Neither is must-carry, although its economic significance is probably greater than controlling indecency on access channels. In contrast, where a truly important set of Internet regulations was tested, there were no significant differences among the justices. I suggest that something under the surface likely explains the pattern of disagreements.

Economic Regulation and Speech Regulation

Under U.S. constitutional law freedom of speech and press get greater protection than do economic freedoms. If the government regulates ordinary market processes, such as contracting or use of property, the regulations will be sustained as long as there is some rational basis for the legislation, and the regulations implement the rational basis to some minimal degree. This test embodies great deference to the legislature, and looks more or less the same regardless of whether the claim is framed under the liberty clause of the Fourteenth Amendment,[129] the Contracts Clause,[130] or even the Equal Protection Clause of the Fourteenth Amendment.[131] If the Federal Power Commission sets field rates for natural gas,[132] or if the Federal Trade Commission sets disclosure standards for gasoline,[133] or if the federal government decides to regulate all wages and prices,[134] the courts will ordinarily not intervene, at least on constitutional grounds.

> Whether embodied in the Fourteenth Amendment or inferred from the Fifth, equal protection is not a license for courts to judge the wisdom, fairness, or logic of legislative choices. In areas of social and economic policy, a statutory classification that neither proceeds along suspect lines nor infringes fundamental constitutional rights must be upheld against equal protection challenge if there is any reasonably conceivable state of facts that could provide a rational basis for the classification. (citations omitted). Where there are "plausible reasons" for Congress' action, "our inquiry is at an end." (citation omitted). This standard of review is a paradigm of judicial restraint. The Constitution presumes that, absent some reason to infer antipathy, even improvident decisions will eventually be rectified by the democratic process and that judicial intervention is

generally unwarranted no matter how unwisely we may think a political branch has acted." (citation omitted).[135]

Although the quoted language focuses on the guarantee of equal protection, exactly the same could be said of other constitutional guarantees. *FCC* v. *Beach Communications*, the case generating the quoted language, upheld some cable regulations by viewing the case as a pure issue of economic regulation.

This approach to reviewing the constitutionality of economic regulations has dominated since at least 1938, when the Supreme Court announced the rational basis test in *United States* v. *Carolene Products Company*.[136] However, in a famous footnote in that case, the Court announced that regulations that appeared to violate individuals' civil rights would get far less deference. "There may be narrower scope for operation of the presumption of constitutionality when legislation appears on its face to be within a specific prohibition of the Constitution, such as those of the first ten amendments."[137] In particular, when the regulations seem to violate the guarantees of freedom of speech or press the Court engages in far more searching review.

We have already seen that content-based regulations must pass the very demanding "compelling state interest" test to survive. Even content-neutral regulations of speech garner more searching review than the rational basis test that is applied to economic regulations. Our hierarchy of constitutional rights represents "Free Speech and Unfree Markets."[138]

This hierarchy is so deeply ingrained that the Supreme Court has had to rely on arguments grounded in property rights and economics to justify even small departures from this arrangement. We have seen that reduced First Amendment protection for broadcasting stands on the myth of scarcity and the consequent structure of federal ownership of the spectrum with licenses granted to individual broadcasters. In cable television it is the franchise—again a type of license—and the consequent bottleneck power, that justifies reduced protection.

Regulation of Cable and Other Communications Media

Regardless of whether the explanation for the speech rights/economic rights hierarchy lies in pure political economy or in pure justification, or in some combination of them,[139] cable regulation subjects the hierarchy to great stress. Cable television systems are large, capital-intensive businesses. They seem to have economies of scale and (possibly) scope that make them resemble electric power distribution companies or natural gas pipeline companies. Regulating the terms of entry, exit, terms of doing business with various classes of customers, product quality, and prices in such businesses is the core of economic regulation to which the Court professes deference. However, cable television is in the business of selling speech, as speech has been understood in the second half of the twentieth century. Regulations of speech should garner great protection and little deference. In sum, cable television regulation should simultaneously garner great deference and little deference from the Court.[140]

The Court has considered regulations of other media that seem quite similar to the cable regulations considered in *Turner* and *Denver* (and *Reno*). It has taken different paths in broadcasting and in print than it has taken in cable television.[141] In broadcasting, as we learned above, the Court has relied upon the myth that spectrum scarcity is different, and hence justifies regulation of broadcasting.[142] Scarcity, a universal condition since our expulsion from the Garden of Eden, supposedly justifies deferential review of broadcasting regulations. Broadcast licensing, as well as something akin to the must-carry doctrines,[143] has been approved in broadcasting. Federal regulatory control over the medium of transmission has been used to justify deferential review of control over virtually all aspects of the broadcasting business.

Print, including newspapers, magazines, pamphlets, and letters, is a medium afflicted with many economies of scale and scope. Daily newspapers, in particular, clearly have regional economies of scale that have driven the majority of major cities to be one-newspaper markets. Economies of scope produce the modern newspaper's varying parts—national news, local news, sports, business, and so on—all bundled together into one product. Pamphlets, on the other hand, produce litter—a classic externality that normally justifies regulation. In the case of magazines and letters, the naturally monopolistic delivery system has been run as a common carrier (U.S. Postal Service), allowing competition to flourish in that segment of the market.

When the government has attempted to regulate the print medium, using its economic characteristics as justifications, the results have been mixed. The Court has a baseline principle that universally applicable economic regulations, such as taxes[144] and antitrust law,[145] apply equally to the media. Where regulations target the print media, however, the Court becomes suspicious, and often refuses to accept the government's justifications. Where taxes apply only to the print media, or, even worse, to *part* of the print media, the Court applies strict scrutiny.[146]

In some print cases the Court has required the government to tolerate inefficiency in the name of freedom of expression. Where a community attempted to ban leafletting, on the theory that it causes litter, the Court struck down the regulation on the theory that freedom of speech required a community to put up with litter and clean up later.[147] And where Florida attempted to force newspapers to carry replies to their candidate endorsements, on the theory that economies of scale had rendered newspapers monopolists, the Court struck down the statute.[148] Newspapers may be monopolists, but the First Amendment's guarantee of freedom still precludes government from regulating newspaper operations. Newspaper editors are to do the editing, reasoned the Court, not the government. In essence, the First Amendment required the government to tolerate the inefficient operation of the market.[149]

The last two cases should be emphasized. Not only did the Court show little deference to the government, it refused to accept the economic theory of regulation, at all. The economic rationales for the regulations— litter and economies of scale—were obviously right, and conceded to be so by the Court. The Court essentially ruled them irrelevant to the First Amendment, at least in the print medium.

Cable Again: What Is at Stake?

Cable television developed during a time when no one was sure if cable operators had *any* First Amendment rights. And when the Supreme Court finally decided that cable operators had some First Amendment rights, the Court refused to explain the extent of those rights.[150] As a result, cable developed in an environment where regulation was more or less effectively unchallenged on constitutional grounds. Local municipalities franchised monopoly cable operators, allowed prices to rise, and captured some of the profits for favored groups.[151] The excess profits attracted attacks, in the courts on antitrust grounds,[152] and in Congress on policy grounds.[153]

In *Public Policy toward Cable Television*, Thomas Hazlett and I estimate the effects of the structure of cable television. Cable television systems appear to have significant amounts of market power.[154] The market power appears to stem, in large part, from the monopoly franchise granted by the municipal government.[155] Our survey of existing literature, combined with our own analyses of the underlying data, indicates that cable operators utilize their market power to raise rates approximately 20 percent above that which would occur in duopolistic competition. The elasticity of demand at this point appears to be somewhere around two. Hence, if the point elasticity is a decent estimate of arc elasticity, dropping price by 20 percent would produce approximately 40 percent increase in penetration. Even if the arc elasticity is less, one would expect at least a 20 percent to 30 percent increase in penetration from dropping to (duopolistically) competitive prices.

But, you ask, hasn't regulation forced prices of monopoly cable operators down to competitive prices? No. In fact, it is difficult to perceive much impact on the price level from periods of regulation and deregulation.[156] We can find a change in the distribution of monopoly profits under regulation, and we can find clear losses in consumer satisfaction during periods of regulation. We can also find that penetration is only 60 percent during regulation, rather than the 72 percent to 80 percent penetration that would be achieved under competitive pricing.

Very little of what we find would give cheer to someone genuinely interested in pursuing the public interest through regulation. And none of this would be tolerated if analogous regulations were applied to print. Imagine, for the moment, that a municipality tried to franchise a monopoly newspaper, kept newspaper rates at the monopoly level, distributed some of the monopoly rents, in kind, to favored groups, and thereby priced newspapers out of the grasp of 20 percent to 30 percent of the market. The Court would quickly strike down these regulations.

Fighting and Lurching toward a New Approach

I suspect that the rather dismal results from unfettered cable regulation have prodded all the members of the Supreme Court to approach cable regulations with something more than the complete deference shown to purely economic regulation. No justice's ideology regards monopolistic exploitation of the cable industry as a good thing. These dismal results, however, do not tell the justices exactly what approach to take in place of full deference.

Consider what might be entailed by applying the print model of the First Amendment to cable television, as O'Connor claimed to be doing in *Turner (II)*. Cities claim to franchise cable systems so as to reduce wear and tear on the streets, enhance safety, reduce the amount of tree trimming needed to accommodate an extra cable on the poles, reduce aesthetic blight, reduce the number of dogs running loose when inadvertently freed from yards by cable servicepeople, and, of course, reduce natural monopoly. Some of these, such as natural monopoly and wear and tear on the streets, could possibly be dismissed out of hand by analogy to the print cases. But others, including aesthetics and safety,[157] cannot easily be discarded. No court would likely accept these arguments as justifying a monopoly franchise. But the arguments might require appraisal after the second or third entrant into the cable market. The courts would have to rule on the importance of the municipalities' claimed interests in each setting. This could be done,[158] but would be slow and expensive. Price controls, must-carry regulations, compulsory leased access, and similar industry regulations would all fall by the wayside, even if competition produced monopoly cable systems, much as we have monopoly newspapers.

Evolving economics of scope in cable television and telephone may put even more at risk. If it turns out that one wide bandwidth cable, carrying video and switched communications, is the most economical approach for the future, then one company may offer video, telephone, security, shopping, and other services. If this cable company has full First Amendment freedoms,[159] then the company might argue that it can decide what sorts of phone messages it is willing to carry. This would be similar to a newspaper arguing that it has the right to reject classified advertising that it deems inappropriate.[160] This cable company also might wish to control other sorts of content on its system, including e-mail, Web sites, and newsgroups.[161] The full-blown print model might protect the private cable company, which would be reason enough to make many justices unwilling to follow this path all the way to the end.

Thus we have the following situation. I have outlined two endpoints on the judicial review spectrum, each likely unacceptable to many justices. The pure economic regulation approach allows for monopoly franchises, exploitation of consumers, high prices, and so forth. The print model would require reviewing a lot of local franchise decisions, negate large amounts of regulation, and possibly allow monopoly phone companies without any common carrier obligations. Neither approach is likely to appeal to the justices. Instead, each justice must grope toward some intermediate approach. Depending on which approach the Court takes, there will be a different allocation of rights between cable companies, individuals, cable suppliers, and regulators. The stakes are big enough to generate strong feelings among the justices.

Because the justices must try to fashion their intermediate approach within the current structure of "Free Speech and Unfree Markets," every approach must be fundamentally flawed. Thus, justices who disagree with any proposed approach will have the motive and the opportunity for a strong attack.[162]

Resolution?

The various opinions in *Turner (I)*, *Turner (II)*, and *Denver* attempt to stake out a position between the unacceptable endpoints. The majority in *Turner (I)* and *Turner (II)* can thus be seen as unwilling to stray very far from the traditional economic regulation model, at least when the regulations look like typical industrial organization stuff. Although these two majorities couched their opinions in the language of First Amendment doctrine, they applied First Amendment doctrine in a way that looked much like the deferential review accorded purely economic regulation. In contrast, Justice Thomas in *Denver* staked out something as close to the pure print model for cable that we have seen. The logic of his opinion would invalidate all access channels. The dissents in *Turner (I)* and *(II)*, as well as the Kennedy opinion in *Denver*, all profess to be applying something like the print model to cable. The *Turner* opinions do so in a way that reveals little of their implications for other cases. The Kennedy opinion in *Denver* gives an indication of how he would avoid the problem of a completely private cable and phone company, exercising editorial control over telephone calls. Justice Kennedy would allow common carrier access and public forum obligations in private systems. He thus seemingly felt free to write the majority opinion in *Turner (II)*. And then there is the Breyer opinion in *Denver*, which is trying not to stake out any position, at all. He explicitly recognizes the importance of the approach for future telecommunications cases, but is not ready to figure out what the best doctrines might be.[163]

We can now see that the intensity of the disputes between the various opinions in *Turner (I)*, *Denver*, and *Turner (II)* stem not from the importance of the regulations at issue in those cases. Rather, the disputes are over what approach to take for the future. And the approach has to fit, somehow, within the overall framework of higher protection for speech than for economic regulation. Because no approach to cable regulation can simultaneously satisfy the demands of high and low deference, every justice's choice will appeared flawed in some fundamental way.

What of *Reno*? Why did the Court suddenly come together? Testing the CDA required none of the justices to confront the dichotomy between economic regulation and speech regulation. Whereas regulations in *Turner* and *Denver* directly affected the regulatory apparatus, the regulations struck down in *Reno* did not attempt to control or change an economic regulatory structure. The highly regulated phone system was left entirely alone by the CDA. Internet users, those whose conduct was directly controlled by the CDA, were not otherwise regulated. Further, there was no hint of an exception, similar to licensing in broadcasting or franchises in cable television, to justify giving less than full First Amendment protection to the Internet. Computers, the hardware needed to make the Internet work, are owned as unregulated private property. And the phone companies, which distribute the messages, are run (for the most part) as common carriers that are uninterested in exercising any First Amendment rights. The Internet distribution technology is already run as a common carrier in the middle and as private property at the endpoints. The common carrier portions did not seek to exercise any First Amendment rights. Those who own the computers as private property did claim rights in conflict with the CDA. Only the government, which claimed no property interest at all, wished to prevent Internet transmissions. Hence, all of the justices could see that, regardless of how they ultimately try to resolve the conflict between regulation and speech rights in cable, the CDA should be tested under strict scrutiny and then fail.

Conclusion

The existing constitutional hierarchy fits cable regulation poorly. The justices are trying to work out some approach to testing cable regulation that will fit within the existing framework and also produce results that are acceptable, where acceptable will mean different things to different justices. Such a task is fundamentally impossible and can only produce flawed results. Cases that highlight the flaws also produce heated disagreements, whereas cases that do not can produce consensus. This difference likely explains the acrimony in *Turner* and *Denver* and the consensus in *Reno*.

Notes

1. *Turner Broadcasting System, Inc.* v. *FCC*, 512 U.S. 622 (1994)(*Turner I*); *Turner Broadcasting System, Inc.* v. *FCC*, 117 S.Ct. 1174 (1996) (*Turner II*).

2. *Denver Area Educational Telecommunications Consortium, Inc.* v. *FCC*, 116 S.Ct. 2374 (1996).

3. *Reno* v. *ACLU*, No. 96-511, 1997 WL 348012 (U.S.) (June 26, 1997).

4. 512 U.S. 622; and 117 S.Ct. 1174.

5. In the 1962 *Carter Mountain* case the FCC denied a microwave common carrier a construction permit because it was building the facilities to serve a cable system. The commission sided with a TV broadcaster which claimed it would be "economically disadvantaged" by the competition from cable. See *Carter Mountain Transmission Corp.*, 32 FCC 459 (1962), reprinted in Frank J. Kahn, *Documents of American Broadcasting*, 3d ed. (Prentice Hall, 1978), p. 298. The 1965 rules against distant signal importation, then codified at 47 CFR § 74.1107(a), were approved by the Supreme Court in *United States* v. *Southwestern Cable Co.*, 392 U.S. 157 (1968). Cable rules were also adopted in 1966, 1968, 1970, and 1972. The history is reviewed in all its inglorious detail in Cable Television Report and Order, Dkt. 18397, 36 FCC 2d 143 (1972). For a review and critique of these rules, see Thomas Hazlett, "Station Brakes: The Government's War against Cable Television," *Reason*, vol. 26 (February 1995), pp. 41–47.

6. *Home Box Office, Inc.* v. *FCC*, 567 F.2d 9 (D.C. Cir. 1977), *cert. denied*, 434 U.S. 829 (1977).

7. See Stanley M. Besen and Robert N. Crandall, "The Deregulation of Cable Television," *Law and Contemporary Problems*, vol. 44 (Winter 1981), p. 77. For early history see Roger G. Noll, Merton J. Peck, and John J. McGowan, *Economic Aspects of Television Regulation* (Brookings, 1973).

8. *Quincy Cable TV, Inc.* v. *FCC*, 768 F.2d 1434 (D.C. Cir. 1985), *cert. denied*, 476 U.S. 1169 (1986).

9. *Century Communications Corp.* v. *FCC*, 837 F.2d 517 (D.C. Cir. 1988), *cert. denied*, 486 U.S. 1032 (1988).

10. Cable Television Consumer Protection and Competition Act of 1992, § 4, 47 U.S.C. § 534 (Supp. V 1993), § 5, 47 U.S.C. § 535 (Supp. V 1993). For useful background, see Kathy L. Cooper, "The Cable Industry: Regulation Revisited in the Cable Television Consumer Protection and Competition Act of 1992," *Commlaw Conspectus*, vol. 1 (1993), p. 109.

11. Hence, the broadcaster gained the right to be carried without compensation on any local cable system, *or* to negotiate for carriage compensation. The prior rules forbade individual station licensing fees.

12. 47 U.S.C. § 555(c)(1–2) Supp. V 1993.

13. *Turner Broadcasting System, Inc.* v. *FCC*, 819 F. Supp. 32 (D.D.C. 1993).

14. *Turner Broadcasting System, Inc.* v. *FCC*, 512 U.S. 622, at 636 (1994) (*Turner I*). This issue was, in theory, settled in *Los Angeles* v. *Preferred Communications, Inc.*, 476 U.S. 488, 494 (1986). However, *Preferred* was such an odd

case, including a remand that never returned, that the issue could have been revisited in *Turner (I)*.

15. 512 U.S. at 656.

16. See Jonathan D. Levy and Peter K. Pitsch, "Statistical Evidence of Substitutability among Video Delivery Systems," in Eli M. Noam, ed., *Video Media Competition: Regulation, Economics, and Technology* (Columbia University Press, 1985) p. 57; Bruce M. Owen and Steven S. Wildman, *Video Economics* (Harvard University Press, 1992), pp. 223–24; and George H. Shapiro, Philip B. Kurland, and James P. Mercurio, *"CableSpeech": The Case for First Amendment Protection* (New York: Law and Business, Inc. 1983), pp. 5–8. The Supreme Court has reaffirmed that this view of cable supports the decision. *Hurley* v. *Irish-American Gay, Lesbian and Bisexual Group of Boston*, 515 U.S. 557 (1995).

17. See Thomas W. Hazlett and Matthew L. Spitzer, *Public Policy toward Cable Television* (MIT/AEI Press, 1997), chap. 3.

18. *Miami Herald Publishing* v. *Tornillo*, 418 U.S. 241 (1974).

19. 512 U.S. at 632–634, 658.

20. Each set of signals would come from a different nearby city.

21. Thomas W. Hazlett, "Changing Channels" (interview with C-SPAN CEO Brian Lamb), *Reason*, vol. 27 (March 9, 1996), p. 37.

22. See Michael G. Vita and John P. Wiegand, "Must-Carry Regulations for Cable Television Systems: An Economic Policy Analysis," *Journal of Broadcasting and Electronic Media*, vol. 37 (Winter 1993), p. 1, reporting data on the effect of must-carry rules consistent with the description in text.

23. See Cass R. Sunstein, "The First Amendment in Cyberspace," *Yale Law Journal*, vol. 104 (May 1995), pp. 1757, 1767–68 (considering the interest group explanation for the must-carry rules).

24. *Turner Broadcasting System Inc.* v. *FCC*, 512 U.S. 512, 637 (1994).

25. See *Widmar* v. *Vincent*, 454 U.S. 263 (1981).

26. See *United States* v. *O'Brien*, 391 U.S. 367 (1968).

27. Usually, but not always. See *Renton* v. *Playtime Theatres*, 475 U.S. 41 (1986) (labeling content-neutral regulations prohibiting motion picture theaters from exhibiting X-rated fare in certain areas, on the theory that the motivation for the regulations was not content based).

28. See generally 512 U.S. at 640–42 (discussing the reasons for the differing levels of scrutiny). All of the justices except for Stevens joined in this discussion.

29. Matthew L. Spitzer, *Seven Dirty Words and Six Other Stories: Controlling the Content of Print and Broadcast* (Yale University Press, 1986); and Thomas G. Krattenmaker and Lucas A. Powe, Jr., *Regulating Broadcast Programming* (MIT/AEI Press 1994).

30. Everything else, such as studios, satellites, cameras, and news trucks, is owned as private property.

31. See *Metro Broadcasting* v. *FCC*, 497 U.S. 547 (1990); *FCC* v. *League of Women Voters of Cal.*, 468 U.S. 364 (1984); *Red Lion Broadcasting Co.* v. *FCC*, 395 U.S. 367 (1969); *NBC* v. *United States*, 319 U.S. 190 (1943); and Thomas G. Krattenmaker and Lucas A. Powe, Jr., *Regulating Broadcast Programming* (MIT/AEI Press 1994).

32. The Court claims that commentators have "criticized the scarcity rationale since its inception." 512 U.S. at 639, citing *Telecommunications Research and Action Center* v. *FCC*, 801 F.2d 501, 508–509 (D.C. Cir. 1986), *cert denied*, 482 U.S. 919 (1987)); Lee Bollinger, *Images of a Free Press* (University of Chicago Press, 1991), pp. 87–90; Lucas A. Powe, *American Broadcasting and the First Amendment* (University of California Press, 1987), 197–209; Matthew L. Spitzer, *Seven Dirty Words and Six Other Stories* (Yale University Press, 1986), pp. 7–18; "Note, The Message in the Medium: The First Amendment on the Information Superhighway," *Harvard Law Review*, vol. 107 (March 1994), pp. 1062, 1072–74; Laurence H. Winer, "The Signal Cable Sends—Part I: Why Can't Cable Be More Like Broadcasting?" *Maryland Law Review*, vol. 46 (Winter 1987); pp. 212, 218–40; and R. H. Coase, "The Federal Communications Commission," *Journal of Law and Economics*, vol. 2 (October 1959), pp. 1, 12–27. As the citations show, the scarcity rationale for regulation fails completely: Broadcast licensing (and content regulation) are not necessary to solve the interference problem. See generally the discussion in Thomas G. Hazlett and Matthew L. Spitzer, *Public Policy toward Cable Television* (MIT/AEI Press 1997), chap. 5 (discussing the use of property rights to solve scarcity and interference problems).

The Court's claim about the timing of commentators' attacks on scarcity is exactly right. As Thomas Hazlett shows in "The Rationality of U.S. Regulation of the Broadcast Spectrum," *Journal of Law and Economics*, vol. 33 (April 1990), pp. 133, 135–37, 147–48. Congress was not so confused as to believe the scarcity story at the time of passing the Federal Radio Act in 1927. Instead, the Supreme Court invented the scarcity story many years later in *NBC* v. *United States*, 319 U.S. 190 (1943). In response, commentators began to attack in the 1950s.

33. *Miami Herald* v. *Tornillo*, 418 U.S. 241 (1974).

34. Again, excepting Stevens.

35. See *FCC* v. *Beach Communications, Inc.* 508 U.S. 307, 315 (1993). [T]he absence of "legislative facts" explaining the distinction "on the record" (citation omitted) has no significance in rational-basis analysis. [E]qual protection "does not demand for purposes of rational-basis review that a legislature or governing decisionmaker actually articulate at any time the purpose or rationale supporting its classification" (citation omitted). In other words, a legislative choice is not subject to courtroom fact-finding and may be based on rational speculation unsupported by evidence or empirical data. "Only by faithful adherence to this guiding principle of judicial review of legislation is it possible to preserve to the legislative branch its rightful independence and its ability to function" (citation omitted).

36. *Turner Broadcasting System, Inc.* v. *FCC*, 512 U.S. 622, 640 (1994).

37. The Court cited *Associated Press* v. *United States*, 326 U.S. 1 (1945), and *Lorain Journal* v. *United States*, 342 U.S. 143 (1951).

38. The Court cited *Cohen* v. *Cowles Media*, 501 U.S. 663, 670 (1991), and *Barnes* v. *Glen Theatre*, 501 U.S. 560, 566–67 (1991).

39. The majority recognized that the provisions regarding carriage of low-power television stations and of otherwise ineligible broadcast stations seemed to be premised explicitly on the "local" content of the stations seeking coverage.

In footnote 6 the Court remanded these portions of the rules to the District Court, for a determination of whether such provisions were content based. 512 U.S. at 644.

There is another theory, not considered by the Court, upon which the act was content based. Section 4 of the act imposes one set of must-carry rules for "local commercial television stations," 47 U.S.C. § 534 (Supp. V 1993), and provides a different set of must-carry rules for "noncommercial educational television stations," ibid. § 535. The latter set of stations is defined, in part, by the content of the broadcasts. See Sunstein, "The First Amendment in Cyberspace," pp. 1767–77.

40. 47 U.S.C. § 312(a)(7) (1988).

41. 47 CFR § 73.1920 (1993).

42. 18 U.S.C. § 1464 (1988).

43. See *Children's Television Act of 1990*. 47 U.S.C. § 303 (Supp. IV 1993).

44. *Turner Broadcasting System, Inc.* v. *FCC*, 819 F. Supp. 32, 58 (D.D.C. 1993).

45. *Turner Broadcasting System, Inc.* v. *FCC*, 512 U.S. 622, 656 (1994).

46. Ibid. at 646.

47. *Cable Television Consumer Protection and Competition Act of 1992*, P.L. 102-385, §§ 2(a)(8)–(11), 106 Stat. 1460 (1992).

48. 512 U.S. at 648.

49. The giant disjunction between the majority's description of broadcasting and reality as lawyers, broadcasters, scholars, and politicians know it has been noted by others. Monroe E. Price and Donald W. Hawthorne, "Saving Public Television: The Remand of Turner Broadcasting and the Future of Cable Regulation," vol. 17 (Fall 1994), pp. 65, 68–73. See also Ashutosh Bhagwat, "Purpose Scrutiny in Constitutional Analysis," *California Law Review*, vol. 85 (March 1997), p. 297 (maintaining that Turner (I) is part of a trend toward looking at underlying purpose rather than means chosen).

50. The Majority also turned away claims that strict scrutiny should apply because "the provisions (1) compel speech by cable operators (2) favor broadcast programmers over cable programmers, and (3) single out certain members of the press for disfavored treatment." 512 U.S. at 653.

51. Ibid. at 622.

52. For a very similar characterization, referring to regulation of speech (highly protected) or regulation of "amplification technology" (not highly protected, unless the speech and amplification technology are regarded as "integrated" speech), see Burt Neuborne, "Speech, Technology, and the Emergence of a Tricameral Media: You Can't Tell the Players without a Scorecard," *Hastings Communication and Entertainment Law Journal*, vol. 17 (Fall 1994), p. 17.

53. The majority used the narrow tailoring language from the strict scrutiny test to characterize the required connection between goals and means.

54. *Turner Broadcasting System, Inc.* v. *FCC*, 512 U.S. 622, 675–77 (1994).

55. The dissent also rejected the must-carry rules, assuming that they were content neutral, as overbroad. Ibid. at 681–82.

56. The Supreme Court made this distinction explicit when it found that the

First Amendment precluded forcing the private organizers of a St. Patrick's Day parade to include a gay and lesbian group. The unanimous Court had no trouble seeing that forcing parade organizers to include unwanted groups forced the parade to "say" unwanted things. Parades, however, are traditional forms of expression, and hence garner great protection. *Hurley* v. *Irish-American Gay, Lesbian and Bisexual Group of Boston*, 515 U.S. 557 (1995). Cable, under *Turner Broadcasting*, was explicitly distinguished. Everyone knows, said the Court, that the cable system is not "speaking" when it carries broadcasters and other signals. It would appear that, as far as the Court is concerned, what "everyone knows" depends on whether the regulations look like traditional economic regulation or not. After all, everyone might "know" that march organizers are not speaking when an organized group participates in the march.

57. Sunstein, "The First Amendment in Cyberspace," p. 1774 (emphasis in original and footnote omitted). Neuborne also believes that *Turner Broadcasting* establishes an intermediate mode of analysis for cable. Neuborne, "Speech, Technology, and the Emergence of a Tricameral Media," p. 35.

Commentators continue to critique *Turner (I)* and subsequent cable cases. Lawrence Winer, "The Red Lion of Cable, and Beyond?—*Turner Broadcasting* v. *FCC*," *Cardozo Arts and Entertainment Law Journal*, vol. 15 (1997), p. 1 (arguing that the Supreme Court should have applied strict scrutiny); Ronald W. Adelman, "The First Amendment and the Metaphor of Free Trade," *Arizona Law Review*, vol. 38 (Winter 1996), p. 1125 (arguing against allowing state interventions into media markets for benign purposes); Ashutosh Bhagwat, "Of Markets and Media: The First Amendment, the New Mass Media, and the Political Components of Culture," *North Carolina Law Review*, vol. 74 (November 1995), p. 142 (terming *Turner (I)* as unworkable, and suggesting a unitary test that allows intervention into cable markets to promote diversity where there are "real" market dysfunctions); Erik Forde Ugland, "Cable Television, New Technologies and the First Amendment after *Turner Broadcasting System, Inc.* v. *FCC*," *Missouri Law Review*, vol. 60 (Fall 1995), p. 799 (contending that the Court should have applied the print model of the First Amendment to cable television).

58. Thomas G. Krattenmaker and Lucas A. Powe, Jr., "Converging First Amendment Principles for Converging Communications Media," *Yale Law Journal*, vol. 104 (May 1995), pp. 1719, 1723. See also Monroe E. Price and Donald W. Hawthorne, "Saving Public Television: The Remand of Turner Broadcasting and the Future of Cable Regulation," *Hastings Communications and Entertainment Law Journal*, vol. 17 (Fall 1994), p. 65.

59. *Denver Area Educational Telecommunications Consortium, Inc.* v. *FCC*, 116 S.Ct. 2374 (1996).

60. *Cable Television Consumer Protection and Competition Act of 1992*, P. L. 102-385, §§ 10(a)–(c), 106 Stat. 1460 (1992).

61. 47 U.S.C. § 532(b). The percentage varies with cable system size.

62. 138 *Congressional Record*, S642-01, *S648.

63. 138 *Congressional Record*, S642-01, *S649.

64. P. L. 102-385, § 10(a)(2), 106 Stat. 1460 (1992), *Cable Television Consumer Protection and Competition Act of 1992.*

65. *Cable Television Consumer Protection and Competition Act of 1992,* P. L. 102-385, § 10(b)(1), 106 Stat. 1460 (1992).

66. The act instructs the FCC to promulgate regulations that will: "enable a cable operator of a cable system to prohibit the use, on such system, of any channel capacity of any public, educational, or governmental access facility for any programming which contains obscene material, sexually explicit conduct, or material soliciting or promoting unlawful conduct." *Cable Television Consumer Protection and Competition Act of 1992,* P. L.102-385, § 10(c), 106 Stat. 1460 (1992).

67. *Perry Educational Association v. Perry Local Educators' Association,* 460 U.S. 37 (1983); and *Hague v. Committee of Industrial Organizations,* 307 U.S. 496 (1939).

68. *International Society for Krishna Consciousness, Inc. v. Lee,* 505 U.S. 672 (1992).

69. *Rosenberger v. Rector and Visitors of University of Va.,* 515 U.S. 819 (1995).

70. *Cornelius v. NAACP Legal Defense and Educational Fund, Inc.,* 473 U.S. 788 (1985).

71. This raises one of the central conundrums of public forum doctrine: do the exclusions from a limited public forum need to be justified under the same standard as regulations of an unlimited public forum? If not, the limited public forum category threatens to swallow the high burden imposed on regulations of unlimited public forums. See Matthew L. Spitzer, "The Constitutionality of Licensing Broadcasters," *New York University Law Review,* vol. 64 (November 1989), p. 990; and Robert Post, "Between Governance and Management: The History and Theory of the Public Forum," *UCLA Law Review,* vol. 34 (June–August 1987), p. 1713.

72. *Denver Area Educational Telecommunications Consortium, Inc. v. FCC,* 116 S.Ct. 2374 (1996).

73. Ibid.

74. Ibid. at 2385.

75. See discussion in text at note 29. 512 U.S. 622 at 636.

76. *FCC v. Pacifica Foundation,* 438 U.S. 726 (1978).

77. 116 S. Ct. at 2403 (opinion of Justice Kennedy claiming no difference in standard for testing broadcast indecency); *Pacifica,* 438 U.S. at 745–48 (opinion of Justice Stevens, holding that indecent materials, at least in a broadcast context, get lesser First Amendment protection).

78. *Butler v. Michigan,* 352 U.S. 380 (1957); and *Cohen v. California,* 403 U.S. 15 (1971).

79. *Sable Communications of California, Inc. v. FCC,* 492 U.S. 115 (1989).

80. In one sense Justice Breyer imports a part of broadcasting law into cable. The Supreme Court has held that broadcast indecency can be regulated because of the pervasiveness of broadcasting in American life and because of the unique accessibility of broadcasting to children. Justice Breyer explicitly refused to state

whether there is a lower standard for reviewing broadcast indecency, *Denver Area Educational Telecommunications Consortium, Inc.* v. *FCC*, 116 S. Ct. 2374, 2378 (1996), because he thought § 10 (a) passed even the most demanding level of scrutiny. Justice Breyer relied on the same considerations used in Pacifica—pervasiveness and accessibility to children—to uphold § 10 (a).

81. Ibid.

82. *Turner Broadcasting System, Inc.* v. *FCC*, 512 U.S. 622 (1994).

83. For a taste of how much may be changing because of the Internet, connection to which is often made through cable television systems, see A. Michael Froomkin, "Flood Control on the Information Ocean: Living with Anonymity, Digital Cash, and Distributed Databases," *Journal of Law and Commerce*, vol. 15 (Spring 1996), p. 395, and Margaret Jane Radin, "Regulation of Computing and Information Technology: Property Evolving in Cyberspace," p. 509; and Norman Redlich and David R. Lurie, "First Amendment Issues Presented by the 'Information Superhighway,'" *Seton Hall Law Review*, vol. 25 (1995), p. 1446.

84. 116 S.Ct. at 2385.

85. Justice O'Connor wrote separately, voting to uphold § 10(c) for the same reasons that Justice Breyer upheld § 10(a). Justice O'Connor agreed with Justice Breyer "that we should not yet undertake fully to adapt our First Amendment doctrine to the new context we confront here." Ibid. at 2403.

86. Ibid. at 2404.

87. Ibid. at 2405–07.

88. Ibid. at 2413–15.

89. Ibid. at 2422.

90. Ibid. at 2421.

91. Although Justice Thomas expressly refused to decide the issue, his argument casts doubt on the constitutionality of the access provisions.

92. *Denver Area Educational Telecommunications Consortium, Inc.* v. *FCC*, 116 S.Ct. 2374, 2421, 2425–26 (1996).

93. *Turner Broadcasting System, Inc.* v. *FCC*, 117 S.Ct. 1174 (1996).

94. Ibid. at 1186.

95. Ibid. at 1187 (internal quotation marks omitted).

96. Ibid. (internal quotation marks omitted).

97. Ibid. at 1188 (internal citations and quotation marks omitted; emphasis added).

98. "Even in the realm of First Amendment questions where Congress must base its conclusions upon substantial evidence, deference must be accorded to its findings as to the harm to be avoided and to the remedial measures adopted for that end, lest we infringe on traditional legislative authority to make predictive judgments when enacting nationwide regulatory policy." Ibid. at 1189.

99. Ibid. at 1192.

100. Ibid. at 1194.

101. Ibid. at 1195.

102. Ibid.

103. Ibid. at 1196.

104. "The question is not whether Congress, as an objective matter, was

correct to determine must-carry is necessary to prevent a substantial number of broadcast stations from losing cable carriage and suffering significant financial hardship. Rather, the question is whether the legislative conclusion was reasonable and supported by substantial evidence in the record before Congress. . . . We have noted in another context, involving less deferential review than is at issue here, that 'the possibility of drawing two inconsistent conclusions from the evidence does not prevent . . . [a] finding from being supported by substantial evidence.' "

Ibid. at 1196. The quoted language came from *American Textile Manufacturers Institue, Inc.* v. *Donovan*, 452 U.S. 490 (1981), which involved the reasonableness of the secretary of labor's regulations controlling the amount of ambient cotton dust in cotton mills. Thus, Justice Kennedy is saying that congressional judgments on cable regulation deserve no more deference than the secretary of labor's choice of purely economic regulations.

105. Ibid. at 1198.

106. "The 5,880 channels occupied by added broadcasters represent the actual burden of the regulatory scheme. Appellants concede most of those stations would be dropped in the absence of must-carry, . . . so the figure approximates the benefits of must-carry as well.

Because the burden imposed by must-carry is congruent to the benefits it affords, we conclude must-carry is narrowly tailored to preserve a multiplicity of broadcast stations for the 40 percent of American households without cable." Ibid. at 1199.

107. Ibid. at 1199.

108. Ibid. at 1199–1202.

109. In particular, I note (and agree) that a cable system, physically dependent upon the availability of space along city streets, at present (perhaps less in the future) typically faces little competition, that it therefore constitutes a kind of bottleneck that controls the range of viewer choice (whether or not it uses any consequent economic power for economically predatory purposes), and that some degree—at least a limited degree—of governmental intervention and control through regulation can prove appropriate when justified under O'Brien (at least when not "content based"). Ibid. at 1204–05.

110. Ibid. at 1210.

111. Ibid. at 1211.

112. Ibid. at 1211–12.

113. Ibid. at 1213–15.

114. "The Court's leap to the conclusion that must-carry is narrowly tailored to preserve a multiplicity of broadcast stations, . . . is nothing short of astounding. The Court's logic is circular. Surmising that most of the 5,880 channels added by the regulatory scheme would be dropped in its absence, the Court concludes that the figure also approximates the 'benefit' of must-carry. Finding the scheme's burden 'congruent' to the benefit it affords, the Court declares the statute narrowly tailored. The Court achieves this result, however, only by equating the effect of the statute—requiring cable operators to add 5,880 stations—with the governmental interest sought to be served." Ibid. at 1215.

115. Ibid. at 1219 (footnote omitted).

116. *Reno* v. *ACLU*, No. 96-511, 1997 WL 348012 (U.S.) (June 26, 1997).

117. "(a) Whoever—(1) in interstate or foreign communications—. . . .(B) by means of a telecommunications device knowingly—(i) makes, creates, or solicits, and (ii) initiates the transmission of any comment request, suggestion, proposal, image, or other communication which is obscene or indecent, knowing that the recipient of the communication is under 18 years of age, regardless of whether the maker of such communication placed the call or initiated the communication; . . . (2) knowingly permits any telecommunications facility under his control to be used for any activity prohibited by paragraph (1) with the intent that it be used for such activity, shall be fined under Title 18, or imprisoned not more than two years, or both." 47 U.S.C.A. § 223(a)(Supp. 1997).

118. "(d) Whoever—(1) in interstate or foreign communications knowingly—(A) uses an interactive computer service to send to a specific person or persons under 18 years of age, or

(B) uses any interactive computer service to display in a manner available to a person under 18 years of age, any comment, request, suggestion, proposal, image, or other communication that, in context, depicts or describes, in terms patently offensive as measured by contemporary community standards, sexual or excretory activities or organs, regardless of whether the user of such service placed the call or initiated the communication; or (2) knowingly permits any telecommunications facility under such person's control to be used for an activity prohibited by paragraph (1) with the intent that it be used for such activity, shall be fined under Title 18, or imprisoned not more than two years, or both." 47 U.S.C.A. § 223(d)(Supp. 1997).

119. 47 U.S.C.A. § 223(e)(5)(B)(Supp. 1997).

120. I treat *Reno* as a cable case for two reasons. First, connection to the Internet is increasingly made through cable systems. Second, the Justices treated the cable cases as directly on point in their opinions in *Reno*.

121. *Reno*, 1997 WL 348012, at *14 (U.S.)(citation omitted).

122. Ibid. at *2.

123. The Court rejected the government's suggestion that indecent sites be "tagged" as a possible solution that is not yet here. A tag is a digital code that would allow users to identify a site as indecent without examining the site's contents. Until such a solution is up and running, the government may not rely upon it to impose criminal liability.

124. The Court regarded the vagueness of the two regulations as increasing the overbreadth of the CDA. *Reno*, 1997 WL 348012, at *18–19 (U.S.).

125. The Court severed part of § 223(a) that applied to indecency and read the statute so as to prohibit only obscene material.

126. *Reno*, 1997 WL 348012, at *18 (U.S.) (quotation marks omitted). The Court also rejected the government's arguments that the "knowledge" requirements of both regulations and the various affirmative defenses saved the regulations. The knowledge is irrelevant to the analysis, and the defenses are all technologically incomplete or too expensive.

127. Justice O'Connor construed 47 U.S.C.A. §§ 223(a)(a)(B) and 223(d)(a)(A) as both doing essentially this.

128. *Reno*, 1997 WL 348012, at *25 (U.S.).

129. "No State . . . shall . . . deprive any person of life, liberty, or property, without due process of law." U.S. Const, Amend XIV, § 1.

130. "No State shall . . . pass any . . . Law impairing the Obligation of Contracts." U.S. Const, Art I, § 10, cl. 1. *Home Building and Loan Association* v. *Blaisdell*, 290 U.S. 398 (1934).

131. "No State shall . . . deny to any person within its jurisdiction the equal protection of the laws." U.S. Const, Amend XIV, § 1.

132. *In re* Permian Basin Area Rate Cases, 390 U.S. 747 (1968).

133. FTC v. *Texaco, Inc.*, 555 F.2d 862 (D.C. Cir. 1977), *cert. denied*, 431 U.S. 974 (1977).

134. *Amalgamated Meat Cutters* v. *Connally*, 337 F. Supp. 737, 745–63 (D.D.C. 1971).

135. *FCC* v. *Beach Communications, Inc.*, 508 U.S. 307, 313 (1993).

136. *U.S.* v. *Carolene Prods., Co.*, 304 U.S. 144 (1938).

137. 304 U.S. 144, 152–153 n.4 (1938). For a discussion of the evolution of the Carolene Products approach, see Erwin Chemerinsky, *Constitutional Law: Principles and Policies* (New York: Aspen Law and Business, 1997), pp. 491–94.

138. Kathleen M. Sullivan, "Free Speech and Unfree Markets," *UCLA Law Review*, vol. 42 (1995), p. 949, represents by far the best review essay on the subject. Sullivan discusses possible justifications for the hierarchy, as well as organizing arguments from the left and the right for bringing the treatment of speech and markets into line with each other.

Where litigants attempt to persuade a court to regard a regulation that appears to be economic as really about speech because the regulation produces substantial burdens on speech, the court will ask if the burdens on speech are direct or incidental. If direct, the regulation will face strict scrutiny. If incidental, the regulation will face far more relaxed scrutiny. Burdens from a seeming economic regulation will, in general, be regarded as incidental. Michael C. Dorf, "Incidental Burdens on Fundamental Rights," *Harvard Law Review*, vol. 109 (April 1996), p. 1175.

139. On how to explain the hierarchy, see Matthew L. Spitzer, "The Economics of Freedom of Expression," entry in the *New Palgrave Dictionary of Law and Economics* (forthcoming). On justifications, see Sullivan, "Free Speech," p. 949.

140. The Court faces a similar problem in other areas of regulation. For example, where the state or federal government regulates speech about economic matters, such as the price of goods or services, the Court must choose whether to approach the matter as economic regulation or speech regulation. *Valentine* v. *Christensen*, 316 U.S. 52 (1942); *Virginia State Board of Pharmacy* v. *Virginia Citizens Consumer Council, Inc.*, 425 U.S. 748 (1976); *Bolger* v. *Young Drug Prods. Corp.*, 463 U.S. 60 (1983); and *Florida Bar* v. *Went for It, Inc.*, 115 S.Ct. 2371 (1995). When trade associations that have been granted special powers by the government, such as the State Bar or a union, use association dues to fund

speech with which some of the members differ, the Court must decide whether to treat the complaint as a speech case or an economic regulation case. See *Keller v. State Bar of California*, 496 U.S. 1 (1990); *Abood v. Detroit Board of Education*, 431 U.S. 209 (1977); and *Glickman v. Wileman Bros. and Elliott, Inc.*, No. 95-1184, 1997 WL 345357 (U.S.).

141. Commentators recognize the central dilemma posed by such cases. John O. McGinnis, "The Once and Future Property-Based Vision of the First Amendment," *University of Chicago Law Review*, vol. 63 (Winter 1996), pp. 49, 91 ("one of the most recurrent and intractable problems in First Amendment jurisprudence [is] the appropriate standard for assessing government regulation of the material property used to transmit information.").

142. See discussion in text at notes 31–32.

143. *Red Lion Broadcasting Co. v. FCC*, 395 U.S. 367 (1969).

144. *Grosjean v. American Press Co.*, 297 U.S. 233 (1936); *Minneapolis Star and Tribune Co. v. Minnesota Commissioner of Revenue*, 460 U.S. 575 (1983); *Arkansas Writers' Project, Inc. v. Ragland*, 481 U.S. 221 (1987). But see *Leathers v. Medlock*, 499 U.S. 439 (1991) (allowing differential taxation of cable television). "Note, Taxation of Cable Television," *Harvard Law Review*, vol. 109 (December 1995), p. 440, argues that *Turner (I)* requires a more exacting review of cable taxation than was applied in *Leathers v. Medlock*.

145. *Citizen Publishing. Co. v. U.S.*, 394 U.S. 131 (1969).

146. *Grosjean v. American Press Co.*, 297 U.S. 233 (1936); *Minneapolis Star and Tribune Co. v. Minnesota Commissioner of Revenue*, 460 U.S. 575 (1983); and *Arkansas Writers' Project, Inc. v. Ragland*, 481 U.S. 221 (1987).

147. *Schneider v. State* (Town of Irvington), 308 U.S. 147 (1939).

148. *Miami Herald Publishing Company v. Tornillo*, 418 U.S. 241 (1974).

149. For an argument that must-carry regulations are really consistent with prior treatment of print regulations, see C. Edwin Baker, "Turner Broadcasting: Content-Based Regulation of Persons and Presses," *Supreme Court Review* (1994), p. 57.

150. *Los Angeles v. Preferred Communications, Inc.*, 476 U.S. 488 (1986).

151. The latest example comes from the city of Troy, Michigan. TCI, the local cable operator, applied for permission to upgrade its cable system. Troy demanded, as a condition of approval, that TCI run a fiber optic backbone through a business development with no cable subscribers. The only use for this spur would be to provide inexpensive telephone service to the businesses. TCI balked and appealed to the FCC. Ted Hearn, "FCC Panel Backs Troy in TCI Dispute," *Multichannel News*, vol. 18 (July 7, 1997), p. 34.

152. *Community Communications Co., Inc. v. Boulder*, 455 U.S. 40 (1982).

153. *1984 Cable Act*; and *Telecommunications Act of 1996*.

154. Thomas W. Hazlett and Matthew L. Spitzer, *Public Policy toward Cable Television: The Economics of Rate Controls* (MIT/AEI Press 1997), chap. 3.

155. We conduct a pair of spreadsheet exercises which demonstrate that with current cost structures most markets could support duopolistic competition. Hazlett and Spitzer, "Public Policy toward Cable Television," pp. 36–38.

156. The reregulatory period following the *1992 Cable Act* would be the exception to this statement. Prices were clearly forced down for awhile.

157. *Metromedia, Inc.* v. *San Diego*, 453 U.S. 490 (1981); *Ladue* v. *Gilleo*, 512 U.S. 43 (1994); *Schenck* v. *Pro-Choice Network of Western New York*, 117 S. Ct. 855 (1997); and *Rubin* v. *Coors Brewing Co.*, 115 S. Ct. 1585 (1995).

158. It has been done by several lower federal courts in monopoly franchise litigation. *Nor-West Cable Communications* v. *St. Paul*, 924 F.2d 741 (8th Cir. 1991); *Preferred Communications, Inc.* v. *Los Angeles*, 13 F.3d 1327 (9th Cir. 1994); *City Communications, Inc.* v. *Detroit*, 888 F.2d 1081, 1090 (6th Cir. 1989) (finding that cable television "burdens public streets, roads and rights-of-way in the same manner as telephone systems or electric utilities, and is subject to City regulation. . . ."); *Video International Production, Inc.* v. *Warner-Amex Cable Communications*, 858 F.2d 1075, 1081 (5th Cir. 1988), *cert. denied sub nom. Dallas* v. *Video Int'l Prod., Inc.*, 490 U.S. 1047 (1989); *Community Communications Co.* v. *Boulder*, 660 F.2d 1370 (1981); *Telesat Cablevision, Inc.* v. *Riviera Beach*, 773 F. Supp 383 (S.D. Fla. 1991). See also *Omega Satellite Prods. Co.* v. *Indianapolis*, 694 F.2d 119 (7th Cir. 1982) (noting in *dictum* that the city could have denied a permit to the SMATV company to put a cable under a street for independent and valid reasons, such as safety hazards).

159. See Fred H. Cate, "Telephone Companies, The First Amendment, and Technological Convergence," *DePaul Law Review*, vol. 45 (1996), p. 1035 (discussing First Amendment rights of telephone companies).

160. There may be limits on the ability of a newspaper to control its classified ads. See *Pittsburgh Press Co.* v. *Pittsburgh Commission on Human Relations*, 413 U.S. 376 (1973) (upholding ban on sex-segregated help wanted ads prior to modern cases bringing commercial speech clearly within protection of First Amendment).

161. The First Amendment could also be used to challenge regulations controlling ownership of multiple media outlets, where concentrated ownership threatens competition. See generally Henry Geller, "Ownership Regulatory Policies in the U.S. Telecom Sector," *Cardozo Arts and Entertainment Law Journal*, vol. 13 (1995), p. 727; "Symposium, The Changing Landscape of Jurisprudence in Light of the New Communications and Media Alliances," *Fordham Intellectual Property, Media, and Entertainment Law Journal*, vol. 6 (Spring 1996), p. 427.

162. At some deep level, every opinion is subject to a strong attack on the ideological underpinnings of its basic assumptions. See Mark Kelman, *A Guide to Critical Legal Studies* (Harvard University Press, 1987). The opportunities for attack in cable jurisprudence lie much closer to the surface.

163. For a review of the traditional regulatory approaches to cable television, each of which could serve as a starting point for First Amendment doctrine, see Daniel L. Brenner, "Ownership and Content Regulation in Merging and Emerging Media," *DePaul Law Review*, vol. 45 (Summer 1996), p. 1009.

CHAPTER EIGHT

Global Communication Policy and the Realization of Human Rights

Marc Raboy

CITIZENSHIP IS TIED to democracy, and global citizenship should in some way be tied to global democracy, at least to a process of democratization that extends some notion of rights, representation, and accountability to the operations of international institutions.[1]

Various textual versions of a human right to communicate have been enshrined in the UN Universal Declaration of Human Rights and dozens of national constitutions. As millions of people around the world can attest, however, these texts in themselves do not actually mean that citizens are necessarily able to enjoy that right.

The problem lies in the way "rights" are actualized in different societies—and, increasingly, in an emerging global society. We can gain some insight into the scope of this problem by reflecting on French semantics.

In the French language, the word *droit* signifies both "rights" and "law." Thus *le droit à la communication* means "the right to communicate," while *le droit de la communication* signifies "communication law." The French Revolution is indeed the precursor to the worldwide modernist tradition of codifying rights in law. But as the French Revolution itself and dozens of subsequent events have shown, the codification of rights in legal texts can be a wonderful camouflage of the social conflicts and relations of power that mark a given society at any point in time.

Under the rule of law, according to Canadian jurist Pierre Trudel, "the law contributes to resolving or attenuating the contradictions that necessarily exist between the interests, claims and rights of subjects." Com-

This chapter will appear in the *Journal of International Communication*, Shalini Venturelli, ed.

munication law is thus the point of encounter between various branches of law and various fundamental rights. It is at one and the same time the site of affirmation and realization of the most basic human rights, as well as the site of arbitration and constraining of various claims. "Which is why it is necessary to put in place institutions for mediation and frank discussion of the relative weight to be attached to different values."[2]

Establishing the spaces in which such mediation and discussion can take place is the domain of communication policy. Policy sits one step removed from law. Through policy, the state and its agencies create mechanisms and take steps for ensuring that the real intentions of legal texts can be met. Policy is, in fact, the expression of the intent of the state. But policy is both more vague and more complex than law. For example, society will still create norms in areas where the law is silent; but the absence of an explicit state policy on a particular question is in fact a policy—the policy not to intervene explicitly in that area, or to do so on a strictly ad hoc basis.[3]

Until quite recently, communication policy was made and executed for the most part by national governments. Countries borrowed and adapted organizational models for structuring and regulating media from one another, but national communication systems by and large reflected the societies within whose national boundaries they operated. Issues requiring international agreement, such as the allocation of radio frequencies, were resolved between governments, with the implicit assumption that those governments were then free to use those resources as they wished.

That general framework has now changed. Communication policy is now made in a global environment where, for the time being, there is no institution equivalent to the national state. National governments have lost important parts of the sovereignty they once enjoyed in communication, and at the global level, accountability is loose, where it exists at all. National communication systems still exist, but they resemble one another more than they ever did, and their evolution is increasingly determined by developments beyond the control of any one government.

This has enormous implications for the question of human rights in general and the right to communicate in particular. The extension and promotion of human rights in general is tied to the proliferation of free, pluralist, democratically organized, and democratically inclined mass media,[4] and the right to communicate depends on access to these media, as well as to the new information and communication technologies that are changing what we mean by "media." In order for these rights to be realized, policy mechanisms will have to be put in place to check the development of the global communication system.

Technologies of communication will play an increasingly important part in every aspect of people's lives in the so-called age of globalization.[5] Whatever we may think of catchphrases like "the information society," something new is going on here.[6] The disintegration of the nation-based policy framework for guiding and orienting the interaction of media and society over the past seventy-five years is at the core of that. If history is a guiding light, we should expect the age of globalization to engender its own structures of governance—among these, institutional and regulatory mechanisms for dealing with technologies of communication.

So what will this new policy framework look like? We should recall that the accumulated benefits of the nation-state-based world system were not the result of anyone's benevolence but of often bitter social struggles, class negotiation, and at certain moments, enlightened political and economic leadership. Communication played a role in this process. From the early beginnings of parliamentary institutions, communication rights were framed as basic social and political rights.[7] Media were used by social actors as sources of empowerment as well as for mobilization and persuasion. Typical of the modern state was the creation of institutions such as public service broadcasting, public telephone and telegraph monopolies (PTTs), and regulatory agencies. Today, the emergence of a global media regime is at once symptomatic of a new type of society in emergence, and a challenge to shaping that society toward a new phase of social progress.

In the era of the nation-state, media were seen as institutions of social cohesion at the national level. One of the characteristics of globalization is the questions it raises about conventional forms of social cohesion, "national" solidarity, and shared values. In fact—as we see with the proliferation of global media—globalization basically transposes to another level the characteristics of societies whose boundaries (and media systems) were once upon a time contiguous with those of the nation-state.

It was only with the invention of the printing press that the nation-state became possible, enabling the consolidation of power and authority within the reach of the official state "gazettes." But the printing press also enabled the proliferation of struggles for freedom of expression, public debate, and democratic institutions. Different types of national states gave rise to different models of mass media.[8] But the separation of state and press was fundamental to the development of the democratic nation-state.

A fundamental shift occurred with the introduction of broadcasting. In the decade following World War I, an activist, interventionist state integrated the sphere of broadcasting to its realm of activity. The discourses of legitimation for the regulation of broadcasting ranged from the scarcity of frequencies to the idea that broadcasting was a cultural and educational resource too important to be left to the marketplace. In the name of social values and the public interest, institutional structures were set up in the 1920s in most countries of northern and western Europe as well as in many of their colonial dependencies such as Canada and Australia. Nationally based public broadcasting, for example, continues to serve as an inspirational model for democratically inclined communication in many parts of the world.[9]

Now we are on the verge of a new shift. National states are seeking to redefine their raison d'être. It is clearly too early to write them off entirely, but they will no longer exercise the kind and degree of sovereignty they knew for the past 300 years or so. What is taking their place? On the one hand, conventional mass media activity as well as trade and commerce is centered in vastly more autonomous transnational business enterprises tied into the world capitalist system; on the other hand, new and intricate communication networks have begun operating across boundaries in manners as yet uncontrolled and, some say, uncontrollable.

In response, new structures of governance are beginning to emerge to complement the nation-state, at the global, regional, international, subnational, and local levels. As these structures consolidate, they will inevitably give rise to new mechanisms for media regulation. The nature of these is in no way predetermined. The media structures of the year 2000 and beyond will emerge from the convergence of a range of social struggles, entrepreneurial strategies, geopolitical developments, and diplomatic negotiations. They will also be tied to prevailing communication technologies and, most important, to the uses to which those technologies will be put.

One can argue about how much space there is to maneuver with respect to this historical process, and about where that space is. But the key starting point to such a necessary argument is to recognize that we are indeed engaged in a historical process, and like all historical processes it will be marked by both continuity and change with respect to what came before. If we are concerned with the evolution of the relationship between communication and human rights in this context, we have to ask ourselves what forms of media regulation might be appropriate to integrating communication into the overall project of a just and equitable global society.

Toward a Global Public Space

Where can we begin to discuss questions such as how to transpose the media policy issues which have occupied national agendas since the invention of the telegraph to the transnational level—where, to all intents and purposes, the most important issues are henceforth being played out?[10]

The global media system is developing according to its own logic, requirements, protocols, and rules. National governments and groups of states are trying to influence the activities of this transnational system in their own countries or regions as best they can. But global issues require global approaches, and global problems call for global solutions. Where can we begin looking for these?

The various dimensions of globalization and the problems it raises are being increasingly well-documented in the work of distinguished scholars in political economy, sociology, anthropology, and international communication.[11] Meanwhile, activists—and I include a handful of academics in that category—are developing new normative perspectives, new programs and proposals, and building and mobilizing new networks of support and promotion of a *global public space* whose outline we are just beginning to make out.

The emergence of a global communication policy environment and the extension of national debates on communication policy to the global level have both limitations and possibilities. Debates on communication policy issues in local (that is, national) contexts are not only constrained but also enhanced by global policy developments. Globalization, I would like to suggest, should be viewed as a policy challenge rather than a justification for "the end of policy" arguments presented in neoliberal, deregulationist discourses—or even the apocalyptic views that often predominate with some obvious justification in progressive circles. In fact, I would go so far as to argue that the struggle to create socially driven communication systems on a global scale is no more nor less than the contemporary version of the nationally based struggles that surrounded the introduction of press, radio, television, and other earlier communication technologies.[12]

All around us there is ample evidence that people have not given up the struggle to appropriate the means of communication in their efforts to influence the course of their own histories.[13] Until we are prepared to write off the value of democratic politics altogether, we have to create and occupy the spaces in which to strengthen the democratic capabilities of communication systems. What is new today is the extent to which this has to be done by finding ways to give expression to local concerns at the global level.

To begin developing a global framework for democratic media, we need to begin thinking about global public policy mechanisms, legislative, regulatory, and supervisory structures for media. We need to establish the parameters of a truly global media framework that supersedes increasingly phony "national" interests while protecting cultural diversity at its own level of expression—be it territorial, linguistic, ethnocultural, or gender based. This framework must empower an emerging global civil society that will otherwise remain disenfranchised at the hands of corporate interests.

I am talking about a framework for democratically developing global media policy and eventually launching and sustaining public interest media on a global scale.[14] This is a *political* project, which will only be accomplished by combining political action at a variety of levels ranging from grassroots organizing and publishing manifestos to international diplomacy. The first step is to force a general debate on the need to create global mechanisms for ensuring the public interest in media; the next will be to create a permanent, democratic forum for developing global media policy.

This is not an easy question to address. In the political arena, various authors, think tanks, and international organizations have begun to look at the need for conceptualizing notions such as global citizenship and developing new modes of governance appropriate to the twenty-first century.[15] But there are no precedents, there is no tradition for dealing with media policy outside the established political frameworks of national states. Many countries do not even have well-anchored national traditions, and where these exist, they are facing serious challenges to their legitimacy. And as there is no appropriate global public forum in which to talk about such questions, the question of global media regulation has yet to be seriously addressed.[16]

Transnational free-enterprise media will need to be countered with global public service media. The structural basis of such institutions is not immediately evident, given that these have traditionally operated exclusively at the national level. Hence, it is all the more important that such questions be discussed in democratic, multilateral forums. The role of existing world bodies such as UNESCO and the International Tele-communication Union (ITU) is crucial to this action, but these will have to be opened up to include participation by a broader range of actors than the present assortment of member states. New structures will need to be developed in order for media to fulfil their potential as the central institutions of an emerging global public sphere.[17]

Credibility will need to be given to the idea that the global media environment, from the conventional airwaves to outer space, is a public resource, to be organized, managed, and regulated in the global public interest. This implies recognition of the legitimacy of public intervention on a global scale. Broadening access will require appropriate transnational regulatory mechanisms, as well as mechanisms for a more equitable distribution of global commercial benefits. There is a need for the international appropriation of some air and space for the distribution outside the country of origin of viable creative products that currently have no access to the new global agora that figures so prominently in utopian discourses on the new information technologies.

The convergence of communication technologies requires a parallel convergence in programs and policies. This is going to require the invention of new models, new concepts, and a general new way of thinking about communication. For example, the notion of "access" has traditionally meant different things in broadcasting and in telecommunications.[18] In the broadcasting model, emphasis is placed on the active receiver, on free choice, and access refers to the entire range of products on offer. In the telecommunications model, emphasis is on the sender, on the capacity to get one's messages out, and access refers to the means of communication. In the new media environment, public policy will need to promote a new hybrid model of communication, which combines the social and cultural objectives of both broadcasting and telecommunications, and provides new mechanisms—drawn from both traditional models—aimed at maximizing equitable access to services and the means of communication for *both* senders and receivers.[19]

The central issue is still who will get to use the full range of local, national, and global media to receive and disseminate messages, and on what basis. Resolution of this issue will depend on a different kind of access: to the processes and points of decisionmaking that will determine the framework in which media are going to develop, that is to say, access to the policy framework of the new global media system.

But meanwhile, the interests promoting the global media system are not standing by idly waiting for this to happen. They are in the front lines, developing their project, mobilizing support, lobbying decisionmakers.

The Globalization of the Context of Communication Policy

The global arena for communication policy was launched in Paris, in 1865, with the first international (interstate) conference on telegraphy. For the next 130 years, international relations in communication were largely focused on managing the environment in which communication resources would be used at the national level, according to the goals and capacities of individual nation-states. From the harmonization of technical standards to the development of a common rate-accounting system, to the allocation of radio frequencies and later geostationary satellite positions, the underlying assumption was that communication was a national affair requiring a minimum of international coordination.[20]

This multilateral framework remained basically unchanged until 1995, when it was radically transformed with the launching of the U.S.-initiated proposal to establish a Global Information Infrastructure (GII), presented by its promoters as a transnational, seamless communication system that would revolutionize human relations and national economies.[21] What was new about the GII was that it proposed a single vision, program, and policy framework for the role of communication technology as a means for achieving an idealized global society. First presented, as an idea, at a meeting of the ITU in Buenos Aires in 1994, the GII became a concrete project in February 1995, with the adoption by the G7 group of countries of an eight-point plan for implementing it.

The GII project emanated from the Clinton administration's 1993 *Agenda for Action*, launching an initiative to build a new national information infrastructure (NII) which it defined as "the aggregate of the nation's networks, computers, software, information resources, developers and producers."[22] The NII has been the object of vigorous debate in the United States, over the contradictions between the development of its public interest and commercial vocations.[23] But trampolined to the global level, it becomes an apparently unproblematic plan for establishing an information- and communication-based utopia.

As outlined before the ITU by U.S. Vice President Al Gore in 1994, the GII project traverses a continuum connecting public purpose and private enterprise by mobilizing such concepts as free trade, industrial development, modernization, and technological progress. After Buenos Aires, U.S. strategy called for bringing its partners in the alliance of advanced capitalist countries aboard under U.S. leadership. In a document prepared as background to the G7 meeting in Brussels, the United States outlined the necessity for international coordination of regulatory policies on competition, interconnectivity, global applications, and content.[24]

The U.S.-stated objectives for Brussels included seeking support for the five basic principles announced in the GII plan—private investment, competition, flexible regulation, open access, and universal service—and identifying "policy actions" likely to advance these principles. But the key objective was to integrate the private sector to the process:

> Consideration of the broad range of policy and technical issues associated with the worldwide integration of information infrastructure at the Ministerial level will help shape the "vision" of the GII, and can constructively create common ground for the further development of the GII. We further believe that, however designed, *input from the private sector will be critical to the success of the conference.*[25]

The role of the private sector would be definitively consecrated in Brussels. In addition, a more complex political dynamic set in, reflecting the range of important specific interests of different G7 members. The need to achieve favorable positioning for their own national representatives at the table of international capital, as well as to reflect key aspects of national policy (and thus speak to domestic public opinion), required negotiation of an acceptable *modus vivendi*. The U.S. version of the GII's original five points was thus expanded with the addition of references to equal access, content diversity, and international cooperation.[26] The new eight-point GII indicated a greater attentiveness to potentially explosive issues such as perceived threats to cultural and linguistic diversity, social justice, and the gap between richer and poorer nations.

The irony of a "global" project originating from a private meeting of the world's most powerful nations has been lost on most mainstream observers. In terms of the changing world system of governance, the Brussels meeting represented a major shift: for the first time under the auspices of the G7, corporate enterprises met around their own separate table, with official status.[27] Groups representing civil society, meanwhile, were relegated to the margins of unofficial intervention—more reminiscent of the masses gathered outside the city gates in medieval Europe, than of the social partners that could be imagined by a naive reading of the GII project.

The GII project has since been further developed in other venues, such as the 1997 World Trade Organization agreement on "market access for basic telecommunications services" signed by all members of the OECD along with some 40 "developing" or "transitional" (that is, east-central European) countries.[28] Under this accord—again, the result of a U.S. initiative[29]—"participants agreed to set aside national differences in how basic telecommunications might be defined domestically." Henceforth, telecommunications infrastructure development in 90 percent of the world market will proceed without regard to national regulatory constraints, particularly concerning domestic ownership requirements.

Indeed, in every respect, the GII project is a harbinger of both a certain emerging global regulatory system in communication and a future system of world governance. It is an imperial project, with enormous implications for the future of democracy and human rights, insofar as it is based on political decisionmaking at a level where there is no accountability, the recognized autonomy of private capital, and the formal exclusion of the institutions of civil society. In terms of international relations, it extends the dependency of the technologically challenged parts of the world. As a social project, it locates human development as a potential benefit of economic investment, rather than as the principal goal.[30]

This is the reality behind the rhetoric of the GII. But is it the only possible reality, or is there an alternative way to imagine the organization of the global information society?

The Limits and Possibilities of Multilateralism

Aside from the minimal regulatory framework of the ITU, international issues in communication were rarely the object of consideration in multilateral forums until the emergence of the New World Information and Communication Order (NWICO) debate that enflamed UNESCO in the

1970s. Focusing on the supporting role of communication in maintaining the inequalities built into the world system, the proponents of that debate sought to develop policy and programmatic approaches to communication in a perspective of democratic, equitable social development.[31]

The NWICO debate highlighted both the possibilities and limitations of seeking to resolve global issues in multilateral fora made up of nation-states. Launched by the nonaligned nations in the context of the bipolar politics of the cold war, the debate was quickly hijacked and derailed by the dominant (U.S. and Soviet) geopolitical agendas. The proposals stemming from the 1980 report of UNESCO's International Commission on the Study of Communication Problems, chaired by Sean MacBride,[32] were never seriously considered, and the subsequent withdrawal of the United States and the United Kingdom from the organization had the effect of chilling out further discussion of communication issues in UNESCO for the next fifteen years.

Preoccupied with the fallout from the NWICO events, UNESCO re-directed its priorities to a "new communication strategy" aimed essentially at providing services in the areas of media development and advising the "transitional" democracies of Africa, Asia, and the post-Soviet bloc on setting up new legal and structural frameworks for their media systems.[33] Adopted in 1989, the "new strategy" has provided a useful basis for service to member states, and a series of UNESCO-sponsored conferences on freedom of the press (held successively in Windhoek, Almaty, Santiago de Chile, and Sana'a) have made important contributions to the cause of media liberalization. For reasons that may be politically and diplomatically understandable, UNESCO has been reluctant to embark on another debate on the global problem of mass communication. Yet UNESCO's credibility is in fact tied to its capacity to act as a forum for such debate.

As for the ITU, it recognized the significance of the worldwide gap in telecommunications infrastructure between rich and poor as early as 1984.[34] Eleven years later, a joint ITU/UNESCO study entitled *The Right to Communicate: At What Price?* wondered to what extent societal goals could be reconciled with commercial objectives in this context.[35] This interagency report represented a rare effort to bridge the gap between technical and sociocultural sectors, insofar as UNESCO could be said to constitute a community of "public concern" for telecommunications services furnished by ITU members. The study noted the detrimental effects of economic barriers to access to telecommunication services; the lack of infrastructures in some countries; and the lack of an international universal telecommunication infrastructure. This is often the result of historical circumstances, political requirements, and monopolistic industry structures, the study recognized. The ITU as well, however, is tied to the agendas of intergovernmental politics.

Organizations such as the World Bank, meanwhile, began paying attention to communication infrastructure issues in the 1980s, relating them to what it would eventually label "knowledge for development in the information age."[36] Information and communication technologies are now being foregrounded on the international development agenda, where they had once been seen as peripheral. But as one observer at the 1997 World Bank/Government of Canada Global Knowledge conference in Toronto put it:

> From now on it appears that telecommunication will be presented as having a role as part of the "infrastructure" of development alongside the provision of electricity and transportation access. While this development may prove to be a bonanza for certain strategically located consulting and technology firms it is less evident that it will be of much immediate benefit to the proposed beneficiaries.[37]

Indeed, the thrust of all this activity at the heart of the UN system was essentially in harmony with that of the GII project and the national policies being put in place in the G7 nations and through regional bodies such as the European Union.[38] This activity has as its central policy to shift the emphasis from the state to the private sector for initiative, innovation, and capital investment to develop the new information infrastructures for global commerce, finance, communication, and social services. The problem with such an approach is that private capital expects a financial return on its investments and structures its activities with this in view. No public policy objective can overrule this basic imperative.

The summary report of a high-level colloquium of policy advisers, regulators, and business leaders organized by the ITU in December 1996 captures the core aspects of this new context.[39] The changing role of government in the sphere of communications, and the changing role of regulation in particular, one reads here, "focuses on the rapid transformation of telecommunications markets and regulation toward market-based, competitive environments and an increasing globalization of all markets and services."[40]

The document goes on to describe "a fundamental 'paradigm shift' away from conventional modes of operation, commerce and interaction" in communication, similar to previous shifts that occurred in the past with the introduction of radio, television, and computer technology. The effects of this shift are being felt globally, although "the wave is only just beginning to build."[41]

> At the same time, there is an equally fundamental evolution occurring in attitudes and assumptions concerning the role of regulation and the definition of the public interest in communications. . . . To the extent there is agreement concerning the desired direction of evolution for communications worldwide . . . it is that market forces should ultimately determine the pace and scope of development of communications infrastructure or conduit, to the extent possible, and therefore that regulation should seek to promote market-based outcomes.[42]

This already says it all, but there is more:

> First of all, it is important to approach communications policy and regulatory issues with a presumption that market-based solutions will be preferable to responses imposed by government. Put another way, we should establish a goal of minimal regulation: no more regulatory intervention than is essential to achieve legitimate public objectives (and to ensure the market works well) in a largely market-driven environment.[43]

But there will still be a need for some regulatory intervention, and the participants in this colloquium foresee it moving from the national to the global level as "institutions and policies relating to telecommunications that are determined at the global level (e.g., international trade agreements, spectrum allocation, standards, regional and bilateral treaties) are coming to supersede national policies and regulatory practices, just as global technological and market trends are beyond the control of national regulators."[44]

It is this process that must absolutely be the focus of efforts for democratization, not only at the national but at the global level. There are some interesting starting points to such a process to be found in a handful of documents that have emerged in the past few years on the fringes of transnational policy bodies. Let us briefly consider one of these.

The World Commission on Culture and Development

The World Commission on Culture and Development (WCCD) was created in 1991 by the United Nations and UNESCO to make "proposals for both urgent and long-term action to meet cultural needs in the context of development."[45] Within the framework of the UN system, it is important to note that this commission had "independent" status, on the one hand providing it with great leeway with respect to the political *rapports de force* governing relations between member states at any given point in time while, on the other hand, freeing the sponsoring organizations from any responsibility for its findings or commitment to implement its recommendations.

The WCCD reported to the UNESCO General Assembly in November 1995.[46] The foreword to its report outlined the critical spirit with which the commission approached its task:

A bipolar order had collapsed, but the implosion of one side was hardly an unalloyed victory for the other. In the affluent world the notion of progress without limits had become an illusion. Value systems and ties of solidarity appeared to be breaking down. The gulf between the "haves" and the "have-nots" appeared to be widening, the scourge of social and economic exclusion disturbing the smooth surface of contentment.[47]

Evoking the unequal and asymmetrical process of globalization that has resulted in a "fragmented global culture," it emphasized that the cultural dimension of development in this context must imply "a new global ethics" based on human rights and responsibilities, democracy and the elements of civil society, the protection of minorities, commitment to peaceful conflict-resolution and fair negotiation, and intergenerational equity.

In a broad review of cultural issues ranging from ethics to the environment, the WCCD proposed an international agenda for developing global policy with respect to cultural development. Several chapters and proposals relating to mass media and new global issues in mass communication were framed by the following question: "How can the world's growing media capacities be channeled so as to support cultural diversity and democratic discourse?"

The WCCD recognized that while many countries were dealing individually with various important aspects of this question, the time had come for a transfer of emphasis from the national to the international level. "There is room for an international framework that complements national regulatory frameworks."[48] While many countries still need to be incited to put in place or modernize existing national frameworks, the justification for the proposed transfer of attention was to be found in a word: globalization.

> Concentration of media ownership and production is becoming even more striking internationally than it is nationally, making the global media ever more market-driven. In this context, can the kind of pluralist "mixed economy" media system which is emerging in many countries be encouraged globally? Can we envisage a world public sphere in which there is room for alternative voices? Can the media professionals sit down together with policy-makers and consumers to work out mechanisms that promote access and a diversity of expression despite the acutely competitive environment that drives the media moguls apart?[49]

The WCCD admitted that it did not have ready answers to these questions, but that answers had to be sought through international dialogue:

> Many specialists have told the Commission how important it would be to arrive at an international balance between public and private interests. They envision a common ground of public interest on a transnational scale. They suggest that different national approaches can be aligned, that broadly acceptable guidelines could be elaborated with the active participation of the principal actors, that new international rules are not a pipe-dream but could emerge through the forging of transnational alliances across the public and private media space.[50]

The WCCD's international agenda contained a series of specific proposals aimed at "enhancing access, diversity and competition of the international media system," based on the assertion that the airwaves and space are "part of the global commons, a collective asset that belongs to all humankind. This international asset at present is used free of charge by those who possess resources and technology. Eventually, 'property rights' may have to be assigned to the global commons, and access to airwaves and space regulated in the public interest."[51]

Just as national community and public media services require public subsidy,

> internationally, the redistribution of benefits from the growing global commercial media activity could help subsidize the rest. As a first step, and within a market context, the Commission suggests that the time may have come for commercial regional or international satellite radio and television interests which now use the global commons free of charge to contribute to the financing of a more plural media system. New revenue could be invested in alternative programming for international distribution.[52]

Competition policies, as exist in many countries, need to be enacted in the international sphere to ensure fair practices. International public broadcasting services need to be established "to help assure a truly plural media space." In general, this calls for a new and concerted international effort, "an active policy to promote competition, access and diversity of expression amongst the media globally, analogous to policies that exist at the national level."[53]

Published only months after the G7 launching of the GII initiative, the WCCD report ventured gingerly onto the terrain of the new communication technologies. A passage regarding access to the information highway did not make it into the final version of the report,[54] which generally endorsed the liberal thrust of the GII project, although an important concern that it be opened up beyond the leadership of industry was voiced: "The Commission also recognizes that, in the context of an open market economy, the development of the new information infrastructure must be ensured through innovative partnerships between international agencies, governments, industry and civil society."[55]

Concretely, the WCCD went no further than to call for two feasibility studies to be conducted under the auspices of the UN system: one to determine the possibility of establishing international alternative broadcasting services, including funding requirements; and a second to investigate "how best to favour a competitive and equitable media environment internationally."[56] These studies would enable exploration of appropriate global mechanisms analogous to national models of public service broadcasting and independent regulatory authorities.

Finally, the WCCD proposed that a Global Summit on Culture and Development be convened to discuss the full gamut of issues raised by its report.

One of the most crucial aspects of this question that needs to be addressed is how to avoid such a discussion becoming yet another debate among states, each representing its own national interest and those of its partners in the private sector, rather than among a global public dealing with global issues, across national borders and in quest of a global public interest.

The Report of the World Commission on Culture and Development, in its tone and its substance, opens the door to this. But its fate is typical of the scope of the problem. Nearly two years after its tabling, the report has attracted almost no attention outside the immediate circle of UN/ UNESCO diplomacy. A handful of national commissions for UNESCO have made timid overtures to publicizing some of its less controversial aspects (steering shy of the media chapter, most notably), and UNESCO itself has been clear to point out the report's "independent," nonbinding nature. Even specialists closely attuned to the various fields covered by the report have been barely touched by it. This in itself constitutes an interesting question for communication scholars with an interest in the formal right to communicate. But there may be something more profound at work here.

In considering the cool reception that has greeted the WCCD report, there is no overlooking the obvious subtext of the deep-rooted politics of the UN system and particularly UNESCO with respect to media. The obvious question that comes to mind is to what extent is this a sequel to the MacBride report of 1980, and is the UN system prepared to entertain a debate of the type that accompanied the preparation and publication of that report. The corollary question is, can such a debate responsibly be avoided?[57]

Resistances or New Beginnings?

The preceding example was presented at some length to illustrate that there already exists an important knowledge base for beginning to elaborate a socially progressive global regulatory framework for mass media, information, and communication technologies. Before such a framework is likely to take shape, however, it will have to find a transnational political constituency.

This constituency will have to be put together piece by piece and it will overlap conventional levels of political activity. The new supranational decisionmaking bodies such as the European Union provide an important intermediary phase between the national and the global. Not surprisingly, information and communication policy is a major sphere of activity for such bodies.

In the European case, an important alternative perspective has been provided recently by the EU's High Level Experts Group (HLEG), set up in 1995 to examine the social aspects of the Information Society. The group's final report was tabled in April 1997 and officially released by Brussels only several months later. This was in remarkable contrast to the highly mediatized appearance of the so-called Bangemann Report of 1994,[58] which immediately became the cornerstone of EU information and communication policy by "urg[ing] the European Union to put its faith in market mechanisms as the motive power to carry us into the Information Age."[59]

In contrast, the HLEG report proposes to refocus debate on communication regulatory issues and social aspects of uses for new information and communication technologies in order to build "a strong ethos of solidarity" in the European Information Society.[60] For example, its ten-point policy agenda emphasizes the key role of the public sector. Rather than the "minimalist" role for public services foreseen by Bangemann, the HLEG sees them as an engine of growth as well as providing access and democratic control. Public administration should take the lead in developing the information society, initiating where appropriate public-private partnerships in key areas like education, health, culture, and media. Public services should be concerned not only with infrastructure but with providing content as well. They should be local, information led, and employment intensive, while private services would be market driven: "The public service sector should be a model of service provision to the public: particularly in combining the utilization of access at a distance through communication technologies with the possibility of human contact for those citizens who desire."[61]

In order to implement such a program, the HLEG sees a need for some transfer of regulatory power to the EU level, where regulation would be coordinated by a European FCC-type regulatory agency: "Today, increasingly, regulation policy must fully reflect the new international agenda formed by the emerging global information infrastructure."[62] A transparent, borderless, global information society can have significant benefits to the world as a whole provided it is socially integrated, says this report: "Just as global transparency is likely to benefit economic welfare in terms of a better international allocation of resources and cheaper prices, it might also increase social welfare bringing about an improvement in social and labour conditions."[63]

This idea of a global welfare state is tied to the notion of a new tax base for financing the social security system in the global information society: the "bit tax," based on intensity of electronic transmission and applied to all interactive digital services. "There is a need to adapt taxation to the changing economic structure of the information society and the increasing importance of information transmission."[64] Clearly, only an international approach, founded on a global enforcement mechanism, could make such a venture possible.[65]

It remains to be seen what sort of response this official report will generate from Brussels. Proposals with a similar social thrust are to be found emanating from the margins of various national information infrastructure policy debates. But the conditions for determining a global policy that would enhance the role of communication in human rights are likely to come only from the efforts of the new global networks of alternative communication.

The 1990s have witnessed an unprecedented growth of projects, groups, and associations of all sorts working in areas that can be clustered under the general heading of democratic communication. Working with shoestring resources, practitioners of conventional alternative media have established important worldwide organisations such as AMARC (community radio) and Vidéazimut (alternative video). The spread of computer-based communication and the Internet has engendered countless information links and "listservs," as well as organizations such as the Association for Progressive Communications. Researchers associated with the NWICO debate have kept the issues it raised alive through the annual meetings of the MacBride Round Table on Communication and a plethora of conferences, books, and journals. In 1996, 300 activists in the U.S. "belly of the beast" launched the Cultural Environment Movement (CEM), which has become an important watchdog and critical policy lobbying organization. AMARC, CEM, and the Malaysia-based

Third World Network are promoting a "people's communication charter" (drafted by Cees Hamelink of the Centre for Communication and Human Rights, in the Netherlands).

In November 1996, these and a number of other like-minded organizations met under the auspices of the World Association for Christian Communication in London, England, to draft a "Platform for Cooperation on Communication and Democratisation." The London Platform, as it has come to be known, is aiming to organize a worldwide "Right to Communicate" event to coincide with the fiftieth anniversary of the UN Declaration of Human Rights in 1998.[66]

On the contribution of communication to the democratisation of society, the London Platform aims for "the right to communicate to be recognised and guaranteed as fundamental to securing human rights founded on principles of genuine participation, social justice, plurality and diversity, and which reflect gender, cultural and regional perspectives."[67]

On the democratization of communication structures, institutions, and processes, it promotes "the need to defend and deepen an open public space for debate and action that build critical understanding of the ethics of communication, democratic policy development, and equitable and effective access."[68]

To what extent can initiatives such as these be said to constitute the embryonic beginnings of a global civil society based on socially oriented uses of information and communication technologies?[69] For the purposes of closing this paper, let us say that the answer will be crucial in determining whether the type of global policy framework we have put forward will ever be established.

Numerous scholars and analysts have convincingly argued that the conventional frameworks for regulating media and communication in order to achieve nonmarket objectives *ought to* be translated into some sort of international mechanisms.[70] I would suggest that this is going to happen only once widespread popular mobilization is translated into political will. Only then will communication play a meaningful role in human rights; only then will the right to communicate be realized.

Notes

1. Richard Falk, "The Making of Global Citizenship," in Bart van Steenbergen, ed., *The Condition of Citizenship* (London: Sage, 1994), pp. 127–40, esp. p. 128.

2. Pierre Trudel, "Le rôle du droit dans les politiques de communication," in Pierre Trudel, ed., *Les politiques de communication et leur mise en oeuvre: Tendances et états de questions* (Montreal: Consortium CRDP/IDDM, 1996), pp. 9–25, esp. p. 9. My translation.

3. It is interesting to consider, for example, the debates on so-called deregulation through this prism. The decision to "deregulate" in a given area is no less a policy decision than the decision to regulate. It simply represents a shift in the relative weight to be placed on the state, the market, and civil society.

4. Peter A. Bruck and Marc Raboy, "The Challenge of Democratic Communication," in Marc Raboy and Peter A. Bruck, eds., *Communication for and against Democracy* (Montreal: Black Rose Books, 1989), pp. 3–16.

5. By globalization, I mean a general context characterized by the diminishing role of national states, the transnational concentration of corporate economic power, the technologically based reduction of constraints of time and space, the questioning of received ideas about national and cultural identity, the emergence of new, locally based, global networks, and the progressive establishment of a new legal and political framework for world governance.

6. Manuel Castells, *The Rise of the Network Society* (Malden/Oxford: Blackwell Publishers, 1996).

7. John Keane, *The Media and Democracy* (London: Polity Press, 1991).

8. John C. Nerone, ed., *Last Rights: Revisiting Four Theories of the Press* (University of Illinois Press, 1995).

9. See Marc Raboy, ed., *Public Broadcasting for the Twenty-first Century* (Luton (UK): John Libbey Media/University of Luton Press, 1996); and *The Media in a Democratic Society*, draft resolutions and draft political declaration, 4th European Ministerial Conference on Mass Media Policy, Prague, 1994, Strasbourg, Council of Europe, MCM-CDMM (94) 3 prov 1.

10. William H. Melody, ed., *Telecom Reform: Principles, Policies and Regulatory Practices* (Lyngby: Technical University of Denmark, 1997).

11. See, for example, Arjun Appadurai, "Disjuncture and Difference in the Global Cultural Economy," in Mike Featherstone, ed., *Global Culture: Nationalism, Globalization and Modernity* (London: Sage, 1993), pp. 295–310; Roland Robertson, *Globalization: Social Theory and Global Culture* (London: Sage, 1992); Immanuel Wallerstein, *Geopolitics and Geoculture: Essays on the Changing World-System* (Cambridge: Cambridge University Press, 1991); and Hamid Mowlana, *Global Communication in Transition: The End of Diversity?* (Sage, 1996).

12. See Robert W. McChesney, "The Internet and U.S. Communication Policy-Making in Historical and Critical Perspective," *Journal of Communication*, vol. 46, no. 1 (1996), pp. 98–124.

13. See Alain His, ed., *Communication and Multimedia for People. Moving into Social Empowerment over the Information Highway* (Paris: Transversales Science Culture, 1996).

14. See Marc Raboy, "Towards a Global Framework for Democratic Media," *CLIPS*, no. 10, 1996.

15. The range of literature emerging around this subject is truly vast. See, for example, The Group of Lisbon, *Limits to Competition* (Lisbon: Gulbenkian

Foundation, 1993); Bart van Steenbergen, ed., *The Condition of Citizenship* (London: Sage, 1994); Richard Falk, *On Human Governance: Toward a New Global Politics* (Oxford: Polity Press, 1995); Daniele Archibugi and David Held, *Cosmopolitan Democracy: An Agenda for a New World Order* (Cambridge: Polity Press, 1995); and Commission on Global Governance, *Our Global Neighbourhood* (Oxford: Oxford University Press, 1995).

16. An important academic exception is to be found in the work of Monroe E. Price. See "The Market for Loyalties: Agenda-Setting for a Global Communications Commission," *InterMedia*, vol. 22, no. 5 (1994), pp. 14–21, and its more extensive earlier version, "The Market for Loyalties: Electronic Media and the Global Competition for Allegiances," *Yale Law Journal*, vol. 104 (1994), pp. 667–705.

17. See John Keane, "Structural Transformations of the Public Sphere," *Communication Review*, vol.1, no. 1 (1995), pp. 1–22.

18. See Marc Raboy, "Access to Policy, Policies of Access," *Javnost/The Public*, vol. 2 (1995), pp. 51–61.

19. See Susan G. Hadden and Edward Lenert, "Telecommunications Networks Are Not VCRs: The Public Nature of New Information Technologies for Universal Service," *Media, Culture and Society*, vol. 17, no. 1 (1995), pp. 121–40.

20. See Armand Mattelart, *La mondialisation de la communication* (Paris: Presses universitaires de France, 1996); and Cees J. Hamelink, *The Politics of World Communication* (London: Sage, 1994). The world's first permanent intergovernmental organization, precursor to the ITU, was set up in 1865 to provide a framework for development of international telegraph and telegram services. Provision was made for private sector participation at the organization's second conference in Vienna in 1868, and nongovernment, corporate members were first admitted as early as 1871. Today's ITU is composed of 184 government and 375 private members. According to its director-general, Pekka Tarjanne, the role of the private sector in the ITU is perhaps the single most important strategic issue it has to face. Pekka Tarjanne, "The Limits of National Sovereignty: Issues for the Governance of International Telecommunications," in Melody, *Telecom Reform*, pp. 41–50.

21. U.S. Government, "The Global Information Infrastructure: Agenda for Cooperation," Washington, 1994.

22. Cited in Brian Kahin, "The Internet and the National Information Infrastructure," in Brian Kahin and James Keller, eds., *Public Access to the Internet* (MIT Press, 1995), pp. 3–23, esp. p. 3. Kahin points out that the U.S. Interstate Highway System, regularly invoked in U.S. public policy discourse as the model for the metaphor of the information superhighway, was in fact constructed entirely with public funds, unlike the new high-speed information networks that will, according to NII design, be left to the private sector to develop (p. 19, note 2).

23. Lewis M. Branscomb, "Balancing the Commercial and Public-Interest Visions of the NII," in Brian Kahin and James Keller, eds., *Public Access to the Internet* (MIT Press, 1995), pp. 24–33.

24. U.S. Government, "U.S. Goals and Objectives for the G7 GII Conference" (Washington: National Telecommunications Infrastructure Agency and Information Administration, 1994).

25. Ibid. Emphasis added.

26. G7, "A Shared Vision of Human Enrichment," chair's conclusions to the G7 Ministerial Conference on the Information Society, Brussels, February 1995.

27. The main transnational companies involved in information and communication technologies (ICT) development formally set up a Global Information Infrastructure Commission (GIIC) to continue pursuing their common interest in this area. Among the companies involved in the GIIC are Mitsubishi, Motorola, Viacom, Time-Warner, Olivetti, Sprint, AT&T, Nokia, Oracle, NEC, Alcatel Alsthom, Teleglobe Canada, and Nippon Telegraph and Telephone (Michel Venne, "Le secteur privé s'interroge: Où mènent les inforoutes," *Le Devoir* [Montreal], February 12, 1995).

28. WTO, "The WTO Negotiations on Basic Telecommunications," news release, Geneva, March 6, 1997.

29. See U.S. Government, "Irving Outlines Benefits of Open Telecom Markets to WTO Negotiators from Developing Countries," National Telecommunications and Information Administration Update, March 15, 1996.

30. See Marc Raboy, "La 'Global Information Infrastructure' (GII): Un projet impérial pour l'ère de la mondialisation," *Communications et stratégies*, no. 25 (1997) pp. 15–32.

31. See Johan Galtung and Richard C. Vincent, *Global Glasnost: Toward a New World Information and Communication Order?* (Cresskill: Hampton Press, 1993); and George Gerbner, Hamid Mowlana, and Kaarle Nordenstreng, *The Global Media Debate* (Norwood N.J.: Ablex, 1993).

32. UNESCO, International Commission for the Study of Communication Problems, chaired by Sean MacBride, *Many Voices, One World* (London: Kogan Page, 1980).

33. UNESCO, "New Communication Strategy," adopted by the general conference at its twenty-fifth session, Paris, 1989. See also UNESCO, *Textes fondamentaux sur la communication—1989–1995* (Paris, 1996).

34. ITU, Independent Commission for Worldwide Telecommunications Development, chaired by Donald Maitland, *The Missing Link* (Geneva, 1984).

35. ITU/UNESCO, *The Right to Communicate: At What Price? Economic Constraints to the Effective Use of Telecommunications in Education, Science, Culture and in the Circulation of Information* (Paris, 1995).

36. See Eduardo Talero, "National Information Infrastructure in Developing Economies," in Brian Kahin and Ernest J. Wilson III, eds., *National Information Infrastructure Initiatives: Vision and Policy Design* (MIT Press, 1997), pp. 287–306.

37. Michael Gurstein, "Global Knowledge for Development '97," University College of Cape Breton, Nova Scotia, Canada. Web posting (mgurst@ccen.uccb.ns.ca), June 1997.

38. One revealing indication of this concordance is to be seen in the cooptation of the "new world order" terminology in the GII literature. For example,

see U.S. Information Agency, *Toward a Global Information Infrastructure: The Promise of a New World Information Order*, USIA pamphlet series (Washington, 1995).

39. ITU, *Regulatory Implications of Telecommunications Convergence: The Changing Role of Government in an Era of Telecom Deregulation* (Geneva, December 1996).

40. Ibid., p. 6.

41. Ibid., p. 8.

42. Ibid., pp. 8, 11.

43. Ibid., p. 11.

44. Ibid., p. 21.

45. This undertaking was part of the UN/UNESCO Decade of Cultural Development, an operation launched in 1988 with the central claim that processes of "development" could not be isolated from their cultural dimension.

46. UN/UNESCO, *Our Creative Diversity*, report of the World Commission on Culture and Development, chaired by Javier Perez de Cuellar (Paris: World Commission on Culture and Development, 1995).

47. Ibid., p. 9.

48. Ibid., p. 117.

49. Ibid., p. 117.

50. Ibid., p. 117.

51. Ibid., p. 278.

52. Ibid., p. 278.

53. Ibid., p. 279.

54. See UN/UNESCO, "Report of the World Commission on Culture and Development," fifth draft, August 30, 1995. Manuscript.

55. UN/UNESCO, *Our Creative Diversity*, p. 280.

56. Ibid., p. 279. Here, the following from the original was dropped: "The question of a coordinated international approach in favour of competition, global equity and fair access would be the focus of the second study. The need for an international and independent regulatory agency should be examined." (UN/UNESCO, "Report of the World Commission on Culture and Development," fifth draft, August 30, 1995)

57. UNESCO has issued a sign of recognition of the importance of this question by organizing the Intergovernmental Conference on Cultural Policies for Development, 1998, Stockholm, on the basis of the WCCD report.

58. European Commission, *Europe and the Global Information Society* (Bangemann Report), *Recommendations to the European Council* (Brussels, May 1994).

59. Ibid., p. 3.

60. European Commission, High Level Group of Experts, chaired by Luc Soete, *Building the European Information Society for Us All*, final policy report (Luxembourg: Office for Official Publications of the European Communities, 1997).

61. Ibid., p. 18.

62. Ibid., p. 15.

63. Ibid., p. 41.

64. Ibid., p. 42.

65. The idea of such a tax is developed in Arthur J. Cordell and T. Ran Ide, *The New Wealth of Nations: Taxing Cyberspace* (Toronto: Between the Lines, 1997). The premise of this Canadian proposal is that the emergence of an information society requires renewal of the tax system that evolved as the fiscal basis for public finance in the age of industrial society. For the purposes of this paper, it can be seen as the basis for a more equitable distribution of wealth and resources at the transnational, or global, level.

66. See "Media Alternatives Forum Launches New Network," *Action* (World Association for Christian Communication), no. 193 (November–December 1996), p. 3.

67. Ibid.

68. Ibid.

69. This question is being addressed in a doctoral dissertation currently being undertaken at the University of Montreal by Alain Ambrosi, one of the founders of Vidéazimut and a central figure in the London Platform movement.

70. For example, Price, "The Market for Loyalties"; Melody, *Telecom Reform*. Wolfgang Hoffmann-Riem, *Regulating Media* (Guilford, 1996); and Eli Noam, "Telecommunications Policy Issues for the Next Century," in "Toward a Global Information Infrastructure," U.S. Information Agency pamphlet series, Washington, 1996.

CHAPTER NINE

Promoting Deliberative Public Discourse on the Web

Bruce Murray

NEW ELECTRONIC communication technology is transforming societies all over the globe. The relentless spread of broadcast radio and TV entices people throughout the world to be ever more focused on current events, dramatizations, and celebrities. Instant opinion generation and manipulation is becoming a significant political factor in many countries, including the United States. This shortening of the collective perspective raises concerns for the future of deliberative democracy and for the wise management of our planet.

At the same time, the explosive growth and evolution of the World Wide Web may offer unprecedented opportunities for deliberative discourse on complex public issues, on both the local and the global scale, thus offsetting somewhat the deleterious effects of mass broadcast communications. To explore such potentialities, a novel hyperforum was developed and demonstrated under Markle Foundation sponsorship. The results and implications of that endeavor are presented here for the first time in the print medium. They suggest the web can play a powerful new role in shaping informed opinion and catalyzing the development of consensus on difficult near-term steps to promote more promising long-term outcomes.

The Coevolution of Humans and Communication Technology

Communications technology has progressively extended individual awareness beyond the face-to-face community since at least Gutenburg. Books, newspapers, transistor radios, cassette players, and video have each contributed to major historical change. Some new communication technologies, like magazines in the late nineteenth and early twentieth centuries, were an integrating social force. Others, like broadcast video, have undermined traditional communities rather than helping to develop new functional communities based on shared values and mutual obligations.

New interactive electronic communications during the early decades of the twenty-first century will strongly affect individuals and groups, perhaps as much as broadcast radio and video have shaped the twentieth century. In the 1994–95 Annual Report of the Markle Foundation, Lloyd Morrisett argued that a renaissance may be in the offing because, "Television and computing are coming together in a digital world of high bandwidth and massive computing power. Multipurpose electronic display devices will mingle motion video, sound, data, graphics, and print. The electronic screens of the future will have much greater resolution than television screens and be able to display print that is crisp and clear."[1]

But will these innovations be for the better or for the worse?

For many years I have been trying to envision the range of future possibilities in order to illuminate what collective actions may promote better, rather than worse, outcomes.[2] In 1992 I was named a Markle Fellow, which enabled me to focus on the pivotal role that new interactive electronic communication technologies may play in shaping the next fifty to a hundred years. One early effort was the organization and leadership (with Charles Firestone of the Aspen Institute) of a wide-ranging Aspen conference funded by the Markle Foundation to examine the potential societal implications of the rapid growth of the Internet. The appendix lists the conference participants. The results of the conference are available on-line at www.cco.caltech.edu/rich/aspen.html. Several hundred viewers have used the site's feedback form to send me comments and relevant examples. Because the report has not been published in the print medium and thus remains unavailable to the print-oriented community, I will draw on it freely and without further attribution here, including some verbatim text.

The Hyperforum Concept

The Aspen effort was followed by a Markle-funded project, which I organized and led, to explore the potentialities of the web for promoting

Table 9-1. *Hyperforum Development Team*

Name	Organization	E-Mail address
Bruce Murray (project leader)	California Institute of Technology	bcm@caltech.edu
Stephen Bankes	Rand Corporation	bankes@rand.org
Shawn Ewald	California Institute of Technology	spe@caltech.edu
Allen Hammond	World Resources Institute	allen@wri.org
Robert Lempert	Rand Corporation	lempert@rand.org
Terry West	Rand Corporation	terry@rand.org

deliberative discourse on complex public issues. With some collaborators, I began developing a hyperforum concept in mid-1995 and worked on its preliminary development through mid-1996. This phase was followed by a lengthy succession of tests and demonstrations culminating in a successful demonstration of the hyperforum concept from January through mid-March 1997, using sustainability as the topic. Extensive evaluation and analysis continued through September 1997. My principal collaborators in this endeavor are listed in table 9-1.

The demonstration hyperforum can only be viewed satisfactorily through a web browser because interactive use of the web at this level of hyperlinking and multiple participation becomes a new and intrinsically independent medium of communication. Extensive analyses and generalizations from that hyperforum experiment are also presented on-line in our final report, and these analyses incorporate extensive hyperlinking to diverse pages within the hyperforum, to evaluation databases, and to graphical experiments (www.hf.caltech.edu/HF/F/FinalReport.html, or directly to the hyperforum home page).

It is obviously necessary to convey those experimental results and conclusions to a print-on-paper audience as well, and it is most appropriate to do so in a volume capturing the breadth of Lloyd Morrisett's pioneering of the study of societal implications of new communication technologies. Recognizing that this objective can be accomplished only imperfectly at best in a printed medium, I include ten specially prepared representations of key screens from the demonstration hyperforum. Extensive captions and supporting text are included to try to help the reader envision the social dynamics of using the hyperforum. Brief examination of the site (www.hf.caltech.edu/hf/) will be a great help in understanding this material.

Visualization of Future Possibilities

Visualization can be evoked by good writing, by graphs and diagrams, and by multimedia techniques. The web offers new ways to combine these components for more powerful and broadly available engagement. What is necessary are ensembles of thoughtful, long-range scenarios, rich with detail, to help participants visualize in their own terms aspects of the future postulated by author/designers.

The challenge for new information technology is to make such collections of scenarios available in easy-to-visualize form—first for specialists and then for broader portions of the world's people. The form must be affordable and widely available, easy to learn, convenient for display and communication of images, and amenable to interactive viewing and interrogation, and it must provide interactive communication among viewers.

Collective visualizations of the future must make high-quality, user-friendly information available to individuals whose views stem from a wide variety of intellectual traditions and life experiences. For such visualizations to be successful, they must go beyond discussions among people who share the assumptions and jargon of a common intellectual discipline or political perspective to provide a forum for people of diverse backgrounds to wrestle with the same data and issues.

What Is a Hyperforum?

After several years of conceptualizing, developing, and operating a demonstration hyperforum, my colleagues and I have refined the following definition and attributes:

A *hyperforum is an interactive multimedia environment for collective visualization and discussion of complex public policy issues to aid the development of consensus through:*

—improvement in the quality of debate through ready access to supporting libraries, data, and interactive models

—progressive refinement of differences of opinion and interpretation and discussion guided by facilitators, leading to syntheses of underlying agreement and disagreement

—movement of discussion toward a working consensus on near-term actions needed for long-term benefits.

A *hyperforum fosters deliberative discourse by being:*

—based on written statements and commentary, not a "chat" zone

—decentralized and nonreal time

—rich in information and interpretations, highly cross linked internally

—identified with a sponsoring community of concerned participants

—individually accountable, with no anonymous participation

—led by respected facilitators drawn from the sponsoring community

—aimed at producing consensus actions, not just discussion.

A hyperforum includes:

—signed pages by multiple authors including divergent views and conclusions

—signed commentary by multiple participants, directly linked to authors' material

—visual displays of information, of hyperforum structure, and of the structure of participant interaction

—practical means for: creating and posting commentary linked thematically; for searching databases; for navigating the site

—on-line archives of all commentary and content.

How Does a Hyperforum Differ from Other Net-Based Discussions?

A hyperforum is most appropriate for deliberative discourse where:

—complex and information-rich topics involve opinions and subjective judgments that are important, as well as facts

—the objective is to promote consensus or at least to develop a collective understanding of the basis of differences in individual views

—there is an interested and decentralized community of potential participants united by a common desire to find practical solutions through deliberative discourse

—the community has access to Netscape Navigator or other web browsers and is comfortable with their use

—individuals known to and respected by the community are available to be facilitators (moderators)

—the community will likely respond to an interactive, task-oriented structure rather than passively browsing

—significant amounts of validated databases and authored projections are available or can be commissioned, and resources are available to put them in useful on-line form

—a viewable archive of the content and commentary of the hyper-forum will be of value.

Deliberative Discourse in the Electronic Age

The biggest event of the second half of the twentieth century was the sudden end of the confrontation between the United States and the USSR. World War III did not occur.

New communications technology helped enable this peaceful transition. From battery-powered transistor radios to broadcast TV to fax machines, communications technology has been too vital for rulers to ignore. Despite the best efforts of secret police everywhere, technology proved to be the ultimate source of seditious attitudes and feelings as brainwashed billions learned about a different "outside" world. The Soviet obsession with controlling the printed word was well founded. Indeed, the global breakdown of governance now unfolding flows from the same wine. All governance has rested to some extent on "belief control" and the suppression of opposing beliefs. All systems of governance—even our most enlightened one—must evolve to be stable in the presence of an extraordinary range of information, misinformation, and disinformation.

The abrupt collapse of the Soviet Union was the most dramatic example of the diminishing power of central governments worldwide—but analogous patterns characterize contemporary America, western Europe, China, Africa, Central America, and Japan. The prevailing global trend now is strongly toward dispersion of authority and responsibility downward and outward. Decentralization, as manifested by privatization of traditional government functions, downsizing of large corporations, and growth of small enterprises worldwide, generates an increasing need for more two-way communication,

Dispersed, self-organizing leadership on an unprecedented scale is required in the post–cold war world. There is a necessity to go beyond just interacting to enhancing positive relationships and problem solving. Communities must offer members bonding beyond shared materialistic needs; they must incorporate subjective values. There is a uniquely modern need to reinvent community with each generation, which is the consequence of the unprecedented rate of social and economic change driven by accelerating technological change.

A primary contemporary need, therefore, is to help individuals in all walks of life to collectively envision and deliberate about the range of future possibilities, including the likely outcome of "business-as-usual" as well as more radical approaches. This is necessary to create a greater willingness to accept change and increased responsibility for the future and thus to allocate public and private resources more for future good and less for immediate consumption. The hyperforum concept was invented to some extent specifically in response to my frustration with the inability of current academic and policy institutions (and their inhabitants) to deal with such issues that transcend political and corporate time scales.

Communities, Communication, and Social Cohesiveness

John Gardner has singled out the unifying notion of "community" as the key to viewing social and individual behavior generally.[3] At the most basic level, members of any community are fundamentally bound by shared values and a sense of mutual responsibility.

Face-to-face communities (the family, extended family, school, neighborhood) are where individuals first learn these shared values and mutual obligations. As individuals mature, they identify to varying degrees with larger, dispersed communities—professional and economic, recreational and sports, ethnic and religious, political and geographic, social and "moral." However, for communities to be harmonious externally as well as internally, they must not only provide a sense of belonging and wholeness for their members, but also incorporate and tolerate diversity.

Leaders need to receive feedback from community members; hence the importance of interactive communications. Interactive links are needed to bind communities large and small, nearby and remote, familiar and strange. It is especially important to find ways for new technology to help promote consensus on complex issues encompassing many different communities and points of view. The hyperforum project thus addresses a central contemporary need.

Social Impact of Broadcast Radio and TV

Technological and economic growth since 1961 has created an intense and all-pervasive media immersion for Americans, which hardly anyone can escape. But the information content in this deluge seems proportionally much smaller than when TV first blossomed in the 1960s. Local television programming has been mandated at the expense of network programming. "Narrowcasting" has vastly expanded distribution capacity through cable channels that now far exceeds the economic capacity to supply quality programming. Experienced professional journalists like Walter Cronkite, Eric Sevareid, Chet Huntley, and David Brinkley have been succeeded by "happy talk" announcers pandering to us on nearly every "news" show. The popular docudrama—sometimes also hyped on news shows—further blurs the viewer's distinction between fact and fantasy. The popular TV magazine format fuels the demand for and dignifies celebrity-oriented tabloid journalism in television, as does every flavor of television talk show.

Can new interactive electronic technologies offset this electronic dumbing-down of America? New technologies inevitably pose the Faustian dualism: will they help or harm the body politic? For example, high-tech exploitation of conventional telephone and cable connections to homes can facilitate the instantaneous assessment of opinions. Could such a new capability drive our governing system so overwhelmingly by short-term mass opinions as to render it incapable of sustained actions toward essential long-term needs? A representative democracy, which traditionally incorporated time for leaders and citizens alike to evolve attitudes and to compromise, may not survive in the face of instant polling and publicizing of those instant opinions.

The Markle Foundation accordingly has devoted substantial resources for more than a decade to probing the potentialities of new electronic communications and their possible effect on voting, polling, and equitable access to information. Our hyperforum study seeks to explore the opportunity for enhancing the development of informed opinion on complex issues through innovative use of rapidly growing web capabilities.

Essential Role of Deliberative Discourse in a Democracy

Lloyd Morrisett stated especially clearly the need for deliberative discourse. "Democracy, government by the people, rests on the fundamental idea that people as citizens are able to act rationally in their own interests. The habits of mind that we associate with reason and rational thought include study, analysis, reflection, contemplation, and deliberation. Yet, in our day-to-day life, these habits of mind receive little support or reinforcement. After formal education has ended, most people depend on the media for their information, education, and entertainment."[4] He also quotes Jeffrey Abramson: "Deliberation is a lost virtue in modern democracies; only the jury still regularly calls upon ordinary citizens to engage each other in a face-to-face process of debate. Although the deliberative model of democracy survives in the jury, even there it is in serious decline."[5] Abramson's analysis *preceded* the O.J. Simpson case, which defined a new low in the pernicious interaction between television and the jury system in high-profile cases.

Morrisett continues by noting: "All the habits of mind that are associated with reason seem to be in decline. Sometimes the blame is put on the educational system, and no doubt the critics of education have some merit in their arguments. Often, blame falls upon our political system with media and ad-driven campaigns, and the imperative of winning at all costs. Citizens themselves are blamed for their self-involvement and lack of concern for the polity. While these and other explanations may have some validity, I believe that we must also look to the nature and characteristics of our system of communications to find out what has been happening to us."[6]

After pointing toward mass broadcasting as a significant part of the problem, Morrisett evinces hope in the promise of the rise of interactive discourse over the Net—specifically e-mail: "The widespread use of e-mail will promote deliberative response over immediate response, and active thought over passive reception."[7] I think the subsequent explosive growth of the web and its multimedia capability reinforces his optimism strongly. He argues specifically that "Quite simply, written language—print—is often the best way to convey information. A written document can be skimmed or studied closely, and reading something almost always takes less time than hearing it or seeing the idea enacted in images. Complex or abstract ideas are notoriously difficult to compress within the framework and time of a television program. A thought that might be well expressed on a single printed page and easily read in five minutes might well prove to be difficult or impossible to convey in an hour of conventional television. In the world of multimedia the ability to intermingle images and print opens up many new production possibilities, using each medium when it is most advantageous."[8]

Returning to the basic issue of deliberative discourse, he notes, "Thomas Jefferson was a champion of reason and rationality, but he also lived in a time when the communications system supported the habits of mind associated with reason and rationality. The printing press made books available as well as newspapers and, despite Jefferson's well-known ambivalence about newspapers, he was a strong exponent of a free press. Aside from printed matter, communications took place in face-to-face conversations or through the exchange of letters. As anyone who writes knows, the act of trying to put your thoughts on paper enforces a certain discipline. In Jefferson's time, the mails were slow and we may surmise that special care had to be taken to say what you meant. The necessity of writing, and the slow mail system forced study, analysis, reflection, contemplation, and deliberation."[9]

Of course we can never go back to the slower, more patterned life of centuries ago. However, our hyperforum experiment illustrates how authored letters in a novel web format can facilitate modern deliberative discourse on complex public matters in a very decentralized and multi-participant setting. Thus we aspire to use the web to facilitate wholeness with diversity, mindful that the traditional alternative to such functioning diversity in political systems has been tyranny or disintegration.

Potentialities of the Web

The web is an unprecedented self-organizing, adaptive social phenomenon, growing incredibly fast and evolving its form and substance virtually without any central planning. It is the hottest new communication technology around. It is almost entirely privatized and is starting to affect nearly every American institution to some extent. Millions of Americans already use this new technology, even though it is only about five years old. Most young Americans will come to use the web in one way or another within the next ten years. Nearly everyone will in time. The web is introducing a new phase in the coevolution of humanity and communications technology.

But what distinguishes the web technically? What makes it so special?

The World Wide Web is an interactive communication system created by the extraordinary confluence of four separate new technologies: the Internet; affordable personal computers featuring graphical interfaces; digital multimedia; and hyperlinking. The unprecedented pull of the web fuels extraordinary growth in the availability and affordability of the component technologies, which in turn leads to even faster growth of the web.

The growth of the Internet, the seamless linking of existing copper wire, optical fiber, and radio communication networks that enables direct digital communication between users virtually anywhere in the world, is a part of the global stampede into integrated digital communications. In 1961, when digital electronics were in their infancy, I became a very junior member of the JPL/Caltech team trying to develop and fly to Mars the first digital camera. The camera was to be operated in conjunction with the NASA/JPL Deep Space Net, the first digital communication network. In July 1965, Mariner 4 broadcast a tenuous stream of bits earthward, where the 270-foot Goldstone antenna in the California desert snatched them out of the ether and relayed them bit by bit *through teletype* to Pasadena. To our dismay we discovered that poor Martian lighting combined with camera difficulties rendered the raw images incomprehensible! Three additional days dragged by while exhausted team members invented and applied new digital image processing techniques. Finally, we could release to the three angry television networks astonishing scenes of a Moon-like Mars, quite unlike the habitable world all had expected.

Everything else in those days was analog. Some things still are—home television sets, VCRs, telephones, cable connections, and video cameras. But they will not be analog for long. The dominant industrial and financial theme of the 1990s is, arguably, the global integration of communication and media companies and their technological capabilities. These titanic battles for power and control stem from the widely shared expectation of the merging of personal computers with television sets featuring much higher-definition screens fed by practically unlimited amounts of dazzling interactive multimedia. The keyboard and mouse will be supplemented by voice-recognition and easy-to-use remote controls. Entertainment, news, information, banking, shopping, personal and professional communication—even deliberative discourse—will be available in the home, office, or mobile location, wireless as well as wired.

Today's web helps enable this technological revolution as much as it will benefit from it. But hyperlinking, the fourth element of the technological confluence that enabled the web (and its static analog, CD-ROM), may in the long run be the most significant addition to the coevolution of humanity and communication technology. Hyperlinking is a fundamentally new way to organize knowledge. Information is organized in terms of its connections to other information and context. For the first time in human civilization, knowledge and information (and human conceptual systems) are no longer slaves to serial systems of categorization and storage such as letters of alphabets, or the ordering of Chinese characters by sequence of strokes, or the classification of books by the Dewey Decimal System. With the web and CD-ROM, all entries are defined by their links to other entries. Einstein would have been intrigued by this ultimate perceptual relativity.

I am struck by the analogy with how the human brain is organized. But in the web individual brain cells are replaced with individual brains!

Regardless of how prophetic these feverish visions of the future prove, the web is already a major element in human affairs and certainly will grow in importance in the coming decades. Thus it is vital that its potential for building informed, deliberative consensus on complex, information-rich topics be explored as we have begun to do with the hyperforum project.

Denial of the Future—The Sustainability Example

We chose a difficult and complex topic for our hyperforum demonstration: sustainability. Why?

Accelerating technological change is the hallmark of the modern world, profoundly transforming life all over the globe in just a few generations. Imagine someone during the first half of the twentieth century trying to visualize the second half. Who could have foreseen that World War II would be followed by the widespread use of nuclear energy for peace and war, by the end of colonialism and the rise of self-determination, and by the global trauma of the cold war? No one anticipated then the transforming cultural impact of transistor radios, broadcast television, and networked-computers leading to revolutionary changes in the workplace and in popular culture, in the status of women and minorities, and in individual life styles and beliefs generally. Who could have imagined that the world population would treble, yet the global economy would grow so much faster as to begin threatening the long-term regenerative powers of Earth itself?

Likewise for us in 1997, it is frustrating and confusing to try to visualize the faceless, uncertain, and somehow threatening middle of the twenty-first century, the world of our grandchildren. Widespread denial of major transformations in our future by scholars and the public alike is the common response, making our descendants ever more hostages to fate.

Such denial by even those who should be most oriented toward the long-range aspects of our collective destiny was illustrated to me most strikingly at the symposium "Visions of a Sustainable World."[10] This three-day symposium was held in October 1991 as the centerpiece of Caltech's centennial celebration. I was one of the organizers, working closely with Murray Gell-Mann, whose encyclopedic knowledge of the leading scholars in relevant disciplines helped us assemble an extraordinary collection of speakers. We recruited leaders in population and demography, economics, ecology, development, energy, technology, governance, and culture and ideology as speakers and panelists. In preparation, we repeatedly advised the participants that the focus of the conference was the world of the next fifty years or more. Major social, political, economic, technological, and environmental transformations were inevitable. Indeed, we organized the program around such transformations. What were their speculations and intuitions about the world of their grandchildren? How should we proceed collectively to be good ancestors?

I had long pursued such questions as a personal and sometimes isolated intellectual quest. Now I hoped to encounter integrated insight and wisdom about this threatening future and how we should work to enhance it.

But that was not to be. Most speakers focused instead on near-term problems and circumstances: "How we should prepare for the Rio Conference (the following June)?"; "Why loss of species diversity is a bad thing"; "Graduate education challenges in the next ten years"; "The current rate of deforestation is unsustainable"; "Rapid population increase is undermining many developing countries"; "The need for more recycling in manufacturing"; and "We need to find practical ways to include the value of public goods in the marketplace." Ten years seemed to be the maximum projection into the future for many. Some even stated that today's problems were so compelling that there was no point in looking much further ahead.

I finally realized that envisioning the future collectively was simply too threatening even for this elite group. Doing so forced many beyond their comfortable zones of acknowledged expertise into vulnerable areas of intuition and speculation. So, some chose denial. It was then that I finally grasped that the central problem about sustainability was getting contemporary thinkers and leaders to engage it. That realization ultimately led me to the original conceptualization of the hyperforum project.

Conventional economists and business leaders often invoke a modern version of Adam Smith's invisible hand asserting that incremental actions of the marketplace ultimately will find practical solutions. Politicians simply shrug their shoulders and emphasize their impotence to influence large-scale processes—"My job is to practice the art of the possible within the understanding of my constituents." Such blocking out of the longer-range needs leads to political and economic emphasis on near-term consumption and investments at the expense of long-range investments and policies—the very opposite of what this and other deficit-financed societies need.

It is simply too painful for many to acknowledge that the world of our grandchildren will be as profoundly different from today's as today is from the world of our grandparents. Ironically, by not thinking about it collectively we unwittingly make our grandchildren—and their grandchildren—ever-greater hostages to fate. Somehow we must find ways to collectively visualize and deliberate over a broad range of future possibilities if we are to work together effectively to avoid the worst and help realize the more desirable by inducing wise near-term actions.

Thus sustainability was selected as the topic for the demonstration hyperforum because it is really central to our times and especially needs deliberative discourse. At a practical level it provided a broad, enduring, and international subject that illustrated well the promise, as well as the challenges and limitations, of the hyperforum concept.

The Experiment to Demonstrate a Hyperforum Using Sustainability as the Topic

Our approach was to focus on innovation at the system level in order to facilitate and encourage effective participation. Existing public domain software components were used wherever possible. Thus our achievements are primarily at the levels of system architecture and social computing, rather than in construction of specific new tools for comment, navigation, search, and management.

As is common in the development of new technology, our task proved more challenging than first envisioned and took considerably longer. We found it necessary to evolve through two distinct early approaches (Beta 1 and Beta 2). Finally, substantial discourse between previously unacquainted participants took place during February–March 1997 (Beta 3), satisfying one criterion for success.

Architecture and Organization

Our first two experimental configurations placed the participant "outside" the hyperforum initially, entering through a gateway (Beta 1) or through a two-dimensional map (Beta 2). A major innovation for Beta 3 was the realization of the importance of a user-centered architecture from the beginning (figure 9-1). Figure 9-2 shows the orientation screen, which is linked to the bottom of figure 9-1. Thus we created the FORUM as the central location (see figure 9-3) containing: the latest information and messages from the facilitator; direct links to the four main parts of the hyperforum; search and comment tools (figure 9-4); and help. Upon completing login, the participant is placed immediately in the FORUM (figure 9-3) to begin the session, and that is where he or she returns each time after visiting other parts of the hyperforum. We found that placing the user in the familiar forum right at the beginning reduced orientation and navigation difficulties for the participants.

THE FOUR-FOLD UNITY: FACTS, PROJECTIONS, GENERALIZATIONS, ACTION. The fundamental organization of the hyperforum evolved into four sequential spaces: "libraries" of reviewed and authenticated information (figure 9-5); "scenarios," authored projections into the future under varying assumptions (figure 9-6 and figure 9-9); "syntheses," generalizations drawn from scenario intercomparisons that illuminate the underlying reasons for differences in perceived plausibility and desirability of different scenarios (figure 9-7 and figure 9-10); and "actions," possible near-term endeavors intended to enhance future outcomes for which a consensus has developed (figure 9-8). This pattern moves from verified facts through authored projections, which inevitably contain a good deal of opinion, into generalizations that are largely opinion assembled in value-laden structures, and finally back into discourse over near-term actions.

We conclude that the four-fold sequential organization—facts (libraries), projections (scenarios), generalizations (syntheses), and action—provides a very useful way to structure discourse concerning contentious issues.

Figure 9-1. *HyperForum Home Page*

What will the world be
like in the year 2050? **HyperForum <u>Final Report</u>**

Registered users may
<u>ENTER</u> directly.

Welcome to the HyperForum
on Long Term Sustainability

The HyperForum architecture is centered around the Forum page, which is the focus of activity and navigation as shown in the following diagram.

SYNTHESES
Overviews of
participant's comments
and debate

SCENARIOS
Descriptions
of possible
futures

FORUM
The activity
hub, message
board, and
nerve center

ACTIONS
Near term
strategies,
seeds of
new policy

LIBRARIES
Supporting materials,
organized by topic

<u>Sponsors</u>

Why Am I Here?

You have been invited because of your interest/expertise in this subject matter and this novel (and still experimental) HyperForum tool. Also because we hope you will help us test this tool by engaging in a dialog about sustainability.

<u>Orientation and Registration</u>

A monotone representation of the introductory screen at www.hf.caltech. edu/hf/. The circular diagram in the center portrays the hyperforum structure. Clicking the mouse anywhere in one of the five sectors (which are characteristically colored on the actual screen) brings up the initial screen for that sector.

The underlined words (brightly colored on the actual screen) are hyperlinks to subsidiary pages. First-time users click on <u>Orientation and Registration</u>, which takes them to the Orientation page (figure 9-2), where they find a hyperlink to <u>Register</u>. Registered users click on <u>ENTER,</u> which links directly to the Forum (figure 9-3), the activity center of the hyperforum.

The hyperlink to Final Report was added after completion of the demonstration.

Figure 9-2. *Orientation*

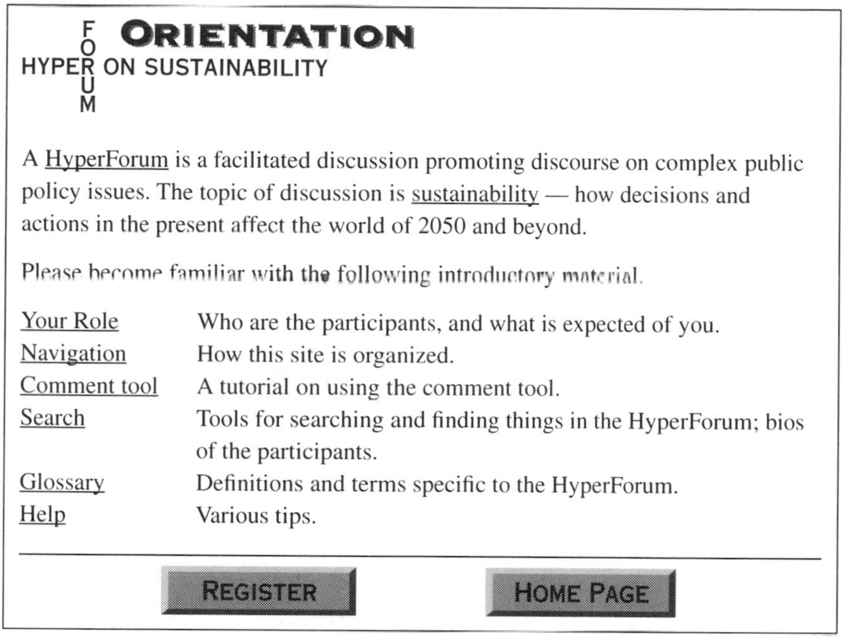

```
F ORIENTATION
O
HYPER ON SUSTAINABILITY
U
M
```

A HyperForum is a facilitated discussion promoting discourse on complex public policy issues. The topic of discussion is sustainability — how decisions and actions in the present affect the world of 2050 and beyond.

Please become familiar with the following introductory material.

Your Role	Who are the participants, and what is expected of you.
Navigation	How this site is organized.
Comment tool	A tutorial on using the comment tool.
Search	Tools for searching and finding things in the HyperForum; bios of the participants.
Glossary	Definitions and terms specific to the HyperForum.
Help	Various tips.

```
REGISTER                    HOME PAGE
```

The sequence of links Your Role through Help provides a short tutorial on using the site. HyperForum and sustainability link to extended definitions of these terms.

HOME PAGE returns to the introductory screen shown in figure 9-1. REGISTER brings up a self-registration form for selecting a login and password and for providing the new participant's name, identification, and e-mail address. That information is automatically incorporated into the BIOS page (not shown), which is always available to all participants.

After completing registration the new user is connected directly to the FORUM (figure 9-3).

IMPORTANCE OF A COMPELLING TOPIC AND A DYNAMIC, TASK-ORIENTED STRUCTURE.   A key requirement for a vigorous hyperforum lies in choosing a topic that captures conflicting views from the outset. Otherwise, the hyperforum may degenerate into an elaborate tutorial (which, however, may still be suitable for some educational applications) or leave the participants confused about the purpose. This was a principal finding, although we never completely met that challenge. A crucial companion conclusion is the importance of an "activity centered" design for the system, particularly the user interface.

Figure 9-3. *Forum*

F **FORUM**
O
HYPER ON SUSTAINABILITY
U
M

Always return to this page for announcements, current activities, and instructions from the Facilitator.

Facilitator's Message

3/3/97
Our Synthesis Discourse really ignited! To review, check "Recent Comments" in the <u>search tool</u> as well as the lengthy threads of commentary following <u>"Co-Evolution of Markets and Governance — Context of the Future"</u> and <u>"Well Said," 2/27/97</u>. This has been a remarkably thoughtful and comprehensive discourse between individuals separated by great distances, and, in most cases, not acquainted personally.

Now on to a new and somewhat different challenge. We ask you to link the synthesis discourse (and also the previous discussions of scenarios) to near-term priority actions by institutions that you think can help steer Planet Earth onto better rather than worse pathways through the middle of the next Century. We have discussed many potentially threatening prospects for the future. So what to do about it? Try to link your action suggestions to the previous discussions, if possible.

Hammond (<u>A Proposal for the Opening Discussion</u>) offers one possible way to begin the discussion of Actions, by returning to the growing disparity between Haves and Have Nots. But Kleeman <u>"Levers for Change," 2/28</u> raises an important transitional issue — which Institutions are likely to have significant leverage in the future. Please look at both, and then add your own thoughts.

Archive of Daily Messages

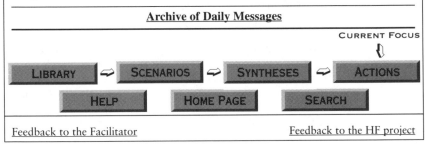

CURRENT FOCUS

| LIBRARY | ⇨ | SCENARIOS | ⇨ | SYNTHESES | ⇨ | ACTIONS |

| HELP | HOME PAGE | SEARCH |

Feedback to the Facilitator   Feedback to the HF project

This screen, from March 3, 1997, depicts the activity center of the hyperforum, which is intended to be the participant's office. A new Facilitator's Message appears every few days directing attention to significant threads of the ongoing discourse and including links to key comments and essays. The <u>Archive of Daily Messages</u> accesses a serial tabulation of previous facilitator's messages, thus providing temporal context for the current deliberations. The two <u>Feedback</u> links at the very bottom enable direct communication to the facilitator (and to the hyperforum project development team for this demonstration).

The seven buttons at the bottom provide direct links to the four main sections of the hyperforum (figures 9-5, 9-6, 9-7, 9-8) and to Help and Search (figure 9-4) and back to the introductory Home Page.

Figure 9-4. *Search*

F
HYPER O SEARCH   FORUM
ON SUSTAINABILITY
U
M

---

5 September 1997

- How much of the site have you seen?

- [Show Recent Comments]   (submitted in the last three days)

- Search Comments By Author, Title, and Recent Dates

- View Comments By Topic:

  All Topics New Version of Viewer, preserves framed format of commentary and scenarios.

       All Topics (old version)

  Library

  Scenarios

  Syntheses

  Actions

- Bios of participants in this HyperForum — those who posted commentary.

A variety of useful search tools developed by the core team is presented on this page, which links directly to and from FORUM.

How much of the site have you seen? brings up a prototype graphical display based on the site access logs. Show Recent Comments provides a display with links to all commentary posted within the past three days. This proved to be especially popular with the participants; it was updated automatically each day.

Search Comments by Author, Title, and Recent Dates searches as appropriate all the commentary headings and then displays links to the actual commentary. All Topics provides the same function on all the topics, as listed in the heading of the commentary. The entire hyperforum or just one of the four sectors can be searched.

Bios originally included all registered participants but was changed after the demonstration was completed to only those fifty or so who actually posted commentary. E-mail addresses there link automatically to message forms that can be sent directly to the individual in question.

Figure 9-5. *Library*

```
F   LIBRARY                              [ FORUM ]
O
HYPER ON SUSTAINABILITY
U
M
```

A `LIBRARY` contains widely agreed upon information. This prototype library contains examples of relevant material about the past, present, and how the world works — that may constrain what we consider to be a plausible future.

You can view a text list of the library's contents by scrolling down this page.

- General Discussion

- CrossCutting Issues

- View All Library Comments

Text List of the Library

Population	Economics
Food	Water
Environment	Security
Land Issues	Energy
Beliefs	Governance
International	Military

Population, Food, Environment, Water, and Energy lead to extensively hyper-linked on-line tutorials located at the World Resources Institute that were prepared under Allen Hammond's leadership. Security leads to an excellent overview article prepared by John Steinbruner of the Brookings Institution. The other unlinked titles illustrate additional potential categories for such a library.

The library content for this demonstration was necessarily quite limited in scope and diversity of sources. In an operational sustainability hyperforum, much larger amounts of reference materials need to be accessible. In addition a powerful tool for searching that content (not just the commentary headings) is necessary.

The button in the upper right hand corner of the page is a standard link back to the FORUM page used throughout the hyperforum.

Figure 9-6. *Scenarios*

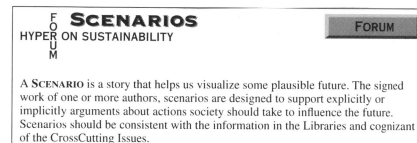

Global Scenarios links to an extensive set of text and graphs describing and comparing ten very different global scenarios (see figure 9-9). The United States scenario is a text-only narrative prepared by Murray; it provoked considerable discussions and reevaluation of views during the second test in October 1996.

The site should be designed to facilitate what it is the designers want the participants to do. For example, in Beta 3 the participants not only were placed in the center of the forum, but were encouraged by the facilitators to focus on specific elements of the discourse with the goal of eventually dealing with some major issue, such as the gap in wealth and income between the rich nations of the world and the developing nations (figure 9-8). Our original designs (Beta 1 and Beta 2) were organized around the information that should be in the site, and around our a priori typology on important things we wanted to see happen. (The RAND group was able to exploit the task-oriented participant structure more effectively on their more focused Defense Advanced Research Project Agency [DARPA] Defense hyperforum.)

THE NONLINEAR DYNAMICS OF DISCOURSE. From a broader point of view, much of our experience can be thought of from the perspective of getting people to engage. The metaphor of fire seems especially appro-

Figure 9-7. *Syntheses*

In this section of HyperForum, we work towards developing points of view that can synthesize the diverse ideas expressed in the scenarios and discussion. This doesn't necessarily mean arriving at consensus, but at least developing a framework that explains the fundamental differences between the contending bodies of opinion.

New, 2/23/97:   **Co-Evolution of Markets and Governance — Context for the Future.**

2/17/97:   **From Scenarios to Syntheses**

A synthesis could be either textual or graphical. Here's an example of a textual synthesis:

- Facilitator's Wrapup (10/31/96): <u>More than values.</u>

Here are some examples of graphical syntheses:

- <u>Change vs. the desirability of outcome</u> suggests that fundamental change is needed if undesirable outcomes are to be avoided.

- <u>Values vs. policy</u> demonstrates that the scenarios are evenly distributed among those looking towards changes in policy and those envisioning changes in social values.

Please comment on the question of the need for fundamental change, and the implications of changes in institutional policy vs. change in fundamental values. You may find it helpful to reference individual scenarios to make your point. And, if you feel inclined to do so, feel free to suggest your own synthesis of our deliberations.

- <u>General Discussion of Syntheses</u>
- <u>View All Syntheses Comments</u>

From Scenarios to Syntheses is an essay by the facilitators posted on 2/17/97 intended to move the focus of the participants beyond criticism and discussion of the scenarios to elucidation of the underlying reasons for disagreement. Co-Evolution of Markets and Governance — Context for the Future was posted by the facilitators six days later to focus the lively discourse emerging concerning the role of markets. It includes links to key commentary posted by participants in the preceding days. The sequence of comments posted is illustrated in figure 9-10.

Figure 9-8. *Actions*

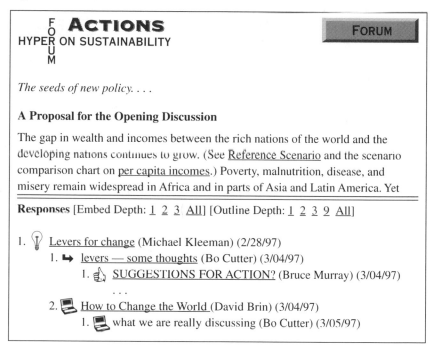

This figure illustrates the use of *frames,* which, in this case, juxtaposes below the opening facilitator's essay the top of a hypernews commentary screen displaying the beginning of a threaded list of the commentary posted in response to that essay. Not shown in this representation are slider bars along the sides of both frames that enable the user to move each set of text up or down for full viewing. The boundary between the two frames can also be moved vertically.

With this arrangement, the participant can first read the opening essay, link to Reference Scenario and per capita incomes as background, then scan the list of authored comments. Comments that are made directly on the essay initiate a new thread; for example, "Levers for Change. . . ." Clicking on that title brings up that comment in full with a new Response link, which can be used to post a new comment on the first comment. The new title is automatically displayed beneath and indented from the first one: "levers—some thoughts. . . ." The small icons just following each number are selected by the participant to convey the general sense of the message. All such commentary is also available through the links at the bottom of the page, as well as through the SEARCH tool (figure 9-4).

Figure 9-9. *Scenarios*

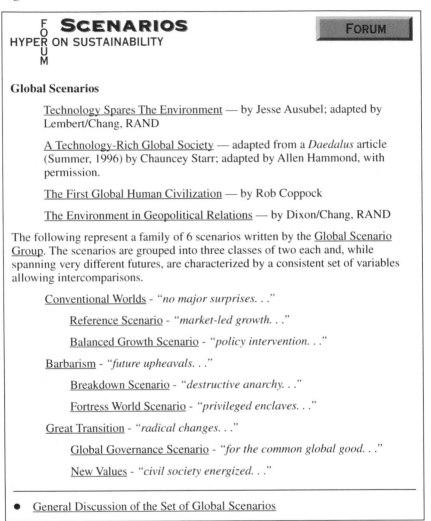

F
O
HYPER **SCENARIOS**
U
M
ON SUSTAINABILITY

FORUM

Global Scenarios

Technology Spares The Environment — by Jesse Ausubel; adapted by Lembert/Chang, RAND

A Technology-Rich Global Society — adapted from a *Daedalus* article (Summer, 1996) by Chauncey Starr; adapted by Allen Hammond, with permission.

The First Global Human Civilization — by Rob Coppock

The Environment in Geopolitical Relations — by Dixon/Chang, RAND

The following represent a family of 6 scenarios written by the Global Scenario Group. The scenarios are grouped into three classes of two each and, while spanning very different futures, are characterized by a consistent set of variables allowing intercomparisons.

Conventional Worlds - *"no major surprises. . ."*

Reference Scenario - *"market-led growth. . ."*

Balanced Growth Scenario - *"policy intervention. . ."*

Barbarism - *"future upheavals. . ."*

Breakdown Scenario - *"destructive anarchy. . ."*

Fortress World Scenario - *"privileged enclaves. . ."*

Great Transition - *"radical changes. . ."*

Global Governance Scenario - *"for the common global good. . ."*

New Values - *"civil society energized. . ."*

● General Discussion of the Set of Global Scenarios

Ten different authored scenarios are linked to this page. Most are further linked to supporting sources. The first three develop different aspects of the view that technology will provide solutions. The fourth emphasizes the interaction of poverty and environmental degradation.

The integrated set of six projections that follows illustrates and compares a broad range of assumptions. These were generously made available in preliminary form by the Global Scenario Group for our use in our prototype.

Each scenario is the subject of a separate hypernews commentary tool, available in framed format like that illustrated in figure 9-8.

Figure 9-10. *Comments in Topic: Syntheses*

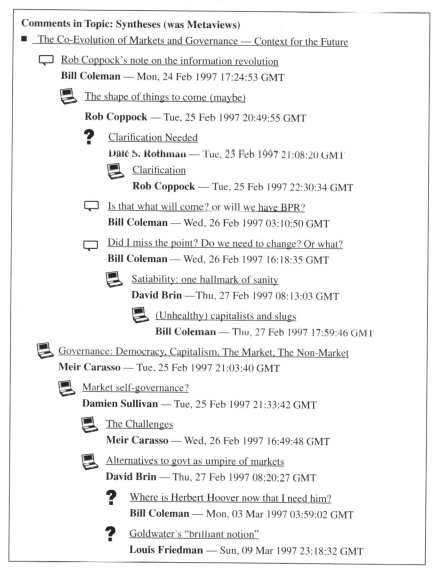

Comments in Topic: Syntheses (was Metaviews)

■   The Co-Evolution of Markets and Governance — Context for the Future

    Rob Coppock's note on the information revolution
    Bill Coleman — Mon, 24 Feb 1997 17:24:53 GMT

      The shape of things to come (maybe)

      Rob Coppock — Tue, 25 Feb 1997 20:49:55 GMT

       ? Clarification Needed
         Dale S. Rothman — Tue, 25 Feb 1997 21:08:20 GMT

         Clarification
           Rob Coppock — Tue, 25 Feb 1997 22:30:34 GMT

      Is that what will come? or will we have BPR?
      Bill Coleman — Wed, 26 Feb 1997 03:10:50 GMT

      Did I miss the point? Do we need to change? Or what?
      Bill Coleman — Wed, 26 Feb 1997 16:18:35 GMT

       Satiability: one hallmark of sanity
       David Brin —Thu, 27 Feb 1997 08:13:03 GMT

        (Unhealthy) capitalists and slugs
        Bill Coleman — Thu, 27 Feb 1997 17:59:46 GMT

  Governance: Democracy, Capitalism, The Market, The Non-Market
  Meir Carasso — Tue, 25 Feb 1997 21:03:40 GMT

    Market self-governance?
    Damien Sullivan — Tue, 25 Feb 1997 21:33:42 GMT

     The Challenges
     Meir Carasso — Wed, 26 Feb 1997 16:49:48 GMT

     Alternatives to govt as umpire of markets
     David Brin — Thu, 27 Feb 1997 08:20:27 GMT

      ? Where is Herbert Hoover now that I need him?
        Bill Coleman — Mon, 03 Mar 1997 03:59:02 GMT

      ? Goldwater's "brilliant notion"
        Louis Friedman — Sun, 09 Mar 1997 23:18:32 GMT

A portion of the threaded commentary responding to the February 23, 1997, facilitator's essay posted in figure 9-7. (Altogether 120 comments were made in the syntheses phase of the hyperforum.) Each title is linked to the actual comment, which, in turn, is displayed in framed format (like figure 9-8) with a new Response link for further commentary.

Each time a new comment is posted, it is automatically forwarded by e-mail to the author of the subject of the comment and is added to such a threaded display.

priate. It is a problem getting the fire to light, and once it is lit, it is a problem to control it. You have to maintain certain conditions to keep it from going out, but on the other hand, stopping it is not always that easy either. And finally, once you have a reliable, controlled blaze, using it to do something like cook your dinner is an additional challenge.

We did a variety of things to manage this nonlinear process. The "activity-centered" design makes it easy for the users to do things besides just look around, which lowers the ignition temperature. The FORUM helped create a spatial focus (a fireplace) to help get ignition and also to provide a better handle on managing and guiding the resulting "heat" (the damper). We also attempted to provide a temporal focus through things like the facilitators' message of the day (figure 9-3) and a clock icon in Beta 2, and by turning what had originally been a four-part typology of information into a four-fold agenda or trajectory for the process. Much of what the facilitators did was to try to get things ignited and then to stabilize and guide the resulting deliberative discourse. Indeed, we actually had to turn off the site to put out the "fire" of determined discourse.

We were surprised at how sharp this nonlinearity was. Much of the art of constructing and operating hyperforums must lie in this challenge of getting people to engage and then getting that engagement to lead somewhere.

NEED FOR A STRONG, INTERACTIVE FACILITATOR. In our earliest conceptualizations, we even considered the possibility of structuring an "automatic," algorithm-based facility to organize and summarize the commentary cogently and without bias. Our subsequent experiences demonstrated to all how naive such thinking is. Indeed, we found the role of the facilitator(s) to be essential to the hyperforum process. The requirements are similar to those for a good moderator in general, but with the additional challenge of motivating and focusing discussion and discourse remotely and asynchronously. The facilitator's task begins with trying to stimulate discussion, then trying to focus it, and finally trying to guide it through the four stages of the hyperforum trajectory. Facilitator bias can be minimized by using facilitator teams. We used groups of two in Beta 3, which also eases the time burden of daily web interaction. However, this teaming approach requires: a previous personal relationship; available time; and a shared commitment to facilitating a stimulating discourse.

Facilitators' tools were available on a restricted page. Prototype tools helped the facilitators determine web site traffic and activity from various Internet-provider addresses. The facilitators need daily to check the access log—it was available to them through a restricted link titled "Statistics"—as well as all the recent commentary. The latter was available conveniently to all through the search tool on the FORUM page (figure 9-4). In fact, many participants developed the habit of checking the "recent commentary" immediately on accessing the forum, and then entering the debate directly.

In Beta 3 we found it very desirable to post a daily facilitator's message at the top of the forum (figure 9-3). The message summarized the commentary thematically, usually directing attention to specific, central comments and supplying active links to those comments. It also provided a means of moving the discourse through the four sequential stages of the hyperforum. Finally, the facilitator's messages were archived sequentially, also available through the forum. Hence, participants who missed several days—even one or two weeks—could recapture and retrace the evolving discourse and catch up.

Nature of Participants and Their Community

A fundamental aspect of any community is each individual's knowledge of the identity of the other individuals composing that community. Of course for the purposes of role playing, individuals may assume psuedo-identities, such as in a traditional masquerade or a contemporary chat room. But for serious, deliberative discourse it is important that each participant feel personally accountable for his or her commentary. Similarly, everyone must be able to know something about the other participants. Thus there must be a "bio" section, or equivalent (figure 9-2). Similarly, all scenarios and other contributions must be authored, either by an individual or by an identified group such as the participants and facilitators of a previous hyperforum.

A subtle but important aspect of the complete mutual visibility of the participants is the increased credibility to all of the active participation of widely recognized individuals. For example, the frequent and provocative comments by science-fiction author David Brin from the beginning of our demonstration aided significantly in keeping the attention of other participants, including those who follow closely the commentary of others but declined to express their own opinions. (Such "lurkers" are visible to the facilitators through access to the activity logs.)

Expectations, Motivations, and Community of Participants

A key attribute of a hyperforum is the nature and degree of cohesiveness of the participants. Our sustainability hyperforum demonstration necessarily involved quite a heterogeneous mixture of mainly unacquainted individuals, a far-from-ideal group. They were generally busy people recruited by the designers on an ad hoc basis, and they received no compensation or explicit professional benefit for their participation. Some were interested in aspects of computation, others in sustainability, and only a few had a professional interest in both. Not surprisingly, the drop-out rate was high, usually with press of business as the explanation, but others were frustrated by the clearly incomplete content or difficulties with the experimental tools and organization. Some of these topics are summarized as part of the "Evaluation."

Despite these limitations, the sustainability hyperforum demonstration successfully met its goals, and some participants (and also designers) found that even this tortured demonstration added to their individual understanding of how sustainability is viewed by differing groups. About fifty individuals actually posted comments during our demonstration.

Generally, any operational hyperforum must define at the beginning who is to compose the community of participants and what their motivations and expectations are. Very useful experience with a more sharply focused hyperforum was acquired by the RAND members of our development team, who participated in a demonstration sponsored by DARPA. The topic was evaluation of the Department of Defense Advanced Technology Plan. The participants there were nearly all involved in related matters and mostly participated professionally. As might be expected, this group was able to reach more definitive results and was able to provide more specific feedback, albeit on a much narrower topic.

Key Functions and Tools

Navigation requires a successful blend of a good functional architecture and an intuitive graphical and visualization scheme. The hypeforum evolved through several distinct navigation schemes, including a 3-D pavilion and a magazine-like design. The intuitive judgment among the members of the development team varied greatly on the evaluation of visual representation. Our experience with purchased consulting services did not bring about internal consensus. What helped most was the user-centered concept that was translated into a very simple graphic. This experience suggests that the basis of a good navigation system lies in the system architecture more than in the style of visual representation (in other words, two rather than three dimensions).

The most common subject of complaint by participants was the comment facility. Clearly a more useful, easier-to-use comment tool really is needed. We used what was available (HyperNews) with only moderate customization, as a matter of development philosophy. Thus we learned about the problem and also did not become dependent upon the proprietary software of some other nonprofit or commercial organization. That might have inhibited distribution and utilization subsequently by the broader community.

The criticisms ranged from obvious impediments—duplicate password/logins, word wrap, slowness—to more sophisticated desires to see the benefits of e-mail (in one's own environment) combined somehow with the visibility and pluralism of a web site for threading and displaying the commentary. The absence of cut-and-paste tools was a serious obstacle to the kind of thoughtful quoting, paraphrasing, and linking we sought.

Thus we concluded that design and acquisition of a much better comment tool is the primary structural software development we need to make the hyperforum approach widely useful. The Caltech group has moved ahead to introduce incrementally significant improvements in HyperNews and to reduce other difficulties reported by the participants in our tests.

A common theme throughout this report is the difficulties created by the absence of a cut-and-paste capability within the hyperforum and within and without the HyperNews commentary tool. This is a serious system-level deficiency that must be addressed in future hyperforums. Some relief may come about through the evolution of available browsers, but customization of individual hyperforums is likely to remain necessary.

Search tools became quite important. We were able to develop adequate search aids for the commentary titles and headings. We did not have tools to search the content of commentary or posted content. Future systems should attempt to provide powerful interactive search-and-display systems for nearly every facet of the hyperforum, especially the libraries and scenarios, which should be dynamic, equipped with powerful search tools like those used for a data base searching generally.

The Outcome and Conclusions of the Experiment

Three project assessment criteria were identified jointly by the project and the Markle Foundation staff in June 1996: assessment by the development team; assessment by the participants in the hyperforum; and amount of follow-up activity by other sponsors.

The development team indeed judged the demonstration to be successful, and its members are therefore pursuing follow-up possibilities collectively and separately. Many complimentary and supportive messages evidence positive net assessment by sophisticated participants. The sustainability hyperforum did become "self-sustaining" in its later phases, which was an internal criterion for success within the project. Indeed, we eventually had to deactivate the site to silence the most determined participants.

However, those who were too busy, were put off by the hyperforum form or substance, were just not interested, or did not respond to an e-mail request for evaluation are not well represented. Such an outcome is nearly inevitable when the diverse participating volunteers are not drawn from some unifying community.

What about the third criterion, follow-up hyperforum efforts under new sponsorship? So far one complete follow-up has been accomplished, by RAND under DARPA support. Another seven or eight possibilities have developed illustrating considerable external interest in a follow-up. However, the absence of downloadable tools, architectural templates, and accessible examples is a significant impediment for new developments. A new hyperforum resource site we are developing is intended to reduce the barriers in moving from our demonstration to other operational applications by providing a rich set of do-it-yourself tools, help, examples, and discourse (www.hf.caltech.edu/HyperForum).

Potential of Horizontal and Vertical Concatenation

It is apparent from our experience that every aspect of the hyperforum should be iterative and interactive. All views and projections (like scenarios) must be authored, and the authors should be willing to participate in the discourse to modify their scenarios (projections) in response to the discourse. Truly factual material in the libraries can be discussed as in any scholarly interchange—based on its consistency and independent sources. But scenarios really are informed opinions and stories to illustrate those informed opinions. In our demonstration, only one author participated deeply in the critique of his scenario and evolved his views accordingly. The absence of serious, flexible participation by other scenario authors probably limited the development of scenario consensus in Beta 3. Conversely, another well-regarded participant who chose to play the sophisticated advocate for markets really helped ignite discourse during the synthesis phase of Beta 3.

Thus a hyperforum could be focused on the development of a set of scenarios based on certain assumptions to incorporate the deliberative discourse of a group of experts and interested parties. The resulting scenario—no longer the static product of a single author—along with the commentary and data that led to the final form—then could become part of the input to a larger topic such as sustainability. This would be helped if one of the facilitators, and some of the participants from the first hyperforum, were also participants in the second. This process would constitute vertical iteration.

Alternatively, the output of a sustainability hyperforum carried out with an initial community (foreign policy experts, for example) could become the input for a second hyperforum using, for example, economists as the main participants, but also including some of the participants and facilitators from the first hyperforum for continuity. This process would represent horizontal iteration. Numerous combinations and variations offer ways to increase the intellectual capital of a sequence of hyperforums well beyond the capacities of any one cycle of a particular group of participants.

Educational Applications

The overriding motivation for the development of a hyperforum has been to engage specialists and opinionmakers in deliberative discourse concerning the longer-range challenges facing this and other societies. Deliberative discourse necessarily must take place among a relatively small number of participants. In our demonstration about fifty actually left comments out of a total of about a hundred who were persuaded to register. A few hundred would seem to be a practical upper limit for effective participation in a single hyperforum, at least of the type we have been developing. Using concatenations such as those described in the preceding section, the number engaged overall could be expanded to, perhaps, 1,000. Subsequent hyperforums could increase the total more or less linearly. This scale of involvement could significantly affect development of enlightened new policies in many areas.

But what about much broader educational impact? How can the hyperforum concept help more broadly in education, both formal and otherwise?

Uncontrolled, open public participation in a hyperforum seems infeasible to me because there would not be a cohesive sponsoring and participating community. How would effective facilitators be recruited? How could progressive *deliberative* discourse take place?

There may, however, be another way to involve many in the dynamics and insights of hyperforums. The archive of a successful hyperforum could, in principle, be "rerun" using stored, recreated epochs from successive stages of the completed hyperforum. If the hyperforum site, with all the then-extant links, were recreated for each day that a new facilitator's message had been posted, it would provide an interesting representation to an after-the-fact viewer of the dynamics and content of that hyperforum. Indeed, such a post-production version linked to a familiar web site might be of interest to numerous other members of the sponsoring community who were not participants in the original hyperforum.

Much broader educational impact seemingly could be possible if the post-production involved purposeful editing emphasizing the development and consensual progress of a single, critical theme. For example, during our demonstration, I found parts of the discourse on markets and governance breaking new ground (for me). A heavily edited version of that demonstration might prove to be a useful web-based supplement to a general course I teach involving aspects of the environment, ecology, and economics. Better yet, if a hyperforum were organized from the start with the objective of producing such supplementary educational materials, and the participants and facilitators were recruited partly with that aim in mind, powerful and widely available educational materials could result. The sponsoring community (for example, the American Association for the Advancement of Science, the National Science Foundation, a professional society, a special-interest nonprofit, or a regional or municipal policy body) could then post links to such viewable discourses on appropriate web sites.

Hyperforum Resource Site

To be widely useful, hyperforums' system architecture and principles, software, formats, and tools must be readily available and easy to use. One participant referred to the need for "just-in-time" tools to be available for nongovernmental organizations to quickly and easily construct hyperforums for their specific, changing needs. We have had many inquiries from nonprofit groups that want to start their own hyperforums—and would we please show them where to download the software! This experience has led us to create a public hyperforum resource site (www.hf.caltech.edu/HyperForum). The objective is to provide a highly visible resource to help to start this process.

The Markle Foundation has supplied modest funds to Caltech for this purpose. We expect that the existence of this public site will lead to considerable sharing of techniques, examples, and software. Ultimately we hope there will be enough diverse experience so that the requisite customizing may be available commercially in an affordable manner and hyperforum and other approaches to deliberative discourse will become part of the mainstream of twenty-first century communications, community, and consensus.

Appendix

Conference on "The Impact of Interactive Communication on Future Attitudes and Behaviors," Aspen, Colorado, August 26–29, 1994
Participants
Edith Bjornson
Program Officer
The John and Mary R. Markle Foundation

Esther Dyson
President
Edventure Holdings, Inc.

David Brin
Encinitas, Calif.

Annie Cohen-Solal
New York, N.Y.

Charles Firestone
Director
The Aspen Institute
Communication and Society Program

John Gaddis
Ohio University

John Gardner
Graduate School of Business
Stanford University

Allen Hammond
World Resources Institute

Lloyd Morrisett
President
The John and Mary R. Markle Foundation

Bruce Murray
California Institute of Technology
Division of Geological and Planetary Sciences

Monroe Price
Cardozo School of Law

Notes

1. Lloyd Morriset, *Annual Report, 1994–95*, Markle Foundation.
2. See for example, Bruce Murray, *Navigating the Future* (Harper and Row, 1975).
3. See John Gardner, "Building Community" (Washington, D.C.: Independent Sector, 1991); and John Gardner, *On Leadership* (New York: The Free Press, 1990), chapter 11.
4. Lloyd Morrisett, "Habits of Mind and a New Technology of Freedom," 1994–95 Annual Report (New York: Markle Foundation).
5. Jeffrey Abramson, *We, the Jury* (Basic Books, 1994).
6. Morrisett, "Habits of Mind."
7. Ibid.
8. Ibid.
9. Ibid.
10. *Engineering and Science*, California Institute of Technology, Spring 1992.

Part Two

Media and Children

CHAPTER TEN

Sesame Street and Educational Television for Children

Daniel R. Anderson, Aletha C. Huston, John C. Wright, and Patricia A. Collins

Big bird is thirty years old in 1999. One of the most beloved characters of American children's television, Big Bird has helped *Sesame Street* become one of the longest running TV shows. If one counts the numerous adaptations and coproductions worldwide, *Sesame Street* is probably the most watched children's TV program in the world, ever.

At its inception in 1969, *Sesame Street* was truly revolutionary in children's educational television. The most fundamental decision that set *Sesame Street* apart was to convey an ambitious curriculum by means of entertaining content using the best professional production techniques employed by commercial television broadcasters. Another decision was to pursue a double premise by making the program entertaining to adults (parents) as well as children. Using the best contemporary knowledge of child development and early education (obtained from numerous seminars attended by numerous advisers), the curriculum was developed. Unheard of previously, Ph.D.'s in child development and education (especially Gerald Lesser and Edward Palmer) played significant roles in developing the series.[1] Intensive formative research became integral to the development of the series, and an unprecedented four pilot programs were produced and studied before the series was first broadcast. Curriculum development, carefully specified goals and objectives, and formative research became parts of an ongoing process as the series continued year after successful year.

We thank Deb Linebarger, Kelly Schmitt, Elizabeth McElroy, and the late Seanna Donley for their assistance on this project. The Recontact Project was funded by a generous grant from the Markle Foundation, which is gratefully acknowledged.

By such measures of success as size of intended audience, worldwide distribution, sale of branded products, and public recognition and support, *Sesame Street* is certainly the most successful children's TV program of all time. But when Joan Ganz Cooney, Lloyd Morrisett, and Ernest Boyer created the concept that eventually led to *Sesame Street*, those were not the forms of success they had in mind. The program would be a success if it reached an audience of young children living in poverty, who would not otherwise be well prepared to enter school, *and* if it taught them the necessary skills and attitudes. The measure of that success can only be based on outcome. How do *Sesame Street* viewers do when they get to school?

Independently conducted summative evaluations during the first two years of the series provided evidence that children were learning school-related skills.[2] The original research designs were field experiments in which children were randomly assigned to a group whose parents were encouraged to have them watch the program or to a control group which received no such encouragement. In the first year of broadcasting, this design was compromised by the initial success of the series; too many "control group" children were attracted to the show. In both groups, however, children who watched the show frequently gained more on tests of preacademic skills than did infrequent viewers.[3] In the second year, the design was successful because studies were conducted in areas for which access to the program required cable or UHF capacity. Families in the experimental group received the necessary equipment as well as encouragement; families in the control group did not. Children in the experimental group gained significantly more from the beginning to the end of the broadcast season than those in the control group.[4]

Nonetheless, these evaluations were eventually criticized on a variety of methodological grounds. In particular, it was argued that "encouragement to view" led parents to take an active role, so that the children's learning could not be attributed solely to watching the program.[5] Questions were also raised about whether the program was reaching the most economically disadvantaged children who were its target audience.

Partly as a result of the success of *Sesame Street*, educational programming for children blossomed in the 1970s. Programs that had begun before 1969, in particular *Mr. Rogers' Neighborhood* and *Captain Kangaroo*, continued to be favorites of young children, and new programs were broadcast on both nonprofit public and commercial television. A wide range of educational content and goals was represented, including problem solving, creativity, prosocial behavior, healthy self concepts, and the value of diversity among people. By the end of the 1970s, there was a fairly wide selection of such programs, particularly for a preschool audience. In the early 1980s, educational programs almost disappeared from commercial stations but remained the mainstay of daytime public television.[6]

Criticisms of Television as an Educational Tool

If the tallest tree in the forest draws the greatest amount of lightning, then *Sesame Street* has been the tallest tree in the forest of children's educational television. Numerous critics have argued that the very factors that make *Sesame Street* a success on the conventional criteria of audience size and appreciation also detract from its potential to be a successful teacher of young children. The qualities that make *Sesame Street* attention-worthy and entertaining, they claim, block the process of education. The basic argument has been that the use of animation, a magazine format, and a variety of video editing devices elicits an involuntary form of attention that functionally blocks useful learning.[7] Some extend the argument to all television, arguing that the medium is by its very nature incompatible with such important skills as careful thought, verbal representation, and symbolic thinking.

Jane Healy has been especially vociferous, arguing that *Sesame Street* teaches inattention to language. Blaming many of the problems of the "TV generation" on *Sesame Street*, she writes that "the worst thing about *Sesame Street* is that people believe it is educationally valuable."[8] (It should be noted that none of these critics has actually done any research which shows either that there is an involuntary form of attention to *Sesame Street* that blocks learning or that *Sesame Street* teaches an inattention to language.)

Attention

Research examining children's cognitive interactions with *Sesame Street* has shown that these critics are wrong. For example, if the program is changed so that it looks the same, but no longer makes sense, then young children stop watching it. Attention of American children declines when shots are randomly rearranged, the dialogue is run backward, or when the language spoken is Greek.[9] Young children's attention to *Sesame Street* is hardly involuntary. No matter how attractive the production, it has to be understandable before preschoolers will watch it.

High levels of attention do not block learning. Elizabeth P. Lorch, Daniel R. Anderson, and Stephen R. Levin found that children showed the best comprehension of the *Sesame Street* segments to which they paid the most attention.[10] In another experiment, a set of educational messages about nutrition was made using animation, strange voices, and other techniques often used in *Sesame Street*. Children were more attentive *and* learned more from these messages than from a parallel set that had identical content, but used live actors and normal voices.[11]

Language

Contrary to Healy's assertions, the language on *Sesame Street* and other educational programs is well suited to the comprehension levels of preschoolers. Objects are shown as their names are spoken; words and phrases are repeated; and other techniques associated with "good" language presentation to preschool children are used.[12] Preschool viewers are sensitive to language on the program. Not only do American children stop looking if the language is incomprehensible (backwards or Greek), they reduce looking when the language is abstract and more suitable for older children or adults.[13]

Children not only comprehend language on television; they learn vocabulary from it. In the first substantial longitudinal study to examine *Sesame Street* viewing and its outcomes, 3- and 5-year-olds from Topeka, Kansas, were studied over a two-year period until they were 5 and 7, respectively. Every six months, parents kept week-long diaries of all television watched by the children and their families. Among other assessments, children's performance on the Peabody Picture Vocabulary Test (PPVT) was assessed at the beginning and end of the study. The PPVT measures receptive vocabulary; it is also strongly related to overall intellectual development and to later school achievement.

Sesame Street viewing from ages 3 to 4 predicted improvement in PPVT score from ages 3 to 5, even after statistically controlling for parent education and a variety of characteristics of the home environment. Viewing noneducational programs did not predict changes in vocabulary. Most important, the detailed pattern of results ruled out the self-selection possibility—that those children who were most attracted to *Sesame Street* were the children with the highest initial vocabulary scores. Rather, the results were most consistent with the interpretation that watching *Sesame Street* increases vocabulary.[14]

Laboratory experiments confirm the power of animated children's programs to teach language skills. Mabel L. Rice and Linda Woodsmall prepared two versions of animated children's stories that were identical except that the 20 common words in one version were replaced with synonyms that were unfamiliar to young children in the other version (for example, "carpenter" changed to "artisan"; "walked" changed to "trudged").[15] Children were able to recognize the correct meaning for many of the unfamiliar vocabulary words after two 15-minute viewing sessions.

In general, studies of young children's cognitive interactions with *Sesame Street* and with educational programming using similar techniques not only provide no support for the critics but typically refute their assertions.[16]

School Readiness

The major goal of *Sesame Street* is to prepare viewers for school. The evidence suggests that it succeeds in teaching basic skills underlying literacy, mathematics, concept formation, and the like. The National Household Education Survey, originally commissioned by the U.S. Department of Education, interviewed a representative sample of adults. A reanalysis of parents' reports, focused on the relations of *Sesame Street* viewing to school readiness, found that preschoolers who were *Sesame Street* viewers were "more likely to be able to count to twenty, identify the primary colors by name, and show other signs of emerging literacy and numeracy than their counterparts who were not current viewers of the program." First and second graders who watched *Sesame Street* before entering school "were more likely to be reading storybooks on their own and less likely to be receiving special help in school for reading problems."[17] These patterns occurred after controlling for a variety of family characteristics.

With respect to the program's goals of helping children from poor families, children from families living in poverty were slightly more frequent viewers than those from more affluent families. The differences in school readiness skills in favor of *Sesame Street* viewers as compared to nonviewers was greater for children of poverty than for middle class children.[18]

More comprehensive evidence that children from low and moderate income families learn from educational television comes from the Early Window study, conducted between 1990 and 1994 by John C. Wright and Aletha C. Huston.[19] Children were given annual tests of school readiness, and parents provided detailed diaries of home television viewing over three years from the time children were age 2 to 5 or, for another group, from age 4 to 7. Detailed observations of children's home environments were collected. Children who viewed *Sesame Street* and other educational programs for children when they were 2 to 4 years old performed better on tests of school readiness, literacy, number skills, and language than their counterparts who rarely watched such programs. The *Sesame Street* viewers were also rated higher than nonviewers on school adjustment by their kindergarten and first-grade teachers. Although frequent viewers had more stimulating home environments than infrequent viewers, educational television made a contribution to learning that was independent of the other educational features of the home environment. The advantage associated with viewing was evident as much as three years later.

These American studies indicate that *Sesame Street* is doing its job of increasing the school readiness of preschool children, especially those from poor families. In addition, studies of international adaptations of the program verify these findings.[20]

A major unanswered question is whether *Sesame Street*, or even preschool educational TV viewing generally, has any longer-term outcome. A longitudinal study in Sweden indicated that exposure to preschool educational TV programs was positively associated with academic test scores in first grade and with high marks in sixth grade.[21] The question here is, does viewing *Sesame Street* and other preschool educational television have a detectable long-term impact on school performance and other educational outcomes?

The Recontact Study

The ideal way to answer this question would be a prospective longitudinal experiment in which *Sesame Street* was randomly made available to some children and unavailable to others. The children's school performance and media use would be assessed at intervals, perhaps until they graduated from high school. Such a study, although approaching a social scientific ideal, would be extremely costly, probably impractical (for example, ensuring that a large group of preschoolers not view the program), and would take fifteen years or more to complete.

An alternative approach was developed in conversations between the authors of this article and Keith Mielke, who was vice president of research at Children's Television Workshop. What if we recontacted children whose TV viewing we had studied in earlier investigations? The CRITC research group, headed by Aletha Huston and John Wright, then at the University of Kansas, had intensively investigated the TV viewing of preschoolers in the early 1980s. The University of Massachusetts research group, headed by Daniel Anderson, had also intensively studied the TV viewing of preschoolers in the early 1980s. It was agreed that we would develop a proposal to the Markle Foundation to recontact and interview the teenagers whose preschool TV viewing was known in detail. The Markle Foundation, headed by Lloyd Morrissett, funded the proposal and the Recontact Study was initiated.

The goal of the Recontact Study is to relate preschool television use to adolescent outcomes. Starting with detailed assessments of early TV viewing available to us from the original studies, we interviewed the adolescents about their academic achievement and academic values, media use, and a variety of other topics.

The Original Studies

In the original Kansas investigation one group of children was followed from age 3 to 5; a second group was studied from 5 to 7.[22] Most relevant to the Recontact Study, the parents filled out viewing diaries for these children (and the rest of the family) at six-month intervals. All the children were given the PPVT at the beginning and end of the study.

In the original Massachusetts investigation 5-year-old children from the Springfield, Massachusetts, metropolitan area were studied.[23] The families completed two 10-day viewing diaries. During the second diary period, time-lapse video cameras were installed in some homes to record television viewing. The children were given the PPVT.

The two research groups were in communication during the development of these studies, and many of the measures were similar or identical. Most important, the Kansas group adopted the viewing diary used by the Massachusetts group. Analysis of the time-lapse videotapes for viewer presence showed that the viewing diaries provided valid records of preschool TV viewing; the correlation between the two measures was .84 for the 5-year-olds.[24]

Recontacting

Viewing diaries at age 5 were available for 655 children from the original studies. The first order of business in 1994 was to locate the children whom we had last seen ten to thirteen years earlier. Starting with the parents' names, original address, and telephone number, we located almost half of the sample in local phone directories. Others were found using national computerized phone directories, by contacting neighbors, people with the same names, last known employers of the parents, and so on. Drivers' license records and high school yearbooks were searched for the children's names. This process was not trivial; nearly 3,000 telephone calls, for example, were made in order to locate the last 10 children from the Massachusetts sample. Of the 655 children, 605 or 92 percent were located and contacted, and 570 or 87 percent agreed to participate in the Recontact Study. The adolescents who were most difficult to locate were those whose mothers were single during the preschool study, probably because many of those mothers had remarried and changed their surnames. The average age of the participants was 17.5, ranging from 15.0 to 19.3 years.

The Interview

All 570 participants were interviewed by telephone in a session that lasted about forty minutes. Of these, 385 were currently in high school; 32 were interviewed in the summer, and the remainder had either graduated or dropped out. Those not in school were asked retrospective questions about their last year in high school. A separate study indicated that these retrospective reports were highly correlated with contemporaneous responses.

Items on the interview included courses taken in high school, grades in English, math, and science, academic expectancies and attainment value, media use, participation in activities outside of school, and creativity, among others. Demographic information was available from the original studies and was updated by a separate interview with a parent (unless the participant no longer lived with parents).

High school transcripts were obtained for 491 or 86 percent of the participants. An analysis of actual grades against self-reported grades indicated that they were closely related but that self-reported grades were slightly inflated. We accordingly adjusted the self-reported grades of those participants from whom we did not obtain transcripts.

It should be emphasized that our participants were largely white and from middle and working class backgrounds. Very few could be characterized as coming from backgrounds of poverty.

Results

At the time of this writing, we are still analyzing the data from this large and complex study. We have, however, reported a number of results at a scientific conference, and we describe them with an emphasis on *Sesame Street*.[25]

Educational Television

One of our major questions was whether preschool exposure to educational programs was related to high school grades. In this report, we focus on the results for *Sesame Street* viewing because it constituted about half of all the time children spent watching educational programs and because it had the most concentrated focus on academic and cognitive skills. For the most part, the patterns reported occurred in analyses of other child informative programs, although the relations were typically not quite as robust as they were for *Sesame Street* alone.

Because family experiences can affect both early viewing and academic achievement, we controlled for two "selection" variables: parents' education level and the child's birth order. Children with better educated parents watched more *Sesame Street* in preschool and had higher grades than those whose parents had less education. Children who were the oldest in their families watched more *Sesame Street* than younger children, and other studies show that first-born children tend to have superior levels of achievement.[26] In some analyses, we also controlled for the child's vocabulary score at age 5 as an indicator of early intellectual competence.

With all of these controls in place, educational program viewing in general and *Sesame Street* viewing in particular was significantly and positively associated with high school grade-point average in core academic subject areas—English, math, and science. Separate analyses of grades in English, math, and science indicated that the pattern holds for each type of subject matter. Children who watched *Sesame Street* and other educational programs often at age 5 performed better in high school than did infrequent viewers, even when individual differences associated with parent education and birth order were taken into account. Perhaps more impressive, frequent viewers had better later grades than infrequent viewers with equivalent vocabulary scores did.

Although the pattern of positive association between viewing and grades held for the entire group of 570 adolescents, it was much stronger for boys than for girls. When we analyzed boys and girls separately, early viewing was a positive and strong predictor of grades for boys, but the relationships for girls, while positive, were no longer statistically significant.

These apparent positive effects of early viewing clearly contradict the critics who argue that all television viewing is deleterious to academic achievement or that rapidly paced educational programs are harmful. Clearly, watching educational programming does not have short- or long-term negative consequences; quite the opposite appears to be the case.

As a practical matter, how large are these effects? One measure of effect size is the statistical notion of percent of variability in an outcome measure accounted for by the variable of interest. By this measure, *Sesame Street* viewing at age 5 accounts for 1 to 2 percent of the variability in high school grades. This may seem small, but it should be obvious that 1) *Sesame Street* does not teach content which is tested in high school, and 2) factors more recent in the adolescents' lives, such as illnesses or distractions, likely have a much greater impact on high school grades.

Another measure of effect size is the amount by which grades increase for every hour per week of viewing, after correcting for parent education, birth order, and 5-year-old PPVT vocabulary score. For boys, GPA increases by .07 grade points for each hour of *Sesame Street* per week viewed at age 5, or .35 for a child who watched five hours per week. A boy who might otherwise have had a 2.75 GPA in high school would have, by this measure, a GPA of 3.10. For girls, the difference (not statistically significant) is .02 grade points per hour viewed—an increase of .10 for a child who watched five hours per week.

It is worth pointing out that these analyses may underestimate the contribution of educational television in the preschool years. Most children reach their peak interest in *Sesame Street* by age 4; viewing has begun to decline by age 5 when our diaries were collected.[27] Hence, our estimates of the overall amount of viewing may have been low compared with those that would have been obtained for the same children at a younger age. Some of the important individual differences among children may have been obscured by this underestimate. For example, a child who was a heavy viewer at age 3 but was in all-day preschool without access to the program at age 5 would be counted as an infrequent viewer.

There is evidence that much of the important learning from the program occurs during the years before age 5. In the Early Window Study, it was viewing from age 2 to 4 that was associated with school readiness. In the Kansas sample for the Recontact Study, the children's vocabulary scores at age 5 were positively influenced by earlier *Sesame Street* viewing.[28] By statistically controlling for PPVT vocabulary, we may have underestimated some of the positive effect of *Sesame Street* viewing on academic competence.

Are our findings mediated by teen TV viewing? For example, was it the case that early educational TV viewing improves the viewing diet during the teen years, and that this improved viewing diet influences school grades? In the Swedish study by Rosengren and colleagues, the positive relation of preschool viewing to sixth-grade marks was mediated by grade school television viewing. That is, children who watched educational programs in the preschool years also watched documentaries and other informational programs in fifth grade; fifth-grade viewing, in turn, was associated with good grades in school in the sixth grade. We had information about how much our teenagers watched documentaries, news, and other informative programs for adults. There was no relation between preschool and teen viewing of educational content. Teen viewing patterns did not account for the positive association of preschool educational viewing with high school grades.

Violent and Entertainment Television

Much of the criticism of television has been directed to the large amount of entertainment programming that many children watch. Children who spend a lot of time viewing noneducational programs designed for children or for general audiences may miss out on other more valuable activities—an assumption supported by an analysis of the time use diaries of young children.[29] Cartoons and other programs containing high levels of violence may, moreover, stimulate children to be aggressive; as a result they may have more difficulty adapting to classroom demands in school and be perceived by teachers as difficult-to-teach students.[30]

For all of these reasons, we examined the frequency of viewing non-educational television programs (for example, cartoons, situation comedies, drama, game shows) in relation to high school grades. Girls who watched noneducational entertainment programs frequently as 5-year-olds had poorer grades in core academic subjects than girls who were relatively infrequent viewers. That is, we did find some evidence for the widespread belief that entertainment television viewing can interfere with the development of academic skills, but this relationship held only for girls.

Two categories within this broad entertainment cluster were further examined because they have high average rates of violence: cartoons and action adventure shows. Cartoons in the early 1980s were almost always designed for a child audience. Action adventure programs included some live action children's programs, but were primarily composed of shows about police, detectives, horror, cowboys, and super heroes. Girls who were heavy viewers of such programs at age 5 had lower high school grades than girls who were infrequent viewers. In fact, the negative relationship of noneducational television viewing to female grades was largely due to programs with violent content.

Future Analyses

The results of our analyses thus far are encouraging but preliminary. In our full-scale technical report of the findings, we plan analyses of viewing "diet," that is, analyses of viewing certain classes of programming which take into account the viewing of other classes of programming. For example, what are the effects of child informative viewing when one takes into account the amount of time the child views non-informative television? We are also examining other outcome variables such as participation in extracurricular activities, creativity, aggression, body self-image and satisfaction, alcohol and tobacco consumption, and identification with media figures.

Discussion and Interpretation

The national discussion about the impact of television on children has, through most of its history, been dominated by the medium's potential for harm. This dominance of the negative view has even led to a movement for a "TV Free America." In contrast, from its beginnings more than forty years ago, a few visionaries thought the medium could be powerfully employed for the benefit of children. The results of the Recontact Study indicate that this vision has been realized. The impact of watching TV programs designed to teach preschool children is apparent even through high school. The more the preschoolers in our study watched such child informative programs as *Sesame Street*, the better grades they got in high school.

Our results support our long-standing argument that it is the content of television rather than the medium as a whole that matters. Viewing educational programs was associated with positive outcomes in high school achievement, but children who spent a lot of time watching violent cartoons and live action programs as well as other noneducational entertainment had relatively poor grades. The great majority of programming available is not informative; our findings suggest that the concern about viewing such programming has some basis.

The fact that viewing any type of television program at age 5 can predict high school grades ten to twelve years later is remarkable when one considers the fact that the content taught at age 5 is not directly applicable to high school core academic subjects. Nothing taught on *Sesame Street* is tested in high school examinations, and whatever direct effects *Sesame Street* had on our participants probably occurred a decade or more earlier! Moreover, even such fairly intense direct preschool experiences as Head Start often have little demonstrable long-term effect on grades.[31] In this context, the size of the effect found in our study is impressive.

How, then, could *Sesame Street* and other child informative television programs have an impact detectable ten years or more later in high school grades? Our view is similar to an argument that has been made about other early interventions with a positive impact. Preschool child informative programs provide the young child with positive attitudes about learning and with information and skills that help to ensure early success in school. A child who enters school with basic literacy and numeracy skills is probably better able to learn the early reading and math skills that are taught in first grade. The result is success that enables the child to progress and that provides a sense of confidence. Among children from poor families these abilities may be especially important influences on teachers' perceptions of the children, which in turn influence the teacher's expectations and teaching techniques with individual children. These early differences in school success, self-confidence, and teacher perceptions begin a process that snowballs over time. Success leads to more success, and failure leads to more failure.

An analogous case can be made about the negative effects on academic achievement of violent content. Children may learn antisocial behaviors and aggression from these programs, which, in the context of school, produce negative interactions with teachers and other children. These negative interactions produce their own cascade of consequences ultimately influencing academic achievement over the long term.

We did not expect sex differences in response to informative and violent programs. The positive effects of educational viewing on achievement were much more pronounced for boys than for girls. This pattern occurred for *Sesame Street* and for other child informative programs. So whatever accounts for this effect is not solely a consequence of *Sesame Street* content. One hypothesis is that child informative programs in the early 1980s were developed primarily for a male audience. For example, *Sesame Street* was criticized because the most attractive characters, such as the Muppets, were male. To us, this hypothesis is unlikely to account for the effect because studies in the 1970s and 1980s of preschoolers' attention to and comprehension of *Sesame Street* almost never revealed effects related to the gender of the viewer. Girls appeared to learn from and appreciate the program as much as boys do. Similarly, boys and girls watch *Sesame Street* and other children's informative programs about equally often at home.[32] When differences do occur, they are slightly in the direction of more viewing by girls than by boys. Moreover, violent programs were even more male dominated, and girls appeared to be more affected than boys by watching them.

A second hypothesis is that girls are simply better prepared for school than boys and that boys are, conversely, more at risk of initial failure. As a consequence, boys benefit the most from preschool exposure to *Sesame Street* and other educational programs. It is a common observation that girls at school entry are physically more mature; they are less physically active and have better self-control; their language skills are better; and their social skills are better developed for the school situation. Teachers of young children, are, moreover, likely to be female. As a consequence, there may be several avenues to school success for most girls.

Conversely, the negative effects of viewing violence and entertainment programs in general were limited to girls. Girls' high school grades were negatively related to viewing violent and entertainment programming as preschoolers; for boys, there was no relation of such viewing to grades. Unlike educational programs that have about equal appeal to girls and boys, cartoons and action adventure programs are clearly more appealing to boys than girls. Boys watch more violence at home, and they name violent programs as their favorites more often than girls do. Hence, boys who watch such programs frequently are "typical" of their gender. Girls who are heavy consumers of cartoon and live violence are less typical of their gender. They may be temperamentally more inclined to activity and aggression, and they may be more susceptible to the effects of exposure to violent programs than girls who rarely choose to watch them.

We do not know whether the sex difference found in this study will generalize to other populations. In their Swedish samples, Rosengren and his associates also found a negative relation of general television viewing to later academic performance for girls, but not for boys, suggesting that this gender difference may be general.

If the positive effects of viewing for boys do generalize to less economically advantaged populations, particularly African-American children, it would be especially encouraging. The achievement gap between boys and girls for minority children living in poverty is much larger than the gap for more advantaged white children. A relatively inexpensive societal investment like *Sesame Street*, which reaches many children in poor families, may help boys in such families to be better prepared for school. Early success in school, in turn, can help produce a cascade of positive outcomes that not only benefit the children themselves, but the society with the wisdom to make and maintain that investment.

The research thus far is nearly unanimous in its indication that the many millions of children who have watched *Sesame Street* and other educational programming have been beneficiaries of a bold concept enacted nearly thirty years ago. As a generation of *Sesame Street* viewers has come of age, some of them are now engaged in producing new kinds of positive and educational programming for children. With *Sesame Street*'s example of the positive potential of television, and with the requirement by the Children's Television Act for broadcasters to provide positive programming, we may be at the beginning of a golden age of children's television. The day may come when, like books, TV programs are criticized on the basis of their content, and not the medium by which that content is transmitted.

Notes

1. G. S. Lesser, "Learning, Teaching, and Television Production for Children: The Experience from 'Sesame Street,'" *Harvard Educational Review,* vol. 42 (1972), pp. 232–72.

2. S. Ball and G. A. Bogatz, *The First Year of "Sesame Street": An Evaluation* (Princeton, N.J.: Educational Testing Service, 1970); and G. A. Bogatz and S. Ball, *The Second Year of "Sesame Street": A Continuing Evaluation* (Princeton, N.J.: Educational Testing Service, 1971).

3. Ball and Bogatz, *The First Year of "Sesame Street."*

4. Bogatz and Ball, *The Second Year of "Sesame Street."*

5. See T. D. Cook and others, *"Sesame Street" Revisited: A Study in Evaluation Research* (New York: Russell Sage Foundation, 1975).

6. D. Kerkman and others, "Television Programming and the 'Free Market Solution,'" *Journalism Quarterly,* vol. 67 (1990), pp. 147–56.

7. Jane Healy, *Endangered Minds: Why Our Children Don't Think* (Simon and Schuster, 1990); K. Moody, *Growing Up on Television: The TV Effect* (New York Times Books, 1980); J. L. Singer, "The Power and Limitations of Television: A Cognitive-Affective Analysis," in P. Tannenbaum, ed., *The Entertainment Function of Television* (Hillsdale, N.J.: Erlbaum), pp. 31–65; and M. Winn, *The Plug-In Drug* (Viking Press, 1977).

8. Healy, *Endangered Minds,* p. 219.

9. D. R. Anderson and others, "The Effects of TV Program Comprehensibility on Preschool Children's Visual Attention to Television," *Child Development,* vol. 52 (1981), pp. 151–57; E. P. Lorch and V. Castle, "Preschool Children's Attention to Television: Visual Attention and Probe Response Times," *Journal of Experimental Child Psychology,* vol. 66 (1997), pp. 111–27; and S. Pingree, "Children's Activity and Television Comprehensibility" (1986), pp. 239–56.

10. E. P. Lorch, D. R. Anderson, and S. R. Levin, "The Relationship of Visual Attention to Children's Comprehension of Television," *Child Development,* vol. 58 (1979), pp. 453–63.

11. T. Campbell, J. C. Wright, and A. C. Huston, "Form Cues and Content Difficulty as Determinants of Children's Cognitive Processing of Televised Educational Messages," *Journal of Experimental Child Psychology,* vol. 43 (1987), pp. 311–27.

12. Healy, *Endangered Minds*; and M. L. Rice, "The Role of Television in Language Acquisition," *Developmental Review,* vol. 3 (1983), pp. 211–24; and

M. L. Rice, "The Words of Children's Television," *Journal of Broadcasting*, vol. 28 (1984), pp. 445–61.

13. Anderson and others, "The Effects of TV Program Comprehensibility."

14. M. L. Rice and others, "Words from 'Sesame Street': Learning Vocabulary While Viewing," *Developmental Psychology*, vol. 26 (1990), pp. 421–28.

15. M. L. Rice and I. Woodsmall, "Lessons from Television: Children's Word Learning When Viewing," *Child Development*, vol. 59 (1988), pp. 420–29.

16. Technical reviews of this and related research may be found in D. R. Anderson and P. A. Collins, *The Impact on Children's Education: Television's Influence on Cognitive Development* (Washington: Department of Education, 1988), J. J. Burns and D. R. Anderson, "Cognition and Watching Television," in D. Tupper and K. Cicerone, eds., *Neuropsychology of Everyday Life: Issues in Development and Rehabilitation* (Boston: Kluwer, 1991), pp. 93–108; G. Comstock and H. Paik, *Television and the American Child* (Academic Press, 1991); A. C. Huston and J. C. Wright, "The Forms of Television and the Child Viewer," in G. Comstock, ed., *Public Communication and Behavior*, vol. 2 (Academic Press, 1989), pp. 103–159; and a less technical discussion is found in M. Chen, *The Smart Parent's Guide to Kids' TV* (San Francisco: KQED, 1996).

17. N. Zill, E. Davies, and M. Daly, *Viewing of "Sesame Street" by Preschool Children in the United States and Its Relationship to School Readiness* (Rockville, Md.: Westat, Inc., 1994), esp. p. 20.

18. Ibid.

19. J. C. Wright and A. C. Huston, "Effects of Educational TV Viewing of Lower Income Preschoolers on Academic Skills, School Readiness, and School Adjustment One to Three Years Later," report to Children's Television Workshop by the Center for Research on the Influences of Television on Children (University of Kansas, 1995).

20. For example, R. Diaz-Guerrero and W. H. Holtzman, "Learning by Televised 'Plaza Sesamo' in Mexico," *Journal of Educational Psychology*, vol. 66 (1974), pp. 632–43; and R. Diaz-Guerrero and others, "Plaza Sesamo in Mexico: An Evaluation," *Journal of Communication*, vol. 26 (1976), pp. 145–55.

21. K. E. Rosengren and S. Windahl, *Media Matter: TV Use in Childhood and Adolescence* (Norwood, N.J.: Ablex, 1989).

22. A. C. Huston and others, "The Development of Television Viewing Patterns in Early Childhood: A Longitudinal Investigation," *Developmental Psychology*, vol. 26 (1990), pp. 409–20.

23. D. R. Anderson and others, "Estimates of Young Children's Time with Television: A Methodological Comparison of Parent Reports with Time-Lapse Video Home Observation," *Child Development*, vol. 56 (1985), pp. 1345–57.

24. D. R. Anderson and D. E. Field, "Online and Offline Assessment of the Television Audience," in D. Zillmann and J. Bryant, eds., *Responding to the Screen: Perception and Reaction Processes* (Hillsdale, N.J.: Erlbaum, 1991), pp. 199–216.

25. P. A. Collins and others, "Effects of Early Childhood Media Use on Adolescent Academic Achievement," A. C. Huston and others, "Early Exposure

to Television Violence as a Predictor of Adolescent Achievement and Aggression," and K. L. Schmitt and others, "Effects of Preschool Television Viewing on Adolescent Creative Thinking and Behavior," all presented at the meeting of the Society for Research in Child Development, Washington, D.C., 1997.

26. M. F. Pinon, A. C. Huston, and J. C. Wright, "Family Ecology and Child Characteristics That Predict Young Children's Educational Television Viewing," *Child Development,* vol. 60 (1989), pp. 846–56; and R. B. Zajonc, H. Markus, and G. B. Markus, "The Birth Order Puzzle," *Journal of Personality and Social Psychology,* vol. 37 (1979), pp. 1325–41.

27. Huston and others, "The Development of Television Viewing Patterns in Early Childhood."

28. Rice and others, "Words from 'Sesame Street.' "

29. Wright and Huston, "Effects of Educational TV Viewing of Lower Income Preschoolers."

30. R. Huesmann and L. Eron, eds., *Television and the Aggressive Child: A Cross-National Comparison* (Hillsdale, N.J.: Erlbaum, 1986).

31. S. Barnett, "Long-Term Effects of Early Childhood Education Programs on Cognitive and School Outcomes," *The Future of Children,* vol. 5 (1995), pp. 25–50.

32. Wright and Huston, "Effects of Educational TV Viewing of Lower Income Preschoolers."

CHAPTER ELEVEN

The Children's Television Workshop: The Experiment Continues

Shalom M. Fisch

"[Television] can teach, it can illuminate: Yes, and it can even inspire. But it can do so only to the extent that humans are determined to use it to those ends. Otherwise, it is merely lights and wires in a box."
—Edward R. Murrow

"And your idea is that the kids are gonna race in from baseball and turn on the educational TV channel to be taught letters and numbers, hmmm?"
—Kermit the Frog

APPROXIMATELY THIRTY years ago, a small group of people embarked on a groundbreaking experiment—to create a television series for preschool children that would blend education and entertainment. The team of people, which included television producers, educators, researchers, and others, would come to be known as the Children's Television Workshop (CTW). The television series would eventually be named *Sesame Street*.

This chapter owes a tremendous debt to Gerald Lesser, Herbert Land, and Richard Polsky for their histories of the early days of the Children's Television Workshop. See Herbert Land, *Children's Television Workshop: How and Why It Works* (Jericho, N.Y.: Nassau Board of Cooperative Educational Services, 1972); Gerald Lesser, *Children and Television: Lessons from Sesame Street* (Vintage Books/Random House, 1974); and Richard Polsky, *Getting to Sesame Street: Origins of the Children's Television Workshop* (Praeger, 1974). I also gratefully acknowledge David Britt, Joan Ganz Cooney, Marjorie Kalins, and Lloyd Morrisett for sharing more recent thoughts and reminiscences about CTW. Nina Elias Bamberger, Charlotte Cole, Hope Davis, James Livesey, Wendy Louie, Linda Rapuano, Beth Richman, and Barbara Stewart provided helpful suggestions and support. Finally, I must thank the talented production staff, content specialists, and researchers who bring CTW's programs and initiatives to life.

In the years that followed, the success of *Sesame Street* exceeded even the high expectations of its creators. Its success would spur CTW on to create numerous other television series for preschoolers, school-age children, and adults, including:

—*The Electric Company*, a school-age series for beginning readers, broadcast on PBS;

—*Feeling Good*, a health series for adults, broadcast on PBS;

—*Best of Families*, a dramatic history of New York for adults, broadcast on PBS;

—*3-2-1 Contact*, a series about science and technology for eight- to twelve-year-old children, broadcast on PBS;

—*Square One TV*, a series about mathematics and problem solving for eight- to twelve-year-old children, broadcast on PBS;

—*Encyclopedia*, a series broadcast on HBO, with each episode focusing on a variety topics beginning with a given letter of the alphabet;

—*Ghostwriter*, a literacy series for seven- to ten-year-olds, broadcast on PBS (followed by a new series, *The New Ghostwriter Mysteries*);

—*Cro*, a Saturday-morning animated series about technology, broadcast on ABC; and

—*Big Bag*, a participatory series aimed at encouraging preschool children's social and cognitive development, broadcast on the Cartoon Network.

Numerous television specials were also broadcast (ranging from an animated Christmas special, *The Wish That Saved Christmas*, to a *3-2-1 Contact* special, *What Children Want to Know about Sex and Growing Up*), public service announcements, informational spots broadcast between entertainment programs on Saturday mornings, and more. Outside the arena of television, CTW also currently produces outreach programs for school and child care settings, books, magazines, software, and other educational products, domestically and abroad.

This chapter traces some of the history of CTW: where it has come from, where it is going, and what it means for children. The first section focuses on the origins of *Sesame Street* and CTW as a whole. In particular, this section focuses on two aspects of *Sesame Street* that represented, perhaps, the series' greatest departures from the state of children's television at the time: its approaches to entertainment and education. The second focuses on the present day—how CTW functions and continues to pursue its mission of simultaneously educating and entertaining children in a world, a broadcast environment, and a funding environment that is very different from that of the late 1960s, when its work began. Finally, the last section presents a brief review of summative research on *Sesame Street* and other CTW television series to assess their educational impact on children.

The 1960s: The Experiment Begins

It is hard to recognize today what a revolutionary departure *Sesame Street* represented from the existing state of children's television in the late 1960s. Although television series for children had been produced and broadcast almost since the medium of television was created, they were markedly different from what *Sesame Street* would become. Creatively, the early series were typically low-budget productions, often aired only locally. Educationally, while some conveyed positive messages to children, none attempted to address specific educational curricula or goals with preschool children. Little was known about television's potential for education, largely because so little had been attempted.

So little was known, in fact, that Cooney received Morrisett's aid in obtaining funding from the Carnegie Corporation to investigate the potential uses of television in educating young children. Cooney spent four months interviewing dozens of cognitive psychologists, preschool educators, television producers, filmmakers, and specialists in children's entertainment, and was encouraged by what she found. It was true that, until that time, no one had attempted a television series as ambitious as the one Cooney envisioned. However, the need for such a series was clear; a widely accessible medium such as television could reach large numbers of children at relatively little cost per child. Moreover, almost none of the experts Cooney interviewed doubted that television could play a potent role in education.[1]

Sesame Street was very different from other existing television for children on a number of levels. First, the quality of production that was made possible by *Sesame Street*'s eight-million-dollar budget far surpassed that of standard children's programs. As Cooney wrote in her report to the Carnegie Corporation, "Because of the constant competition presented by entertainment programs on television, educational material must be just as lively, fast-moving and dramatically presented as standard TV fare, if it hopes to win a sizable audience. . . . I believe that any high quality educational program for children must accommodate itself to that fact, although it means breaking new ground and risking the criticism of educational purists."[2]

To achieve this aim, experienced, top-quality creative people were needed to produce the series; for example, Executive Producer David Connell, Producer/Head Writer Jon Stone, and Producer Samuel Gibbon all had extensive prior experience on children's series such as *Captain Kangaroo*. With producers such as these, as well as other early recruits such as Muppeteer Jim Henson, songwriter Joe Raposo, and educational adviser Gerald Lesser, Cooney "knew we couldn't fail."[3]

Second, *Sesame Street* employed an innovative magazine format, in which each show was made up of a variety of types of segments, including puppet segments, animation, and live action films.

Third, the series featured a multiracial cast with both male and female characters. This blend was exceedingly rare at the time.

Fourth, one of the innovative elements that became most emblematic of *Sesame Street* was its fast pace and use of brief "commercials" and slogans that used the techniques of advertising to teach. As Cooney explained after her initial feasibility study, this decision stemmed from a strong educational rationale:

> If we accept the premise that commercials are effective teachers, it is important to be aware of their characteristics, the most obvious being frequent repetition, clever visual presentation, brevity, and clarity. Probably, then, their success is not due to any magic formula. Instead, television commercials appear to have adopted what have always been effective teaching techniques; unfortunately for our children, many teachers may have forgotten what Madison Avenue, with consummate skill, has cribbed from them.[4]

Executive Producer David Connell summed up the philosophy in describing an early piece of animation to a group of educational advisers: "We're calling these things "commercials" for our own shorthand, and we're planning to treat them essentially the same as a commercial enterprise would create a campaign. But we're trying to sell the alphabet to preschool children."[5]

This approach not only worked but became one of the most recognizable signatures of the series, with catchy songs and familiar phrases such as "*Sesame Street* was brought to you by the letter W and the number 3" passing into common usage.

Finally, unlike most television series for children, decisions about the appeal of the material being produced—what "worked" and what didn't—were not left simply to the instincts of the producers. Rather, an extensive program of formative research was employed to test material directly with children as it was produced. Material that was found appealing to children was included in the series as it was seen on the air. However, material that proved to be unappealing to children was redone, edited, supported by other surrounding material or simply cut from the series before it was broadcast.

Blending Entertainment and Education: The CTW Model

In her initial report to the Carnegie Corporation, Joan Ganz Cooney recommended several possible areas for *Sesame Street*'s educational curriculum, including language skills, letters and numbers, visual discrimination and logical classification, science and nature, music and art, and "teaching children about themselves" (for example, feelings, conflicts, and everyday problems). Attempting to address such subjects via television was a highly ambitious objective. Yet, there was little precedent upon which anyone could rely to provide guidance for appropriate ways to establish formal goals for *Sesame Street* or embed educational content in a way that would have an impact on viewers without interfering with the entertainment value of the series.

Thus, early on, the *Sesame Street* team realized that it would need substantial involvement by experts in education and early childhood on an ongoing basis. This realization led to the adoption of what would eventually come to be called the *CTW model*, an interdisciplinary approach to television production that brings together content experts, television producers, and educational researchers, who collaborate throughout the life of the project.[6] This collaboration would not be trivial, nor would it be limited to occasional memos or telephone conversations. As Cooney described it, "*We are talking about a marriage—* not researchers to work as consultants to producers. . . . We were by then talking about a product that would come out of a marriage—living together, dealing together, drinking together, eating together until they all would absolutely understand what the product looked like."[7]

Such an idea was wholly unprecedented in television; as Executive Producer David Connell and Research Director Edward Palmer observed,

"If *Sesame Street* was an experiment—and it very definitely continues to be one—this notion of broadcaster/researcher cooperation was the most bold experiment within it."[8] Understandably, the novelty of the idea was, at first, somewhat threatening to producers, who were used to relying entirely upon their own opinions and instincts. Looking back, Connell recalled,

> My background was in commercial television, where we felt we had developed a pretty good sense of instincts about what kind of show would appeal to children at any given age. I frankly was skeptical about the idea of researching every moment of a television show, and certainly of being told how to design it. There was the risk of intellectualizing the material to death and ending up with a program most notable for its monumental boredom. It would be like trying to analyze the elements of a joke, only to find that when we had isolated all the pieces, there was nothing learned and nothing to laugh about . . . . I kept thinking of the biologists who crossbred a crocodile with an abalone in hopes of getting an abadile. Only something went wrong and they ended up with a [crock a' b'loney].[9]

It was not long, however, before the production team began to recognize the value in having access to experts who could help them understand the nuances of *Sesame Street*'s educational goals and how to actualize them, or who could gather actual reactions from children to inform production decisions, rather than having to rely on subjective "best guesses." Certainly, as in the case of the production team recruited for *Sesame Street*, much of this conversion was directly attributable to the skills, expertise, and personalities of the researchers involved. At the time *Sesame Street* was being developed, very few academic researchers had any experience in studying (or even thinking about) television and children. One of these, Gerald Lesser, was a professor at the Harvard School of Education who became the chairman of *Sesame Street*'s board of advisers, as well as a key figure at CTW. Another was Edward Palmer, who had been working with the Oregon State Division of Higher Education, where he was developing measures of children's attention to television; Palmer became the first research director for *Sesame Street* and CTW's first vice president for research. Under the guidance of Lesser and, subsequently, Palmer and his research staff, seminars were held to establish concrete goals for *Sesame Street*, a "writers' notebook" was assembled to help writers understand the goals and how to address them, and an ongoing program of formative research was launched to inform the production of the series.

CURRICULUM SEMINARS. Once work began in earnest on *Sesame Street*, one of the first steps was to establish educational goals for the series. To this end, Lesser recruited educational advisers and consultants who

> would not act to "kosher" a project created by others but actually would contribute substantially to the design and implementation of the project. With only a few tremors of shocked surprise by board members over being asked to provide more than window dressing, the board was formed, went to work, and began to deliver ideas about educational goals and methods that provided a base from which a creative television staff could begin to operate.[10]

Much of this work took place in a series of five three-day seminars that brought together more than one hundred leading educational theorists and practitioners, developmental researchers, preschool teachers, filmmakers, animators, musicians, and children's book authors. Each seminar focused on a different theme: social, moral, and affective development; language and reading; mathematical and numerical skills; reasoning and problem solving; and perception.

The task before the group in each seminar was to define a set of goals that would not only be educationally and developmentally valid, but also be appropriate for a television series as opposed to a classroom. This was, of course, not an easy task, as the producers did not come to the seminars with a deep understanding of the educational issues involved and the advisers did not come equipped with a deep understanding of the constraints of television. Lapses into technical jargon, too, could pose barriers to discussion; as Lesser recalled, "Confrontations over language occurred at each seminar, sometimes on several occasions.... These exchanges never were allowed to continue for long, but they exceeded the patience of some nonacademics who asked, in one form or another, 'Why don't you speak English?'"[11]

Despite such obstacles, however, the end result of the seminars was a set of objective, concrete goals for the series. The seminars provided a

Table 11-1. *Subset of Goals for* Sesame Street

Symbolic representation
   The child can recognize such basic symbols as letters, numbers, and geometric forms and can perform rudimentary operations with these symbols.

Letters
1. Given a set of symbols, either all letters or all numbers, the child knows whether those symbols are used in reading or counting.
2. Given a printed letter, the child can select the identical letter from a set of printed letters.
3. Given a printed letter, the child can select its other case version from a set of printed letters.
4. Given a verbal label for certain letters, the child can select the appropriate letter from a set of printed letters.
5. Given a printed letter, the child can provide the verbal label.
6. Given a series of words presented orally, all beginning with the same letter, the child can make up another word or pick another word starting with the same letter.
7. Given a spoken letter, the child can select a set of pictures or objects beginning with that letter.
8. The child can recite the alphabet.

forum for extensive discussion and give-and-take that allowed these goals to be educationally appropriate and achievable through television.[12] (A small sample is presented in table 11-1.)

WRITERS' NOTEBOOK. The work of helping the production team to actualize these goals did not end with the initial seminars. The goals set the groundwork for creating such material, but the production team still needed help in translating the goals into terms they could use and applying them in creating material for the series.

Much of this help came from the ongoing process of collaboration between researchers and producers. Another important tool was the writers' notebook. Assembled by the research staff, the writers' notebook presented several child-centered, real-life situations in which each goal could be played out. Writers were not required to build sketches or stories around these situations (although they were free to do so). Rather, the suggested situations were used to clarify the meaning of each goal and serve as a possible spur for ideas.

FORMATIVE RESEARCH. Another vital component of the process was formative research, that is, empirical testing of material that is conducted with children during production, to inform the development and revision of the material. Such research examines the material from the standpoint of comprehension and appeal, so that strengths can be identified (and built into future segments or shows) and weaknesses can be corrected before the series is broadcast.

The use of formative research in developing educational television was unprecedented when it was first employed for *Sesame Street*. Indeed, even the term "formative evaluation" had been coined only a short time earlier.[13] The absence of any prior research literature meant that no time-tested methodologies existed for examining the appeal or comprehensibility of television programs for preschool children. Thus, the research staff, under the guidance of Edward Palmer, had to develop new methods and assessments that would provide valid and reliable answers to a broad range of production issues.

One of the chief methods that Palmer developed was known as the *distractor method*. Palmer reasoned that television viewing typically occurs in a home environment that presents many distractions that compete with the television for the viewer's attention. Thus, in the distractor method, viewers were seated within view of both a television set that showed the material being tested and a slide projector that displayed a new slide every eight seconds. Researchers recorded the children's viewing—whether they were watching the television or the slides at any given moment. Thus, the method provided a moment-by-moment portrait of the degree to which a given segment or show held children's interest and fine-grained indicators of the precise features of the material that gained or lost that interest.[14]

Formative research provided empirical answers to myriad production questions. For example, Palmer and Producer Samuel Gibbon later recalled, "Field studies were conducted to determine the effect of various schedules of repetition and spacing, of providing the child with preliminary or follow-up explanation, of presenting different approaches to a given goal separately or in combination, and of the relative effectiveness of adult vs. child voice-over narration."[15]

The results of such testing could lead to concrete changes in material for the series. For example, tests of an early animation concerning the letter J were encouraging, but showed that children attended more to the animated characters in the segment than to the stationary letter itself, thus interfering with comprehension. To draw viewers' attention back to the letter, the production team subsequently redesigned the segment so that the J itself would move via animation.[16] This technique was also incorporated into later segments and is still often used today.

In some cases, difficulties were more pronounced and material was simply discarded. For example, an early series of segments called "The Man from Alphabet" concerned a bumbling detective-spy aided by a brilliant seven-year-old who actually solved the team's mysteries. Although the segments seemed like a good idea initially, they performed poorly with children, largely because they featured lengthy periods of dialogue with little action (thus losing children's interest). Based on these data, Executive Producer David Connell recommended that they be acknowledged as "Connell's folly" and cut from the series before they aired.[17] Such a decision in the face of the money spent on producing the segments required great conviction from their creator, but benefited the series in the long run.

An even more extreme, but equally valuable, risk was taken in producing five one-hour test shows that would be tested with preschool children. If the results had proven negative, the staff was fully prepared to scrap all five hours, despite the $230,000 investment that had been required to produce them.[18] However, the results of the test were generally very positive; children showed evidence of learning from the shows, and their appeal was as high as any other television programs that had been tested. These results spurred the team on to create the remainder of the first season of *Sesame Street*.

Still, not everything within the test shows was equally appealing. In particular, children tended to enjoy the animations and Muppet insert segments more than the live-action segments set on the "Street" set. The lower appeal of these "first-draft" street segments was largely due to the fact that, because advisors had recommended against blending reality and fantasy, Muppets appeared in their own segments but not alongside the humans in the street segments. The appeal of the human characters on the street by themselves was simply not as high as the appeal of the Muppets or animations. Thus, to boost the appeal of the street segments, the *Sesame Street* team decided that they would include Muppets on the street after all, and created two new Muppets expressly for this purpose: Oscar the Grouch and Big Bird.

As these examples demonstrate, formative research can play an extremely valuable role in the production of educational television. While producers and researchers can attempt to look at material with a child's perspective in mind, the fact remains that they are adults and may not accurately capture a child's reactions. Formative research provides a means by which the voice of the child can itself be brought into the production process.

A Product of Its Time

Certainly, the early success of *Sesame Street* and CTW is attributable almost entirely to the talent and dedication of a small group of people. However, it is also important to recognize that *Sesame Street* was very much a product of the political and social atmosphere in which those people found themselves. Funding for the series might have been far more difficult to obtain if it were not for the fact that, in the mid-1960s, a great deal of attention was being focused on the needs of preschool children and means of enriching their educational experiences (an atmosphere that also gave rise to projects such as Head Start). Lloyd Morrisett recalled that, through his involvement with the Carnegie Corporation, he had become aware that "we were dealing with a big problem affecting millions of children, but we were financing [educational efforts] that were dealing with only a few thousand at the most, maybe only a few hundred."[19] Television provided a medium for reaching preschool children on a larger scale.

At the same time, the desire by those involved in *Sesame Street* to have a positive impact on children was clearly influenced by the social optimism of the time. As Cooney put it, "The *zeitgeist* was this highly idealistic period, where Bobby Kennedy was running for President, the antiwar movement was huge, and civil rights was very much on the front burner."[20]

Indeed, even the tragedies of the time sometimes served as galvanizing forces. When the men who would become *Sesame Street*'s initial key producers—David Connell, Jon Stone, and Samuel Gibbon—were first approached, all three were reluctant. All of them had left the field of children's television and were not eager to reenter it. However, as Cooney recalled, at least one was moved to reconsider his decision by a public tragedy: "Martin Luther King was shot, and that was an event that sort of got the attention of everybody. You had the sense that the country was kind of falling apart because you had all the riots and fires following it. And Sam Gibbon called me right away and said, "I'll come aboard. It's done. [I] can't say no under these circumstances."[21]

Thus *Sesame Street* and CTW grew out of a combination of two key factors: talented people and a supportive environment. In many ways, then, CTW was a matter of people and timing—the right people being in the right place at the right time.

The 1990s: The Experiment Continues

If CTW was a product of its time, then an obvious question is how the Workshop continues to function in a world that has changed dramatically since the late 1960s. As Cooney recently observed, CTW is still "the same place in terms of values . . . [but] almost everything else has changed."[22] David Britt, who succeeded Cooney as CTW's chief executive officer in 1990, agreed: "[CTW remains] the same in that the sense of experimentation, the sense of 'We can do anything we set out to do,' the sense of mission in the broad sense of that word are, at their heart, fundamentally unchanged.[23]

A Changing World

Yet, while CTW's mission may be the same, the current broadcast environment, the funding environment, the regulatory environment, and even technology itself are all very different than those that existed when CTW was founded. To continue to accomplish its mission in a changing world, CTW has had to change.

THE BROADCAST ENVIRONMENT. When *Sesame Street* first went on the air, most stations were not yet broadcasting twenty-four hours a day. Broadcast television consisted primarily of three commercial networks (CBS, NBC, and ABC), PBS, and independent stations that served local communities. Even PBS did not cover the entire United States, and the PBS stations in many areas were broadcast on UHF, which led to poor reception of PBS broadcasts in those areas. Cable television was still in its infancy, often used more for the purpose of improving television reception than for providing access to a greater number of stations.

Children's programming, too, was very different from the present day. Networks often did not broadcast children's programs on weekdays, concentrating their efforts on Saturday mornings. The relatively small number of children's programs on the air, coupled with their weekend scheduling, meant that weekday airings of *Sesame Street* frequently were the only children's programs airing in those time slots.

Today's broadcast environment bears little resemblance to that of thirty years ago. In recent years, broadcast television has seen the birth of three new networks (Fox, WB, and UPN), causing severe reductions in the number of local, unaffiliated television stations. The widespread growth of cable television and advent of other delivery systems such as satellite television have increased viewers' choices from ten or twelve channels to fifty, sixty, or more. New media, such as videocassettes, laser discs, and video games, also compete with television viewing. As a result, the audience for any given television program may be far more narrowly defined and fragmented than would have been the case in the past.

At the same time, children's programming has changed as well, expanding in some ways while it has contracted in others. Until the 1980s, children's programming on weekdays was largely the province of PBS and independent commercial stations; that changed when the still-new Fox network began to air a block of children's programming on weekday afternoons (while Disney started producing a popular "Disney Afternoon" block for syndication). Entire child-oriented networks, such as Nickelodeon and the Cartoon Network, have emerged. Indeed, even the landscape of PBS's children's programming has shown significant change in the past ten years. As CTW's senior vice president for production, Marjorie Kalins, noted,

> When *Sesame Street* came along, for whatever reason, despite all of the success *Sesame Street* had, there was never a bandwagon reaction for people to go out and try to compete with it. . . . Along comes [the financial success of] *Barney*, and . . . everybody then said, "There's so much money to be made in the kids' business, let's get into the kids' business." So the kids' business has proliferated among producers who were never in it, especially major studios. At the same time, everybody wanted to get on PBS.[24]

This heightened competition has been accompanied by a simultaneous reduction in the outlets through which independent television production companies can reach children. Fox's increasing success on Saturday mornings has led competitors such as NBC to move away from broadcasting children's programs and placing adult- and teen-oriented programming in its place. Mergers between networks and production companies (such as Disney's recent acquisition of ABC) have led broadcasters to rely more on in-house children's production and less on outside production companies. Even on PBS, the suddenly fierce competition for space has resulted in instances of producers providing programming at little or even no cost to PBS itself, in the hopes of recouping production costs through merchandising. Thus, there is less incentive for PBS to purchase or provide significant funding for children's television programs.

The impact of all of these developments on CTW is that, as Kalins observed, "you've got a broadening of the business and, at the same time, a shrinking of the people to whom we could potentially sell what we do."[25]

THE REGULATORY ENVIRONMENT. Over the past two decades, the regulatory environment concerning children's television has resembled a tremendous pendulum. Under the Reagan/Bush administrations, the 1980s were a time of great deregulation, when various rules and bans concerning children's television were lifted. More recently, the pendulum has swung back in the opposite direction, with heated public debates over federal regulations on topics such as ratings to indicate the content or age level of television programming, or new technology such as the V-chip that could allow parents to block out undesirable programs from their families' televisions.

Perhaps one of the most visible sets of developments regarding children's television in the public policy arena has centered around the Children's Television Act of 1990. Among the provisions of the act was the requirement that broadcasters must serve "the educational and informational needs of children through the licensee's overall programming, including programming specifically designed to serve such needs."[26]

When first passed, the act did not lead to significant increases in the number of educational programs being aired; instead, many broadcasters responded to the act by redefining existing entertainment programming as educational.[27] Indeed, although a station survey conducted by the National Association of Broadcasters showed increases in the average amount of children's educational programming on television, the Federal Communications Commission (FCC) concluded from a cursory review of license renewal applications that these figures were inflated.[28]

To strengthen the guidelines of the act, the FCC voted in 1996 to set a minimum requirement of three hours of such programming per week.

However, the FCC did not simultaneously narrow its original, broad definition of television "that serves the needs of children"—that is, programs that "further the positive development of the child in any respect, including the child's cognitive/intellectual or emotional/social needs."[29] Given the breadth of this definition, it is too early to determine whether the FCC's quantified guidelines for programming will result in increases in educational programs, or simply in further redefining of entertainment programs as educational.

THE FUNDING ENVIRONMENT.   The entire cost of the first season of *Sesame Street* was covered by grants from public and private sources. Approximately one-half of the eight-million-dollar budget was covered by the U.S. Department of Health, Education, and Welfare (including the Office of Education and Office of Economic Opportunity, among others), with the remainder supplied by the newly created Corporation for Public Broadcasting and private foundations such as the Carnegie Corporation, the Ford Foundation, and others.

Yet, even during its initial success, Morrisett cautioned others at CTW that such sources could not be relied upon for long-term funding. As he noted in 1972,

> From the beginning we have gone under the assumption that we could not count on continued foundation support in the long run. . . . Once the project became successful, we were convinced that we had to find ways of generating income of our own. We would also like to diminish the government's share of that to as little as possible. If we could become completely self-supporting, that would be what we would want to do.[30]

Morrisett's prophecy proved well founded. The Department of Education began to phase out its funding of *Sesame Street* in 1978, and awarded its last grant to the series in 1982. Faced with government cutbacks throughout the 1980s and an economic recession that discouraged corporate and foundational support, CTW needed to find other sources of revenue to fund its efforts.

Adapting to the Environment

Faced with the extensive challenges detailed above, it quickly became clear that CTW, too, would have to evolve and change in order to survive, let alone grow. The changes that followed can be divided into several broad categories: finding new ways to reach children "where they are" (for example, via Saturday-morning cartoons and cable television, materials for child care settings, or new media such as home video and interactive technology); expanding the domestic audience for CTW's educational efforts (to include not only preschool children but also, for example, school-age children, parents, teachers, child care providers, and other adults) and the subject matter addressed; pursuing international efforts to address both "universal" educational needs and needs that are more specific to particular countries, cultures, or regions; developing new sources of revenue to make CTW as self-sufficient as possible (for example, by licensing products based on *Sesame Street* and other series); and modifying and streamlining the process described by the CTW model itself, both to capitalize on CTW's accumulated past experience and to reduce production costs as much as possible.

REACHING CHILDREN WHERE THEY ARE. As noted above, changes in the broadcast environment have led to an increasing fragmentation of the television viewing audience, with viewers spread across an increasing number of broadcast and cable television channels. Simultaneously, new media, such as home videos, interactive software, computer games, and on-line services also compete for children's time and attention. To be effective in reaching children, then, CTW has had to broaden the means and the media by which it has pursued them.

In fact, while CTW is often associated with PBS in the minds of the public, the workshop has also been involved with commercial television since its inception. A prime-time *Sesame Street* "preview" special was aired on NBC two days before the series premiered on PBS, and a specially created *Sesame Street/Electric Company* special called "Out to Lunch" was broadcast on ABC in 1974.

Over the years, however, CTW has increased its emphasis on commercial television. As cable television has grown, CTW created *Encyclopedia* for HBO (in the 1980s) and *Big Bag* for the Cartoon Network (in the 1990s). In the arena of broadcast television, a 1990 analysis of Nielsen ratings showed the greatest concentration of children to be watching broadcast television on Saturday mornings.[31] Since then, CTW has created series such as *Cro* for ABC's Saturday-morning schedule in the early 1990s and, more recently, the *New Ghostwriter Mysteries* for CBS.

Simultaneously, CTW has expanded outside television to reach children via other media as well. The Workshop's Interactive Technology division has produced numerous pieces of educational software for children, including CD-ROMs based on *Sesame Street* for preschoolers and others based on *3-2-1 Contact* for school-age children. Its Publishing group produces magazines and books for preschool and school-age children, based on series such as *Sesame Street, Big Bag, Ghostwriter, 3-2-1 Contact*, and others. The Community Education Services department has been producing materials for child care settings since the earliest days of the workshop, in an attempt to reach disadvantaged children; this effort has become even more important as increasing numbers of preschool children are placed in child care at young ages.[32] In a parallel effort, the Schools group develops and produces materials appropriate for classroom use. Home videos, toys, and other products serve as additional vehicles for carrying educational materials and messages to children. *Sesame Street*–based activities on the Prodigy service brought CTW into the Internet, and at the time of this writing, work is under way in developing a broader CTW on-line service for families. Indeed, CTW has expanded into so many different media that it has almost reached the point where, as David Britt put it, "if I were naming CTW today, I would not name it the 'Children's *Television* Workshop' any more than the 'Children's Publishing Workshop' or 'Online Workshop.'"[33]

In many ways, the common thread in all of these efforts is actually quite similar to the thinking that underlay the original creation of *Sesame Street*. Much of the motivation for *Sesame Street* stemmed from the realization that large numbers of children were already watching television, and that the conventions of television could be used to benefit them. In the same way, these subsequent efforts have also sought to go "where kids are" (be it physical locations such as schools or child care settings, television channels and timeslots that attract large concentrations of viewers, or media such as the Internet) and use the conventions of these settings or contexts to educate and enrich children.

EXPANDING THE DOMESTIC AUDIENCE AND SUBJECT MATTER. When CTW first began, its focus was fairly narrowly limited to the production of *Sesame Street* and attempting to help disadvantaged children enter school with the preparation necessary to put them on an even footing with their higher peers of higher socioeconomic status. Yet, even older children do not all excel in school; the need for informal educational material to motivate children and supplement their more formal class-room instruction does not end when children enter first grade.

For this reason, when *Sesame Street* was experiencing its first flush of success and Lloyd Morrisett raised the question of what would come next, the eventual answer was to follow the reading curriculum begun by *Sesame Street* with a complementary series for school-age children, *The Electric Company*. As Morrisett recalled in 1997, there were two reasons for choosing school-age literacy for the workshop's next endeavor: "One was that literacy and reading were very important on the public agenda at the time, and there was no effective national response to the problem. Secondly, in terms of what we were trying to do—that is, get children ready to go to school—we were teaching letters and numbers in the preschool period. Reading was a natural next step for that."[34]

The Electric Company was built on the same spirit as *Sesame Street* and achieved a similar level of success. It was produced for six years, with repeats broadcast for eight more. During and after that time, CTW would continue to pursue television series for both preschool and school-age audiences, to handle school-age topics such as mathematics and problem solving (*Square One TV*) and science and technology (*3-2-1 Contact* and *Cro*), as well as to encourage preschoolers' socioemotional and cognitive development (*Big Bag*) and pursuit of challenges (the upcoming *Dragon Tales*). At the same time, *Sesame Street*'s educational curriculum also continued to expand, to incorporate topics as diverse as ecology, nutrition, and race relations for preschool children.

In addition, the years brought with them an increasing emphasis on creating materials for adults. While some CTW television efforts in the 1970s, such as *Feeling Good* or *Best of Families*, attempted to reach adult audiences, most of the Workshop's adult-oriented materials have attempted to help parents, caregivers, and educators better serve their children. The need for such efforts is twofold: on the one hand, while children certainly can and do learn from television (see the review of summative research below), a broadcast television series cannot provide a child with individualized feedback or conduct hands-on activities at the child's own pace; in this way, adult involvement can enrich an educational television experience immeasurably. On the other hand, many parents do not recognize the role they can serve in teaching their children.[35] The motivational power of well-produced educational television can be of great benefit to teachers and child care providers; in this way, hands-on materials and activities that grow out of television (or CTW-produced magazines such as *Sesame Street Parents* or *Creative Classroom*) can serve as rich additions to parents' and caregivers' repertoires.

EXPANDING INTERNATIONALLY. At the same time that CTW has expanded its efforts in domestic U.S. television, it has also broadened its reach to children internationally. To date, *Sesame Street* has aired in more than 140 countries around the world.

In some countries, *Sesame Street* has been seen in its original English-language form or dubbed into other languages. Still others have been coproductions; under this model, producers and educators native to a particular country work in partnership with CTW to create a version of *Sesame Street* that is culturally, as well as linguistically, appropriate to children in their country. Thus, for example, the Mexican *Plaza Sesamo* is set in a typical Latin American plaza, a setting that is familiar to the diverse population of children in the area.

To some degree, the educational goals of these international coproductions map directly onto those of the American *Sesame Street*; for example, almost every coproduction involves teaching letters and numbers. However, these curricula often include additional goal areas that are more specifically tailored to the needs of the country being served. For example, recent coproductions in Russia and Poland attempt to provide children with knowledge and skills they will need in their new, open societies (for example, critical thinking, conflict resolution, culture and diversity), and a significant portion of the curriculum for a joint Israeli-Palestinian coproduction (now being produced) centers on mutual respect.

The collaboration between native producers, educators, and researchers and their American counterparts from CTW helps to ensure that the final product that is broadcast is true to both the culture and needs of the native culture and to the style and philosophy of *Sesame Street*.

NEW SOURCES OF REVENUE. As noted earlier, it was not long after *Sesame Street* premiered that CTW personnel (led by Morrisett) recognized that the Workshop's existing government and foundation support would not be available at that level for long. Thus, while CTW continues to draw on such support to this day (for example, approximately one-half of the cost of *Cro* was covered by the National Science Foundation), there has been an ongoing effort to reduce CTW's dependence on outside funding and make the workshop more self-sufficient.

One of the primary means that has been used is a highly active program of product licensing. Beginning in the early 1970s, CTW established a Products group (then called the Nonbroadcast Materials division) to license books, records, and other products based on *Sesame Street*. In the years since then, the Products group has expanded tremendously, to license clothing, dolls, school supplies, developmental toys for infants, and a host of other products based on *Sesame Street* and other CTW television series around the world. In keeping with CTW's nonprofit status, any profits from these products (along with proceeds from the CTW magazines, interactive technology, and international television sales) are fed directly back into a pool that helps to support the production of *Sesame Street* and other CTW efforts.

In recent years, CTW has also attempted to draw income more directly from its extensive library of television programs by marketing existing television series internationally (as described above) or selling series that have gone out of production into domestic syndication. The first major inroads in domestic syndication came in 1996, when existing episodes of *Ghostwriter* (which had originally aired on PBS) were syndicated to commercial television stations across the United States.

At the same time, in producing new series and nontelevision projects, CTW has turned increasingly to partnerships with outside organizations that can help to share in the overhead entailed in developing and producing these projects. For example, the upcoming series *Dragon Tales* (expected to air on PBS in 1999) is being produced in partnership with Columbia TriStar Television. Taking this concept even further, *Big Bag* has been produced in partnership, not only with the Cartoon Network (which broadcasts the series), but also several foreign producers who have supplied or coproduced animated segments in collaboration with CTW.

These types of efforts in licensing, sales, and partnerships have been instrumental in keeping CTW in business and *Sesame Street* on the air fifteen years after *Sesame Street*'s last government grant from the Department of Education. As Cooney concluded, without the income that these efforts have provided for new television production, "*Sesame Street* would be a happy memory."[36]

STREAMLINING THE CTW MODEL. Naturally, all of the above points affect the process by which material is produced. For example, reductions in available funding mean that the production process itself must be made less expensive; in addition, the schedule for development of a new series on commercial television may be too short to allow for the kinds of lengthy, initial investigations described earlier. Therefore, just as it has been important to find new sources of revenue and to expand into new media and new outlets within television itself, it has been equally important to find ways to make the production process as efficient and inexpensive as possible. The challenge, then, has been to find a way to accomplish this without simultaneously lessening the quality or educational power of the final product.

In many ways, this has been made possible by *Sesame Street* and other CTW television series themselves. Recall that when *Sesame Street* was first being developed, no one had experience in creating this type of educational television; indeed, it was not even certain whether television could be effective as an educational tool for young children. Today, thanks to CTW's long history with *Sesame Street* and other series, such questions have long since been answered, and the Workshop has accumulated a great deal of expertise in creating entertaining, educational television series. Drawing on experiences with past projects to inform current efforts can help to make the process of development and production more efficient and economical.

As a concrete example, let us contrast the creation of *Sesame Street* with that of another, more recent CTW series, *Big Bag*. Like *Sesame Street*, *Big Bag* is a magazine-format television series for preschoolers that combines Muppets, live-action studio segments, music, and animation. Unlike *Sesame Street*, however, *Big Bag* was created for a commercial cable channel, the Cartoon Network, and it was created after CTW had accumulated more than twenty-five years of experience in educational television.

In many ways, *Big Bag* was produced under the same CTW model that had characterized the creation of *Sesame Street*. There was extremely close collaboration between production and research staff at all stages of the project, including the selection and development of characters and recurring formats, the writing of stories and scripts, production and editing of segments, and assembly of segments into finished shows. Like *Sesame Street*, *Big Bag* required the creation of specified educational curriculum goals, and a program of formative research informed the creation of material for the series.

At the same time, however, the process that characterized the creation of *Big Bag* was far less extensive than that for *Sesame Street*. At the earliest stages of development, the fact that television's potential for education had already been proven meant that *Big Bag* did not require the sort of feasibility study that Cooney had conducted in the mid-1960s. Additionally, while personnel needed to be recruited for *Big Bag* (just as had been done at the beginning of *Sesame Street*), much of the search could be conducted in-house. Many of the key production and research staff of *Big Bag* came to the project after working on other CTW series, including *Sesame Street*, *Square One TV*, *Cro*, and others. These staff people brought extensive experience to the project, along with a great deal of knowledge about the kinds of elements that were likely to work or not work in the new series. In addition, this experience meant that although much of the key personnel on *Big Bag* had not worked together before, they were already very familiar with the close collaboration prescribed by the CTW model.

As conceived by its creator, Executive Producer Nina Elias Bamberger, every episode of *Big Bag* would incorporate several four- to eight-minute animated series, most of which would be coproductions between CTW and various foreign animation producers. During the initial stages of development, Bamberger held a series of meetings to solicit opinions from in-house CTW staff on the direction of the series, from the standpoint of production, education, and international use. Simultaneously, a small production team (Bamberger and one associate producer, supported by Senior Vice President for Production Kalins) reviewed more than one hundred animation proposals and pilot films to select contenders for inclusion in the series.

Meanwhile, a three-person research team was at work assembling an advisory board and educational curriculum for the series. To ensure that the new series would complement, rather than compete with, *Sesame Street* on an educational level, it was decided that the primary focus of *Big Bag* would be on socioemotional development, rather than preacademic skills. Yet, *Big Bag* would work on a deeper level than most of the socioemotional programs on television; for example, where other series might tell children that it is good to share, *Big Bag* would show them *how* to arrive at a fair division or trade. In addition, the series incorporated a focus on the development of thinking skills such as imagination, investigation, and divergent thinking.

For reasons related to both production and education, the *Big Bag* team also decided to build a strong focus on viewer participation into

Table 11-2. *Goals of* Big Bag

1. To nurture preschoolers' socioemotional development by presenting positive models and examples (regarding, for example, cooperation, conflict resolution, responsibility)
2. To nurture preschoolers' developing cognitive skills, with a particular emphasis on fostering basic problem-solving skills and a disposition to think imaginatively, to risk failure when reasonable, and to be curious about one's surroundings
3. To invite viewers to be active participants, via stimulating, enjoyable activities (both physical and mental)

the series. From the standpoint of production, the use of participation would help to differentiate *Big Bag* from the many other preschool series on the air since, at the time, no other series placed as strong an emphasis on participation. From an educational standpoint, participation seemed to be a likely means to help draw viewers into the series more deeply, so that its educational messages might be even more powerful.

Even the process of assembling advisers and creating a curriculum was made considerably more efficient than had been the case in creating *Sesame Street*. Because *Sesame Street* was created in a vacuum, the input of more than eighty educational experts (including prominent academics, theorists, and preschool teachers) was needed to help shape its curriculum. Given the fact that *Big Bag* could be built off the success and experience of *Sesame Street* (and *Big Bag*'s significantly smaller resources), an exercise this extensive was neither possible nor necessary. Approximately one dozen candidates for the advisory board were screened to select a final board of six leading experts, almost all of whom had prior experience consulting for CTW; in fact, one of the advisers was Gerald Lesser, who had played a pivotal role in developing *Sesame Street*.

These six advisers were chosen because their fields of expertise complemented each other and, among them, spanned the final goals that were developed for *Big Bag* (see table 11-2; note that each of these broad goals is also divided into a number of subgoals). Apart from Lesser, one adviser was one of the world's leading authorities on children's social and moral development; one was an expert on creative thinking from Harvard's Project Zero; one had extensive experience in both multicultural education and the impact of television on children; one was a specialist in early education and storybook reading; and one was an expert on issues related to the Latino community (which was particularly important because one of the planned animations was set in the context of a Latino family).

The input that this handful of advisers brought from their various perspectives was invaluable in helping to develop the curriculum and shape material being created for the series. In contrast to the series of five three-day seminars that brought together advisers for *Sesame Street*, however, the *Big Bag* advisers were brought together only once, for approximately one and one-half days to help prepare for the first season of *Big Bag*. In the interest of efficiency (and minimizing travel costs), most of the interaction with advisers took place via telephone conversations with individual advisers on issues pertaining to their particular expertise, as well as their more general reactions to the materials as a whole. The larger advisory board meeting that brought all of the advisers together served primarily to allow the advisers an opportunity for debate and give-and-take among themselves and for firsthand interaction among advisers, producers, and writers.[37]

Efficiencies were able to be made in formative research as well. Throughout the first season of *Big Bag*, *Sesame Street*'s director of research served as an additional "unofficial adviser" to the project, answering questions and reviewing materials as needed. As a result, to the degree that questions that arose for *Big Bag* were similar to ones that had already been answered for *Sesame Street*, there was no need to conduct new formative research to rediscover the same answers. The approximately two dozen formative research studies that were conducted during the first season of *Big Bag* could thus be reserved for issues that were particular to the new series, such as comparing the appeal of potential animated coproductions or designs for new characters, or finding means of promoting viewer participation while watching (an area that is not emphasized on *Sesame Street*). (Conversely, some of the curriculum development and formative research methods developed for *Big Bag* have subsequently helped to inform later work on *Sesame Street* as well.)

All of the above efficiencies helped make it possible for *Big Bag* to be produced under the constraints of its funding, schedule, and available resources. Yet, it is equally important to note that, at the core of the series, there was the same commitment to quality (from the standpoint of both production and education) that underlay the success of *Sesame Street*. These efficiencies were arrived at, not by compromising the quality of the series, but by capitalizing on an accumulated body of knowledge and experience that contributes to the quality of all of CTW's new and continuing projects.

Conclusion

This section began with the observation that the world of the 1990s is very different than that of the 1960s when *Sesame Street* and CTW were first created. Today, the Workshop faces challenges related to competition, technology, and funding realities that could barely be imagined thirty years ago. Faced with such issues and constraints, it would be very easy for CTW to compromise its principles and cut back on the quality of the material it produces.

The challenge for CTW, then, has been (and continues to be) finding ways to remain true to its mission of both educating and entertaining children while continuing to function in a changing world.

Summative Research: The Impact of Educational Television

For producers of noneducational television, the ultimate standard by which success is measured is the number of viewers a program attracts, as measured by Nielsen ratings. By this standard, CTW has had considerable success; for example, *Sesame Street* continues to be one of the most highly rated preschool series on television, nearly thirty years after its creation.[38]

Because of CTW's educational mission, however, its standard for success lies not only in a series' popularity among viewers, but also in the educational impacts it exerts on those viewers. This impact is measured through *summative research*, conducted after a series has been produced to assess its impact on children's knowledge and/or attitudes regarding the educational content of the series. Summative research studies have been conducted to examine many of the series produced by CTW. Some of these studies are reviewed below.

Television and School Readiness: Sesame Street

Sesame Street is, perhaps, the most heavily researched series in the history of television. More than one thousand studies have examined *Sesame Street* and its power in areas such as literacy, number skills, and promoting prosocial messages, as well as formal features pertaining to issues such as children's attention. In the interest of space, this review will focus on only a few landmark studies.

EARLY SUMMATIVE RESEARCH. The educational impact of *Sesame Street* was first documented in a pair of studies conducted by the Educational Testing Service (ETS).[39] The first of these studies, conducted after the first season of production was completed, tested *Sesame Street*'s impact on a variety of cognitive skills. A geographically and ethnically diverse sample of nearly one thousand children aged three to five (most of whom were considered to be from disadvantaged backgrounds) were either encouraged or not encouraged to watch *Sesame Street* (at home or at school) during a twenty-six-week period; across the sample, exposure ranged from zero times per week to more than five. Before and after this twenty-six-week exposure, the children were tested via an extensive battery of measures that covered several dimensions: knowledge of the alphabet and numbers, names of body parts, recognition of forms, knowledge of relational terms, and sorting and classification skills.

The results of the study indicated that exposure to *Sesame Street* had the desired educational effects. Those children who watched the most showed the greatest pretest-posttest gains, and the areas that showed the greatest effects were those that had been emphasized the most in *Sesame Street* (for example, letters). These effects held across age (although three-year-olds showed the greatest gains, presumably because they knew the least when they came to the series), sex, geographic location, socioeconomic status (SES) (with low-SES children showing greater gains than middle-SES children), native language (English or Spanish), and whether the children watched at home or in school. Indeed, even when Thomas Cook and his colleagues conducted a reanalysis of these data that controlled statistically for other, potentially contributing factors such as a mother discussing *Sesame Street* with her child, the above effects were reduced but remained statistically significant.[40]

The second ETS study consisted of two components.[41] One was a replication of the earlier study, using season II shows that had been produced under a revised and expanded educational curriculum; this study confirmed the earlier results, finding effects in many of the same areas and in new areas that had been added in the second season (for example, roles of community members, counting to twenty rather than ten).

The second component was a follow-up study that examined 283 of the children from the season I study, about one-half of whom had begun school in the interim. Teachers were asked to rate all of the children in their classes on several dimensions (for example, verbal readiness, quantitative readiness, attitude toward school, relationship with peers), without knowing which ones had been *Sesame Street* viewers or were participating in the study. Results showed that, contrary to the claims of critics of *Sesame Street*, viewers were not bored, restless, or passive when they entered a formal classroom experience. Rather, frequent *Sesame Street* viewers were rated as better prepared for school than their non- or low-viewing classmates.

RECENT SUMMATIVE RESEARCH. The above results are echoed and extended by several recent studies of the effects of viewing *Sesame Street*. A three-year longitudinal study, conducted at the University of Kansas, examined the impact of *Sesame Street* on school readiness by tracking approximately 250 low-SES children from either two years to five years old or from four years to seven years old.[42] The study took into account, not only viewing of *Sesame Street*, but viewing of all television, as well as nontelevision activities (for example, reading, music, use of video games) and numerous contextual variables that have been found to affect academic achievement (for example, parents' own level of education, native language, preschool attendance). At regular intervals over the three years, children were tested with a broad range of measures, including standard tests such as the Peabody Picture Vocabulary Test and the Woodcock-Johnson Letter-Word Recognition Test.

The results of the study indicated that preschool children who watched educational programs—and *Sesame Street* in particular—spent more time reading and engaged in educational activities. In addition, these children performed significantly better than their peers on tests of letter-word knowledge, math skills, vocabulary size, and school readiness on age-appropriate standardized achievement tests. These differences remained significant even after the effects of various moderator variables (for example, parents' educational level, primary language spoken at home) were removed statistically. In addition, long-term effects were found when children subsequently entered school; for example, consistent with earlier data, teachers more often rated *Sesame Street* viewers as well adjusted to school.[43]

A second study was a correlational analysis of data from a national survey of the parents of approximately 10,000 children, originally collected for the U.S. Department of Education's National Household Education Survey in 1993.[44] This analysis found that preschoolers who viewed *Sesame Street* were more likely to be able to recognize letters of the alphabet and tell connected stories when pretending to read; these effects were strongest among children from low-income families, and held true even after the effects of other contributing factors (for example, parental reading, preschool attendance, parental education) were removed statistically. In addition, when they subsequently entered first and second grade, children who had viewed *Sesame Street* as preschoolers were also more likely to be reading storybooks on their own and less likely to require remedial reading instruction.

It is important to note that, because the data from this study are correlational, they do not conclusively indicate a causal relationship between *Sesame Street* viewing and these various educational outcomes. Nevertheless, they are highly suggestive and consistent with data from the University of Kansas study.

Finally, the longest-ranging evidence for the impact of *Sesame Street* is a "re-contact" study conducted at the University of Massachusetts at Amherst and the University of Kansas, reported in chapter 10 in this volume. To recap briefly here, this 1996 study examined high school students who either had or had not watched *Sesame Street* as preschoolers. Results indicated that viewing *Sesame Street* as a preschooler was significantly related to performance in high school; high school students who had watched *Sesame Street* as preschoolers had higher grades in English, mathematics, and science. They also used books more often, showed higher academic self-esteem, and placed a higher value on academic performance. These differences held true even after the students' early language skills as preschoolers and family background variables were factored out.

CONCLUSION. Together, these studies stand as powerful evidence of *Sesame Street*'s potential for helping to prepare children for school. This is not to say, of course, that *Sesame Street* is the only tool that should be used; certainly, hands-on experiences provided by parents and caregivers are vitally important and cannot be replaced. Nevertheless, preschool viewing of *Sesame Street* has been shown repeatedly to exert an impact on children, both immediately and once they enter school. Indeed, it appears that viewing *Sesame Street* can even contribute toward children's developing an ongoing love of learning that can stretch as far as high school.

Television and Literacy:
The Electric Company *and* Ghostwriter

CTW has produced two television series that attempted to promote literacy among school-age children too, *The Electric Company* and *Ghostwriter*. *The Electric Company* was a humorous, half-hour series that employed a magazine format, in which a number of short segments (typically comedy sketches, songs, and animations) made up a complete show. Among the more familiar elements of the series were "Letterman," a super hero who changed the letters in words (and thus, the objects that the words described, such as a "broom" into a "groom") to solve problems, and a series of "Silhouette Blends," in which silhouettes of two profiles faced each other, with print appearing on screen as the actors pronounced partial and complete words (for example, "bl-," "-ack," "black").

Ghostwriter was a very different series than *The Electric Company*, although it, too, was designed to promote literacy among school-age children. Launched in the fall of 1992, *Ghostwriter* was designed from its inception, not just as a television series, but as a multiple-media initiative that included efforts in television, outreach materials, magazines, books, promotional activities, software, licensed products, and videos for home and school (although the present discussion focuses on the television component). The *Ghostwriter* television series featured a multiethnic team of children who used literacy to plot their way out of jeopardy and solve mysteries. The team was aided by Ghostwriter, an invisible ghost who could communicate with them only via reading and writing.

Apart from the surface differences between the two series, there were differences in their underlying educational philosophies as well, for two basic reasons. One reason concerned the target age groups addressed by the two series; *The Electric Company* was aimed at poor readers in the second grade, while *Ghostwriter* was aimed at an older audience of seven- to ten-year-olds. A second reason was that nearly twenty years had elapsed between the creation of *The Electric Company* and *Ghostwriter*, and in that time, the state of the art in literacy education had changed. Leading educational practice in the early 1970s had been based in phonics instruction, so much of the focus of *The Electric Company* lay in demonstrating the correspondence between letters and their associated sounds. By the 1990s, educators' focus had shifted greatly. As a result, *Ghostwriter* focused more on strategic approaches to reading and writing (for example, taking a second look, rewriting) than on letter sounds. Despite these different foci, however, research data demonstrated that both television series had significant impacts on children within their respective areas and age groups.

THE ELECTRIC COMPANY.   After the first season of *The Electric Company* was produced, researchers from the Educational Testing Service conducted an experimental/control, pretest-posttest study in which more than 8,000 first- through fourth-grade children participated.[45] Approximately one-half of the children were shown *The Electric Company* in school for six months, while the remaining children were not. Before and after the six-month exposure period, all of the children completed a paper-and-pencil battery of assessments that addressed all of *The Electric Company*'s nineteen goal areas (for example, the ability to read consonant blends, digraphs, sight words, and final E, among others); a subset of more than one thousand children were also tested orally in one-on-one sessions with researchers.

The data showed that exposure to *The Electric Company* resulted in significant gains in almost all of the nineteen goal areas, thus covering a broad range of reading skills associated with phonics instruction, as well as gains in children's ability to read for meaning. These gains were greatest for younger children (first and second graders), presumably because they had shown the lowest initial performance in the pretest. (Recall also that *The Electric Company*'s target audience was poor readers in the second grade.) The effects held across sex, ethnicity, and native language (English or Spanish).

A follow-up evaluation of *The Electric Company* was conducted after its second season.[46] Participants in the study were more than 1,700 children, including children who had participated in the 1973 study when they were in first or second grade; the measures were largely identical to those used in the earlier study.[47]

Data from the pretest (that is, before children saw any additional episodes of *The Electric Company*) indicated that the effect of viewers' initial exposure sustained itself, even though the children could not have watched the series during the several-month interval between studies, because it was not on the air in those cities. The effects of viewing season

II parallelled those of season I (although they were not as pronounced), but the effect of viewing two seasons was not considerably greater than the effect of viewing one. Thus, it seemed that the major impact of *The Electric Company* came from the children's initial six-month exposure to the series, and this impact was sufficiently long-term to sustain itself several months after viewing.

GHOSTWRITER. To date, there have been no experimental/control studies of the impact of *Ghostwriter*. However, many of the findings from existing *Ghostwriter* research point to its success in encouraging positive attitudes toward reading and writing, and in providing children with compelling opportunities to engage in such behaviors.

On the most basic level, children's initial engagement with *Ghostwriter* itself provided numerous opportunities to become involved in reading and writing. A central component of the *Ghostwriter* television series was print on screen (for example, in the form of messages to and from Ghostwriter, a variety of print-based clues, and characters' recording information in their "casebooks"). Several studies have shown that viewers typically read this on-screen print; one survey found that 83 percent of respondents said they read along, and an additional 8 percent "sometimes" did so. Many viewers also kept *Ghostwriter* casebooks in which they recorded clues along with the characters on screen; one study found that approximately 25 percent of the girls who viewed *Ghostwriter* kept casebooks, and about 20 percent of the children said they regularly wrote in code.[48]

Yet, perhaps the clearest evidence of *Ghostwriter*'s impact on children's pursuit of literacy activities comes from the tremendous numbers of children who wrote letters to *Ghostwriter* and participated in mail-in contests that required them to engage in complex activities such as writing songs or creating their own original super-heroes. Such activities were almost completely self-motivated on the part of children, and many reported that it was the first time they had written a letter. Thus, children's participation in such activities required substantial effort—not only in writing the letters themselves, but also in learning how to address an envelope, obtaining the necessary postage, using zip codes, and so on. Despite all of these potential obstacles, more than 450,000 children wrote letters to *Ghostwriter* during its first two seasons.[49] The fact that so many children chose to engage in these types of activities stands as powerful evidence of *Ghostwriter*'s ability to motivate children to become engaged in reading and writing.

Television and Mathematics: Square One TV

Square One TV was a series about mathematics and problem solving, aimed at eight- to twelve-year-old children. The magazine-format series incorporated studio sketches (featuring a seven-player repertory company), game shows (using real children as contestants), short films, music videos, animation, and an ongoing mathematical detective serial, "Mathnet." The goals of the series were to promote positive attitudes toward mathematics, promote the use and application of problem-solving processes, and present sound mathematical content in an interesting, accessible, and meaningful manner.

Over the life of the series, several summative studies were conducted to gauge its impact.[50] The most powerful of these studies was an experimental/control, pretest-posttest comparison of viewers and nonviewers of *Square One TV*, which assessed the series' impact on children's problem-solving behavior and attitudes toward mathematics.[51]

In this study, fifth graders in two public elementary schools in Corpus Christi, Texas (where *Square One TV* had not been broadcast), viewed thirty episodes of *Square One TV* over a period of eight weeks, while their counterparts in two other schools did not. A subsample of forty-eight children (twenty-four viewers and twenty-four nonviewers), individually matched for sex, SES, ethnicity, and performance on a standardized mathematics test, participated in extensive, task-based interviews before and after the eight-week viewing period. The CTW interviewers and coders did not know which children were viewers and which were not, and the children did not know of the interviewers' connection to *Square One TV*.

The interview consisted of two components, one of which assessed the children's problem-solving ability and the other of which gauged their attitudes toward mathematics. Pretest-posttest comparisons of viewers and nonviewers showed significant positive effects in both areas.

Problem solving was tested via several hands-on, nonroutine mathematical problem-solving activities (PSAs), each of which could be solved through a number of approaches. For example, one set of problems presented children with a mathematical game and asked them to figure out what was wrong with the game and how to fix it. (In fact, the problem lay in probability—one player had a much greater chance of winning—and there were several valid ways to fix it.) From pretest to posttest, viewers showed significant gains in the number and variety of problem-solving actions and heuristics they used to solve problems (for example, looking for patterns, transforming problems); at the posttest, viewers used a significantly greater number and variety than nonviewers. At the same time, viewers showed significant gains in the mathematical completeness and sophistication of their solutions; that is, their solutions to two of the three sets of PSAs became significantly more complete and sophisticated after watching the thirty episodes of *Square One TV*, while nonviewers showed no significant change. Thus, exposure to *Square One TV* affected both the ways children worked on problems and the solutions they reached, effects that occurred regardless of the children's sex, ethnicity, SES, or performance on standardized mathematics tests.

Effects on attitudes fell within several domains. Some noteworthy effects were the following: viewers showed a broader conception of what "math" is (that is, beyond basic arithmetic) than nonviewers, a greater desire than nonviewers to pursue challenging mathematical tasks, and significantly greater gains than nonviewers in the number of times they spontaneously talked about enjoying mathematics and problem solving throughout the interview (that is, without being asked directly about enjoyment). Again, there was no consistent effect of sex, ethnicity, or SES.

Thus, the data indicated that *Square One TV* was successful in exerting a significant effect on children's problem-solving behavior and attitudes toward mathematics. In particular, the series exerted a significant effect on girls and minority children, two populations that have been considered to be "at risk" for mathematics education.[52]

Television and Science: 3-2-1 Contact and Cro

To date, CTW has produced two television series to address science and technology for school-age children. The first was *3-2-1 Contact*, a magazine-format series that relied heavily on live-action minidocumentary segments in which teenage hosts investigated scientific topics or interviewed real scientists in a variety of fields and settings. In addition, the series also included animations, songs, and a dramatized mystery serial called "The Bloodhound Gang." Each week of shows was built around a specific theme, such as scaling, electricity, or outer space, with many of that week's segments corresponding to some aspect of that theme.

The second series, *Cro*, was very different. *Cro* was a half-hour, Saturday-morning animated series about technology that featured the humorous adventures of an 11-year-old Cro-Magnon boy, his Neanderthal "family," and the talking woolly mammoths who were their friends, as they used a variety of scientific concepts and simple machines to overcome the obstacles of their prehistoric world. The main body of each show was set in the Ice Age, with relatively brief framing sequences (starring a Latina scientist, an African-American boy, and a well-preserved mammoth) set in the present.

Though very different in their execution, both series were found to have a significant impact on their viewers.

3-2-1 CONTACT. Research on the impact of *3-2-1 Contact* is somewhat limited by the methodologies used; almost all of the studies that have been conducted rely largely on paper-and-pencil (typically multiple-choice) quizzes to assess comprehension and on pencil-and-paper checklists (for example, concerning occupations that children would like to have or that they believe involve science) to assess impact on science interest, rather than on interview methods that might provide richer portraits of children's knowledge and attitudes.

Despite this limitation, however, a consistent pattern of effects has been observed with regard to comprehension. Studies have varied in the number of episodes presented to children (from ten to more than forty). At all levels of exposure, these studies have been unanimous in demonstrating that viewing *3-2-1 Contact* resulted in positive effects on children's comprehension of the science topics presented, as reflected in significant increases in viewers' performance on pencil-and-paper quizzes.[53]

Moderate, and less consistent, effects have been observed on children's interest in science and images of scientists across these studies, although it is not clear whether *3-2-1 Contact* had less impact in this area, or whether the more moderate effects were a function of the relatively limited measures used.

The effects of *3-2-1 Contact* were often strongest among girls, one of the populations that has often been found to demonstrate lower levels of science achievement.[54]

CRO. Perhaps the strongest evidence for the effects of *Cro* comes from a summative study conducted after its second season.[55] This study adopted an experimental/control, pretest/posttest design in which children who viewed eight episodes of *Cro* were compared with nonviewers, who watched eight episodes of another animated educational series that did not concern science (*Where on Earth Is Carmen Sandiego?*). The study used multiple measures (including pencil-and-paper measures, in-depth interviews, and behavioral observations of children as they chose to engage in technology-related vs. -unrelated activities) to examine *Cro*'s impact on children's interest in and understanding of science and technology.

The results showed significant differences between viewers and nonviewers in their understanding of the technology content of four episodes of *Cro* (that is, all of the episodes tested for comprehension). As in the case of *3-2-1 Contact*, these effects were often strongest for girls, one of the populations deemed to be "at risk" for dropping out of science.

Cro was also found to produce a variety of significant effects concerning interest. Some of these were: *Cro* viewers showed significantly greater pretest-posttest gains than nonviewers in their interest in doing *Cro*-related technology activities (for example, making a catapult), exhibited greater interest in learning more about the technology content of particular episodes, and were significantly more likely to engage in hands-on activities connected to two of the episodes when given a choice among these activities and other, nontechnology activities.

Conclusion

Taken together, these studies provide a strong and compelling answer to Lloyd Morrisett's 1966 question of whether television could be used to educate children. The effects of educational television have been found to be powerful for both preschool and school-age children, and to span a broad range of subject areas, including school readiness, literacy, mathematics and problem solving, and science and technology. In addition, the few studies that have evaluated series longitudinally have shown their effects to be long-lasting as well.

As Edward R. Murrow observed in the quotation that began this chapter, television has the potential to teach, illuminate, and inspire. It needs merely to be used . . . and used well.

The Future

For many reasons, the first season of *Sesame Street* was referred to as the "first experimental season," and it is significant that the season currently in production (at the time of this writing) is referred to as the "twenty-ninth experimental season." CTW began as an experiment, and that experiment continues. Throughout its history, CTW has survived and succeeded by adapting to its changing environment while, at its core, remaining true to its mission of educating and entertaining children. As David Britt put it, "This organization made its mark by putting [educational media and the marketplace] together without losing its way or compromising its principles."[56]

Naturally, this balance is not easy to maintain. Considerable time and effort have been spent on a continuous basis to help ensure that CTW's efforts are sufficiently responsive to the current state of the broadcast or funding environment while not sacrificing the elements that are vital to meeting the company's educational goals. For example, consider CTW's two series about science and technology, *3-2-1 Contact* and *Cro*. *Cro* was produced as a Saturday-morning, animated series for a commercial broadcaster, which meant that it was subject to very different constraints (for example, smaller budget, shorter production timeline) than *3-2-1 Contact*, which had premiered a decade earlier on PBS. Yet, despite these different constraints and the different demands they placed on production, summative research showed both series to hold significant educational benefits for children, promoting their knowledge of science and technology and (where tested) their attitudes as well.

At the time of this writing, no one can know what the future of television and other mass media will hold. The rapid growth of cable, satellite television, and the Internet (to name but a few) raises more questions than it answers; will one of these become the dominant consumer medium of the future, or will it be something else entirely? The opportunities are great, and the challenges are, too. Still, whatever form the media landscape takes, one thing is relatively certain: CTW will continue to adapt, using any means at its disposal to help meet the needs of children.

Notes

1. J. G. Cooney, *The Potential Uses of Television in Preschool Education: A Report to the Carnegie Corporation of New York* (New York: Carnegie Corporation, 1966).
2. Ibid., p. 38.

3. Personal communication, 1997.

4. Cooney, *The Potential Uses of Television*, p. 10.

5. *Sesame Street* sales tape (New York: Children's Television Workshop, 1969).

6. See, for example, K. W. Mielke, "Research and Development at the Children's Television Workshop," *Educational Technology Research and Development*, vol. 38 (Winter, 1990), pp. 7–16.

7. Quoted in H. W. Land, *The Children's Television Workshop: How and Why It Works* (Jericho, N.Y.: Nassau Board of Cooperative Educational Services, 1972), p. 34.

8. D. D. Connell, and E. L. Palmer, "Sesame Street: A Case Study," in J. D. Halloran and M. Gurevitch, eds., *Broadcaster/Researcher Cooperation in Mass Communication Research* (Leeds, England: Kavanagh and Sons, 1971), p. 67.

9. Connell and Palmer, "Sesame Street: A Case Study," p. 67.

10. G. S. Lesser, *Children and Television: Lessons from Sesame Street* (Vintage Books/Random House, 1974), pp. 42–43.

11. Ibid., p. 54.

12. A complete listing of the original goals for *Sesame Street* can be found in Lesser, *Children and Television*.

13. M. Scriven, "The Methodology of Evaluation," *AERA Monograph Series on Curriculum Evaluation*, vol. 1 (AERA, 1967), pp. 39–83.

14. Like *Sesame Street* itself, the methods used in formative research have also undergone continual reevaluation and refinement. In subsequent years, the distractor method was streamlined to an "eyes-on-screen" methodology that eliminated the need for slides. In this method, visual attention to television is set against the naturally occurring distractions present in the room where testing occurs (typically a day care center or other child care setting). More recently, researchers have begun to experiment with "engagement ratings" that take into account not only visual attention but also other behavioral indicators of engagement with televised material.

15. S. Y. Gibbon and E. L. Palmer, *Pre-reading on Sesame Street* (New York: Children's Television Workshop, 1970), p. 9.

16. Lesser, *Children and Television*.

17. Ibid.

18. Ibid.

19. Personal communication, 1997.

20. Personal communication, 1997.

21. Personal communication, 1997. As a more recent, parallel example of the positive potential of public tragedies, Israeli Prime Minster Yitzhak Rabin was assassinated during a 1996 series of curriculum seminars for a joint Israeli-Palestinian coproduction of *Sesame Street*. Despite the political realities of the region, the assassination of Rabin (who had been a central figure in the Mideast peace process) galvanized the group and motivated them to set aside their differences and push the project forward.

22. Ibid.

23. Personal communication, 1997.

24. Personal communication, 1997.

25. Ibid.

26. Sec. 103 [a] [2].

27. Condry and others, "Children's Television before and after the Children's Television Act of 1990," poster presented at the Society for Research in Child Development, New Orleans, 1993; and D. Kunkel and J. Canepa, "Broadcasters' License Renewal Claims regarding Children's Educational Programming," *Journal of Broadcasting and Electronic Media*, vol. 38 (Fall 1994), pp. 397–416.

28. Federal Communications Commission, FCC Notice of Proposed Rule Making, FCC 95-143 (Washington, 1995), p. 11.

29. Federal Communications Commission, "Report and Order: In the Matter of Policies and Rules concerning Children's Television Programming," *FCC Record*, vol. 6 (April 1991), pp. 2111–27.

30. Quoted in Land, *The Children's Television Workshop*, p. 204.

31. Nielsen Media Research, *National Television Index* (Northbrook, Ill., 1990).

32. Children's Defense Fund, *The State of America's Children, 1991* (Washington, 1991).

33. Personal communication, 1997.

34. Personal communication, 1997.

35. For example, Children's Defense Fund, *The State of America's Children*, p. 80.

36. Personal communication, 1997.

37. It is noteworthy that the extensive use of multiple curriculum seminars is still used in creating new international coproductions of *Sesame Street*. While the International Television group within CTW has also, certainly, accumulated a great deal of expertise over the years, the CTW model is a new process to virtually every new coproducer. Many indigenous producers may come to process with little experience in creating educational television for children, let alone extensive collaboration with educators and researchers. Thus, these more extensive curriculum seminars can serve the same purpose for coproducers that they served for the original *Sesame Street* team in the United States, and the process can later be streamlined in subsequent seasons.

38. Nielsen Media Research, *National Television Index* (Northbrook, Ill., 1997).

39. S. Ball and G. A. Bogatz, *The First Year of Sesame Street: An Evaluation* (Princeton, N.J.: Educational Testing Service, 1970); and G. A. Bogatz and S. Ball, *The Second Year of Sesame Street: A Continuing Evaluation* (Princeton, N.J.: Educational Testing Service, 1971).

40. T. D. Cook and others, Sesame Street *Revisited* (New York: Russell Sage Foundation, 1975).

41. Bogatz and Ball, *The Second Year of Sesame Street*.

42. J. C. Wright and A. C. Huston, *Effects of Educational TV Viewing of Lower Income Preschoolers on Academic Skills, School Readiness, and School Adjustment One to Three Years Later: A Report to the Children's Television*

Workshop (University of Kansas, Center for Research on the Influences of Television on Children, 1995).

43. Bogatz and Ball, *The Second Year of Sesame Street*.

44. N. Zill, E. Davies, and M. Daly, *Viewing of Sesame Street by Preschool Children and Its Relationship to School Readiness: Report Prepared for the Children's Television Workshop* (Rockville, Md.: Westat, Inc., 1994).

45. S. Ball and G. A. Bogatz, *Reading with Television: An Evaluation of The Electric Company* (Princeton, N.J.: Educational Testing Service, 1973).

46. Ball and others, *Reading with Television: A Follow-up Evaluation of The Electric Company* (Princeton, N.J.: Educational Testing Service, 1974).

47. Ball and Bogatz, *Reading with Television*.

48. Nielsen New Media Services, *Study, Wave II: May, 1993* (Dunedin, Fla., 1993); and KRC Research and Consulting, *An Evaluative Assessment of the Ghostwriter Project* (New York, 1994).

49. Children's Television Workshop, *Learning from Ghostwriter*: Strategies and Outcomes (New York, 1994).

50. For example, T. Peel and others, *Square One Television: The Comprehension and Problem Solving Study* (New York: Children's Television Workshop, 1987); and L. Schauble and B. Peel, *"Mathnet" Format on Square One: Children's Informal Problem Solving, Understanding of Mathematical Concepts, and Ideas and Attitudes about Mathematics* (New York: Children's Television Workshop, 1986).

51. E. R. Hall and others, *Children's Problem-Solving Behavior and their Attitudes toward Mathematics: A Study of the Effects of Square One TV*, vols. 1–5 (New York: Children's Television Workshop, 1990); and E. R. Hall, E. T. Esty, and S. M. Fisch, "Television and Children's Problem-Solving Behavior: A Synopsis of an Evaluation of the Effects of *Square One TV*," *Journal of Mathematical Behavior*, vol. 9 (October 1990), pp. 161–74.

52. For example, National Research Council, *Everybody Counts: A Report to the Nation on the Future of Mathematics Education* (Washington: National Academy Press, 1989).

53. A. Cambre and D. Fernie, *Formative Evaluation of Season IV, 3-2-1 Contact: Assessing the Appeal of Four Weeks of Educational Television Programs and Their Influence on Children's Science Comprehension and Science Interest* (New York: Children's Television Workshop, 1985); J. Johnston, *An Exploratory Study of the Effects of Viewing the First Season of 3-2-1 Contact* (New York: Children's Television Workshop, 1980); J. Johnston and R. Luker, *The "Eriksson Study": An Exploratory Study of Viewing Two Weeks of the Second Season of 3-2-1 Contact* (New York: Children's Television Workshop, 1983); and S. Wagner, *Evaluation of the Fourth Season of 3-2-1 Contact* (New York: Children's Television Workshop, 1985).

54. T. Levin, N. Sabar, and Z. Libman, "Achievements and Attitudinal Patterns of Boys and Girls in Science," *Journal of Research in Science Teaching*, vol. 28 (January 1991), pp. 31–328.

55. A. L. Fay and others, *Children's Interest in and Their Understanding of Science and Technology: A Study of the Effects of Cro* (Pittsburgh, Pa. and New

York, N.Y.: University of Pittsburgh Children's Television Workshop, 1995); and S. M. Fisch and others, "Can Television Increase Children's Interest in Science and Technology?: The Impact of *Cro*," poster presented at the sixty-second annual meeting of the Society for Research in Child Development, 1997.

56. Personal communication, 1997.

CHAPTER TWELVE

Children's Television in European Public Broadcasting

Jay G. Blumler

Europe offers fascinating terrain at present for students of the interplay between established broadcasting systems and powerful currents of media change and social change. As is well known, in most European countries television was almost entirely in the hands of public broadcasting organizations until the 1980s. But since that time, their broadcasting systems have been transformed by (still ongoing) impulses of multichannel expansion; the introduction of private terrestrial, cable, and satellite services; the ever-intensifying competition for audiences and revenue to which all players, public and private alike, have been subjected; and increasing attempts by global entrepreneurs to tap European markets through both ownership of transnational services and program sales.

The responses of national policymakers to these developments have varied from country to country, but few wished to abandon their public service broadcasting systems entirely to the commercial wolves. Many were aware of certain values, which those systems had been created to support, and which still deserved some institutional embodiment or protection. Only France went so far as to privatize a public television channel. Germany, however, has guaranteed its public service broadcasters' roles and rights in almost constitutional terms. In Britain too, the BBC has been assured of an important role and access to public funds for some years ahead, while its main advertising-funded competitor (ITV) must meet defined programming obligations (for news, current affairs, regional, religious, and children's programs) under a relatively detailed regulatory regime.

Even so, all European public broadcasters have been on the defensive in this period, though in different degrees and on different fronts. Audience shares have fallen, and adaptive programming and scheduling strategies have been followed. Afraid to leave untended any hours of the day or night in which their commercial rivals were transmitting, many increased the amount of time they were on air—by over a quarter on average between 1991 and 1995 according to one survey (see below). This aggravated their financial problems, which were already worsening owing to shrinking real-term revenues and rising production costs. Analyses of European public broadcasters' schedules suggest that the program profiles of some have also been changing—with higher proportions of entertainment and fiction, serious programs moved out of prime time or tabloidized, and more program imports.

In the European public service broadcasting scheme of things, children's television long had a special place—and one that was quite different from its cartoon-dominated, advertising-permeated, and toy-ridden U.S. counterpart. Children were to be treated not as commercial consumers but more as all-round developing personalities and future citizens. This meant that broadcasters should devote a significant part of their output to children; that such programming should span a broad range of genres, including drama, news, awareness-building documentaries, introductions to the arts and ways of life in other lands, and so on; and that they should take account of differences in children's stages of development, offering programs suited specifically to toddlers as well as for children at school and adolescents. Children's programming fashioned by such principles could even be regarded as central to and a supreme expression of the basic public service philosophy. Children's television is therefore an interesting and important test case of the survivability of the public service idea in these highly volatile and pressured times

Professor Daniel Biltereyst of the University of Leuven and I recently conducted a pan-European survey.[1] The results have shed some light on this issue. In autumn 1996 we sent a questionnaire to the heads of the children's programming departments of all public broadcasters who belonged to the European Broadcasting Union. Among other things, this covered the amount of programming the departments provided for children, how it is scheduled, whether and how it is targeted at children of different ages, the range offered (that is, how it is distributed across informational programs, drama, animation, and other entertainment), proportions of domestic and imported productions screened, recent trends in audience share, responses to competition, creation of Web sites, and whether the future looked hopeful—and why. On the whole, a good response was received from twenty-five organizations in seventeen countries providing programs for children on a total of thirty-nine channels, amounting to 55 percent of the contacted departments.

The evidence from this survey was enriched by linkages to two other sources of data. One afforded a perspective on key developments across a recent period of time. The other enabled significant influences on the work of children's television providers to be identified, stemming from differences in their broadcasting systems and environments.

Possibilities of cross-time analysis arose from an earlier questionnaire-based survey, which Bilterreyst had conducted for the European Broadcasting Union in 1994, asking about the provision of children's television in 1991 and 1993. This covered thirty-five television channels of twenty-two broadcasters, about a half of whom also participated in our 1996 study. And it allowed us to calculate key trends over time—from 1991 to 1995—in the amount of children's programming that European public broadcasters provide and the proportion of domestically made programs in the output for children.

The second additional data source was the 1996 European Audiovisual Observatory *Statistical Yearbook: Cinema, Television, Video and New Media in Europe.* From information available in it we compiled a set of eleven of what we called "external variables" about the broadcasting organizations to which the children's departments belonged. Those variables dealt with such matters as their market shares, exposure to commercial competition, how far they were funded from public or commercial revenues, and overall programming profiles. We also divided the departments by the cultural regions in which they were located—Nordic, Anglo-German, Romance, and eastern Europe—and by country size (singling out respondents located in the large countries of the United Kingdom, Germany, and France from the rest).

This is not the place to present our findings in detail.[2] Instead, I highlight those parts of the evidence that illustrate the fate, in today's new media conditions, of public television for children in Europe.

Where the Tradition Stands Firm

From one perspective, these children's services look as principled as ever. At a philosophic level, many respondents wrote eloquently when asked about their departments' goals and objectives and about their commitments to diversity of provision, respect for young viewers as developing human beings and members of society, presenting their national value systems and cultures in terms that children can understand, and maintaining high standards of program quality overall.

The response was backed up by several tangible indicators of such policies in practice. For example, most of the departments target their programs to meet the needs of different groups, typically fine-tuning the child audience into as many as three or four age categories (including, in all cases except two, materials designed to serve the low-audience group of preschoolers). Most departments are responsible for substantial programming and therefore air time—amounting on average to 9.5 percent of their parent broadcasters' total transmission time. Typically, that programming is provided, not only on Saturday and Sunday morning but also every weekday—often in the late afternoons when children have returned home from school. If one criterion of a good children's television service is provision when children are available to view, this part of the European public service record is still positive.

Moreover, the status of children's television in Europe's public broadcasting organizations seems relatively high. This is not to suggest that they can rival the bigger battalions of broadcast news, fiction, and sport or that they are sheltered from internal problems, challenges, and struggles for resources. In pressured times, senior executives may subordinate their interests to those of the larger organization. Nevertheless, the survey showed that most children's programming is provided by dedicated departments, staffed by heads and producers who have specialized in this area of work. Most of them also enjoy a significant say in how their programs are scheduled. Only three of the responding departments reported that this was out of their hands.

But perhaps the most striking sign of vibrancy emerged from the respondents' answers to a question about whether on balance they were "hopeful" or "pessimistic" about "the future prospects for children's television in your country." Despite all the problems and uncertainties of children's television today and all the pressures from a surging commercial sector, almost all said they were hopeful compared with only three who felt pessimistic. This is an important result, suggesting that most of the departments still draw confidence from the distinctiveness and social importance of a principled public broadcasting service for children.

Trends over Time

The picture changes, however, when we look at how the children's programming of Europe's public service broadcasters has evolved over time. Two significant trends emerged from our longitudinal data analysis, comparing 1991 with 1995. One concerned the amount of children's programming supplied by the departments. The other concerned the relative weight of domestic and imported materials in the output.

First, there has been a Europewide expansion in the amount of children's programming in the public broadcasters' schedules. It should be recalled that from 1991 to 1995 the number of clock hours covered by Europe's public broadcasters had increased by over a quarter (in our sample by 29 percent on average). The figures from our respondents for children's programming specifically show that this increase had kept pace with overall programming time, having increased by 28 percent in the same period. This trend applied without exception to all the broadcasters who responded to both surveys, ranging from a low of a 9 percent increase (for the BBC and Channel 4 in the UK) up to highs of 66 percent (Czech television) and even 96 percent (one of the Dutch channels). Thus, programming for the child audience was not marginalized in these increasingly competitive years. On the contrary, it appears that children's television came to play a central part in the public broadcasters' strategic response to the new media environment, facilitating the overall extension of time, filling new time slots, and combating the commercial competition.

In this context, the second main trend is startling. Despite the increased number of hours devoted to children's television, domestically produced children's programming actually declined from 1991 to 1995— absolutely and not just proportionately. This was almost a universal phenomenon, the only exceptions being ZDF (a German broadcaster), Danish R/TV, and Channel 4 in the United Kingdom. As an average for the entire sample, domestic production was down from 203 hours per department in 1991 to 177 hours four years later. The same period witnessed a heavy increase in imports—from an average of 202 hours in 1991 to 340 hours in 1995. Put another way, reliance on domestically made children's programming fell from an average of about 45 minutes of the total offer of 75 minutes in 1991 to about 33 minutes of the 105 minutes scheduled in 1995. That is a drop from approximately half of the total children's output to about a third.

It is true that in 1995 domestic material was still the most important source of children's programs for most European public broadcasters. But imports from the United States were now a close second. The sources of programming were as follows: domestic production, 37 percent; United States, 29 percent; other European countries, 18 percent; Australia, 7 percent; Japan, 2 percent; and other, 6 percent. Six of the twenty-five respondents were even screening more U.S.-made children's programs than domestic production, namely BRTN (Flemish-speaking Belgium), France 2, RTE (in Ireland), Romanian Television, TSI (the Italian Swiss broadcaster), and Channel 4.

It also seems that these trends—in the amounts and origins of children's programming—are related to and probably responsible for a third.

Program Range

Diversity of provision is often regarded as a core feature of public service television for children. As noted above, it took pride of place in many respondents' ideas about the policies that they should be pursuing.

But how does the programming practice of European public television match up to this ideal? Unfortunately, no longitudinal data are available on this point for our sample of broadcasters. What we do have is their estimates of the proportions of their children's programming hours that were devoted to drama, animation, other entertainment and factual material, respectively, in 1995. The full results, which appear broadcaster-by-broadcaster in table 12-1, are sobering. Three main points stand out from these data.

First, one is struck by enormous variations in the mix of program types offered to children by the different European public broadcasters. Each profile is virtually unique. The amount of animation provided, for example, ranges from 17 percent or less of the output (seven organizations) to 20–40 percent (six), to 45–60 percent (five) and more than 60 percent (among three broadcasters, registering 61 percent, 80 percent, and 85 percent, respectively).

Second, although most respondents probably offer a more diverse pallet of children's television than do their commercial competitors or than do the big U.S. suppliers, their commitments to range seem less impressive than might have been expected. Of course, there is no objective measure of what counts as a sufficiently diverse program offer. But if we define a diverse children's schedule as one in which no category takes up 50 percent or more of programming time and no category falls below 11 percent, then only about half of the respondents reached that standard. And if the figures are converted into the average number of hours devoted by the whole sample of European broadcasters to each of the four program genres, animation tops the list:

	Average yearly output	
	Hours	Percent
Animation	206	40
Other entertainment	107	21
Drama	104	20
Factual	99	19

This presumably reflects the fact that in competitive conditions, animation has many advantages: appealing to a broad all-age audience, easy to schedule, and amply available at low cost on the international market.

Third, there are big regional variations in European public broadcasters' approaches to the range of children's programming. The Nordic stations perform particularly well as far as range is concerned. These broadcasters are strongly drama oriented (35 percent of the children's output), while animation accounts for less than a fifth. At the opposite end of the spectrum, we find the Romance stations with a huge share of animated material (56 percent) and only a tenth reserved for information. The Anglo-German stations rely quite heavily on animation as well (43 percent), but they also devote a larger proportion of their children's output to factual programming (23 percent) than do the broadcasters in the other regions.

	Program profiles by region (%)			
	Nordic	Romance	E. Europe	AngloGerman
Drama	35	18	25	15
Animation	17	56	29	43
Other entertainment	27	16	25	19
Factual	20	10	20	23
	99	100	99	100

We also suspect that children's programming in European public television has become less diverse than it used to be, though no direct evidence is available on this question. But reduced diversity could be a

Table 12-1. *Program Range by Cultural Region*

Region and broadcaster	Percent of children's output according to type of program[a]			
	Drama	Animation	Other entertainment	Factual
Nordic				
YLE Finland	20	30	30	20
SVT Sweden	49	14	20	17
NRK Norway	25	15	40	20
DR/TV Denmark	35	15	25	25
Anglo-German				
BBC UK	13	30	25	32
ITV UK	15	33	33	20
Ch. 4 UK	10	80	—	10
RTE Ireland	5	55	35	5
ZDF Germany	30	30	15	25
NOS Netherlands	17	17	15	51
BRTN Flemish Belgium	25	61	13	10
Romance				
F2 France	20	60	13	7
F3 France	10	85	4	1
TSR Sw. Fr.[b]	40	45	15	—
TSI Sw. It.[c]	23	10	44	22
RTP Protugal	12	51	18	18
East European				
MTV Hungary	10	—	50	40
RTV Romania	35	30	15	20
CT Czech.	42	26	7	25
Rost Russia	20	50	15	15
AR Croatia	—	10	75	15

a. Broadcasters' estimates for 1996.
b. French-speaking Swiatrland.
c. Italian-speaking Switzerland.

consequence of the other two trends manifest in our longitudinal data: the increase in the number of hours devoted to children's television (diluting range thereby); and the steep decline in the amount of domestically produced programming for children (entailing more recourse to imported animation).

Indeed, two empirical associations within our survey data are in line with our suspicions.

First, it turns out that the amount of children's television provided by the departments in 1995 was closely correlated with its range. That is, those broadcasters with the highest output of children's programming (over 1,000 hours annually) relied predominantly on animation (for

53 percent of their output) in contrast to the skimpiest programmers (scheduling 500 hours or less) who devoted only 16 percent of their output to animation.

Second, a similar relationship obtains between reliance on domestic production and the balance of genres offered to children. When, for example, our 1995 sample was dichotomized between high and low providers of domestically made programmes, we found that 50 percent of the former were high in factual output compared to only 11 percent of the latter; that 50 percent of the former were also high in dramatic provision compared with only 33 percent of the latter; and that only 30 percent of the former were high in animated output compared with 56 percent of the latter.

The most plausible rationale behind this web of relationships is that scheduling more children's programming has driven Europe's public broadcasters into those categories that are most prominently on offer in the international marketplace. The provision of more children's programming has thus been a two-edged sword: although it gives children more to view, it threatens diversity both in genre (more animation) and in origin (more U.S. imports).

A European Patchwork of Differentiated Provision

Although this chapter has dealt with a number of pan-European influences, European public television is not in fact a homogeneous category. Even though our survey covered only one source of children's television— that provided by public broadcasters—it has disclosed big differences among the responding organizations in, for example: the amount of children's programming provided, how it is scheduled, the ages catered to, the range of programming offered, reliance on domestic production, and the countries from which imports are drawn.

This chapter cannot do justice to the influences responsible for such differentiation, but three may be briefly mentioned.

One (as shown by table 12-1 above) is what we have called cultural region. Of course this may be less a geographical factor and have more to do with different cultural and broadcasting traditions. From this perspective, the Nordic stations seemed most "pure" in conformity to the traditional public service model, while some of the "Romance" stations seem almost to have adopted a commercial model. Anglo-German providers were situated somewhere in the middle, while the east European channels, which in 1995 were clearly in a phase of transition, showed themselves to be least modernized (with relatively low amounts of children's programs but a broad range in genre).

Another discriminator turned out to be country size, though this again probably refers less to a geographic criterion than to a pattern of different economic and industrial conditions related to home market size. Public broadcasters in the small countries offered less programming for children, less of it domestically made, a reflection perhaps of their tight budgets. Public broadcasters in the three larger countries were better off in children's programming volume as well as the amount and share of domestic production, but they also seemed to face keener competition in their markets. Thus, more of the British, French, and German departments reported having altered their production and program purchasing practices in response to increased competition than did the small-country ones.

A particularly important discriminator, however, was how the public broadcasters were funded. Whereas some organizations, like the Scandinavians and the BBC, depend almost entirely on license fee revenue, many, like ARD and ZDF in Germany and most east European broadcasters, supplement such public funds with sales of advertising. And among the latter there is considerable variation in dependence on commercial income, ranging in proportions from as low as 9 percent (for ARD) and 16 percent (ZDF) up to 61 percent for RTE in Ireland and 67 percent for RTP in Portugal.

A key finding in our study was that a lower level of public finance was associated with a more "Americanized" mode of provision. That is, the broadcasters with higher levels of commercial income tended to show more children's programs, less domestic material, more U.S. imports, and more animation. Our study cannot establish why this should be so, but two reasons suggest themselves. One is that a more commercial spirit permeates a broadcasting organization that sells advertising. The other is that children's departments are constrained to ensure that their programs satisfy advertisers' ratings needs. Some support for the latter explanation emerged when our sample was divided into three categories: those organizations that sold no advertising, those that sold advertisements but excluded them from the children's schedules, and those that allowed commercials to appear in and around children's programs. Only the last group clearly displayed the "Americanized" pattern of high animation, low information, high imports from the United States, and so on.

Some Implications

What lessons may be drawn from this survey? Its results are most relevant of course to European policymakers, regulators, broadcasters, and media-aware citizens. But there may be implications for Americans to ponder as well.

For Europeans interested in public service values and high-quality children's television, the findings of this study are profoundly mixed. On the one hand, they disclose a programming sector that is impressively supported by fine traditions, dedicated personnel, and much service-inspired production. On the other hand, gripped by the tides of multi-channel expansion, competition, commercialization and internationalization, it is evidently drifting away from some of its crucial standards. "Survivability" (to return to a question raised in the introduction to this chapter) is not an imminent issue yet, except perhaps in those Romance countries where it is becoming quite difficult to see the difference between public and private patterns of provision for children. Elsewhere, however, the responses of the children's programmers to the new media environment varyingly combine disparate elements of preservation (of what applied in the past); of adaptation (to new conditions, including changes in the social world that youngsters inhabit today); and of near-capitulation (to powerful internal organizational and external market pressures).

But in such mixed conditions it makes sense to contemplate and take steps to counter capitulation and drift. For Europeans, then, some of the policy implications are the following:

—To recognize what is happening—since inattention can only favor more erosion.

—Inside public broadcasting organizations, to set concrete targets for program range and domestic production and allocate sufficient budgets for children's departments to meet extra scheduling demands without resorting to floods of cheap imports.

—Resistance by national policymakers in governments, parliaments, and regulatory agencies to any further commercialization of public broadcasting finance.

—Vigilance by concerned civic groups to put pressure on decision-makers, opposing drift and supporting constructive measures.

—Action by European institutions—the European Union, the Council of Europe, and the European Broadcasting Union—to support more co-production and cross-border program exchanges by public service broadcasters and the firm regulation of television advertising to children.

—Continual monitoring of trends in children's programming by some suitable agency that would regularly disclose the results for public discussion.

For thoughtful Americans, the study results may merit consideration from three points of view.

First, they challenge two assumptions of faith that underpin much of the U.S. media system. One is the quantitatively expansionist criterion that more communication is always better. For European children's television, at least, this has not been entirely so. "More" has thinned resources and encouraged imports to fill gaps in the schedules. The other pet presumption is that full-scale commercialism invariably enhances choice. But as Europe's broadcasting economies have become more responsive to the market, the range of its children's programming has narrowed, and the provision has been least diverse among those public broadcasters who were most commercialized in the sense of being most dependent on income from advertising and sponsorship.

Second, it is worth noting that regulation (a "boo" word for many American policymakers) can still be an effective tool for curbing commercial excesses. For example, the children's programming of those public broadcasters, who were not permitted either to sell advertising or to place it in children's television slots, was markedly more diverse in genre and origin than that offered by those whose commercials could appear in and around programming for kids. The potential efficacy of regulation is also illustrated by the record of UK Independent Television in this survey. Although it is 100 percent financed by advertising, its children's programming profile in 1995 was actually among the most diverse in Europe (table 12-1). This very likely reflects the fact that, as a licensing condition, it is required by the Independent Television Commission to provide at least ten hours of children's programming a week, including "a range of entertainment, drama and information programmes."

A third set of implications may follow from how we interpret the sources of the erosion that European children's television has been suffering recently. Our evidence suggests that the threats to its diversity may have been more indirect than direct. That is, they have stemmed less from having been plunged into competitive cockpits nationally, and more from their exposure to certain powerful transnational trends of broadcasting change and reorganization. This suggests that how the global media economy develops can have deleterious knock-on effects for national media systems. And that implies in turn that U.S. policies of unconditional support for open markets and free information flows may be increasing the difficulties that other societies face in trying to realize goals they deem important for their media systems. Those conflicts are not, and should not be treated as, just issues of trade barriers and opportunities, but as a broad set of communication values as well.

Notes

1. The research was financed by the Center for Media Education (1511 K Street, NW, Washington, DC 2005, USA) with additional support from the UK Broadcasting Standards Commission.

2. A fuller account can be consulted in a research monograph by Jay G. Blumer and Daniel Biltereyst, *The Integrity and Erosion of Public Television for Children: A Pan-European Survey* (European Broadcasting Union, 1998).

CHAPTER THIRTEEN

Media Content Labeling Systems

Donald F. Roberts

T HE PAST SEVERAL years in the United States have witnessed a re-markable debate over whether and how to control media content. The discussion has included most of the media—film, television, popular music recordings, computer games and video games, and of course, the Internet and the World Wide Web (traditional print media have been largely ignored), and has ranged from arguments about whether controls are needed at all, to what kinds of controls best fit U.S. political and social needs. One recent upshot of this debate, although hardly the end of the discussion, has been federal legislation mandating that a V-chip be installed in virtually every new television set sold in the United States, the industry announcement of a companion TV rating system in January 1997, and a remarkable outpouring of public and government dissatisfaction with that system, leading to its modification less than a year later.

This chapter considers why the content rating issue has gained such momentum, briefly reviews empirical research on current portrayals of violence on television and on consequences of exposure to such portrayals, and discusses what the V-chip is and how it works. It proceeds to argue that an informational content labeling system is preferable to a judgmental and restrictive rating system such as the one recently adopted, at least for the time being, by the U.S. television industry, and closes with a description of such an informational advisory system.

Earlier versions of this chapter were delivered as the Wally Langenschmidt memorial lecture at the South African Broadcasting Corporation in Johannesburg, Republic of South Africa, August 28, 1996, and as an invited address to the Korean Broadcasting Commission, Seoul, Korea, June 3, 1997.

Protecting Children

Children are presumed, quite justifiably, to be different from adults—to be more vulnerable, less able to apply critical judgmental standards, more at risk.[1] As a consequence, attempts to do anything about media content, whether to label it, restrict access to it, or censor it totally are generally justified in terms of keeping children from harm.

Such arguments are not new. Consider these comments by a psychiatrist, Edward Podolsky, to a U.S. Senate subcommittee on juvenile delinquency. He spoke following the committee's viewing of excerpts from several televised crime shows.

> Seeing constant brutality, viciousness and unsocial acts results in hardness, intense selfishness, even in mercilessness, proportionate to the amount of exposure and its play on the native temperament of the child. Some cease to show resentment to insults, to indignities, and even cruelty toward helpless old people, to women and other children.[2]

I selected that particular quote because it implicates several of the consequences I discuss in this chapter—and because of its date—1954. I suspect the programs that committee viewed forty-four years ago would elicit smiles or yawns if they were held up as examples of television violence today.

Here is another statement about children and the mass media:

> The tendency of children to imitate the daring deeds seen upon the screen has been illustrated in nearly every court in the land. Train wrecks, robberies, murders, thefts, runaways, and other forms of juvenile delinquency have been traced to some particular film. The imitation is not confined to young boys and girls, but extends even through adolescents and to adults.[3]

That is taken from a now-defunct periodical entitled *Education*, commenting on the new mass medium—film . . . in 1919.

I could continue moving back through history in hundred-year chunks, presenting similar expressions of concern about media content referring to each and every new medium—including print. But let me end with one final quote: "Then shall we simply allow our children to listen to any story anyone happens to make up, and so receive into their minds ideas often the very opposite of those we shall think they ought to have when they are grown up?"

The classicists may recognize that this is Plato, giving his justification for censorship as a necessary condition for building the ideal citizen to inhabit the Republic. My point is simply that fear of what the media may do to children is nothing new. Humans have always wrestled with the issue of what kinds of media content might be inappropriate for children—and what should be done about it.

Calls for Content Labeling

Responses to the question seem always to have ranged from "do nothing" at one extreme, to "burn the books" (films/games/records—authors!) at the other. A middle ground, in the United States at least, has taken the form of calls for implementation of some kind of content labeling or rating system—that is, some means to identify the appropriateness of media content for children, and then to use that system to empower parents, to control children's access, or some combination of the two. Most of us are familiar with motion picture ratings. In the United States, they have been around since at least 1931, when the Hayes Production Code went into effect and have been continued since 1968 in the form of the Motion Picture Association of America's (MMPA) movie classification and rating system.[4] So why the recent upsurge in concern and debate?

Why have ratings become such a social and political issue in the 1990s? There are probably many reasons that public concern with "doing something" about media content has reached such a crescendo in the past few years. In the United States, two of the more important factors are that several negative social trends began to peak at the same time that advances in communication technology enabled popular media to present content in new and more disturbing ways than ever before. Just when our society was experiencing dramatic (and unconscionable) increases in teenage violence and crime, in teenage pregnancies and venereal disease, and in just plain incivility, at just that time, the media also began to portray violence, sex, and incivility in what seemed to be greater proportions.[5] (Actually, levels of television violence have remained remarkably constant for more than twenty years.)[6] More important, violence is portrayed more graphically than ever before. (I suspect that increased graphicness feeds the perception of an increase in amount of violence portrayed.) Film and television have now developed techniques to make bodies explode and blood spray right before—if not into—audience eyes; video games now reward kids for the number of on-screen enemies they can decapitate, with bonus points for extra blood and gore; some popular music lyrics, Web sites, and premium cable channel films make available—indeed, make almost commonplace—sexual content that, in the United States at least, once resided almost exclusively within "brown paper wrappers."

Given that adults have always worried that the messages media bring from "outside" may exert undue influence on children, it is not surprising that the co-occurrence of these two trends led to a perception that the mass media are "obviously" having a negative impact on society, and, therefore, that controls or restrictions are needed.[7] Given the complexity of devising regulation that satisfies the First Amendment guarantee of freedom of expression, one of the few viable options for exercising some kind of control seems to lie with a content labeling or rating system—*so long as it is not implemented by the government.* A *New York Times* poll published in July 1995 found that over 80 percent of all adult Americans and 91 percent of all parents favored the establishment of a rating system for television; 80 percent of parents believed that music recordings should be rated; 86 percent of parents thought video tapes and video games need ratings.[8]

Research on Media Violence

Before considering the kinds of rating systems that have been proposed and implemented in the United States, I want to define some boundaries, make clear a premise or two, and briefly consider several of the issues that have been discussed in the ongoing debate about ratings, issues that I believe are central to understanding what a good content labeling system will look like. For the most part (though not exclusively), I focus on television and television content—especially violent content—because that has been the most consistent subject of relevant scientific research. Nevertheless, and this is a basic premise that should be explicit, is *a screen is a screen is a screen.* Viewers, especially children, do not respond differently to movie screens, television screens, and computer screens;

what holds for one probably holds for the others. In other words, in terms of how members of the audience are affected, the issue is the nature of the content, not the channel by which the content is delivered. My second premise is that most of the psychological principles that guide human responses to screen portrayals of violence, also guide responses to portrayals of any other kind of behavior, from sexual to altruistic to how to kick a football. The same kinds of things that increase the likelihood a child will learn a violent act from television also increase learning of an altruistic act or any other kind of act. Obviously there are some differences across media and across types of content, but on the whole the evidence indicates that the similarities are far more important than the differences.

It is also important to note at the outset that I distinguish between content labeling systems and content rating systems. The two terms are not interchangeable; they refer to quite different approaches to content advisories. Indeed, the distinction between the two is at the heart of this chapter's argument. For me the fundamental difference is one of providing information about content and allowing consumers to make decisions (good or bad) versus imposing restrictions or prohibitions on potential consumers based on someone else's evaluation of the information and judgment about the capabilities and/or vulnerabilities of potential consumers.

Given those caveats and assumptions, let us look at some of the issues in the debate over whether ratings are needed, and if so, what form they should take. First, we need to spend a few minutes looking at what the research tells us about the impact of screen violence on children's beliefs, attitudes, and behavior, and about what is currently portrayed on U.S. television.

Most research on the consequences of exposure to media violence has focused on viewers' learning of aggressive behaviors or attitudes through exposure to entertainment violence. Several exhaustive reviews of the hundreds of scientific studies conducted during the past forty years lead to the unequivocal conclusion that exposure to mass media portrayals of violence contribute to aggressive attitudes and behavior in children, adolescents, and adults.[9] Obviously media violence is not the only cause of violent social behavior, but few social scientists any longer debate that it plays a contributory role. As long ago as 1982, a National Institute of Mental Health report on television and behavior concluded: "In magnitude, television violence is as strongly correlated with aggressive behavior as any other behavior variable that has been measured."[10] Studies conducted in the intervening fifteen years have not altered that judgment.[11] More often than not, those who continue to claim that there is no evidence for such a causal connection tend to be associated with the media industry—or simply have not read (or choose to ignore) the scientific literature.

What the past decade and a half of research has added, however, is evidence that exposure to media violence can have negative consequences beyond increasing the likelihood of viewers' aggressive behavior. We now know that prolonged violence viewing can also lead to emotional *desensitization*, engendering callous attitudes toward real-world violence and decreasing the likelihood of helping real victims. In addition, a third consequence of violence viewing is *increased* fear of becoming a victim, which in turn leads to such things a mistrust in others and to increases in self-protective behavior. In short, research evidence confirms that excessive exposure to media violence can lead to learning aggressive behavior, to desensitization, and to fear, and that several of these outcomes might occur simultaneously.[12]

Given that such consequences of viewing violence are well documented, the more interesting research questions (particularly when faced with developing a content labeling system) concern identification of the contextual factors within media content that seem to make a difference. In other words, what are ways of portraying violence that increase or decrease the likelihood of a negative effect? Both intuitively and on the basis of scientific research, we know that some violent programs are more problematic than others, that some ways of displaying violence are likely to increase learning, fear, or desensitization, but that other depictions are quite likely to decrease these outcomes. It does not take a scientific background to sense that the consequences to viewers of the violence in a film like *Schindler's List* (in which a man saves numerous Jews from the Nazi concentration camps during World War II) are probably quite different than the consequences of the violence in a film like *Natural Born Killers* (in which young adults blast a bloody swath across the United States). Both films portray brutal violence, both show a number of killings, both are relatively graphic—yet one is generally thought of as an antiviolence statement while the other has been accused of celebrating violence. The interesting question is: "Why?" What are the differences in how each portrays violence that make the two films so different? If we are to design a content rating system that will differentiate between two such different media portrayals, such questions are critical. A simple body count will not do the job.

Fortunately, as part of a massive content analysis of violence in U.S. television, Barbara Wilson and her colleagues reviewed the experimental research on media violence with an eye to identifying contextual factors that make a significant difference in how viewers respond to violent content.[13] Nine factors emerged from the experimental research literature: (1) the nature or qualities of the perpetrator; (2) the nature or qualities of the target or victim; (3) the reason for the violence—whether it is justified or unjustified; (4) the presence of weapons; (5) the extent and/or graphicness of the violence; (6) the degree of realism of the violence; (7) whether the violence is rewarded or punished; (8) the consequences of the violence as indicated by harm or pain cues; (9) whether humor is involved. Although the amount of research on each individual factor varies (we know a great deal about the role of rewards and punishments but not a great deal about the role of humor), Wilson and her associates contend that there is adequate evidence safely to conclude that each identified factor either increases or decreases the probability that a violent portrayal poses a risk to viewers on at least one of the three outcomes: learning, desensitization, or fear. When these contextual elements are mapped over the three outcomes, the matrix shown in table 13-1 results. The arrowheads show what experimental research says about how each contextual factor affects each outcome. Thus, for example, when violence is rewarded we expect an increase in both learning and fear; when violence is portrayed as unjustified, we expect a decrease in learning but an increase in fear; humor should increase both learning and desensitization; and so on. The spaces where no arrowhead occurs indicate a lack of adequate evidence concerning how that particular contextual factor affects that particular outcome. For example, no research examining how harm and pain cues affect either fear or desensitization was located.

Television Content: The National Television Violence Study

The matrix in table 13-1 served to guide the content analysis component of the National Television Violence Study (NTVS), an ongoing, three-

Table 13-1. *Predicted Impact of Contextual Factors on*
Three Outcomes of Exposure to Media Violence

	Outcomes of media violence		
Contextual factors	Learning aggression	Fear	Desensitization
Attractive perpetrator	⇑		
Attractive target		⇑	
Justified violence	⇑		
Unjustified violence	⇓⇓	⇑	
Presence of weapons	⇑		
Extensive/graphic violence	⇑	⇑	⇑
Realistic violence	⇑	⇑	
Rewards	⇑	⇑	
Punishments	⇓⇓	⇓⇓	
Pain/harm cues	⇓⇓		
Humor	⇑		⇑

Source: Adapted from *National Television Violence Study*, 1994–1995 Executive Summary, (Studio City, Calif.: Mediascope, 1996). Predicted effects are based on review of social science research on contextual features of violence. Spaces indicate that there is inadequate research to make a prediction.
⇑ = Likely to increase the outcome.
⇓ = Likely to decrease the outcome.

year study of violence and U.S. television. Although the overall study includes several different components, description of the work is limited here to its examination of the nature of violent television entertainment content.

Each year the NTVS researchers sample and analyze the content in a *representative week of U. S. entertainment television.* I include the italics to emphasize the magnitude of the task. For example, for the 1994–95 season, they sampled twenty-three channels of television available in the Los Angeles area, including broadcast networks, independent channels, public television, basic cable, and premium cable channels. For each channel they randomly selected two daily, half-hour time slots between 6:00 A.M. and 11:00 P.M. over a period of twenty weeks, ultimately taping a total of 3,185 programs. After eliminating news programs, game shows, religious programs, sports, instructional programs, and "infomercials" (none of which fell within their contracted definition of entertainment programming), they were left with a sample of 2,693 programs—2,737 hours of programming.[14] This resulted in a representative seven-day composite week of programming for each of the twenty-three channels, the largest and most representative sample of entertainment television content ever collected.

The coding scheme in this study is equally detailed and comprehensive. Violence is defined as:

> any overt depiction of a credible threat of physical force or the actual use of such force intended to physically harm an animate being or a group of animate beings. Violence also includes certain depictions of physically harmful consequences against an animate being that occur as a result of unseen violent means. Thus there are three primary types of violent depictions: credible threats, behavioral acts and harmful consequences.[15]

But more important than the definition of violence per se, precise definitions have been developed for all of the contextual factors listed in table 13-1. That is, coding instructions were created to enable coders reliably to identify such content elements as harm, pain, humor, justification for violence, attractiveness of the target of violence, and so forth. Thus, rather than simply counting how often violence occurs in current entertainment television programming, the NTVS analysis provides a detailed picture of the contextual features associated with portrayals of violence. Finally, the coding scheme operates at three distinct levels— that of the overall program, of the scene, and of the individual violent act (that is, violent interaction), enabling independent inferences about the nature and context of violent acts, violent scenes, and violent programs. Such a multilevel approach is necessary if one is to be able to differentiate between programs that glorify violence and those that condemn violence. For example, although a program with an antiviolence theme may depict as many violent scenes as a program that glorifies violence, the more global antiviolence message may emerge only at the program level. If analysis were to be limited to individual acts or scenes, this point might be lost.

Obviously, a study of this magnitude produces results far too extensive to detail here. Nevertheless a brief summary of a few of the findings will help form the foundation of my argument about what kind of content labeling system will best serve the television audience.

The first conclusion from the NTVS study is not surprising—there is a great deal of violence on U.S. entertainment television. Indeed, in 1994–95 more than half of all entertainment programs—58 percent—contained violence (the comparable number for 1995–96 was 61 percent).

Table 13-2. *Selected Findings from National Television Violence Study*

58% of all entertainment programs contained violence
Violent programs
33% contained 9 or more violent interactions
51% portrayed violence in realistic settings
16% showed long-term consequences of violence
4% had an antiviolence theme
Scenes within violent programs
15% of violent scenes portray blood and gore
39% of violent scenes use humor
73% of violent scenes portray violence as unpunished
Interactions within violent scenes
25% of interactions employed a gun
35% of interactions depicted harm unrealistically
44% of interactions showed violence as justified
58% of interactions *did not* depict pain

Source: Adapted from *National Television Violence Study*, Executive Summary, p. 11.

More interesting than the total amount of violence, however, is its nature—that is, the context in which it is portrayed and the attributes with which it is associated. Table 13-2 summarizes a few of the contextual results.

For the most part, the table speaks for itself. Although a substantial proportion of U.S. entertainment television contains no violent content whatsoever, over half of the programs do portray violence. Moreover, when violence does occur it is often portrayed in ways that are more likely than not to increase the chances of some kind of negative effect on viewers. Violence often goes unpunished, seldom results in either immediate pain or negative long-term consequences, and is often portrayed as something to laugh about. Over a third of violent interactions depict harm unrealistically, almost 45 percent portray violent acts as justified, and well over half fail to depict any associated pain. These are all factors that have been shown to increase the likelihood of viewers learning to be more aggressive, or becoming more fearful, or becoming more desensitized. In other words, the contextual factors characteristic of much (not all, but much) U.S. television programming are just those that *increase* the likelihood of negative consequences among youthful viewers. Indeed, the results of the NTVS content analysis read like a primer on how *not* to produce programming for children.

The V-Chip

In February 1996, President Bill Clinton signed into law the Telecom-munications Act of 1996, a far-reaching piece of legislation that is des-tined to change the face of U.S. telecommunications. One small part of that legislation was intended to empower parents by providing a way for them to control the television content to which their children can have access. This was accomplished by mandating that within two years of the signing of the bill (February 1998), all new television sets sold in the United States must contain a V-chip, and that within one year (February 1997) the television industry must have developed a system to implement V-chip capabilities (otherwise, the Federal Communications Commission would appoint an independent committee to do it for them). Now what does this mean? What is the V-chip, and what is the system designed to implement it?

Briefly, a V-chip is simply a piece of hardware, a very tiny piece of hardware, that will be included in the electronics of new TV sets (or added to existing TV sets). It allows consumers to block programs de-pending on how their content is labeled or rated. The chip reads a signal that is not visible to viewers (it is embedded in the vertical blanking interval, the portion of the television signal that currently carries "closed caption" services for the hearing impaired). That signal, which is to be included within every television program, will carry information about the content of the program. The consumer can program the chip to recognize and respond to any particular rating or level of intensity, or other kind of information embedded in the signal. Programs that fail to meet the selected criteria, whatever they might be, are blocked. Thus, for example, a show might be labeled somewhere between $V = 0$ (for no violence) to $V = 4$ (for a great deal of violence). Or, using the television rating system employed from December 1996 through September 1997, it might be rated anywhere from TV-G (General Audience), through TV-PG (Parental Guidance Suggested) or TV-14 (Parents Strongly Cau-tioned), to TV-M (Mature Audience Only). On the basis of such a label or rating, parents decide what kinds of shows are to be allowed in their home and set the V-chip to block anything in excess of (or not conform-ing to) the selected criteria. Once that selection is made, the chip auto-matically decodes the signal embedded in each program and acts in ac-cordance with parental (or other consumer) decisions. If the program exceeds the rating, the V-chip picks up the signal and the screen goes blank. In short, the chip is simply a device that enables consumers to decide what kinds of television content they want to allow into their homes at any given time and to block out any content that does not meet their standards.

Several other things about this technology are important to note: the V-chip is capable of accommodating any one of a number of different labeling or rating systems; the chip can accommodate several different systems simultaneously (there is no requirement to settle on a single approach); a single program can have independent ratings for different kinds of content (that is, there can be one rating for violence, another for sex, and another for language, all pertaining to the same program); the chip can be turned on or off, or reprogrammed, at any time. For all these reasons, I believe the chip has been misnamed. Initially the V was appended to indicate "violence chip," but since it can do much more than respond to violence levels, I think a more appropriate name would be C-chip, standing for "choice chip." To make it a real choice chip, however, requires giving consumers the necessary information to make reasoned choices—what I call an informational content advisory.

Informational versus Judgmental Systems

An informational content labeling system posits that information contained in an advisory helps consumers direct their behavior by telling them what is in "the package"—that is, what is contained in the program, film, or game they are considering. The usefulness of the information depends on how clear, specific, and relevant it is to a given consumer. For example, assume one wishes to avoid—or select—content depicting violent or sexual behavior. In this case, a label explicitly describing the kind and amount of either behavior is more helpful than content-free proscriptions that simply warn the content may be problematic but do not state why (for example, TV-14). In other words, informational systems assume that the primary function of content advisories is to inform viewers about what to expect, and that the more fully they do this, the better. An informational system leaves open both the question of appropriateness and the selection decision.

Judgmental approaches—for example, the Motion Picture Association of America's (MPAA) Film Classification System—generally do not provide much descriptive information. Rather, such systems make judgments about what is or is not appropriate for particular audiences—specifically, for different age groups of children. Thus, a TV-14 rating tells consumers that somebody has made a judgment that something about the content is inappropriate for children younger than 14, but says little or nothing about what that content is (for example, violence, sex, inappropriate language, and so on). In the most extreme cases, such judgments become proscriptions. For example, in the United States, youngsters under 17 years old are prohibited from attending an R-rated film unless accompanied by an adult. In other words, judgmental approaches hand over to someone other than the consumer the question of what is appropriate, and in some cases, the selection decision. Usually the judgment is made by some relatively anonymous ratings board.[16]

Typically, two rationales are offered for adopting a judgmental as opposed to an informational approach. First, it is argued that given the thousands of hours of media content produced each year, there is no way to develop a descriptive system complex enough to identify the kinds of content differences that proponents of informational systems would like to describe, but still simple enough to be employed by whomever is charged with the task of labeling. Second, even if an informational system could be developed, proponents of judgmental systems say that it would be far too complex for most consumers to use. Rather, they argue, parents are more likely to use a system that only requires them to make a single, simple, age-based choice.

By now it should be clear that I favor informational content labeling systems over judgmental systems. There is, of course, the possibility of combining the two approaches—of both telling the consumer what is in the package *and* providing judgments about its age appropriateness. But even that, I think, is a mistake. Not only do judgmental systems take fundamental decisionmaking power away from parents, but they also increase the risk of attracting children to the very kinds of content from which we would like to protect them. Even though content advisories are intended to help parents monitor and guide their children's media consumption, we cannot lose sight of the fact that youngsters also see and respond to these ratings. Nor can we ignore that content decisions are under control of at least some children most of the time and of most children at least some of the time. It follows that how content advisories affect children also warrants careful consideration.

Boomerang Effects

Unfortunately, evidence is mounting that advisory labels can boomerang, attracting youngsters to inappropriate content—a kind of "forbidden fruit" effect.[17] And although both informational and judgmental advisories have been found to boomerang sometimes, the effect is more general and more consistent with judgmental rating.[18]

To the extent that informational systems attract children to "forbidden fruit," they do so because they identify content which youngsters seek because of some need or interest independent of the labeled content. For example, youngsters interested in sex or violence for whatever reason will read the advisory to determine whether a given program can satisfy their interest and act accordingly. Children not interested in these topics may either ignore or actively avoid the program, also depending on the information in the advisory. It is no different than when people who are interested in gardening read program listings to locate programs about gardening. For better or worse, information is used to guide choices; not approving of the choice a person might make on the basis of information is not a legitimate reason to withhold information.

The boomerang effect associated with judgmental ratings, on the other hand, is not primarily a function of fulfilling a child's information needs; judgmental ratings provide little information. Rather, when children are drawn to content rated as inappropriate by a judgmental system (for example, when a 12-year-old chooses a TV-14 program), it is primarily because they are reacting against what they perceive to be someone attempting to control their media choices; such a reaction is quite independent of what the content may be. Reactance theory posits that a perceived threat to individual freedom motivates humans to restore freedom by actively seeking to engage in the proscribed behavior.[19] Thus, to the extent that children perceive content advisories as attempts by some "authority" to limit their access to content or otherwise impose control or censorship, the theory predicts that they will strive to consume the proscribed material *regardless of the nature of the content*. Several studies indicate that youngsters perceive labels proscribing content on the basis of age or appearing to put control in the hands of others—particularly parents (for example, an advisory such as "Parental Discretion Advised")—as highly restrictive, and that they react strongly against them. At least three experiments have shown that the MPAA film classification system is particularly likely to engender reactance and a boomerang effect among children.[20]

Of course, the informational and the judgmental models are not entirely independent. Simply the fact that any rating is assigned—whether a single letter icon (for example, "R") or a descriptive phrase (for example., "Humans killed; blood and gore")—indicates that someone hopes to control at least some consumers' access to the content, thus creating some potential for reactance. Similarly, even the most "content free" label usually elicits consumer inferences about the nature of the proscribed material. For example, when asked what an MPAA "R" stands for, most young adolescents in the United States will refer to sex and/or violence. Moreover, both mechanisms may operate simultaneously. A 12-year-old boy might seek out an R-rated film both because he has been told he can't see it (reactance) and because he believes it may portray activity about which he is curious (information seeking). Whether a particular rating or advisory provides information or elicits reactance, then, is a matter of degree. When concerned with children's responses to ratings from a practical point of view, the question is better phrased in terms of which systems are less likely to cause reactance and more likely to provide useful information.

The Recreational Software Advisory Council Content Labeling System

Let me turn, then, to the issue of whether it is possible to design an informational system complex enough to give relatively fine-grained information about a program but still simple enough for both labelers and parents to use. I shall describe a content advisory system I helped devise a few years ago and start by describing some questions we addressed from the beginning of the project.

First, consider how satisfied a parent would be with a system that rated programs with either a simple G (good for children) or NG (not good for children). Prior to viewing, that's all one would know about the program—either it's G or NG. Would the situation be better if there were four or five ratings level—say from 0 to 5, or from TV-G through TV-PG, and TV-14 to TV-M (the TV Parental Guidelines)? My experience has been that most parents would prefer either of the latter options to the simple G or NG. But is that enough? Wouldn't the "parent" want to know what the rating means by the term "children?" That is, would it help to know if G-NG referred to 7-year-olds, 10-year-olds, or 14-year-olds? Would your answer to the questions change depending on who gave the rating, on whether, for example, the G (for "good") or NG (for "not good") was assigned by a leader in your public educational system or by a youthful college dropout marking time as a television content rater while awaiting a "real" job? What if the rating was always assigned by one of two educators, one of whom was obsessed with keeping violence off television while the other made keeping children safe from nudity his life's work—but you never knew which gave a particular rating? Would it make a difference which one assigned the rating? Are you more concerned with portrayals of violence than with portrayals of sex? Do you have different feelings about depictions of nudity? Of vulgar language? And even if you decide which kind of content concerns you most, are you certain about how any particular portrayal should be rated? Perhaps what you see as brutal violence someone else will judge to be little more than a friendly tussle. Indeed, consider the wide range of answers the preceding questions are likely to elicit from a large, diverse group of parents.

The importance of such questions began to emerge for me when I was asked by the Software Publishers Association to help develop a parental advisory system for computer games.[21] In 1994, in response to the release of several particularly violent and bloody video games, some members of the U.S. Congress brought pressure to bear on both the video game and computer game industries to develop some kind of parental advisory label to be placed on game packages.[22] At minimum, the argument went, parents should have some indication of what is in a game before they purchase it for their children. I won't detail the history of that particular debate, except to note that in order to preclude threatened government action, each of the two industries (video games and computer games) developed its own system, and the one produced for computer games took an informational approach. Ultimately, when the computer game content labeling system was completed, it was turned over to a nonprofit advisory board independent of the computer game industry—the Recreational Software Advisory Council (RSAC), and became known as the RSAC system. Over the past two years a slightly revised version of the system, called the RSACi system (i for Internet) has gone into effect on the World Wide Web, and over 60,000 Web sites currently use it to label content.

Several factors influenced the shape of the RSAC content labeling system. Most important was the issue of whether an advisory should be judgmental or informational (evaluative or descriptive). That is, should a content advisory make an evaluative judgment about what a child should see, or should it provide descriptive information about what is in the game, allowing parents to make the evaluative judgments appropriate to their personal beliefs and value systems? Is it better to label a program as "inappropriate for children under 13 years," or to say "this game depicts violence that goes unpunished and that results in injury to humans," asking parents to decide whether their children should play? When I talked to parents about the Motion Picture Film Classification System, I found that many objected to age-based, judgmental ratings because they believed that often such ratings were not appropriate for their own children. Some felt their 10-year-olds were perfectly capable of handling some kinds of content likely to get a PG-13 rating, but not other kinds; some felt that their 14-year-old should not see a PG-13 movie, but had a great deal of trouble defending their position in the face of such "expert" ratings; most complained that the simple lettering system simply did not tell them enough to enable them to exercise informed judgment. They believe that a PG-13 rating can be assigned to a film on the basis of violence, or sex, or language, but they often are uncertain about what particular kind of content is at issue in any given film—sometimes even after they have seen the film. Many parents indicate that all they really know when faced with a PG-13 rating is that someone has made an evaluative judgment that the content is "inappropriate" for younger children.

Of course, to the extent that an advisory provides descriptive information and an age-based judgment, parents can make a decision based on descriptive information combined with the additional knowledge of someone else's evaluative judgment about appropriate age levels. That evaluative judgment, however, is or is not valuable to the parent depending on who that someone else is and what the criteria underlying the judgment were—information that is not currently available for the MPAA system.[23] Moreover, in some circumstances that judgment can override a parental decision; that is, parents cannot decide to have their 16-year-old attend an R-rated film absent the company of an adult.

In any case, given (a) parents' expressed desire for more information; (b) game developers' antipathy toward others making evaluative judgments about their products; and (c) reactance theory's prediction that age-based content restrictions are likely to boomerang, we opted for informational content labeling as opposed to judgmental ratings. Ultimately, we took as our model the U.S. food labeling system, which requires food packagers to list the ingredients in the package. Consumers are not told what they should or should not eat; rather, they are given adequate information and the consumption decision is left to them. The RSAC content labeling system used the same principles.

Another important factor that shaped the final form of the RSAC system was logistical. The nature of computer games makes it very difficult to require that they be screened by independent raters. Unlike films or videotapes which can be viewed in ninety minutes or so, it can take upwards of one hundred hours to review a computer game (make that two hundred hours if you are over 40 years old). Given the hundreds of games that need to be labeled each year, it would be extremely expensive and impractical to require independent coders to describe or rate each game. We decided, therefore, to develop a self-rating system—that is, a system whereby the game developers themselves rate their own games. This, of course, created a new problem. To ask a game developer to label his or her own game, particularly when many developers tend to believe that labels or ratings indicating higher levels of violence (or sex, or vulgar language) may decrease sales, is like asking the fox to guard the hen house. It would seem to invite the developers to bend the rules. Thus, we had to find a way to keep game developers accurate and honest as they labeled their own games, and equally important, a way that would also assure the public that such self-administered ratings are, in fact, accurate and honest. Ultimately, the solution turned out to be quite simple. We took the norms and canons of science and moved them into the public arena. That is, we developed a content labeling system that is reliable and public, and those two attributes largely solved the problem.

A reliable system means that any two individuals using the coding procedures correctly will describe or rate a game identically. This requires concrete, highly detailed definitions of everything to be described, and a set of questions about the content based on those definitions that ask for nothing other than yes/no responses. The idea is that no matter how different the individuals, if they use the same objective definitions correctly, and answer the questions honestly, they cannot help but assign the same label or rating to a game.

A public system means open to public oversight; that is, anyone and everyone has access to the system, its definitions, and its procedures. To the extent that open access to a reliable system is guaranteed, then anyone should be able to check the label or rating given to any game at any time. The idea underlying this requirement is that if it is easy for anyone in the public to raise questions or objections in those instances when they do not agree on the rating (using, of course, the same rating system), the threat of such checks keeps game developers honest. If the game developers misuse the system, they face loss of their rating (which can cost them access to retail outlets) and heavy fines. (A public system can also provide increased flexibility in that, over time, public input can be used to sharpen or modify questions and/or definitions, keeping the system in step with cultural norms.)

Finally, there remained the question of what to label and how to label it. Both public opinion and prodding from Congress dictated advisories addressing each of four content dimensions—violence, sex, nudity, and language (ultimately, the labels combine sex and nudity, but the two kinds of content are still rated separately). Here, however, I will focus on violence.

We decided that there would be five levels of intensity for each content area—that is, from 0 for no violence to 4 for the most potentially harmful portrayals of violence. We reviewed the research literature on the effects of media violence, identifying content dimensions—what Barbara J. Wilson and others called contextual factors—that were most likely to increase negative effects and that seemed most appropriate to the content of games.[24] (Since games do not have the kinds of story lines found in dramatic narratives, their content labels focus on slightly different dimensions than might be the case for television programs.) By this procedure we settled on five primary features that would make a difference in the level of the advisory:

—The nature of the target (victim)—that is, is the target human-like, nonhuman, or an object?

—The stance of the target (victim)—that is, is the target threatening or nonthreatening?

—Consequences to the target (victim)—that is, death versus injury versus disappearance versus no consequences?

—Depiction of blood and gore; and

—Consequences to the player—that is, is the player rewarded or not rewarded for aggressive behavior?

To the extent that one or more of these attributes occurs within a computer game, the advisory of the level of violence increases. For example, if the game portrays a threatening human attacked but not injured, the game gets a 1 for violence; if the threatening human is injured, it gets a 2, and so on. Combinations of these various dimensions result in the logic chart shown in table 13-3, which illustrates the various attributes in a computer game that result in different violence advisories.

Of course, the person judging the content is not required to make his or her way through that chart. Rather, there is a set of highly concrete, highly objective definitions for every term used in the chart, and a parallel set of yes/no questions employing those definitions. For example, one question asks: "Does the software title depict blood and gore of sentient beings?" That question results in a straightforward yes or no response from the person doing the labeling because the terms "depict," "blood and gore," and "sentient beings" are each explicitly and extensively defined. (Terms such as "sentient beings" would never be used in a descriptive label but are included in the definitions in order to cover the wide array of creatures inhabiting the world of computer games—from realistic humans, to animated space aliens, to killer frogs.) Here, for example, is part of the definition of "blood and gore":

> Blood and Gore: Visual Depiction of a great quantity of a Sentient Being's blood or what a reasonable person would consider as vital body fluids, OR a visual Depiction of innards, and/or dismembered body parts showing tendons, veins, bones, muscles, etc., and/or organs, and/or detailed insides, and/or fractured bones and skulls.
>
> The depiction of blood or vital body fluids must be shown as what a reasonable person would classify as flowing, spurting, flying, collecting or having collected in large amounts or pools, or the results of what a reasonable person would consider as a large loss of the fluid such as a body covered in blood or a floor smeared with the fluid. . . . etc.[25]

There are dozens of pages of such definitions and associated examples, one for every important term in each of the questions.

The questions are arranged in a branching format and are typically administered on a computer. Depending on the response to any given question, the system either gives an appropriate content label or determines what the next question should be. Depending on the amount and nature of violence in a given game, whoever does the labeling may respond to as few as two or as many as fifteen questions. The same procedure is followed for sex/nudity and for language. Finally, depending

Table 13-3. *RSAC Methodology Logic Chart*

Attributes	0ª	1	2	3	4
Maximum violence					
Rape					X
Wanton and gratuitous violence					X
Blood/gore				X	
Human threatening victims					
No apparent damage/no death		X			
Damage with or without death			X		
Death/no damage			X		
Human nonthreatening victims					
Damage/no death					
Player not rewarded (unintentional act)			X		
Player rewarded				X	
Death with or without damage					
Player not rewarded (unintentional act)			X		
Player rewarded (gratuitous violence)					X
Nonhuman threatening victims					
No apparent damage/no death		X			
Damage with or without death		X			
Death/no damage		X			
Nonhuman nonthreatening victims					
Damage/no death					
Player not rewarded (accidental)		X			
Player rewarded (intentional)			X		
Death with or without damage					
Player not rewarded (accidental)		X			
Player rewarded (intentional)				X	
Natural/accidental violence					
Damage/death, human victims			X		
Damage/death, nonhuman victims		X			
Blood/gore (humans and nonhumans)				X	
Objects (aggressive and acidental violence)					
Damage and/or destruction of symbolic objects	X				
Realistic objects					
Disappear without damage or implied social presence	X				
Disappear without damage with implied social presence			X		
Damage with or without destruction			X		

Source: Recreational Software Advisory Council.
a. "0" means suitable for all audiences.

Figure 13-1. *Two Recreational Software Advisory Council Labels for Hypothetical Computer Games*

Example 1

Example 2

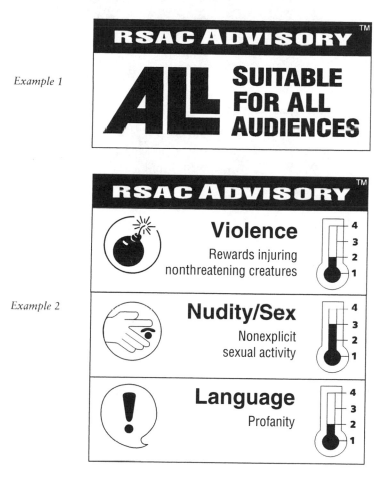

Source: Recreational Software Advisory Council (RSAC), Lexington, Mass.

on how the questions have been answered, the program determines what the advisory icon should be (figure 13-1) and what information is to be used to explain that icon. In other words, the final label consists of an icon and associated number (from 0 to 4) indicating the level of violence, and a descriptive phrase explaining why that number was assigned. As shown in table 13-1, the content description associated with any given level may vary. For example, there are six different reasons a game can receive a violence score of 2 and four different reasons it could earn a

Figure 13-2. *RSAC Label for "Doom," a Computer Game*

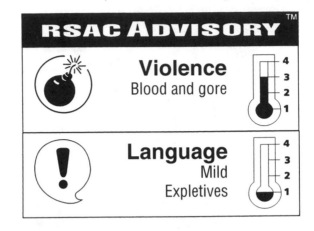

Source: RSAC.

violence score of 3. In all cases, the advisory informs the consumer about the specific kind of content underlying each level of violence assigned. Note, for instance, the descriptive information in the violence section of the RSAC advisory label displayed in figure 13-1. The hypothetical game described by that label received 2 for violence level because it "rewards injuring nonthreatening creatures" (for example, the player scored points for shooting living creatures that posed no threat to other figures in the game). Another descriptive phrase paired with a level 2 violence advisory might have been simply: "Humans injured." Finally, figure 13-2 shows an advisory label assigned to one of the more violent games available in the United States a year or so ago (even more violent games have since reached market), a game called "Doom." As you can see, the game received the next to highest advisory for violence—in this case because it portrayed blood and gore—and a very mild rating for language (mild expletives). There were no instances of sex or nudity in the game.

Content Labeling and Television

Now, how might something such as the RSAC content labeling system relate to a TV content labeling system to implement the V-chip? Clearly, some modifications would have to be made in the dimensions employed and in some of the questions required to assign a label. (The contextual features identified in the NCTV study would be a good place to begin developing the appropriate dimensions for television content.) But for the most part, such an informational approach seems ideal for the new V-chip technology. It would be inexpensive and quick, because the producers and writers of each television show would rate their own product with the understanding that the rating procedure is public. More important, it would serve the consumer well because it has the advantage of being descriptive and informational rather than judgmental.

Joel Federman concluded his recent book on media ratings with the recommendation that whatever rating system is adopted, it should make every effort to maximize information and minimize judgment.[26] Of course, "informational" and "judgmental" are relative terms. Since even the act of choosing to label content implies evaluation, no rating system can be purely informational. Nevertheless, because something like the RSAC content labeling system leans far more in the direction of description than evaluation, it has several valuable advantages over evaluative systems. First, and most important, it puts the decisionmaking power in the hands of the parents rather than some outside agency with which the parent may or may not agree. It presumes that children are different from one another and that parents know the needs and capabilities of their own children far better than anyone else can. Second, it has the advantage of consistency because the criteria for labeling any content are objective, concrete, and public. And this in turn means that it can be used in highly flexible ways. Parents whose primary concern might be media violence and parents whose primary concern might be language or sexuality can all use the system with confidence, adapting it to fit each of their different needs.

There is probably no such thing as a perfect solution to the problem of protecting a highly vulnerable audience such as children while simultaneously protecting people's right to speak, write, film, and program freely. Nevertheless, providing parents with descriptive information on which they can based informed decisions would be a big step in the right direction—a step that attempts to respond to the needs and right of all concerned parties.

Notes

1. D. F. Roberts, "Adolescents and the Mass Media: From 'Leave It to Beaver' to 'Beverly Hills 90210,' " *Teachers College Record*, vol. 94 (Spring 1993), pp.

629–43; and D. F. Roberts, "From Plato's Republic to Hillary's Village: Children and the Changing Media Environment," in R. P. Weissberg and others, eds., *Trends in the Well-Being of Children and Youth* (Sage, 1998).

2. Steven Starker, *Evil Influences: Crusades against the Mass Media* (New Brunswick, N.J.: Transaction Publishers, 1989), p. 137.

3. Ibid.

4. Joel Federman, *Media Ratings: Design, Use and Consequences* (Studio City, Calif.: Mediascope, 1996).

5. F. M. Hechinger, *Fateful Choices: Healthy Youth for the 21st Century* (New York: Carnegie Council on Adolescent Development, Carnegie Corporation of New York, 1992).

6. G. Gerber and N. Signorelli, "Violence Profile, 1967 through 1988–89: Enduring Patterns," Annenberg School of Communications, University of Pennsylvania, 1990; and *National Television Violence Study* (Studio City, Calif.: Mediascope, 1997).

7. Roberts, "From Plato's Republic to Hillary's Village."

8. "Sex and Violence in Popular Culture," *New York Times,* July 23–26, 1995, p. 6.

9. See, for example, George Comstock, with Haejung Paik, *Television and the American Child* (San Diego, Calif.: Academic Press, 1991); A. C. Huston and others., *Big World, Small Screen: The Role of Television in American Society* (University of Nebraska Press, 1992); and H. Paik and G. Comstock, "The Effects of Television Violence in Antisocial Behavior," *Communication Research*, vol. 21 (August 1994), pp. 516–46.

10. National Institute of Mental Health, *Television and Behavior: Ten Years of Scientific Progress and Implications for the Eighties, vol. 1, Summary Report* (Washington: Government Printing Office, 1982).

11. Comstock with Paik, *Television and the American Child.*

12. For reviews see Comstock with Paik, *Television and the American Child*; and B. J. Wilson and others, "Television Violence and Its Context: University of California, Santa Barbara Study," in *National Television Violence Study*, Scientific Papers (Studio City, Calif.: Mediascope, 1996), pp. 5–268.

13. *National Television Violence Study, 1994–1995* (Studio City, Calif.: Mediascope,1996); and *National Television Violence Study*, vol. 2, *Executive Summary* (Sage, 1997); and Barbara Wilson and others, "Content Analysis of Entertainment Television: The Importance of Context," paper presented to the Duke University Conference on Media Violence and Public Policy, 1996.

14. The National Cable Television Association, which funded the study, determined which kinds of programming would be included in the content analysis.

15. *National Television Violence Study, Content Analysis Codebook, 1994–1995*, p. 3.

16. Federman, *Media Ratings.*

17. P. G. Christenson, "The Effects of Parental Advisory Labels on Adolescent Music Preferences," *Journal of Communication*, vol. 42 (Winter 1992), pp. 106–13.

18. See B. J. Bushman and A. D. Stack, "Forbidden Fruit versus Tainted Fruit:

Effects of Warning Labels on Attraction to Television Violence," *Journal of Experimental Psychology: Applied*, vol. 2 (September 1996), pp. 202–36; J. Cantor and K. Harrison, "Ratings and Advisories for Television Programming," in *National Television Violence Study, 1994–1995*, Scientific Papers, pp. III.1–III.50; J. Cantor, K. Harrison, and A. Nathanson, "Ratings and Advisories for Television Programming," University of Wisconsin study, in *National Television Violence Study 2*, vol. 2, pp. 267–322; P. G. Christenson, "The Effect of Videogame Ratings: Is There a Boomerang Effect?" paper presented at the annual meetings of the International Communication Association, 1997; J. Morkes, H. L. Chen, and D. F. Roberts, "Adolescents' Responses to Movie, Television and Computer Game Ratings and Advisories," paper presented at the annual meeting of the International Communication Association, 1997.

19. J. W. Brehm, *Responses to Loss of Freedom: A Theory of Psychological Reactance* (Morristown, N.J.: General Learning Press, 1972).

20. Cantor and Harrison, "Ratings and Advisories"; Cantor, Harrison, and Nathanson, "Ratings and Advisories," University of Wisconsin study; Morkes, Chen, and Roberts, "Adolescents' Responses"; and Bushman and Stack, "Forbidden Fruit."

21. The design team consisted of Glenn Ochsnreiter of the Software Publisher's Association, Washington, D.C.; Jim Green of Shareware Testing Laboratories, Indianapolis, Ind.; and me.

22. Federman, *Media Ratings*.

23. Ibid.

24. Wilson and others, "Television Violence and Its Context."

25. The entire rating system of the Recreational Software Advisory Council (RSAC), including all definitions, can be found through www.RSAC.org.

26. Federman, *Media Ratings*.

Part Three

Communications Policy

CHAPTER FOURTEEN

The Evolving Politics of Telecommunications Regulation

Elizabeth E. Bailey

THE MATRIX DEVELOPED by James Q. Wilson to describe the nature of political competition is taught in nearly all courses concerned with business-government relations.[1] In Wilson's scheme, policy proposals are evaluated in terms of the perceived distribution of their costs and benefits. Costs and benefits can be widely distributed or narrowly concentrated. The four polar cases of political competition, as he describes them, include *majoritarian* politics (both costs and benefits are widely distributed); *entrepreneurial* politics (costs are concentrated, benefits are widely distributed); *client* politics (benefits are concentrated, costs are widely distributed); and *interest group* politics (both costs and benefits are narrowly concentrated). This chapter explores these four polar cases in some detail and relates each to a particular policy change surrounding telecommunications regulation. As we will see, the policy change cases are striking, but not pure. Some features of other boxes in the Wilson 2X2 matrix are present in each of our examples, as indeed happens whenever the Wilson theory is applied in the real world.

Client politics describes the situation in 1910 when Theodore Vail, then president of American Bell, crafted the regulated monopoly compromise that would govern telecommunications regulatory policy for over half a century. Entrepreneurial politics portrays the activity of the Department of Justice when it filed its antitrust case against the American Telephone and Telegraph Co. (AT&T) in 1974 and settled the case through divestiture in 1984. Interest group politics characterizes the policy changes in the Telecommunications Act of 1996, including the political activity leading up to and trailing its passage. Finally, majoritarian politics summarizes the politics of the 1997 World Trade Organization's massive international telecommunications liberalization.

It is extremely useful pedagogically that students learn to classify the nature of political competition for an industry in its evolution over time. They learn that political competition surrounds issues rather than an industry. The exercise trains students to observe current political processes and to characterize the nature of ongoing political competition. They find that the Wilson matrix is useful beyond merely its ability to classify. The framework also offers strategic guidance that better enables decisionmakers to achieve desired political outcomes.

The Wilson Matrix

Figure 14-1 displays the Wilson matrix. The matrix focuses on the economic status of those who will be affected by a public policy change. The distributional aspect of the costs and benefits—whether they are narrowly concentrated or widely distributed—is taken to be especially relevant to political action. If a particular industry is negatively affected by a proposed policy change (narrowly concentrated costs), it will have an incentive to engage in political action to block the initiative. If legislators, whose consent may be needed for the adoption of a regulatory proposal, view the proposal as unfair or inequitable, that industry cannot hope to be successful without engaging in further political activity. Therefore, this portrayal of the Wilson matrix includes the classification framework itself, and also describes, within each of the four end-points of political competition, some key concepts that are important to understanding what elements are necessary if that political action is to be successful.

Each of the four types of political competition is considered in turn. When both costs and benefits are widely distributed so that all of society expects to gain and all of society expects to pay, the politics are said to be *majoritarian* in nature. The policy change must be perceived to be in the broad public interest if it is to achieve passage. Not all issues that offer net gains to society as a whole are successfully passed, however. As indicated within the box, there must be a policy window or focusing event that enables the proposal to get onto the political agenda. People must agree that it is legitimate for the government to take action. Ideological objections to the propriety or feasibility of the policy change must be overcome.

Figure 14-1. *Nature of Political Competition*

Distribution of benefits from policy change

	Narrowly concentrated	Widely distributed
Distribution of costs from policy change Narrowly concentrated	*Interest group politics* • Some business expects to benefit at expense of another; zero sum game. • Public does not believe it will be much affected. • Legislation, if passed, often has something to please each affected party.	*Entrepreneurial politics* • Energy originates in public sector. • General benefits conferred at cost to be borne by a business group. • Politician must mobilize latent public sentiment, put opponents of plan publicly on defensive, and associate legislation with widely shared values.
Widely distributed	*Client politics* • Energy for policy change originates in private sector. • Some businesses expect to capture a disproportionate share of benefits. • Business must organize a coalition and/or lobby to change perception of new policy's effects and/or to justify effects.	*Majoritarian politics* • All or most of society expects to gain; all or most of society expects to pay. • Issue must get onto political agenda. • There must be agreement that it is legitimate for government to take action. • Ideological objections must be overcome.

Source: Based on the Wilson matrix in James Q. Wilson, "The Politics of Regulation," in *The Politics of Regulation* (Basic Books, 1980), pp. 357–95.

When the distribution of both costs and benefits are narrowly concentrated, the politics have an *interest group* cast. A subsidy or regulation may benefit one industry player at the expense of another comparable industry player. Because of the zero-sum nature of the competition, each side has an incentive to organize and exercise political influence. Since consumers may not think they will be much affected one way or another, they are unlikely to weigh in strongly. In many, but not all, examples of interest group politics, there is something in the final legislation to please each affected party.

Client politics occur when some business or industry group expects to capture a disproportionate share of the benefits of a proposed policy change. Usually, the politics are originated and energized by the activity of the business or industry group that sees itself as the beneficiary. The general public is likely to sit on the sidelines, often because it is unaware of the policy change or believes the policy change will have few, if any, negative effects. When the issue is more visible, however, and is perceived to have some negative consequences, business must organize a circle of friends and make an effort to change the perception of the new policy's effects or to justify them if it is to achieve political victory. Client politics are best thought of as approximating the producer-dominance model of regulation rather than the public interest model.[2] In Wilson's words, client politics are associated with "backstairs intrigue and quiet lobbying."[3]

Finally, a policy may be proposed that will confer general benefits at a cost to be borne by a particular business or industry group. When this is attempted, usually by a politician, the politics are said to be *entrepreneurial*. The political leader must be a skilled entrepreneur because the incentive to voice opposition is strong for the industry that will be harmed by the policy. The politician must be able to mobilize latent public sentiment, put the opponents of the proposal publicly on the defensive, and associate the legislation with widely shared values. The entrepreneur serves as a vicarious representative of the ordinary citizen, who is not directly a part of the legislative process. The entrepreneur may be helped if the issue has gotten onto the political agenda, perhaps by a scandal or crisis. Sometimes, indeed, the hearing process is used to generate the public outrage needed to overcome the lobbying effects by industry.

It is important to emphasize that our description of the Wilson 2X2 matrix focuses on the four end-points. In almost all cases, there are mixes of these four political characterizations. Moreover, the extent to which interests get mobilized on both sides is to some degree in control of advocates of policy reform. That is, the way reforms are packaged affects the degree to which they become salient to some constituencies.

Thus, the four polar cases are ideal types that do not completely characterize any real reform. Rather, they are often useful for capturing the essence of the debate or illustrating how a particular pivotal political player became mobilized. Political scientists almost never (as is the case with most of the chapters in Wilson's 1980 book) try to explain the outcomes of the process using this model. Their focus is almost always horse-race-like—who won the battle for control of the policy. This chapter emphasizes as well the packaging aspect, so as to better understand how political strategy can influence outcomes.

While the above discussion of the Wilson matrix has focused primarily on legislative change, it should be understood that both the judicial branch and the executive and agency branches of the government have roles to play, as do international policymaking organizations. Some of these interplays will become evident in the telecommunications applications discussed below.

Client Politics: The Vail Compromise

The telephone was invented in 1876. By 1900 some 1,002 of 1,051 U.S. towns with populations over 4,000 had telephone service.[4] During these years, telephone service was local, that is, calls were made within limited geographic areas or exchanges. The monopoly rents from telephony were granted to the holders of the patent rights to the invention of A. G. Bell (albeit after a Court struggle over these patent rights). The expiration of these patents in 1892–93 ushered in a new era of competition to the American Bell Company. As a result, prices were lowered in virtually all of the exchanges, and profit margins eroded. By 1907, most of the assets of the American Bell Company were in the hands of investment bankers. They selected Theodore N. Vail to head the company. In the words of Gerald R. Faulhaber, Vail instituted the first revolution in telecommunications: "the transformation from an industry based on highly competitive local markets for a business/luxury good based on a readily available technology, to an industry based on a regulated monopoly of a national market for a mass consumer good based on high technology."[5]

Figure 14-2 identifies the politics engaged in by Theodore Vail as *client* politics. The key elements of these politics, as they appear in the enlarged client politics box, are highlighted. First, Vail saw the need for a change in the current regime. From his perspective, there was simply too much local competition. Vail was living in an era which had seen concern with "destructive competition" in the railroads, followed by a legislative solution to those problems with the passage of the Act to Regulate Commerce in 1887. He could use this regulatory solution for his own purposes by analogizing that similar oversight by a regulatory agency might meet the public purpose in telecommunications. Specifically, there was destructive competition in certain rail corridors; for example, by 1880 twenty different railroads were in operation between St. Louis and Atlanta. Not surprisingly, there were fierce rate wars in those sections of the country

Figure 14-2. *Client Politics: The Vail Compromise*

Distribution of benefits from policy change

	Narrowly concentrated	Widely distributed
Distribution of costs from policy change Narrowly concentrated	*Interest group politics*	*Entrepreneurial politics*
Widely distributed	*Client politics* • Vail wants to restore American Bell profits after patents expired in 1892–93; cites "destructive competition" in local markets. • Vail provides impetus to improve public perception of local monopoly franchise; focus on universal service, mass local availability. • Vail needs control of day's high technology, radio, vacuum tubes, switching, to introduce long distance service, mass national market. • Vail meets populist concern over monopoly, trusts, through regulation; idea is to trade protection from competitive entry in return for price controls. • Motto: One System, One Policy: Universal Service.	*Majoritarian politics*

Source: Based on Wilson matrix.

where there was so much competing rail service. In order to attract business from competitors, prices would be bid down toward short-run operating costs where excess capacity among competitors existed. Where competition was absent, railroad charges were set as high as the market would bear. Small businesses, small communities, and farmers were particularly disadvantaged. These practices were in direct conflict with the public policy goals of equity, universality of services, and economic development of the entire country. The 1887 act required the railways to make their rates public by filing them with a commission, the Interstate Commerce Commission (ICC). The act ruled out undue preference or advantage to any person, place, or kind of traffic, but made no mention of price discrimination among different commodities. Thus, rate structures were to be such that railroads would treat shippers fairly similarly with respect to their size and location, while receiving high margins on high-value manufactured commodities and relatively low margins on low-value bulk and agricultural commodities. These principles of "reasonable and just rates" reflected the strong political influence of the farmers.

The desired government policy toward telecommunications, as articulated by Theodore Vail in the American Telephone and Telegraph (AT&T) annual report of 1910, was:

> The telephone systems should be universal, interdependent and intercommunicating, affording opportunity for any subscriber of any exchange to communicate with any other subscriber of any other exchange . . . that some sort of connection with the telephone system should be within the reach of all . . . that all this can be accomplished . . . under such control and regulation as will afford the public much better service at less cost than any competition or governmental-owned monopoly.

Thus, in the creation of the nation's communication network, Vail aligned his own interests with the public's desire for universal service. He also saw that in order to create and keep the telephone monopoly strong, he would need to generate patents in long-distance service based on the high technology of the time: radio, vacuum tubes, switching, and so on. His strategy was to dominate long-distance service by promising rapid deployment to all areas of the country. Local services were to be licensed to one subsidiary in any geographical location so as to avoid the uneconomic duplication of facilities that had characterized railroad expansion. Both local and long distance would be available to the mass market. This transformation of telephones fit well with industry trends and consumer desires of the time, such as Henry Ford's Model T for the masses.

However, Vail realized that he would have to pay a price for his vision of a monopoly franchise. The American public had grown suspicious of the large railroad and other trusts. Such trusts brought in their wake cartel-like behavior of industry magnates, financial manipulation and speculation in stocks, as well as the destructive competition noted above. Vail saw that his monopoly rights would not be granted unless he could alleviate the populist concern with the new form of massive capitalistic enterprises. Vail's strategy was to coopt these public concerns by forging a compromise in which the Bell System was protected from competitive entry in return for price controls. The regulation was to take place both at the state level (for local exchanges) and at the federal level (for interstate).

The Mann-Elkins Act of 1910 gave the ICC authority to determine "just and reasonable" rates for interstate wire communication and the power to eliminate rate discrimination. The ICC would continue to be of special aid to remote areas. The same agency was given authority over interstate communications as well as transportation. The concept was that the commission, an expert body, would aid Congress in planning regulatory policy, and would be more responsive and flexible than the alternative of Court processes. The rate regulation principles for telecommunications were to be similar to those applied to the railroads, but little explicit price regulation was undertaken in the early years of telephony.

The motto adopted by Bell System was: "One System, One Policy: Universal Service." The motto worked in that it committed the Bell System to a social mission, and it united Bell System managers and ICC regulators in a common mission. Government policy concerned itself with inefficiency through division of the market and duplication of facilities. For the telephone industry, this meant that a regulated Bell System was given control of all long distance service. In terms of the politics, it is interesting that the independent telephone systems of this period seemingly ceded the long-distance services to Vail. Vail's vision of the future viewed long-distance service as having far greater importance than was seen by the independents, whose focus was local, and whose lobbying was concerned more with the interconnection issue than the monopoly issue. Thus, what could have been an example of interest group politics—if Vail and the independents had both fought to control long distance—instead became client politics.

It is worth noting that the antitrust authorities did not buy into the Vail vision as fully as did the ICC. The explicit threat of antitrust action in 1913 brought an end to Vail's vigorous purchases of local exchanges. The Bell System agreed at that time to stop taking over telephone companies and to interconnect with independent systems. The interconnection issue was particularly important because refusal to interconnect cut off independents from other cities. During 1909–11 the Bell System took over Western Union but was forced to divest it in 1913. Again, this governmental activity outside the legislative arena served as a check and balance to the client politics that had successfully taken place in that arena. In retrospect, it appears that the very strategy that worked so well for legislators—focus on one universal system—raised the hackles of the antitrust authorities whose mandate was to promote competition.

The next analysis of telecommunications politics takes place in 1974; some of the intervening political history is worth discussion. By the end of the Great Depression in 1939 the Bell System had assets of about $5 billion, which at that time made it the largest company in the history of private enterprise. It controlled 83 percent of all telephones in service in the United States, 98 percent of all long-distance wires, and 100 percent of all transoceanic radio telephony. Its subsidiary, Western Electric, manufactured 90 percent of all telephone equipment. By 1965 the Bell System could claim to be serving 85 percent of all households in the areas where it operated, compared with 50 percent in 1925.[6] Between 1920 and 1960 the number of phones increased from 8 million to 90 million. Thus, the promise of universal service was delivered.

Federal regulation gained broad powers with passage of the Communications Act of 1934. The Federal Communications Commission (FCC) took over regulation of all interstate long-distance telephone service and of local and intrastate service to the degree they affected interstate service. The FCC had a development mandate similar to Vail's: "to make available, so far as possible, to all people of the United States a rapid, efficient, nationwide and worldwide wire and radio communication service." Rate regulation and common-carrier obligations formed the core of the regulatory regime. Passage of the act displayed many aspects of interest group politics, particularly with respect to manufacturers who wanted competition in telephone equipment. The act contained a requirement that the FCC report back in five years about how to promote equipment competition. After World War II, the FCC's manufacturing report became the main basis for the 1947 antitrust against Western Electric. Finally, the act was basically neutral about entry, and it allowed the FCC to eventually promulgate the Above 890 and Specialized Common Carriers decisions. Telecommunications regulation also changed a great deal after World War II. The main form of federal regulation of public utilities became the so-called rate-base rate-of-return regulation (this happened primarily after the *Hope Natural Gas Case* of 1944). Federal price regulation of telecommunications tended to leave price structure to the suppliers to decide. Price levels trended downward due to technological advances and growth of the system.

Concern for equitable price regulation came more from state than from federal pressure. Over time, state commissions began to sanction statewide average pricing rules, such as equal charges for equal mileage regardless of cost differences, and, as a result, rate averaging held prices low in rural areas even though connection distances made costs high for such areas. And as new technology greatly reduced long-distance costs, local regulators sought to allocate more of the local plant to long-distance service. Their aim was to hold down local rates without requiring an increase in long-distance rates. This was possible because of the increasing importance of interstate services and their high rate of return. From 1921 to 1925, for example, AT&T was calculated to earn 7.16 percent on local service investment, but 19.21 percent on investment in long lines.[7] Over time, the resulting cross-subsidy meant that long distance rates became very high relative to the low costs made possible by advancing technology.

Entrepreneurial Politics: The Bell System Breakup

As a lead-in to motivate the Bell System breakup, the commercial development of two related technologies, microwave transmission and solid state electronics, is described next. The advent of microwave substantially undermined the natural monopoly argument for long-distance service. Providers no longer needed to own continuous rights-of-way, nor did they need to engage in trenching to protect the cable. Instead, all that was required were radio relay towers at twenty-five mile intervals (line of sight) with suitable electronics at either end and suitable alignment of antennae along the route.[8] Microwave radio enabled long-distance telecommunications to become wireless. Thus, the stage was set for a group of potential competitors to ask the FCC for permission to enter the industry. Separation agreements between federal and state authorities and the rate-averaging philosophy had led to long-distance rates so far above the costs of service in dense markets as to make entry seem attractive even to an inefficient supplier. By the late 1950s numerous companies were granted microwave licenses for their internal use. This success of the competitors to enter some markets through the FCC reflects interest group politics. By the 1960s the FCC began to permit similar competition in long-distance service. Companies began to push for entry into the telephone equipment business as well, both at the customer level and for equipment used by telephone companies.

By the early 1970s, society became convinced that the "heavy hand" of regulation was contributing to inflation and inefficiency. The inherent flaws of the independent regulatory structure began to be recognized. There was a concern that regulatory agencies were being "captured" by the firms they regulated to the detriment of both potential competitors and consumers. The regulatory system had fostered protection of the current set of competitors (however inefficient) rather than enhancing overall competition. Moreover, the policies initiated by the government years before had met the needs for equity and universality. Just as industrial competitiveness was seen as important for other industries, efficiency in the regulated industries was now given high priority.

In 1974 the Department of Justice (DOJ) filed an antitrust suit against the Bell System. The DOJ's theory was that the markets for long-distance service and telephone equipment were potentially competitive. Local service was still a natural monopoly. Ownership by AT&T of all three segments could cause distortions if long distance and equipment markets were removed from regulatory jurisdiction. AT&T could insist, for example, that its local service subsidiaries buy all of their telephone equipment from Western Electric. Or, the local operating companies could favor AT&T long distance services over those of its rivals. The remedy sought by the DOJ was that AT&T's local operating companies be divested from its other activities. The first seven years after the filing of the suit were filled with legal maneuvering. As figure 14-3 shows, this DOJ case represented *entrepreneurial* politics since any remedy would impose concentrated costs on AT&T, while the public at large would benefit if competition replaced monopoly in the long-distance portion of the industry. AT&T attempted to head off both regulatory reform and the antitrust complaints by getting favorable legislation passed—an example of client politics that very nearly worked twice (1976, 1981).

Judge Green issued an opinion following presentation of the DOJ case in 1981. He denied a request by AT&T that the case be dismissed and gave the impression that the DOJ case had a great deal of merit. AT&T began to negotiate a settlement in the form of a consent decree that was announced on January 8, 1982. The agreement was officially known as the Modification of Final Judgment in that it vacated and replaced the Final Judgment of 1956, which ended an earlier antitrust suit filed by the government in 1949; that earlier decree prohibited the telephone com-

Figure 14-3. *Entrepreneurial Politics: The Bell System Break-Up*

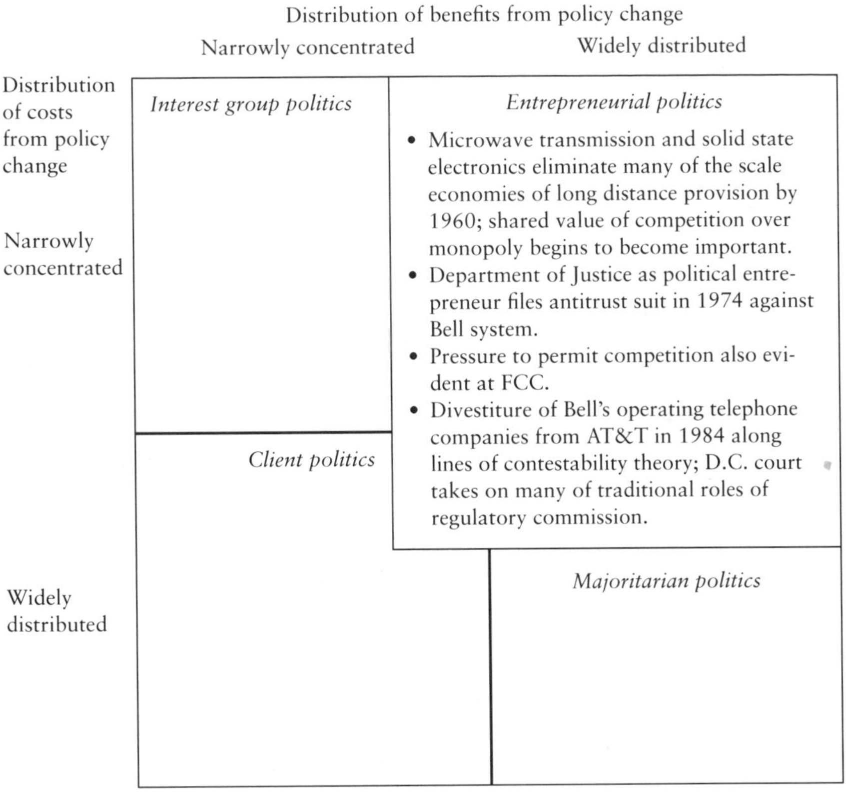

Distribution of benefits from policy change

	Narrowly concentrated	Widely distributed
Distribution of costs from policy change **Narrowly concentrated**	*Interest group politics*	*Entrepreneurial politics* • Microwave transmission and solid state electronics eliminate many of the scale economies of long distance provision by 1960; shared value of competition over monopoly begins to become important. • Department of Justice as political entrepreneur files antitrust suit in 1974 against Bell system. • Pressure to permit competition also evident at FCC.
	Client politics	• Divestiture of Bell's operating telephone companies from AT&T in 1984 along lines of contestability theory; D.C. court takes on many of traditional roles of regulatory commission.
Widely distributed		*Majoritarian politics*

Source: Based on Wilson matrix.

pany from participating in unregulated industries, such as data processing. The 1984 settlement achieved virtually all of the relief requested by the DOJ. Thus, the twenty-two Bell operating companies controlling the local, bottleneck facilities were separated from AT&T, leaving their parent with long-distance service, Western Electric, and Bell Laboratories.

The locals were restructured into seven regulated monopolies. Restrictions were placed upon them that were similar to those that had previously been applied to AT&T. Thus, they were prevented from entering any line of business other than telecommunications exchange access. The seven operating companies could choose which company to buy terminal equipment from, and were permitted (after a modification of the decree) to market (but not manufacture) terminal equipment. AT&T was forbidden to enter local service. The environment for long-distance and terminal equipment was at least partially deregulated. Individuals can choose the long-distance carrier they wish to serve them. This choice is enhanced further by the equal access provisions of the decree, which require that all long-distance companies get the same connection to local networks as that afforded to AT&T. In return, the government has removed the restrictions limiting AT&T to provision of common carrier services and has permitted AT&T to enter the information systems arena. The D.C. court and Judge Green became the public players who provided enforcement to the new competitive regime.

In many ways, the AT&T divestiture reflects the contestability literature in the economics of regulation and antitrust. Contestability theory, as put forth most fully in William Baumol, John Panzar, and Robert Willig, provides the framework that serves as a guide for deregulatory change. Intuitively speaking, the theory of contestable markets builds on the tradition of Harold Demsetz, who first pointed out that sunk costs, not economies of scale, constitute the barrier to entry that confers monopoly power.[9] It is primarily the risk involved in expending large sums of money in order to acquire sunk cost facilities that deters new entry when an otherwise profitable entry opportunity arises. Potential competition becomes an ever more effective force as the extent of large irretrievable entry costs declines. Similarly, incumbent firms, even those who have borne the burden of acquiring the sunk cost facility, are a problem for public policy only to the extent that they have permanent or exclusive access to that facility. Consequently, the single most important element in the design of public policy for monopoly should be the design of arrangements that render benign the exercise of power associated with operating sunk facilities.

One way to avoid the exercise of monopoly power is to have the sunk costs borne by a government or municipality—as they are in U.S. highway systems or airports—or by mandating that sunk costs be shared by a consortium—as is to some extent true of international broadcasting satellites—rather than to have the sunk costs incurred by the firm that is supplying the services. Virtually any method will do as long as there are contractual or other arrangements that are nondiscriminatory and permit easy transfer or lease or shared use of these cost commitments. The theory tells us that when sunk costs are borne exclusively by a serving natural monopoly, as are local telephone loops, then there may be a need for some form of government intervention to assure society that no excessive monopoly rents are earned from those facilities. By detaching sunk costs from the serving firm, much of the need for traditional economic regulation of the industry disappears. Fixed costs are not, according to the theory, a villain unless they also happen to be sunk. For example, although airplanes and barges might be individually costly, their mobility from market to market and their ability to be resold renders this cost unimportant as an entry barrier to a particular route. Technological economies may be such that only one firm can actually serve in the market at any one time, but without exclusive rights or stickiness in entry or exit from airports or terminal facilities, the firm cannot expect to extract monopoly rents.[10]

In the case of the Bell System break-up, it was recognized that AT&T still had an enormous market share of long-distance services, yet this market power was downplayed, focusing instead on the possibility of entry. Evidence has shown that the advocates of competition were proved right about the ability of entrants to challenge AT&T in its long distance services. Between 1982 and 1995, AT&T's share of long distance traffic dropped from 90 percent to the mid 50 percent range. At least part of this entry success, however, has been due to a more stringent continued price regulation as applied to AT&T versus its rivals. It was not until mid 1995 that the FCC removed AT&T's "dominant" status and burdens, so that deregulation was evenly available to all carriers.

Interest Group Politics: The Telecommunications Act of 1996

Since divestiture, telecommunications politics has been of an *interest group* character, as is evident in figure 14-4. The newly formed regional operating companies have not wanted to stay in the local monopoly box created for them under the Modified Final Judgment. They have continually sought relief from line of business and geographic restrictions imposed upon them. The most dramatic efforts along these lines are the announced mergers between Bell Atlantic/NYNEX and SBC/Pactel, both of which have been cleared by DOJ. The local operating companies also sought waivers to enter long-distance service, which were not granted by Judge Green.

The Telecommunications Act of 1996 is designed to further break down the telephone monopoly. This time the focus is on the local phone monopoly. The goal is to have full-scale competition in telephony so that

Figure 14-4. *Interest Group Politics: The Telecommunications Act of 1996*

Distribution of benefits from policy change

	Narrowly concentrated	Widely distributed

Distribution of costs from policy change	*Interest group politics*	*Entrepreneurial politics*
	• Regional operating companies refuse to stay in local monopoly box; they seek relief from line of business and geographic restrictions; they announce mergers.	
Narrowly concentrated	• AT&T still regulated; prices held above those of competitors; regulation gradually moved from rate-of-return to price caps; it seeks relief from regulation.	
	• Consumers see long distance rates decline; local rates increase. State Public Utility Commissions attempt to prevent erosion of local cross subsidy.	*Majoritarian politics*
	• Telecommunications Deregulation Act of 1996 opens entry to long distance after local entry is opened.	
Widely distributed	*Client politics*	

Source: Based on Wilson matrix.

consumers can not only choose between several long-distance options but also between several local operators. Ultimately, consumers could also choose between several combined local and long distance options. As in the 1984 divestiture, there is a technology now available—cellular radio telephone service—which offers the promise of dismantling the monopoly features of local service. Unfortunately, until the new act, the development of this mode was left in the hands of the local telephone companies who had the incentive to develop cellular technology as a complement to, rather than as a substitute for, their existing service. The 1996 act provides for local service the same type of formula that divestiture provided for the long-distance service. By changing the regulatory environment, it was hoped that the market for local telephone service could be subject to the discipline of competition, bringing down prices and increasing choice for consumers.

The act attempted to balance the divergent interests of the regional Bell operating companies (RBOCs), the long-distance carriers, and cable TV operators. Its main focus is to encourage further competition. Competitors to the RBOCs, including the long-distance carriers, cable television providers, and other new entrants, were encouraged to enter local-service markets. The RBOCs are permitted entry into long distance once they can demonstrate that there is adequate competition at the local level. New competitors (including the RBOCs) are encouraged to provide competition to the cable TV companies. The goal of the legislation was to reduce the scale and scope of regulation in all these areas.

However, the act itself has led to further interest group politics as the FCC has sought implementation rules. In describing the interest group activity recently played out before the FCC, Kirk Victor quotes Roy M. Neel, president of the United States Telephone Association (representing local telephone companies) as saying, "This is the big enchilada. This is where all the money gets divided—it's where the commission can arbitrarily pick winners and losers."[11] Indeed, the rules put forward by the FCC in August of 1996 have been stayed by the Courts. State regulators have been protective toward the RBOCs, and sought the stay because of the feature that new entrants be permitted to lease all required facilities from the RBOCs at prices below costs that reflect current cross-subsidies. Another issue is whether states or the FCC can set the terms and conditions of local entry. Yet, without local competition in place, the RBOCs will not be allowed to provide long distance and therefore one-stop shopping services (both local and long distance).

So, as of the spring of 1997, there is still an interest group stand-off. AT&T has made a number of moves indicating its intention to move into local services. It has separated its computer and network systems businesses, and spun off Bell Laboratories into Lucent Technologies. It has recently unveiled a new fixed wireless technology that allows customers to use the same phone in the home and on the road, and also promises high-speed data service capability. Several states are also trying new approaches that would free the RBOCs to enter new markets more quickly. The idea is that entry can be opened faster if states have more effective enforcement mechanisms against anticompetitive practices. Fortunately, throughout this process of competitive entry, there is evidence that universal service will survive and indeed that most consumers will achieve net benefits from a competitive communications environment.[12]

Majoritarian Politics: The World Trade Organization Deal of 1997

In February of 1997, an accord was reached among sixty-nine countries under the World Trade Organization (WTO) that opens the global telecommunications market. The agreement gives U.S. and foreign companies global market access to offer telephone services. It ensures that these companies can acquire stakes in foreign communications firms, and it adopts regulations to promote competition. The scope is very broad. It opens the three largest telecommunications markets—America, the European Union, and Japan—to domestic and international competition in 1998. Fifteen other countries will also be opened immediately, while sixteen others will be opened more gradually over the next seven years. The agreement offers an example of majoritarian politics, as depicted in figure 14-5.

In order to understand why the benefits are taken to exceed the costs of this new global telecommunications regime, it is necessary to go back in history to understand the nature of the status quo. For decades, the world's telephone monopolies have operated under a regime in which they deliver each other's international calls for a prearranged fee, one which greatly exceeds the cost of provision. Many foreign governments use these fees to cross-subsidize their postal or transportation services. At the end of each year, there is a settlement. For the United States the annual deficit in telephone services has risen from $0.3 billion in 1980 to some $2.4 billion in 1989. In order to avoid these high rates, multinational firms began leasing private lines to their offices in other countries, avoiding the cartel. The United States and the United Kingdom began permitting telephone firms to "resell" capacity making their countries cheap hubs for international telephone traffic. Consumers wanted access to the same low prices offered businesses, so "call-back" services let them avoid expensive countries' telephone rates by seeming to originate their calls at cheaper American rates.

The WTO agreement can be viewed as a grudging recognition of the fact that advancing technology and the move toward international liberalization are making global changes in governmental policy inevitable.

Figure 14-5. *Majoritarian Politics: The World Trade Organization Deal of 1997*

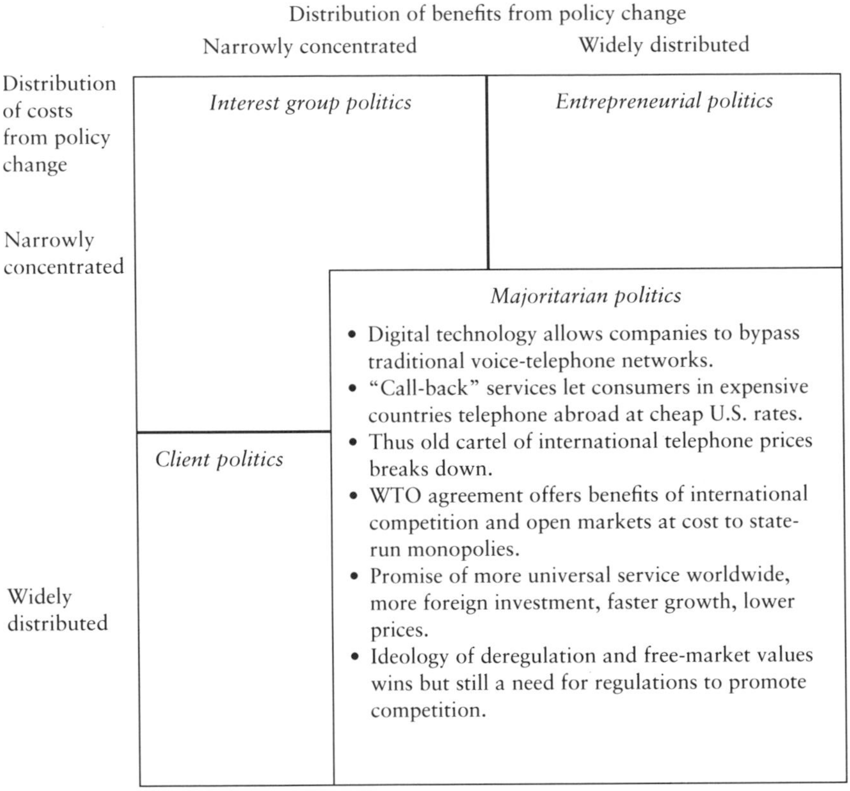

	Distribution of benefits from policy change	
	Narrowly concentrated	Widely distributed
Distribution of costs from policy change Narrowly concentrated	*Interest group politics*	*Entrepreneurial politics*
Widely distributed	*Client politics*	*Majoritarian politics* • Digital technology allows companies to bypass traditional voice-telephone networks. • "Call-back" services let consumers in expensive countries telephone abroad at cheap U.S. rates. • Thus old cartel of international telephone prices breaks down. • WTO agreement offers benefits of international competition and open markets at cost to state-run monopolies. • Promise of more universal service worldwide, more foreign investment, faster growth, lower prices. • Ideology of deregulation and free-market values wins but still a need for regulations to promote competition.

Source: Based on Wilson matrix.

The deregulation movement in the United States has its counterparts internationally. Britain, New Zealand, and most of the Scandinavian countries have already opened most of their markets. Much of European Union telephony was already scheduled to liberalize and privatize in 1998. Even Japan has been bringing some domestic competition to NTT to match its somewhat opened long-distance markets. Without such changes, a WTO agreement might never have been possible. The agreement will boost international alliances, such as that of Sprint Corporation with the national phone carriers of France and Germany. It will be similarly advantageous to British Telecommunications PLC, which is in the process of acquiring MCI Communications Corporation.

The WTO accord offers benefits not only to the telephone giants but also to emerging economies. Developing countries are projected to require tens of billions in capital investment each year for telecommunications, and a vast majority of this investment will need to come from private sources. However, as service moves from the state to the private sector, the countries will be needing to establish a dependable regulatory system. At a minimum, the WTO accord offers a degree of safeguard to the private capital since it will be enforceable under the rules of international trade.

In the interest of a balanced presentation, it should be mentioned that the WTO as majoritarian politics leaves out an important part of the story: the nature of what the WTO means by "open" telecommunication markets, and the boundary between "national" and "international" for purposes of defining openness. It does not require countries to let foreign firms own local telephone companies or to make local access competitive, or even to end ownership of telephones by the local carrier. It requires open procurement, foreign participation in international connections, and equal access to national networks. The WTO rules still permit a country to operate much of its telecommunications as a nationalized entity, subject primarily to local client and interest group politics.

Conclusion

Over the past two hundred years, there has been a shifting balance in public sector priorities toward telecommunications. The earliest priority was for universal service. The next political imperative was for equity: that communications services be reasonably priced, and that all localities receive service. No person or locality should be charged too high or unreasonable a price. Thus, it made political sense for both state and local governments to buy into Vail's *client politics* vision of a regulated monopoly that would do everything possible to improve the availability and lower the cost of communications.

During the last two decades, the federal government has been concerned not just with universal service and equity, but also with industrial competitiveness. The government has sought to improve competitiveness and productivity through deregulation. In telecommunications, the *entrepreneurial politics* of the DOJ attempted to separate the by then potentially competitive long-distance portions of the business from the still local monopoly portions. Recent further innovations in technology have seen the hope of competition in the local markets as well. *Interest group politics* has characterized the fight over how to divide the pie between the interstate carriers and the RBOCs as both seek to enter each other's markets. Most recently of all, there has been a major step forward in liberalizing international telecommunications policy through a *majoritarian politics* accord crafted by the WTO.

These are the politics this chapter has characterized. But there are political and economic issues that the paper has not addressed. Most importantly, the extent to which the salient political issue of the time was really at stake or was just symbolic has not been discussed. Would the United States have achieved universal service much more slowly if competition had prevailed? Would long distance and manufacturing competition have been materially different today without divestiture? Will the Telecommunications Act of 1996 actually bring about local competition sooner than it otherwise would have? Will the WTO agreement hasten international competition—or would the U.S. policies about call-back and international calling rates have killed off international cartels anyway? Clearly, a full political analysis would be enriched by deeper exploration of just how much the outcomes of the Wilsonian political competition have mattered.

Notes

1. James Q. Wilson, "The Politics of Regulation," *The Politics of Regulation* (Basic Books, 1980), pp. 357–95.

2. See, for example, Roger G. Noll, "Economic Perspectives on the Politics of Regulation," in R. Schmalensee and R. D. Willings, *Hardbook of Industrial Organization,* vol. 2 (Elsevier Science Publishers, 1989), pp. 253–1287, chapter 22.

3. Wilson, "The Politics of Regulation," p. 369.

4. John Meyer and others, *The Economics of Competition in the Telecommunications Industry* (Oelgeschlager, Gunn and Hain Publishers, 1980).

5. Gerald R. Faulhaber, "Public Policy in Telecommunications: The Third Revolution," *Information Economics and Policy,* vol. 7 (September 1995), pp. 251–82, esp. p. 253.

6. John Brooks, *Telephone: The First Hundred Years* (Harper and Row, 1975), pp. 205, 266.

7. Stephen Breyer, *Regulation and Its Reform* (Harvard University Press, 1982), p. 296.

8. See Faulhaber, "Public Policy in Telecommunications."

9. William Baumol, John C. Panzar, and Robert D. Willig, *Contestable Markets and the Theory of Industry Structure* (Harcourt Brace Jovanovich, 1982); and Harold Demsetz, "Why Regulate Utilities?" *Journal of Law and Economics*, vol 11 (April 1968), pp. 55–65.

10. See also Elizabeth E. Bailey and William J. Baumol, "Deregulation and the Theory of Contestable Markets," *Yale Journal on Regulation*, vol. 1, no. 2 (1984), pp. 111–37.

11. Kirk Victor, "The Biggest Enchilada," *National Journal*, July 20, 1996.

12. Frank A. Wolak, "Can Universal Service Survive in a Competitive Telecommunications Environment? Evidence from the United States Consumer Expenditure Survey," *Information Economics and Policies*, vol. 8 (September 1996), pp. 163–203.

CHAPTER FIFTEEN

Telephone Subsidies, Income Redistribution, and Consumer Welfare

Robert W. Crandall

T HE FEDERAL COMMUNICATIONS Commission (FCC) has been engaged in a struggle to adjust its general policies toward the pricing of telephone service as it prepares for the new competitive era ushered in by the 1996 Telecommunications Act. Among its early targets has been the decades-old policy of allowing long distance rates to cross-subsidize local residential rates. State regulators have pursued the same policy with intrastate long distance rates and have added to these price distortions by keeping local telephone rates below cost while allowing telephone companies to charge business subscribers and some urban residential subscribers local rates that are above cost. None of these policies will be able to survive in a world in which competition, not the politics of regulation, determines how much we pay to use the telephone network.

Behind the crazy quilt of regulatory cross-subsidies erected by the FCC and state regulators over several decades is the notion that the number of households who subscribe to the network is enhanced by keeping local rates low and allowing the price of *using* the network to be kept artificially high. Ending this practice, regulators fear, would therefore threaten "universal service" among the poor and our rural brethren. Even more threatening to politically sensitive regulators is that moving telephone rates toward cost would create a revolt of the populists who would rail against higher local rates even if long distance charges fell dramatically.

This chapter is based on current research on universal service policies being conducted by Leonard Waverman and me at the Brookings Institution. Support for this research has been provided by Ameritech, Bell Atlantic, and the Markle Foundation. The author is indebted to Lin Lin for research assistance.

This pricing policy has extremely unfortunate side effects because it restricts communication by making the use of the network expensive and by creating the imperative for continuing regulation while providing additional inducement to households to subscribe to telephone service. Even more distressing is that so little income redistribution from wealthy to less wealthy households occurs as the result of such a policy. Many of the alleged beneficiaries of subsidized local rates use substantial amounts of long distance service that is deliberately overpriced to keep their local rates so low. It is as if sandwiches were subsidized by keeping the price of bread below cost and recovering the required subsidy from the meats and cheeses used to fill them. Some consumers who like to eat plain bread or thin sandwiches might benefit from such a policy, but the cost of the policy would be substantial in terms of nutrition and consumer welfare.

In this chapter, I use recent data drawn from a sample of household telephone bills to measure the degree to which the current system of cross subsidies redistributes income among income classes. I then use these data, published information on local rates, and estimates of the cost of providing telephone lines to residences in areas of different population density to estimate the degree to which state regulators subsidize rural residences at the expense of urban households and business subscribers.

Who Pays for Telephone Service?

The residential customer typically buys its local telephone service and long distance service from different suppliers. The local telephone company provides the line up to the residence, connects local calls, provides long distance service over a limited nearby area, and supplies a variety of "vertical services," such as call waiting, messaging, and number-identification. In the United States, most residential service is offered with unlimited local calling—in other words, local calls are priced at zero, a price that is surely below cost during periods of peak usage. In addition, residential lines and even some business lines are priced below cost, but long distance service and the vertical services are generally priced above cost. Traditionally all such services have been heavily regulated, but protected to varying degrees from entry by the regulators.

Long distance service outside the local companies' local access and transport areas (LATAs) is provided by national carriers (AT&T, Sprint, MCI, and others) or regional carriers. These carriers must pay the local companies access charges to connect their calls. Because these connection charges are designed by regulators to recover 25 percent of the local companies' fixed (nontraffic-sensitive) costs, they are now between $0.0275 and $0.03 a minute on each end of the call, or between $0.055 and $0.06 a minute for a normal voice call[1] even though the actual cost of delivering these calls to and from the long distance carriers is perhaps $0.005 to $0.01 a conversation These charges now account for about 34 percent of the total price of a call.[2] The difference between access rates and the cost of originating and terminating a long distance call—about $0.05 a minute—is quite simply a subsidy from long distance to local service.[3]

In addition to the per-minute access charges, long distance carriers are also assessed nearly $6.50 per subscriber line per year to subsidize low-income and rural subscribers. Less than $1.20 of these charges is directed toward state lifeline and link-up programs that subsidize monthly line rentals or new connections (installation charges) for low-income subscribers. The remainder—or about $800 million a year—goes into a "high-cost" fund to subsidize rural telephone carriers.

Finally, state regulators erect a variety of cross-subsidies through the intrastate rate structures that they control. Residential rates for local service are typically less than half the rates charged to small and medium businesses even though the cost of residential service is typically little different from that of business service.[4] In addition, the monthly rates for local service typically fall slowly as one moves from center cities in large urban areas to the suburbs and into rural areas despite the fact that the cost of extending such service rises with declining population density. In some states, regulators have allowed a uniform pricing policy for local service across the state, reflecting a movement in the right direction, but no state requires rates to rise to reflect the additional costs of extending wires to more remote subscribers.[5] These cross-subsidies from urban to rural areas and from business to residential subscribers amount to perhaps $6 billion to $8 billion a year, but they have not been fully quantified because regulators have not been interested in knowing their magnitude until the recent passage of the 1996 Telecommunications Act.

A Look at Household Telephone Expenditures

Until recently, we had very little data on the distribution of telephone expenditures across households. As a result, we could not measure with

Figure 15-1. *Average Expenditures, Sample Month, 1995*

Dollars per month

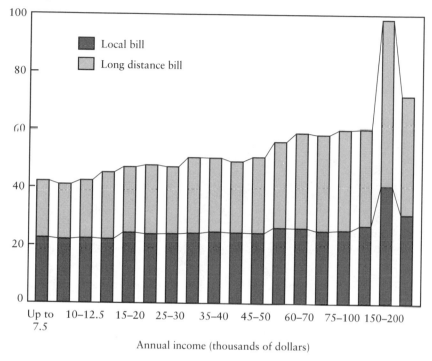

Annual income (thousands of dollars)

Source: PNR, Inc., Phila., 1995.

precision the effects of the regulatory pricing strategy on households of different income groups or in different locations. To remedy this deficiency, a private market-research firm has been employed to collect the telephone bills of a stratified random sample of 10,000 households.[6] These data have been made available to me for ongoing research on the effects of universal-service policies. They provide some rather startling initial conclusions about the effects of the cross-subsidies of local service from excessive long distance rates and access charges.

First, in every income category, the average long distance bill is a rather large share of total telephone expenditures. Even in the lowest-income households, those with less than $10,000 a year in annual income, more than 45 percent of the average bill is for long-distance calls (figure 15-1). Indeed, every income class above $30,000 spends

Table 15-1. *Average Spending on Long Distance Service by Deciles within Income Classes*

Dollars per month

Decile	Less than $10,000	$10,000–$20,000	$20,000–$40,000	$40,000–$75,000	$75,000+
10	0	0	0.15	0.37	0.77
20	0.22	0.95	2.53	3.62	5.09
30	1.74	3.69	5.89	8.00	9.92
40	4.02	6.78	9.52	12.17	15.41
50	7.22	10.10	13.47	16.92	21.09
60	11.14	14.28	18.15	22.37	26.83
70	16.42	19.88	23.86	28.76	34.84
80	23.35	27.73	31.83	38.28	45.96
90	36.77	42.27	45.13	53.43	64.75
100	91.12	91.41	93.07	104.31	135.68

Source: PNR, Inc., *Bill Harvesting II* (Philadelphia, Pa.: 1995).

more on long distance services than on all local services, including vertical services. Long distance calling is not simply an indulgence of the rich.

Second, within each income category, there is enormous variance in the number of long distance calls per month. The top 10 percent of households with incomes below $10,000 spent more than $90 on long distance calls in our sample month (table 15-1)! Any attempt to keep monthly bills low by charging *them* more for long distance calls is surely not a desirable redistribution of income.

Third, more than half of high-income households—those with more than $75,000 in annual income—have long distance bills below $25 a month. As a result, they pay less to the cause of "universal" service than do 20 percent of the poorest households.

Finally, the subsidy to residential lines is absorbed disproportionately by higher-income households who lease more than one line. There are about 109 million residential lines but only 95 million telephone households because many households now have two, three, or more lines to accommodate numerous family members, fax machines, and computer modems. The higher-income households are clearly the most intensive users of such lines as figure 15-1 shows. Their local bills average $30 or more, despite the fact that the average residential telephone line costs only about $20 a month, in part because they lease more lines than do those in the lower-income classes.[7]

The Effects of Reducing Long Distance
Access Charges to Incremental Cost

The average price paid for long distance service is remarkably constant across income levels. Low-income households pay about $0.14 a minute for the shorter intraLATA calls provided mainly by their local telephone company. High-income households pay an average of $0.13 a minute.[8] Similarly, for the longer interLATA calls, low-income and high-income households pay about the same price—$0.18 a minute—although the higher income households tend to make calls that average slightly more than 600 miles while low-income households average about 500 miles.

Were regulators to eliminate the cross-subsidy flowing from *residential* long distance calls to local services, they would essentially reduce access charges by $0.05 a minute.[9] This reduction, in turn, should reduce long distance rates by about the same amount—or by 30 percent. If this reduction were to occur for residential customers, the local companies would suffer an immediate loss of $11.7 billion on the roughly 235 billion residential calls,[10] or about $100 per residential line a year. Since lower long distance rates would stimulate greater calling, the net loss to local companies would likely be about $10 billion, or $90 per line per year.[11] At the same time, the increase in local rates would reduce the number of subscribers by a few percentage points, but most of those disconnecting would likely be customers that are now unprofitable. Thus, a $7.00 a month increase in local rates would probably be sufficient to recover the lost access revenues. Put another way, the cross-subsidies flowing from residential long distance to residential local service is about $7.00 a month per line.

What if the FCC and the state regulators were to attempt to rebalance at least residential long distance and local rates by reducing the former by $0.05 a minute and raising the latter by $7.00 a month? Would "consumers" suffer? Would low-income consumers suffer more than high-income consumers? Figure 15-2 provides the bare elements of an answer. Comparing figures 15-1 and 15-2 reveals surprisingly little average change in telephone bills across consumer groups.

In figure 15-3, I display the change in total telephone spending per month as a result of this "drastic" rebalancing. No income class suffers as much as a $5.50 average increase a month. But the increase in consumer welfare—the value of telephone service to the consumer—rises by

Figure 15-2. *Average Expenditures after Repricing*

Dollars per month

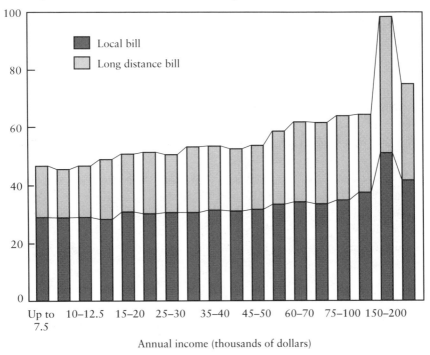

Annual income (thousands of dollars)

Source: Author's calculations based on data from PNR, Inc., 1995.

more than the increase in spending on average for all but the three lowest income classes, and even these lowest income classes suffer only an average loss of between $0.39 and $0.79 a month per household, or $4.68 to $9.48 a year. For instance, those with annual incomes between $7,500 and $10,000 suffer losses equal to about 0.1 percent of their annual income. On average, each household gains more than $15.00 a year, for a total gain to the economy of more than $1.5 billion a year.[12]

The Effects of Rate Rebalancing within Income Classes

The results shown in figures 15-1 through 15-3 fail to come to grips with the substantial differences in long distance spending *within* income classes. The average residential long distance bill in the sample month

Figure 15-3. *Effects of Repricing on Households*

Dollars per month

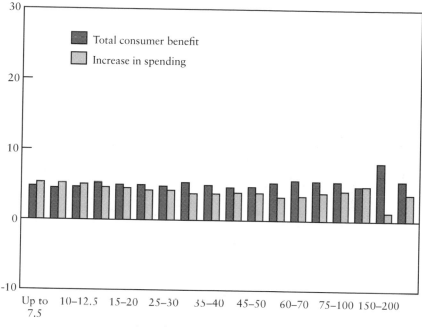

Annual income (thousands of dollars)

Source: Author's calculations based on data from PNR, Inc., 1995.

was $25.00; however, as table 15-1 shows, *most* households in *every* income group spent less than $25.00 This skewness in the distribution of long distance calling is well-recognized within the industry, but these data show that it exists in every income category. It may also help to explain why the "universal service" policy of subsidizing local rates from long distance services is politically popular. One-third of all households account for more than half of residential long distance spending, which in turn accounts for only 47 percent of all long distance expenditures. Business spending on long distance accounts for the other 53 percent. Thus, two-thirds of the nation's residential consumers account for less than one-fourth of total long distance spending.

The impacts of local/long distance rate rebalancing on each of the five income classes shown in table 15-1 may be seen in figures 15-4 through 15-8, which array households in terms of their monthly long distance bills (see table 15-1). In the two lowest income classes, each decile except

Figure 15-4. *Effect on Households: Income under $10,000*

Dollars per month

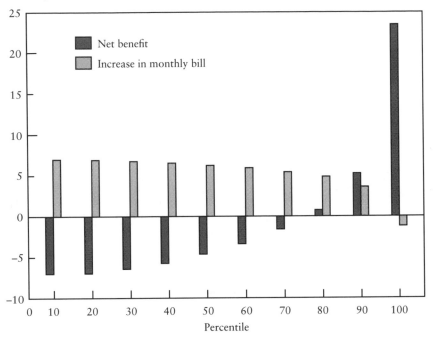

Source: Author's calculations based on data from PNR, Inc., 1995.

for the highest experiences an increase in its total monthly telephone bill from the repricing of local and long distance service. However, the three highest deciles in the lowest income class (less than $10,000 in annual income) actually realize an improvement in their economic welfare from their increased long distance calling that is facilitated by lower access charges.

In every other income category, the top 40 percent of households in terms of long distance expenditure gain while the bottom 60 percent suffer some losses. Ironically, the largest losers in our analysis are wealthy households with very little long distance spending because we assume that households with $75,000 in annual income or more have an average of 1.5 local lines per residence. Once again, every income class other than the lowest income class gains on average, but there are very large gains from rebalancing among the heaviest long distance users and generally

Figure 15-5. *Effect on Households: Income $10,000–$20,000*

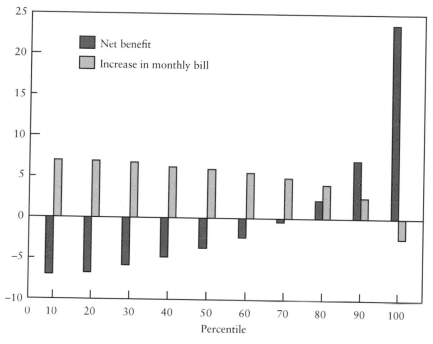

Source: Author's calculations based on data from PNR, Inc., 1995.

moderate losses for the rest owing to the increase of local rates toward cost.

Telephone Subscription by Income Class

The preceding analysis demonstrates that while low-income households are less intensive users of long distance services on average, there are many among these lower-income households who consume substantial amounts of long distance. Surely, it is not equitable to require these heavy long distance users to subsidize those in all income classes who use little long distance service.

The remarkable constancy of household spending on local service across incomes, shown in figure 15-1, demonstrates that the extremely

Figure 15-6. *Effect on Households: Income $20,000–$40,000*

Dollars per month

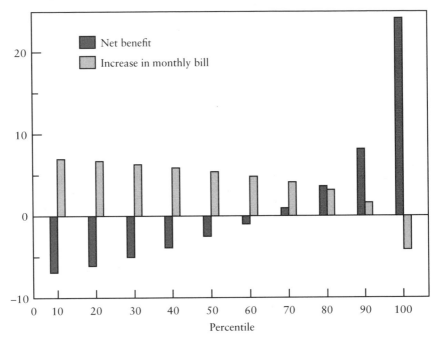

Source: Author's calculations based on data from PNR, Inc., 1995.

elaborate system of cross subsidies erected by regulators of telephone service has not reduced local rates for lower-income households. All residential rates and particularly all rural residential rates are kept artificially low by regulators, but not for the particular benefit of poorer households.

One might ask if there is any need to subsidize telephone connections for low-income households. Table 15-2 displays the trends in telephone subscribership across income levels for the 1984–96 period. Because the data in table 15-2 are displayed for categories of nominal income, they understate the degree to which lower-income households have increasingly connected to telephone service. In 1996 a nominal income of $15,000 was equivalent in real terms to a nominal income of $10,000 in 1984. Thus the increase in telephone subscribership among persons with real incomes of less than $10,000 has undoubtedly been far greater than the 5.3 percentage-point gain shown in table 15-2. But even table 15-2

Figure 15-7. *Effect on Households: Income $40,000–$75,000*

Dollars per month

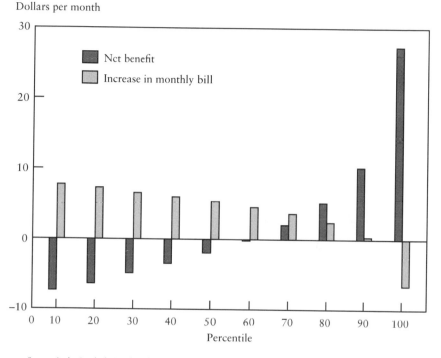

Source: Author's calculations based on data from PNR, Inc., 1995.

shows that the telephone has now become virtually ubiquitous for households with incomes above $20,000.

Given the Lifeline and Link-up subsidy programs that have existed for ten years or more, all but a few states have some form of subsidy program directed at various categories of low-income households. The Lifeline program provides matching funds for state programs that reduce the monthly charge for eligible households while the Link-up program provides matching funds for reducing the installation charges for these households. Both programs are funded from taxes on long distance services, but Lifeline receives about seven times the federal funding that is directed to the Link-up program.

There is at best only a modest possibility that low-income subsidies of monthly telephone connection charges are very successful in increasing subscribership among these households. A variety of interviews and anecdotal evidence suggests that a large share of the low-income households

Figure 15-8. *Effect on Households: Income above $75,000*

Dollars per month

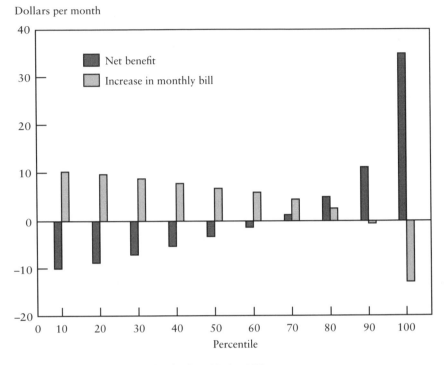

Percentile

Source: Author's calculations based on data from PNR, Inc., 1995.

without telephone service do not currently subscribe because they have run up large long distance bills in previous months. Unable to pay these long distance charges, their entire telephone service is disconnected. Lower local monthly rates would not ameliorate their condition, but lower installation charges might. Thus, there is a much more significant case for Link-up subsidies than for the Lifeline program.

Recent estimates of residential telephone demand for telephone service conclude that the price elasticity of demand is extremely low, perhaps as low as −0.01 to −0.03.[13] These results do not provide much support for a program, such as Lifeline, that is directed at lowering the already-subsidized monthly residential rates. A very recent study by Christopher Garbacz and Herbert G.Thompson Jr. finds that the price elasticity of residential demand is between −0.001 and −0.026, but that the elasticity with respect to the initial *connection charge* is between −0.007 and −0.046.[14] Thus, if a subsidy were to be designed for maximum impact,

Table 15-2. *Telephone Penetration by Nominal Income Class,
Selected Years*

Percent

Income	1984	1990	1996
Less than $10,000	80.1	82.9	85.4
$10,000–$19,999	90.8	91.9	93.0
$20,000–$29,999	95.9	96.3	96.5
$30,000–$39,999	98.3	98.4	97.6
$40,000 or more	98.6	99.1	98.5

Source: Alexander Belinfante, *Telephone Penetration by Income by State*, Industry Analysis Division (Federal Communications Commission, March 1997). (Data from the Current Population Survey.)

it should be directed at the connection charge, not the monthly rate. But with residential subscription rates above 85 percent for even the very lowest-income households, the marginal effect of subsidizing either rate is meager indeed.

Our own research on the determinants of residential subscription to telephone service is at an early stage. However, we tentatively conclude from analyzing 1990 Census data for 1,600 communities and 1995 Current Population Survey (CPS) data for the lower forty-eight states that local monthly rates have little or no statistically significant effect on subscriptions, but that connection charges have a small, but highly significant effect.[15] It is therefore our preliminary conclusion that local monthly rates could rise without any noticeable effect on telephone subscriptions.

Do Local Rate Structures Result in Favorable Income Redistribution?

Until recently, virtually every state required local telephone companies to offer lower rates with declining population density despite the fact that the fixed (nontraffic-sensitive) costs of serving rural subscribers is much higher than the cost of serving urban customers. In recent years, some states have moved to a uniform, statewide rate for residences and a higher one for businesses. In addition, several states have introduced mandatory usage-sensitive rates, particularly for business subscribers. However, no state has implemented a rate structure that reflects the incremental costs of connecting and serving its diverse subscriber base. In every state, rural subscribers pay no more than urban subscribers,

Figure 15-9. *Average Local Rates, December 1994*

Dollars per month

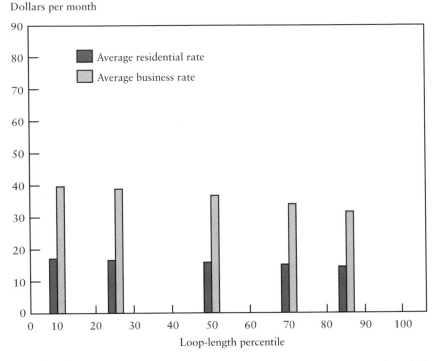

Loop-length percentile

Source: National Association of Regulatory Utility Commissioners, *Bell Operating Companies' Exchange Service Telephone Rates*, December 31, 1994; and author's estimates.

and business subscribers pay more than similarly located residential subscribers.

The residential rate structure clearly favors rural subscribers as shown in Bell Company rate data arrayed in figure 15-9. As the size of the wire center (where the central office is located) declines, the length of the loop connecting the subscriber rises. Despite the fact that the marginal cost of wire is clearly positive, the monthly flat rate declines modestly with the length of the loop. Surprisingly, the 1995 bill-harvesting data show no relationship at all to population density. A simple linear regression of the monthly bill for local service is directly related to household size and income (because larger, wealthier households have more lines and vertical services), but it does not rise or fall with population density in the community in which the household resides. On the other hand, when metropolitan statistical area (MSA) size is substituted for population density,

I find that the average price paid in the largest markets is about $0.80 to $1.60 higher than in the smaller markets, or about 4 percent to 8 percent of the national average local rate, holding family size and income constant.

Loop length decreases with population density. The precise relationship between density and the cost of local service may be deduced from recent cost models proffered to the Federal Communications Commission and state regulators by contesting parties for the purpose of establishing the wholesale rates for unbundled local network elements.[16] The two major models—the long distance companies' Hatfield model and the incumbents' Benchmark Cost Proxy model—differ greatly as to the *level* of costs, but both provide similar estimates of the effects of density on costs. An analysis of the state-by-state results for each model suggests that an equation of the form:

$$(1) \qquad C = a(16,500 - 163P)^{-0.4}$$

approximates the relationship between density and cost where C is the cost per line per month and P is the percentile of density, arrayed from the most dense to the least dense areas.

The parameter a in (1) may be chosen to reflect one's assumptions about investment costs, the cost of capital, and operating costs. For instance, I use $a = 575$ to calibrate the cost model to generate total costs approximately equal to total residential revenues from basic service in 1995. This calibration allows me to show a revenue-neutral restructuring of residential rates toward relative costs (figure 15-10). This restructuring suggests that the monthly rate should be $11.87 for the households in areas with the top 1 percent of population density and $54.41 for households in areas with the lowest 1 percent of population density if rates were proportional to the actual cost per loop. Obviously, rates would have to be proportionally higher for all households if local rates were structured to recover the entire cost of providing local service. The results from inserting $a = 575$ into (1) are broadly consistent with the Hatfield model's predictions except at the very tail of low population density. However, it is now unreasonable to assume that households in the most remote areas should receive telephone service through wires rather than through wireless facilities. Hence, this truncation of the prediction for extremely low-density areas is appropriate.

In figure 15-10, I reproduce the cost-per-loop estimates from (1), calibrated to generate an integral of total costs approximately equal to

Figure 15-10. *The Subsidy to Rural Subscribers, 1994*

Dollars per month

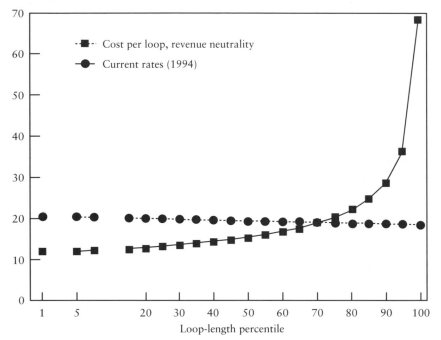

Source: Author's calculations based on FCC (1996) and Hatfield model.

current residential local-service revenues. The degree to which local residential rates cover estimated costs on average is arrayed by loop length. I also assume that local rates average $19.50 a month, the FCC's estimate for a single line in 1995.[17] In addition, I assume that rates fall linearly but gradually from $20.50 a month for the most dense areas to $18.50 in the least dense areas, a result consistent with the average Bell Company rate data. Under these assumptions, figure 15-10 shows that roughly 70 percent of households pay more than their share of the costs allocated to local service while the 30 percent of the population in the least dense areas pay less than their share The transfers are modest for most households—the average transfer from the 70 percent who overpay is about $4 a month, but the gains for those in the 90th to 100th percentile of loop lengths (least dense areas) are very large, ranging from $10 to more than $50 a month. The total wealth transfer is approximately $3.3 billion

Table 15-3. *Income and Poverty by Size of MSA, 1990*

Population of MSA	Percent of total U.S. households	Average household income ($)	Percent of persons below poverty level
Non-MSA	22.5	29,049	16.3
50,000–249,999	8.7	33,244	13.7
250,000–499,999	8.6	35,263	13.4
500,000–999,999	10.2	37,164	12.2
1,000,000–2,499,999	16.5	39,077	10.9
2,500,000 +	33.5	47,103	11.1
Total	100	38,478	12.8

Source: U.S. Bureau of the Census, *1990 Census of Population* (Department of Commerce, 1990).

from those in the most densely populated areas to the 30 percent of the population in the least densely populated areas.[18]

Does the favoritism shown toward rural subscribers translate into a favorable redistribution of income? The answer is mildly in the affirmative because average household incomes rise mildly with the size of the metropolitan area (MSA), and poverty declines slightly with the size of the MSA (table 15-3). The results above are broadly consistent with a conclusion that households in MSAs with more than 250,000 people are forced to shift more than $3 billion a year through local telephone rates to those living in areas with fewer than 250,000 people. The average income of households in areas paying proportionately more than their share of costs is $42,200 while the average income in areas receiving these transfers is $30,200. However, it is obvious that many relatively low-income subscribers live in large MSAs and many wealthy households are in rural areas. Hence, this crude form of income redistribution results in punishing many at the lowest end of the income scale while subsidizing wealthy residences in small towns and rural areas as well as affluent owners of ski condominiums and hunting lodges. Because the price elasticity of demand for local service is so very low, the geographic rate distortions in basic, local rates do not constitute a major source of economic welfare loss. Were this the only subsidy embedded in the telephone rate structure, the cost to the country would not be large even if the cost to urban subscribers is substantial. However, with competition being ushered in by the 1996 act, even these distortions are in peril. As a result, the FCC is in the process of reconfiguring the universal-service subsidy mechanism to one of a common, indirect tax on all telephone services.

Conclusion

The cross-subsidization of local residential service through supracompetitive residential long distance rates is a very expensive policy that costs consumers about $1.5 billion a year in economic welfare. The cost of keeping all long distance rates—including those paid by businesses—artificially high through these cross-subsidies is much greater since businesses account for more than half of all long distance calling. The political imperative to keep local rates low raises long distance charges to low-income and high-income consumers alike. The net cost of this policy to a large share of consumers—those who use long distance services most intensively—is extremely high, but the benefit to those consumers who use little long distance is relatively low. Even the lowest-income consumers—those with less than $10,000 in annual income—gain only about $6 to $8 a year on average from this policy. Paying $1.5 billion or more per year for such limited income redistribution is clearly a bad bargain. Direct subsidies to truly needy consumers, paid visibly and directly, wold be far more efficient and effective in stimulating "universal" service, for it is only those with extremely low incomes who are not universally connected to the network.

In addition, the current universal-service policies transfer enormous rents from urban to rural subscribers with little or no positive benefit on overall telephone subscriptions. Urban residences are not universally wealthy, and rural residents are not universally poor. Indeed, many poor inner-city residents now pay proportionately more than their share of costs for local service to allow middle-income and wealthy rural residences to enjoy low monthly rates. The transfer from densely populated areas to the 30 percent of households living farthest from a telephone central office is more than $3 billion a year, and it achieves very little in terms of increasing telephone subscriptions or helping needy Americans.

Notes

1. Federal Communications Commission, Common Carrier Bureau, Industry Analysis Division, *Telephone Trends Report* (Washington, annual editions).

2. Bureau of the Census, *Annual Survey of Communications, 1995* (Depart-

ment of Commerce, 1995). Long distance revenues were $81.3 billion in 1995, and network access charges paid by business firms were $27.9 billion. These data include all types of long distance services—800 services, private-line services, ordinary switched services, and so on—as well as switched and "special" (dedicated-line) access revenues.

3. I use the term "subsidy" in its popular sense; however, it may even satisfy the narrower, economists' definition of the term in that access charges may be above the stand-alone costs of providing long distance connections to some subscribers and residential rates may be below long-run incremental costs.

4. Businesses are generally closer to the telephone company switching center, thereby requiring less copper wire per line than for residences, but business subscribers typically have more busy-hour calls than do residences, thereby requiring more switching capacity per line. These two factors offset each other, resulting in rather similar costs for local business and residential service.

5. For evidence on the extent of these cross-subsidies, see Robert W. Crandall and Leonard Waverman, *Talk Is Cheap: the Promise of Regulatory Reform in North American Telecommunications* (Brookings, 1996), chap. 3.

6. This data base has been collected by PNR for a number of telecommunications firms. We have been able to obtain PNR's 1995 sample of bills for one month.

7. They are also likely to subscribe to more "vertical" local services, such as call-waiting, than are lower-income households. Unfortunately, we cannot separate these charges from line-rental charges in the PNR data base.

8. PNR, Bill Harvesting II, 1995.

9. I assume that the long-run incremental cost of originating and terminating long distance calls through the local companies' end-office switches is no more than 0.5 cents a month.

10. The Census Bureau reports that residential long distance revenues in 1995 were $38.3 billion. At an average price of $0.163 per minute, this suggests that total residential calling was 235 billion minutes in 1995.

11. Assuming that the demand for long distance service has a constant elasticity of −0.7, a decline in rates from $0.163 to $0.113 per minute would increase long distance minutes from 235 billion to 304 billion. This additional calling would generate an additional $0.7 billion in access charges for the local companies plus additional revenues from long distance services they provide—primarily intraLATA services today. If the local companies account for 30 percent of these services and if they yield another $0.05 to $0.07 cents a minute, the total increase in LEC revenues from demand stimulation is in the range of $1.7 to $2.1 billion a year.

12. This gain is much smaller than some earlier estimates, including our own (*Talk is Cheap*, Brookings, 1996), because we exclude business calls from the calculation and do not address the benefits from greater competition in long distance services. Nor does this estimate include the effects of the distortions in the *structure* of local rates.

13. Lester D. Taylor, *Telecommunications Demand in Theory and Practice* (Dordrecht: Kluwer Academic Publisher, 1994), chap. 5.

14. Christopher Garbacz and Herbert G. Thompson, Jr., "Assessing the Impact of FCC Lifeline and Link-Up Programs on Telephone Penetration," *Journal of Regulatory Economics*, vol. 11 (1997), pp. 67–78.

15. Using two-stage least squares, we estimate a demand equation of the form: $Log(PEN/(1 - PEN)) = a + bP + cI + dY + ...$, where *PEN* is the share of households with a telephone (penetration), *P* is the monthly flat rate, *I* is the installation charge, and *Y* is median household income. A number of other demographic variables are also included: the proportion of black households, the proportion of Hispanic households, the proportion of persons below the poverty level, and average family size. The rates are carefully matched to the individual towns in the 1990 Census sample, a procedure that is not possible with statewide data used in other studies. In general, installation charges are the same throughout a state. The results generally find that poverty, black, and Hispanic population shares are inversely related to telephone subscription and that the elasticity of subscription with respect to the installation charge is about -0.05. However, there is no systematic relationship between penetration and monthly subscription rates. The statewide CPS data for 1995 provide broadly similar results.

16. In the new era of telephone regulation spawned by the 1996 Telecommunications Act, regulators must (for the first time) set wholesale rates for local facilities on the basis of cost. As a result, the entrants (particularly, the long distance companies) and the incumbent local companies have developed two competing cost models. The entrants' model is the "Hatfield model," and the incumbents' model is the "Benchmark Cost Proxy model."

17. FCC, *Statistics of Communications Common Carriers, 1995/96* (Washington, 1996), p. 328.

18. This is not to say that any of these households pay the full long-run incremental cost of their local service through these monthly rates. All rates my be below LRIC, but the current rate *structure* finds the 30 percent of households in the most rural areas paying far less than their share of the costs that are now recovered from local rates while their urban brethren pay $3.3 billion more than their share. See figure 15-9 for evidence that residences pay far less than small, multiline business subscribers.

CHAPTER SIXTEEN

Electronic Substitution in the Household-Level Demand for Postal Delivery Services

Frank A. Wolak

T HE PAST DECADE has witnessed a dramatic increase in the number of available modes of interpersonal communication and in the range of quality of these modes in terms of speed, reliability, and flexibility. Many of these modes have experienced substantial price reductions over this same time period; for instance, the price of long distance telephone service has fallen continuously; both the purchase price of FAX machines and the cost of using these machines have declined; on-line information services such as America Online or CompuServe, which charge a zero price for incremental messages sent to other subscribers to their service and to users of the Internet, have experienced explosive growth in the number of subscribers. All of these modes of communication provide attractive alternatives to traditional postal delivery services supplied by the United States Postal Service (USPS).

The relative attractiveness of long distance telephony, FAX communication, and electronic mail is enhanced by the steadily increasing price of postal delivery services over the past decade. From January 1, 1986, to January 1, 1995, the price of a one-ounce first-class letter increased from $0.22 to $0.32, a more than 45 percent increase in nine years. This combination of higher prices for postal delivery services and the growing number of viable alternative modes of communication has led to dire predictions about the future demand for postal delivery services. However, aggregate pieces delivered by the USPS have continued to increase

I would like to thank Matt Shum for outstanding research assistance. Financial support for this research was provided by the Markle Foundation and the National Science Foundation.

steadily up to the present time. Of 166.4 billion pieces delivered in 1992, growth in pieces delivered was 2.9 percent in 1993 and 3.4 percent in 1994. For 1994 the percentages of the various classes by volume are first class, 54 percent; second class, 6 percent; third class, 39 percent; and all other classes, 1 percent. Third class, principally advertising circulars and mail-order catalogues, has steadily increased its share of pieces delivered. The number of first-class pieces delivered has continued to grow, but the bulk of this growth has come from presorted first class. In fact, from 1993 to 1994, single-piece volume fell by 0.2 percent, but a 6.8 percent increase in presorted first class resulted in a net 2.4 percent increase in total first-class volume.[1] The increasing share of pieces delivered going to third-class mail and presorted first class, both of which are used primarily by businesses, seems to signal a shift by households away from the consumption of postal delivery services.

The purpose of this paper is to quantify this shift in the household-level demand for postal delivery services from 1986 to 1994 and determine the extent to which it can be attributed to the appearance of alternative modes of communication versus the concomitant increasing relative price of postal delivery services. Specific questions addressed are the following: what are the own-price, cross-price, and expenditure elasticities of household-level demand for postal delivery services, and how have these magnitudes changed over time? What is the impact of the increasing penetration of home-computing technology on postal demand? What household characteristics predict differences in household-level postal demand? How has the aggregate demand for postal delivery services by U.S. households changed over this time period?

To perform this analysis, I use the Bureau of Labor Statistics (BLS) Consumer Expenditure Survey (CES), which is a national probability sample of U.S. households generated from the 1980 Census 100 percent detail file. The BLS administers two distinct surveys to different samples of households: the Quarterly Interview Survey and the Diary Survey. These surveys differ in the number of goods that they cover, the length of time they survey a household, and the kinds of background questions asked about the household. For the Diary Survey, each household is requested to keep two one-week diaries of all expenditures over consecutive weeks. For the Interview Survey, the household is interviewed every three months over a fifteen-month period; this survey also asks questions about durable goods holdings—cars, housing, and personal computers. Both surveys collect information on household characteristics—hours of work of the head and spouse, occupation of the head and spouse, age and race of the head and spouse, marital status of the head, number of children, dwelling type and income. This information can be used to link durable goods holdings across the Interview Survey sample and the Diary Survey sample.

The Diary Survey is the source of data on household-level consumption of postal delivery services. The Interview Survey is used to estimate a probit model of the probability of personal computer ownership as a function of household characteristics common to both surveys. Each of the 49,089 households from the Diary Survey for the years 1986 to 1994 is then assigned an estimated probability of computer ownership using the coefficient estimates from the Interview Survey probit model using the common household demographic characteristics across the two surveys.

Because the purchases of each household in the Diary Survey are only recorded for two weeks, a household's purchases of postal delivery services can differ substantially from its consumption of these services. For example, a household can purchase and store these services in the form of blocks or rolls of stamps, using these stamps later to consume postal delivery services. The fact that, for the sample period, approximately 67 percent of all households do not purchase any postage during the two-week Diary Survey period attests to the empirical relevance of this difference. The distinction between consumption and purchases within the two-week sample period creates various complications for the proper recovery of the structure of household-level demand for postal delivery services. The observed purchases of postal delivery services are the combination of actual (but unobserved) consumption and a frequency of purchase process.

A considerable amount of across-household heterogeneity exists in the demand for postal delivery services. The probability of computer ownership affects both the consumption of postal delivery services and the frequency of purchase of postage. A higher household-level probability of computer ownership predicts a decreased amount of consumption of postal delivery services and a reduced probability of postage purchase during the two-week Diary Survey period by that household. The results from estimating the model of postage expenditures pooling all of the years in the sample imply substitutability between the consumption of telecommunications services and the consumption of postal delivery services.

In order to investigate how the structure of postal demand changed from 1986 to 1994, I estimate the model allowing for changes over time in the parameters determining the own- and cross-price and expenditure elasticities of household-level demand for postal delivery services. Perhaps the most surprising result to emerge from this analysis is a substantial increase in the absolute value of the own-price elasticity of demand for postal delivery services over time. For example, the own-price elasticity in 1986 is approximately -0.76, but by 1994 this magnitude is -1.3. This trend toward a more price-elastic demand has potentially dire consequences for the ability of the USPS to raise revenues from households through future postage price increases. These results yield an expenditure elasticity of demand decline from 0.36 in 1986 to 0.25 in 1994, indicating that higher-expenditure and -income households are increasingly substituting away from postal delivery services as their preferred mode for interpersonal communications. There is also an increasing degree of substitutability between postal delivery services and telecommunications services, indicating that, to a greater extent in recent years, declines in the price of telecommunications services should bring about decreases in the household-level demand for postal delivery services. When I quantify how the impact of personal-computing technology and Internet use on the household-level demand for postal delivery services changes over time, I find that, for most years in the sample, a higher probability of ownership of a personal computer is associated with an increased demand for postal delivery services. However, particularly in 1993 and 1994, when subscribership to on-line services and access to the Internet in general became widespread, an increased probability of computer ownership predicts a decline in the household-level demand for postal delivery services.

Because I have a weight giving the number of households in the United States represented by each household in the Diary Survey sample each year, I can use these weights to compute estimates of the aggregate household-level demand for postal delivery services as well as the aggregate price elasticities of the demand for postal delivery services. This enables me to assess the likely revenue consequences to the USPS from future postal price increases given the aggregate demand relations I have estimated. I find that, for a 10 percent increase in the price of postage, the most recent year's aggregate own-price elasticity estimate implies a 2.7 percent reduction in the revenues that the USPS can expect to receive from U.S. households. I can also compute an aggregate elasticity of household-level demand for postal services with respect to the probability of computer ownership. Using the aggregate elasticity estimate for 1994, and assuming a 17 percent increase in the probability of computer ownership for all households in the sample (a plausible increase given that the estimated penetration of personal computers in the household sector has more than tripled from 1988 to 1994), yields a 2.7 percent decline in the aggregate demand for postal delivery services, or a 2.7 reduction in annual household-level revenues, the same percentage decline in revenues brought about by the 10 percent price increase.

Predicting Computer Ownership and Trends in Postage Expenditures

In this section I first discuss the two major data sources used in the analysis. This is followed by a presentation of the estimates of the probability of computer ownership models estimated using the Interview Survey data. These models are then used to impute a probability of computer ownership for each household in the Diary Survey. The parameter estimates are of some independent interest given the rapid increase in the fraction of households owning personal computers—from 7 percent in 1988, the first year in which the Interview Survey collected this information, to 25 percent in 1994, the last year of data currently available. To motivate the household-level demand estimation results presented later, summary statistics on household postage and telephone consumption from 1986 to 1994 are given. Finally, I describe the annual changes in the percent of U.S. households owning personal computing technology up to 1994.

As noted above, the Diary Survey is the source of data on postage consumption. This survey collects all expenditures for each sampled household for two consecutive one-week periods. Each sampled household completes a weekly diary document listing every purchase, the good and the amount, made within that one-week period (except expenditures incurred while away from home overnight, or longer). Every year the Diary sample is redrawn, with each day of the week having an equal probability of being the first day of the reference week for a sampled household. With the exception of the last six weeks of the year, when the Diary sample size is doubled to increase the coverage of expenditures

Figure 16-1. *Postage Purchases over Two-Week Period*

Percentage of total observations

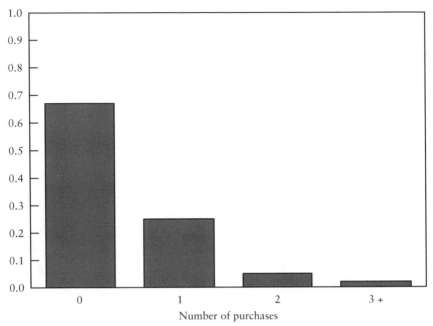

Source: Author's calculations.

unique to the holiday season, the number of Diary Surveys administered is uniformly distributed throughout the year.

For my analysis, total postage expenditures for each household is the sum of all purchases of postage during the two-week sample interval. Figure 16-1 presents a histogram of the number of purchases of postage during the two-week diary period. From the figure it is clear that the vast majority of households that purchase postage during their Diary Survey period only make one purchase. For this reason, the subsequent empirical analysis focuses on the decision to purchase within the two-week period, rather than on the number of purchases made.

The Interview Survey is the source for computer ownership data at the household level. Beginning with the 1988 survey, households were asked whether they owned a personal computer. Because the Diary Survey and Interview Survey collect the same household characteristics, these variables can be used to match households that share these characteristics across the Interview Survey and Diary Survey samples. The Interview

Survey is used to collect information on major expenditure items on a retrospective basis. Each household selected to appear in this sample is interviewed quarterly for five consecutive quarters for these major expenditures and the above household characteristics in addition to its income. As a result of this sampling scheme, 20 percent of the Interview Survey sample is rotated each quarter.

The probability of computer ownership model utilizes all available household characteristics variables that are common to the Interview and Diary Surveys to predict the probability of computer ownership using a probit model. Let X_i denote the vector of household characteristics for the ith household in the Interview Survey. Let y_i^* denote the latent propensity of household i to own a computer. I assume that the household owns a computer if $y_i^* \geq 0$ and does not if $y_i^* < 0$. The event of computer ownership is denoted by the indicator variable y_i, which takes on the value 1 if the household owns a computer and zero otherwise. The propensity to own computers is determined by $y_i^* = X_i'\beta + \epsilon_i$, where ϵ_i is an independent identically distributed $N(0,1)$ random variable across households. The log-likelihood function for this model is:

$$L(\beta) = \sum_{i=1}^{N} y_i \ln[\Phi(X_i'\beta)] + (1 - y_i)\ln[1 - \Phi(X_i'\beta)],$$

where N is the number of households in the Interview Survey during the year under consideration and $\Phi(t)$ is the standard normal distribution function. Given the maximum likelihood estimate of β, an estimate of the probability of computer ownership as a function of X_i can be computed as $\Phi(X_i\hat{\beta})$, where $\hat{\beta}$ is the maximum likelihood estimate of β. Taking the values of X_i for each observation in the Diary Survey for the same year as the Interview Survey, I compute $\Phi(X_i'\hat{\beta})$, the estimated probability of computer ownership for that Diary Survey observation. This estimated probability is used in the model for postage expenditures to measure the extent of electronic substitution in the consumption of postal delivery services.

Table 16-1 gives the maximum likelihood estimates of the elements of β for 1988, the first year this information was collected in the Interview Survey, and for 1994, in order to quantify the changes in these probit coefficient estimates over time. This same probit model is estimated separately for each year from 1988 to 1994. To compute the probability of computer ownership for each household during each year of the Diary

Table 16-1. *Selected Results from Computer Ownership Probits*

	1988 estimates		1994 estimates	
Variable	Estimate	Standard error	Estimate	Standard error
Constant	−3.03e+00	4.62e−01	−2.14e+00	3.14e−01
February	−5.79e−01	1.80e−01	−8.05e−02	5.16e−02
March	−1.95e−01	1.40e−01	−1.14e−01	5.10e−02
April	1.18e+00	1.19e−01	4.82e−02	7.48e−02
May	1.17e+00	1.18e−01	1.84e−01	7.50e−02
June	1.33e+00	1.16e−01	1.03e−02	7.42e−02
July	1.20e+00	1.17e−01	6.51e−02	7.65e−02
August	1.23e+00	1.16e−01	5.23e−02	7.37e−02
September	1.31e+00	1.13e−01	4.64e−03	7.40e−02
October	1.31e+00	1.13e−01	8.30e−02	7.20e−02
November	1.35e+00	1.14e−01	5.00e−02	7.35e−02
December	1.46e+00	1.13e−01	1.26e−02	7.56e−02
Northwest	2.27e−01	1.26e−01	−7.50e−02	8.32e−02
Midwest	1.54e−01	1.27e−01	−7.84e−02	8.30e−02
South	1.38e−01	1.27e−01	−7.33e−02	8.31e−02
West	2.34e−01	1.25e−01	1.19e−01	8.26e−02
SMSA	−7.28e−02	8.83e−02	−2.02e−01	6.27e−02
Homeowner	5.90e−02	2.55e−01	2.35e−01	1.21e−01
Renter	−5.75e−02	2.55e−01	9.18e−02	1.21e−01
Dorm resident	2.37e−01	3.18e−01	1.19e+00	1.66e−01
Family size	−8.15e−02	5.38e−02	−7.62e−02	3.48e−02
Persons < 18	1.63e−01	5.68e−02	1.42e−01	3.76e−02
Persons > 64	5.03e−04	9.04e−02	−4.19e−02	5.79e−02
Number of earners	5.85e−02	4.95e−02	1.28e−01	3.26e−02
Number of vehicles	5.97e−02	1.59e−02	5.99e−02	1.09e−02
White	−2.93e−01	2.16e−01	−6.42e−02	2.00e−01
Black	−4.23e−01	2.32e−01	−2.91e−01	2.06e−01
Male	1.16e−01	6.22e−02	6.07e−02	3.76e−02
Married	−2.91e−01	1.90e−01	−2.31e−01	1.19e−01
High school grad	2.29e−01	8.89e−02	3.81e−01	5.86e−02
> High school, < college	5.66e−01	8.84e−02	8.61e−01	5.85e−02
College grad	8.14e−01	9.18e−02	1.15e+00	6.03e−02
Age	1.05e+00	1.24e+00	2.46e+00	7.20e−01
Age²[a]	−2.26e+00	1.43e+00	−2.91e+00	7.74e−01
Spouse's age	1.62e+00	1.00e+00	1.84e+00	6.11e−01
Spouse's age²[a]	−1.43e+00	1.27e+00	−1.78e+00	7.50e−01
Professional occupation	1.98e−01	6.67e−02	1.01e−01	5.13e−02
Technical occupation	5.18e−02	6.86e−02	−9.97e−02	7.88e−02
Self-employed	1.51e−01	9.64e−02	−1.06e−01	1.11e−01
Retired	−4.99e−03	1.44e−01	−2.57e−02	6.42e−02
Hours of work	−2.28e−03	1.78e−03	−2.38e−04	1.08e−03
Spouse's hours of work	1.11e−03	1.87e−03	1.37e−03	1.28e−03
Positive income	3.59e−02	1.04e−02	5.10e−02	6.28e−03
Negative income (dummy)	1.38e−01	8.05e−02	7.02e−02	5.57e−02
Log-likelihood function value	−1881.159		−4554.942	
N	10,122		9,967	

Source: Author's calculations.
a. Age² = Age *Age = (Age)²; spouse's age² = (Spouse's age).²

Survey, I use the probit model parameter estimates from that same year's Interview Survey data. Because computer ownership information was not collected for 1986 or 1987 in the Interview Survey, the parameter estimates from the model estimated for 1988 are used to compute estimated probabilities of computer ownership for all observations from the Diary Surveys in 1986 and 1987.

I now describe the time series behavior of the sample averages of household-level postage purchases and telephone expenditures from the Diary Survey database. Table 16-2 gives the sample average, minimum, and maximum household level purchases of postage, and local and long distance telephone services during the two-week interview period for each year from 1986 to 1994 in nominal dollars. This table shows an initially increasing average consumption of postal delivery services from 1986 to 1989 and then a steady decline from 1990 to 1994. On the other hand, telephone consumption shows a steady increase throughout the sample period. This table also gives these same magnitudes as shares of total nondurable goods expenditure during the two-week Diary Survey time interval. Viewed relative to total nondurable goods expenditures, the downturn in household-level postage expenditures is even more pronounced. Figure 16-2 plots the monthly Consumer Price Index (CPI) price indexes for postage and the composite of local and long distance telephone services, nonseasonally adjusted and normalized to have January 1986 equal to one. This figure shows the large relative price increase in postage versus telephone service over the sample period. These increases in the price of postage later in the sample period, and the accompanying reduction in average household-level purchases, is indicative of a price-elastic demand which brings about reductions in total expenditures in response to a price increase. On the other hand, telephone services expenditures increase over the sample, despite a slight upward trend in the telephone services price index over time.

Table 16-3 gives the sample average percent of households in the Interview Survey that own computers for each year from 1988 to 1994. This percentage nearly quadrupled over the eight-year sample period. This magnitude almost doubled from 1988 to 1989, the same time period in which average household-level expenditures on postal delivery services began to decline. The inverse relation between these two trends suggests the importance of accounting for the relationship between computer ownership and the consumption of postage delivery services in constructing an econometric model of household-level postage expenditures.

Table 16-2. *Average Expenditures and Shares by Year for*
Postage and Telephone Service

Year	Share	Mean	Standard deviation	Minimum	Maximum
1986	Postal share	0.01	0.02	0.00	0.62
N = 5,839	Postal expenditure ($)	2.34	6.67	0.00	200.58
	Telephone share	0.04	0.08	0.00	0.82
	Telephone expenditure ($)	16.00	32.76	0.00	400.00
1987	Postal share	0.01	0.03	0.00	0.77
N = 6,024	Postal expenditure ($)	2.61	9.51	0.00	399.98
	Telephone share	0.05	0.09	0.00	0.84
	Telephone expenditure ($)	17.62	34.96	0.00	401.94
1988	Postal share	0.01	0.03	0.00	0.75
N = 5,264	Postal expenditure ($)	2.80	8.33	0.00	357.78
	Telephone share	0.05	0.09	0.00	0.82
	Telephone expendiure ($)	18.21	35.53	0.00	429.65
1989	Postal share	0.01	0.03	0.00	0.89
N = 5,317	Postal expenditure ($)	3.02	8.20	0.00	214.00
	Telephone share	0.05	0.08	0.00	0.93
	Telephone expenditure ($)	19.36	38.26	0.00	584.94
1990	Postal share	0.01	0.02	0.00	0.39
N = 5,446	Postal expenditure ($)	2.90	6.62	0.00	87.00
	Telephone share	0.05	0.09	0.00	0.78
	Telephone expenditure ($)	20.29	41.07	0.00	551.00
1991	Postal share	0.01	0.02	0.00	0.46
N = 5,550	Postal expenditure ($)	2.51	7.08	0.00	120.55
	Telephone share	0.05	0.08	0.00	0.78
	Telephone expenditure ($)	20.79	41.87	0.00	518.72
1992	Postal share	0.01	0.02	0.00	0.75
N = 5,436	Postal expenditure ($)	2.56	7.57	0.00	222.78
	Telephone share	0.05	0.09	0.00	1.00
	Telephone expenditure ($)	23.66	45.78	0.00	729.16
1993	Postal share	0.01	0.02	0.00	0.31
N = 5,299	Postal expenditure ($)	2.23	6.85	0.00	122.37
	Telephone share	0.05	0.09	0.00	0.86
	Telephone expenditure ($)	23.74	47.63	0.00	742.00
1994	Postal share	0.01	0.02	0.00	0.72
N = 4,914	Postal expenditure ($)	2.13	6.76	0.00	157.32
	Telephone share	0.05	0.09	0.00	0.90
	Telephone expenditure ($)	25.55	48.83	0.00	520.00

Source: Author's calculations.

Figure 16-2. *Movements in Postage and Telephone Prices*

Monthly prices: Jan. 1986 = 1

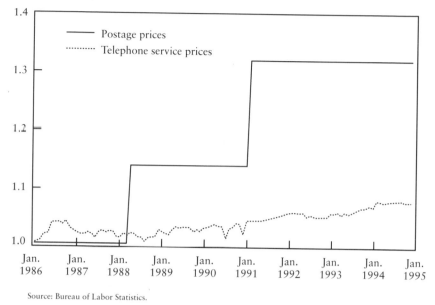

Source: Bureau of Labor Statistics.

Econometric Model of Postal Delivery Services Expenditures

The econometric model of household-level postage expenditures accounts for the infrequency of purchases of postal delivery services within the two-week sampling interval of the Diary Survey, yet is still consistent with the basic features of consumer demand theory. This model is specified with postage expenditures as a share of total nondurable expenditures within the two-week Diary Survey period as the dependent variable. The range of real (in January 1986 dollars) total nondurable goods expenditures in the two-week Diary Survey period for all years in the sample is $20 to $1,700, so there is a considerable variability across households in the share of total expenditures going to postal delivery services. This model gives rise to a joint distribution of postal expenditure shares across all of the households during the sample period, which is then used to estimate the parameters of the econometric model by maximum likelihood techniques.

In order to describe the details of the model, I require the following notation. Let y_i^* denote the share of total nondurable expenditures going

Table 16-3. *Annual Sample Percentages of Personal Computer Ownership for Interview Survey Sample*

Year	Number of households	Percent owning personal computer
1988	10,122	7.0
1989	9,907	14.5
1990	10,015	16.2
1991	9,878	17.4
1992	10,028	19.1
1993	10,097	22.3
1994	10,011	24.9

Source: Author's calculations.

to postage *consumption* and y_i the share of total nondurable goods expenditures going to postage *expenditures*, by the ith household for the two-week interval. Let x_i equal the vector of ratios of the logarithm of prices to total nondurable goods expenditures—$\ln(p_j/M)$, where p_j is the price of the jth good and M is total nondurable goods expenditures—and other demographic variables assumed to shift postage consumption across households. I enter prices and total nondurable goods expenditures as ratios in order to impose the theoretical restriction of homogeneity of degree zero of the resulting demand function in prices and total nondurable goods expenditures. Let w_i denote the indicator random variable that equals 1 if the household purchases postage within the two-week interval and 0 otherwise. The purchase probability can be written as $pr(w_i = 1) = \Phi(z_i'\theta)$, with z_i equal to the vector of household characteristics that shift the propensity to purchase postage; $\Phi(t)$, the standard normal distribution function; and θ, a vector of parameters to be estimated.

Assume that $\log(y_i^*) = x_i'\beta + \epsilon_i$, where $\epsilon_i \sim N(0,\sigma^2)$ and $y_i = w_i\,y_i^*/\Phi(z_i'\theta)$. The relation $y_i = w_i\,y_i^*/\Phi(z_i'\theta)$ implies that if a purchase of postage occurs in the two-week interval ($w_i = 1$), the household buys the inverse of its postage purchase probability in that two-week interval ($1/\Phi(z_i'\theta)$) times its unobservable demand for postal delivery services for the two-week interval, y_i^*. Consider a simple numerical example to illustrate this aspect of the econometric model. Suppose the household's unobservable two-week demand for postal delivery services is $10.00 and its probability of purchasing postage within any two-week interval is 0.5. This implies that when it does purchase postage, it will buy $20.00 = $10.00/0.5 worth to maintain its rate of consumption given its purchase frequency.

Because $\log(y_i^*)$ is assumed to be normally distributed, y_i^* must therefore only take on positive values. This model assumes that all households consume a nonzero (although it can be extremely small) amount of postal delivery services within a two-week time period. Let Y equal the vector of all postal expenditure shares, $(y_1, y_2, \ldots, y_N)$, where N is the number of households in the sample. The demand for postal delivery services function and the equation relating consumption to purchases via the purchase probability function yields the log-likelihood function for Y:

$$\log L(Y) = \sum_0 \log(1 - \Phi(z_i'\theta)) + \sum_+ [-\log\sigma + \log\Phi((\log(y_i)$$

$$+ \log\Phi(z_i'\sigma) - x_i'\beta)/\sigma) + \log\Phi(z_i\theta) - \log y_i)].$$

Variants of this model are discussed in work by Richard Blundell and Costas Meghir and Angus Deaton and Margaret Irish.[2] In previous work I considered three other forms for this combination purchase frequency and latent demand for postal delivery services model of postal expenditures that differ in terms of their assumptions about the unobserved demand for postal delivery services.[3] Because all four competing models give rise to joint densities of Y, nonnested hypothesis testing techniques developed by Quang Vuong can be used to determine which model provides a statistically significantly superior description of the underlying data generation process.[4] These nonnested hypothesis testing results find that this *log infrequency of purchase* model, which implies nonzero consumption of postal delivery services for all households, provides a statistically superior description of the observed household-level expenditure patterns relative to the other three models.[5] Other reasonableness checks of the four models found further support for the superiority of the log infrequency of purchase of postal delivery services model considered here.

Variables Entering Demand and Purchase Probability Functions

Consumer theory provides a strong guide as to what should enter x_i, the determinants of the demand for postal delivery services. Because $y_i^* = \exp(x_i'\beta + \epsilon_i)$ is an expenditure share demand function, it follows that the own-price, the prices of all other goods consumed by the household and total nondurable expenditures, should enter x_i. Consequently, I enter the logarithms of the price of postage, the price of telephone services, an index of the prices of other nondurable goods besides postage and telephone services, and total nondurable expenditures. I also enter demographic variables describing the characteristics of the household that should alter its consumption of postal delivery services, such as race, number of children, marital status, education, occupation, and age of the head, and the probability of computer ownership.

Economic theory provides less guidance for what variables should enter in z_i, the determinants of the purchase probability. There are a number of reasons why the probability of purchasing postage should differ across households. A major determinant of these differences is the opportunity cost to the household of making a purchase. If it were costless to purchase postage, then all households would purchase only when at least one household member actually consumed postal delivery services. Under these circumstances, the purchase probability within the two-week sample interval would exactly equal one for all households consuming any postal delivery services during this time interval. Consequently, I expect household characteristics that predict the opportunity cost of purchasing postage to be important predictors of this probability—the geographic area in which the household resides, the number of children in the household, the marital status of the head, the education of the spouse and head, the occupation, age, and hours of work of the head and spouse, household income, and the probability of computer ownership. Table 16-4 presents the sample mean, standard deviation, minimum, and maximum of the variables entering x_i and z_i.

Table 16-5 gives estimates of the parameters of this two-equation model for postal expenditures. As noted above, I impose homogeneity of degree zero in price and total expenditure on the share equations by requiring that the coefficient on the logarithm of the price index for other nondurable goods equal the sum of coefficients on the prices of postage and telephone services minus the coefficient on the logarithm of total nondurable expenditures. (Table 16-6 gives a list of the variable definitions used in all of the models.) The household demographic variables significantly improve the predictive power of the model, indicating the presence of deterministic differences in postage consumption and frequency of purchase across households based on these observable characteristics. The standard error estimates in table 16-5 are computed using the misspecification-robust standard error estimates derived by Halbert White.[6] Using these covariance matrix estimates makes the inferences drawn robust to various forms of misspecification of the distributional assumptions used to derive the joint density of Y.

Table 16-4. *Consumer Expenditure Diary Survey Summary Statistics*[a]

Item	Mean	Standard deviation	Minimum	Maximum
Postage purchase indicator	0.33	0.47	0.00	1.00
Nondurable expenditures	393.26	289.79	20.00	1698.08
Postage expenditures	2.57	7.60	0.00	399.98
Telephone expenditures	20.46	41.00	0.00	742.00
Number of postage purchases (in 2 wks.)	0.45	0.78	0.00	11.00
Postage expn. share	0.01	0.02	0.00	0.89
Telephone expn. share	0.05	0.09	0.00	1.00
Nondurables prices (Jan. 1986 = 1)	1.15	0.11	0.96	1.30
Telephone price (Jan. 1986 = 1)	1.04	0.02	1.00	1.08
Postage price (Jan. 1986 = 1)	1.18	0.13	1.00	1.32
Computer ownership probability	0.16	0.16	0.00	0.98
Northwest	0.19	0.39	0.00	1.00
Midwest	0.23	0.42	0.00	1.00
South	0.26	0.44	0.00	1.00
West	0.21	0.41	0.00	1.00
SMSA	0.19	0.39	0.00	1.00
Homeowner	0.64	0.48	0.00	1.00
Renter	0.33	0.47	0.00	1.00
Dorm resident	0.01	0.10	0.00	1.00
Family size	2.61	1.50	1.00	16.00
Persons < 18	0.74	1.13	0.00	12.00
Persons > 64	0.29	0.60	0.00	5.00
Number of earners	1.44	1.00	0.00	9.00
Number of vehicles	1.65	1.13	0.00	21.00
White	0.89	0.31	0.00	1.00
Black	0.10	0.30	0.00	1.00
Male	0.65	0.48	0.00	1.00
Married	0.58	0.49	0.00	1.00
High school graduate	0.31	0.46	0.00	1.00
> High school, < college	0.23	0.42	0.00	1.00
College graduate	0.25	0.43	0.00	1.00
Age	0.47	0.17	0.15	0.90
Spouse's age	0.25	0.25	0.00	0.90
Professional occupation	0.22	0.42	0.00	1.00
Technical occupation	0.18	0.39	0.00	1.00
Self-employed	0.07	0.25	0.00	1.00
Retired	0.15	0.35	0.00	1.00
Hours of work	31.69	20.54	0.00	90.00
Spouse's hours of work	14.66	19.59	0.00	90.00
Positive income	2.66	2.65	0.00	48.64
Negative income (dummy)	0.12	0.33	0.00	1.00
December (dummy)	0.14	0.34	0.00	1.00

Source: Author's calculations.
a. Number of observations: 49,089.

Table 16-5. *Log Infrequency of Purchase Model*

Variable	Share equation		Purchase probability	
	Estimate	Standard error	Estimate	Standard error
Constant	−6.35e+00	1.76e−01	−6.12e−01	9.78e−02
Log price$_{post}$	−5.59e−02	1.93e−01		
Log price$_{tel}$	8.95e−02	1.08e−01		
Nondur. expn.	6.82e−01	1.29e−02		
Northwest	2.66e−02	5.33e−02	−3.33e−02	3.05e−02
Midwest	−5.13e−02	5.27e−02	−4.88e−02	3.01e−02
South	−8.43e−02	5.30e−02	−8.29e−02	3.02e−02
West	2.89e−02	5.44e−02	−5.92e−02	3.10e−02
SMSA	−1.93e−01	4.12e−02	−5.21e−02	2.33e−02
Family size	−1.90e−02	1.70e−02		
Persons < 18	−3.82e−02	1.89e−02		
Persons > 64	4.85e−02	2.02e−02		
Number of earners	−1.35e−02	1.45e−02		
White	−3.38e−03	1.06e−01	3.66e−03	5.91e−02
Black	−3.64e−01	1.13e−01	−1.43e−01	6.24e−02
Male	−1.85e−01	2.60e−02	−5.42e−02	1.49e−02
Married	2.46e−01	4.89e−02		
High school graduate	3.19e−01	3.13e−02	1.65e−01	1.77e−02
>High school < college	4.52e−01	3.55e−02	2.73e−01	2.04e−02
College graduate	6.48e−01	4.05e−02	3.89e−01	2.32e−02
Age	1.22e+00	9.28e−02	1.64e−01	4.65e−02
Spouse's age	3.40e−01	9.67e−02	5.12e−01	3.19e−02
Professional occupation	1.95e−01	3.19e−02	1.38e−01	1.91e−02
Technical occupation	1.06e−01	3.09e−02	9.40e−02	1.80e−02
Self-employed	5.29e−02	4.65e−02	−1.28e−02	2.59e−02
Retired	1.43e−01	3.78e−02	7.03e−02	2.29e−02
Hours of work			−2.02e−04	3.58e−04
Spouse's hours of work			3.63e−04	3.22e−04
Positive income			1.03e−02	2.65e−03
Negative income (dummy)			−1.52e−01	1.73e−02
Computer ownership probability	−4.15e−01	1.08e−01	−7.90e−01	6.15e−02
December	3.94e−01	2.85e−02	5.67e−02	1.73e−02
σ	9.80e−01	5.32e−03		

Source: Author's calculations.
Note: Standard errors are heteroscedasticity-consistent in sense of H. White, "Maximum Likelihood Estimation of Misspecified Models," *Econometrica*, vol. 50 (1982), pp. 1–26. Log-likelihood function value: 19070.6.

Table 16-6. *Variable Definitions*

Variable name	Definition
Northwest	1 if household resides in Northwest Census region
Midwest	1 if household resides in Midwest Census region
South	1 if household resides in Southern Census region
West	1 if household resides in Western Census region (omitted category is rural residents in all regions)
SMSA	0 if household resides in a Census SMSA; 1 if not
Famsize	Number of members in household
Persons < 18	Number of persons < 18 yrs of age in household
Persons > 64	Number of persons > 64 yrs of age in household
Number of earners	Number of earners in household
White	1 if household head is white
Black	1 if household head is black (omitted category is Nat. Americans and other ethnic groups)
Married	1 if household head is married
Male	1 if household head is male
High school graduate	1 if household head is high school graduate
> High school, < college	1 if household head has some college education
College grad	1 if household head is college graduate (omitted category is high school noncompleters)
Age	Age of household head
Spouse's age	Age of spouse (if applicable)
Professional occupation	1 if household head is a professional
Technical occupation	1 if household head is in a technical occupation
Self-employed	1 if household head is self-employed
Retired	1 if household head is retired
Hours of work	Weekly hours of work for household head
Spouse's hours of work	Weekly hours of work for spouse (if applicable)
Positive income	Household's income, if >0
Negative income (dummy)	1 if household income is negative
Computer ownership probability	Imputed computer ownership probability (details in text)
December	1 if survey month is December

Figure 16-3 plots the smoothed density of household-level expected postal delivery services consumption within the two-week period for the log-infrequency of purchase model.[7] There is a large range in the density of expected two-week consumption of postage, with a significant positive skew. Figure 16-4 plots the smoothed density of household-level purchase probabilities from this model. Although this density of purchase probabilities is centered at 0.32, many households have estimated purchase

Figure 16-3. *Density Estimate of Postage Expenditures*

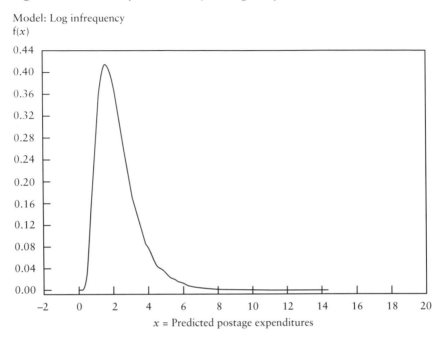

Model: Log infrequency

x = Predicted postage expenditures

frequencies above and below this value. Table 16-7 gives the probability derivatives associated with the postage purchase probability for this model. This table shows that increases in the probability of personal computer ownership significantly reduce the purchase frequency of postal delivery services.

Table 16-8 gives the sample mean household-level elasticities of postage demand with respect to the prices of postage, telephone services, other nondurable goods, and total nondurable expenditures. The structure of the log infrequency of purchase of model implies price and expenditure elasticities that do not vary across households. The last row of table 16-8 gives the sample mean of the elasticity demand with respect to the probability of computer ownership. Because this elasticity varies across households, the sample standard deviation of the household-level elasticities is reported below it. This mean elasticity implies that increases in the probability of computer ownership bring about reductions in the demand for postal delivery services at the household level.

To address the question of the impact of the increasing number of

Figure 16-4. *Density Estimate of Purchase Probabilities*

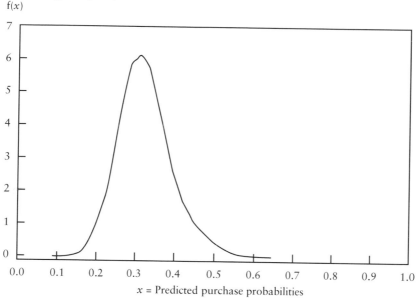

Model: Log infrequency
f(x)

x = Predicted purchase probabilities

Source: Author's calculations.

low-cost alternatives to postal delivery services and the increasing price of postal delivery services over the past decade on the demand for postal delivery services, I enlarge the specification of the demand function to allow for time-varying own- and cross-price elasticities, total nondurable expenditure elasticities, and elasticities with respect to the probability of computer ownership. This requires interacting each of these five variables—$\ln(p_{postage})$, $\ln(p_{phone})$, $\ln(p_{other})$, ln(total nondurable expenditures), and the probability of computer ownership—with an annual time trend and including these variables in the vector of regressors, x_i, for the log-consumption share equation. An annual time-trend is also interacted with the probability of computer ownership in the purchase probability equation. The remaining parameters in the consumption share equation and the purchase probability equation are assumed to be fixed over time. For these variables, the resulting parameter estimates are very similar to those reported in table 16-5. There are changes in the coefficients on log-prices, log-total nondurable expenditure, and probability of computer owner-ship variables that reflect the fact that I have included these variables

Table 16-7. Purchase Probability Derivatives for
Log Infrequency Model

Variable	Mean dP/dX	Standard error
Constant	−2.34e−01	2.02e−02
Northwest	−1.18e−02	1.01e−03
Midwest	−1.72e−02	1.48e−03
South	−2.93e−02	2.52e−03
West	−2.09e−02	1.80e−03
SMSA	−1.84e−02	1.58e−03
White	1.29e−03	1.11e−04
Black	−5.05e−02	4.35e−03
Male	−1.92e−02	1.65e−03
High school graduate	5.83e−02	5.02e−03
> High school < college	9.64e−02	8.30e−03
College graduate	1.37e−01	1.18e−02
Age	5.80e−02	4.99e−03
Spouse's age	1.81e−01	1.55e−02
Professional occupation	4.88e−02	4.20e−03
Technical occupation	3.32e−02	2.86e−03
Self-employed	−4.51e−03	3.88e−04
Retired	2.48e−02	2.14e−03
Hours of work	−7.12e−05	6.13e−06
Spouse's hours of work	1.28e−04	1.10e−05
Positive income	3.64e−03	3.13e−04
Negative income (dummy)	−5.37e−02	4.62e−03
Computer ownership probability	−2.79e−01	2.40e−02
December	2.00e−02	1.72e−03

Source: Author's calculations.

interacted with a time trend in the model. The full set of parameter
estimates is reported in table 16-9.

Table 16-10 gives estimates of the sample average price, expenditure,
and probability of computer ownership elasticities for each year in the
sample implied by this model. Recall that the only demand elasticity that
varies across households is the one with respect to the probability of

Table 16-8. Sample Mean Household-Level Elasticities from the
Log Infrequency Model

Elasticity		Log infrequency
ϵ_{pp}		−1.06
ϵ_{pt}		−7.64e−02
ϵ_{po}		6.48e−01
ϵ_{pm}		3.18e−01
$\epsilon_{p,comp}$	mean	−6.87e−01
	st. dev.	6.55e−02

Source: Author's calculations.

Table 16-9. *Log Infrequency Model with Time Trends*

Variable	Share equation		Purchase probability	
	Estimate	Standard error	Estimate	Standard error
Constant	−6.50e+00	1.76e−01	−7.28e−01	9.85e−02
Log price$_{post}$	2.42e−01	5.33e−01		
(yearly trend)*log price$_{post}$	−6.36e−02	1.32e−01		
Log price$_{tel}$	−1.22e−01	2.21e−01		
(yearly trend)*log price$_{tel}$	2.88e−02	4.67e−02		
log nondur. expn.	6.15e−01	2.09e−02		
(yearly trend)*log expn	8.70e−03	4.80e−03		
Northwest	6.54e−03	5.32e−02	−4.97e−02	3.05e−02
Midwest	−6.17e−02	5.26e−02	−5.78e−02	3.01e−02
South	−9.52e−02	5.29e−02	−9.16e−02	3.02e−02
West	−3.96e−03	5.44e−02	−8.67e−02	3.11e−02
SMSA	−1.87e−01	4.12e−02	−4.95e−02	2.33e−02
Family size	−1.42e−02	1.70e−02		
Persons < 18	−4.19e−02	1.89e−02		
Persons > 64	5.19e−02	2.02e−02		
Number of earners	−2.28e−02	1.45e−02		
White	1.05e−01	1.07e−01	9.47e−02	5.99e−02
Black	−2.41e−01	1.13e−01	−4.23e−02	6.32e−02
Male	−2.04e−01	2.60e−02	−7.35e−02	1.50e−02
Married	2.24e−01	4.89e−02		
High school graduate	3.12e−01	3.13e−02	1.60e−01	1.77e−02
>High school < college	4.07e−01	3.59e−02	2.35e−01	2.06e−02
College graduate	5.56e−01	4.17e−02	3.11e−01	2.39e−02
Age	1.31e+00	9.31e−02	2.50e−01	4.70e−02
Spouse's age	3.22e−01	9.66e−02	4.83e−01	3.19e−02
Professional occupation	1.45e−01	3.23e−02	9.55e−02	1.94e−02
Technical occupation	8.85e−02	3.09e−02	7.83e−02	1.80e−02
Self-employed	3.34e−02	4.65e−02	−3.18e−02	2.60e−02
Retired	1.36e−01	3.80e−02	6.44e−02	2.28e−02
Hours of work			−3.16e−04	3.58e−04
Spouse's hours of work			−9.02e−05	3.24e−04
Positive income			7.79e−03	2.66e−03
Negative income (dummy)			−1.60e−01	1.74e−02
Computer ownership probability	1.09e+00	1.76e−01	7.22e−01	1.02e−01
Yearly trend*comp. ownership	−2.16e−01	2.40e−02	−1.81e−01	1.19e−02
December	3.55e−01	2.87e−02	2.42e−02	1.75e−02
σ	9.79e−01	5.32e−03		

Note: Standard errors are heteroscedasticity-consistent in sense of White, "Maximum Likelihood Estimation." Log-likelihood function value: 19195.2.

Table 16-10. *Sample Mean Elasticity Estimates: Log Infrequency
Model with Time Trend*

Year	ϵ_{pp}	ϵ_{pt}	ϵ_{po}	ϵ_{pm}	$\epsilon_{p,comp}$
1986	−7.58e−01	−1.22e−01	5.18e−01	3.62e−01	1.18e−01
1987	−8.21e−01	−9.29e−02	5.66e−01	3.48e−01	9.19e−02
1988	−8.85e−01	−6.41e−02	6.15e−01	3.34e−01	7.06e−02
1989	−9.49e−01	−3.53e−02	6.63e−01	3.20e−01	6.64e−02
1990	−1.01e+00	−6.51e−03	7.12e−01	3.07e−01	3.81e−02
1991	−1.08e+00	2.23e−02	7.61e−01	2.93e−01	1.79e−03
1992	−1.14e+00	5.11e−02	8.09e−01	2.79e−01	−4.09e−02
1993	−1.20e+00	7.99e−02	8.58e−01	2.65e−01	−9.94e−02
1994	−1.27e+00	1.09e−01	9.06e−01	2.51e−01	−1.68e−01

Source: Author's calculations.

computer ownership. Consequently, the last column in this table presents the sample means of these elasticities estimates for each year. The own-price elasticity begins at −0.758 in 1986 and ends in 1994 with a value of −1.27. These two price elasticities have very different implications for the ability of the USPS to raise revenues from U.S. households through postage price increases. In general, an X percent price increase of a product with a demand elasticity of ϵ increases total revenue from the sale of that product by $X(1 + \epsilon)$. Consequently, if the absolute value of ϵ is less than one—the product is inelastically demanded—total revenue will increase as a result of this price increase. This is the case for household-level demand for postal delivery services for all years up until 1989. If, as is the case for the years following 1989, the elasticity of demand is greater than one in absolute value, price increases will bring about total revenue decreases. A natural question to ask is: how much revenue is lost from reductions in the household-level use of postal delivery services by these price increases?

A first step in answering this question is an estimate of annual aggregate household expenditures on postage. Table 16-11 gives estimates of the aggregate annual amount of postage expenditures computed using the sample of households for each year and the corresponding weights giving the number of households in the United States represented by each household in the sample. The documentation to the Diary Survey Public Use Tape describes the procedure I use to estimate annual aggregate household expenditures. The second column of this table gives estimates of the average annual expenditures per household on postage, using the procedure to compute this magnitude given in the Diary Survey Public Use Tapes documentation. For the sake of comparison, the third and

Table 16-11. *Postal Revenue and Estimated Annual Household Expenditures*

Year	Estimated aggregate postage expn. ($, billion)	Estimated average postage expn. ($)	Estimated aggregate telephone expn. ($, billion)	Estimated average telephone expn. ($)	Total USPS annual revenue ($, billion)	Revenue share of households (%)
1986	5.07	58.19	36.70	421.67	29.12	17.39
1987	5.83	66.89	41.32	474.22	30.50	19.11
1988	5.85	65.87	42.64	480.38	33.92	17.23
1989	6.69	74.26	45.63	506.51	36.67	18.24
1990	6.38	69.88	50.11	549.16	37.89	16.83
1991	5.80	62.71	52.16	563.45	41.92	13.85
1992	6.06	64.20	59.79	633.04	44.72	13.56
1993	5.90	62.75	60.82	647.07	45.91	12.85
1994	5.05	54.35	64.19	690.65	47.75	10.58

Source: Author's calculations.

fourth columns repeat these same two calculations for telephone services. The behavior of average annual household-level postage and telephone services expenditures over time is similar to the behavior of the sample means of the two-week expenditures on postage and telephone services given in table 16-2.

Using these numbers and the elasticity estimates, I consider the revenue implications of the January 1, 1995, increase in the price of a one-ounce first-class letter from $0.29 to $0.32, a little more than a 10 percent price increase. Estimated annual aggregate household postage expenditures in 1994 are approximately $5 billion (table 16-11). Using the above equation and the own-price elasticity of -1.27 for 1994 yields a 2.7 percent reduction in annual aggregate expenditures, or approximately a $135 million reduction in annual revenues from sales of postal delivery services to U.S. households. To put these figures into perspective, I should note that, according to these estimates, sales to households is 10 percent of total USPS mail delivery revenues in 1994. Table 16-11 also gives total USPS revenues for each fiscal year, and the last column of the table gives the fraction of these revenues that come from expenditures by households. From 1987 to 1994, the share of annual revenues coming from expenditures by households approximately halved. Given the revenue loss calculation from reduced sales to households owing to the recent first-class postage price increase, further declines in the share of revenues coming from sales to households can be expected in the future.

To assess the impact of personal computing technology on the demand for postal delivery services, I perform a similar calculation assuming an equal percentage change in the probability of computer ownership across all U.S. households. Suppose that, as a result of the explosion in services offered via the Internet, the probability of computer ownership increases by 17 percent for all U.S. households. In 1994 the fraction of households owning a personal computer is 0.249 (table 16-3). A 17 percent increase in this magnitude would make it $1.17 \times 0.249 = 0.29$, a reasonable increase in the penetration of computers over the course of a single year. There is a substantial amount of heterogeneity in the probability of computer ownership across households, so that the actual final probability of computer ownership (as result of this uniform 17 percent increase) for each household could be greater or less than this magnitude, although the average probability over all U.S. households would be equal to approximately 0.29. To illustrate this heterogeneity in estimated computer

Figure 16-5. *Density Estimate of Computer Ownership Probabilities, 1994*

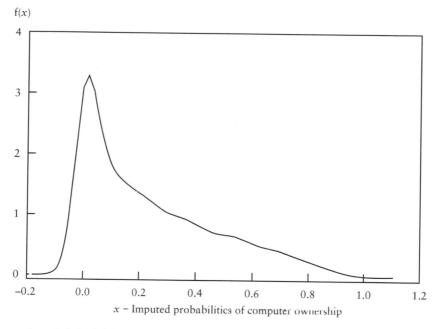

f(x)

x – Imputed probabilities of computer ownership

Source: Author's calculations.

ownership probabilities, figure 16-5 plots the smoothed density estimate of the probability of computer ownership for the 1994 Diary Sample. Although the sample mean of the probability of computer ownership is 0.24, there are values substantially above and below this value.

Using the U.S. population average elasticity of demand with respect to the probability of computer ownership for 1994 of -0.158 (computed by taking the average of the estimated household-level elasticities, weighted by the Diary Survey weights, over all of the households in the 1994 Diary Survey) implies a 2.7 percent decrease in the demand for postal delivery services. Assuming no accompanying change in the price of postal delivery services, this nationwide increase in the probability of personal computer ownership implies a 2.7 percent reduction in revenues from household-level postage expenditures, which is exactly the same reduction in revenues brought about by the 10 percent increase in the price of postal delivery services discussed above. Consequently, for the aggregate demand for postal delivery services by U.S. households, the increasing penetration of personal computing technology and the accompanying more widespread access to the Internet should have significant adverse impacts on the revenues generated from households that rival those from substantial postage price increases.

The other elasticities in table 16-10 show plausible trends over the sample period. For example, there appears to be an increasing degree of substitutability between postal delivery services and all other nondurable goods from 1986 to 1994. The expenditure elasticity shows a downward trend from 0.362 in 1986 to 0.251 in 1994. Another interesting result to emerge from this table is the initial slight complementarity between telephone services and postal delivery services, which shifts toward substitutability between these two goods from 1991 onward.

Conclusions and Direction for Future Research

The two major results to emerge from this analysis are that postal price increases of the magnitude enacted on January 1, 1995, should lead to significant reductions in aggregate household-level expenditures on postal delivery services; and annual increases in the pervasiveness of personal computer technology at historical rates should lead to reductions in aggregate household-level expenditures on postal delivery services that are at least as large as those that would result from a postal price increase on the order of 10 percent.

Clearly, there are many caveats associated with these results. One obvious direction for future research is to investigate alternative functional forms for both the demand for postal delivery services and the frequency of purchase model. An additional extension would be to investigate models that explicitly utilize the number purchases made within the two-week Diary Survey period. These kinds of models can allow own- and other prices to affect the decision to purchase and the amount to consume. The relatively small number of multiple purchases observed may imply that multiple purchases in the two-week period occur primarily for noneconomic reasons. Neveretheless, this appears to be a fruitful direction for future research given the potential large payoff in terms of a richer model for expenditures on postal delivery services.

Notes

1. U.S. Postal Service, *The 1994 Annual Report of the Postmaster General* (Washington, 1994).

2. Richard Blundell and Costas Meghir, "Bivariate Alternatives to the Tobit Model," *Journal of Econometrics*, vol. 34 (1987), pp. 179–200; and Angus Deaton and Margaret Irish, "Statistical Models for Zero Expenditures in Household Budgets," *Journal of Econometrics,* vol. 23 (1984), pp. 59–80.

3. Frank A. Wolak, "Changes in the Household-Level Demand for Postal Delivery Services from 1986 to 1994," in M. A. Crew and P. Kleindorfer, eds., *Managing Change in the Postal and Delivery Industries* (Kluwer Academic Publishers, 1997), pp. 162–91.

4. Quang Vuong, "Likelihood Ratio Tests for Model Selection and Nonnested Hypotheses," *Econometrica*, vol. 57 (1989), pp. 307–34.

5. Wolak, "Changes in the Household-Level Demand."

6. H. White, "Maximum Likelihood Estimation of Misspecified Models," *Econometrica*, vol. 50 (1982), pp. 1–26.

7. All smoothed density estimates use a kernel density estimator with a Gaussian kernel. The automatic bandwidth selection procedure described in B. W. Silverman, *Density Estimates for Statistics and Data Analysis* (London: Chapman and Hall, 1986) is used to determine the amount of smoothing.

CHAPTER SEVENTEEN

Public Harms Unique to Satellite Spectrum Auctions

Charles L. Jackson, John Haring, Harry M. Shooshan III, Jeffrey H. Rohlfs, and Kirsten M. Pehrsson

A FTER DECADES OF discussion, in 1993, spurred by budget considerations, Congress authorized the Federal Communications Commission
(FCC) to use competitive bidding systems (including auctions) to decide
among mutually exclusive applications for radio licenses. The FCC has
conducted several such auctions and has indicated a strong predisposition
to auction radio licenses whenever possible.

Spectrum auctions are an efficient administrative tool in many circumstances. If, however, auctions become an end in themselves, there may
be unfortunate and unintended consequences. The incentive might arise
to restrict the use and supply of spectrum inefficiently in order to drive
up its price and resulting auction revenues. This outcome could conflict
with public-interest obligations and with the FCC's clear statutory mandate to provide for a fair, efficient, and equitable radio service.

Before undertaking any additional satellite auctions, the FCC should
consider whether what has worked in the past cannot continue to work
in the future. Are auctions for every radio license appropriate? If not,
when are auctions appropriate?

This chapter considers these general questions and the specific question
of whether auctions are appropriate for satellite systems, especially given
the history of the FCC's successful satellite licensing efforts. Although
much of this discussion is framed in terms of a U.S. context, the analysis
applies generally to most single-country satellite auctions.

Auctions are one way of choosing the licensee when there are more

This chapter is based upon a study originally prepared for the Satellite Industry Association. The authors thank Clayton Mowry for helpful discussion and advice on this topic.

applicants than licenses available. The FCC historically has often taken steps to avoid scarcity in the satellite industry and thereby has obviated the need to choose among competing applicants. For example, the FCC has used the combination of strict eligibility requirements, more efficient technical rules (for example, reduced orbital spacing), and expanded frequency bands to accommodate growth in the satellite industry. As a result, the industry has adopted new technologies that permit more satellites to operate. These efficiency improvements have paid great dividends in terms of services to consumers and in terms of job creation within the satellite industry.

The FCC's track record here constitutes a significant accomplishment, though one that has not received the attention afforded revenue-producing spectrum auctions. The combined efforts of the satellite industry and the FCC have expanded satellite capacity by a substantial amount. There has been substantial growth in both in-orbit satellite capacity and spectrum exploitable for fixed satellite service. Worldwide capacity of operating satellites has increased enormously in the past thirty years. This growth has been accommodated through a combination of technological advance and more efficient use of spectrum. In the latter regard, adoption of cross-polarized transmissions and the move from four-degree to two-degree satellite spacing *each* have allowed a doubling of capacity in geostationary C-band services. It is also interesting to contrast satellite services with cellular/PCS. In cellular, licensing began ten to fifteen years after the service was technically feasible; the corresponding lag in satellites was about three to five years. Additional spectrum was made available for PCS thirteen years later; in contrast, a second satellite band was operational four years after the first band.

The Satellite Industry: Historical Background

The commercial satellite industry grew from modest and fairly slow beginnings to today's industry composed of almost 200 commercial satellites providing services around the globe. In this section we quickly describe the evolution of the satellite industry and examine the economic and regulatory factors that spurred the rapid technological evolution in this industry.

Technological Development

The United States and Canada began their domestic satellite programs in the early 1970s. Initial plans for domestic communications satellite service in the United States were announced in 1966, but regulatory review by the FCC delayed active development until 1972. The 1972 Open Skies order permitted any qualified legal entity to construct a satellite system offering specialized services.[1] Meanwhile, the USSR had began operation of the nongeostationary *Molniya*.[2] Canada's *Anik A* series provided the first non-Soviet domestic satellite system in 1972. In the United States, the Open Skies policy stimulated RCA's introduction of the first domestic service in 1973 using leased *Anik A-2* channels. The first U.S. carrier to launch its own satellite was Western Union, which launched *Westar* in 1974. A joint venture between Germany and France deployed experimental *Symphonie* satellites in 1974 and 1975. RCA developed its own *Satcom* series of satellites by 1975, the first satellites domestically or internationally to provide spectrum reuse, using orthogonal antenna polarization to achieve increased channel capacity and more efficient spectrum utilization. This approach was next used by AT&T/Comsat with the 1976 launch of the first large *Comstar*. Indonesia used technology and designs developed by Hughes to become the fourth nation to deploy a domestic communications satellite system with the launch of its first *Palapa* satellite in 1976.

Sparked by rapid growth of domestic systems based on C-band technology, Ku-band systems were developed. These new systems were motivated by the need for additional spectrum capacity and the economies of smaller earth terminals located at the user site. The first hybrid satellite (using both Ku-band and C-band) was the Canadian *Anik B*, launched in 1978. The first all Ku-band satellite—*SBS*—was launched in 1980. Intelsat began deploying hybrid *Intelsat V* spacecraft in 1980. U.S. domestic satellite service burgeoned in the 1980s. GTE, American Satellite, and Hughes joined the competition of RCA/GE Americom, Western Union, AT&T, and Satellite Business Systems (SBS). Today, there are about 160 geostationary satellites serving the world's nonmilitary communications needs.

Evolution of Satellite Services

Fiber optic systems eroded some of the earlier satellite business (particularly long distance telephony), but other services were developed that compensated for that loss. Satellite technology's accessibility in remote areas, its distance insensitivity, and its rapid deployment capability encouraged use for specialized applications. Highly important is the ability of satellite systems to serve one to many communication needs efficiently. A number of applications involve the use of very small aperture terminals (VSATs). VSAT usage was spurred as customers expanded individual networks by installing VSAT networks for intracorporate data, video, and voice communications. VSATs are used particularly heavily for relay of point-of-sale credit authorization and inventory control data among multiple remote locations. In the United States, automotive, retail, and financial services industries are particularly heavy VSAT users.

Regulation of a Growing Industry

Regulators have used a variety of tools to assure that consumers receive technically efficient services from competitive suppliers in the satellite industry. The FCC and the satellite industry have not had to resort to exclusive choice mechanisms for decades while compiling an enviable record of output growth and innovation. This section describes some of the reasons for this outcome and describes the various approaches the FCC has taken to avoid mutual exclusivity. More important than any single element on the list is the philosophy underlying it—cooperative planning by government and private interests can accommodate the needs of the satellite industry while benefiting consumers.

The FCC has used several policy tools in the past to accommodate all applicants. Some of these policy tools are universal (for example, better technology) and can be applied to any satellite service. Others have proven themselves in specific satellite services and processing rounds[3] in the past; application to other satellite services and processing rounds is unclear.

Five proven policy tools are as follows:

—Encouraging better technology. The FCC's rules have always encouraged the satellite industry to adopt more efficient technology and have thus expanded the usable capacity of the orbital arc many times over. Openness to innovation has allowed the FCC to accommodate more satellite systems and more traffic at any given time.

—Expanding the spectrum available to satellite systems. Historically, the FCC and International Telecommunication Union (ITU) have expanded the spectrum bands available for use by satellite services. Originally, satellites were restricted to the C-band. Eventually, the Ku-band and the Ka-band were also made available. Today, the L-band and S-band are slated for use by the mobile satellite service (MSS) and digital audio radio service (DARS). The commission has had success in encouraging population of the higher-frequency bands. It has also managed to promote bandsharing between satellite and terrestrial systems by constructing rules of operation that accommodate both technologies (for example, that constrain power output and signal direction).

—Imposing due diligence milestone requirements on licensees and other policies to deter speculation and warehousing. The FCC has several policies to deter speculation and ensure that satellite licenses are available to serious operators. For example, the imposition of milestone requirements ("use it or lose it" rules) is a proven means of discouraging those who would seek licenses simply in an effort to exploit future scarcity rents. Given the expense of satellite systems, a milestone requirement imposes substantial costs on anyone seeking to hold a purely speculative license. Conversely, a milestone requirement imposes little or no cost on those firms that obtain licenses for the purpose of actually building and launching a satellite.[4] Besides discouraging the submission of speculative license applications, the FCC also has used due diligence milestones to prevent licensees from warehousing scarce orbital locations with in-orbit satellites that have reached the end of their useful lives.

—Authorizing multiple systems using a "build and coordinate" rule. A complementary approach, which has been deemed appropriate for some kinds of satellite systems, is to authorize systems using a "build and coordinate" rule—a form of closely-monitored dynamic sharing. Such an approach is currently used for LEOs using Code-Division Multiple Access (CDMA) technology. The heart of this approach is to select a set of authorized operators and then establish deadlines for construction and launch. Each authorized operator must disclose its construction progress to the other operators, and all operators must cooperate to develop coordination procedures. Similarly, all operators must employ technology that allows flexible use and sharing of the relevant band. Milestone requirements prevent licensing for speculative purposes. Disclosure requirements permit every firm to better understand the likely frequency-sharing and competitive regime they will be entering. Once the satellites are launched, each operator receives a prorated share of the spectrum. A variation of this approach was utilized in both the Big LEO and Little LEO processing rounds. In both cases, the applicants developed a means of sharing the available spectrum, thus permitting grant of most of the pending applications.[5]

—Authorizing shared platforms. Another approach is to encourage resource sharing or consolidation so as to avoid mutual exclusivity. The FCC used fractional licenses in its early stage of licensing the DBS service. In this service, the U.S. rights to the orbital-spectrum resource were already well defined by international agreements. Defining license rights by DBS channels was a natural step. The FCC faced a surplus of channel applications over availability in DBS services. It resolved the issue in its 1989 *Continental*[6] order, in which it granted each DBS application only to the extent that it was possible to award an equal number of channel reservations to each applicant. Another example of this approach is American Mobile Satellite Corporation (AMSC), which was formed when the FCC ordered formation of a consortium to offer geostationary mobile satellite services. Although the deliberations leading to that decision caused some delay, a protracted applicant selection process was averted. Today, DIRECTV and USSB offer competing (and complementary) DBS services operating from shared spacecraft in their common orbital slot. Customers who buy an earth station and point it at that satellite can subscribe to one or both services using the same equipment.

We conducted an informal survey of several individuals who were well informed about the FCC's satellite policies and also had broad experience in telecommunications policy. The universal response of these individuals was that satellite policy is an area where the commission has an excellent record.[7]

For example, the commission's Open Skies satellite policy in the early 1970s helped set the stage for the broader revolution in telecommunications services competition that was to follow. The recently enacted Telecommunications Act of 1996 effectively extended that competitive, open policy to all telecommunications markets. As a result of the FCC's policies, the satellite industry has been characterized by innovation and output expansion.

Perhaps equally important, the satellite industry itself has supported the move toward more efficient operation and additional entry. Why has the industry done so? The following attributes of the satellite industry facilitate the adoption of more efficient regulations and technology:

—New satellite technology is more economically productive than old. (Added capacity requires some additional costs, but also shares common costs of spacecraft bus, launch and launch services, and insurance.)

—Satellites wear out (expend station-keeping fuel) and must be replaced.

—The satellite industry (unlike some other spectrum-based industries) is going after a market with rapidly growing demand, and expanded capacity translates into more sales.

—Satellites are very expensive (several hundred million dollars for spacecraft and launch services) and take time to build; consequently, launching a satellite into service is a weighty and deliberate decision.

—The natural scale of the industry requires system operators to maintain high technical capabilities in the firm.

The fact that satellites must be replaced creates a natural opportunity for technology upgrades. The enormous fixed costs of launch services and the spacecraft bus create strong incentives to install the most productive equipment in each satellite. Satellite systems serve a variety of communications needs and compete in many communications markets. Installation of additional capacity by one satellite operator does not automatically translate into reduced sales for other satellite system operators. This is an important and essential point. Satellite system operators whose services compete in significantly broader telecommunications markets and who are well positioned to exploit added satellite capacity would be expected to support expanded orbital arc capacity. In contrast, if the satellite industry were only the war of one satellite firm against another, it would be less likely that the industry would support capacity additions. Historically, the satellite industry's support for expanded orbital arc capacity may also have grown, in part, from the participation of manufacturers in the industry.

Negative Impacts of Satellite Auctions

Although we believe that auctions are a valuable tool for spectrum management, they are not a cure-all for every ill that besets regulatory policy. Next, we first discuss the conditions under which spectrum auctions work well and work poorly. Then we consider the specific environment under which satellite auctions by a single nation would take place and identify some disabilities that appear to be unique to satellite auctions.

When Should Auctions Be Used?

We believe that auctions of radio licenses can serve a valuable purpose, and we were early proponents of the use of auctions and market mechanisms in spectrum management.[8] Nevertheless, one should recognize that auctions are a tool for spectrum management and are only a means to an end—making fair and efficient radio services available to the public—not an end in themselves. Treatment of auction revenues as a goal might lead to inefficient restriction of the use and supply of spectrum in order to drive up its price and the resulting auction revenues.[9] In addition, arguments against auctions in the satellite industry uniquely extend beyond traditional arguments against auctions, because of some disabilities posed in this context. Auctioning satellite licenses can be usefully contrasted with, for example, auctioning a PCS or cellular license in San Francisco. Satellite-license auctions could lead to preassignment of spectrum by international regulatory bodies; no such danger exists with PCS or cellular. Auction of satellite spectrum raises the specter of multiple fees or sequential auctions whose complexity and unpredictability could stifle industry growth; there is no parallel danger of sequential auctions for PCS or cellular. We discuss these dangers in more detail in the next section.

Auctions provide a good means for assigning licenses when certain conditions exist. The more completely each of the following conditions hold, the better the case for auction is likely to be:

—The specific radio technology requires exclusivity or other usage limitations to control interference;[10]
—There are more applicants than spectrum available;
—There are no serious problems posed by incomplete markets, market failures, or other "second-best" considerations;
—There are no negative international consequences; and
—Auctions have no other perceived deleterious effects.

Consider PCS—a case where many of these conditions did exist. In PCS, the FCC defined technical rules that created large regions (in bandwidth and geography) where a single firm could internalize interference decisions. PCS still required coordination between firms at the boundaries of license regions to control interference. Under these rules, practical exclusivity could be provided. At the same time, there were no serious market failure considerations arguing against auctions and no apparent disabilities of an auction per se. Thus, auctions in that context could be anticipated to, and indeed did, supply an administratively efficient tool to determine which entity obtained each specific resource block.[11]

In contrast, consider the early days of AM broadcasting. The FCC was faced with mutually exclusive applications with vastly different potential impacts on consumers. Suppose that the FCC received two mutually exclusive AM broadcasting applications—one for the first service to a town of 30,000, the other for the second service to a town of 100,000. It is quite possible to imagine that an auction would have assigned the license to the larger city, whereas considerations of consumer welfare and fairness would assign the license to the smaller city.[12] Of course, the optimal solution might be to require each potential broadcaster to modify its technical design and operating parameters so that both could operate without interference.[13] Indeed, in the case of satellites, technical solutions have been used to resolve mutual exclusivity, thus permitting the market to be served by a larger number of firms. Technical solutions, as well as market competition, have brought about extensive innovation in the satellite industry.

The Harms Created by Satellite Spectrum Auctions

Auctions of rights to operate satellite systems run the risk of harming both the interests of the licensing nation and the interests of others around the world. First, auctions in one country could prompt authorities in other countries to impose auctions for landing rights in each country, thereby creating the potential for extortion and promoting uncertainty and inefficiency in the satellite industry.[14] These harms could affect systems authorized by one nation that do not yet have all the licenses and spectrum assignments needed in other countries. Second, a move to auctions could temper the strong push for expanded output and increased efficiency that has historically been the touchstone of satellite policy.[15] One of the greatest harms that could come from auctions would be a move to extensive a priori planning of the orbital arc. The United States has consistently opposed such a priori planning, arguing that it would limit technology and harm consumers by limiting output.[16] Third, some highly negative consequences in the international spectrum-management community could be reasonably anticipated. Fourth, the delay and uncertainty of auctions would harm consumers by delaying or denying services.

HARMS FROM SEQUENTIAL AUCTIONS. Satellite auctions in any one nation may induce other nations to hold auctions for the assignment of spectrum and rights to transmit and receive signals in that country (spectrum assignments, or "landing rights"). The incidence of sequential auctions to collect all the necessary international rights provides an opportunity for extortion by individual countries and would promote inefficiency and uncertainty in the satellite industry.

Sequential auctions may deter system operators from beginning operations. It is important to recognize and appreciate that satellite operations require securing a bundle of rights rather than a single right. Authorization of a spacecraft to orbit at a particular location, granted through national licensing and ITU coordination of the space segment, is one of those rights. This authorization is required to control interference and otherwise manage the orbit-spectrum resource. Rights to transmit signals to and receive signals from the satellite in each individual country reachable by the satellite (spectrum assignments, or landing rights) are separate. Procurement of such rights is an important aspect of the *economics* of satellite licensing. The potential for individual countries to withhold such rights in demand for payment provides an opportunity for sequential auctions—that is, separate negotiations with each country covered by the satellite "footprint." As a result, although sequential auctions do not yield *technical* obstacles to satellite operation, they could well yield *economic* obstacles of such magnitude as to stifle an enterprise entirely.

Potential harms from sequential auctions can be easily illustrated. Consider a simple example. Suppose that a firm has identified a satellite service that will generate net profits with a discounted present value of $50 million.[17] Further suppose that this service will be offered using a single satellite system (costing $200 million)[18] that provides service to both the United States and Canada and that the revenues will be generated equally by sales in the United States and Canada ($125 million in each country). Further assume that the technology comes in lumpy chunks. A satellite built just to serve the U.S. market costs negligibly less than a satellite built to serve the combined U.S. and Canada market. Thus, operating a successful business requires permission to operate in each nation.

Consider how an auction might proceed. First, the FCC auctions off the right to serve the United States from a particular orbital slot, and the firm wins with a bid of $20 million. But, let us further assume (realistically) that the Canadian government is smart. It recognizes that this system is very valuable in Canada, so it sets a minimum bid of $30 million in the auction for landing rights. Under our assumptions, the company will make no profit at the minimum bid. But without the Canadian market it loses money. So the firm bids $30 million and only breaks even. Of course, the Canadians may set the reservation price in the auction higher—say $49 million. At this point, the company will lose $19 million if it meets the Canadians' minimum bid. But, if it drops out it will lose $20 million (the sunk cost of the winning bid paid in the United States). The company would still choose to meet the Canadians' terms; the company's best strategy becomes no-bid in the auction in Canada and absorbs the loss of the $20 million it bid in the United States only if the Canadians raise their minimum bid to $51 million. Notice that, if the order of bidding were reversed, the United States could set its reservation price at $49 million and extract the maximum amount.

The problem here is not unlike that facing a real estate developer who wishes to buy up a block of smaller properties and build an office building. In an extreme case, each holdout can halt the project. If we assume that there are not just two nations that must give a go-ahead before the project can be profitable, but ten such nations, then uncertainty is multiplied and incentives to invest are reduced. Consider a satellite application that requires approval from ten nations. The approval of the system by the first nation isn't worth much to the system operator—because nine more nations must approve. In contrast, the approval of the system by the tenth nation takes the system from unviable to viable. The added value of the last approval is equal to all the value created by the system. Every nation faces the same incentives to be last in line and thereby confer the most value. But these incentives will slow the process and hinder efficiency.

In the above two-nation example, the bidding process in the United States is complicated by considerations of how other nations will run their auctions. Even in a simple example with only two nations, rational behavior by the second nation to conduct the auction in the fashion that maximizes its financial benefits can seriously distort the decisionmaking process. A company should not bid $20 million in the United States if it anticipates a good chance that the auction process in other nations will impose costs of greater than $30 million.

In the more general case, there would be several system operators, each proposing a slightly different system with different costs and benefits associated with operations in each country. There would also be several different countries, some of which would be essential to a satellite system's economic viability while others would not be essential.

Of course, the administration in the second country may take an entirely different tack. It may wait until the system is operational and the investment in the space segment is sunk. Once the space segment is in place, an opportunistic second country could set a spectrum fee (or minimum bid in a landing rights auction) that takes into account the marginal profitability of the satellite business—ignoring any sunk costs. In the above example, the entire $125 million in revenues from the second country is at risk if fees are assessed after the space segment is in place. If the company has spent the $200 million to launch, then an "auction" payment of $50 million is far better than being denied access to the second country's market and losing $125 million.

To recapitulate, a major potential source of harm to consumers from such sequential auctions would be the delay created as satellite system operators tried to contend with the increased uncertainty flowing from multiple auctions. In addition, one can easily envision scenarios where attempts by individual nations to maximize their own revenues from the auction process make satellite projects unprofitable. One can also envision scenarios where auctions in multiple countries could create confusion and delay such that some companies might be compelled to forgo or abandon projects.

AN ASIDE: THOUGHTS ON SEQUENTIAL AUCTIONS. The outcome of sequential auctions for the rights to operate a single satellite communications can have a wide variety of outcomes depending upon the characteristics of the satellite technology, the end-market served by the satellite, the rules adopted by each nation regarding its auctions, the transferability of the licenses it issues, and the number of firms that are capable of operating such satellite systems. A few examples will show how sensitive the outcome can be to slight changes in these factors.

In each of the following examples we will assume that each bidder acts independently without coordination of behavior with other bidders, that auction rules are known to all bidders in advance, that there is no uncertainty about the value of the satellite system authorization, that all bidders share the same complete information about values, that the sequence of auctions is known, that there are sufficiently many qualified bidders that the outcome is competitive, and that the rules are fixed before the beginning of the first auction. We label the countries auctioning their license rights as Country 1, Country 2, Country 3, in the order they hold their sequential auctions. We label the bidders B_1, B_2, B_3 . . . according to the order in which they win auctions. That is, Bidder B_1 wins the first auction (and perhaps some others), B_2 wins the first auction B_1 doesn't win, and so on.

Example 1—Two countries and no transferability. Consider the simplest example, a two-country case and a satellite technology that is uneconomic unless permission is granted by both countries to operate the system. Further assume that licenses are not transferable.[19] With permission from both countries, the satellite system is worth 10 units. Country 1 holds its auction. B_1 wins with a bid of x units. (We will come back shortly and solve for x.) Country 2 then holds its auction. Because of the technical constraints and the lack of transferability, the license is worthless to anyone else but bidder B_1. Consequently, B_1 wins the second auction with a bid only slightly higher than zero. Knowing this, we can solve for the amount of the bid, x, in the first auction. x is clearly 10, if we assume that the auction is competitive. This result is so bad for Country 2 that it can hardly be called an equilibrium. One must expect Country 2 to change the rules. This motivates example 2.

Example 2—Two countries, no transferability, and reservation prices. This example is the same as Example 1, above, except that Country 2, thinking through the analysis above, adds a reservation price of 6 to its auction. This reservation price is known in advance of both auctions. As before B_1 will win both auctions. But, B_1, knowing that the price in the second auction will be at least 6 units, will only bid 4 in the first auction.

Notice that the each country has an incentive to set a higher reservation price and thereby get a higher share of the auction revenues. If, however, the reservation prices are set too high, they will raise the sum of the minimum bids above the value of the satellite rights and no one will bid.

Example 3—Two-countries and transferability. This is the same as Example 1, except we drop the assumption that licenses are not trans-

Table 17-1. *Outcomes of Two-Country Sequential Auctions under Different Rules*

Auction rules	Payment to country 1	Payment to country 2	Total payments
No transferability	10	0	10
No transferability, reserve price set by country 2 of x units	$10 - x$	x	10
Transferability	$5 -$ risk premium	5 (center value of bargaining range)	<10

ferable. Country 1 holds its auction. B_1 wins with a bid of x units. (Again, we will come back shortly and solve for x.) Country 2 then holds its auction. This transferable license is worth 10 units to B_1 and gives anyone else who purchases it the right to engage in a bilateral monopoly negotiation with B_1 for the total package of rights needed to operate the system. As is well known, the outcome of such a bilateral negotiation is uncertain. A plausible value to assign to it is the midpoint 5 between its highest (10) and lowest (0) values. In what follows, we assume that the competitive market does value such a bargaining opportunity at 5. It is important to recognize that this midpoint is an uncertain value which depends upon the negotiating strengths of the firms involved. If B_1 is risk averse (as most entities are), then B_1 will prefer paying a certain quantity than an uncertain quantity with the same expected value. So B_1 will win the second auction with a bid of 5 and thereby avoid a negotiation with the same expected outcome. If so, the most B_1 will pay in the first auction, x, is 5 also. Notice, however, that a prudent investor might avoid these auctions altogether. There may exist a speculative bidder who believes that he can do better in the bilateral monopoly bargaining than the midpoint value. If so, then the price in the second auction will rise higher than 5. More generally, uncertainty about the outcome of the second auction and any subsequent transfers would reduce the value delivered in the first auction and in the two auctions considered together.

Table 17-1 summarizes the results of a simple sequential auction involving two countries and slightly different rules.

Let us consider a few more examples, this time with three countries.

Example 4—Three countries and no transferability. The rules in this case are the same as in the first example, but there are three countries rather than two. The satellite technology is uneconomic unless permission is granted by all three countries to operate the system; licenses are not transferable. With permission from all countries, the satellite system is worth 10 units.

Country 1 holds its auction. B_1 wins with a bid of x units. Country 2 then holds its auction. Because of the technical constraints and the lack of transferability, the license is worthless to anyone else but bidder B_1. Consequently, B_1 wins the second auction with a bid only slightly higher than zero. Similarly for the third auction. As before, x is clearly 10.

Example 5—Three countries, two needed for economic viability, no transferability. This example has the same rules as Example 4 with the exception that the technology can serve any two but only two of the countries. A system operator needs to get permission from only two of the three possible countries in order to realize the value 10. Assume that B_1 wins the Country 1 auction with a bid of x units. Consider now the auction by Country 2. If another bidder B_2 wins that auction, then B_1 and B_2 enter an auction for an item worth 10 units to each of them. The likely outcome of such an auction is that either B_1 or B_2 will win the auction at a price of 10 units. Thus, if B_2 wins the third auction, he still is a net loser—by the amount he paid in the second auction. Similarly, if B_2 loses the auction, he is a net loser by the amount he paid in the second auction. Hence, he is better off by not bidding in the second auction. So the second auction goes to B_1 for a low price. As before x, the price reached in the first auction, is 10. This solution, in particular, has a knife-edge flavor. If there is are differences among the bidders about valuations, results could vary enormously.

Example 6—Three countries, two needed for economic viability, transferability. This is the same as Example 5, except that licenses are transferable. B_1 wins the Country 1 auction with a bid of x units. Assume that another bidder, B_2 wins the Country 2 auction with a bid of y units. If the Country 3 auction begins, each firm gains 10 units of value if it wins the auction. The outcome is that either B_1 or B_2 will win the Country 3 auction with a bid of 10. This outcome turns each of them into net losers. An alternative exists: before the Country 3 auction begins, B_2 can sell his right to provide service in Country 2 to B_1. At any price less than 10 units, this side transfer is more attractive to B_1 than is entering the Country 3 auction. So a transfer is likely to take place—the outcome of a bilateral monopoly negotiation between B_1 and B_2. If we make the same assumptions about the value of bilateral monopoly agreements as we did in Example 3, then the outcome of the Country 2 auction is that B_1 wins with a bid of 5 units. Note the strong pressures the structure of this auction creates for firms with partial rights to join together to eliminate the uncertain effects of later auctions.

In the real world, many of the assumptions of these simple models cannot be expected to hold. Some deviations from these assumptions make outcomes more uncertain. Countries can change their rules during the sequence of auctions (raising the reservation price, for example), participants have imperfect knowledge of the value of the rights offered, transferability is neither prohibited nor frictionless, and so on. The threat that one of the nations that conducts its auctions later will raise its reservation price or engage in other equivalent conduct (such as stimulating a "national champion" bidder in its auction) appears to us to be the element of such sequential auctions that creates the greatest uncertainty and disincentives for investment.

Nevertheless, one of the most striking results of these simple models is the vast differences among the outcomes at various stages of the auctions depending upon the rules selected. Sequential auctions create great uncertainty and thus could make multinational satellite systems harder to bring into operation.

OUTPUT RESTRICTION. The condition of mutual exclusivity is critical to any consideration of auctions. In the satellite industry the national regulators have been resourceful in promoting output expansion while also accommodating new entrants, thus reducing or avoiding conflicts over exclusivity. Worldwide satellite capacity has burgeoned during the past thirty years. Complex trade-offs between power, bandwidth, and satellite spacing make it difficult to precisely quantify progress in satellite technology, but it is enormous by any measure. For example, the first-generation satellites could support only about 240 voice circuits while the latest generation can support 112,500 voice circuits. Satellite equipment costs have fallen, and technological innovations allow more satellites to operate within the same orbital space. These factors have combined to place 2,105 C- and Ku-band transponders in orbit worldwide, as estimated by Arianespace in 1995.

To accommodate the U.S. share of this vast growth, the FCC has historically employed two primary means to reconcile conflicting demands in the satellite industry.

First, it has encouraged the industry to adopt more efficient technology. Use of more efficient technology has, in turn, permitted rapid expansion of output and multiplied the number of satellite orbital locations as well. Industry-government cooperation in resolving spectrum conflicts has made the satellite industry more competitive with terrestrial systems, made each satellite vendor a stronger competitor, and, simultaneously, avoided the delay and economic arbitrariness of comparative hearings or lotteries in the choice of satellite system operators.

The history here is quite remarkable. The U.S.'s first domestic satellite was *Westar 1*—a 12-transponder C-band bird. Today's C-band satellites typically carry 24 transponders and are packed twice as tightly together— for a fourfold increase in efficiency in the C-band. To promote the use of more efficient satellite communications technologies, the commission approved the use of spread-spectrum technology and small-diameter earth stations in the C-band as well as the Ku-band—a step that was important in the growth of the VSAT industry.

The second means the commission has utilized to provide efficient satellite services has been timely release of substantial additional spectrum resources. The FCC has opened up the Ku- and Ka-band, DBS spectrum, L-band for MSS, and digital audio broadcasting satellites at the S-band.

The history of the satellite industry reflects the commission's overriding interest in the provision of an efficient satellite service. The history of the satellite industry includes many firms and projects that failed to prosper: SBS, Comsat's DBS, National Exchange, and Equatorial Communications, to name a few. These commercial failures should be counted as commission successes in terms of its spectrum management functions. In an environment more like the computer industry than most of the telecommunications industry, firms were permitted to enter the market and test their products and market ideas. Some succeeded; others failed. The FCC gave them all room to try.

One of the dangers of moving to auctions for satellite licenses is to reduce or eliminate the incentives that have driven spectrum regulators to induce efficient growth and output expansion in the satellite industry.[20] Because satellites wear out approximately every fifteen years, the FCC has the opportunity to require operators to adopt new, more efficient technology and to coordinate their systems with new and existing operators. Auctions may limit moves to require new technology by generating greater renewal expectancy. For example, a recent Heritage Foundation study has called for auctions with flexible spectrum use (that is, auction winners can use spectrum for whatever purposes and via whatever technology desired)—such an approach would interfere with the renewal process. In the simplest case, one can envision government decisionmakers saying, "Why worry about pushing increased capacity? Auctions and markets will solve the problems."[21]

Auctions can *resolve* demand conflicts but not *solve* them. Relaxation of scarcity constraints through increases in the supply of spectrum and improvements in the technologies utilized to harvest the spectrum resource are what ultimately solve the problem.

There is a danger that resorting to auctions may relieve pressure to promote efficiency or, worse, distort incentives so as to promote ineffiÂ ciency. While policymakers assert that auctions are merely an assignment mechanism and that auctions should not affect the development of policy, the ability of auctions to raise money has been the focal point of community and political interest. But raising money can be the enemy of efficiency. Consider a future regulator facing a choice between two satellite plans. Industry support is roughly divided between two plans: *Plan A*, which will accommodate six new systems and *Plan B*, which will accommodate eight new systems. A decisionmaker might well take into account the fact that an auction of six satellite slots might raise more revenues than an auction of eight satellite slots, understanding that scarce resources are more valuable. Indeed, to the extent that the commission is gaining positive publicity and being otherwise rewarded by its success in raising revenues, it may possess incentives to create higher auction revenues.

INTERNATIONAL REPERCUSSIONS. Auctions of the right to operate satellite systems by any one nation could elicit numerous other international repercussions.

First, auctions will disrupt existing dynamics of the international regulatory regime. Currently, numerous frequency bands allocated internationally for satellite services are managed under an international coordination and registration process based, to a large measure, on a principle of first come, first served. Thus as international satellite spectrum (except for the Broadcast Satellite Service) is currently treated, it is not allocated as the property of any nation to auction. One needs to consider that international regulation of spectrum is not a static process. Increasingly, within the International Telecommunication Union (ITU), a United Nations agency that allocates frequencies internationally and adopts principles for their use, countries have sought to revise the system of first come, first served. This dynamic arises out of concerns of many countries that the developed world, and the United States in particular, is garnering the lion's share of the economic and other benefits under the current system. As a result of pressure from such countries, a priori plans have already been devised for certain frequency bands and satellite system services. These plans do not afford the technical, operational, and market flexibility that has characterized U.S. regulation. In fact, the planned satellite bands are lightly used relative to spectrum available for evolutionary implementation of satellite systems.

The implementation of auctions for satellite licenses will almost surely fuel the pressure for change in the international allocation and regulatory regime for satellite communications. If much of the world perceives the larger developed nations as taking auction revenues from assignment of satellite spectrum and orbital locations, it will seek to change the regulatory regime so as to secure more revenue for other countries. One possibility is more a priori planning (as with DBS), which would sharply limit access to spectrum/orbit. Another is adoption of an international licensing and/or auction process (even for domestic systems) with the proceeds to be used by or divided up in accordance with the political imperatives of the international organization. Yet another possibility is establishment of high fees for international notification, coordination, and registration.

Second, we can expect system operators to choose to operate under administrations that offer less onerous licensing mechanisms. There would be little incentive for a prospective satellite operator to seek an operating license from its home country if it could obtain an operating license more cheaply from another country. Consider an example:

Suppose a firm is considering building a satellite system to serve the Pacific. Suppose further that, after studying markets and technology it determines that a satellite operating anywhere on the arc from 160° W Longitude to 160° E Longitude will reasonably serve its business purpose. The firm has a choice of administrations through which to obtain a license—many nations lie in view of the proposed satellite. Suppose it narrows candidate administrations to two—the United States and the Philippines. Although the United States has substantially more experience with satellites, both administrations have the necessary technical capabilities and are familiar with the ITU process. Suppose, further, that the U.S. subjects applicants to an auction while the Philippines will attempt to accommodate as many applicants as possible, using rules similar to those of the ITU coordination process.

Which administration should the firm choose? If it elects to apply through the United States, it is certain to face an auction; only after that expense, delay, and risk can it proceed to ITU coordination with others who seek to operate in the same part of the arc. However, the firm runs only a risk of an auction if it chooses to apply through the Philippines. If no auction occurs, it can begin the ITU coordination process sooner.

Over time, the satellite is authorized by the Philippines at 160° W Longitude and is properly registered at the ITU. The firm desires to provide service to and from points in Alaska, Hawaii, and some of the western continental United States. Is it now viable for the FCC to auction off the rights to provide service from that slot? No—a downlink signal is already operating from that slot. No other entity could use those same frequencies for a different satellite without creating interference with the incumbent satellite services. Similarly, no one can use the uplinks except people taking service from the satellite. Relevant spectrum management decisions have now been made by the Philippines administration and the ITU process. At this point, it would be hard, probably impossible, to define an additional economically valuable satellite service to operate at 160° W Longitude that would not interfere with service from the Philippines-sponsored satellite. As a result, the FCC has no valuable spectrum right to auction and so has effectively dropped out of the coordination process. In this example, institution of a U.S. auction of 160° W Longitude satellite service rights has actually served to reduce or preclude U.S. input into efficient spectrum management decisions.

Third, auctions in one nation are likely to change the incentives of other administrations. Currently, authorization of a satellite system that serves markets outside the authorizing nation does not deny the administrations in those other nations any revenue. If a system is registered with the ITU, then any other nation that tries to auction off the same slot (or the right to use that slot in their jurisdiction) will run into the interference problems alluded to in the example described above. With the advent of auctions, however, other nations may try to stake their claim to prospective auction revenues by claiming slots through "paper applicants" that never actually come to be built.

Fourth, auctions may pollute the current cooperative environment to the extent that all satellite and spectrum coordination reverts to the ITU. One rational approach to preventing races among jurisdictions is to pre-allocate the orbital arc. The ITU could engage in a priori planning for *all* satellite services in the same fashion that it does in the DBS and certain

FSS frequency bands. This would ensure that each nation would get its "fair share" of revenues from the auctions. Of course, auction revenues can be counted on to be higher if the technical plans adopted restrict entry and create scarcity rents. International auctions and preallocation would replace the pressures that exist today to increase technical efficiency with pressures to increase scarcity rents. With expanded a priori planning nations would not compete with each other for the right to auction any specific slot. Any such move towards monopoly and away from competition is suspect. In fact, a major basis for the historical opposition of the United States to a priori planning is the inefficiency inherent in any plan that freezes technology.

An alternative response to prevent races among jurisdictions or sequential auctions would be for the ITU itself to hold global auctions. Even then, two economic problems arise. First, how are the proceeds to be distributed? Second, would the ITU have the proper incentives to encourage efficiency? Or would the ITU, lured by the prospect of additional revenues, restrict the supply of spectrum in order to increase auction revenues?

We judge that expanded a priori planning is a more likely result than a global auction run by the ITU. A priori planning has been used before. It would ensure each nation of a share of the bounty. The greatest harms to consumers would come from the rigidity of a priori plans, which restricts innovation and stifles expansion, and from any ITU restriction on supply.

DELAY AND DENIAL OF SERVICE. Auctions of satellite rights in any one nation also create incentives that may harm consumers by delaying and denying service. Suppose sequential auctions do occur. What then is the decision process facing a system operator? How can it estimate the total costs of a project until landing-rights auctions have been conducted in all countries? If the economic feasibility of a project depends upon the service revenues in other countries, then firms must wait until all (or at least many) nations have completed their authorization process before they safely forecast the profitability of the project. Clearly, five or fifteen nations cannot conduct their auctions as quickly as one nation. This will cause delay in services, at the least. Moreover, because it will be impossible to calculate the costs associated with these sequential auctions, firms cannot forecast the total system cost or whether a system will be profitable. This uncertainty may make it more difficult for firms to obtain financing or cause cancellation of the venture entirely.

SYNOPSIS. Auctions in one nation for satellite operating rights will likely spill over into the international community. This spillover will harm consumers by creating incentives to restrict output and by creating institutions that will delay decisionmaking and could impose incalculable costs. There are other options available to national regulators for licensing satellite systems that have substantial benefits and avoid the risks created by auctions.

Conclusions

The FCC has taken steps to overcome scarcity constraints and thereby has obviated the need to choose among competing applicants. The FCC's track record in this respect has been remarkable. The combined efforts of the satellite industry and the FCC have substantially expanded satellite capacity, brought new services to market rapidly, and provided substantial benefits to consumers.

A critical factor that sets this area apart from others is that satellite communications systems are inherently international. Consequently, each nation's approach to regulation of satellite systems necessarily has international implications.

Given the successful history of accommodating entry, and in light of the international implications, decisionmakers should ponder carefully the implications of auctions for awarding satellite spectrum, especially since regulators possess a variety of tools to avoid the need for auctions.

Notes

1. Domestic Communications Satellite Facilities, 35 FCC 2d 844 (1972). See also *Network Project* v. FCC 511 F. 2d 786 (District of Columbia Cir.) 1975.

2. The *Molniya*'s unique twelve-hour elliptical inclined orbit with northern apogee afforded coverage of high-latitude areas, though ground antenna tracking and satellite "hand-over" were required.

3. The FCC has frequently accepted multiple applications for satellite systems and then worked to find a set of assignments that satisfy many or all of the

applicants. Such processing of a block of satellite applications is known as a processing round.

4. Because a firm's preferred schedule for building a system may deviate from that imposed by the commission, the possibility exists that a milestone requirement would impose some costs even on firms that did intend to build satellite systems.

5. See Report and Order in CC Docket No. 92-76, 8 FCC Rcd 8450 (1993) (*NVNG MSS Order*) and 9 FCC Rcd 5936 (1994) (Big LEO Order).

6. *Continental Satellite Corp.*, 4 FCC Rcd 6292, 6299 (1989), *partial recon. denied*, 5 FCC Rcd 7421 (1990).

7. Some went on to attribute the soundness of the commission's policy to the guidance it had received from the White House's Office of Telecommunications Policy.

8. For early examples of such advocacy, see Charles L. Jackson, "Technology for Spectrum Markets," Ph.D. thesis, MIT, 1976, or House Commerce Committee, "Improving Use of the Spectrum," Staff Options Paper (Government Printing Office, 1977). Jackson was also an architect of the spectrum market plan in New Zealand. The New Zealand plan led to the world's first significant spectrum rights auctions but recommended against auctioning satellite spectrum. See *Management of the Radio Frequency Spectrum in New Zealand* (Ministry of Commerce, November 1988), p. 166. More recently, Jackson testified to the House Commerce Committee: "Let me offer a warning. The pendulum may have swung too far. A few years ago it appeared that auctions of radio licenses were politically unthinkable. Now, the budget process puts strong pressure on this committee to find large amounts of spectrum for further auctions. While I feel auctions are generally sound, and I applaud the Committee for its contributions in putting that policy in place, we should not let the budget process force bad spectrum policy." House Commerce Committee, *Federal Management of the Radio Spectrum*, serial 104-35 (Washington, September 7, 1995), p. 15.

John Haring served on the staff and then as chief of the FCC's Office of Plans and Policy (OPP) during a formative period in which that office espoused the administrative efficiency of spectrum auctions and their revenue-producing potential. Early OPP papers on this topic include: Evan Kwerel and Alex D. Felker, *Using Auctions to Select FCC Licensees*, Working Paper 16, May 1985, and John O. Robinson, *Spectrum Management Policy in the United States: An Historical Account*, Working Paper 15, April 1985.

9. In fact, the statute states that such treatment of auction revenues as a goal is prohibited. 47 U.S.C. Section 309(j)(7)(A).

10. In fact, the commission is permitted to conduct auctions only where there are mutually exclusive applications: "If mutually exclusive applications are accepted for filing for any initial license or construction permit which will involve a use of the electromagnetic spectrum described in paragraph (2), then the Commission shall have the authority, subject to paragraph (10), to grant such license or permit to a qualified applicant through the use of a system of competitive bidding that meets the requirements of this subsection." See 47 U.S.C. § 309 (j)(1).

11. See, for example, Peter Crampon, "The FCC Spectrum Auctions: An Early Assessment," University of Maryland, JEL D44 (Auctions) (Telecommunications), July 15, 1996; or Thomas J. Duesterberg and Peter K. Pitsch, "Wireless Services, Spectrum Auctions and Competition in Modern Telecommunications," *Hudson Institute Outlook*, vol. 1 (May 1997).

12. It is easy to define simple examples with the above properties. The key point is that radio stations are advertiser supported and that advertiser support only weakly reflects consumer preferences. The second radio station in a town of 100,000 might have an average potential audience of 50,000 while the first radio station in a town of 30,000 would have a potential audience of 30,000. Auction prices would likely reflect these potential audiences. If listeners value their first broadcast channel significantly more than their second, then welfare would be maximized with one station in each town.

13. In the late 1920s, when these decisions were first started, the (Federal Radio) Commission had only limited tools available to implement this option.

14. The commission recently amended its rules to allow domestic satellite systems to provide international service. Similarly, providers that had previously been limited to providing international service may now provide domestic service. See "Amendment of the Commission's Regulatory Policies Governing Domestic Fixed Satellites and Separate International Satellite Systems," FCC 96-14, Washington, January 22, 1996 at pg 7. The analysis contained in this report turns on economic issues and consumer impacts and does not delve into fundamental issues of international property rights law. Even so, it is perplexing that the FCC could auction rights to systems that may not even serve points in the United States.

At least one country appears to be considering the auction of uplink frequencies associated with an existing satellite. See Decree 807, El Salvador, 1997.

15. This is certainly true in the United States and probably true worldwide.

16. For an example of this U.S. position, see "U.S. Proposal for WARC Malaga-Torremolinos," Spain, 1992. Reprinted in Office of Technology Assessment, *The 1992 World Administration Radio Conference: Issues for U.S. International Spectrum Policy—Background Paper* (GPO, November 1991), appendix D.

17. For simplicity, further assume that the firm has unique technology and that other potential users of the satellite capacity will generate significantly less profit. Thus we focus on the options facing the two governments.

18. For simplicity's sake, all costs are expressed in net present value terms.

19. Or equivalently, that the legal costs and delay of inquiries by the competition policy and regulatory agencies in the two countries into any such transfer will impose costs greater than the value of the license.

20. Although such a revenue maximization approach seems unlikely at the FCC, it's far more likely in Congress and some international forums.

21. This view ignores the fact that markets will trade in the units defined by the FCC. For example, there is no easy market transaction that leads to moving from four-degree to two-degree spacing (yielding increased capacity), but the

FCC was able to effect this transition in the C- and Ku-bands. More generally, for a market to work, the rights assigned have to be mutually exclusive, collectively exhaustive, and reasonably matched to the technology. But we may well lack knowledge of the appropriate boundaries for the satellite technologies of thirty years from now.

CHAPTER EIGHTEEN

Keeping Competitors Out: Broadcast Regulation from 1927 to 1996

Charles R. Shipan

T HE 1996 TELECOMMUNICATIONS ACT is widely seen as a watershed achievement, and for good reason. The regulatory framework for communications policy, set forth in the 1934 Communications Act, was nearing senior citizen status. Although Congress had modified the 1934 act several times, its attempts to pass a law that provided for a wholesale revamping of the policy area had always fallen short.[1] Indeed, even the deregulation of telecommunications that took place during the 1960s, 1970s, and early 1980s was accomplished mostly through judicial decisions and initiatives undertaken by the Federal Communications Commission.[2]

While the 1996 act represents a major break from the past, in some important ways the song remains the same, especially for broadcasters. In this chapter I demonstrate that in the 1996 act, just as in the 1934 act and the Radio Act of 1927, broadcasters sought—generally successfully—to protect their interests. In addition, I show that one of the subtle ways in which they did so was by pushing for the inclusion of specific administrative and judicial procedures that they knew would benefit them.

Then and Now: 1927, 1934, and 1996

How does the 1996 act differ from its predecessor, the 1934 act (which in turn had evolved, at least in terms of its provisions for broadcasting,

I would like to thank David Furth and Roger Noll for helpful comments and discussions.

from the 1927 Radio Act)? First, and most obviously, it addressed a communications field that was vastly more complicated. In 1934 radio broadcasting was still a fledgling industry, barely ten years old. The "phone company"—AT&T—was the sole (or at least dominant) provider of most telephone services and equipment. And except for telegraph, there was little else.

By 1996 the landscape had been completely transformed. "Ma Bell" was no longer around, having been broken up into several pieces as a result of the 1982 settlement of the government's antitrust case against AT&T. Long distance telephone service was provided not only by AT&T but also by MCI, Sprint, and a host of smaller companies. Local phone service was provided by the regional Bell operating companies (RBOCs), which were also actively involved in a variety of other business activities. With the advent of television, cable, and satellite broadcasting, radio was no longer the sole medium for broadcasting. And perhaps most important, technological advances had almost completely blurred the distinctions among many of these industries.[3]

Second, the 1934 act was conceived during the New Deal, an era that was host to the greatest burst of regulatory creation and activity ever seen in the United States, an era fundamentally different from anything that had preceded it.[4] Indeed, the years surrounding the creation of the FCC also witnessed the birth of the Securities and Exchange Commission, the National Labor Relations Board, the Federal Maritime Commission, and the Civil Aeronautics Board, as well as the revamping of the Federal Power Commission and the Federal Trade Commission and the birth of a host of other agencies that are no longer with us. The FCC was thus created during an era that looked favorably toward regulation and regulatory agencies.

The 1996 act, however, was written and enacted by the most deregulatory Congress since the advent of the New Deal. Instead of being part of a tidal wave of regulation enacted by a Congress dominated by pro-government Democrats, the 1996 act was instead passed by a Republican Congress whose ideology veered much more toward the support of free markets, a Congress that earlier had dismantled the Interstate Commerce Commission (ICC), the longest-lived of the independent regulatory agencies. While the 1996 act cannot realistically be described as a purely deregulatory bill, it certainly took more steps in that direction than had any earlier attempts at telecommunications reform.

Yet while the differences between the 1996 act and the acts of the

1920s and 1930s are clear, there are also some strong similarities between the new act and the older laws. For one thing, in both cases legislators were forced to make decisions regarding policy areas about which they had little substantive knowledge and in which technological development was taking place at a dizzying pace. While the level of technological achievement today dwarfs that of the 1920s and 1930s, this difference must be kept in perspective. Radio in the 1920s was an entirely new medium, the likes of which had never before been dealt with by Congress and which inspired a mixture of admiration and confusion. There is little doubt that today few members have expertise in understanding the technology involved in satellite transmission or digital technology. And proof that members of Congress seventy years ago were just as unfamiliar with the technology of the time can be found in one member's concern, voiced on the House floor, that if radio equipment were to be installed in Congress, some anarchists "would send something through it and blow us all out of here."[5]

In addition to the uncertainty about technology and its actual and potential uses, both the earlier acts and the 1996 act were subject to intense scrutiny and pressure from interested groups. Today, of course, the pressure comes from a wider panoply of groups. But just as observers of the earlier era noted the unmatched ability of broadcasting groups to mobilize support and place pressure on Congress—in one instance, for example, more than 170,000 letters were submitted as evidence in a congressional hearing—so, too, have today's observers.[6] William Safire, for example, in describing the tactics of broadcasters with regard to the potential auctioning of some of the broadcast spectrum, quipped, "Members of Congress soon felt the hometown heat that the vaunted gun lobby wishes it could generate—not only from the network mega-mergers, but from suffering 'mom-and-pop broadcasters,' some worth as little as $100 million."[7] Because of the huge stakes involved, as well as the importance of the medium to reelection-minded members of Congress, today, as in the past, telecommunications groups like the broadcast industry are able to place an incredible pressure on members of Congress.

Finally, both the 1996 act and the 1927 and 1934 acts provide wonderful examples of how regulation—or deregulation—is political, and can be used by political actors, such as interest groups, to further their goals. In this chapter I argue that, in 1996 as in the 1920s and 1930s, the most important battles were about *entry*—that is, about who got to enter what lines of business. For if politics is about who gets what, when, and how, then the battles in these regulatory acts revolve in large part around who gets *to do* what, when they get to do it, and how they get to do it. In the area of broadcasting, as I will show, existing stations use regulation—or deregulation—as means by which to prevent competitors from gaining a foothold and to increase their own options.

There are a couple ways an interest group can improve its ability to enter new markets while impinging on its opponents' ability to do the same. The group might seek direct congressional approval (or disapproval) of entry. Alternatively, it might seek to affect entry through the use of more subtle, but not unimportant, procedural and structural mechanisms. In what follows I will focus on these administrative and judicial procedures and structures.

Because I want to draw parallels between the two eras, for the most part I will stick to a discussion of commercial broadcasting. In first looking at regulation in the 1920s and 1930s, and then looking at some of the issues in the 1996 act, I will show that provisions which might appear to be merely procedural are in fact very consistent with the desires of the relevant and powerful groups. And in some cases, there is direct evidence that existing stations lobbied for the inclusion of such provisions in legislation.

Theoretical Background

Before examining the importance of procedural provisions in the communications acts of 1996, 1934, and 1927, some theoretical perspective is needed. First, it needs to be understood that regulation is not purely a public interest phenomenon, and that it can provide significant benefits to an industry by preventing the industry's competitors from entering its lines of business. Second, we need to see that procedures and structures that are specified in legislation are not merely "details" but are important political variables in their own right.

Regulation, the Public Interest, and Entry

Regulation is often seen as being undertaken in "the public interest"; and in fact that was, and continues to be, the guiding standard for regulation of broadcasting.[8] According to such a perspective, regulation is undertaken to correct some sort of defect, most commonly arising from market imperfections. Thus, most textbooks on regulation, business, and administrative law typically include a section that lists the various abuses of economic power, such as price gouging and fraudulent advertising, and the market imperfections, such as the existence of monopolies, imperfect information, and externalities, which necessitate regulation in the public interest. While these sorts of factors undoubtedly contribute to the need for regulation, the passage of laws, and the creation of regulatory agencies, at the same time they understate the degree to which regulation is also *political.*

The notion that regulation could be viewed exclusively through the lens of the public interest first took a major hit when political scientists began to study the workings of different agencies and noted that these agencies were not serving the public interest. The ICC, for example, was described as a "marasmus" because of its steady movement away from regulation in the public interest and toward regulation that benefited the railroads.[9] The FCC was similarly described as contributing to the private interest of broadcasters at the expense of the public.[10] This movement away from the public interest and toward the private interest was generalized in the notion of a "life cycle" for regulatory agencies, which posited that such a movement was inexorable.[11]

While these studies cast shadows over the idea that regulation could be nonpolitical, they still essentially accepted the notion that regulation began in the public interest. Only with the passage of time, and because of the heavy pressure from interest groups, did regulation began to favor private interests over public ones. That is, regulation was initially intended to benefit the public, but then over time the agencies were (inevitably) *captured* by the industries they were intended to regulate.

The idea that regulation was initially in the public interest was turned on its head by the Chicago School of economists, most notably George Stigler.[12] Rather than starting with the premise that regulation was initially undertaken in the public interest and then later subverted by interest groups, Stigler asserted that regulation was actually requested by such groups and was meant to serve their interests. Among the most important of the benefits that regulation can confer on groups, noted Stigler, is control over entry, for preventing such entry by potential competitors helps guarantee that the market need not be divided into ever smaller pieces.

Procedural Details and Political Control

Roughly fifteen years after Stigler's article was published, a variety of political scientists and economists began to analyze the importance of the procedural and structural mechanisms specified in legislation. The concern of these authors was in many ways different from that of Stigler—they were interested in examining the mechanisms of political control over agencies, whereas Stigler was more interested in demonstrating that regulation was designed for the benefit of powerful interests. Yet at the same time, Stigler's work can be seen as a forerunner of these more recent studies of political control, with these later studies attempting to fill in the political and institutional details that Stigler omitted.[13]

Goal-oriented political actors seek to obtain outcomes that are consistent with their interests. Powerful groups thus will push elected politicians to make sure that policy outcomes are in line with what the groups want. How might these politicians attempt to ensure such favorable outcomes? One option they have is to wait for agencies or courts to make decisions, and then to "correct" any decisions they know that their supporters will not like. Thus, members of Congress respond *ex post* to the actions of agencies and courts.[14] Or they might also attempt to influence such decisions before corrective action is needed. Such influence need not be direct, nor need it be overt. Instead, because of the powers that they have over agencies (and, to a lesser extent, courts), including the ability to change policy *ex post*, the president and members of Congress can influence policy outcomes even without taking direct action to overturn such actions.[15]

In addition to the power to influence policy *ex post* and as it is being made, there is one additional way that groups can get their political friends to influence agencies and courts. They can push for the inclusion in legislation of specific administrative and judicial procedures and structures that help produce policy outcomes consistent with their goals. That is, they can act *ex ante* in an attempt to affect the policies that will be created by courts and agencies.

What sorts of procedures and structures might groups push for in order to gain an advantage? They might seek to ensure that they have standing before the agency, or that their opponents are denied standing.[16] Or they might seek to specify the burden of proof, standing, reviewability, which courts have jurisdiction, and other aspects of judicial review.[17] More generally, groups might seek to ensure that their achievement in enacting legislation is long-lived by creating decisionmaking processes that stack the deck in their favor or that mirror the balance of power that exists at the time the law is passed. In some cases they may even seek to place the agency beyond the reach of politicians.[18]

Empirical research is providing more and more evidence that such actions exist and that procedural choices are strategically chosen in order to confer political advantage. The Environmental Protection Agency, the Occupational Safety and Health Administration, and the Consumer Product Safety Commission were created after pitched battles about structural and procedural details, as were the ICC and the FCC.[19] Amendments to the Clean Air Act have likewise been the scene of numerous battles over administrative and judicial procedures.[20] In all these cases, and doubtless in many more, because groups were aware of the substantive importance of these procedural and structural details, they lobbied for the inclusion (or exclusion) of specific provisions.

The notion that procedural and structural details are political instruments that can be used strategically to increase the likelihood of some outcomes while decreasing the likelihood of others can be tied to the argument that one of the primary ways in which regulation benefits powerful groups is by prohibiting their opponents from entering. Procedural and structural details can be used to confer political advantage, and one of the primary ways in which this advantage is realized is by raising the barriers to entry for competitors or lowering the bar for yourself. Legislation can thus be expected to contain specific procedural provisions that will benefit some groups at the expense of others. And we will often see evidence that groups lobbied for such provisions. In the following sections I focus on the communications acts of the 1920s and 1930s as well as the 1996 act to demonstrate that the broadcasting industry used regulation to inhibit their opponents' ability to enter, and that in many instances they relied on procedural mechanisms to do so.

Broadcasters, Procedures, and Radio Regulation in the 1920s and 1930s

As mentioned at the outset of this chapter, communications policy in the 1920s and 1930s essentially consisted of regulating AT&T's monopoly over telephone and organizing the development of radio. Although this chapter cannot undertake a systematic investigation of the origins of regulation during this time, or of the importance of all procedures, it can present some examples of the importance of procedures.[21] To do so, however, we first must have an understanding of the situation faced by, and the goals of, commercial broadcasters at this time.[22]

Background

The first commercial broadcasting license was issued to Pittsburgh station KDKA (owned by Westinghouse) in September of 1921. In the next two months this station was joined by four other newly licensed stations. Then, in December of 1921 alone, 23 new station licenses were issued. This rapid increase represented just the beginning of the explosion. By the end of 1922, 576 stations were licensed and the Department of Commerce estimated that between 600,000 and 1,000,000 people owned radios, compared with fewer than 50,000 one year earlier.[23]

This rapid rate of growth overwhelmed the simple licensing scheme that existed and, more generally, threatened to undermine the development of radio. In response, Secretary of Commerce Herbert Hoover, with the cooperation of members of the radio industry, initiated a series of radio conferences, beginning in 1922, to deal with the growing problem of congestion. These conferences, which convened yearly, resulted in a number of legislative proposals and eventually in the creation of an independent commission, the Federal Radio Commission (FRC), to regulate—at least temporarily—the more than 700 stations in existence.[24]

Not surprisingly, the groups with the strongest interest in the regulation of radio were those that wished to use the radio spectrum. Amateurs, educational and religious organizations, labor, other government agencies (such as the U.S. Navy and the Post Office), and commercial broadcasters were involved at every step of the development of regulation from the 1910s through the 1930s because of their keen interest in the development of regulatory policy. In part their interest was spurred by the opportunity to broadcast their views to the public; this was especially true for ideological groups. Ultimately, however, their interest was motivated by financial concerns. The monetary stakes involved were huge; in 1931, for example, broadcasters received over $77,000,000 for rental of their facilities.[25]

Because of the huge financial opportunity presented by the radio industry, by far the most attentive of these groups were the commercial broadcasters. This potential financial gain led, in the eyes of the FRC's early critics, to excessive interest group influence.[26] Either by working directly with the agency or indirectly through members of Congress, these groups brought pressure on the agency. And the pressure could be enormous.[27]

The National Association of Broadcasters

The main organization through which the commercial interests made their desires known was the National Association of Broadcasters (NAB).[28] This organization, which came together as a result of Hoover's radio conferences, was the main force agitating for federal regulation in the 1920s. Although it had opposed the creation of the FRC, it soon found it was able to exert far greater influence on this agency than it would have been able to on the Department of Commerce.

The members of this group fought relentlessly for two goals: *keeping their licenses* and *preventing new stations from being created*.[29] This statement is borne out by a careful reading of the *Broadcasters' News Bulletin* (and later the *NAB Reports*), the trade journal of broadcasters. Time and again during the 1920s and early 1930s, these reports issued calls-to-arms for existing stations to join together to protect themselves against the potential incursions of newcomers. The following passage is representative of the viewpoint expressed in these reports:

> Broadcasting is the most regulated business in the world. . . . Interests that have stood passively by and were unwilling to bear the trials of pioneering are now endeavoring to *invade the broadcast band at the expense of existing stations*. While broadcasters throughout the United States are busily engaged at home performing the exacting duty of developing programs for the public, those who are designedly seeking to enter the broadcasting field are effectively organized in Washington. . . . Broadcasters must unite or they cannot withstand the impending onslaughts. Broadcasters must organize for self-preservation.[30]

This refrain was quite common in these reports. The NAB constantly argued in newsletters and special bulletins that existing stations needed to band together to protect their interests; and the rivals that broadcasters sought protection from were potential entrants.[31]

Even after the chaos of the industry in the 1920s subsided, commercial broadcasters still fought ardently to keep their licenses and to prevent new entry. Despite the efforts of the FRC, which often acted in concert with the NAB, the airwaves were still congested. When existing stations wanted to expand, perhaps in the hopes of attracting more advertising dollars, they generally did so not by starting up *new* stations, but rather by buying *existing* stations. Reduction of interference, which could in part be accomplished by making it more difficult for potential stations to get licenses, continued to be a primary goal of most commercial broadcasters.

Judicial Review in the 1927 Act

While in retrospect it is clear that commercial radio broadcasters had many reasons to be highly satisfied with the work of the FRC, it should be remembered that they could not have known in 1927 that their experiences with an independent regulatory commission would be so positive. Indeed, many observers, and the industry itself, found several reasons to oppose the creation of such an agency. The commercial broadcasters needed some additional assurance that eventual policy decisions would be favorable to them, and they obtained this assurance through the provisions for judicial review.

First, the 1927 act expressly allowed station owners whose licenses had been revoked by the FRC, or whose licenses had not been renewed, to appeal the revocation or denial to the courts. This clearly benefited existing stations by giving them a second chance when agency decisions did not go their way. In addition, after some worries that the law's provisions might not allow them to challenge the FRC in court if the agency approved a license on terms other than those they had sought, the broadcasters were comforted by a court ruling that guaranteed them the right to review under such circumstances.[32]

Standing was limited, too. In some ways, this limitation hurt broadcasters. The 1927 act gave standing to only those persons or companies whose application was denied or whose license was revoked. This limitation was potentially damaging to existing broadcasters, as it was entirely possible that, owing to congestion, the awarding of another license might affect the ability of their stations to be heard clearly. At the same time, however, this provision prevented those who opposed a license renewal from seeking the reversal of a renewal decision in the courts. That is, if a license renewal was approved, another company that coveted that license could not appeal the agency's decision in the hopes that the decision might be overturned and it might get the license.

Most importantly for the existing stations, the courts were given a broad scope of review and in fact were allowed to review de novo the actions of the agency. This was the biggest bonus for the existing stations. As the 1927 act was being written, broadcasters were extremely uncertain about how the agency might act. At the same time, they knew that the courts of the era were strongly predisposed to protect private interests and property. Combined with the provisions that limited their opponents' ability to challenge their licenses, this broad scope of review helped to ensure that even if existing broadcasters did not receive favorable treatment from the agency, they were likely to receive such treatment from the courts. Evidence of broadcasters' preferences over judicial review in this act is extremely limited, but an understanding of the effects of these provisions and of the goals of the station owners makes it clear that the review provisions were beneficial to them. The judicial review provisions of the 1927 act helped broadcasters to keep their licenses while raising barriers to entry.

The Choice of Judicial Venue and the 1934 Act

As has been well-recounted elsewhere, the 1934 Communications Act was constructed by combining the regulation of telephones and telegraphs, which previously had been the responsibility of the ICC, with the features of radio regulation that had been arranged by the 1927 Radio Act.[33] Few provisions of the act generated controversy. However, one of the issues over which there was a great deal of controversy was the exact specification of judicial review.

In fact, much of the discussion over S. 2910, a forerunner of the 1934 act, focused on how the review provisions of this act might adversely affect existing stations. In testimony before Congress, E. O. Sykes, the chairman of the FRC and a friend to the commercial broadcasting industry, worried about the effects of the review provisions on existing stations. In addition, Henry A. Bellows, the chair of the NAB's Legislative Committee, argued even more forcefully that the review provisions needed to be sensitive to the needs of the existing stations. The concern of these two witnesses centered around the *lack* of review, under certain conditions, that might be afforded to *existing* station owners.

In addition, the radio interests fought heavily for vesting review only in the District of Columbia's Court of Appeals. At first impression, this preference seems illogical: existing stations would probably receive more favorable treatment from local courts, which are generally seen to favor local interests, than from a court located in Washington, D.C. However, the NAB argued strongly for having appeals centralized in one court.

Certainly some credence needs to be given to the argument, expressed during congressional hearings by the NAB, that the D.C. Court had built up a great deal of expertise on radio law.[34] But at the same time, the NAB knew that anyone who opposed a license application might have more trouble affording the costs of a hearing in Washington, D.C., than a hearing in their hometown, and that potential new stations would similarly have a harder time dealing with the costs of a judicial appeal in Washington, D.C. This tactic had been used to good effect in the nascent years of the FRC, when the FRC would kill low-budget and noncommercial new stations by requiring them to come to Washington, D.C., and it promised to work to good effect if placed in the new legislation.

Congress was skeptical of such claims, and in the end allowed certain decisions to be reviewed in the district courts.[35] At the same time, however, it allowed for review of a broader range of issues than had been provided for in S. 2910, thereby placating the broadcasters. The point is not that broadcasters were always able to get their way with respect to such provisions, but rather that they sought to gain advantage through procedural mechanisms. Allowing a broad range of issues to be reviewed would have helped existing stations keep their licenses, while placing review authority entirely with the D.C. Court would have both benefited existing stations that were familiar with this court and imposed a greater financial hardship on their opponents and new stations.

Back to the Present

The 1996 Telecommunications Act, as noted earlier, presented Congress with a very different situation from the 1934 act. In particular, because of technological advances, barriers between what previously had been seen as separate areas of telecommunications were rapidly falling away, while the legal framework still maintained separation between these areas. Although this is not the place for a complete description of this act, a brief overview should be helpful in understanding the importance of procedural provisions.[36]

A Brief Overview of the 1996 Act

Because of the nature of the companies involved, it should come as no surprise that this bill was heavily lobbied—"the most lobbied bill in history," according to Senator Larry Pressler, a veteran of legislative battles over health care and tax reform.[37] The communications industry represents approximately one-sixth of the nation's economy, so it is obviously home to a wide range of powerful and wealthy companies. In addition, the industry is extremely important to members of Congress, who rely heavily on television in their bids for reelection, and whose constituents have strong expectations about prices and service for television, telephones, and cable.[38]

The keys to the 1996 act were *deregulation* and *competition*. This can be seen most conspicuously in the preamble to the act, which states that its goal is "to promote competition and reduce regulation in order to secure lower prices and higher quality services." In addition, it can be seen in reading press accounts of the bill, which consistently noted that some of the most strenuous objections raised during the bill's year-long journey to passage came from House Republicans, who wanted the bill to be as deregulatory and procompetitive as possible. And finally, it can be seen in the words of Reed Hundt, the chairman of the FCC, who in speeches given since the passage of the act has used the word *competition* as a sort of mantra, or perhaps as a talisman.

Yet as many close observers recognized, while there are deregulatory provisions in this bill, there is also a fair amount of new regulation. Some barriers to entry have been removed, but others have been erected. And while some industries have seen some regulatory hurdles lowered, those same industries and others have seen the imposition of new regulations. In a very important sense, most of the important battles fought in this act, with the most notable exception of the Communications Decency Act, centered around barriers to entry. Each industry wanted to prevent competitors from encroaching on its turf while at the same time each sought to enter other lines of business.

To some extent, such restrictions on and allowances of entry can simply be mandated by Congress. Thus, the act permits the RBOCs to enter the long distance market. At the same time, the act also contains a large number of procedures that are designed to either restrict or enhance opportunities for entry. It is these procedural provisions that often provoked fighting, as once the broad outlines of competition and entry became apparent, groups continued to fight tooth-and-nail for every last bit of advantage; and it is to these procedural provisions that we now turn.

The Renewal of Broadcast Licenses

There are two views on the inclusion in the act of provisions relating to broadcasting. One holds that Congress, because it was undertaking a wholesale revamping of communications policy, simply trained its lens on each area of communications and tried to bring current law up to date with current technological realities. Another view holds that the act was spurred almost entirely by concerns over the archaic, anticompetitive barriers between the RBOCs, the long distance carriers, and the cable television companies. Broadcasters, seeing the deregulatory fervor with which many member of the House approached their task, knew a golden opportunity when they saw it and pushed to be included in the rewrite of the 1934 act.[39]

Whichever view one finds most convincing, there is no doubt that the issues that occupied most of Congress's time—and that attracted the most attention from interest groups and the press—were those centering around the various phone companies.[40] In fact, it would be possible to peruse all press accounts of the act and barely see any references to the fact that the procedures for broadcast license renewals were changed.[41] There was almost no mention of the changes in the broadcast media, and even such respected journals as *Congressional Quarterly Weekly Report* and *National Journal* paid very little attention.

But changes were made. To begin with, stations are now allowed to hold on to their licenses for a longer period of time. In addition, restrictions on the number of stations a company can own were relaxed. And finally, what had been known as the "comparative renewal hearing" procedure was replaced by a new procedure that is more favorable to existing licensees.

Prior to the 1996 act, a radio station license was granted for five years and a television license for seven. The act increased these terms to eight years for both radio and television. This change is admittedly not major. Nevertheless, it does marginally enhance the value of receiving a license by increasing the amount of time that a station owner can be guaranteed to receive the benefits of a license and by reducing the average annual cost of the renewal process. It represents an incremental step in the direction of a more implicit property rights approach to licensure. Furthermore, an increase in the term of each license make it that much more difficult for new companies to enter the market.

Similarly, while the relaxation of ownership rules was not major, it was something for which existing stations lobbied. The owners of radio stations are no longer limited in the number of stations they can own nationally. The new law also increased the number of radio stations that could be owned within a single market. The rules for television followed a similar pattern. Television broadcasters are no longer limited in the number of stations they can own nationally, although the stations they own are not allowed to reach more than 35 percent of the nation's population.[42] The act also liberalizes the rules for co-ownership of radio and television stations and for station mergers.[43] Again, none of these are sea changes, but all at least marginally increase the value of existing licenses and make it less likely that newcomers will enter the market.

Most important, Congress created new procedures for the renewal of broadcasting licenses, procedures that again will favor existing stations at the expense of potential entrants. Prior to the 1996 act, license renewals took place through a comparative hearing process in which the FCC would hear not only from the station seeking renewal of its license, but also from any potential competitor for the license and, since the *United Church of Christ* decision in 1966, from any citizens who sought to intervene in the process. The FCC would then compare the applicants and make a decision, based, as required by the 1934 act and interpreted in various court decisions, on which applicant could best serve the public interest.[44]

The comparative hearing process is now dead. Indeed, Congress could not have buried it any deeper. In a section bluntly entitled "Competitor Consideration Prohibited," the law states that "the Commission shall not consider whether the public interest, convenience, and necessity might be served by the grant of a license to a person other than the renewal applicant."[45] Furthermore, there is no longer any burden of proof upon the existing licensee to demonstrate that its station had served the public interest. Instead, there is now a three-step procedure for license renewals. First, the FCC must determine whether the station has served the public interest. Second, it must ascertain that the station has not seriously violated any rules and regulations. And third, it must determine that the station has not engaged in a pattern of abuse with respect to the agency or the terms of its license. If a station is found to be in violation of these standards, the commission *may* deny the application. However, the act explicitly states that the commission also has the option of *granting* the renewal in such cases, and even goes on to instruct the commission to search for "mitigating factors [that] justify the imposition of lesser sanctions" before issuing a denial![46]

How important is this change in procedure? Some might argue that it matters little. The most commonly heard argument in this vein is that such a revision in the renewal process would have little effect since the FCC rarely turned down application for license renewals.[47]. A more subtle argument holds that the new procedure actually opens to door for stricter scrutiny on behalf of the commission.[48]

While there is undoubtedly something to both of these arguments, at the same time it seems clear that existing stations benefited from this procedural change and potential stations were hurt by it. First of all, the burden of proof no longer falls on the existing station to demonstrate its public worth and to show that it is *better* than a potential competitor. A station no longer needs to prove that it is worthy of a license; rather, it needs only to make sure that the FCC does not find that it is *un*worthy. Even if it does not achieve such a minimally satisfactory level of performance, it *still* might receive a renewal. In any event, the new procedure reduces the incentives for a potential entrant to challenge an existing station because it lowers the odds that such a challenger will receive the license.[49]

Second, even though few license renewals were denied by the commission, there was always the specter of the competitive hearing process. Countering a challenge before the FCC could result in major costs to the incumbent station. The chance that a license renewal application might be turned down during the competitive hearing doubtlessly affected the actions of the incumbent station owners, regardless of the infrequency of such rejections.[50] Furthermore, the numbers involved are not necessarily that small—during the 1970s, the commission revoked or denied renewal of more than sixty television and radio station licenses.[51] The comparative hearing process could, and sometimes did, lead to the demise of existing stations.

In the end, how should the changes be evaluated? Sixty-two years passed between the 1934 act and the 1996 act. In the interim, television and then cable were developed and regulated by the FCC. Yet the concerns of the broadcasters remain the same: they seek to retain their licenses while making it harder for others to get new licenses. Longer terms for licenses and the changes in the procedures that stations must follow in order to get a license renewed help increase the probability that stations will achieve these goals.

The Spectrum Giveaway

The most hotly debated of the provisions in the 1996 act concerning broadcasting dealt with the issue of giving new portions of the spectrum to existing broadcasters. Alone among the broadcasting features of this act, the spectrum giveaway ignited a controversy that attracted the attention of a wide range of observers. Not only was it debated at the level of congressional hearings, floor speeches, op-ed pieces, and on innumerable web sites, it also became a part of the presidential campaign when Bob Dole raised the issue and characterized it as a "big, big corporate welfare project."[52]

This issue had its genesis in the late 1980s and early 1990s, when the FCC foresaw that in the not-so-distant future television station owners would be able to make use of new digital technologies to broadcast programs.[53] This newer technology would have the advantage of producing pictures that are, by the standards of today's analog television signals, startlingly clear. The drawback that the FCC foresaw was that existing television sets could not receive these digital signals. In order to smooth the transition from analog to digital broadcasts, the FCC reserved a portion of the spectrum so that existing stations would be able to broadcast both analog and digital signals during the years when consumers were slowly switching over to televisions that could receive the digital signals. After the transition had been completed, the broadcasters would return the portion of the spectrum they previously had used for their analog signals, and this older spectrum could then be auctioned off.

While such a transition promised benefits, technological advances soon changed the terms of the discussion. According to the FCC's plan, each station was to be given 6 MHz on which to broadcast its digital signal, which was the same amount needed for the current analog signals. However, because of developments that allowed the digital signals to be compressed, only a small portion of the 6 MHz was needed for these signals, thus freeing up the rest for other uses. Broadcasters could now use this new spectrum not only for their digital signals but also at the same time could use it for such profitable ventures as data delivery, paging, wireless telephone service, and pay television. Estimates of the value of this "gift" ranged wildly, but the most conservative estimates held that the new spectrum was worth $10 billion, and more liberal estimates reached as high as $70 billion.

Opposition to giving the broadcasters this new portion of the spectrum quickly sprang up from both sides of the political spectrum. Conservatives saw the huge pecuniary value of the new spectrum and argued strenuously that the new spectrum should be auctioned off up front, with the money perhaps being used to pay for deficit reduction or tax cuts. Liberals, however, argued against the broadcasters' contention that there should be "spectrum flexibility," meaning that none of the uses of this spectrum other than digital technology should be subject to the public interest standard. These liberals argued that in return for such a gift, stations needed to be subject to even stronger public interest regulation and needed to supply a quid pro quo of free air time for political candidates and increased children's and educational programming.

This issue proved to be contentious enough that when Senator (and presidential contender) Dole made his speech in January of 1996 it contributed to a growing pessimism that the current bill, like all of its predecessors in recent decades, was doomed. Representative Thomas Bliley, the most important congressional supporter of the broadcast industry, responded to Dole's criticism by contending that without the free use of this spectrum, free television would no longer exist. The NAB fired all its guns, seconding Bliley's argument and adding that an up-front auction would kill digital television, increase interference to the point of making analog TV unwatchable, disproportionately disadvantage small and rural stations, and generate far less revenue than expected. This was all brought home to members of Congress even more strongly when Robert Wright, chairman of NBC and the strongest and most visible network supporter of the bill, threatened to withdraw his support if the spectrum were auctioned off.[54]

In the end, Congress felt the pressure from the broadcasters and decided not to call for an up-front auction. Nor did they heed Dole's call to deal with the issue separately. Instead, they inserted some procedural language in the bill to deal with the issue. According to the bill, if the FCC "determines to issue additional licenses for advanced television services" it is required to "limit the initial eligibility for such licenses to persons that, as of the date of such issuance, are licensed to operate a television broadcast station."[55] In other words, if the FCC decides to give the spectrum away, as it was already on record as favoring, it could do so without objection (although it informally agreed to wait to see if

Congress would first address this issue). And the sole beneficiaries would be existing stations.

The new law clearly stacked the deck in favor of existing stations. Dole was "blindsided" when other Republican leaders agreed to move forward on the bill without calling for auctions, and even admitted that he had been rolled. The bone that was thrown to supporters of auctions—that the FCC would wait a short time before moving ahead with the distribution of the spectrum—was seen as merely a face-saving gesture.[56] The procedure designed by Congress allows an FCC that favored the giveaway to decide whether the spectrum should be distributed. In essence, broadcasters wanted, and received, the spectrum without having to incur any additional public service obligations and without having to bid for it, thus preventing competitors from using it.

A postscript on this issue: in April 1997 the FCC went ahead and distributed the spectrum, at no charge, to the nation's 1,600 television stations. They also passed a rule calling for the return of these new channels in 2006, giving stations nearly ten years to make the transition from analog to digital transmission. However, bills being considered in both the House and the Senate would make this distribution of the spectrum even more of a gift than its opponents had feared. At the urging of lobbyists for the broadcast industry, in July 1997, House and Senate budget conferees agreed to allow broadcasters to keep their second channels indefinitely in any city where more than 15 percent of homes lack access to digital signals, a condition that most industry experts expect to last for years.[57]

At the same time, the Senate Commerce Committee has lessened the requirement that stations must begin using the new channels to transmit digital signals by the fall of 1999. Broadcasters had agreed to this rule, which had been established by the FCC. Again, however, industry lobbyists pushed for—and received—a relaxing of the rule. According to a bill passed by the Senate Commerce Committee, stations are only *encouraged*—not *required*—to meet this deadline. In the meantime, they are free to use these channels for other, potentially more profitable, ventures.[58]

Conclusion

In 1934 Congress passed the Communications Act, which was based in part on the previous decade's Radio Act. In 1996 Congress completely revamped telecommunications policy by passing a new law to act as the legal framework of the industry. Although this latter bill is often characterized as being deregulatory, it is clear that it contains many regulatory features and therefore is also an intensely political act. One of the goals of industries affected by the act is to use the political, regulatory process to enhance their own position and to disadvantage their competitors by, among other things, limiting their competitors' ability to enter and survive in new markets. And one way in which industries can achieve such a goal is by obtaining procedural provisions in legislation that favor them. This strategic importance and use of procedural provisions is evident in the judicial review provisions that existed in the 1927 act, just as it is apparent from the battles over regulatory authority and judicial review in the 1934 act, and just as it is apparent in the actions the 1996 act takes with regard to broadcasting.

The strategic use of and political battles over procedures are not limited to broadcasting, of course. The regional Bell operating companies (RBOCs) had been pushing for years to enter new markets, such as long distance. The long distance companies had been fighting for just as long to prevent the RBOCs from doing so. Even though it became clear early in 1995 that the RBOCs had more firepower in this battle and had more support from more important members in Congress, the long distance companies did not simply give up. Rather, even after it was generally conceded that the RBOCs would be allowed to enter new lines of business, the battles continued. They simply shifted to a new battleground, one in which the various groups fought over the procedures that would allow the RBOCs to enter these new businesses. Not surprisingly, the more regulatory-minded White House wanted any RBOC seeking to enter the long distance market to be subject to existing competition and to receive explicit approval from the Department of Justice (DOJ). The RBOCs, on the other hand, preferred that the DOJ be kept out of the process and that they need only demonstrate that they are "open" to competition. In the end, the RBOCs prevailed on some of these issues, and the long distance companies on others.[59]

Procedures are not merely details, even when political actors claim that they are. Procedures often define who wins and who loses and as such are the subject of much political debate during the writing of legislation. Groups try to obtain procedures that will help them and that will hurt their opponents. This is a simple fact of politics, as true for the "deregulatory" bills passed today as it was for the regulatory bills passed more than sixty years ago.

Notes

1. Glen Robinson, "The 'New' Communications Act: A Second Opinion. *Connecticut Law Review*, vol. 29 (Fall 1996), pp. 289–329. By one count, Congress had amended the 1934 act 113 times. Prior to the 1996 act, the bills that came the closest to effecting major changes in telecommunications law were those pushed by Representative Lionel Van Deerlin in the late 1970s and by various member of the House in 1994.

2. See, for example, Martha Derthick and Paul J. Quirk, *The Politics of Deregulation* (Brookings, 1985). It is important to note, however, that Congress could have—but did not—disapprove of the deregulatory decisions.

3. Thomas G. Krattenmaker, "The Telecommunications Act of 1996," *Connecticut Law Review*, vol. 29 (Fall 1996), pp. 123–77.

4. Robert L. Rabin, "Federal Regulation in Historical Perspective," *Stanford Law Review*, vol. 38 (May 1986), pp. 1189–1326.

5. Susan Smulyan, *Selling Radio* (Washington: Smithsonian Press, 1994), p. 142.

6. Pendleton E. Herring, *Public Administration and the Public Interest* (McGraw-Hill Book Co., Inc., 1936), p. 165.

7. See William Safire, "Stop the Giveaway," *New York Times*, January 4, 1996, p. A21.

8. Glen O. Robinson, "The Federal Communications Act: An Essay on Origins and Regulatory Purpose," in Max D. Paglin, ed., *A Legislative History of the Communications Act of 1934* (Oxford: Oxford University Press, 1989).

9. Samuel P. Huntington, "The Marasmus of the ICC," *Yale Law Journal*, vol. 61 (April 1952), pp. 467–509.

10. James M. Herring and Gerald C. Gross, *Telecommunications, Economics, and Regulation* (McGraw-Hill, 1936).

11. Marver H. Bernstein, *Regulating Business by Independent Commission* (Princeton University Press, 1955).

12. George Stigler, "The Theory of Economic Regulation," *Bell Journal of Economics and Management Science*, vol. 2 (Spring 1971), pp. 3–21; Richard A. Posner, "Theories of Economic Regulation." *Bell Journal of Economics and Management Science*, vol. 5 (Autumn 1974), pp. 335–58; Sam Peltzman, "Toward a More General Theory of Regulation." *Journal of Law and Economics*, vol. 19 (August 1976), pp. 211–48; Gary S. Becker, "A Theory of Competition among Pressure Groups for Political Influence," *Quarterly Journal of Economics*, vol. 98 (August 1983), pp. 37–400. From a very different perspective, see Gabriel Kolko, *Railroads and Regulation, 1877–1916* (Princeton University Press, 1965). Kolko also argues that regulation was never intended to serve the public interest.

13. Timothy Amato and Charles R. Shipan, "Regime Changes and Regulatory Policy: Measuring Political Influence on the Bureaucracy," presented at the annual meeting of the American Political Science Association, 1994.

14. William N. Eskridge Jr., "Reneging on History? Playing the Court/Congress/President Civil Rights Game," *California Law Review*, vol. 79 (May 1991), pp. 613–84.

15. Terry M. Moe, "Regulatory Performance and Presidential Administration," *American Journal of Political Science* , vol. 26 (May 1982), pp. 197–225; Barry R. Weingast and Mark J. Moran, "Bureaucratic Discretion or Congressional Control: Regulatory Policymaking by the FTC," *Journal of Political Economy*, vol. 91 (October 1983), pp. 765–800; and John Ferejohn and Charles R. Shipan, "Congress and Telecommunications Policymaking," in Paula R. Newberg, ed., *New Directions in Telecommunications Policy*, vol. 1 (Duke University Press, 1989).

16. Mathew D. McCubbins, "Legislative Design of Regulatory Structure," *American Journal of Political Science*, vol. 29 (November 1985), pp. 721–74.

17. Charles R. Shipan, *Designing Judicial Review: Interest Groups, Congress, and Communication Policy* (University of Michigan Press, 1997).

18. Mathew D. McCubbins, Roger G. Noll, and Barry R. Weingast, "Administrative Procedures as Instruments of Political Control," *Journal of Law, Economics, and Organization*, vol. 3 (Fall 1987), pp. 243–77; John A. Ferejohn, "The Structure of Agency Decisions," in Mathew D. McCubbins and Terry Sullivan, eds., *Congress: Structure and Policy* (Cambridge University Press, 1987); and Terry M. Moe, "The Politics of Bureaucratic Structure," in John E. Chubb and Paul E. Peterson, eds., *Can the Government Govern?* (Brookings, 1989).

19. Moe, "The Politics of Bureaucratic Structure"; Stephen Skowronek, *Building a New American State* (Cambridge University Press, 1982); Morris P. Fiorina, "Legislator Uncertainty, Legislative Control, and the Delegation of Legislative Power," *Journal of Law, Economics, and Organization*, vol. 2 (Spring 1986), pp. 33–51; Ronald A. Cass, "Review, Enforcement, and Power under the Communications Act of 1934: Choice and Chance in Institutional Design," in Max D. Paglin, ed., *A Legislative History of the Communications Act of 1934* (Oxford University Press, 1989); Shipan, *Designing Judicial Review;* and Charles R. Shipan, "Interest Groups, Judicial Review, and the Origins of Broadcasting Regulation," *Administrative Law Review*, vol. 49 (Summer 1997), pp. 549–83.

20. McCubbins, Noll, and Weingast, "Administrative Procedures"; and Joseph Smith, "Congressional Management of Judicial Policy Making: The Case of Environmental Policy," presented at the annual meeting of the Midwest Political Science Association, 1997.

21. The best histories of the politics of radio in the 1920s and 1930s are Thomas W. Hazlett, "The Rationality of U.S. Regulation of the Broadcast Spectrum," *Journal of Law and Economics*, vol. 33 (April 1990), pp. 133–75; Thomas Streeter, *Selling the Air* (University of Chicago Press, 1996); Ronald A. Coase, "The Federal Communications Commission," *Journal of Law and Economics*, vol. 2 (October 1959), pp. 1–40; Philip T. Rosen, *The Modern Stentors: Radio Broadcasters and the Federal Government, 1920–1934* (Greenwood Press, 1980);

and Robert W. McChesney, *Telecommunications, Mass Media, and Democracy: The Battle for the Control of U.S. Broadcasting, 1928–1935* (Oxford University Press, 1994). See also the wealth of information contained in Max D. Paglin, *A Legislative History of the Communications Act of 1934* (Oxford: Oxford University Press, 1989), especially the essays by Glen O. Robinson and Ronald A. Cass.

22. For an elaboration of the themes and arguments presented in this section, see Shipan, *Designing Judicial Review.*

23. These figures come from Herring and Gross, *Telecommunications*, p. 244; Lawrence F. Schmeckebier, *The Federal Radio Commission: Its History, Activities, and Organization* (Brookings, 1932), p. 4; and Jora R. Minasian, "The Political Economy of Broadcasting in the 1920's," *Journal of Law and Economics*, vol. 12 (October 1969), pp. 391–403, esp. p. 401.

24. See Rosen, *The Modern Stentors*, for an account of the battles over the location of regulatory authority over radio.

25. Herring, *Public Administration and the Public Interest*, p. 170.

26. Herring, *Public Administration and the Public Interest.*

27. One observer noted that "probably no quasi-judicial body was ever subjected to so much congressional pressure as the Federal Radio Commission." See Schmeckebier, *The Federal Radio Commission*, p. 54.

28. There were, of course, other organizations, but the NAB was by far the most important for commercial broadcasters: "To be sure, NAB is not the only radio association. Some of the others are worth noting, if only to observe how little impact they have had on the medium as a whole." Llewellyn White, *The American Radio* (University of Chicago Press, 1947), p. 85.

29. Hazlett, "The Rationality of U.S. Regulation."

30. *Broadcasters' News Bulletin*, no date, 1931; emphasis added.

31. To be sure, commercial broadcasters also went on the offensive against non-commercial broadcasters. And they were aided by a willing, even compliant, agency that issued orders and procedures that made it almost impossible for educational and other non-commercial stations to stay on the air. Despite FRC claims to the contrary, many non-profits blamed the Commission for their demise: "The Commission may boast that it has never cut an educational station off the air. It merely cuts off our head, our arms, and our legs, and then allows us to die a natural death," quoted in McChesney, *Telecommunications, Mass Media, and Democracy*, p. 31.

32. *Federal Radio Commission v. General Electric Company*, 281 U.S. 464 (1930).

33. Thomas Porter Robinson, *Radio Networks and the Federal Government* (Columbia University Press, 1943); and McChesney, *Telecommunications, Mass Media, and Democracy.* McChesney, however, demolishes the notion that the construction of the 1934 act was simply an act of cutting and pasting.

34. Not coincidentally, the existing stations had done well in this court, as demonstrated by R. J. Nordhaus, "Judicial Control of the Federal Radio Commission," *Journal of Radio Law*, vol. 2 (July 1932), pp. 447–72.

35. See in particular the exchange between Bellows and Rep. Cole (D-MD), in which Bellows argued for placing all appeals in the hands of the D.C. Court

(where "a very sound body of law has been built up"). Cole countered that such "Under the bill before us, the radio companies that have several stations on the Pacific coast, or in other parts of the country . . . would have to come all the way here to Washington. . . . that is a pretty good monopoly for the lawyers of Washington, but too much of an imposition on the people in the rest of this country." See House Committee on Interstate and Foreign Commerce, *Hearings on H.R. 8301*, 73d Cong. 2 sess., April 10, 1934, pp. 107–08.

36. For an excellent overview of the 1996 act, see Krattenmaker, "The Telecommunications Act," who argues that the primary impetus for the act was the clash between technological convergence and legal balkanization. See also the excellent comments on the article, especially the following: Thomas W. Hazlett, "Explaining the Telecommunications Act of 1996: Comment on Thomas G. Krattenmaker," *Connecticut Law Review*, vol. 29 (Fall 1996), pp. 217–42; Matthew L. Spitzer, "Dean Krattenmaker's Road Not Taken: The Political Economy of Broadcasting in the Telecommunications Act of 1996," *Connecticut Law Review*, vol. 29 (Fall 1996), pp. 353–72; Lili Levi, "Not With a Bang But a Whimper: Broadcast License Renewal and the Telecommunications Act of 1996," *Connecticut Law Review*, vol. 29 (Fall 1996), pp. 243–87; Michael I. Meyerson, "Ideas of the Marketplace: A Guide to the 1996 Telecommunication Act," *Federal Communications Law Journal*, vol. 49 (March 1997), pp. 252–87; and Peter W. Huber, Michael K. Kellogg, and John Thorne, *The Telecommunications Act of 1996: A Special Report* (Little, Brown and Co., 1996).

37. *Congressional Quarterly Weekly Report*, December 23, 1995, p. 3881.

38. As Gigi B. Sohn, executive director of the Media Access Project, has pointed out, "each broadcaster has incredible control over how much a politician gets access to his constituency. It's the local broadcaster who decides whether a particular senator is worthy of news when he cuts a ribbon at a shopping center." Leslie Wayne, "Broadcast Lobby's Formula: Airtime + Money = Influence," *New York Times*, May 5, 1997, p. C1.

39. Henry Geller, "The 1996 Telecom Act: Cutting the Competitive Gordian Knot," *Connecticut Law Review*, vol. 29 (Fall 1996), pp. 205–15.

40. The two primary exceptions to this are the Communications Decency Act (again) and the matter of how to distribute portions of the broadcast spectrum, which is discussed in the following section.

41. Levi, "Not with a Bang," p. 245.

42. The more pro-deregulation House had initially proposed the higher limit of 50 percent.

43. Meyerson, "Ideas of the Marketplace."

44. For an excellent discussion of the renewal process and the changes it underwent over the years, see Levi, "Not with a Bang." In the 1960s and 1970s the commission had tried to relax the requirements of a comparative hearing, only to have its actions struck down by the courts. See especially *Office of Communication of the United Church of Christ v. FCC*, 359 F.2d 994 (D.C. Cir. 1966).

45. See sec. 204 (a) (4) of the 1996 Act.

46. 1996 Act, sec. 204 (a) (3).

47. John A. Abel, Charles Clift, and Frederic Weiss, "Station License Revocations and Denials of Renewal, 1934–1969," *Journal of Broadcasting*, vol. 14 (Fall 1970), pp. 411–21; and Frederic Weiss, Ostroff, and Charles Clift, "Station License Revocations and Denials of Renewal, 1970-1978," *Journal of Broadcasting*, vol. 24 (Winter 1980), pp. 69–77.

48. Levi, "Not with a Bang." See, however, Huber, Kellogg, and Thorne, *The Telecommunications Act of 1996*, who argue that in the absence of comparative hearings the FCC will be less able to scrutinize the performance of licensees. And see Daniel P. Carpenter, "Adaptive Signal Processing, Hierarchy, and Budgetary Control in Federal Regulation," *American Political Science Review*, vol. 90 (June 1996), pp. 283–302, for a demonstration that the frequency of rejections was influenced by political signals from Congress. In addition, some economic research has shown that the FCC was less likely to renew licenses for stations whose primary goals were social or political (as opposed to economic). For a theory of programming choices of profit maximizing owners, see Matthew L. Spitzer, "Justifying Minority Preferences in Broadcasting." *Southern California Law Review*, vol. 64 (November 1991), pp. 293–46. More generally, see the discussions and analyses of license renewals in Roger G. Noll, Merton J. Peck, and John J. McGowan, *Economic Aspects of Television Regulation* (Brookings, 1973); and Thomas G. Krattenmaker and Lucas A. Powe Jr., *Regulating Broadcast Programming* (MIT Press, 1994).

49. Spitzer, "Dean Krattenmaker's Road Not Taken."

50. Since the early 1970s broadcasters have sought legislation to guarantee the renewal of their licenses. See Robinson, *Radio Networks*. Such legislation would both reduce the costs of hearings and decrease the probability of denials.

51. Weiss, Ostroff, and Clift, "Station License Revocations."

52. See William Safire, "Stop the Giveaway," *New York Times*, January 4, 1996, p. A21. Not surprisingly, however, broadcast television stations devoted almost no air time to discussions of this issue. See James H. Snider and Benjamin I. Page, "Does Median Ownership Affect Media Stands? The Case of the Telecommunications Act of 1996," presented at the annual meeting of the Midwest Political Science Association, 1997.

53. A good, if admittedly one-sided, introduction to this issue can be found in a report on the Media Access Project's web site. See Gigi B. Sohn and Andrew Jay Schwartzman, "The Great Spectrum Giveaway of 1995; Issues and Options," http://campaign.com/maprojec.html.

54. *Congressional Quarterly Weekly Report*, January 27, 1996, p. 220. The NAB's position on this subject is presented at http://www.nab.org/on-line/spectrum.html.

55. *1996 Telecommunications Act*, sec. 336 (a) (1).

56. *National Journal*, February 10, 1996, p. 318.

57. Deborah Shapley, "Broadcasters Get Extra Time for TV Changeover," *New York Times*, July 28, 1997, p. C5.

58. FCC Chairman Reed E. Hundt characterized these moves as follows: "what a result that would be: Give the digital television licenses to broadcasters so no competitors could get them; tell broadcasters they don't really have to

build the digital television systems and then tell broadcasters their reward for not using this incredibly valuable property is that they never have to give back the analog licenses." Ibid, p. C3.

59. More specifically, the DOJ plays only an advisory role; the RBOCs need only open their facilities to competition; and the RBOCs need to clear the procedural hurdle of a 14-point checklist, to be approved by the FCC, before entering the long distance market. Interestingly, in its first opportunities to examine RBOC entry into the long distance market, the DOJ recommended that Ameritech and SBC Communications be prohibited from providing long distance service in Michigan and Oklahoma, respectively (*New York Times*, June 26, p. C1).

CHAPTER NINETEEN

Regulatory Standards: The Effect of Broadcast Signals on Cable Television

James N. Dertouzos and Steven S. Wildman

ALTHOUGH DEBATES concerning the regulation of firms and industries tend to reflect both political and economic concerns, policymakers have always at least paid lip service to the principle of relying primarily on market forces to work for the common good and resorting to government intervention only in clearcut cases of market failure.[1] Indeed, much of the deregulatory fervor of the 1970s can be attributed to a growing recognition that regulation is beset by its own peculiar types of "failures" and inefficiencies. In addition to the direct costs of setting up and maintaining the regulatory apparatus, there is a general belief that regulators may be unable to define and replicate competitive outcomes, even in the short run. Furthermore, regulation will impede market responses to changes in demand and cost conditions and the opportunities posed by new technologies. There are also agency problems that arise from the fact that regulators may have personal goals that conflict with those of their nominal constituents. Finally, regulation may introduce a political element to economic decisionmaking that does not always serve the interests of consumers and society.

However, critics of the deregulatory movement of the 1970s and early 1980s argue that an obsessive focus on the problems of regulation lead policymakers to discount the well-known deficiencies of markets where firms exercise monopoly discretion over prices and product qualities. Regardless of who, if anyone, can be proven right in this debate over the appropriate extent of regulation, the debate is primarily a disagreement over where to draw the line determining where regulation is and is not appropriate. Most participants on both sides of the debate now accept the principle that regulation should not be employed casually and that the decision to regulate should be based on reasonable criteria for distinguishing between situations in which regulation may improve consumer welfare and economic efficiency and situations in which competitive forces are most effective in achieving their goals.

Congress implicitly recognized these trade-offs in the Cable Communications Policy Act of 1984 by charging the Federal Communications Commission with the responsibility of distinguishing between situations in which regulation was needed and situations in which competition rendered service and price regulation unnecessary. In 1985 the commission instituted a three-broadcast signal standard of effective competition, which reflected its assessment of the state of competition to cable in the mid-1980s. Under the three-signal standard, a cable system was exempt from price regulation if all viewers in its service area had available at least three off-air television channels, where availability was defined as residing within a station's grade B broadcast reception contour.

Pressure to either revise the 1984 act or replace it entirely was building ever since it became fully effective at the end of 1986. At the heart of the ongoing debate over cable policy was the question of whether over-the-air (OTA) broadcasters could effectively prevent the exercise of market power by cable operators, and, if so, how many stations were necessary. Advocates of a more restrictive regulatory approach cited continuing price increases and a growing proportion of U.S. households subscribing to cable as evidence of monopoly power.[2] Some proponents of regulatory reform argued that cable services have become sufficiently unique that it is no longer possible to force cable operators to price competitively with broadcast competition alone, regardless of the number of television stations available to viewers off-air. Both the National League of Cities and the United States Telephone Association, for example, claimed that the absence of competitive multichannel providers (such as another cable company) made price regulation necessary in most local markets.[3] This perspective prevailed with the passage of the 1992 Cable Competition Act that scrapped the three-signal OTA standard in favor of a new policy that established price regulation in markets not served by multichannel providers, regardless of the number of available, free, over-the-air broadcast signals.[4]

This chapter presents an econometric study of the nature and strength of broadcast competition to cable systems and compares these effects with those resulting from more direct competition among local cable operators. Summarized briefly, the results of this study support the following conclusions. First, off-air signals do constitute significant competition to cable service. This is reflected in the effect of local broadcast signals on subscriber counts, program service offerings, and prices of these services. Second, three broadcast signals are not sufficient to achieve the maximum competitive effect. However, additional signals beyond five have no discernible effect on the behavior of cable operators. Finally, economic outcomes in markets that receive five or more OTA signals are quite similar to those observed when consumers are served by directly competitive cable operators. Although these results do not prove that local areas receiving a full complement of over-the-air signals fully achieve some competitive "ideal," they do indicate that broadcast competition significantly restricts the market power of some cable operators. Given the costs and unproven efficacy of price regulation, this finding suggests that current standards for effective competition should be expanded to consider the important influence of broadcast signals on the cable industry.

An Economic Framework for Analyzing Competition to Cable

Analysis of competition to cable must allow for a variety of responses to substitute products. If multiple firms attempt to supply substitute products to the same group of consumers, then each firm is affected directly by the others' decisions regarding prices, output, and product specifications and will consider the availability of substitutes in setting its own prices and in designing its products. The intensity of competition may be reflected in a firm's prices, sales, level of product quality, and product positioning. Holding other things such as quality and product variety constant, we generally expect a firm facing competition to have lower prices and, because it loses customers to competitors, to make fewer sales than it would if there were no competition. Firms may also respond to competition by changing their products, either to alter the quality or to reposition their products relative to competing products. This complicates the interpretation of price changes. A study of the state of competition in a market should examine all four variables to the extent possible.

There has been a strong tendency in the debate over cable policy to focus on price as an indicator of competitiveness to the exclusion of the other three variables. This is a serious oversight that could lead to the misclassification of competitive situations as uncompetitive and vice versa. Studies examining the extent to which broadcast signals compete with cable commonly compare prices for basic service in a variety of markets with varying numbers of television stations available off-air or compare price levels at different points in time.[5] This is one component of the study described in the next section of this chapter. However, with this type of data alone it may not be possible to distinguish between highly competitive and monopoly situations. This is because firms may change other product or service dimensions in response to competition.

One possibility is for firms to change the quality of their products in response to competitive pressures. From the consumer's perspective, there could be a welfare-enhancing reduction in a quality-adjusted price, resulting in more value per dollar. Alternatively, increased competition may affect some other product dimension such as advertising or demand for premium services. There may be fewer incentives to keep the price of basic cable low, since the marginal advertising and premium service revenues associated with additional subscribers are diminished by the increased competition to cable. Clearly, an analyst focusing on the nominal price patterns for basic service alone may incorrectly conclude that cable operators are insulated from competition from other market participants.

When it is possible to vary product characteristics and consumers differ in their preferences among variants of a product, competitive industries commonly respond by offering consumers a diversified menu of choices. The differentiation produced by the competitive process generally works to the advantage of consumers by making it possible for individuals to find products more closely matched to their personal preferences than would otherwise be possible. Product differentiation, like changes in quality, complicates the interpretation of price changes. In many cases, it is difficult to disentangle changes in quality from increased differentiation. Consumers whose preferences are better served by a repositioned product will tend to see the change as quality enhancing. When products are differentiated so that consumers have distinct preferences among them, the demand curve for each product will be downward sloping, even if competitive entry has driven profits to zero.[6] Entry in markets with differentiated products may affect the demands for established products in two ways. Demand will almost certainly shift inward as consumers who find the entrants' products more to their liking switch from their old suppliers. All else equal, sellers will lower prices if their demand curves shift inward. However, if marginal costs fall with increased output, sellers will be faced with higher marginal costs as de-

Table 19-1. *Size Distribution of Sample for Cable Systems Operation*

Size (thousands)	Sample Systems	Sample Subscribers (thousands)	Industry Systems	Industry Subscribers (thousands)	Percent of indusry Systems	Percent of indusry Subscribers
50 +	66	5,843	168	15,771	39.3	37.0
20–50	54	1,580	379	11,722	14.2	13.5
10–20	30	431	495	6,951	6.1	6.2
3.5–10	40	211	1,049	6,250	3.8	3.4
.5–3.5	110	148	2,912	4,043	3.8	3.7
.25–.5	20	7	1,265	456	1.6	1.5
0–.25	20	2	2,225	305	0.9	0.7
Unknown	0	0	513	n.a.	0.0	n.a.
Total	340	8,814	9,006	45,509	3.8	19.4

Source: *Television and Cable Factbook* (Washington, D.C.: Warren Publishing, 1989).
n.a. Not available.

mand curves shift inward, which could cause prices to rise. The slopes of demand curves may also change, becoming more or less elastic depending on differences in the demands of customers lost and customers retained. Increasing elasticity will reduce prices, but prices will rise if the demands for individual products become less elastic.

The upshot of this discussion of quality variation, multiple service offerings, and product differentiation is that prices may rise, fall, or stay the same in response to increased competition. Therefore, price evidence alone is not sufficient for evaluating the extent to which competition from other media is effective in limiting the potential market power of cable systems. Changes in service quality, output, and prices of related products must all be considered in a thorough investigation of this issue. Below we report the results of an econometric study of cable systems' responses to broadcast competition and compare those outcomes to those observed in markets served by multiple cable operators.

Empirical Analysis

For the first set of analyses, we utilized information describing the operations of 340 cable systems during 1989. Table 19-1 describes the size distribution of the stratified sample utilized.[7] Cable systems were randomly chosen within the size categories indicated. The sample systems represent about 3.8 percent of the industry's 9,010 systems. However, these systems represent nearly 20 percent of the nation's cable subscrib-

Table 19-2. Description of System Data

Variable	Mean	Minimum	Maximum
Endogenous variables			
Basic subscribers	24,111	32	298,445
Cable networks carried on basic	16	10	24
Basic price	15.18	6.50	31.90
HBO price	10.35	4.95	14.00
System characteristics			
Miles of system	413	1	3,697
Homes passed	44,503	39	438,403
Age of headend (years)	15.2	1	41
Capacity (channels)	39.9	12	120
Multiple system operator (million plus subs)	.390	0	1
Market demographics			
Hispanic population (percent)	5.2	0	99.6
Black population (percent)	8.5	0	68.5
Employment (all local counties)	202,382	427	3,482,629
Income median	26,415	9,499	64,518
Home ownership (percent)	69.3	8.4	86.6
VCR penetration (percent)	63.4	10.6	74.4
Projected population growth	6.2	−9.8	28.9
Southern region	.308	0	1
Pacific region	.135	0	1
Northeast region	.182	0	1

Source: A. C. Nielsen CODE data base, 1989.

ers. For each of these systems, information describing the cable system, prices and services offered, and local market characteristics was compiled. Table 19-2 describes the variables used in the statistical analysis and provides means and ranges of values.

Endogenous Variables

Four measures of system performance were the focus of the statistical analysis. The number of basic subscribers had an average value of 24,111, ranging from 32 to 298,445 households. Owing to the stratification in favor of big systems, the mean sample size is considerably larger than the industry average of just over 5,000 subscribers. In addition, data were collected on the number of "top-20" cable networks plus four superstations included in basic services.[8] On average, the sample systems carried about 16 of these networks. They ranged from zero to the maximum of 24. Price data were also collected for basic and premium services. For basic, the average price was just over $15.00 and ranged from $6.50 to almost $32.00. For Home Box Office (HBO) or some alternative movie channel, the monthly fee averaged a little over $10.00. For the majority of the systems, the monthly subscription price for HBO was employed. When HBO was not carried by the system, an alternative, such as Showtime, was used instead.

Cable System Characteristics

Information describing the cable systems was also gathered. These variables, considered exogenous to the short-run decisionmaking process, include the miles of cable, the number of homes passed, the age of the headend, the total capacity of the system, and whether or not the franchise was owned by a large multiple-system operator.[9] The average number of households passed was over 44,000. About 40 percent of the sample was affiliated with MSOs having greater than one million total subscribers.

Table 19-2 also describes other exogenous factors that are likely to affect local cable operations via effects on market demand.[10] Included in the statistical analysis are the population percentages of blacks and Hispanics, as well as the median family income. Also included are the projected five-year population growth, and the household penetration of video cassette recorders (VCRs) in the larger media market (Designated Market Area) where the system is located. Finally, dichotomous variables indicating location in the south, Pacific coast, or northeast regions of the country were compiled.

Off-the-Air Television Signals

To assess the effect of off-the-air (OTA) television competition, information on the number of grade-B signals, commercial and educational, received by households located in a cable system's franchise area was collected. A summary of these data, tabulated by system size, is provided in table 19-3. About 15 percent of the systems in the sample received fewer than three OTA signals. Another 60 systems, or 18 percent, received three or four broadcast signals. Over one-quarter received grade-B signals from 10 or more commercial and educational broadcast stations. The data also indicate a positive correlation between the system size and the number of signals carried. For example, 9 of the 66 systems having greater than 50,000 subscribers are subject to price regulation

Table 19-3. Off-the-Air Signals by System Size

System subscribers (thousands)	Total	Number of signals				
		<3	3–4	5	6–9	10+
50+	66	0	5	10	22	29
20–50	54	2	8	6	14	24
3.5–20	70	9	11	8	20	22
1–3.5	55	12	16	12	9	6
.5–1	55	21	6	10	14	4
0–.5	40	7	14	3	13	3
Total	340	51	60	49	92	88

Sources: The Compucon data base, *Broadcasting/Cable Factbook* (Washington, D.C.: Warren Publishing, 1989); and *Cable and Station Coverage Atlas* (Washington, D.C.: Warren Publishing, 1989).

because they receive fewer than three signals. Over 90 percent of these systems receive at least six OTA signals.

Estimated Effects of Broadcast Competition

To assess the impact of off-the-air signals on the market power of cable operators, we estimated log-linear models that related variations in basic subscribers, basic programming, and three price measures to the exogenous demographic and market factors described earlier. The parameter estimates along with standard errors are reported in table 19-4.

Basic Service Subscribers

The first column of table 19-4 provides the results of an OLS regression of the natural log of basic subscribers as a function of the independent variables. Not surprisingly, the most important factor for explaining the number of subscribers is the number of homes passed in a cable franchise. The estimated elasticity is significantly greater than zero and less than 1.0. More households purchase cable when market income is higher. If other factors are held constant, mature systems and those located in the Northeast appear to penetrate a greater percentage of homes. Systems with less dense populations also have greater numbers of subscribers as the number of system miles is positively related to subscriptions. In addition, the employment levels of counties served by the system is inversely correlated with the number of basic customers. Holding the number of households constant, higher employment generally indicates that the area

Table 19-4. *Empirical Model of Cable Subscribers, Networks, and Prices*

Variable	Basic subs	Basic networks	Basic price I	Basic price II	HBO price
Intercept	−1.648	−1.715	1.618**	2.020**	1.056*
	(1.367)	(1.048)	(0.724)	(0.678)	(0.462)
Log(miles)	0.073*	0.006	0.040*	0.040*	0.017
	(0.042)	(0.034)	(0.022)	(0.021)	(0.014)
Log(homes)	0.852**	0.003	−0.044*	−0.043*	−0.035*
	(0.049)	(0.039)	(0.026)	(0.024)	(0.016)
Log(age)	0.118**	0.033	−0.000	−0.008	−0.006
	(0.035)	(0.029)	(0.018)	(0.018)	(0.012)
Log(income)	0.186**	0.122**	0.160**	0.147**	0.122**
	(0.098)	(0.042)	(0.052)	(0.052)	(0.033)
Log(capacity)	0.024	0.926**	0.182**	. . .	0.067
	(0.146)	(0.119)	(0.082)		(0.054)
Log(capacity <15)	−0.331	0.589**	0.055	. . .	0.193**
	(0.211)	(0.171)	(0.116)		(0.075)
Log(capacity >25)	0.381	−1.213**	−0.155	. . .	−0.367**
	(0.284)	(0.231)	(0.149)		(0.100)
Log(employment)	−0.043**	−0.030*	−0.014	−0.008	−0.023**
	(0.021)	(0.017)	(0.011)	(0.011)	(0.007)
Hispanic population %	−0.026	−0.027	0.010	0.015	0.005
	(0.030)	(0.024)	(0.016)	(0.016)	(0.010)
Black population %	−0.010	0.023	−0.016	−0.020*	0.004
	(0.023)	(0.018)	(0.012)	(0.012)	(0.008)
Log(VCR %)	0.023	−0.067	−0.053	−0.042	0.028
	(0.243)	(0.197)	(0.127)	(0.126)	(0.080)
Home owners %	−0.065	0.085	−0.197**	−0.213**	−0.058
	(0.113)	(0.082)	(0.059)	(0.059)	(0.038)
Future population growth	−0.002	0.009**	−0.002	−0.003	−0.000
	(0.004)	(0.004)	(0.002)	(0.002)	(0.002)
South	0.027	−0.079	0.055	0.069*	−0.010
	(0.074)	(0.060)	(0.039)	(0.038)	(0.025)
Pacific	−0.002	−0.097	−0.033	−0.019	0.031
	(0.090)	(0.073)	(0.047)	(0.046)	(0.029)
Northeast	0.150**	0.008	−0.023	−0.026	0.063**
	(0.066)	(0.053)	(0.034)	(0.034)	(0.022)
Log(networks), predicted	. . .	. . .	. . .	0.175**	. . .
				(0.059)	
MSO > million	0.035	0.092**	−0.041*	−0.060**	0.024
	(0.049)	(0.040)	(0.026)	(0.026)	(0.016)
Regulated	−0.046	0.024	0.001	−0.006	0.012
	(0.080)	(0.065)	(0.042)	(0.042)	(0.027)
5 TV signals	−0.194**	0.158**	−0.010	−0.043	−0.066**
	(0.080)	(0.064)	(0.043)	(0.041)	(0.026)
6 plus TV signals	−0.205**	0.129**	−0.019	−0.044	−0.047**
	(0.067)	(0.055)	(0.035)	(0.036)	(0.023)
R-squared	0.966	0.571	0.168	0.168	0.237

*Significant at 10 percent.
**Significant at 5 percent.

is an urban center. Other demographic and system characteristics did not have significant effects.

As stated earlier, increased competition in a market should diminish the demand for cable services, thereby reducing the number of basic subscribers. This decrease would occur regardless of cost relationships or changes in the shape of the demand schedule relating quantity demanded to price. In table 19-4, we report the effects of receiving fewer than three OTA signals (recall, these markets are subject to price regulation), five OTA signals, and six or more signals, all compared to the base case of three or four broadcast signals. As reported, the number of basic subscribers in cable system areas served in regulated markets having fewer than three signals is not significantly different from those receiving three or four. However, subscriptions in markets served by five OTA television signals are significantly lower by about 19 percent. In markets having greater than five signals, the predicted number of subscribers is also reduced but by an amount that is not significantly lower than in five-signal systems.

Models that analyzed less aggregate measures of signal availability provided no additional information. The coefficient estimates for dichotomous variables representing two, three, four, five, six, and greater numbers of signals are reported in table 19-5 for this model and each of the four others discussed below. For two-, three-, and four-OTA signal markets, the effects of additional competition are insignificantly different from zero though the high standard errors preclude making strong inferences. However, the pattern of effects for markets having greater competition is consistent with the estimates of the previous specification of the model. That is, there is a significant fall in subscribers for franchise areas receiving five TV channels. For systems facing competition from six or seven plus stations, the subscriber decline is not statistically different from the decline in markets receiving five signals.

Basic Network Programming

One measure of product quality is the number of cable networks available on the basic tiers. The second column of table 19-4 documents the results of the OLS regressions of the log of the number of basic networks on the set of exogenous factors described earlier. The most important explanatory variables were measures of channel capacity. In order to allow for nonlinearities, separate elasticities were estimated for systems having fewer than 15 channels and those having greater than 25.[11] For systems with fewer than 15 channels, the elasticity of basic programming with respect to capacity is equal to the sum of the coefficients on log(capacity) and log(capacity < 15). The elasticity of 1.5 (.926 + .589) implies that smaller systems expand the number of basic networks rapidly with increases in channel capacity. As capacity grows beyond 15, the percentage change in basic offerings increases less rapidly. At higher levels of capacity, there is no discernible rise in the number of major basic networks offered as the number of available channels increases. These results indicate a high degree of uniformity across cable systems in their valuation of basic cable networks. Systems with little capacity beyond what is required to carry local OTA signals tend to fill what capacity is available almost entirely with selections from the list of top 20 basic networks and four superstations employed in this study. However, for most systems 25 channels are sufficient for OTA carriage and to complete desired selections among the most popular services.

Holding other factors constant, systems in urban areas, indicated by high levels of employment relative to households, provide fewer cable program services. Franchises in markets with projected increases in population carry more programming as do those owned by MSOs with one million or more total subscribers. This latter result could reflect scale economies associated with the centralized procurement of programming.

As suggested earlier, a likely response to the existence of increased competition would be the enhancement of product quality. In comparison with systems in areas receiving fewer signals, systems in areas served by five grade-B broadcast signals provide over 15 percent more basic networks. Markets receiving greater than five OTA signals also supply more programming, but the parameter estimate is not measurably different. As indicated in table 19-5 this pattern is less precisely estimated but also apparent in the models that utilized more disaggregate definitions of signal reception.

Basic Cable Prices

The third and fourth columns of table 19-4 present results from two sets of regressions on basic cable fees. In the first model, we regress the predicted log of basic cable subscription prices on the same set of explanatory variables. In the second, we control for the level of product quality in a two-stage least-squares regression.[12] The estimated elasticity

Table 19-5. *Effect of TV Signals on Cable Systems*

Number of TV signals	Subscribers	Networks	Price per channel	Premium price
2	−.117 (.118)	.105 (.097)	−.011 (.111)	−.026 (.039)
3	.085 (.106)	.085 (.086)	−.054 (.095)	−.001 (.036)
4	−.053 (.109)	−.034 (.088)	.075 (.097)	−.046 (.037)
5	−.183* (.106)	.183** (.081)	−.157* (.089)	−.090** (.033)
6	−.198** (.116)	.166* (.085)	−.102 (.105)	−.063* (.039)
> 6	−.201** (.097)	.142* (.079)	−.136* (.087)	−.075** (.032)

*Significant at 10 percent.
**Significant at 5 percent.

of the basic fee with respect to program offerings was .175. That is, adding a single channel to a typical system's menu of 15 offerings would enable the operator to raise the monthly price by 20 cents.[13] For other explanatory variables, the two approaches provided very similar results. Basic prices are somewhat higher in high-income markets and seem to be negatively related to the number of homes in the system. In addition, prices charged by systems owned by large MSOs are slightly lower. As in the case of large local cable systems, this may reflect scale efficiencies. On the other hand, some large MSOs earn significant ancillary revenues via advertising sales. Clearly, such systems would have greater incentives to promote large potential audiences by lowering basic cable prices.

As suggested in an earlier discussion, the effects of competition on basic prices is theoretically indeterminate. This is because competition can simultaneously increase product quality, diminish the number of subscribers, and reduce demand elasticity.[14] Indeed, if marginal costs diminish with the number of subscribers, a price increase in more competitive markets would be entirely plausible. As a result, estimated price differences cannot be viewed as a necessary condition for demonstrating the existence of monopoly power. In addition, the statistical results for prices were much less precise than those for subscriber and programming models. In part, this may be because of the aforementioned theoretical indeterminacy. In addition, operators may be constrained by the residual effects of previous pricing limitations, the franchise renewal process, or uncertainty about the appropriate profit-maximizing level and mix (installation fees, basic tiers, premium prices, and pay-per-view) of prices.

Keeping these caveats in mind, the statistical results for basic cable pricing were not inconsistent with the existence of enhanced competition at the five-signal level and beyond. Basic monthly fees were slightly lower, though not significantly, in markets receiving five or more signals. When one controls for the competitive effects on product quality, the price changes are somewhat larger (as high as 4 percent) but still not significantly different from zero.

HBO Subscription Prices

The final model examined variations in the monthly price charged for a premium movie channel, usually HBO. The final column of table 19-5 reports coefficient estimates and standard errors. As in the other models, channel capacity and location in northeastern and urban areas influence the price. Once again, there appear to be strong competitive effects of increased numbers of television signals. Systems in areas served by five stations charge prices that were about 7 percent lower than those located in areas receiving fewer OTA stations. As reported in table 19-5, this result is insensitive to less aggregated characterizations of signal reception. Additional competitors do not reduce prices further.

Estimated Effects of Face-to-Face Cable Competition

In this section, we conducted an empirical analysis that compared the operations of 28 cable systems that were identified by the Federal Communications Commission as facing face-to-face competition with other local operators. Data describing these "overbuild" markets were gathered and merged with the 340-system sample described earlier. The characteristics of these systems are described in table 19-6.

The overbuild system averages described in table 19-6 can be compared with those provided in table 19-2 for the overall sample of 340 systems. The average system facing direct competition is slightly larger (about 15 percent more subscribers) and has more channel capacity (44.7 versus 39.9) than the overall sample. Given the oversampling of large systems, this implies that the typical overbuild system is considerably larger than typical cable systems. Overbuild systems charge similar prices for premium movie channels and basic cable services. These operators, however, offer 18.7 networks, on average, fully three more than

Table 19-6. *Data Describing Overbuild Systems*

Number of systems	28
Homes passed	48,571
Subscribers	29,617
Median income	30,002
Age	11.7
Channel capacity	44.7
Northeast (%)	10.7
Pacific (%)	3.5
Cable networks	18.7
Basic price	$14.98
HBO price	$10.08
Large MSO (%)	53.5
6 plus TV signals	71.2

Source: Federal Communications Commission, *1989 Television and Cable Factbook* (Washington, 1989).

the systems in the original sample. Overbuild systems are less likely to be located in northeast or Pacific states and are more likely to be owned by a large MSO. Over 70 percent of these systems are in markets that receive six or more off-the-air signals. This is similar to the 340-system sample but is almost twice the percentage for the industry at large. Unfortunately, information on the complete set of exogenous variables was not available for the overbuild sample. However, our empirical results, though somewhat affected by left-out variable biases, were quite similar to those from the more complete data set. Thus, we believe that our results for the effects of overbuild competition are reliable for purposes of comparison.

Utilizing the merged data sets, including the overbuild sample of 28 systems, we regressed the national log of subscribers, networks, and basic cable prices on the subset of available independent variables listed in table 19-6. Overall, the results were quite similar to those reported earlier. In table 19-7, results for the variables indicating maximum broadcast competition (greater than five signals) and the existence of a face-to-face overbuild competitor are provided. We were unable to obtain identical information on the number of FCC grade-B contour signals within the geographic markets for the subset of overbuild systems. Instead, we utilized data provided to us from the *Television Factbook* that included some fringe signals that are not carried by the local cable operators.[15] We compared the two measures for the original subset of 340 stations and found that the *Factbook* information typically overstates the number of signals received by one. Thus, for purposes of comparison with the earlier estimates, the indicator variable representing more than five sig-

Table 19-7. *Estimated Effects of Competition:*
Broadcasting versus Cable Overbuilds

Dependent variable	More than 5 OTA Signals	Competition from cable overbuild
Log(subscribers)	−0.155**	−0.142**
	(0.034)	(0.048)
Log(networks)	0.065**	0.077**
	(0.027)	(0.038)
Log(basic cable price)	−0.050	−0.109
	(0.057)	(0.081)

*Significant at 10 percent
**Significant at 5 percent.

nals (as defined in the *Factbook*) corresponds with the previous standard of five or more OTA signals actually received.

As indicated, competitive effects of overbuilds are very similar to those provided by a large number of free off-the-air broadcast signals. There are similar reductions in the number of subscribers who purchase services (down by about 14 percent) as well as increases in cable networks provided (up by about 8 percent). Basic cable prices also appear to fall, though these estimates are imprecise and not significantly different from zero.

Summary and Conclusions

These results support the conclusion that free broadcast signals provide important competition to cable operators. However, the pre-1992 standard for effective competition, based on a minimum of three signals, is not appropriate. There are demonstrable competitive benefits to increasing the number of competing signals to five, although no benefits seem to occur from additional signals beyond this number. It is not the case, as some critics of the cable industry claim, that only the presence of a second multichannel competitor can provide true competition to cable services.[16] Indeed, our results suggest that broadcast competition can be just as effective as that provided by the face-to-face competition from cable operators serving the same local markets.[17] Clearly, it is not possible to conclude on the basis of this type of study alone that free broadcast signals or multiple cable operators provide sufficient competition to maximize consumer welfare. Even under the best of circumstances, oligopoly markets are unlikely to generate fully competitive outcomes. Although suggestive, the absence of any measurable effect of adding additional signals beyond five is not definitive. With the growth of additional broadcast networks (other than ABC, CBS, Fox, NBC, and PBS), it could very well be true that consumers would benefit from receiving more than five free signals.

Even if room for improvement exists, it is unlikely that price regulation is the solution. First, we have seen that basic prices are only marginally lower in competitive markets. Other outcomes are equally or even more important. Also, evidence indicates that regulation does not improve matters and may even worsen them. For example, Adam B. Jaffee and David M. Kanter found no significant appreciation in the value of cable systems following cable deregulation in 1984.[18] Yasuji Otsuka demonstrated that quality adjustments in the face of price regulation can actually diminish consumer welfare.[19] In the empirical analyses presented earlier, we found that systems subject to local regulation before 1992 (located in markets receiving fewer than three signals) did not exhibit measurably different outcomes. Of course, these findings could reflect inefficiencies of cable regulation at the local level. Mark A. Zupan has argued that there are substantial inefficiency costs associated with local cable regulation and that these are reflected in the prices of cable services.[20] However, in an informal phone survey in 1992, of 39 (out of 51) systems in our sample that were potentially subject to rate regulation because they competed with fewer than 3 broadcast stations, only 3 stated that their prices were actually regulated by local authorities. For many communities, particularly small ones unable to develop or hire the requisite expertise, the potential payoff to regulation may not be large enough to justify the costs.

The significance of broadcast competition coupled with the dearth of any solid evidence that price regulation works lend support to the following conclusions. At the very least, the standards for effective competition should be relaxed to include cable systems that compete with five or more broadcast signals. Such competition is just as effective as face-to-face competition with multichannel providers, and there is no justification for treating such markets, representing almost 60 percent of all systems, any differently. Government policies should instead focus on the promotion of new competition by removing many of the artificial barriers to effective entry in video programming markets by telephone and satellite providers.

Notes

1. Roger G. Noll and Bruce M. Owen. *The Political Economy of Deregulation: Interest Groups in the Political Process* (Washington: American Enterprise Institute for Public Policy Research, 1983); and Sam Peltzman, "Toward a More General Theory of Regulation," *Journal of Law and Economics*, vol. 19 (August 1976), pp. 81–91.

2. See, generally, *Comments Submitted in the Matter of Competition, Rate Deregulation, and the Commission's Policies Relating to the Provision of Cable Television Service*, FCC89-345, MM Docket No. 89-600, Notice of Inquiry, December 29, 1989.

3. *Comments of the City of New York, National League of Cities and United States Conference of Mayors before the Federal Communications Commission in the Matter of Reexamination of the Effective Competition Standard for the Regulation of Cable Television Basic Service Rates*, MM Docket No. 74, April 6, 1990; and *Comments of the United States Telephone Association before the Federal Communications Commission in the Matter of Reexamination of the Effective Competition Standard for the Regulation of Cable Television Basic Service Rates*, MM Docket No. 74, March 1, 1990.

4. In addition to the multichannel competition requirement, systems having market penetrations of under 30 percent of the local households were also exempted from price regulation. For a critique of this alternative penetration standard, see James Dertouzos and Steven Wildman, "The Problems with Penetration Standards for Cable Regulation," *Journal of Communications Law and Policy* (forthcoming).

5. Kenneth R. Dunmore and Mark Bykowsky, "Cable Television Demand and Its Implications for Cable Copyright," Office of Policy Analysis and Development, National Telecommunications and Information Administration (Department of Commerce, September 1982); John W. Mayo and Yasuji Otsuka, "Demand, Pricing, and Regulation: Evidence from the Cable TV Industry, *RAND Journal of Economics*, vol. 22 (Autumn 1991), pp. 396–410; Patricia L. Pacey, "Cable Television in a Less Regulated Market," *Journal of Industrial Economics*, vol. 34 (September 1985), pp. 81–91; Robin Prager, "Firm Behavior in Franchise Monopoly Markets," *RAND Journal of Economics*, vol. 21 (Summer 1990), pp. 211–25; and Robert Rubinowitz, "Market Power and Prices Increases for Basic Service since Deregulation," *RAND Journal of Economics*, vol. 24 (Spring 1993), pp. 1–18.

6. Edward H. Chamberlin, *The Theory of Monopolistic Competition*, 7th ed. (Harvard University Press, 1956); and Michael A. Spence, "Product Selection, Fixed Costs, and Monopolistic Competition," *Review of Economic Studies*, vol. 43 (June 1976), pp. 217–35.

7. This data set was provided by the National Cable Television Association. The sample size was limited by resource constraints, and it was decided to overrepresent larger systems. A more representative size distribution (holding the

sample size constant) would have resulted in very few observations from the largest size categories. Owing to strong correlations between firm size, broadcast competition, ownership structure, and market demographics, it was desirable to have sufficient data variation within size category groupings. This would not have been possible without the stratification.

8. Networks included ESPN, CNN, USA, the Family Channel, the Nashville Network, Nickelodeon, MTV, Discovery Channel, Lifetime, Arts and Entertainment, the Weather Channel, Financial News Network, C-SPAN, Headline News, Turner Network Television, Video Hits One, Black Entertainment Television, and the Learning Channel. Including the four superstations, TBS, WWOR, WGN, and WPIX, the number of basic networks totaled 24.

9. For about 25 percent of the systems, at least one of these variables was missing from data provided in records compiled for 1989 by Nielsen Media Research. To fill in the gaps, predicted values based on regressions of these variables on all other exogenous variables were utilized. This procedure enabled us to use all 340 observations. However, regression results based on the subset of systems for which complete data were available invariably gave similar results.

10. In an exploratory data analysis, several other demographic variables were utilized. Those that failed to explain variation in any of the five endogenous variables (subscribers, networks, basic price, basic price per channel, and HBO price) were dropped from the analysis. These excluded exogenous variables were education levels, age distributions, family composition, single-unit residences, population mobility, industrial composition, local work force characteristics, and media market ranking.

11. Other results were insensitive to the choice of where to place the "spline" or change in the coefficient representing the elasticity of basic programming with respect to channel capacity.

12. The first-stage prediction is based on the model reported in column 2 for basic networks. Note that the capacity measures are excluded in the second stage, thereby permitting the identification of the parameters of this two-equation system.

13. Interestingly, the average cable subscriber received about twice the number of popular basic networks, including superstations, in 1989 in comparison with 1984. This estimation was based upon changes in the aggregate number of households receiving the top 25 cable networks in 1984 and 1989. The sum of these audiences increased by about 140 percent over this time period. Since cable penetration also increased by 30 percent, this implies that the average cable household received twice the number of basic network stations in 1989 (140 percent/1.30 = 108 percent increase). Given our elasticity estimate of .175, we can infer that a 20 percent rise in the price of basic cable can be attributed to the increase in the availability of basic programming. The actual effect of improved basic services could, of course, be greater owing to the increased quality of the programming available on cable networks.

14. Theoretically, it is possible to specify and estimate a full structural model of cable system operations that is capable of separating and controlling for all these countervailing effects. For example, see James N. Dertouzos and William

B. Trautman, "Economic Effects of Media Concentration: Estimates from the Model of the Newspaper Firm," *Journal of Industrial Economics*, vol. 39 (September 1990), pp. 1–14, for an illustrated methodology applied to the case of daily newspapers. The modeling complexity necessary to perform such an analysis was beyond the scope of this study.

15. *Television Factbook* (Washington: Warren Publishing, 1991).

16. *Comments of the United States Telephone Association.*

17. Steven S. Wildman and Bruce M. Owen. "Program Competition, Diversity, and Multichannel Bundling in the New Video Industry," in Eli M. Noam, ed., *Video Media Competition: Regulation, Economics, and Technology* (Columbia University Press, 1985), pp. 244–73, show that it is not possible to determine on theoretical grounds alone whether several single-channel firms would provide more or less effective competition to a multichannel service like a cable system than would a second multichannel service. Either may be more effective in different circumstances. This issue must therefore be resolved empirically.

18. Adam B. Jaffee and David M. Kanter, "Market Power of Local Cable Television Franchises: Evidence from the Effects of Deregulation," *RAND Journal of Economics*, vol. 21 (Summer 1990), pp. 226–34.

19. Yasuji Otsuka, "A Welfare Analysis of Local Franchise and Other Types of Regulation: Evidence from the Cable TV Industry," *Journal of Regulatory Economics* (March 1997), vol. 11, pp. 157–80.

20. Mark A. Zupan, "The Efficiency of Franchise Bidding Schemes in the Case of Cable Television: Some Systematic Evidence," *Journal of Law and Economics*, vol. 32 (October 1989), pp. 401–56.

CHAPTER TWENTY

Public Policy and Broadband Infrastructure

Gerald R. Faulhaber

T HE EXTREMELY RAPID emergence of the Internet as a mass communications service and its concomitant commercialization has stirred great
interest in creating a broadband infrastructure, both in the United States
and worldwide.[1] The concept of a national, even global, network linking
citizens and governments, friends and neighbors, customers and firms,
schools and students appears new and exciting, almost unprecedented to
many. Whether this will occur and how it will play out appear as great
uncertainties.

In fact, networks are nothing new. "Hard" networks, such as road
and rail systems, power grids, and water and gas distribution networks,
have been with us for a century. These networks connect customers to
suppliers (or other customers) with physical facilities. "Soft" networks,
such as computer hardware and software, and automobile service and
parts systems, depend upon shared standards and protocols to link products and their uses and are a barely noticed part of our lives. Telecommunications networks have also been with us for a century, from early
telephone networks, local in scope, to the emergence of the current globally connected telephone system. In the 1920s, radio networks emerged,
followed by television networks in the 1940s and 1950s. Somewhat later,

I wish to thank the Annenberg School's Public Policy Center for its financial support
for this project. I have also benefited from comments by Christiaan Hogendorn, Wharton
School, on an earlier draft. I am also indebted to my colleagues at INSEAD's Business
Economics Seminar, Fontainebleau, France, for their comments. An earlier version of this
paper has been published in the *Journal of Law and Public Policy*. Internet: faulhaber
@wharton.upenn.edu; WWW: rider.wharton.upenn.edu/faulhabe.

cable television networks grew, slowly at first, but now passing over 90 percent of U.S. homes. In other countries, satellite TV distribution networks perform much the same role. More recently, cellular telephone networks have also grown, illustrating the point that telecommunications networks, though "hard" in the sense used above, can be wireless links, without a continuous physical connection.

In this broader network context, why the sudden interest now in broadband networks, and what is unique about them? For those familiar with this technology, the surprise is that it took so long. Engineers and communications specialists have been predicting the coming of broadband systems with confidence and regularity over the last thirty years. There have been numerous "false dawns," such as teletext and videotext, and more successfully, Minitel in France. However, despite the enthusiasm of engineers and telephone companies, consumers did not have a question to which broadband data networks were the answer.

But given the rich context of existing telecommunications networks, what is so special and unique about broadband data networks? The fact that they are broadband is nothing special; coaxial cable and broadcast TV are broadband. However, both these media are inherently one way: they are designed to carry video content from a producer of that content to customers of it. Recent attempts to refit cable systems for two-way traffic, though successful, reinforce the point that this system was designed to deliver a specific product, and attempts to modify it are quite costly. These are specialized systems. The fact that broadband networks are interactive is also nothing special; the telephone network has been two way for a hundred years. But again, this is a network designed to deliver a specific product, and that is two-way simultaneous voice; and it will not be easily modified to do much else. This too is a specialized system. What is special is that broadband data networks are both broadband and interactive, and this conjunction of attributes creates the power broadband networks: just about *any* electronic signal can be sent *from* anybody *to* anybody else. Rather than the design of the network tying it to a specific purpose, it is a general system, with the potential for its use to be shaped and tailored by the needs and desires of its users.

However, all this power is of little interest unless there are persons capable of using it who find it of value to them. Before, say, 1992, this defined a small community of scientists, computer literate, widely dispersed among the world's universities and research institutions, who

Figure 20-1. *Number of Internet Hosts*

Millions of Internet hosts

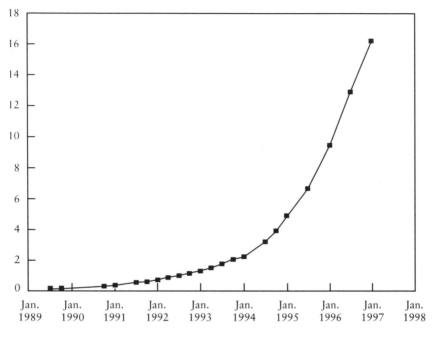

Jan. 1989 Jan. 1990 Jan. 1991 Jan. 1992 Jan. 1993 Jan. 1994 Jan. 1995 Jan. 1996 Jan. 1997 Jan. 1998

Source: ftp://ftp.genmagic.com/pub/internet/MIT-DC-v7.ppt

place a high value on communicating with one another and with access to large data sets for experimental purposes. For this group, the Internet became integral to their research efforts. For everyone else, the Internet was virtually unknown.

Nevertheless, the Internet grew at an extremely rapid rate since the late 1980s and as of this writing, shows no sign of diminishing (figure 20-1). This extremely rapid and sustained growth has generated the enormous attention that the Internet has received in the press and by many corporations.

What was the cause of this sudden growth spurt? There is no definitive answer, of course. However, by 1993, a number of *necessary* conditions were in place:

—The World Wide Web (WWW) was invented at Conseil Européen

pour la Recherche Nucléaire (CERN) in 1989 and in general use by this time;

—More than 30 percent of U.S. households owned personal computers, generally with an easy-to-use graphic interface (Windows or Macintosh);[2]

—An easy-to-use graphics "browser" for the WWW was available; first Mosaic followed shortly by Netscape Navigator; and

—Sufficient information was available on the WWW (data, graphics, programs, and so on) to make it worthwhile for people to browse.

This list is certainly not exhaustive; it merely enumerates the more obvious necessary conditions that must have been present to support the observed growth spurt.

During 1993 there was a growing corporate involvement in the potential for "multimedia," a catch-phrase that included video-on-demand and other entertainment options. Several very large mergers were proposed, the most publicized being the Bell Atlantic–TCI deal, only some of which were consummated.[3] These mergers were predicated, at least in part, on the future market potential of broadband network entertainment delivery systems.[4] But during this year, the Internet and WWW were still perceived by most communications, entertainment, and software firms as at best a predecessor to, and at worst a distraction from, the true Information Superhighway.

By 1994 the sustained growth of the Internet attracted more and more users and corporations. The number of ".com" sites (indicating a commercial user) exceeded the number of ".edu" sites (indicating an educational user) for the first time in Internet history.[5] Total traffic and total number of hosts on the Internet exploded during 1994.

Nevertheless, the Internet continued to be viewed by most large corporations throughout 1994 and 1995 as something of a fad, the "oat bran muffin of the 1990s." Nor was their skepticism unwarranted; having seen several "false dawns," the unruly hackers' paradise of the Internet hardly looked like the engine of commerce and entertainment that large corporations envisioned as the Information Superhighway.

The highly publicized launch of Windows 95 by Microsoft in August 1995 also introduced the Microsoft Network (MSN), the world's largest software firm's much anticipated entrée into on-line services. Microsoft's early experience with MSN coupled with their assessment of the traditional on-line services market apparently was not entirely satisfactory; in

December Microsoft announced a major shift in strategy that would focus its considerable resources on the Internet. This acknowledgment by the most influential software firm in the world that it was more profitable to cooperate on the Internet rather than compete with it marked a turning point in both public and corporate perceptions of the future of the Internet: this was no longer seen as another false dawn; the Net appeared to be here to stay. By 1996 Microsoft had announced plans "to eliminate proprietary interfaces altogether and move entirely to Web-based content."[6]

In sum, it now appears that the long-anticipated mass deployment of broadband data networks is at hand, with the Internet and WWW forming the basis of this growth. How fast this will occur, what fraction of households, businesses, schools, and governments will eventually become active users, what technologies will be used, and what they will be used for are subject to great uncertainty. A wide range of possibilities exists, from "small impact on a few enthusiasts" to "a fundamental change in the way we all live and work."

However, which route is taken, and how fast it develops, will almost surely be deeply affected by public policy decisions being made now regarding government involvement in infrastructure development, either through direct encouragement, even investment, or through regulation, possibly with universal service mandates.

The Historical Context of Convergence

For three decades, engineers and communications specialists have spoken of the convergence of the telecommunications, computers, and entertainment industries, coming together around the technologies of broadband networks to produce a new, integrated industry, serving a new set of customer demands. Convergence does seem to be what is happening; telecommunications firms are seeking partners in the entertainment business, computer firms, both hardware and software, seek content providers, and cable TV companies are looking for telephone companies and for entertainment distribution channels. Whether such pairings will be consummated, and if consummated be successful, is highly uncertain. Mergers or alliances among established firms may indeed be how convergence is realized, but there are other routes as well.

Complicating matters is the Internet "industry" itself: noncommercial, based on cooperative arrangements among (largely) academics, supported (until quite recently) by the federal government research establishment. For good or ill, the Internet Society and the Internet Engineering Task Force currently control the destiny of the only existing broadband data network in the United States, indeed the world.

Each of these industries approaches this convergence with very different expectations of what convergence actually means and very different skills and attitudes toward markets and technology. From the perspective of this chapter, however, the most important difference among these industries is the degree and kind of government intervention into their market. This chapter addresses two fundamental hypotheses:

—The convergence of these industries into a single new industry leads ineluctably to the convergence of the public policy models for these industries into a single new public policy model overarching this emerging market; and

—The speed and direction of the market convergence will be closely coupled with speed and direction of the public policy convergence.

Each of these industries is briefly (and somewhat arbitrarily) characterized below, with particular but not exclusive attention to the history of government intervention.

Computer Hardware and Software

Since the early 1980s, the computer business has undergone extraordinary changes, driven largely by extraordinary improvements in the price and performance of microelectronics devices and the conversion to open architectures. From a highly specialized corporate market for proprietary systems dominated by a few firms, the industry has moved toward a mass commodity market for open systems with many competitors in nearly every market segment. The industry is *technology and market driven*, highly competitive and rivalrous. There has been very little government intervention into this market. Even though IBM dominated the industry in the 1960s and 1970s, and Microsoft has approached that dominance in the late 1980s and 1990s, no government antitrust suit was prosecuted to completion against either firm. The industry is and always has been completely unregulated. Even its standard setting has been negotiated without government intervention. The worldview of this industry is highly competitive, that is, the firm that best manages technology and its markets wins. Government intervention, although occasionally requested by smaller players fearful of dominant firms, is virtually nonexistent.

Entertainment

Entertainment is a high-risk business in which vertical relationships among content providers (for example, Disney, Paramount) and distributors (for example, NBC, HBO) are shifting and generally contentious. The industry is *deal driven*, highly competitive, and individualistic. Government intervention has often been sought by some players to gain a competitive advantage within their value chain. For example, intervention was sought by entertainers at the height of the power of network broadcasters to ensure that their rights to syndication royalties could not be bargained away. Generally, government power has been viewed as a mechanism to advance one's own commercial interests, not as a constraint on behavior.

Telephone

Historically, a highly stable industry with an enormous capital base and very large cash flows. Dependability and quality of service characterize this industry; it has historically been *operations driven*. This is the most tightly regulated of all the converging industries, with state or federal regulators controlling price, quality, investment, and entry into many aspects of this industry. The process of deregulation, begun so tentatively with the break-up of the Bell System in 1984, has only modestly freed this industry to behave competitively in certain sectors.[7]

Cable TV

An industry that spent its early years in battle against the Federal Communications Commission and the broadcast networks, cable has had a somewhat "rough and tumble" history. The late 1970s were a period of substantial growth based on municipal franchising, an often questionable process, followed by full deregulation by Congress in 1984. Rapidly increasing rates and decreasing quality of service led to voter demand for relief, which was delivered by Congress in 1992 in the form of re-regulation of the industry. Cable is *short term, finance-driven*, often dominated by the need for short-term cash flow to meet substantial debt payments with less attention paid to longer-term issues.[8]

Internet

Few would characterize the Internet as an "industry" at all; until recently, the backbone network of the U.S. Internet was owned by the National Science Foundation. The midlevel networks, which served universities, schools, governments, not-for-profits, and some technology based firms in local geographic areas (often multistate) were owned and managed by consortiums of universities and technology firms operating in a cooperative mode. The objective of the network managers was to support research and education, and until quite recently, commercial traffic was not permitted on the network for fear of compromising the cooperative, not-for-profit spirit of the Internet. Nor was there much attempt to make the Internet easy to use; the target market was scientists and computer experts well versed in high-end computing, little interested in (indeed, antagonistic to) graphic interfaces or "easy to use" tools. The Internet was *research and education driven*. Government intervention was generally in the form of financial support with only those regulations that the Internet community generally supported, such as the ban on commercial use. Indeed, the privatization of the Internet in 1994 (but announced earlier) occasioned great concern that the Internet community was being abandoned by the National Science Foundation, perhaps being left to the not-so-tender mercies of the FCC.[9]

As should be evident, each of these industries about to converge has quite different histories, expectations, and perspectives on government intervention. As of this writing, there is ample evidence that none of these industries has much understanding of the others. The Internet community and the telephone industry, to name just one example, are in conflict over the appropriate technology to use for very high-speed connections, a capability both industries want and need.[10] Other examples abound; though this topic is not germane to this chapter, it is worth noting that convergence is apt to be characterized by contention and misunderstanding among the principal players.

There are other industries, of course. Cellular telephone, direct broadcast television, and other wireless technologies will no doubt affect, and be affected by, this convergence. But the four listed above are most likely to be the major participants.

Public Policy: Problems and Context

What are the public policy issues associated with electronic network infrastructure? Generally, the economic issues that draw governmental attention are the following. One, is the service available and affordable to all citizens? This is generally referred to as "universal service." Two, is the service efficiently provided at a reasonable quality? This is generally referred to as "quality of service." Three, is the provider earning excess profits from abuse of a monopoly market position? Four, is the distribution system available to all content providers? I consider each in turn.[11]

The Problem of Universal Service

Each of these four industries mentioned above is network based. Each has achieved substantial penetration of the mass market.[12] For example, more than 94 percent of households have telephones, more than 98 percent of households have television, more than 90 percent of households are passed by cable, about two-thirds of which subscribe to the service, and about 40 percent of households have personal computers.[13] Most every desk and workstation in U.S. industry has a computer on it, and almost all the growth is now coming from sales to homes, where growth rates are still high. Other related industries have also achieved relative ubiquity, such as VCRs.[14]

Each industry has arguably achieved, or is about to achieve, "universal service"; those customers who want the service are generally able to afford it. And yet the routes they followed to achieve universal service have differed. In the cases of television, cellular phones, VCRs, and personal computers, competitive markets drove prices down and market penetration up. In the case of cable TV, the laying of cable in all neighborhoods was generally a condition of the franchise that granted each company a geographic monopoly on wireline video delivery. For the telephone, universal service was an objective of both the old Bell System and its regulators since the early years of this century, not to be realized until about 1960. In cable and telephone, universal service was an explicit public policy objective, but different instruments were used to achieve it. In telephone, active regulation was the chosen instrument; in cable, the contract terms of the franchise was the chosen instrument.

The Price of Mandated Universal Service

In both cable and telephone, however, the price of publicly mandated universal service was monopoly. To make it feasible (so it was claimed) for a firm to serve everyone, profitable and unprofitable, the government had to forbid entry by competitors into the firm's market area. Why should this be? The universal service mandate of regulators has traditionally gone beyond ensuring that service is available to all; it is rather that service should be *affordable* by all. To achieve this objective, regulators have traditionally insisted on pricing practices that involve subsidies:

—Prices for service should be the same for all (or based on simple criteria such as distance), regardless of cost. For example, telephone service in rural areas where it is more costly to provide is priced no higher than service in suburban areas where it is less costly to provide. Long distance telephone service rates depend only upon distance between the two parties having the conversation, whether the call uses very expensive sparse routes across rugged terrain or relatively cheap, dense routes across a plain.

—Prices for basic services, such as telephone access or basic-tier cable TV, are often subsidized by "premium" services, such as long distance and international telephone or premium cable channels, in order that they be "affordable," especially for the poor.

These pricing practices are not unique to the United States but occur in publicly regulated or publicly owned networks throughout the world.

However, such practices cannot be sustained in the presence of competitive entry. New firms could enter only those markets in which prices are held above cost in order to subsidize other customers, forcing incumbents to respond competitively with price decreases or lose the business altogether. In either case, the source of internal subsidy would eventually disappear, and the incumbent could no longer afford to serve unprofitable (though allegedly deserving) customers. Therefore, to maintain the subsidies that most regulators use to achieve universal service, regulators restrict competitive entry, either by regulatory fiat or by the granting of franchise monopoly.

As a matter of logic, a public policy of universal service need not necessarily lead to franchise monopoly. For example, the market could be open to competition, but some form of direct subsidy from the government, either to customers (such as "telephone stamps" to poor or rural subscribers) or to firms (such as the small-city subsidies that the Civil Aeronautics Board [CAB] gave to serving airlines), would also achieve universal service. However, this situation has two political drawbacks: this is an explicit on-budget government expenditure, rather than an implicit industry-implemented internal subsidy; and it would make the subsidy more explicit and thus subject to potential criticism. Few regulators have used this mechanism (save the CAB in a previous era), favoring the less visible, industry cross-subsidy approach.

The costs of regulated monopoly have been well documented elsewhere, including reduced incentives for efficient operation, reduced incentives for innovation, excessive resources devoted to "rent-seeking" through the regulatory process, and so forth.[15] There is no question that paying the price of monopoly is quite high; is it really necessary in order to achieve universal service?

Several scholars have disputed the assertion that the granting of monopoly franchises was necessary to induce cable operators to enter the market and provide ubiquitous coverage.[16] They argue that granting monopolies is simply bad public policy. Of course, any firm would like a monopoly and will demand that one be given to it as a condition of investment, but is it necessary in order to get cable deployment? These scholars marshal evidence that there are cities in which cable operators compete, and it seems to work. Others argue that the risks of extensive infrastructure investment are just too great to be left to the competitive market, and that no firm will take that risk unless assured of a reasonable return.

The core of the universal service problem for "hard" network infrastructure, however, is simply the magnitude of the investment required. This investment is best conceived as having a network component (switching, transmission, computers, head-end, long-haul satellite, and so on) and an access component (local loop, inside wire, and so on). The network component is typically a shared resource; many users make use of switches and transmission systems. The access component is typically not shared but dedicated to a single household.[17] Moreover, the access component, sometimes referred to as "the last mile," may account for as much as half the total investment in the network. The capital cost of a traditional telephone access line is typically estimated at around $1,000. Every customer, therefore, represents a substantial financial commitment by the serving firm.

The Problem of Quality of Service

In a market with some form of competition, the expectation is that quality of service will take care of itself. Firms will provide the level of quality that customers demand and are willing to pay for, and competition will ensure their responsiveness to customers. In the case of monopoly, however, the incentives for the firm to provide appropriate quality levels may be diminished, so that quality of service may suffer. The most salient examples of quality of service problems in these network industries have occurred in the more monopolistic industries: cable TV and the Internet.

The recent congestion on the Internet is less a problem of monopoly than it is of growth outstripping the Internet's governance structure. WWW users have been experiencing agonizingly slow download times from graphics-intensive web servers, and the delays from the United States to European or Asian sites are extremely long. Since the network uses shared resources, increased demands cause those shared resources to become congested. Management of this situation is at once everyone's problem and no one's problem; both demand and supply of all network components, not just a few, must be managed to solve this quality-of-service problem.

The decline of service quality of another kind was observed by many customers of the cable TV industry during the late 1980s and gave rise to demands on Congress for a solution. That solution was the Cable Reregulation Act of 1992. However, the political demand grew out of what many customers perceived as shoddy treatment in handling requests and complaints and failure to provide reliable, outage-free services.

In principle, regulators generally have the legal power to coerce firms to provide the "right" service level. In practice, this is more difficult, as is borne out in Oliver Williamson's well-known analysis of cable TV franchise bidding.[18] Additionally, it is not clear that regulators are good at assessing the quality level that customers would demand in a more competitive market. For example, in the precompetitive airline market, most scholars agree that airlines overprovided schedule quality, at the cost of higher fares, as a result of the CAB's regulatory practices. After deregulation, schedule quality "deteriorated" to that for which customers were willing to pay. Another example occurred in telephone; before the deregulation of terminal equipment, the Bell System (with regulatory approval) provided rather simple telephones that were virtually indestructible. After deregulation, it became clear that most customers preferred telephones with many more features and a shorter life; the telephone soon became another consumer electronics product. In both cases, regulation led to an inappropriate quality level (as measured against the competitive standard).

The Problem of Monopoly

Many consider network infrastructure a "natural monopoly," an industry in which competitive markets would naturally lead to a single supplier as the most efficient alternative. In such cases, antitrust actions to break up a monopoly would be ineffective, as market forces would eventually lead to the remonopolization of the industry. Some form of regulation may be justified as a means to control the abuse of monopoly power in such industries, and this is the rationale given by many observers for the creation of regulated monopolies in network industries. Others argue that these monopolies may not be so natural but are in fact products of the regulation that seeks to control them. This latter view is somewhat more compelling, in that virtually all regulators protect regulated monopolies with entry prohibitions. In the words of Alfred Kahn, "If the monopoly is so natural, why does it have to be protected?"[19] In fact, the protection is necessary to maintain subsidizing price structures, which are indeed a product of regulation. In any case, regulators find that control of monopoly power is added to their list of responsibilities, be that monopoly natural or created. Generally, much regulatory attention is devoted to determining if a firm is abusing its market power. In the classic regulated monopoly, this concern takes the form of ensuring that the firm's earnings are not "excessive," that is, exceed the cost of capital. In regulated monopolies operating in some markets subject to competition, this concern takes the form of ensuring that power in monopoly markets is not being used to subsidize operations in competitive markets. Both tasks are extremely difficult, but concern for cross-subsidy is virtually impossible. For example, as telecommunications competition slowly increased during the 1970s and early 1980s, the Federal Communications Commission devoted very substantial efforts to develop a standard by which to judge whether or not Bell System rates involved cross-subsidy, without success.

The Problem of Vertical Integration (Content versus Conduit)

The "network" of a network industry is a distribution system, a conduit over which something else, *content*, is sent. In telecommunications, this something is telephone calls; in cable, it is video programming; in electric utilities, it is power. In computing, it is possible to think of hardware as conduit and software (which actually delivers what customers want) as content. In both regulated and competitive markets, an important economic issue is the vertical integration of content and conduit.

In some markets such as telephone, content and conduit are separated as a matter of law, generally on First Amendment grounds. In other related markets such as cable and broadcast television, content and conduit can be and generally are integrated within each firm.[20] For example, a subscriber to a particular cable firm can only buy material that the cable firm chooses to make available. In contrast, anyone can use the telephone network to distribute any information (such as 800 or 900 services); the telephone company has nothing to say about it.

The computer industry provides a prime example of how competitive markets evolve. Before the early 1980s, virtually all computer companies bundled hardware and software together. An IBM customer had to buy IBM proprietary software, because no other commercially available software ran on IBM machines. This was the era of closed computer architecture. In contrast, the PC ushered in the era of open architecture, in which hardware vendors encouraged provision of software by as many sources as possible. The result was a flowering of hardware and software, with thousands of companies, many no more than a single person, pumping out tens of thousands of software titles. Many have credited this open architecture with the extraordinary growth and richness of the computer industry of the 1980s and 1990s, compared with the relatively stately pace of innovation in the closed architecture era.[21] However, many software firms have complained that Microsoft, the firm that controls the dominant PC operating system (the conduit), has used its operating system (OS) control to unfair competitive advantage in the applications (content) market, such as word processors, spreadsheets, and presentation graphics. After considering such complaints, the Department of Justice did not prosecute, reaching a relatively mild agreement with Microsoft that it cease certain practices. No one seriously suggests that

Microsoft should not be permitted to compete in the applications software market. However, the example brings home the fact that vertical integration of content and conduit is certain to give rise to contention of market abuses, if not actual abuses, and constitutes a public policy problem, either regulatory or antitrust.

In sum, universal service with appropriate service quality, the control of monopoly pricing, and open architectures can be achieved with competitive markets, at least in some cases. However, regulation and franchise control have traditionally been the chosen instruments in virtually all electronic network infrastructure industries. In the case of broadband networks, the question is, which is the more appropriate means of achieving the public policy objectives?

Public Policy: What Needs to Be Done?

The four issues raised in the previous section present an interrelated set of problems for which various interest groups expect a public policy response. Fortunately, the U.S. Congress, in the Telecommunications Act of 1996, has established a procompetitive context in which state regulators and legislators, as well as federal regulators, can respond. However, control of telecommunications in the United States is fragmented among fifty-two local jurisdictions plus the federal level, suggesting that progress within this framework and the policies adopted may be quite varied, even contradictory. The process by which the individual states and the nation as a whole come to understand what needs to be done is likely to be drawn out over the better part of a decade, after which there will no doubt continue to be some variation among jurisdictions. The focus of this chapter is the economic issues, not the jurisdictional issues.

Universal Service

The universal service issue for broadband two-way networks is currently relatively quiescent. A federal-state joint board (of FCC and state regulatory commissions), which is charged with considering universal service issues in the light of the Telecommunications Act of 1996, has on its agenda the Clinton administration's proposal to provide "basic" service at 1.54 Mbps to the nation's schools, clearly a broadband issue.[22] Generally, however, few have supported a universal service concept of a broadband link into every home in the United States, an enormously capital-intensive venture. Restricting the universal service concept to below-cost provision of broadband to schools (and possibly libraries) ensures that this event will be a nonissue.

However, this situation may change if the demand for broadband in rural areas or from disadvantaged groups increase substantially. This demand would translate into political action that could redefine universal service to include broadband, possibly fiber, to the home (or curb). Should this occur relatively soon, before the industry has had a chance to form, there could well be public intervention to ensure that all suppliers were required to provide fiber service to all households and businesses. In fact, if municipalities are permitted to limit broadband fiber providers by monopoly franchising, as has been done in cable TV, this outcome is highly likely. Even more likely is that those firms who believe they have a good chance of winning such monopoly franchises may press legislators toward universal service as a means of justifying monopoly. It could be argued, as above, that only monopoly can ensure that everyone will be served.

Should this occur, it will almost surely be a substantial loss to the nation, for the following reasons:

—The track record of regulated/franchised monopoly in fostering product innovation has been particularly poor. In the emerging broadband network industry, this form of innovation will be particularly important. Since no one now knows what services will emerge that will capture the interests of consumers, it is essential that firms be permitted to explore the possibilities, that consumers have the maximum choices, and that the market be permitted to evolve in as free and open a fashion as possible. Imposing regulation or franchised monopoly on this market will surely throttle this needed innovative process, substituting (whether intended or not) the visible hand of government for the invisible one of the market.

—There is an existing infrastructure for delivering Internet-type services to everyone. Most schools and libraries have some form of access, and most households have telephones, which permit 28.8 Kbps access, which is satisfactory if not perfect for Internet access at least at present.

—There is little evidence that broadband access from the home (as opposed to broadband access from the school, or 28.8 Kbps access from the home) constitutes an essential tool for all Americans to achieve equal opportunities, either in the political or economic marketplace. It could, of course, become a valued entertainment distribution channel, but this is hardly a public policy reason to subsidize universal service.

If regulated monopoly is a poor policy choice, is it at least better than competition? A unique feature of the emerging broadband technologies is that there are so many of them. Although much attention has been focused on fiber, satellite delivery as well as various "add-on" technologies for telephone and cable are also competitors to fiber for broadband.[23] This potential for *intermodal* competition changes the nature of the market alternative to franchised/regulated wireline monopoly.[24] Recent research on competition for broadband access has shown the following results:[25]

—For "reasonable" estimates of cost and demand for broadband distribution, it appears likely that major metropolitan areas may support more than one fiber distributor but not until demand levels are approximately double present levels.

—However, competitive deployment of fiber may occur in "rings," in which the areas of densest population are served by n fiber distributors, the less dense areas are served by $n-1$ distributors, until the final ring, which is served by only one provider. Prices within each ring would reflect competitive conditions. In high-density cities, fiber is likely to serve the entire metropolitan area. In low-density cities, fiber will not extend to outlying areas.

—In low-density cities, satellite services are likely to be an important competitive factor, serving all customers in the metropolitan area, though with a service that is somewhat inferior.[26] These services would cover all the population, thus achieving universal service through competition.

However, at least some legislators and regulators find it difficult to refrain from intervention if only to "help" competition to achieve public policy objectives. Some have suggested an intermediate approach that would permit public policymakers to show a commitment to universal service while encouraging competition. Municipalities could offer nonexclusive franchises, with the condition that franchise holders would be required to provide universal service. Entry would require a franchise, but anyone could obtain a franchise for the asking. This could encourage competition among broadband fiber firms, all of whom would be forced to serve all customers. In this way, not only would everyone enjoy the benefits of broadband, they would also enjoy the benefits of competition as well.

Unfortunately, this happy outcome may never occur. The requirement for universal service imposes a fixed cost on entrants that would constrain the number of fiber providers who would be willing to enter with a universal service constraint. Simulation analysis suggests that the imposition of a universal service constraint to make service available to (say) 95 percent of households in a metropolitan area will increase the cost of providing fiber sufficiently that initial entry, as well as competitive entry, is only feasible at greater demand levels than would otherwise be the case.[27] The reason is that the cost of supplying fiber infrastructure to unprofitable customers may be greater than even duopoly profits from the profitable markets. Thus, imposing the universal service obligation may lead, at certain demand levels, to monopoly, even if unconstrained competition could support multiple fiber vendors. Of course, the price charged under this scenario would be a monopoly price, substantially higher than most customers would pay under unconstrained competition. The only constraint on monopoly pricing in this scenario would be the presence of satellite services, should satellite vendors choose to (and be permitted to) compete.

On balance, then, it would appear that competitive provision of broadband access is far superior to any form of regulation or franchising. Further, unless there is significant pressure of rural or disadvantaged groups for below-cost provision of broadband access to the home, it should be relatively easy for legislators, regulators, and municipalities to resist vendor demands for monopoly franchises. The policy direction established by the Telecommunications Act of 1996 should provide a rationale for policymakers to take the competitive option.

It is important to realize, however, that it is unlikely that two or more fiber providers will enter the market simultaneously. It is more likely that a single firm will enter, possibly expanding its service area over time, most likely competing with satellite providers. The second fiber firm may not enter for several years, when demand levels are sufficiently high to support two providers. During this interim period, the temptation to regulate the monopoly may be quite strong. It is critical that this temptation be resisted, as efficient and innovative competitors are unlikely to emerge in a regulated environment.

Quality of Service

The evolution of the Internet into the two-way broadband network of the future has been exciting and painful. The network itself, its administrative support, and its governance structure were all designed for a much different environment. Institutions and infrastructure designed to meet the needs of university researchers around the world are quite unsuitable for the high-growth, high-volume, commercialized mass market service the Internet has become in the last year. What is amazing is not that the Internet is congested (which it clearly is); it is that it has not collapsed under the crushing weight of unprecedented traffic volumes.[28] The problem is clear: investment in Internet capacity has not kept pace with the growth of demand, leading to a slowdown of the Internet. In some places (such as transoceanic traffic) and for some uses (such as telnet and real-time video), this increase in congestion has made the Internet almost unusable.

Does this call for a public policy intervention? The Clinton administration has established an Information Infrastructure Task Force, with committees, working groups, events, speeches, and testimony.[29] The current Internet Engineering Task Force is comfortable working with government agencies, so this may help. However, any long-term solution will clearly involve three factors:

—An overhaul of the Internet's governance structure. While research and education should continue to have strong representation in governance, commercial users and vendors will eventually take on more governance responsibility.

—Pricing and revenue sharing. This is probably the most immediate need of the Internet in order to ensure that those who own facilities, such as transmission pipes, servers, and routers, have sufficient incentive to invest in new capacity to handle increased traffic volumes.[30] Such arrangements exist in virtually every commercial network industry in which multiple entities are responsible for different parts of a single network. Railroads and telecommunications are two obvious examples. Such arrangements need to be adopted by the Internet, and relatively quickly.

—Interconnected Internets. Internets may develop and coexist, interconnected with gateways that limit the impact of congestion between networks. In October 1996 a group of American universities announced their intention to set up Internet II, as a means of avoiding increased congestion and ensuring that this network would enable them to meet their education and research objectives. Other groups may wish to do the same in order to meet their objectives. Certainly the recent trend toward corporate "intranets" is best viewed in this light; that is, networks that share the protocols of the Internet without sharing its congestion and lack of security.

Clearly, government can play a role in helping this development. It is most likely that the existing institutions can evolve toward the above solutions, though with some pain and contention. Government can play a supporting role here. However, should government attempt to play a directive role, it is more likely to be the problem, not the solution. In the early 1990s, the National Science Foundation correctly perceived that its role in providing the NSFNet backbone was over, and that this role should be taken over by the private sector. Despite many protestations from the Internet community, NSF implemented this privatization successfully. It would be inappropriate if the government were to step back into a directive role, having had the good sense to withdraw from such a role some years ago.

Monopoly and Vertical Integration

There is a reasonable chance that limited competition in broadband may emerge. Not only may there be more than one fiber provider, there is likely to be satellite coverage too. Further, existing infrastructure providers are currently developing technologies that increase the effective bandwidth of their infrastructure. Cable firms are experimenting with cable modems, which promise in-bound speeds of 10 Mbps, although there is some concern over how much bandwidth cable systems have for heavy Internet usage. Telephone companies are experimenting with ADSL, a technology that will permit 10 Mbps in-bound over existing telephone lines. All these technologies will compete with each other, provided they are deployed.

And therein lies the concern. It is possible (some would say likely) that after all the grand announcements, alliances, initial public offerings (IPOs), and other fanfare, only the telephone companies will actually lay fiber to the curb and thereby control the one broadband, two-way distribution channel into the home. In that case, two problems confront public policymakers. The first is the classic problem of monopoly: a firm takes advantage of its market position to charge prices higher than costs. The second is the problem of access control: the monopoly firm chooses the content its users can access, which limits its customers as well as potential suppliers. Monopolies tend to be closed architecture systems, with a limited choice controlled by the "bottleneck" supplier.

On balance, it is likely that the second problem would be more serious than the first. If it is the case that the market can only support a single supplier, then it is likely that monopoly prices are not very much higher than total costs; if they were, then the market could support more than one supplier. Of course, it could be that the monopoly may be a temporary one, until other firms can deploy resources to compete. In this case, it is particularly important that antitrust authorities be alert to attempts by the incumbent to raise potential rivals' entry costs, or other anticompetitive behavior. In any case, this would appear to be a problem of the antitrust authorities.

The second problem is somewhat more difficult. Should a single firm be the monopoly supplier of broadband distribution, it is likely to control content, increasing its profits through price discrimination among content providers. By analogy with the IBM-dominated computer market of the 1970s, we would expect proprietary content provision in a closed architecture, without the profusion of content and access that a more competitive market would provide. If such a monopoly emerges, or emerges even temporarily, how should policymakers respond?[31]

The problem is closely related to two issues in telecommunications today: encouraging local telephone competition, a market now dominated by the regional Bell operating companies (RBOCs), and ensuring that RBOC provision of video services are open to non-RBOC content providers. Both issues are before regulatory commissions as of this writing, and broadly similar approaches are being taken. In the case of local competition, RBOCs are being required by the Telecommunications Act of 1996 to open their networks to potential competitors who wish to lease facilities to provide local service. Originally, the FCC mandated wholesale rates at which the RBOC would be required to provide local facilities; however, this requirement was struck down on challenge from state regulators on jurisdictional grounds.[32] However, state regulators are arbitrating agreements between RBOCs and potential competitors for wholesale rates close to the FCC guidelines, around 20 percent discounts from retail. The concept of the act was to mandate resale of bottleneck facilities to encourage competitive supply of local telephone service.

Similarly, the FCC was concerned that the provision of broadband fiber services to residential areas could become a distribution monopoly, with the fiber becoming a bottleneck facility. To address this problem, the FCC has adopted the Open Video Systems approach, in which telephone companies (indeed, any OVS supplier) providing video distribution to the home is required to provide access to any content provider that wished to use the supplier's capacity under the same terms and conditions that it supplies its own content provider. In this model, the facilities supplier is not enjoined from providing content; but it is required to make its facilities available to other content providers under the same terms and conditions it offers its own content provider.[33] Although this approach is not without problems, it does represent a regulatory approach to convert an otherwise bottleneck facility into an open architecture system.

In fact, this is a good example of a regulatory intervention that opens up markets to a far richer supply structure than would otherwise obtain and certainly far richer than would obtain under traditional rate-based, rate-of-return monopoly regulation. Should temporary monopoly of two-way broadband facilities become a problem, then this relatively light touch of regulation designed to open access to any content provider is an effective solution to that problem.

Summary and Conclusion

The history of network infrastructure supply in the United States (and indeed the world) is one of unrelenting regulated monopoly. I have argued in this chapter that adopting such a model for two-way broadband networks is likely to throttle innovation and deliver only a very small fraction of the content that would be interchanged in a more open market. Ensuring that this historical public policy solution is not imposed on this exciting and uncertain enterprise is perhaps the most important public policy issue for the electronic age of the next decade.

Fortunately, the Telecommunications Act of 1996 set a highly pro-competitive strategic direction for public policymakers, which federal and state regulators, as well as state legislators, appear to be following. Calls for broadband universal service appear to be limited to schools and libraries, an enterprise well within the capabilities of the emerging industry to handle. The FCC's OVS approach to handling bottleneck broadband facilities shows promise of providing more open architectures even under conditions of facilities monopoly. The willingness of state regulators to permit competition with "their" local telephone companies is a welcome break from the past. Competition among broadband access providers appears possible; whether municipalities are willing to give up franchise control of video distribution has yet to be tested.

Indeed, this trend toward open competition, which appears so robust as of this writing, is likely to be rather fragile, cutting against the historical grain of American regulation of network infrastructure. Past attempts at deregulation in this industry have not fared well. Cable TV, deregulated in 1984, is the best example of how an industry made reregulation an attractive option to a country steeped in the tradition of competition. A major setback, a public relations fiasco, or overly aggressive monopolists could reverse this current trend toward reliance upon competitive markets, leading the nation back to regulated monopoly, which may well smother this exciting and promising but infant industry in its crib.

Notes

1. I use the term "broadband" to refer to an electronic signal (or the facilities designed to transmit that signal) carrying information substantially greater than voice, such as video or high-speed data. For the more engineering oriented, I consider ISDN to be more than voice but less than broadband. Generally, a useful if not wholly accurate benchmark would be signals of 10 MHz or above. Note that modern compression technologies may eventually permit the practical carriage of such signals across telephone lines originally designed for voice.

2. Andrew Freeman, "Technology in Finance Survey," *Economist*, October 26, 1996, pp. 19–31.

3. See John Huey and Andrew Kupfer, "What That Merger Means for You," *Fortune*, November 15, 1993, pp. 82–88. See also Andrew Kupfer, "The Baby Bells Butt Heads," *Fortune*, March 21, 1994, pp. 76–82.

4. Andrew C. Barrett, "Shifting Foundations: The Regulation of Telecommunications in an Era of Change, "*Federal Communications Law Journal*, vol. 46 (December 1993), pp. 39–62.

5. Mark K. Lottor, *Internet Domain Survey*, Network Wizards, Inc., October 1994 (http://nw.com/zone/www–9410/distribution.html).

6. Todd Spangler, "The Net Grows Wider: Internet Services," *PC Magazine*, November 19, 1996, pp. 147–89.

7. See, for example, Gerald R. Faulhaber, *Telecommunications in Turmoil* (Ballinger Publishing, 1987).

8. This appears to be a characteristic of many privately funded infrastructure projects. The early railroads, the Chesapeake Bay Bridge-Tunnel, and the Channel Tunnel have all had difficulties managing a crushing debt burden.

9. See, for example, B. Kahin, ed., *Building Information Infrastructure* (McGraw-Hill, 1992), for early discussions and concerns about the (at the time) coming privatization of the NSFNet backbone network.

10. Steven Steinberg, "Net-Heads vs. Bell-Heads," *Wired Magazine*, vol. 4, October 1996 (http://www.hotwired. com/wired/ 4.10/features/atm.htm).

11. There are a host of noneconomic issues that legislators and regulators consider in infrastructure services, such as limiting distribution of material seen as socially pernicious (pornographic material, instructions for making bombs, foreign content, and so on) and encouraging the distribution of material seen as socially beneficial (for example, access to the Library of Congress, educational television, local and neighborhood content). While I recognize the importance of these issues, I do not consider them in this chapter, which is focused on economic issues only.

12. With the exception of the Internet, of course; however, its phenomenal growth rate suggests it may eventually stabilize at relatively high penetration rates (see figure 20-1).

13. See Gerald R. Faulhaber, "Public Policy In Telecommunications: The Third Revolution," *Information Economics and Policy*, vol. 7 (September 1995), pp. 251–82, for supporting material.

14. Even cellular telephone, once thought to be a product targeted to wealthy stockbrokers phoning in buy-and-sell orders from their BMWs, has achieved a market penetration substantially beyond that originally predicted. In 1995 the cellular market grew by 36 percent to 32 million subscribers (compared with 145 million land-line telephone subscribers). See Federal Communications Commission, Industry Analysis Division, "Trends in Telephone Service" (Washington), table 39. Today, a person using a cellular phone next to you in a traffic jam is just as likely to be driving a pickup truck as a BMW.

15. For an early reference (among many others), see Ronald Brauetigam and Bruce Owen, *The Regulation Game: Strategic Use of the Administrative Process* (Ballinger Publishing, 1978).

16. See, for example, Tom Hazlett, 1990, "Duopolistic Competition in Cable Television," *Yale Journal of Regulation*, vol. 7 (1990), pp. 65–119; and Stanford Levin and John Meisel, "Cable Television and Competition," *Telecommunications Policy* (December 1991), pp. 521–22.

17. This is much less of a problem with connections to medium to large businesses, in which businesses provide substantial "cooperating" investment in telephone equipment on their own premises, so that a dedicated access circuit group to a business is a less risky investment for the local telephone company. For households, however, the access investment is often made before the household makes consumption choices or cooperative investments.

18. Oliver Williamson, "Franchise Bidding for Natural Monopolies—In General and with Respect to CATV," *Bell Journal of Economics*, vol. 7 (1976), pp. 73–104.

19. Alfred Kahn, *The Economics of Regulation* (John Wiley and Sons, 1970).

20. This is not to say that cable or broadcast firms actually *produce* their own content (although broadcasters do produce their own news shows), but rather

they *control* the content, which they generally purchase from outside entertainment suppliers.

21. See, for example, M. Kapor, "Building the Open Road: The NREN as a Test-Bed for the National Public Network," Electronic Frontier Foundation, RFC 1259, September (www.uio.no.elund/rfc/1259.txt).

22. Pamela Mendels, "FCC Moves to Ensure Net Access for Schools," *New York Times*, November 13, 1996, p.C1.

23. See David Strom, "Breaking the Internet Speed Barrier," *Windows Sources*, June 1996 (http://www.zdnet.com/wsources/960617/feature.html).

24. It is also worth noting that developing countries in Latin American and Southeast Asia, poised to expand their telephone networks, do not plan on using wireline technology to provide universal service but intend to rely on (indeed, are relying on) cellular and other wireless services to provide services to rural areas. The presence of both wired and wireless modes has changed the nature of the universal service problem in these countries.

25. Gerald R. Faulhaber and Christiaan Hogendorn, "Public Policy and Broadband Networks: The Feasibility of Competition," presented at "Bridging Digital Technologies and Regulatory Paradigms" conference, University of California, Berkeley, 1997.

26. Recently, Direct Broadcast Satellite (DBS) distribution of video entertainment, a direct competitor to cable television, has had some success in penetrating markets already served by cable. Satellite can be used for broadband distribution *to* the customer. However, without expensive transmitting equipment (and much more bandwidth than is currently available), customers would be required to transmit signals *from* the home via telephone lines. This service would be *broadband in, narrowband out*, compared with fiber, which can handle two-way broadband. However, fiber to the curb is not yet a reality, while satellite systems delivering a 400Kbps downlink can be purchased today. See Jeffrey G. Witt, "Hughes Networks on the Final Frontier," *PC Magazine*, June 25, 1996, pp. NE 23–24.

27. Faulhaber and Hogendorn, "Public Policy and Broadband Networks."

28. See, for example, "Why the Net Should Grow Up," *Economist*, October 19, 1996, pp. 17–18.

29. As befits such an organization, its primary point of contact is its website: http://iitf.doc.gov.

30. See, for example, "Too Cheap to Meter?" *Economist*, October 19, 1996, p. 23.

31. This analysis draws on James Kaplan, "Integration, Competition, and Industry Structure in Broadband Communications," University of Pennsylvania, Wharton School Advanced Study Project Paper, 1996.

32. FCC Docket 96-98 Interconnection Order.

33. FCC Report and Order and Notice of Proposed Rulemaking, Docket 96-99, March 11, 1996.

CHAPTER TWENTY-ONE

Public Interest Regulation in the Digital TV Era

Henry Geller

T ELEVISION, INCLUDING terrestrial and direct broadcast satellite (DBS), cable television, multichannel multipoint distribution systems (MMDS), and local multipoint distribution systems (LMDS), is moving into the digital era. Former Federal Communications Commission Chairman Reed Hundt has called for clearly defined and heightened responsibilities for commercial television;[1] he has also indicated the desirability of symmetrical regulation of the principal electronic media subject to the FCC's jurisdiction. The White House, led by Vice President Al Gore, has established an advisory group to study and recommend what the nature of the public interest obligations of digital broadcasters should be.[2] The major focus of this chapter is on that issue.

Trends and Guiding Principles

It is not my purpose here to trace in detail the trends in television. It suffices for the purposes of this chapter that we are heading for an era of digital television, of great abundance, of many delivery systems, of continuing fractionation of the audience, of greater competition for that audience, the advertising dollar, and popular programming.[3] Cable television is certainly a great success story, serving 63 percent of the nation's households,[4] with hundreds of channels of programming; DBS has made a strong entry with its 150 or more channels of digital television; and commercial television is flourishing because it continues to be *the* local outlet for television advertising and on a national level the only way to garner the large audience sought by many advertisers.[5] There is no way to predict with any certainty the impact of future video delivery systems such as LMDS, the local telephone companies (telcos), and most important of all, the Internet, through high-speed data (including video) directed to either digital TV receivers or personal computers (PCs).[6]

Against this trend background, the following principles should guide policy in this area:

—Continue and expand the policy of open entry. Such entry contributes to the diversity of programming and of sources, thereby markedly serving the public interest and the First Amendment.[7]

—Promote open, nondiscriminatory access for information providers and the public. This principle is closely related to the open entry policy, and indeed, with a plethora of effective distribution channels, no government intervention, such as requiring general (telco) or partial (cable) common carriage, may be needed.

—Maintain and promote vigorous competition. In light of the trends, this principle may require a balance of conflicting considerations, namely, a need to consider economies of scale against the desirability of diversification and competition, especially at the local level.[8]

—While the market should thus be given the fullest possible play, there is the need to ensure against deficiencies and thus to promote high-quality public service programming that contributes to an educated and informed citizenry in a manner that is effective; reaches all Americans and deals with the have/have not problem; is consistent with the First Amendment; and reduces First Amendment strains by developing structural approaches that truly facilitate the achievement of goals without behavioral regulation. Television is increasingly important to the nation: it is a child's window on the world, and most people now obtain their news and information from television. Therefore, television should also provide educational, cultural, and in-depth informational programming. The government's role here, as in the case of schools and libraries, is of great importance.

—Avoid unnecessary regulation and to the extent possible, adopt like regulation for like services so as not to tilt the playing field.

The Current Regulatory Schemes

The following are the current regulatory policies, especially for broadcasting.

BROADCASTING: PUBLIC TRUSTEE REGULATION. Because the number of people who want to use the spectrum, and in particular to broadcast, exceeds the number of available frequencies or channels, the Communications Act of 1934 establishes a system of short-term broadcast licenses to be awarded to private parties who volunteer to serve the public interest—to be a fiduciary or trustee for all those who were kept off the air by the government. The act imposes several public service requirements—that the broadcaster serve local needs and interests, called "community issue-oriented programming" today[9] (section 307[b]); that the broadcaster contribute to an informed electorate through informational and political broadcasts (section 315[a]; 312[a][7]); and that because children are so important to the nation and watch so much television, television broadcasters are required to serve the educational and informational needs of this audience with programming specifically designed for that purpose (section 303b[a]; 104 Stat. 997 [1990]).

Requirements such as the above clearly involve content regulation, and thus their constitutionality would normally be judged under the strict scrutiny standard of First Amendment jurisprudence—that the government has the heavy burden of showing that the requirements are narrowly tailored (that is, the least restrictive means) to serve a compelling interest.[10] But the Supreme Court has consistently held that because of the above allocational scarcity, broadcasting requirements such as delineated above do not come under traditional heightened First Amendment jurisprudence but rather the more liberal standard set out in the *Red Lion* and *NBC* cases[11]—if the regulation is reasonably related to the public interest, it is permissible under the First Amendment.

Finally, there is the matter of the efficacy of the public trustee scheme. It is a failure. Indeed, the commission has effectively deregulated broadcasting.[12] With one exception (the 1990 Children's Act [herein CTA], discussed within), the FCC receives no programming information from which it might assess the public service efforts of its licensees nor does it monitor the industry generally or through specific random inspections that evaluate public service efforts. Although the FCC requires broadcasters to maintain files indicating significant treatment of community issues, along with illustrative programs, broadcasters do not have to submit this material to the FCC. Instead, they send the commission postcards stating that the relevant material may be found in the public file at the station. As a result, the FCC must rely solely upon the public to bring to its attention stations that are not fulfilling their public service obligations.

This reliance is wholly misplaced, as the seventeen-year experience with postcard renewal shows: Even though people may send letters complaining about the disappearance of a favorite program or some content feature, they can hardly be expected to go to a station, examine its files, analyze the data, and then file a petition to deny. Postcard renewal simply permits the FCC to avoid consideration of public service issues. That is why it is aptly termed, Deregulation of Radio (or Television).

In 1976 Glen Robinson, former commissioner, echoing Nobel Prize economist Ronald Coase, described FCC regulation of broadcasting as a charade—a wrestling match full of fake grunts and groans but signifying nothing.[13] Today, with postcard renewal, the charade continues but is more starkly apparent. This is not to say commercial broadcasters render no public service, but with the one exception of the CTA, such service has nothing to do with regulation. The point is that the FCC public trustee regime is, and has long been, a failure.[14]

CABLE TELEVISION. Cable comes under a different regulatory and constitutional regime than broadcasting. Because it has a large capacity for many channels of programming, it has never been regulated as a public trustee required to provide public service content in categories like children's television or informational programming. Indeed, the act specifically bars such content regulation.[15] Instead, the policy is geared to providing access for so-called PEG (public, educational, or governmental) channels on a noncommercial basis or for commercial leased channels. (See sections 611, 612.) These access channels are designed to promote the *Associated Press* principle, by freeing some significant amount of cable capacity from the control of the cable operator in order to diversify the sources of information coming to the cable subscriber.[16]

In *Turner*, the Court unanimously rejected the government's argument for application of the *Red Lion* standard to cable television. It held that *Red Lion* is based on the unique and distinguishing characteristic that broadcast frequencies are a scarce resource that must be allocated among many more applicants than there are available frequencies, and that cable does not have such inherent limitations. Rather, the Court found that in light of technological developments, there is no practical limitation on the number of speakers, nor is there any danger of interference between two cable speakers.[17]

It follows that regulation of cable speech comes under traditional First Amendment jurisprudence—if content based, strict scrutiny;[18] if content neutral, the intermediate standard of *O'Brien*.[19] It seems clear, therefore, that extending *Red Lion* requirements such as the provision of educational or informational programs would not pass constitutional muster. There is simply no "compelling interest" or "extremely important" or "extraordinary" problem. Indeed, in light of cable's many channels of programming (for example, The Learning Channel; Discovery Channel; Nickelodeon; Arts and Entertainment Channel; CNN and the new news channels; C-SPAN; the PEG channels), there is no problem at all, and no policy reason for government intrusion.[20]

There is a question as to the efficacy of the access provisions. Although they constitute a sound approach in my view, their implementation at both the national and local levels has been flawed. A large number of franchising authorities do not require PEG channels or, if they do, fail to ensure adequate financial support.[21] As to commercial leased channel operation, Congress recognized in the 1992 Cable Act that this requirement of the 1984 cable law has been a failure. It therefore added a provision requiring the FCC to determine the operator's maximum rates for commercial leased channel use, and to establish reasonable terms and conditions.[22] The commission has acted, with several parties appealing its order as inadequate to remedy the situation.[23] So on this score also, the matter is unsettled both as to legality and efficacy.

DBS. The 1992 Act (sec. 25) contains two public interest provisions concerning DBS. Section 335(a) directs the FCC to initiate a proceeding to impose public interest requirements on DBS providers of video service (at a minimum, the access provisions of sec. 312(a)(7) and the use provisions of sec. 315). Section 335(b) requires the provider to reserve 4 percent to 7 percent of capacity for noncommercial programming of an educational or informational nature, with the prices not to exceed 50 percent of the total direct costs of making such an channel available, and with the DBS provider having no editorial control over any video material offered under the section. The FCC has not imposed any public interest requirements beyond those specified in the act under section 25(a) and has a proceeding under way to determine how both section 25(a) and (b) should be implemented.[24]

Because DBS uses scarce spectrum, the court held that *Red Lion* is applicable and on that basis sustained the constitutionality of section 25.[25] The case points up the unique nature of the Supreme Court's broadcast jurisprudence. The provision requiring 4 percent to 7 percent for noncommercial educational or informational purposes is reasonably related to a public interest purpose and thus can be said to come under *Red Lion*. But if the provision were tested under traditional First Amendment jurisprudence, it would raise substantial constitutional issues. First, there is the question whether the regulation is content neutral. In the case of cable, the access provisions do appear to be content neutral (commercial leased access, and noncommercial access in the form of public and governmental (a local C-SPAN; the educational channel is more problematic but might be swept along with the others). In the case of DBS, the emphasis is on educational and informational, similar to the CTA (and further, DBS is not a bottleneck multichannel provider like cable). If the DBS provision is not content neutral and thus comes under strict scrutiny, there is the question whether a compelling or extraordinary problem is being dealt with. DBS, like cable, carries a plethora of educational and informational programming (albeit most with commercials), and is eager to carry noncommercial PBS programming (and does into areas not served by local PBS stations). If there is a problem in this area, it is really with the financing of such noncommercial channels of programming—a matter left in limbo by the statute. Significantly, MMDS, which is now commencing digital operation, and LMDS, which is about to be authorized, do not come under statutory (or administrative) requirements such as section 25. In my view, this is sound, as both these services need to establish themselves. While DBS is more advanced, it seems to me that with a service reaching only roughly 5 percent of the U.S. households and still in an emerging state, section 25 should be implemented with the lightest regulatory hand at this time (that is, only the 4 percent to 7 percent requirement which is statutorily required); if DBS does become a strong, profitable video provider, there is time enough to consider what public interest requirements are called for.

Sound Regulatory Policies for Digital Broadcast Television

The 1996 Telecommunications Act specifically provides that the public interest standard is applicable to television broadcasting in the advanced (digital) era.[26] Chairman Hundt has called for "clearly defined guidelines for all uses of the airwaves [that come under the] public interest [standard]"[27] and has applauded the executive branch commission to study broadcasters' public interest obligations in a digital age.[28]

The Need for Clearly Defined Guidelines

First, so long as the act requires the application of the public interest standard, the chairman's position calling for clearly defined guidelines is sound. For public service, without further definition, is a vague concept. Commercial broadcasting is a business of fierce and ever-increasing competition.[29] In these circumstances, it is understandable that the commercial broadcaster very largely focuses on the bottom line—on maximizing profit.

The situation is similar to the issue of pollution: some businesses will be good citizens and not pollute the water, land, or air, but many others, driven by strong competition, will take the profit-maximizing route and do great damage to the environment. To prevent a Gresham's Law pattern from taking over the whole situation, the government adopts specific regulations applicable to an entire industry. It does not say to the industry: "Do right and avoid undue pollution."

But with the exception of its recent action in the area of children's television, the FCC has never adopted effective, objective guidelines for local or informational programming—that is, quantitative guidelines for these categories during prescribed times (for example, 6 a.m. to midnight and during prime time).[30] Because the FCC was proceeding under vague, "marshmallow" standards,[31] there was no effective enforcement of the public interest requirement. In 1973 FCC Chairman Dean Burch told a broadcast industry group: "If I were to pose the question, what *are* the FCC renewal policies, and what are the controlling guidelines, everyone in the room would be on equal footing. You couldn't tell me, I couldn't tell you—and no one else at the Commission could do any better."[32]

With such "mushy" standards, it is most difficult for the agency to single out some station for denial of renewal; after all, the station is in the dock because it was given no guidelines by the FCC as to what was to be expected to gain renewal. But this failure to act on an ad hoc basis compounded the problem. An action taken against one station, however unfair and perhaps subject to challenge on that score, would nevertheless serve as an example to the entire industry, with an effect comparable to that of a general regulation. The FCC, however, shirked this responsibility, even when confronted with the most serious violations.[33]

As noted, the FCC effectively deregulated broadcasting in the 1980s by adopting postcard renewal. So instead of moving in the direction of making the public interest requirement effective, it boldly undermined the whole concept, as a practical matter. Most significantly, Congress never even held a hearing on this action, much less moved to set it aside.

Congress did revise one facet with its passage of the 1990 Children's Television Act, requiring the broadcaster to serve the educational and informational needs of children, including with programming specifically designed to do so, and stating that a showing at renewal must be made as to this obligation; the postcard would not suffice in this respect. The history of the implementation of this act demonstrates the need for clearly defined guidelines.

The act became effective in October 1991. In March 1993 the FCC issued a Notice of Inquiry, because after examining renewal applications then on file, it found the following:

—No increase in the number of hours of educational and informational programming. The number of standard-length programs was at times very limited, with many licensees relying substantially on public service announcements (PSAs) and vignettes to meet the CTA obligation.

—No real change in the time slots devoted to children's programming, with CTA proponents' claims that broadcasters have slotted educational programs before 7 a.m. when the child audience is minimal.

—Some licensees are proffering such animated programs as *The Flintstones* and *GI Joe* as educational, asserting that such programs include a variety of general, pro-social themes.[34]

Another way to illustrate the need for quantitative guidelines is to examine the performance of Los Angeles VHF station, KCAL-TV, operated by the premier family and children's entertainment company, Disney. For over a year after the effective date of the CTA, KCAL-TV presented only one core educational program (that is, a program specifically designed to educate or inform children), a half-hour show at 5:30 a.m., subsequently augmented by another half-hour show at 6 a.m. After the FCC issued its notice and moved forward to implement a three-hour quantitative guideline for such core programming, KCAL-TV rapidly increased its effort to meet that guideline.[35]

The National Association of Broadcasters (NAB) argues that the approach of clearly defined guidelines for public service violates the First Amendment—that the amendment bars governmental action "requiring broadcasters to air particular types of programs."[36] But the act itself requires broadcasters to air particular types of programs—to serve as a local outlet (with indeed the entire allocations scheme based on this obligation); to present informational programming, including political broadcasts and children's educational programs.[37] The NAB is really arguing that the public trustee scheme of the act is unconstitutional. If it believes that, the question that immediately comes to the fore is why it does not challenge the constitutionality of the act, and specifically the CTA.[38]

The answer is that the NAB welcomes being called a public trustee, so long as the obligation is left vague and therefore unenforceable. If the NAB were to lose that public trustee status, it would be subject to spectrum auctions for the new digital spectrum (the law now exempts broadcast from such auctions) and spectrum usage fees. For example, in the 103d Congress, the administration, seeking to raise needed revenues, proposed a $5 billion spectrum usage fee on broadcasters (beginning at 1 percent and rising to 5 percent). The NAB successfully opposed this effort, and used the argument that the fee scheme would "change the landscape of communications policy" by eliminating broadcasters' commitment to serve the public interest in exchange for free use of the spectrum. "Broadcasters have always supported that compact, [NAB President] Fritts says. This proposal, however, puts it at risk, he says."[39]

The NAB's position is truly astounding—that it accepts the public service obligation but that any attempt to implement it by adopting quantitative guidelines as to some prescribed category such as the CTA is unconstitutional. The guideline is just that—a reasonable guideline or "safe harbor" ensuring renewal by the staff, with the renewal applicant having the right under the CTA and the FCC's rules to make further showings as to why renewal is in order.[40] If, to take an egregious case, an applicant sought renewal with only a half-hour or one hour of programming at a very early morning hour, the FCC could constitutionally deny renewal on an ad hoc basis. So the issue is why does it not serve the public interest and the First Amendment to give applicants some reasonable notice of what is required for renewal. As the court stated in the *Greater Boston* case, administrative discretion to deny renewal must be "reasonably confined by ground rules and standards."[41]

This is not to say that there are no First Amendment difficulties in the implementation of the public trustee scheme. There clearly are. Thus, the Supreme Court, while affirming the constitutionality of the scheme, has acknowledged that the scheme necessarily entails First Amendment strains—that the role of the government as "guardian of the public interest" and the role of the licensee as a "journalistic 'free agent' call for a delicate balancing of competing interests. . . . The maintenance of this balance for more than 40 years has called on both the regulators and the licensees to walk a 'tightrope' to preserve the First Amendment values written into the . . . Communications Act."[42]

Whatever public service program categories are used, for example, local, informational, nonentertainment, community issue-oriented, or "specifically designed to [educate or inform children]," definitional problems arise, particularly at the margins.[43] Take the latter category, called core educational programming.[44] Educational or informational programming for children contains a strong entertainment component, and trying to separate the two components is neither possible or appropriate. Further, it can have a social purpose instead of being cognitively directed (see n. 70). This can result in the claim that *The Little Mermaid* meets the definition of core educational programming because it shows little girls how to be leaders or assertive. Controversy can and has arisen over programs like NBC's *NBA Inside Stuff*, with the network disputing the criticism that this was not core educational fare by citing the support of two educational psychologists who assisted in its preparation.[45] This means that the act must be implemented reasonably, and specifically by affording broad programming discretion to the licensee.[46] But as shown, it clearly does not mean that there should not be clearly defined, reasonable guidelines as to the public service categories.

The Appropriate Guidelines for the Digital TV Broadcast Operation

Since the 1996 act explicitly makes the public interest standard applicable to the digital era, it is sound policy to consider what clearly defined, reasonable guidelines are appropriate for that era.[47] But before doing so, it makes sense to ask what are the sound guidelines to be adopted today as to the present analog operation. This is so for two reasons: (1) That operation will continue to dominate broadcasting for at least another decade and perhaps longer (the FCC's target date for full industry transition to digital operation is 2006); and (2) as discussed within, there is a substantial possibility that the digital operation may very largely resemble the analog one as far as guidelines are concerned.

As noted, the commission has adopted quantitative guidelines only in the area of children's television programming. The broadcast licensee remains under a general public interest obligation to serve its area through community-issue oriented programming but there are no guidelines, and indeed the renewal applicant sends only a postcard to the FCC. If the FCC were really serious about obtaining a reasonable amount of public service, it would specify some quantitative guideline in this respect. For example, the guideline ensuring renewal in television might be 15 percent of the broadast day (6 a.m. to midnight) devoted to local programming (including 15 percent in prime time), and 18 percent devoted to informational (nonentertainment) programming (including 18 percent in prime time and the three-hour core programming guideline in children's educational/informational programming).[47] In radio, the guideline might be 8 percent of the time (6 a.m. to midnight) to be devoted to nonentertainment (community issue-oriented, by another name) programming (but with an exception for specialized stations like those presenting very largely classical music—perhaps there a requirement of only 2 percent.)[49]

Such an approach would be directed at the three main content thrusts of the Communications Act—local, informational, and children's educational programming.[50] It is not a new approach but, on the contrary, resembles past failed efforts along the same line.[51] Further, there could be new refinements to this general approach. Thus, another facet of the informational requirement stressed in the act is the provision of time for political broadcasts.[52] It has been suggested that there should be a guideline of twenty minutes (in four five-minute segments, one in prime time, all on a sustaining [free] basis) to be devoted to appearances of candidates during the thirty days prior to the general election (or fifteen days in off-year elections)—that this would promote a core value of the public interest.[53]

The above proposal is directed to that value and has nothing to do with campaign reform and indeed would not in any way alleviate the need for such reform.[54] Chairman Hundt has put forward a proposal for substantial amounts of free time during the presidential general election, specifically to effect needed campaign reform.[55] Such proposals would be along the lines of the British system, whereby the parties receive free broadcast time (with the candidate appearing) and cannot purchase any additional time (in the United States, this bar would be the condition for accepting the free time, in order to meet the constitutional requirements of *Buckley* v. *Valeo*).[56] While the proposal is most worthy and certainly of the greatest pertinence to the issue of public trustee obligation, I do not pursue it further here because it is integrally involved with campaign reform rather than simply the broadcast reform issue. Stated differently, such reform is clearly for Congress, not FCC, which is a pity, since Congress, despite the recent scandalous conduct of election campaigns, so far seems most loath to act.[57]

Finally, there are undoubtedly other public interest avenues that could be explored. I do not develop this area, because while it is certainly germane and important in light of the continued applicability of the public interest standard, I strongly favor a different course as is developed later in this chapter.

Guidelines for the Digital (Advanced) Operation

Each existing TV broadcaster has been assigned a 6 MHz digital television (DTV) channel in addition to its current analog channel. The commission has not specified that the broadcaster must use the channel for high definition television (HDTV). Rather, the DTV rules provide that so long as the broadcaster provides at least one free, over-the-air service throughout the broadcast day, it can decide upon the package of digital services that it wishes to provide. The 6 MHz channel really should be thought of as 19.3 Mbs; that 19.3 Mbs can be used almost entirely for HDTV, which does require an enormous stream of data; or because of the availability of digital compression techniques, the broadcaster can now offer four to six telecasts (sacrificing some amount of definition as the number goes up); or it can use some of the capacity for digital ancillary services such as paging (see sec. 336(a)(1), (b)(1), (e) of the 1996 Telecommunications Act). The decision is for the broadcaster to make, obviously based on its business judgment.

How that decision turns out can dramatically affect the formulation of public interest guidelines for DTV. Thus, if the emerging pattern is very largely HDTV operation (with only one or two MHz for ancillary endeavors), the DTV situation does not differ from the present analog one. If, however, a multichannel operation results, there is an opportunity for greatly changed guidelines. For example, the guideline might then call for the devotion of three Mbs for public service operation. I discuss below the nature of such a guideline, but here what needs to be emphasized is that it is premature at this time to make any judgment as to which way the business decision will go. No one can now say whether the operation will be very largely HDTV or multichannel.

It might be thought the broadcaster will surely opt for very extensive multichannel operation in order to meet the challenge of multichannel competitors like cable or DBS. But that might be a bad strategy in the so-called 500 channel universe. Robert Wright, the President of NBC, has stated his belief that the broadcast networks (and their affiliates) will continue to flourish so long as they each command a share around the 12 mark.[58] This view certainly seems to be borne out by present prices for TV advertisements.[59] And for this reason, it may not be wise strategy for the broadcasters (network or local) to send out multiple programs and thus end with a share like the cable channels.[60] Further, CBS Chairman Michael Jordan and Fox Chairman Rupert Murdoch have expressed great doubt that there is advertising support for such multichannel operations.[61] This is not to say with any certainty that broadcast DTV will be largely HDTV; trade and newspaper reports indicate that there is great confusion among the broadcasters as to how to proceed.[62] My point is that it is premature to now formulate public interest guidelines for the future DTV operation when the nature of that operation is so much in doubt.

That could be the conclusion of my essay—wait and hope. But however the decision comes out—very largely HDTV or multichannel, in my view there is no real possibility for a good solution to the public interest question, and therefore a wholly different route should be taken (discussed below). This can be shown by analysing an optimum multichannel DTV public interest approach, and showing that it is still inadequate.

Suppose that in a 19.3 Mbs multichannel operation, three Mbs were required to be used for a public service channel. Such public service might be left to the discretion of the licensee and thus could include public affairs, news documentaries, political broadcasts, educational/information programming for children (in addition to any three hour guideline), and so on. Further, to insure that the broadcaster's incentive is only public service and not profit maximizing, the channel would be entirely sustaining—that is, without any commercials.[63]

The arrangement would thus reflect the original channel 3–channel 4 pattern in the United Kingdom, where channel 4 was supported by a portion of the advertising revenues garnered by channel 3. Here the public service channel would be supported by the commercial operation operation of the remaining 17 Mbs—probably four channels of commercial broadcasting.

Finally, if the broadcaster did not want to devote the three Mbs to this public service channel, it could retain the three Mbs for commercial operation, but then it would have to pay a significant sum for to a public television trust fund.[64] This "play or pay" option would reflect the thrust of sec. 303b(b) of the CTA, which was initially promoted by the FCC but then really discarded in the final decision and is not employed today, to any significant extent.

This would be a very ambitious and optimum public service approach—difficult to achieve practically and politically. But it is set forth here because analysis of it demonstrates the need for a wholly different scheme. First, if the broadcaster decided to "play" in order to avoid a significant payment, the result would very likely be adjudged a dismal failure. For, with no revenue coming in, why would the broadcaster expend the considerable sums needed to produce high-quality programming? Again, if we use children's programming as a focal point because of its central importance to the public interest, the commercial broadcaster would be most unlikely to devote the substantial sums needed to present quality children's programming. The tendency would be to "slough." Indeed, the broadcaster would regard any diversion of its audience to the "public service channel" as a loss of viewers for its advertiser-based channels. Once again, regulation is trying to force a business—one under fierce competitive pressure—to act against its driving interest to maximize profit.[65]

If the broadcaster should pay instead of play, this could contribute significantly to the production and distribution of high-quality programming by the public television community. Indeed, it is the approach that I advocate (as will be seen below). But this leads to an obvious conclusion: Since sound policy is served only by the pay rather than play option, policy should be aimed solely at obtaining that payment.

If the operation were very largely HDTV, this would, in effect, mean that the past inadequate scheme of public interest regulation would be applicable. But even if that scheme were improved along the lines suggested above, so that there were quantitative requirements for public service, such as 15 percent local, 18 percent informational (including the three-hour guideline for core children's educational programming), and so on, there would still be strong arguments militating for a new approach.

First, in the real world, public service programming is not a numbers game. The aim should be to deliver a reasonable amount of high-quality programs that educate, inform, present the classic and new drama, advance culture, serve minority interests, and so on. But in the U.S. regulatory world, any content behavioral approach must be limited to quantitative guidelines and must eschew all qualitative focus. Whether some program is good or high quality is a subjective judgment that government could address only by violating the First Amendment (and the no censorship clause of the act, 47 U.S.C. 326).

In its deregulation decisions in the 1980s, the FCC did state that it intended to emphasize "the quality of a broadcaster's efforts, not the quantity of its non-entertainment programming."[66] Thus, in its Radio and Television Deregulation reports, the commission stated:

A station with good programs addressing public issues and aired during high listenership times but amounting to only 3 percent of its weekly programming may be doing a superior job to a station airing 6 percent of entertainment little of which deals in a meaningful fashion with public issues.

The focus of our inquiry in the petition to deny context can be expected to be whether the challenged licensee acted reasonably in choosing the issues it addressed in its programming. Assessing the reasonableness of a licensee's decision will necessitate an ad hoc review to examine the circumstances in which the programming decision was made.[67]

Nothing is more chilling or inappropriate than the FCC casting itself as the national nanny for broadcasters' decisions on issues, or examining program quality to determine whether a given program is good or bad because it fails to address issues in a meaningful way. Such a regime would flagrantly violate the First Amendment and the act, and the commission has, of course, never implemented such a bizarre scenario. The whole deregulation policy, including postcard renewal, amounts to little more than a smoke screen for inaction.

There may be a great difference in quality between a *Sesame Street* and a commercial children's program that is geared largely to entertainment centered on a toy and has a claimed social purpose—between PBS *News Hour* or *Frontline* and the commercial newscasts or documentaries with "tabloid" emphasis.[68] The government is wholly and soundly precluded from considering such differences through content regulation. But since the provision of high-quality programming in the public service areas is of great importance, the government should adopt a scheme that promotes such provision rather than one in which it correctly has no say on quality and the presentation of such programming may be against the driving business interest of the commercial broadcaster.

That scheme is the one detailed below—and emphatically not the quantitative prescription of public service for HDTV. Significantly, Chairman Hundt, in commenting on the Annenberg study, observed: "The studies show that virtually all the programs aired for children on PBS were judged to be of high quality and educational; only a third of those aired on the 'Big Three' networks fell into the same category. This statistic about PBS is not surprising."[69] It is not surprising because PBS has no commercial motivation and wants solely to deliver high-quality educational programs.

Second, there are First Amendment strains in the latter approach because there will always be difficult questions at the margins, whatever the definition of public service may be. As noted, this again is best illustrated in the children's area, with its definition of core educational programming[70]: To attract the young child, the programming must have a strong entertainment quotient and the commission has wisely determined that there is no way to draw a line as to the amount of such entertainment fare (for example, that the program must be "primarily" educational rather than entertaining). When this consideration is combined with a program that purportedly seeks to teach children a lesson as to some social goal,[71] the FCC can end up reviewing content in a most sensitive area.[72] This is the "tightrope" or "delicate balance" referred to in the Supreme Court decisions. And while it is constitutional under *Red Lion*, it is also good policy to avoid or reduce such First Amendment strains, if it is possible to do so and still obtain the public service sought. It is therefore a decided plus for the approach urged below, which indeed does provide high-quality, public service programming even more effectively, that it eliminates these significant First Amendment strains.

Third, it is also good policy to avoid, as much as possible, asymmetric regulation of the various means of distribution television programming. (See "Trends and Guiding Principles" earlier in this chapter.) Because the media are so different in nature, that is not always feasible or desirable. For example, the main regulatory problem in cable is to deal with its bottleneck monopoly,[73] and in light of its great and growing channel capacity as it moves into digital delivery, access provisions like commercial leased channel and PEG are sound policy; such access provisions are not feasible as to broadcast HDTV, with its single channel of operation.[74]

But it is possible to treat over-the-air broadcasting and cable, its main and growing competitor, in a like fashion as to content regulation. Cable does not face content regulation as does broadcasting. (See "Cable Television" earlier in this chapter.) Because of cable's use of the public streets, the franchising authority can require a franchise fee of up to 5 percent, and thus financing for cable's public service (the PEG channels) is available.[75] With the approach recommended below, over-the-air broadcasting would be treated much like cable—no content requirements like provision of community issue-oriented programming (including the CTA requirements) but because broadcasting uses the public spectrum, there would be a modest spectrum usage fee to support the provision of high-quality public service through its contribution to a trust fund for public telecommunications.

Fourth, even if the quantitative guidelines suggested above were adopted, experience points up the impermanence of any behavioral scheme. As noted, prior to the FCC's deregulatory actions in the 1980s, there were a number of public interest rules and policies, including the quantitative renewal guidelines and the fairness doctrine. All these rules and policies were sloughed aside because of the policy bent of the then chairman of the FCC and his associates (indeed, Chairman Fowler referred to television as a "toaster with pictures" and asserted that at renewal the broadcaster had no obligation to children for which the FCC would hold it responsible).[76] An approach such as advanced below is much more likely not only to be effective but to persist.

The Sound Approach

In lieu of the public interest obligation, substitute a spectrum usage fee that is used to directly achieve public service goals. The sound alternative approach has been foreshadowed in the above discussion. Improving the public trustee regulatory regime, while clearly needed if that regime is retained, is not the best way to proceed. The public trustee regime will always remain a behavioral content scheme that seeks, with First Amendment strains, to make the broadcaster act against its business interests by providing much less remunerative public service and and cannot deal with the need and desirability of promoting high-quality public service programming.

The new approach would substitute a modest spectrum usage fee for the public fiduciary obligation. Congress could reasonably establish such a fee based on a percentage of gross advertising revenues, for example, 1 percent for radio and 3 percent for television. This fee might then be set in a long-term contract, for example, fifteen years, between the FCC and the broadcaster, so that it would be exempt from the effects of government policy changes toward the media.[77] The sums so garnered would go into a trust fund for public telecommunications. For the first time, we would have a policy working for the achievement of public service goals.

The focus so far has been on television, but the far-reaching benefits of the alternative approach are pointed up by considering its application to broadcast radio. There are over 11,500 radio broadcast stations. All of the large number of commercial radio stations are considered public trustees. But as far as the regulatory scheme is concerned, this is the charade previously noted. The commission has no knowledge as to their public service efforts (community issue–oriented programming). It receives only a postcard at renewal. It has never monitored the performance of these stations through community, regional, or individual spot-checks. As a practical matter, this is truly deregulation.

There are market deficiencies in radio. Commercial radio does not now supply in-depth informational programs, dramatic fare, programming for the blind, and so on. Noncommercial radio does, but it is inadequately funded. With a 1 percent spectrum fee, $130 million would be available,[78] with roughly $80 million for public radio and the remainder going to fund political broadcasts over radio, if a free-time trust fund were established as part of campaign reform.

If this new approach were adopted, the policy structure would actively promote public service goals for the first time. The commercial radio system would continue to do what it already does—deliver a variety of entertainment formats, often interspersed with brief messages—and the noncommercial system would have sufficient funds to accomplish its goals.

Significantly, this approach is much sounder than any effort to provide clearly defined guidelines for public service in radio. It gives the most promise of securing high-quality public service programming and avoids all First Amendment strains. Indeed, as shown by FCC experience under the processing guidelines in the 1970s, there can be adverse consequences in radio from the quantitative guideline approach. Because radio stations can choose a specialized format like classical music, they can have difficulty meeting even the generous guideline of 8 percent nonentertainment, and in the circumstances of major market operation, should not have to."[79]

Further, the use of public interest criteria to choose among competing appplicants in comparative hearings has been thoroughly discredited, and the whole process is now at a standstill because of court action.[80] With the new approach, all new frequencies would be auctioned, and the sums obtained (probably not too great in view of the dearth of available frequencies in larger markets) would be contributed to the same trust fund for public telecommunications.

This same approach should be applied to broadcast television. It would markedly help facilitate the production and presentation of high-quality programming like educational programming for children, in-depth informational programming such as the *News Hour* or *Frontline*, and cultural fare. It would contribute most substantially to solving the perennial funding problems of public telecommunications, which are extensively documented in *Quality Time?*, a recent report of the Twentieth Century Fund Task Force on Public Television. The most arresting statistics in the report show the amounts spent per capita by various nations for public broadcasting: In 1992, the United States spent only about $1.06; Japan spent $17.71; Canada spent $32.15; and the United Kingdom spent $38.56.[81]

To continue the example of children's educational programming because of its importance, if 1 percent of the spectrum usage fee were dedicated to this purpose (about $280 million), the Corporation for Public Broadcasting[82] could then fund production of such programming by a PBS station or an independent producer like Children's Television Workshop or for the Ready to Learn Channel.[83] The funds might also be directed to local noncommercial stations working with community groups to activate the educational channel on the local cable system, with some of the programs so produced then broadcast or shared with the local library system to become an electronic educational clearinghouse.[84]

It has been argued that there is no need for the public service contribution of public television in light of cable's multichannel development. The above report establishes the continuing need for the public service contribution of public broadcasting, especially in the area of education. That discussion, while relied upon here, will not be repeated. Again, just to give one example, there is a clear need not just for the excellent preschool fare on public television but also for the strong development of programming aimed at the school-aged child, five to eleven years old. There is no basis for the assumption that cable will fill this need. Further, cable is a pay service and is not received in roughly one-third of all TV households.[85]

This then is the concept for the new approach. There are of course many details to be resolved in its implementation.[86] There are several ways that the funds could be transferred—for example, to accumulate in the trust fund until $4 billion is reached, and at that point the federal support ceases. Or the funds could be divided between the trust fund for public telecommunications and another fund for free political time.[87] Again, such considerations, while of great importance, must await progress or agreement on the main concept—to move forward to replace the public trustee scheme.

Aside from the merits, there are other large obstacles. The commercial broadcasters will strongly oppose the reform, because they would much rather "play" than pay 1 to 3 percent of gross revenues. As has been noted by congressional leaders,[88] the commercial broadcasters are a most powerful lobbying force. But just as campaign reform is difficult to achieve but nevertheless most worthy of being fought for this year and every year, the same thing is true of reform of the public trustee scheme. It took many years of effort to reform transportation or the common carrier scheme in the 1934 act, but those efforts eventually paid off. The same effort should be made here.

Another obstacle is the need for revenues to achieve a balanced budget. This has resulted in the billions obtained through the spectrum auction process all going to deficit reduction,[89] and indeed skewing the auction process.[90] So, here again, Congress could decide on a spectrum usage fee but use the revenues for its own deficit purposes—and thus not to provide high-quality public service over an adequately funded public telecommunications system. But the monies here are being uniquely generated—replacing the public trustee obligation precisely to obtain funds to provide more effectively the needed public service. If the concept is adopted on this ground, the funds should and would go to public telecommunications.

Policies for the Other Main Electronic Media

There is no need for extended discussion on this point. The new electronic delivery systems, telco, LMDS, digital MMDS, Internet video streaming (or other computer delivery systems), all should not come under *Red Lion* content regulation as a matter of policy (wholly aside from most serious constitutional issues). These nascent video delivery systems should be allowed to develop with no intrusive content regulation, in many cases forever, but certainly at this time.

Cable is well established, is a most powerful force in video, and will become even stronger as it enters the digital era. As noted, *Red Lion* cannot constitutionally be applied to cable, which comes under the traditional First Amendment jurisprudence. Congress has soundly eschewed *Red Lion* content regulation, and that policy should continue.

There is a problem as to the PEG channels in light of inadequate support at the local level in many instances. In the circumstances, including the political or practical considerations, it would appear that this problem will have to be solved over time at the local level. Stated differently, if, for example, some communities develop strong and effective local C-SPANs, this may well put pressure on other communities to ensure that resources are available to duplicate that kind of strong service in their own localities. As just noted, efforts to strengthen the local public television station may also be helpful in promoting a stronger PEG effort.

As for the problem with commercial leased access, the move to digital should mean that there is a significant amount of new leased channel capacity available (since the 15 percent requirement would be applicable to the new digital channels). It is to be hoped that the FCC's recent revision as to reasonable pricing for leased channel will be effective. In my view, it would be better policy simply to require the cable operator to engage in last-offer arbitration if no agreement on terms is reached after a stated brief period.[91] Under this scenario, the programmer would obtain immediate access during the arbitration period after posting a bond to ensure financial performance. This would track the market better than authorizing the government to set prices and terms, and it would have offered a practical prerequisite to success for any programmer—prompt access to distribution—instead of a government proceeding.

The other substantial video distributer is DBS, with 5 percent penetration of U.S. TV households, and the prospect of about 10 percent by 2000. As stated, there should be no action to implement sec. 25(a) (other than rules such as equal time for candidates). As for the 4 percent to 7 percent set aside for noncommercial educational and informational access, the real problem here is the lack of financial support for the production of programming. In that respect, the above spectrum usage approach should be most helpful, since the funds thus made available are for public *telecommunications* and thus would foster distribution over DBS for noncommercial educational-informational material produced with the markedly enhanced financial support.

Conclusion

My main focus has been on appropriate governmental policy for DTV because there is now such great focus on that issue at the White House, Congress, and the FCC. What is remarkable is that with the one exception noted below, the focus is confined to how the public interest standard should apply in the digital era. Thus, the approaches of the executive branch and the FCC appear to give no consideration at all as to whether that standard should continue to apply, or whether it should be replaced by a approach such as here advocated.

In the 1996 Telecommunications Act, Congress considered the common carrier approach that had been used for decades (from 1910 on) and drastically reformed the regulatory scheme. But as noted, the same act continues the basic broadcast regulatory scheme that has been applied since 1927. The House Telecommunications Subcommittee, under Chairman Billy Tauzin, is raising the issue of its continuance. His proposal would substitute a spectrum usage fee for the public interest obligation of the commercial broadcaster, with the sums so obtained going to a trust fund for public broadcasting. It is to be hoped that this is the beginning of a long overdue debate on what the sound governmental policy for broadcasting is as the nation moves into the next century.

Notes

1. See, for example, speech before the Cellular Telephone Industry Association (CTIA) convention, March 4, 1997, app. 3; and *Broadcasting and Cable Magazine*, March 3, 1997, pp. 32–33. After the preparation of this article Reed Hundt resigned in late 1997 and was replaced by the former general counsel William Konnard. It is widely believed that Konnard will largely follow the same policies as Hundt in the broadcast field.

2. See statement of the Vice President on Public Interest Obligations in a Digital Age, February 5, 1997; and executive order 13038, issued March 12, 1997, establishing the Advisory Committee on Public Interest Obligations of Digital Television Broadcasters.

3. See Robert Pepper, "Broadcasting Policies in a Multichannel Market-place," in Charles M. Firestone, ed., *Television for the 21st Century: The Next Wave* (Washington: Aspen Institute Communications and Society Program, 1993), p. 120; and Henry Geller, *1995–2005: Regulatory Reform for the Principal Electronic Media* (Washington, D.C.: Annenberg Washington Program, November 1994), pp. 7–8.

4. *Television Digest*, May 12, 1997, p. 2.

5. See "Network TV Sales Head Skyward as Audience Size Remains a Lure," *Wall Street Journal*, June 5, 1997, p. B12, and "Why TV Ad Prices Are Rising as Viewship Is Falling," June 12, 1997, p. B1.

6. The telcos do not appear to be a substantial factor in the near term, but they must eventually turn to broadband transmission (and indeed, several are proceeding with expansive fiber programs). The Internet, while it faces considerable obstacles today for video distribution, may well be a most important future factor. See, for example, *New York Times*, June 10, 1997, pp. D1, D5; and "Here Come the Computers," *Broadcasting and Cable Magazine*, April 9, 1997, p. 6.

7. See *Metro Broadcasting, Inc.* v. *FCC*, 497 U.S. 547, 566–67 (1990), quoting *Associated Press* v. *U.S.*, 326 U.S. 1, 20 ("widest possible dissemination of information from diverse and antagonistic sources is essential to the welfare of the public").

8. Ibid. Thus, the proposal to allow newspaper to own television stations in the same area (*Broadcasting and Cable Magazine*, June 9, 1997, p. 20) or to permit duopoly ownership of local TV stations goes markedly against the diversification principle. People rely on TV stations and the newspaper for information on local issues, and therefore these powerful media should be in separately owned hands. While DBS, cable television, and other media may contribute to informing as to national issues, they are not relevant to local issues. This area, while of the greatest importance, is not treated further in this chapter.

9. Deregulation of Radio, 84 FCC2d 968, 969, 978, 982 (1981), aff'd *UCC* v. *FCC*, 797 F.2d 1413, 1426–30 (D.C. Cir. 1983); Commercial TV Stations, 96 FCC2d 1076 (1984).

10. *Turner Broadcasting System, Inc.* v. *FCC*, 114 S.Ct. 2445 (1994).

11. *Red Lion Broadcasting Co.* v. *FCC*, 395 U.S. 367 (1969); *NBC* v. *U.S.*, 319 U.S. 190, 226–27 (1943).

12. See note 9.

13. Cowles Florida Broadcasting, Inc., 60 FCC2d 371, 439 (1976).

14. For a fuller discussion of this long pattern of failure, see Geller, *1995–2005*, pp. 12–17.

15. See section 624(f)(1), 47 U.S.C. 544(f)(1).

16. See note 7.

17. *Turner*, 114 S. Ct., 2457. The Court, while agreeing that the cable market reflects dysfunction, also rejected the extension of Red Lion on that basis, holding that the physical, rather than economic, characteristics of the broadcast market, underlie the Court's broadcast jurisprudence, and that the claim of market dysfunction "is not sufficient to shield a speech regulation from the First Amendment standards applicable to nonbroadcast media," p. 2458.

18. In *Denver Area Telecommunications Consortium* v. *FCC*, 116 S. Ct. 2374 (1996), involving the constitutionality of provisions dealing with indecent programming over PEG and commercial leased channels, a plurality led by Justice Breyer, used a new standard instead of strict scrutiny, called "close judicial scrutiny" (pp. 2385–86). Under that test, the plurality substitutes "extremely important" problems (or "extraordinary problems") for "compelling interest" and "sufficiently tailored" or "appropriately tailored" (p. 2397) for "least restrictive means." The five other members adhered to *Turner* and employed strict scrutiny.

19. *U.S.* v. *O'Brien*, 391 U.S. 367, 377 (1968). Under this standard, a content-neutral regulation is valid if it "furthers an important or substantial governmental interest; if the governmental interest is unrelated to the suppression of free expression; and if the incidental restriction on alleged First Amendment freedoms is no greater than is essential to the furtherance of that interest."

20. The constitutionality of the PEG and commercial leased channel provisions was sustained under intermediate (*O'Brien*) analysis in *Time Warner Entertainment Co., L.P.* v. *FCC*, 93 F.3d 957, 967–973 (D.C. Cir. 1996).

21. For a full discussion of this and the leased channel problems, see Geller, *1995–2005*, pp. 28–31.

22. See section 9 of the 1992 Act; 47 U.S.C. Sec, 532.

23. Second Report and Order on Leased Commercial Access, 62 Fed. Reg. 11364 (March 12, 1997), appeal pending, *Value Vision Int., Inc.* v. *FCC*, D.C. Cir. No. 97-1138.

24. Implementation of Section 25 of the Cable Television Consumer and Competitive Act of 1992, MM Docket 93-25.

25. *Time Warner Entertainment Co., L.P.* v. *FCC*, 93 F.3d, 973–77, reh. denied, February 7, 1997 (five judges voting for rehearing and stating their belief that the DBS provision is unconstitutional, three voting against rehearing, and two recusing themselves).

26. See section 336(d) of the 1996 Telecommunications Act, 47 U.S.C. 335(d).

27. See speech before the CTIA, 1997.

28. Statement of Chairman Hundt, February 5, 1997. Chairman Kenard has also stated his interest in obtaining "advice from the vice president's advisory committee on public interest obligations in the digital age." *Broadcasting and Cable Magazine*, February 2, 1998, pp. 6–7.

29. See, for example, "Losing Viewers to Cable, Again," *New York Times*, May 22, 1997, p. B6.

30. See *National Black Media Coalition* v. *FCC*, 589 F.2d 578 (D.C. Cir. 1978). From 1973 to the early 1980s, the FCC had processing guidelines governing nonentertainment programming and local programming for its renewal staff, so that the staff could grant renewal under delegated authority. See *UCC* v. *FCC*, 707 F.2d 1415, 1420–21 (D.C. Cir. 1985).

31. Testimony of Chairman Dean Burch, Hearings on Broadcast Renewal License before the House Subcommittee on Communications, 93d Cong. 1 sess. (Government Printing Office, 1973), ser. 93-36, pt. 2, p. 1120; En Banc Pro-

gramming Inquiry, 44 FCC2d 230 (1960); Ascertainment of Community Problems by Broadcast Applicants, 57 FCC2d 418 (1976); Revision of FCC Form 303, 54 FCC2d 750 (1976).

32. Dean Burch, address to the International Radio and Television Society, September 14, 1973, FCC Memo 06608, p. 3.

33. See, for example, *Lamar Life Broadcasting Co.*, 38 FCC 1143 (1965), rev'd, *UCC v. FCC*, 359 F.2d 994 (D.C. Cir. 1965); 425 F.2d 543 (D.C. Cir. 1969); *Kord, Inc.*, 31 FCC2d 85 (1961); *Moline Television Corp.*, 31 FCC2d 263 (1971); *Herman Hall*, 11 FCC2d 344 (1968).

34. See Notice of Inquiry, 8 FCC Rcd 1841, 1842.

35. See Petition of CME, et al., to Deny Applications for Consent to Transfer of Control of Broadcast Licenses Held by Capital Cities/ABC to the Walt Disney Company, File Nos. BTC, BTCH, and BTCCT-950823KA-960823LI, pp. 29–30. For the definition of core educational programming, see note 70.

36. *Broadcasting and Cable Magazine*, April 7, 1997, p. 36, response of President Edward Fritts, National Association of Broadcasters.

37. See "Trends and Guiding Principles" early in this chapter.

38. The allocational scarcity on which the public trustee scheme rests persists today, with no channels or frequencies available in most markets and with stations being sold at very high prices because of the scarcity. See Geller, *1995–2005*, p. 11, n. 16.

39. K. McAvoy, "Dingell May Be Set to Derail Onerous Spectrum Fee," *Broadcasting and Cable Magazine*, June 13, 1994, pp. 42–43; and *Multichannel News*, May 23, 1994, p. 130 (where an industry spokesman warned that if the fee were implemented, the public service obligation would have to be removed).

40. See CTA, sec. 303b(b); FCC Report on CTA, FCC 96-335, par. 135 (1996).

41. *Greater Boston Television Corp. v. FCC*, 444 F.2d 841, 854 (D.C. Cir. 1970), cert. denied, 402 U.S. 1007 (1970).

42. *CBS v. DNC*, 412 U.S. 94, 117–18 (1973): "A licensee must balance what it might prefer to do as a private entrepreneur with what it is required to do as a 'public trustee.' To perform its statutory duties, the Commission must oversee without censoring."

43. For a full discussion of this proposition, see Henry Geller, "Broadcasting," in P. Newberg, ed., *New Directions in Telecommunications Policy* (Duke University Press, 1989), pp. 125–54.

44. See note 70.

45. Thus, in the *1997 State of Children's Television Report: Programming for Children over Broadcast and Cable Television* (Annenberg Public Policy Center of the University of Pennsylvania, June 9, 1997) (hereafter *Annenberg Report*), there is the finding (p. 4) that "one quarter of the commercial broadcasters' E/I [educational/informational] programs could not be considered educational by any reasonable bench mark." This finding included network shows like *NBA Inside Stuff*; ABC, *New Adventures of Winnie the Pooh*; and CBS, *Secrets of the Crypt-keeper's Haunted House*. *Broadcasting and Cable Magazine*, June 16, 1997, p. 21.

46. *CBS* v. *DNC*, 412 U.S., 110 ("Congress intended to permit private broadcasting to develop with the widest journalistic freedom consistent with its public obligations").

47. See "Sound Regulatory Policies for Digital Broadcast Television" in this chapter.

48. The two figures would overlap since, for example, local news would of course also count towards the informational guideline. Chairman Hundt's proposal of a "modest 5 percent of programming time on digital TV" for public service is too modest, in my opinion. See speech to the International Radio and Television Society, October 18, 1996, p. 1.

49. See "Radio Ad Sales Rise Amid Consolidations," *Wall Street Journal*, June 20, 1977, p. B7.

50. See "The Current Regulatory Schemes" early in this chapter.

51. For a detailed discussion of such efforts, see Bill F. Chamberlin, "Lessons in Regulating Information Flow: The FCC's Weak Track Record in Interpreting the Public Interest Standard," *North Carolina Law Review*, vol. 60 (June 1982), pp. 1057, 1083–86, 1093–94.

52. See sections 312(a)(7); 315; S. Rept. No. 92-96, 92d Cong. l sess., p. 28.

53. For a full discussion of this concept, see Petition of Common Cause, et al., for Inquiry or Rulemaking to Require Free Time for Political Broadcasts, filed October 21, 1993. It should be acknowledged that the author is one of two attorneys on the petition. No action has ever been taken on the petition.

54. See above Petition, pp. 6 (n.7), 8, 18.

55. See, for example, Paul Taylor, "Superhighway Robbery," *New Republic*, May 5, 1997, p. 22.

56. 424 U.S. 1 (1976). See the recent speech of former Chairman Newton Minow to the Economic Club of Chicago, April 16, 1997 (*Congressional Record*, April 19, 1997, p. E774) for a fuller exposition of the approach. It is necessary to impose the above condition because otherwise the candidates would accept the free time and still engage in expensive purchases of additional time, so that the need to raise huge sums of money would not be tempered at all. See note 57.

57. See interview with Senator John McCain, chairman of the Senate Commerce Committee, *Broadcasting and Cable Magazine*, March 3, 1997, p. 20: "I don't believe that anything is going to happen which gives free television time to candidates unless it's part of an overall campaign reform package, which will have to be legislation passed by Congress. . . . Congress would naturally rebel if Mr. Hundt said, 'Well, OK, we're going to give this time to candidates without the rest of a reform package being passed.' It would be a total non-starter. . . . Because unless you had some restraint on campaign spending, that would just be another freebie for candidates."

58. *Broadcasting and Cable Magazine*, March 6, 1995, p. 6.

59. See, for example, "Why TV Ad Prices Are Rising Even as Viewership Is Falling," *Wall Street Journal*, May 12, 1997, p. B1: "As TV watchers spread their viewing over several, if not dozens, of the nation's 200-plus cablechannels . . . advertisers have found it nearly impossible to reach the sort of mass audiences

they crave. Broadcasters say it is this fracturing of the market that has made broadcast television so valuable."

60. Thus, Michael Jordan, CBS chairman, has stated that the TV audience already is saturated with program choices from multichannel providers, so "real competitive advantage for broadcasters will be HDTV rather than multichannel standard definition." *Television Digest*, June 16, 1997, p. 8.

61. Ibid.; and *Washington Post*, April 28, 1997, p. A10. See also *Broadcasting and Cable Magazine*, March 17, 1997, p. 18.

62. For example, *Communications Daily*, May 29, 1997, p. 2 (ABC has questions about DTV but no answers yet).

63. As to children's programming, no toy could be spun off for commercial sale until the passage of some substantial period—say, eighteen months to two years.

64. I use the term public television, but the operation would more aptly be described as public telecommunications, using all methods of video distribution (for example, over-the-air terrestrial, DBS, cable, MMDS, LMDS, cassettes).

65. It could be argued that all this stems from the ban on advertising on the public service channel. But if that ban is lifted, we face the same problems already described—the drive to gain advertising support by emphasizing the entertainment/social purpose aspect of children's programming; the resulting First Amendment problems; and so on.

66. *UCC v. FCC*, 779 F.2d 702, 710 (D.C. Cir. 1985).

67. Radio Deregulation, 84 FCC2d, p. 991; Commercial TV Stations, 98 FCC2d, p. 1095, par. 39.

68. See, for example, Steven Stark, "Local News: The Biggest Scandal on TV," *Washington Monthly*, June 1997, p. 38.

69. See note 45; and *Television Digest*, June 16, 1997, p. 7. The *Annenberg Report* necessarily involved both "objective and subjective measures" (p. 11), and therefore cannot be looked to for precise statistics. The figures are properly relied upon as rough indications made by an independent and responsible academic organization. Thus, in the example in the text, even if the figures are not precisely accurate, the great disparity between PBS and the three networks is being soundly portrayed.

70. Core educational programs are defined in the Report on CTA, FCC 96-335, par. 4 (1996) as those that (i) are specifically designed for children age 16 or under; (ii) have serving the educational and information needs of children as a significant purpose; (iii) are regularly scheduled, weekly programs of at least 30 minutes; and (iv) are presented between the hours of 7 a.m. and 10 p.m. On the crucial element, (ii), the FCC looks to "content that would further the development of the child in any respect, including the child's cognitive/intellectualor emotional/social needs." See *Annenberg Report*, pp. 11, 15.

71. See Report on CTA, p. 14, n. 70. The *Annenberg Report* notes (pp. 20–21) that the "most common 'primary lesson' in the broadcasters' educational programs was one that emphasized social/emotional skills (42.7 percent), and that "nearly all of the network-provided programs had prosocial messages as

their primary educational goal," because such programs garner higher ratings than those with a primary cognitive/intellectual message.

72. Thus, it might have to review the one-quarter of E/I programs as to which the *Annenberg Report* concluded "could not be considered educational by any reasonable benchmark" (p. 4). In this context, Chairman Hundt acknowledged that "this definitional issue is . . . the crux of our rules and by far the most difficult." *Television Digest*, June 16, 1997, p. 8. One industry spokesman complained that the process "comes very close to putting someone [from government] in my program department" (p. 8).

73. See *Turner,* 114 S.Ct., 2466, 2468.

74. If broadcasting in the digital era did operate in a multichannel mode, it might be possible to impose some reasonable access requirement on the public service channel (three Mbs) discussed before.

75. Before the 1984 Cable Act, the franchise fee had to be used for cable-related purposes, such as support of the PEG channels. This was changed in the 1984 Act. See Geller, *1995–2005,* pp. 28–29, for a discussion of this change and its result. It is now a matter of discretion with the franchising authority whether adequate support is given to the PEG channels.

76. See Henry Geller, "The FCC under Mark Fowler," COMM/ENT, *Hastings Journal of Communications and Entertainment Law,* vol. 10 (Winter 1988), pp. 521, 530–31.

77. Administrations have become hostile to the broadcast media because of what they regarded as too critical a press attitude. See Henry Geller, "The Comparative Renewal Process," *Virginia Law Review,* vol. 61 (1975), pp. 471, 498; and F. Friendly, "Politicizing TV," *Columbia Journalism Review* (March–April 1973), p. 9 (threatening actions of the Nixon administration).

78. See "Radio Ad Sales Rise amid Consolidations," *Wall Street Journal,* June 20, 1977, p. B7.

79. To give one example, KIBE-AM, a San Francisco classical music station, bowing to the FCC dictates, substituted a 6:00 a.m. talk show for a baroque music program, in order to gain renewal without going through an expensive hearing that it could ill afford. See Letter of April 6, 1976, from Edward Davis, station manager, to the author. In this way, it did the least damage to its schedule. But the audience, which could turn to several other stations if it wanted "talk," lost a program which it enjoyed. The regulatory pattern, when so applied, does not serve the public interest.

80. See *Bechtel* v. *FCC,* 10 F.3d 875 (1993); "Mixed Signals," *Wall Street Journal,* June 18, 1997, p. A1 (quoting Chairman Hundt as saying, "We're in gridlock" and describing the comparative hearing as "cumbersome," one "of subjective judgment [which is] a recipe for lawyering deals"). In section 3002 (a) (3) of the Budget Act of 1997, Congress, in order to end the gridlock, gave the FCC the authority to use competitive bidding if there is no settlement among the parties.

81. *Quality Time?* The Report of the Twentieth Century Fund Task Force on Public Television (Twentieth Century Fund Press, 1993), p. 152. As a member of the task force, the author fully agreed with the report and its recommendations.

82. *Quality Time?* recommended several important changes in the governance of the public broadcasting system. See pp. 35–39.

83. Commendably, Congress created the Ready to Learn Channel to which parents could reliably turn for children's programming; unfortunately, it has never adequately funded this undertaking.

84. *Quality Time?* pp. 20–21.

85. Chairman Hundt opposes the above approach because he believes that "educational programming needs to be on the most popular channels, where viewers will see the show"; he "likened the placing of such shows on a separate channel to creating 'an educational ghetto.'" *Broadcasting and Cable Magazine*, June 16, 1997, p. 20. But as noted, the PBS educational programs are consistently of high quality, are not so heavily weighted toward social goals, and are viewed by a substantial child audience (and with increased funds for marketing to parents, would be able to increase such viewing). Further, the governmental goal must be to ensure the availability of the high-quality programming to all age groups; it is a plus—not a disadvantage—that the parent can turn to noncommercial channels and direct the child's viewing to such channels. If the parent abdicates and does not supervise the child's viewing, the child will turn to the "most popular channels" and will find "low-quality" programs "full of violence and devoid of any educational value." *Annenberg Report*, p. 29.

86. Broadcasting would be subject to government regulation of obscene material and would continue to face the problem of indecent broadcasts, because this regulation is not based on the public trustee concept. See *FCC v. Pacifica Co.*, 438 U.S. 726 (1978). But enforcement would no longer involve denial or revocation of license but only forfeiture.

Further, broadcasters would still have to follow sponsorship identification provisions, multiple ownership rules, rigged quiz or payola restrictions, and so on, all of which would be enforced by cease and desist and/or forfeiture rulings. The equal opportunities provisions (including no censorship) would continue, although in my view equal opportunities should apply only to paid time. I do not discuss these points further because however difficult or important a particular aspect may be, the primary focus must be on the need to replace the public trustee scheme. The devil may be in the details, but without agreement on the central issue, we shall never arrive at the details.

87. See the proposal of Paul Taylor, "Creating a TV Time Bank," *New Democrat*, vol. 9 (May–June 1997), pp. 14–15.

88. Thus, Senator McCain stated that broadcasters were the most powerful lobby that he had encountered in Washington. *Washington Post*, February 16, 1997, p. H5.

89. Chairman Hundt has recognized public broadcasting's need for "significant, long-term, reliable funding" (*Television Digest*, June 16, 1997, p. 7), but believes that such funding should come from spectrum auctions rather than the spectrum usage fee approach urged here. See *Broadcasting and Cable Magazine*, June 16, 1997, p. 20. That solution has been proposed for years and is simply not going to happen because of Congress's drive for deficit reduction, with all

the auction funds committed for many years to that purpose. To advance it yet again in 1997 is a "cop-out."

90. See Peter Passell, *New York Times*, February 6, 1997, p. C2.

91. In last-offer arbitration, the arbitrator chooses between the final offers of the two parties, forcing them to be realistic and thus closely emulating the market bargaining process.

CHAPTER TWENTY-TWO

Toward a Better Integration of Media Economics and Media Competition Policy

Steven S. Wildman

W HILE THE PRINCIPLES of economics are general, their application to any given industry is not necessarily transparent. Much of the challenge and joy of studying the economics of specific industries lies in the process of discovering the subtle and diverse ways that basic economic forces are manifest in the workings of different markets and industries. This is certainly the case with the economics of the mass media and with the use of economics to guide the development of media policy. In fact, it is fair to say that much of our current understanding of the economics of the mass media was developed as economists attempted to address various media policy issues of the day.

Examples of how the economic study of media industries has been stimulated by attempts to address prominent communication policy issues are many. Peter Steiner's seminal paper on how advertiser-supported broadcasters selected their programming, which contrasted monopoly and competitive solutions, was developed at a time when the wisdom of relying on competitive broadcasters rather than a monopolized industry to deliver programs to viewers was far from a settled matter.[1] Roger Noll, Merton Peck, and John McGowan's influential study of television regulation examined the implications of the new regulations on broadcast networks' relationships with their affiliates and program suppliers that were being debated in the 1960s and early 1970s.[2] Approximately a decade later, an extensive FCC-sponsored study of the economics of the television industry and television regulation laid the analytical groundwork for the nearly wholesale dismantling of these regulations that has occurred since.[3] More recently, economists have responded to issues raised by the deregulation of cable television in the 1980s and its subsequent reregulation in the early 1990s with a series of books examining the economics of cable television.[4]

Although the economic perspective on media policy has not always been widely appreciated, today the benefits of incorporating economic analysis in the development of media policy are accepted almost without question. The goals of economic regulation are often economic in intent, and even when not, compliance with and the consequences of regulations are influenced by economic incentives. However, because economic thinking is continually evolving and advances in economic thinking are typically incorporated in policy design with a substantial lag, the process of integrating economic perspectives in media policy is never complete. This chapter offers three suggestions for better aligning media competition policy with the underlying economics of media industries, with emphasis on applications to competition policy for video services.

The first suggestion is that what economists know about the economics of public goods be better integrated into the development of policies for media industries. The content of a media product is what economists call a public good, which means roughly that it is not used up as it is consumed. The fact that fifty million households have already tuned in to the Super Bowl does not diminish the amount of the program available to the fifty million and first household. Because content drives the demand for media products and typically accounts for a substantial fraction of their costs, an understanding of the economics of competition in public goods is essential to an informed analysis of competition in media industries. Unfortunately, while the basic framework for analyzing the effects of competition on media firms' content expenditures was presented in the economics literature approximately a quarter of a century ago, and was used to address important communication policy issues of that time, this perspective was never incorporated as part of the standard economics tool kit for media policy analysis.[5]

The second suggestion is that attempts to assess the effectiveness of competition in video advertising markets explicitly recognize certain unavoidable links between the markets that supply programming to viewers and the markets that sell advertisers the opportunity to present their messages to viewers. Because a viewer's decision whether to watch a program or not is based in part on the split of program time between commercials and the program content, programming suppliers who derive some portion of their revenues from the sale of advertising, as is the case for television and radio stations, all broadcast networks, and most cable networks, have no choice but to consider both viewers' and advertisers' responses to the amount of ad time they sell if they want to maximize their profits. Implications for competition policy of the fact that these two markets are linked by viewers' responses to the amount of commercial time they encounter in television programs are developed below. The analysis builds on earlier work by James Rosse that modeled the interaction between subscriber demands and advertiser demands for newspapers.[6] Again, the perspective applied is not new to the economics literature, but it has been largely ignored in the development of competition policies for media industries.

The chapter also looks at how markets are defined for purposes of assessing the intensity with which video programming services compete in the supply of audiences to advertisers and finds that the current approach, which calculates programming suppliers' shares of aggregate national audiences, is often at odds with the way that advertisers assess their options for getting their messages to viewers. The suggestion here is that the goals of media competition policy would be better served if relevant markets were defined and the vigor of competition assessed by examining the options available to advertisers for purchasing access to individual viewers, rather than viewers in the aggregate.

Public Goods and Competition in the Supply of Media Products

The distinction between what economists call private goods and public goods is critical to the analysis of competition in media industries. A product or service is a private good if the nature of the good is such that one person's consumption of a particular unit of that good precludes its consumption by someone else. Most nonmedia products are private goods. Two people cannot eat the same hamburger, drive the same car (at the same time), or play with the same tennis racket. By contrast, one person's consumption of a public good does not preclude its consumption by another individual. National defense is a commonly used example of a public good. All citizens of a country are defended in equal measure, and one person's consumption of national defense does not diminish the extent to which another is defended against foreign enemies. Media products typically have both public and private good elements. Paper, ink, celluloid, videotape, and compact disks are all private goods. However, the content of a media product is a public good. The number of people who can enjoy the works of Shakespeare in the future is undiminished by the number of people who have read or seen his plays in the past.

The demand for a media product is determined largely by its content, which is a public good, and content creation typically accounts for a large, and often dominant, share of the costs of media products. Therefore, to accurately model competition in media markets it is necessary to understand the nature of competition in public goods. Of critical importance is the fact that the demand for a media product is a function of the amount spent to create its content. While the outcome is by no means certain, on average a media firm can attract a larger audience and collect more from the members of its audience if it budgets more for content creation. For example, films and television programs typically attract larger audiences if they are cast with the major stars who command the highest salaries (which is why their salaries are so high). Similarly, by spending more money a producer can hire more talented directors and writers and can create more spectacular special effects, all of which contribute to audience appeal and, ultimately, to revenue.

The fact that the basic appeal of a media product is a choice variable to the firm that sells it complicates the task of designing policies that improve the policy performance of media industries in several ways. Two related to economic efficiency are addressed here.[7] The first relates to the fact that consumers are likely to differ in the benefits they perceive in media firms' expenditures on content. In this situation, it is unlikely that a media firm will set its content expenditures at the level that maximizes the value created for consumers net of content costs. This observation is not specific to media products but applies to all products for which producers' investments in product quality confer benefits on all of their customers. The likelihood of departures from optimality in quality and content investments was first pointed out by A. Michael Spence in an article that laid out the profit calculus implicit in the choice of product quality.[8] Spence's insight was that in calculating the return to an extra dollar spent improving quality, a firm that has to set a common price for all its customers focuses on the impact of that dollar on the revenue it can collect from the marginal customer served, that is, the consumer who is just indifferent between taking the product or not. However, there is no reason why the value of a small change in quality to the marginal consumer should closely approximate the value of the same small change in quality to inframarginal customers whose decisions to take the product are unlikely to be influenced by a small change in quality.

Subsequent work has shown that when consumers differ in how much they value product quality, competitors may differentiate themselves by offering products with different levels of quality.[9] This is not necessarily an optimal solution to the quality setting problem, however, because in segmenting the market competitors sacrifice economies of scale in the production of quality to achieve a better matching of product quality to variation in the intensity of consumer preferences for quality. However, the problem of the marginal consumer having too much influence on the quality/content expenditure decision should be ameliorated to the extent that firms can find ways to successfully segment markets and charge prices that reflect variation in the values different consumers attach to quality/content improvements. For this reason, the various mechanisms that media firms employ to segment markets, such as releasing films at different prices in different distribution channels (for example, cinema, video cassettes, cable networks, and television stations), probably improve the efficiency with which media markets function.

For the most part, economists studying media industries have approached the quality/content expenditure decision from a different perspective, focusing on factors that influence the level of content expenditures, rather than on whether these expenditures are set at optimal levels. R. W. Crandall and R. E. Park, in their studies of the prospects for a fourth commercial television network, were the first to incorporate the content expenditure decision in a formal model of competition among profit-maximizing media firms.[10] Similar models were later developed by economists studying the international trade in media products, particularly films and television programs.[11]

Both sets of studies showed that factors under the control of policy-makers could significantly influence the content expenditures of media firms by altering the returns to content investments. The Crandall and Park analyses predicted that one consequence of new competitors in television markets would be a reduction in content expenditures by incumbent firms. Because an expanded range of choices for viewers makes it more difficult for individual competitors to increase their audiences by spending more on content, the profit maximizing response to increased competition is to reduce content expenditures. While the Crandall and Park models were specific to ad-supported broadcasters, subsequent work by David Waterman showed that this result generalizes to situations where consumers pay for media products.[12]

Waterman's analysis also demonstrates the possibility that the number

of firms in a competitive equilibrium may exceed the number that maximizes economic benefits, because, beyond a certain point, the loss in
consumer surplus attributable to incumbent firms' reductions in content
expenditures as they respond to increased competition more than offsets
the surplus contributions of the products introduced by the entrants.
Waterman's model is not general enough to support a claim that the
equilibrium number of firms in a competitive media market always exceeds the welfare-maximizing number,[13] but the finding that there is a
cost associated with increased competition in the form of reduced spending on the content of media products is general and should be reflected
in media competition analyses.[14] This is not to say that in the current
environment consumers would or would not benefit on net from increased competition in media markets; but the fact that competition
comes with a cost as well as the traditional benefits of greater diversity
and a heightened incentive to produce efficiently means that the optimal
number of competitors is lower than it would be without this cost.

A similar caution applies to other policies that affect the revenue media
firms can extract from media markets. An important focus of the research
on the international trade in media products has been on the effect of
domestic market size (where markets are defined by either nationality or
common languages) on the budgets for films and television programs.
One of the findings of this research is that the larger are the potential
revenues that might be earned in a market, the more media firms spend
competing for shares of these revenues. Compared to films and programs
produced in other languages, English language productions have very
large production budgets, and, owing in large part to their high production values, they sell very well in other markets. However, English language productions have also benefited in the international arena from
the fact that, until recently, the revenue available in the domestic markets
for films and programs produced in other languages has been artificially
reduced by government restrictions on advertising and various forms of
pay television. A clear implication of the media trade studies is that, like
increased competition, policies that reduce the revenue media firms can
realize on the sale of their products are also likely to have a cost in terms
of reduced expenditures on content valued by viewers. This cost should
also be considered along with whatever benefits, such as lower prices,
are anticipated from policies that reduce media firms' earnings.

Unfortunately, while the basic analytical framework for considering
the effects of increased competition and policies restricting revenues was

developed and published nearly twenty-five years ago, this perspective has never been incorporated in the standard economic tool kit applied to media competition issues. This is reflected in the following quote from the third of the annual FCC reports (the *1996 Report*) on the state of competition in video programming delivery mandated by the 1992 Cable Act, which discusses the implication of concentration in markets for the delivery of video services.

> In both the *1994* and *1995 Reports*, we concluded that the local markets for the delivery of video programming were highly concentrated and characterized by high barriers to entry by potential distributors. In general, sellers in highly concentrated markets may be able to coordinate their conduct, lessen competition, and increase their rates of return. As a result, a high degree of concentration accompanied by substantial barriers to entry may result in prices above competitive levels and sub-optimal product quality, innovation, and service.[15]

The *1996 Report* goes on to note that, on average, concentration measures suggest that local video delivery markets remain concentrated and to cite recent research by Robert Crandall and Harold Furchtgott-Roth that suggests that, where it has occurred, consumers have benefited from overbuild competition through lower prices and enhanced services (more channels of programming), even though duplication of distribution plant increases the total cost of providing service.[16]

This is basically the same type of argument and supporting evidence the FCC used to justify the new cable rate regulations the FCC developed to implement the 1992 Cable Act. To assess the extent to which prices for cable service exceeded competitive levels, the commission compared prices for cable service in monopoly markets to prices charged for cable service in markets that either had two or more cable companies competing with each other in the same geographic territory (known as overbuild competition) or met one of two other criteria for effective competition as specified in the 1992 Cable Act.[17] Working on the assumption that prices in these markets were at the competitive level, the commission decreed first that a 10 percent reduction in prices was warranted. The mandated price reduction was subsequently increased to 17 percent, based on a revised study that focused on those markets where there was overbuild competition.[18] It is important to note, however, that the overbuild markets constituted considerably less than 1 percent of all U.S. cable markets.

The problem with relying on the difference between prices in markets with overbuild competition and markets in which cable systems faced no significant, direct competition from other multichannel services as evidence of what prices should be is that the same networks were available to cable systems in both sets of markets, so the quality of programming inputs was necessarily the same in both markets. But this quality was supported by the prices cable networks could command from cable system operators in the overwhelming majority of markets where there was no direct competition.

Whether the Cable Act of 1992 improved the lot of cable television subscribers on balance is unclear. Gregory Crawford's study probably provides the most comprehensive assessment of the consumer welfare consequences of the act.[19] His work, which compares estimates of the consumer surplus attributable to cable service before and after the 1992 act, shows that many cable systems were able to largely offset the negative effects of the mandated rate reduction on their revenues by repackaging and repricing existing services and introducing new ones. While cable bills fell in many markets, they actually increased following the act in approximately one-third of the markets sampled. While consumer surplus increased slightly in those markets where cable bills fell, after allowing for the effects of restructured service offerings, he estimated that consumer welfare fell in 42 percent of all cable markets. Averaged across all markets, he estimated a mean welfare loss of eight cents per subscriber per month. So this pre- and post-act comparison suggests that most cable subscribers received about the same level of benefits from their cable service after the act as they did before. However, this is not the same as comparing consumer surplus after the act to what it would have been had the act not been passed. If consumer surplus from cable services would have risen in the absence of the act, then the act actually made consumers worse off. However, consumers benefited if consumer surplus would have fallen without the act.

Crawford does estimate that consumer surplus would have increased by 83 cents per subscriber per month had prices fallen by 10 percent under the act. So this is one estimate of the benefits the 1992 Cable Act might have generated had it been implemented differently. However, this estimate also assumes that the quality of cable programming services would have been maintained at its pre-act level despite a reduction in the revenues available to cover programming costs.

What is clear from a review of the major FCC Reports and Orders implementing the 1992 Cable Act is that the act was implemented without seriously considering the implications of significant cable rate reductions on the quality of programming offered viewers.[20] This is not because the issue was willfully disregarded, but because it did not come naturally to mind. While it would be hard to argue that failure to ask this question resulted in any serious disaster for either consumers or the cable industry, this is not a justification for ignoring it when similar issues must be addressed in the future. A well-designed media competition policy requires that all of the economic implications of prospective media regulations be considered before they are implemented.

The Importance of the Link between the Advertising and Consumer Markets for Media Products

Media firms who sell advertising compete simultaneously in two markets: a market for the supply of media content to consumers and a market for the sale of access to the consumers in their audiences to advertisers. These markets are connected by two important relationships that make it impossible to maximize profits if activities in the two markets are not coordinated. One is the effect of its content expenditures on the size of the audience a media firm can sell to advertisers. This relationship was examined in the earlier discussion of the public good characteristics of media products and will not be considered further here. Rather, the content expenditure decision will now be treated as a given to better focus on the market for television advertising.

The second relationship connecting the two markets is the effect that commercials inserted in television programs have on the satisfaction viewers derive from watching those programs. For the most part, the formal models of competition among television programming suppliers, such as stations and networks, developed by economists have incorporated the assumption that commercials do not affect viewers' enjoyment of programs.[21] This assumption is typically justified as an analytical convenience that has little if any impact on the qualitative conclusions of the analysis for which the model is employed. However, while this assumption has served the purpose facilitating modeling that yielded new insights into how media markets work, its validity cannot simply be taken for granted in assessing the efficiency of real world advertising markets.

If viewers truly dislike commercials on television, as many would undoubtedly say they do, then commercials should be treated as another cost of viewing and this cost should be reflected in attempts to evaluate the economic performance of media industries. More generally, as long as viewers are not simply indifferent to commercials and are influenced in their choices among programs (and programming services) by the amount of commercial time they contain, policy analysts run the risk of serious error in assessing the benefits of competition in video industries if they don't take consumers' responses to commercial time into account both because the spillover benefits or costs for viewers (depending on whether they like commercials or not) of competition in the sale of television ad time will be ignored and because the competitive dynamics of media markets are likely to be misspecified.

Rosse's econometric study of newspaper firms provided a dramatic demonstration of the importance of recognizing the links between consumers' and advertisers' demand functions if one is to understand the economics of newspaper firms and markets.[22] Rosse's estimates of the subscriber and advertiser demand functions faced by newspapers showed that subscribers valued newspapers more highly the more advertising they contained, and that advertisers were willing to pay more for ad space the larger a paper's circulation was. This created a positive feedback loop through which events in one market could affect purchase decisions in the other, which in turn would reinforce the effect of the triggering events in the first market, which then might have a second round impact on the second market, and so on. Because of amplification through this feedback process, apparently small initial events may have significant consequences for the financial health of a newspaper firm. Thus, for example, a small initial loss of advertisers to other media, such as television, is likely to lead some of a paper's marginal subscribers to cancel their subscriptions. But following this loss of readership, the paper is likely to experience an additional loss of advertisers, which may lead still more subscriber cancellations, followed by the defection of yet more advertisers, and so on. By the time this process works itself out, advertising linage is likely to have fallen by several times the initial drop, and there could be a substantial loss of subscribers as well. To be true to reality, any attempt to model the competitive strategies of newspaper firms and assess their performance from a welfare perspective must reflect an understanding of this link between its consumer and advertising markets.

Similarly, efforts to assess the efficiency and competitiveness of markets for television advertising should allow for the possibility of feedback processes linking the market that supplies programs to viewers (hereafter the viewer market) with the market in which viewers are sold as audiences to advertisers (the advertiser market). While it is commonly assumed that viewers dislike commercials within their programs, which would imply a negative feedback between the two markets in contrast to the positive feedback found by Rosse for newspapers, it is important to recognize that the evidence that viewers dislike commercials is largely introspective and anecdotal (such as the widely observed phenomenon of viewers picking up the remote to surf other channels during commercial breaks). Neither the sign nor the magnitude of this effect has been determined with the empirical rigor Rosse brought to his study of the newspaper industry. Nevertheless, the standard assumption that viewers dislike commercials will be maintained throughout most of the analysis presented below. The intent, however, is to show that, whether the feedback is positive or negative, it is important to allow for the possibility that the advertiser and viewer markets are dynamically linked in assessing the extent to which competition in the market for television advertising serves the public interest in economic efficiency.

To illustrate the potential importance of feedback between the advertiser and viewer markets in assessing competition in video markets, consider a single television station, station A, that competes with other stations in a local television market, and the effects on its competitors of a decision by station A to increase the amount of advertising time it sells. Both the prices and audiences of its competitors may be affected by station A's action, and I will examine each effect independent of the other, before considering them in combination.

Assume initially that station A suffers no loss in viewership for increasing its ad time. If advertisers consider ad time on station A to be a substitute for ad time on other stations in the market, the increase in time sold by station A would force all stations in the market to lower the prices at which they sell their ad time. Thus, through its effect on stations' ad time prices, station A's decision to increase the amount of ad time it sells reduces the profits of its competitors. Similarly, increased time sold by its competitors would reduce A's profits.

Because each station's ad sales impose a cost in reduced profits on its competitors that is not reflected in its own profit calculus, the amount of commercial time that will be sold by the market's stations collectively will exceed the amount that would maximize their joint profits unless they cooperate (collude) in determining how much ad time each will sell. It is generally accepted that the likelihood that competitors will be able to successfully coordinate their strategies declines as markets become less concentrated, both because the cost of coordination increases with the number of competitors and because the difficulties inherent in monitoring numerous competitors increases the incentive to cheat on collusive arrangements. Thus, if we ignore viewer responses to changes in the amount of commercial time in programs, we would expect less concentrated markets to exhibit lower advertising prices (measured in cost per viewer delivered) than more concentrated markets. This is the standard analysis of the effect of increased competition on price and output underlying much of competition policy.

Now assume that viewers respond to an increase in the ad time on station A by spending more of their time watching programs on other stations, but that the price advertisers pay for access to viewers is unaffected. The shift by viewers to other stations makes it possible for station A's competitors to sell larger audiences to advertisers, which increases their profits. In this case, A's competitors will want it to sell more commercial time than it would be inclined to sell acting purely on its own behalf, because A's calculation of the costs and benefits of selling more commercial time does not include the positive effects of its ad sales on its competitors' profits. Similarly, A would prefer that its competitors sold more ad time than they would be inclined to sell on their own. In this circumstance, collusion on ad sales would result in more ad time being sold, not less, as coordination by competitors would lead each to reflect the benefits realized by the others from increases in its own ad time.[23]

Of course, if viewers do prefer programs with fewer commercials, then both of the effects of an increase in the time sold by one station on its competitors just discussed would operate simultaneously. If the ad price effect dominates, we would expect to see a positive correlation between ad prices and market concentration, because competitors would be more successful in reducing the market supply of ad time and raising prices in more concentrated markets. If the audience diversion effect dominates, however, stations in more concentrated markets should sell more ad time and charge lower prices than stations in less concentrated markets. Thus we should observe a negative correlation between ad prices and concentration. In this situation, advertisers are beneficiaries of collusion. (Of course, if viewers prefer programs with more commercials, ads would attract viewers from competitors and stations would have a double incentive to collude to restrict the amount of time sold.)

Note, however, that advertisers' interests are opposed to those of viewers who prefer programs with fewer commercials at least when the ad time is sold by broadcast television stations and networks for whom advertising is the sole source of support.[24] This further complicates the welfare analysis of competition in markets for television advertising. Nevertheless, these complications must be addressed if policymakers are serious about promoting economic efficiency in media markets.

To date, the possibility that suppliers of television programming might consider viewer responses (whether positive or negative) in determining how much time to sell has simply not been a factor given serious consideration in the official policy assessments of the state of competition in video services markets. This is also reflected in the design and interpretation of what is probably the most influential piece of research on the effectiveness of competition in the sale of television advertising, Gary Fournier and Donald Martin's study of the relationship between concentration and the price of advertising in local television markets.[25]

Fournier and Martin used four separate measures of concentration in metropolitan television markets to study the relationship between the price per viewer per thirty seconds of commercial time at which stations sold ad time and concentration in local television markets. Regressions using two of the concentration measures found no relationship between concentration and the price of ad time, while the regressions employing the other two concentration measures generated weak evidence that prices were inversely correlated with concentration. That is, there was weak evidence that stations in more highly concentrated markets sold their time for less money than stations in less concentrated markets. Collectively, the coefficient estimates from the four sets of regressions were interpreted as evidence that most of the benefits of competition were already being realized even in local markets that were highly concentrated by traditional antitrust standards, and that increasing the number of stations in a market made no discernible contribution to ad pricing efficiency. The two regressions indicating an inverse relationship between concentration and price were dismissed as meaningless because it made no sense that prices would fall if sellers were able to collude more effectively. The more informed analysis presented above shows that this is not an unreasonable expectation. Therefore, an alternative interpretation of the Fournier and Martin study is that they provided weak evidence that stations in more concentrated markets were more successful at coordinating their pricing strategies than those in less concentrated markets; but this coordination led them to sell more commercial time rather than less because the audience diversion effect of increased ad time dominated the price effect. Whether this is good or bad, given the implications for consumer welfare, is less clear.

Defining Advertising Markets for Media Policy Analysis

Implicit in the discussion of competition in advertising markets was the assumption of a well-defined market in which programming services compete in the sale of audiences to advertisers. Here I argue that the way in which advertising markets have traditionally been defined for purposes of assessing competition in media markets is at odds with the way that advertisers evaluate and compare the audiences that can be purchased from programming suppliers.

The way video advertising markets have traditionally been defined for media competition policy analyses is illustrated by the debate over concentration in television advertising markets in the FCC's 1995 proceedings over whether to preserve or eliminate the Prime Time Access Rule.[26] A report submitted by economists working on behalf of the Association of Independent Television Stations, King World, and Viacom International, all of whom wanted to retain the Rule, presented data on shares of the national television audience during prime time, including the access period, to show that the major broadcast networks accounted for the preponderance of that audience.[27] Economists hired by the major broadcast networks, who wanted the Rule repealed, submitted a report that showed that the three largest networks' collective and average shares of total national television advertising sales for all dayparts, defined to include sales of national spot advertising, broadcast network advertising, advertising sold in nationally syndicated programs, and national cable advertising, were not terribly large.[28] In support of its order to strike the Rule, the FCC accepted the broader market definition and argued that because the average share for one of the three largest networks in this market had fallen to only 14.5 percent by 1995, it was unlikely that the broadcast networks retained any market power in the sale of national television advertising.[29]

For competition policy purposes, the products offered by two or more sellers are considered to be in the same market if their customers consider them to be sufficiently close substitutes for each other that the ability of one of the sellers to unilaterally raise its price is substantially constrained by its customers' willingness to purchase from the other seller(s) instead. Therefore, implicit in the use of the concentration statistics by the parties to the PTAR debate was the assumption that advertisers viewed the audiences sold by the programming services identified as competing in these markets as substitutes for each other. The validity of this assumption was taken as self-evident, however, and not subjected to independent validation. But absent evidence on the substitutability of different programs' audiences for each other, measures of concentration in audiences and advertising revenues can tell us very little about the extent to which competition disciplines the prices at which television audiences are sold.

To ascertain the substitutability of one programming service's audience for another's, we need to look at these audiences from an advertiser's perspective. To an advertiser, each viewer is a prospective customer. And it is the profit potential an advertiser sees in viewers as potential customers, combined with the perceived effectiveness of its ads in converting viewers of those ads into actual customers, that determines how much an advertiser is willing to pay to get its ads before viewers. It is important to note, however, that this does not imply that an advertiser will view ad exposures to two viewers with similar profit potential to be substitutes for each other. Each viewer represents an independent source of profit and thus has a value to the advertiser that is independent of the terms at which the advertiser is able to purchase access to the other viewer. To restate this very important point, from an advertiser's perspective two (or any number of) demographically identical viewers are not economic substitutes for each other because having access to one does not diminish the value to an advertiser of having access to the other.

If different viewers are not substitutes for each other, firms who can't sell access to the same viewers are not competitors in a common market. Therefore, the only consistent approach to defining in which advertisers purchase access to viewers is to treat the sale of access to *each* viewer as a separate advertising output market and to treat competition among media firms to get viewers to watch their programs as competition on the input side of this market. Media firms compete with each other on the output side of these markets to the extent they can offer advertisers exposure to the same viewers. They compete with each other on the input side of this market to the extent that they offer viewers programming options that the viewers see as close substitutes for each other.

This provides us with the framework needed to determine whether the audiences of different television programs are substitutes for each other. If advertisers value advertising access to each viewer individually and acquire that access by purchasing ad time on television programs, then the audiences of different programs are economic substitutes from an advertiser's perspective only to the extent that they provide access to the same viewers. While the traditional approach to advertising market definition in media policy has been to treat different audiences as substitutes if their viewers look alike (are demographically similar), the approach that is appropriate for competition policy analysis is to treat them as substitutes only if their viewers literally are the same. The degree to which different programs' audiences are substitutes for each other is now seen to be a matter of the degree to which their audiences duplicate each other. The extent to which per viewer per minute ad prices for different programs are forced to converge because of buyer arbitrage in the marketplace is thus a function of the degree to which their audiences overlap. If different groups of demographically similar viewers watch entirely separate sets of programs, there is no necessary reason why ad time providing access to the different groups would have to be sold at comparable per viewer per minute prices.

It is not uncommon for radio listeners to settle on one or two stations to which they listen almost exclusively. In a study of per listener per minute prices for radio advertising based on radio station rate cards, S. S. Wildman and D. J. Cameron showed there was substantial variation in stations' ad rates, with stations broadcasting to large geographic regions charging systematically lower rates per listener than smaller stations, even when format, which should correlate closely with listener demographics, was controlled for.[30] While not dispositive, this evidence is consistent with the argument advanced above, that market forces do not necessarily compel media firms to sell demographically similar audiences at similar prices. Similar but separate audiences can sell at very different prices because advertisers do not view them as substitutes for each other. It is possible that more varied viewing patterns by television viewers may make stations, networks, and syndicators more direct competitors in the sale of access to viewers and thus produce greater uniformity in television advertising rates. If so, this would provide empirical support for the practice of treating firms whose programs attract demographically similar audiences as direct competitors in a common advertising market. But the empirical evidence required to justify such a claim has not yet been produced.

Finally, if we accept that program services that don't reach the same viewers are not competitors in the same market, regardless of the demographic similarities of their audiences, it must be acknowledged that cable networks do not compete with broadcast networks in selling access to the approximately one-third of television households who still pull their television programs off the air. While the broadcast networks' national advertising prices should reflect competition from cable and Direct Broadcast Satellite (DBS) services for viewers hooked up to these alternative delivery systems who typically have access to off-air services as well, their national rates should also reflect the conditions under which they compete in selling access to viewers who rely solely on rabbit ears and roof-top antennas. That is, the broadcast networks' national advertising rates should be weighted averages of per viewer rates that reflect competition from cable networks and DBS services for the sale of advertising access to multichannel service subscribers and rates that reflect competition only from other terrestrial broadcasters competing in the sale of access to viewers who get all their programming off-air.

This means that the current practice of lumping cable audiences and broadcast audiences (or advertising revenues) together to determine the degree of concentration in a single national advertising market implicitly errs by assigning cable services and satellite services positive shares as competitors who can supply access to viewers who don't subscribe to these pay services, and by assigning these services too little weight in the competition to provide advertisers access to viewers who do subscribe to cable and DBS services. Even this bifurcation of the advertising market is an oversimplification, since it assumes that all broadcast services can provide access to the same broadcast-only viewers and that all broadcasters and pay services can provide access to the same pay service subscribers. In reality, there are likely to be clumpings of viewers who watch small subsets of the available services. In this case, services that are part of the same subset would be closer substitutes to each other than to services outside of that subset, so that market power would be greater than what a strict calculation of shares of broadcast-only viewers and viewers who subscribe to pay services would suggest.

Summary and Conclusions

The public good characteristics of media products, combined with feedback from events and strategies employed in advertising markets to markets for content supplied to consumers and vice versa, give competition a very different look in media markets than in markets for most other goods and services. This is part of the challenge of developing economic policies for media industries. Over time, media competition policy has been improved by incorporating new advances in economic thinking and by the efforts of economists to develop a more complete understanding of how media industries work. This has been most evident in the development (or abandonment) of policies regulating vertical relations among media firms and their suppliers and customers. Media competition policy would be further improved if the ways the nature and merits of competition in media markets are currently assessed were modified to more fully incorporate economists' insights into the nature of competition in goods with important public good characteristics. Similarly, media competition policy would benefit from a better understanding of the ways in which the markets for viewers and the markets for the sale of access to viewers interact with each other. Finally, the current approach to defining relevant markets for television advertising is inconsistent with the way that advertisers evaluate the audiences media firms offer for sale. The current approach should be replaced with one that focuses on the sale of access to individual viewers as the fundament unit of analysis. It is hoped that media competition policy in the future will be based on a model of media market competition that better accounts for the distinctive characteristics of media products and markets outlined in this chapter.

Notes

1. P. O. Steiner, "Program Patterns and Preferences, and the Workability of Competition in Radio Broadcasting," *Quarterly Journal of Economics*, vol. 66 (1952), pp. 194–223.

2. R. G. Noll, M. J. Peck, and J. J. McGowan, *Economic Aspects of Television Regulation* (Brookings, 1973).

3.The findings of this study are reviewed in S. M. Besen and others, *Misregulating Television: Network Dominance and the FCC* (University of Chicago Press, 1984).

4. See, for example, R. W. Crandall and H. Furchtgott-Roth, *Cable TV Regulation or Competition?* (Brookings, 1996); L. L. Johnson, *Toward Competition in Cable Television* (MIT Press, 1994); T. W. Hazlett and M. L. Spitzer, *Public Policy Towards Cable Television: The Economics of Rate Control* (MIT Press, 1997); and D. Waterman and A. A. Weiss, *Vertical Integration in Cable Television* (MIT Press, 1997).

5. R. F Park, *New Television Networks*, Report R-1408-MF (Santa Monica: Rand Corporation, 1973), and "New Television Networks," *Bell Journal of Economics*, vol. 6 (1975), pp. 607–20; and R. W. Crandall, "The Economic Case for a Fourth Commercial Network," *Public Policy*, vol. 12 (1974), pp. 513–36.

6. J. N. Rosse, "The Evolution of One-Newspaper Cities," *Proceedings of the Symposium on Media Concentration*, vol. 2 (Washington: Federal Trade Commission, 1978), pp. 429–71.

7. While economic efficiency is the focus of the discussion that follows, concern with media content also figures importantly in the debate over how well profit-motivated media firms serve the interests of a democracy in free speech and a well-informed citizenry.

8. A. M. Spence, "Monopoly, Quality and Regulation," *Bell Journal of Regulation*, vol. 6 (Autumn 1975), pp. 17–29.

9. See, for example, A. Shaked and J. Sutton, "Relaxing Price Competition through Product Differentiation," *Review of Economic Studies*, vol. 44 (1982), pp. 3–13; and N. M. Hung and N. Schmitt, "Quality Competition and Threat of Entry in Duopoly," *Economics Letters*, vol. 27 (1988), pp. 287–92.

10. Crandall, "The Economic Case for a Fourth Commercial Network"; and Park, *New Television Networks*, Report R-1408-MF, and "New Television Networks," *Bell Journal of Economics*.

11. C. Hoskins and R. Mirus, "Reasons for the U.S. Dominance of the International Trade in Television Programmes," *Media, Culture, and Society*, vol. 10 (1988), pp. 499–515; D. Waterman, "World Television Trade: The Economic Effects of Privatization and New Technology," *Telecommunications Policy* (1988), pp. 141–51; S. S. Wildman and S. E. Siwek, "The Privatization of European Television: Effects on International Markets for Programs," *Columbia Journal of World Business*, vol. 22 (1987), pp. 71–76, and *International Trade in Films and Television Programs* (Ballinger, 1988).

12. D. Waterman, "Diversity and Quality of Information Products in a Monopolistically Competitive Industry," *Information, Economics and Policy*, vol. 4 (1989–90), pp. 291–303.

13. Work on models of competition among firms with differentiated products for which quality is not variable is similarly ambiguous in its conclusions on the optimality of a competitive equilibrium. The number of firms in a competitive equilibrium may exceed or fall short of the optimum number, depending in part

on how consumer demand is specified. See, for example, D. Besanko, M. K. Perry, and R. H. Spady, "The Logit Model of Monopolistic Competition: Brand Diversity," *Journal of Industrial Economics*, vol. 38 (1990), pp. 397–416.

14. On the other hand, to the extent that reduced expenditures on content are reflected in lower prices paid to factors of production that would be employed anyway, quality as perceived by consumers will not suffer. See J. R. Woodbury, S. M. Besen, and G. Fournier, "The Determinants of Network Television Program Prices: Implicit Contracts, Regulations and Bargaining Power," *Bell Journal of Economics*, vol. 14 (1983), pp. 351–65. This study of the renegotiation over license fees that takes place after new network programs have proven themselves successful suggests that a substantial fraction of the higher than expected economic value of hit shows is captured by the talent employed in producing these programs in the form of higher wages and salaries.

15. *Third Annual Report in the Matter of Competition in the Market for the Delivery of Video Programming*, CS Docket 96-133, adopted December 26, 1996, released January 2, 1997, pp. 62, 63.

16. Crandall and Furchtgott-Roth, *Cable TV Regulation or Competition?*; and *Third Annual Report*, paragraph 202.

17. Municipally owned systems and systems with less than 30 percent penetration of homes passed were also defined to be subject to effective competition by the act.

18. Seventeen percent was an average figure that did not apply to all systems. Systems whose prices were sufficiently close to specified competitive benchmark prices that a less than 17 percent rate reduction would bring them to the benchmark were only required to reduce prices to benchmark levels.

19. Gregory S. Crawford, "The Impact of the 1992 Cable Act on Consumer Demand and Welfare: A Discrete-Choice Differentiated Products Approach," paper presented at the Twenty-Fourth Annual Telecommunications Policy Research Conference, Solomons, Md., 1996.

20. See, in particular, FCC 93-177, *Rate Order and Further Notice of Proposed Rule Making*, MM Docket 92-266, released May 3, 1993 (published May 21, 1993); and FCC 93-428, *First Order on Reconsideration, Second Report and Order, and Third Notice of Proposed Rulemaking*, MM Docket 92-266, adopted August 27, 1993 (released August 27, 1993).

21. For example, this is true for the vast bulk of the articles in the substantial literature on how competing stations and networks select programs, beginning with Steiner's seminal paper in 1952 and including the influential article by A. M. Spence and B. M. Owen, "Television Programming, Monopolistic Competition and Welfare," *Quarterly Journal of Economics*, vol. 91 (February 1977), pp. 103–26, which employed a sophisticated model of monopolistic competition to examine competition among television programming suppliers. An exception is Wildman and Owen's extension of the Spence-Owen model to allow for the possibility that viewers preferred programs with fewer commercials. See S. S. Wildman and B. M. Owen, "Program Competition, Diversity, and Multichannel Bundling in the New Video Industry," in E. M. Noam, ed., *Video Media Com-*

petition: Regulation, Economics, and Technology (Columbia University Press, 1985).

22. Rosse, "The Evolution of One-Newspaper Cities."

23. Another way of looking at this is that if viewers lost by one station as it increases its ad time are picked up by other stations, all stations can increase ad time without losing viewers if all increase ad time at the same time and by the same amount. To the extent that some viewers stop watching television entirely as the amount of ad time increases, this cost would be shared by all stations if they set cooperatively the amount of commercial time to be sold.

24. The case for this claim is less clear for programming services, such as basic cable networks, that benefit from fees paid by viewers and from the sale of advertising. If advertising is viewed as a cost by viewers, but a source of revenue to program services, program services should find it profitable to lower subscription fees to attract larger audiences to sell to advertisers. Given the trade-off between ad time and subscription fees, it is not clear whether viewers would benefit or not from reduced ad time on these channels. See B. M. Owen and S. S. Wildman, *Video Economics* (Harvard University Press, 1992), chap. 4, for a more rigorous description of the trade-off cable services face between subscription fees and ad time.

25. G. M. Fournier and D. L. Martin, "Does Government-Restricted Entry Produce Market Power? New Evidence from the Market for Television Advertising," *Bell Journal of Economics*, vol. 14 (Spring 1983), pp. 44–56.

26. The FCC's Prime Time Access Rule restricted the affiliates of ABC, CBS, and NBC to showing network programs during no more than three of the four nightly prime time hours. The intent was to create room in network affiliates schedules for programs provided by nonnetwork suppliers.

27. J. A. Clifton, R. S. Hartman, and S. S. Wildman, *The Economic Effects of Repealing the Prime Time Access Rule: Impact on Broadcasting Markets and the Syndicated Program Market*, report submitted In re: Review of the Prime Time Access Rule, Section 73.658(k) of the Commission's Rules, MM Docket 94-123, March 7, 1995.

28. Economists Incorporated, *An Economic Analysis of the Prime Time Access Rule*, report submitted In re: Review of the Prime Time Access Rule, Section 73.658(k) of the Commission's Rules, MM Docket No. 94-123, March 7, 1995.

29. FCC 95-314, Report and Order, MM Docket 94-123, adopted July 28, 1995, released July 31, 1995, paragraph 37.

30. S. S. Wildman and D. J. Cameron, *Competition, Regulation and Sources of Market Power in the Radio Industry*, Working Paper (Northwestern University, 1989).

CHAPTER TWENTY-THREE

The Future of Television:
Understanding Digital Economics

Bruce M. Owen

T HE PROPHECY OF convergence is commonplace: that television sets, telephones and computers, and the networks that bind them are, or will become, the same. The *Economist* tells us that "the day is coming when virtually all media are transmitted in a digital stream, and processing those ones and zeros involves the same basic technology, regardless of whether they represent a movie or a telephone call."[1] Convergence implies a fundamental competitive struggle for survival among existing media, including some that do not compete today. It also suggests the possibility that surviving media may enjoy economic and other forms of power if they can control what becomes the chief means of communication. How are we to understand what convergence is and what, if anything, it portends for broadcasting? That is, what are the characteristics that define successful, surviving media in a world of technological change?

The idea of convergence usually is taken to suggest that a revolution in digital technology will greatly reduce the cost of communicating information, with the result that the communications industry's output will greatly expand. Meanwhile, the much-reduced price of delivered information will change everyone's life in various fundamental ways. Not least among these changes is that we will spend much more time consuming information, as we would any good whose price falls.

From the point of view of digital communication technology, "information" is a "bit stream" of zeros and ones, just like an old-fashioned

Portions of this chapter are drawn from Bruce M. Owen, *Airwaves to Bits: The Battle for the Future of Television* (Harvard University Press, forthcoming).

telegraph code. Digital technology is transparent to content. Anything that can be digitized can be transmitted on a digital medium to one and all. And virtually any image can be digitized, including books, newspapers, paintings, movies, TV programs, music, personal conversations, speeches, political cartoons, brainwaves, and three-dimensional objects. Further, almost any current electronic communication medium is or can be made into a digital medium, including telephone systems, TV broadcasting systems, cable television systems, and geosynchronous communication satellites. It is easy to see why convergence is a focal concept: all information or messages can be digitized; all communications media are or will be digital; therefore everything seems headed in a certain direction very rapidly. But what direction is that?

There are literally hundreds of possible configurations of communication technologies already available today. Each configuration of technical attributes is associated with a technically defined or constrained set of creative possibilities for the structure of content. Each has its costs. Together, characteristics and costs tell us much about which media are efficient. As to the future, the number of possibilities is endless. Which ones will succeed, and why?

This chapter focuses on the future of television broadcasting in this digital future. Will broadcasting, obviously a successful medium in the analog world, continue to succeed in the digital world, and if so how? Or will digital "multimedia" drive out television?[2] This is a question that can usefully be addressed in the context of the general factors that explain successful media.

Many perspectives can illuminate the search for understanding of successful media. For example, how and why did our present media (print, radio, television) overtake rival technologies? What are the scientific and technical functions of communication media, and how are these affected by invention and innovation? What are the economic factors and processes that determine whether one communication medium or another will be widely adopted? How is the act of consuming communicated content related to media success, and how is content itself shaped by and determinative of media forms? How does one medium successfully harness the power of government to protect and promote itself at the expense of rivals?

As the preceding litany suggests, no single factor "explains" how one medium comes to be successful while others whither away. The success or failure of a medium occurs because of the convergence of many factors, only some of which are under the control of those affected. Those with economic and other stakes in various failed media are legion. Indeed, it is still very possible that even the much-hyped Internet will fail, in the sense that it will stop growing before it becomes a mass medium. Hopes for an explosive Internet future are based not only on falling costs but on the possibility of simpler interfaces; that the second can be achieved is far from obvious.

An understanding of successful media must come from several directions. On the supply side, technology provides us with a set of feasible media forms, and economic analysis can assess their costs. Further, economic outcomes feed back on R&D incentives. On the demand side there are three forces. First, in the television industry, government is paramount. Through regulation and legislation, frequently at the invitation of those it regulates, the government defines and constrains what the television market is permitted to provide. Second, advertisers and merchandisers have well-understood demands for audiences of various types and sizes. Finally, there is consumer demand itself—the willingness of consumers to pay for new media services and forms—about which we can say little except through analogies with past behavior.

Why and How Did Our Present Media Succeed?

Narrowcast and broadcast are the two basic kinds of communication. Narrowcast communications involve one-to-one or one-to-a-few two-way communicants. Broadcast messages are one-way, one-to-many. The special features of broadcast communications are the following. One, the content is a public good; production costs do not increase when viewers are added. Therefore, larger audiences mean lower unit costs. Two, the message is valued in part because it is shared, and near-simultaneity of receipt is an enhancement or feature of sharing.

Broadcast communications can take various forms, each dictated by the technology of the medium, and each influencing the content of the message. A newspaper may broadcast much the same message as television, yet the two forms are very different and make for a different consumption experience. A fundamental distinction among broadcast media is whether the medium is itself a public good. A newspaper, even though it is a broadcast medium, is not in its physical form a public good. Each reader gets his or her own copy. Only the content is shared. Similarly, video "broadcasts" on today's Internet are not public goods, because identical, separate streams of packets must be sent to every viewer. In contrast, over-the-air broadcasts, satellite broadcasts, and certain computer network topologies permit public good transmission of content.

In order to be successful, a transmission medium must perform a given function more cheaply than alternative media or (because of its form) offer an opportunity for the transmission of more valuable content. A brief review of media history illustrates this point.

In the nineteenth century newspaper and magazine publishers invented mass communication by discovering (in the case of newspapers) that low reader prices and mass-appeal content could be used to generate advertising revenue that would support all or nearly all of the costs of publication. Magazine publishers discovered the rewards of tailoring content to the tastes of special-interest readers with respect to whom there was corresponding special-interest advertising demand. However, print media are very inefficient in their reliance on making and transporting a separate, identical copy to every reader. Despite this, and in contrast to early electronic media, the printed form is extremely convenient for readers: it need not be consumed in real time, is portable, and is its own storage medium. These attributes form the touchstone against which electronic media must compete.

The first important electronic mass medium was radio. The central economic feature of radio was that the transmission medium was itself a public good, the first mass medium with this characteristic. This gave radio a tremendous economic advantage over print media in reaching large audiences for the sale of advertising. No print medium could reach so many consumers so cheaply as radio. Radio had an additional advantage: low or zero latency. Newspapers cannot convey real-time events. Radio can cover real-time events, provided program origination facilities are present at the event; RCA founder David Sarnoff came to understand this advantage by playing virtual witness to the *Titanic* disaster. Further, consumption of real-time events enhances the value of the medium because of the consumer satisfaction arising from shared experiences.

In the early 1920s the radio industry was inchoate. There were a few experimental stations and a few thousand radio receivers. No one had clear rights to use the broadcast spectrum. No one knew what sorts of broadcasts might induce people to buy radio sets. Some potential manufacturers of radio sets calculated that they might need to supply free programming to stimulate demand. Others considered charging listeners an ongoing fee. The potential of advertising support was apparent to few. Out of this chaos a few entrepreneurs, such as David Sarnoff and William Paley, made decisions and took risks that turned out to be highly profitable. They promoted the idea of government ownership of the spectrum to bring order and predictability to their industry and to control excessive competition. They invented networks. They discovered the enormous advantage of radio advertising over print and tapped into the industry's chief future source of revenue. Many people in the early 1920s might have seen all of these as possibilities, but only as among many other possibilities. The Internet today, at least when viewed as a potential entertainment medium, is in much the same position.

Of course, radio lacked some useful aspects of the print medium. Indeed, it is by focusing on these differentiating factors that print media survive electronic competition. Until the invention and development of the transistor, radio was not portable. Before tape recorders, radio did not permit listeners to select the time at which consumption of any given program would take place; radio was not a storage medium. Beyond these relative physical disabilities, the form of a radio transmission—chiefly the fact that consumption and production take place in real time—ruled out radio as a means of transmitting certain kinds of information, such as want ads. While there is no technical reason that a radio announcer could not convey the entire textual content of a newspaper, such a broadcast would be of little value to most listeners. The form of radio dictates less detailed and shorter messages—it is not an interactive medium.

Television, on one level, is nothing but radio with pictures. That is, the television medium shares all the advantages and disadvantages of radio, vis-à-vis print media. Of course, it turned out that pictures were very important to consumers, highly valued and consumed in vast quantities. Part of the attraction is that, compared with radio, television has a great deal of redundancy, for any given form of content, which makes it easier to consume. Long sequences of frames in a television broadcast tend to be identical or at least very similar, providing the viewer with some opportunity to dwell on the information, or in effect to have some control over the pace of consumption. In this respect television has some of the attributes of print that radio lacks. In sum, television does the same things that radio did, but much more expensively; therefore it could have succeeded only by adding new features that increased its value to consumers (or, in principle, to advertisers) in line with its added cost.

Cable television provides an interesting contrast in that it was very far from a revolutionary addition to the mass media family. Cable television provides exactly the same service as over-the-air television insofar as any given program is concerned. That is, it is technically possible, and even common, for viewers not to able to distinguish a cable program from a broadcast program. There are really only two respects in which cable television provides features superior to over-the-air television: it has far more channels, and it permits viewers to "vote with dollars" for the programs they prefer. What is most interesting about these two features is that they are, from a technical point of view, equally available on over-the-air broadcasts. There is no technical reason why the number of over-the-air TV channels could not be as great as the number on cable, and there is no technical reason why stations could not charge viewers by scrambling their signals, for example.

Not only is there no technical reason why over-the-air broadcasters could not match these cable features, there probably is no economic reason. The cost of building (around $1,000 per household) and running (around $15 per household per month) a cable system of given channel capacity in large markets certainly exceeds the cost of building and running a similar number of over-the-air broadcast stations and arranging to collect viewer subscriptions to individual channels. If this is so, over-the-air television trumps cable television as a mass medium, and there is no technical or economic or product differentiation reason for the existence of cable television systems, at least in urban areas.

Why then is cable television an important industry, not only in the United States but also in a number of other countries? The answer is straightforward: the U.S. government (and governments in other countries as well), through control of the radio spectrum and licensing of broadcast stations, prevented broadcasters from offering services for which there is a substantial consumer demand. Specifically, the number of broadcast stations has been severely limited, and broadcasters are not permitted to charge viewers directly, thus limiting the resources available for program development. By restricting output, the government has acted as if it were a cartel manager, seeking to drive up the value of licenses. It is no accident that cable television is as old as the television broadcasting industry. From the beginning, the market has found a very expensive and still incomplete way around restrictive government policies, somewhat reducing the burden of these policies on consumers.

It follows that in a free market, one in which broadcasters could buy spectrum as needed to satisfy consumer demand for programming, there would have been no cable television industry, simply because the same service could have been supplied more cheaply over the air. Cable is a giant arbitrage play.

There are less straightforward examples of the application of this approach to explaining media successes and failures. Storage media such as blank video cassettes are interesting chiefly as means to augment the television medium rather than as media in their own right. The VCR brought viewers the ability to "time shift"—that is, to record programs for later viewing. Obviously, this provided television with a feature that had previously distinguished it from print media. But time shifting was no more than a modest success. One reason for this is that television broadcasters had already compensated by adopting a mode of programming that minimized the disadvantages of having to consume television in real time. For many viewers, apparently, one television show of current quality is a pretty good substitute for another, and few shows are sufficiently better than the average to be worth the effort of mastering the difficult task of programming a VCR. Accordingly, most VCR use is limited to playing prerecorded movies.

One could regard the physical distribution of prerecorded cassettes for sale or rent to consumers as a mass medium. What advantages or disadvantages does tape distribution have, vis-à-vis print and conventional television? Cassette distribution is at least as expensive as print distribution and far more costly per unit delivered than over-the-air broadcasts. The content of the tapes is, or could readily be, available over the air. Being able to charge consumers directly is an advantage but only because of the artificial constraints faced by over-the-air television. Prerecorded tapes have very little value to advertisers because the timing and context of their consumption cannot be measured or controlled. Tapes do have the advantage of being a storage medium, which is clearly of value to those consumers who purchase rather than rent. In a rental context, the fact that tapes are somewhat durable is incidental (the business would not be much different if a tape could be used only once and was manufactured to order in the store). However, it is true that durability provides consumers with the opportunity to consume the product on their own schedule rather than in real time. In short, for many purposes it appears that the videotape rental "medium" exists largely on the same basis as cable: as a path by which consumers' demand for video entertainment can be satisfied despite FCC regulations attempting to limit supply.

Digital Transmission

On the technical side media have much in common. All transmission media, from newspapers to radio to the Internet, involve trade-offs among *channel capacity (bandwidth)*, *storage*, and *computing power* (or among the nonelectronic analogs of these attributes, such as newspaper press capacity). Each combination of these three attributes (and other, less important, ones) has a unique form that conditions message content, determines creative scope, and underlies consumer preferences. A given combination defines a particular medium. Efficient media reflect combinations of these attributes that minimize cost for any given level of information delivered to the consumer. The effect of recent rapid changes in technology has been to

—Introduce new digital media with far greater capacities in all three dimensions at much lower costs,

—Change the technical relationships among these three attributes in sudden hard-to-predict jumps, and

—Shift the relative prices of the three attributes.

The structure or "topology" of a communications network also helps define the messages it can effectively carry. Three important distinctions are useful. A broadcast, defined as a one-to-many, one-way communication path, can take place over the air, in print, or on the Internet. But if the object is to make a broadcast communication, then a network like the Internet is much closer to print than to over-the-air broadcasting. In print media, the public good (the message) is conveyed by means of a private good (the book, magazine, or newspaper itself). In over-the-air broadcasting, both message and medium are public, a fact that typically conveys a substantial cost advantage. Internet "broadcasts" are exactly like print "broadcasts"—separate but identical messages are sent to each member of the audience. Finally, there is "interactive" video. This can take forms such as video programming called up on demand (VOD), or videoconferencing. The key is that the video message arrives in response to a request from the user; therefore the message goes to only one user and is not broadcast.[3] In this sense, a video rental store is "interactive video." The Internet is interactive in a sense because all users can send and receive messages. However, the Internet was not designed to be interactive in real time, and it does not reserve an open channel to ensure prompt delivery of requested messages. In short, the Internet has what is called a "latency" problem that makes it unsuitable for many video applications, whether interactive or broadcast.

The technology of any medium determines its suitability for broadcasting or for interactive video. Over-the-air television (whether terrestrial or from space) is an especially cheap way to transmit video broadcasts, taking advantage of the public good character of transmissions. All of the advantages that digital technology brings to the Internet are also available to over-the-air broadcasters and satellite operators. A medium such as the telephone system makes much more sense, however, topologically speaking, if the video delivery service is to be interactive, and even more so if the senders as well as the receivers are widely scattered in space. Unfortunately, the telephone network lacks sufficient bandwidth or processing power at present, and it is unclear whether or when consumer willingness to pay will exceed the cost of upgrading.

The Internet is a convenient word to describe a disparate and changing collection of technologies and services accessed through personal or other computers. The range and changing nature of Internet technology are so broad that it may already be said to encompass more narrowly defined media, such as telephony, radio and television, and even newspapers, all of which now are supplied, in some form, over the Internet. In other words, television, or a version of it, already is part of the Internet, considered as the ubiquitous digital communication infrastructure. However, that the Internet can, or even does, deliver television pictures does not mean that conventional (noninteractive) broadcast digital television will not coexist with it.

Any message traveling from one human to another at a distance must be impressed upon a medium (paper, carrier wave, and so on) by encoding (typesetting, digitizing, modulating, and so on) to suit the features of the medium and then decoded or transformed back into terms accessible to human senses. For a long time electronic communication has used analog modulation for this purpose, because it happened to be the most cost-effective way to get the job done. In recent years the cost of digital computers has fallen greatly, and such computers can be used to lower the cost of communicating any given amount of information, if the information is in digital form, by conserving relatively expensive bandwidth. Indeed, digital coding is, at the moment, still more expensive than analog coding, but this disadvantage is overcome by the bandwidth savings. (Wired bandwidth is extremely expensive because its supply to the home requires installation of conduits, cables, or fibers at substantial labor cost. Wireless bandwidth is relatively expensive at the moment for several reasons, although its price is falling. The FCC has been increasing the supply of bandwidth available for broadband digital communication by auction and otherwise. Such spectrum rights previously were unavailable at any price except by transfers of licenses from incumbent broadcasters.)

The form of the Internet medium, and hence the form of its content, is determined (on the supply side) by a set of trade-offs and constraints such as the trade-off between bandwidth and compression. What is so exciting about this moment in history is that *all* these trade-offs are changing in ways that are difficult to predict. Thus, the form of electronic communication in the next decade (and in the next century) depends greatly on whether the costs of data storage fall faster than the costs of data transmission, and also on whether the costs of data processing fall faster than either storage or transmission.

If data storage prices fall more rapidly than the prices of other components, on account of digital videodisks (DVD) (the successor to compact discs) and follow-on technologies, then entertainment and information images may be called up from local storage in pieces, as needed, at the demand of instructions sent over "narrow" transmission pipelines. This possibility is explored in the radio station example below.

If the price of processing power falls more rapidly than the prices of other components (it has been falling by 50 percent every two years), then the use of digital compression will further increase (it is already about 10:1 in some video applications and climbing), substituting for increased bandwidth and local storage. Digital compression and decompression takes time, even with fast processing, creating delays, or "latency," in responding to user commands. Latency tends to undermine the quality of real-time video services. Put differently, an increase in computing power and hence compression may save bandwidth and storage costs, but it probably will not support interactive video services without increases in either bandwidth or storage.

A brief excursion into the meaning of the term "information" is helpful at this point, because it underlies the trade-offs among bandwidth, compression, and storage. From the point of view of the consumer at whom a bit stream is directed, not all bits are news. That is, some bits comprise content that is already known; these bits are redundant. This notion can be carried to great lengths. Suppose a radio announcer says, "We will now broadcast Beethoven's Ninth Symphony." From the perspective of a listener who (a) believes this statement and (b) already owns a decent and handy recording of the Ninth, nothing is accomplished by the subsequent broadcast. The broadcast is a waste of electrons, or bandwidth, that could be better used for other purposes, at least from the point of view of that listener.

Suppose all the radio stations in a city collaborated on the distribution to all listeners of a set of compact disks containing all the music that would be played in the next month. Then all but one or two of the stations could go off the air, and the remaining stations need only broadcast instructions (perhaps automatically to CD players) specifying the next play in each format. In effect, the one or two broadcast stations would only be needed for this highly "compressed" signal, functionally equivalent from the listener's point of view to the traditional one, plus whatever real-time broadcasting was desired. The bandwidth reserved for the remaining radio stations could be used for cell phones or some other real-time function. There is nothing in this example that requires digital media; it could be done with present-day analog broadcasts.

In the radio station example, there is a clear trade-off between bandwidth and storage. Another way to look at what has happened is to say that the radio broadcasts have been greatly compressed, into a signal consisting of commands that instruct the receiver to *reconstruct* the full message. The reconstruction can take place, as in the radio station example, by calling material up from storage. But if the signal is digital, it can also take place by means of computation. That is, the transmission may be a set of instructions that cause a digital signal processor (in effect, a computer) to construct or create an image or a sound.

We can continue with the radio example. At some point in the Ninth, among the other things that are going on, a solo violin sustains an E-note for six seconds. That sound is digitized (sampled) and broadcast as a stream of identical bits lasting six seconds. The sound can be compressed by sending a very brief series of bits telling the digital signal processor at the receiving end to "play" an E-note for six seconds. These instructions can be sent in less than one second. The five seconds saved can be used to send other information. Virtually all music (and TV images) contain large amounts of redundant information that can be compressed in such fashion. In this way, a channel that once carried only the Ninth could broadcast all nine symphonies at once. Thus, nine radio stations can be replaced by one by means of data compression. Bandwidth can be conserved by storage or by compression or both.

Economic Factors

Products and services do not become available to consumers merely because a clever scientist or engineer thinks of a new way that something can be done. In a market economy, goods and services are available because someone expects to make a profit and is therefore prepared to pay the costs and to undertake the risks of production. New technology, however exciting, cannot come to market if it does not produce, or at least promise to produce, profits.

Further, the very development of technology itself is responsive to economic incentives. Research and development are often very expensive. Not every idea can be developed. Generally, only the ideas that seem most likely to be profitable *are* developed.

Television exists to sell audiences to advertisers. Television also exists to provide entertainment that entices viewers, with or without viewer fees. The television medium, like any, is a collection of technologies, standards, and government regulations. The economics of television is the process by which producers, advertisers, and viewers, by interacting with each other and with the technology, seek private advantage. Commercial television content is the outcome of this self-interested interaction.

One implication of the public good nature of broadcast television is that there are very large economies of scale with respect to audience size. The bigger the audience, the lower the cost per viewer to make the program. Hence two programs with the same production costs and the same inherent attractiveness can have very different profits, depending on which has access to the larger audience. Because of these economies, the producer with the larger potential audience can profitably offer lower prices to viewers and advertisers. So, other things being equal, media that reach larger potential audiences have substantial advantages over those with less reach. In the case of broadcast television, both the program content and the airwave broadcast have these public good characteristics.

Transaction costs are the costs that buyers and sellers face in trying to trade goods or services for money. For example, if merchants face substantial losses because of bad checks, they will insist on cash. Both bad checks and the need to carry cash to buy goods increase the costs of making transactions and thereby diminish the number and value of transactions. Transaction costs are especially important for broadcast television when viewers are paying. In the early years of television (and before that, radio), transaction costs for collecting money from viewers (listeners) were so high that no one considered it; all television was supported by advertising. This unremarkable, expedient business decision of the early broadcasters has, curiously, given rise to present-day claims that the public has a "right" to free over the air television broadcasts. Congress seems prepared to enforce this right.

One problem with charging viewers for programming has been that it is awkward to monitor viewing of broadcast television. Even cable television traditionally has sold the service as a package, with little attempt to monitor usage. Monitoring and charging is not, and never has been, impossible. But the cost of monitoring has remained high, on a per transaction basis, relative to the prices that viewers are willing to pay for individual programs. Even though viewers are generally willing to pay far more than advertisers for a given program delivered to a particular household, it has not been profitable until recently to try to collect that money. Instead, where television is sold directly to viewers, it has been generally sold in packages, without usage-sensitive pricing.

The problem of high transaction costs also plagues the Internet. At this point the Internet is already a somewhat useful source of information, and in many cases people would be willing to pay a small sum to obtain an item of information or for the right to search a database. Many Internet information publishers have been offering service for free as a marketing experiment, but eventually they are going to want to charge. Unfortunately there is as yet no accepted mechanism by which small sums can be collected efficiently and reliably from thousands or millions of users and distributed to information suppliers. Instead, suppliers are beginning to offer monthly subscriptions for wholesale access to their data bases, again without usage-sensitive pricing.

Transaction costs are not the only reason that television programs, like Internet services, frequently are offered as packages. For users or viewers to search out, select, and then arrange for delivery of preferred material is itself a costly process. Consumers value packaged material, like a daily newspaper, that embodies the services of an editor. Nowadays the Internet offers many customized news delivery services, where the user selects from certain categories of news, or news containing certain keywords. Tailored e-mail messages then deliver news items from those categories. These so-called push Internet services offer an alternative to editorial services embodied in a daily newspaper or a daily television news broadcast. In neither case does the consumer engage directly in sorting through the thousands of news stories that are available each day.

Television programs were originally "packaged" within a single channel-through-time. NBC, for example, offered a program schedule designed to attract and keep certain large categories of viewers (viewers attractive to advertisers). The concept of "audience flow" meant that like program followed like program, so that viewers need never, in the days before remote controls, leave their seats to change the channel. Like the editor of a daily newspaper, NBC selected from among the hundreds of program ideas before it chose a menu designed to be attractive to its viewers, or at least one that was not so offensive as to bring viewers to their feet. More recently, as the number of television channels has multiplied, we see specialized channels.

Offering packages of programs or channels for a single price does have two attractive features. First, in some circumstances it may permit the supplier to extract a larger fraction of the consumer surplus or willingness to pay of users, and therefore (in a competitive market) to increase output. Second, it is clear that many consumers place a value on not having to worry about usage; these consumers would be willing to pay something to avoid having a per unit charge for their consumption of certain services. This, together with transactions costs, may explain the popularity of flat-rate pricing of local phone service. America Online (AOL) in 1996 apparently believed that it would gain new subscribers by eliminating usage charges and changing to a flat monthly rate independent of usage. AOL was correct, but the decision came close to scuttling the company as usage immediately far exceeded available capacity, and quality of service deteriorated accordingly.

In many markets an understanding of such supply and demand factors as those discussed above would be sufficient to make predictions. In ordinary markets supply and demand are linked by prices, which serve as impersonal signals to reconcile producer and consumer interests. Communication media markets are more complex, in part because of network effects. Network effects link one consumer to another, making each consumer's demand for any given medium dependent on how many others have accepted it. Further, partly because of network effects, new media may not be successful solely on their merits. Superior media may be excluded from the market simply because some other medium, perhaps less worthy, got there first and enjoys a first-mover advantage, or because the now-superior approach was extinguished earlier, at a time when another approach seemed better. (The example of electric streetcars, which were developed at the same time as gasoline-powered automobiles, is sometimes used in this context.)

As a result of economic forces such as network effects, path dependency, first-mover advantages, and economies of scale, it is likely that the very best ideas do not get implemented all the time, or even most of the time, or as soon as they could be. This notion is very worrisome to Internet entrepreneurs. But there is almost nothing that can be done about it. Government interventions in such matters as standard-setting tend to make matters worse, not better, because the government has no more clue to the right outcome than the market and because government "solutions" are much harder to change than market outcomes. In no case is this more apparent than in the government's sustained and successful effort to dictate or control broadcast technical standards, the effect of which almost certainly has been to keep TV technology a decade or more behind computer technology. Of course, the government must control technical standards, because technology might otherwise offer the market additional ways around the government's inefficient economic controls.

Network externalities exist when my use of a particular service is worth more to me because you use the same service. My fax machine, for example, would be worthless if no one else, or only a few people, had such machines. Subscribing to a telephone service provides consumer value only because others also subscribe, either to the same service or to an interconnected service. As the example of interconnected telephone systems suggests, network externalities do not necessarily imply that the service is a natural monopoly. Similarly, all fax machines need to be able to speak to one another, but they need not all be made by the same company.

Network externalities have several implications. First, there may be a "critical mass" that is necessary before a service can "take off" and begin to grow rapidly. Such was the case with fax machines, and such may apply to the Internet. Second, there are certain obvious business advantages that lie in taking advantage of network externalities. Microsoft increases the demand for its operating system software (such as Windows 95) each time it produces a new application (such as Microsoft Word) that relies on that system, and vice versa. Third, while it may be to the advantage of individual business enterprises to do otherwise, interconnection and compatibility provides consumers and producers with an opportunity to capitalize on network externalities without the burden of monopoly.

Demand Factors

Despite the hype, it appears that fewer than half of American households own a computer, and at this writing only 20 percent of them have access to on-line services. Of those who use the Internet, the majority limits itself chiefly to e-mail services. In short, only a tiny fraction of Americans use or know how to use the World Wide Web as a domestic service. Even at the office, Internet usage is chiefly e-mail.

The major reasons for such low penetration are the cost and difficulty of setting up and using the equipment. Simply put, most people do not own or know how to use a computer, much less want to watch TV on it. If a modern PC, even a Mac, were built into new TV sets, most people would not want to buy them. That computing costs will fall is a given. That the unit cost of digital TV and the Internet will fall is likewise a given. But it certainly is not a given that someone will design an interface that permits ordinary people—people who are unwilling to learn to program their VCRs—to make effective use of a computer, or that someone will think of an entertainment format that will make ordinary people want to use a computer for that purpose.

Uncertainty over the fate of television cannot be resolved until the creative community discovers the form(s) that make(s) sense of the new digital media; yet the new medium itself continues to evolve so rapidly that there is little time to explore its potential. The result is a period of chaos and uncertainty that will greatly increase the risks facing investors while providing nearly unlimited opportunities for entrepreneurship and creativity. In short, the situation greatly resembles that of radio broadcasting in the 1920s.

If consumers are willing to pay enough, almost anything may happen; if they are not, stunning breakthroughs on the supply side will be fruitless. It will be the task of the creative community (perhaps but not inevitably the one that now produces TV programs) to invent formats that take advantage of the strengths of the new medium. One sees this most clearly in the burgeoning and diverse industry of web page designers. Clearly, unless greater strides are made in simplifying interface designs, Internet use will not become a mass medium no matter how cheap it becomes.

Advertisers, of course, matter too, although their aggregate demand for audiences is a small fraction of aggregate consumer willingness to pay for traditional video content. None of the new digital media, whether "conventional" in format like geostationary satellites (GEOs—such as DirecTV or Primestar) or "new," like the World Wide Web, will support delivery of mass audiences. Because of their great capacity to offer specialized content, digital media fragment audiences; they do not aggregate them. Thus, advertisers will have to deal with the equivalent of small, specialized magazines. It will be easier to advertise golf balls and harder to advertise soap. However, advertisers pay more for audiences made up chiefly of likely purchasers of their products. Thus, in the aggregate, Web advertising may have a bright future despite fragmentation; further, the advance of Web advertising will continue to leave room for conventional mass media capable of delivering large audiences to advertisers seeking such audiences.

What is the "right" format: which images of information and entertainment will succeed in making the Internet a video broadcast medium, or a medium that displaces video broadcasts? An economist can only speculate, but it seems doubtful that underlying content will be much different than now or in the past: news, weather, pop entertainment, classics, documentaries. The kinds of stories that we tell each other will not change, but the form in which they appear must change. Suppliers of digital content will come to discover what *forms* best suit their medium. That is, they will discover what unique combinations of animation, resolution, download time, and other interface characteristics make the most attractive form of delivery for Internet information and entertainment. There is no reason to suppose this format is present-day video.

The Role of Government

The future is not just a question of technology and economics: there is government regulation, which despite recent reforms continues to pick commercial winners and losers, and to tax winners. As noted, government has the potential to derail the evolutionary process through such policies as cross-subsidies and encryption controls. But also, through research subsidies, government can continue to stimulate groundbreaking new technologies. Such subsidies were responsible for the Internet itself.

Both television and a large part of the Internet (especially telephone access lines and any radio-based transmissions) continue to be subject to FCC regulation. Therefore the habits and vices of the Federal Communications Commission (or, more generally, the government) are going to be central to the development of new forms of video delivery. At this moment, the government is subsidizing the Internet by exempting access providers from certain fees that logic might dictate they should pay. Sooner or later, the government will want something in return.

Broadcasters face a particular problem in settling on a business plan for exploiting their new digital airwaves assignments, and they do so heavily constrained by the political baggage that goes with continued FCC regulation. For example, the broadcasters will likely be required to maintain some form of free over-the-air television service, and they are likely to face significant restrictions on their ability to combine their airwave assignments into local units of efficient scale, in order to offer a service with bandwidth comparable to that of competing media such as satellites and wireless cable. As with cable, any new digital broadcast service will require substantial investments in consumer equipment. Traditionally, consumers themselves must be persuaded to make this expenditure. But the pace of change now is so rapid, and the uncertainty over the surviving format so great, that it may be necessary for broadcasters (and other providers) to offer the equipment at heavily subsidized prices in order to induce consumers to subscribe. Of course this raises the financial stakes enormously.

Conclusion

While one can ask whether Internet hardware and software is *capable* of delivering television as we know it today, that is almost certainly the wrong question to ask. (The answer is yes, it can be done, although poorly and expensively.) The real issue is what *transformation* of the current video medium will make it most suitable for Internet transmission. That is, how can the content now impressed on the broadcast television medium most effectively be impressed on the digital Internet medium in combination with nonvideo content, if at all? Who will discover how to make video at 5 or 10 frames per second (compared with

28 for standard television) in a two-inch square window on a computer screen an effective means of delivering entertainment? Will it be Ken Burns who will discover this transformation and make a fortune from its exploitation? Maybe there is no form that is still recognizably "television" that can survive in competition with the yet-to-be-invented digital formats.

As already noted, a key perspective on form and content is interface design. The World Wide Web and the modern browser are chiefly responsible for the growth in demand for Internet services. Yet these revolutionary inventions added *nothing whatever* to the functions performed by the Internet; they merely made it easier enough to use so that within a few years tens of millions began to use it. But most people still do not have a clue. The Internet is not yet, and may never be, a mass medium. Another leap forward into simplicity is needed. Indeed, advances in interface design may substitute for better transmission and computing hardware in defining a successful digital medium; lower costs mean nothing if the service has no value to users.

Cable companies, broadcasters, telephone companies, and others in business to deliver video entertainment to the home today are paralyzed with indecision as they brood over investments running into the tens of billions of dollars. The hesitation of investors is not based merely on the issue of which technology will deliver conventional video channels most cheaply or what the government may require or permit; it is also and perhaps mostly based on a lack of understanding of the best form in which to deliver the video. The answer to that question turns in great part on what kind of hardware people will be using to view television (or whatever it is going to be called), and on what kinds of content consumers and advertisers will be willing to pay for.

While the hesitation of television investors goes on, the Internet does not wait. It grows and changes based on the supply and demand for a range of nonvideo information and entertainment services aimed largely by and at an elite minority of the population. As transmission pipelines into the home increase in size only slowly, Internet commercial interests invent ever more clever ways to make the best use of limited bandwidth, substituting processing power, storage, and adaptive content. As they do so, the Internet becomes increasingly a *substitute* for television viewing, rather than a *means* of television viewing.

As for television itself, two things are clear: The FCC's artificial scarcity of spectrum will cease to be a central defining factor in the television industry, and the days when most viewers do not pay for most programs are numbered.

If, contrary to the tacit assumption of the present analysis, the price of bandwidth falls more rapidly than the prices of other components, the future of the Internet and television will depend on who owns rights to the technology. Unlike storage and processing, which are supplied by competitive, decentralized industries, transmission facilities are often highly concentrated. The single most important (expensive) link in the transmission chain is the one that ends in the home. If it should turn out that the key transmission technology is controlled by local telephone companies, for example, the future will be very different (and much slower in arriving) than if one form or another of digital broadcasting turns out to be dominant. The digital assignments recently awarded to existing TV stations may provide an efficient broadcast path, but other possibilities include "wireless cable" (MMDS, LMDS, and 38 gigahertz systems), geosynchronous communication satellites (GEOs), and low-earth orbit satellites (LEOs) such as the $8 billion Teledesic system that Bill Gates and Craig McCaw have started to construct.

After the problem of interface design and entertainment format, cost is the most important unknown factor affecting the future of digital media. The cost characteristics of these media break down into two categories: network costs and terminal equipment costs. Terminal equipment is the new box that sits on the TV or next to the computer, and perhaps the antenna that goes with it. Network costs are those related to building and launching satellites, fiber optic cables, or radio transmitters. Essentially all of the scenarios involve rather expensive new terminal equipment, and there is enough uncertainty about the cost of this equipment to say that all the scenarios are about the same in this respect. Network cost characteristics, however, are very different. A geosynchronous direct broadcast satellite—or even a LEO system—has huge upfront costs but then virtually no variable costs up until 100 percent channel capacity utilization is reached. The same is true for the Internet backbone. Such networks have substantial common costs, shared by many users, thus reducing the cost per user. At the other extreme is the telephone system with its star-shaped networks. Expanding the capacity of any subscriber line is just like adding terminal equipment, and the costs quickly become astronomical.

Satellite broadcasting (for example, DirecTV) obviously enjoys enormous public good transmission advantages. Insofar as national programming is concerned, the comparison above between cable and terrestrial broadcasting can simply be extended to satellites.

Assuming equal quality service, satellites, wireless cable, or even DVD could drive cable out of the market but in turn be unable to survive in competition with conventional broadcasting. But quality is not equal. Digital broadcasts are of remarkably high reception clarity, and there are more than 200 channels plus "near" video on demand on each of the major new systems. Cable can match this only by investing even more per subscriber in digital upgrades to its systems. Terrestrial broadcasters cannot match this by any means at present because of the FCC restrictions, and although future digital broadcast systems may present some useful opportunities, there will still be a capacity disadvantage.

Telephone companies could supply TV signals over existing copper wires to households today, using digital technology. A separate pair of wires would be required for each TV set in the home, but telephones and television could share lines. There is no serious limit to the number of channels that could be made available, because although only one channel could be on the wire at a time, the node serving each neighborhood could be supplied, via fiber, with a full complement of cable networks and "near" or even actual video-on-demand channels. Consumers would be able to select which channel came over the wire and to change that selection easily. The cost of doing all this, however, is in the same range as the cost of installing or upgrading cable systems. Although these costs will fall, competitors have access to the same underlying technology and so their costs also will fall.

Currently deployed and future terrestrial multichannel wireless cable systems such as MMDS and LMDS could offer the same quantity and quality of channels as satellites but only by using very expensive subscriber converter boxes to accommodate highly compressed video broadcasts. Assuming that these end-user costs were as low as those of satellite end users, the issue is whether wireless cable systems operating in every local area would cost more or less, in the aggregate, than a system that can reach all the same viewers from a single satellite. A wide range of uncertainty exists about all of these cost figures and about the extent of demand.

The arrival over the next few years of digital television sets will do little to separate the winners from the losers among media. The advantage of the sets is that they eliminate the need for most or all of the expensive electronics in the present set-top converter boxes. However, they probably do this for all the competing media, so no single medium gets a particular boost from digital TV sales. This occurrence assumes that the new media interests, including cable, succeed in convincing the FCC or Congress to impose a compatibility requirement on TV set manufacturers.

Now which if any of these video media will succeed? Of course no one knows, and the reason why no one knows is interesting: the different approaches all seem to cost about the same, within the range of uncertainty, and they all seem to offer features and suffer handicaps that are very hard to evaluate. Analysts with the latest engineering and marketing information can get out their spreadsheet programs and do the calculations, but the uncertainty about the assumptions overwhelms any attempt to conclude that one of these media clearly is superior to (more profitable than) the others, especially in light of changing technology and the effects on costs of network externalities. For example, a relatively small improvement in compression technology (such as digital subscriber lines) could possibly make narrow-band telephone (the present system) the long-term medium of choice for both Internet and even conventional video. No supplier wants to be in the middle of a multibillion-dollar investment project, only to have a small change in the technology make its efforts obsolete. So both the risks and the stakes remain enormous.

Notes

1. "Boot Up the Television Set," *Economist*, June 28, 1997, p. 63.
2. The term "multimedia" is imprecise. The dictionary definition is, "The combined use of several media, such as movies, slides, music, and lighting, especially for the purpose of education or entertainment." But what most people seem to mean in practice is a computer that can show TV images and sound effects.
3. Of course anything that goes out over the airwaves, even if intended for a single recipient, can be received by all those suitably located and equipped.

Contributors

DANIEL R. ANDERSON
University of Massachusetts,
Amherst

ELIZABETH E. BAILEY
University of Pennsylvania

BENJAMIN R. BARBER
Rutgers University

JAY G. BLUMLER
University of Leeds

PATRICIA A. COLLINS
University of Massachusetts,
Amherst

ROBERT W. CRANDALL
Brookings Institution

JAMES N. DERTOUZOS
Rand Corporation

ROBERT M. ENTMAN
North Carolina State University

GERALD R. FAULHABER
University of Pennsylvania

SHALOM M. FISCH
Children's Television Workshop

HENRY GELLER
Markle Foundation

JOHN HARING
Strategic Policy Research, Inc.

ALETHA C. HUSTON
University of Texas

CHARLES L. JACKSON
Strategic Policy Research, Inc.

ELIHU KATZ
University of Pennsylvania

ELLEN MICKIEWICZ
Duke University

BRUCE MURRAY
California Institute of Technology

ROGER G. NOLL
Stanford University

BRUCE M. OWEN
Economists, Inc.

KIRSTEN M. PEHRSSON
Strategic Policy Research, Inc.

MONROE E. PRICE
*Benjamin N. Cardozo
   School of Law*

MARC RABOY
University of Montreal

DONALD F. ROBERTS
Stanford University

JEFFREY H. ROHLFS
Strategic Policy Research, Inc.

CHARLES R. SHIPAN
University of Michigan

HARRY M. SHOOSHAN III
Strategic Policy Research,Inc.

MATTHEW L. SPITZER
University of Southern California

STEVEN S. WILDMAN
Northwestern University

FRANK A.WOLAK
Stanford University

JOHN C. WRIGHT
University of Texas

Index